AN
AUTOBIOGRAPHY
of
AMERICA

63

Edited by Mark Van Doren

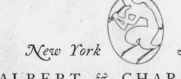

New York   *Mcmxxix*

ALBERT & CHARLES BONI

Printed in the United States of America

ACKNOWLEDGMENTS

ACKNOWLEDGMENT is gratefully given the following authors for permission to quote from their works, or from works edited by them:

William Cabell Bruce, for the Randolph-Morris correspondence from "John Randolph of Roanoke"; Worthington C. Ford and the Massachusetts Historical Society, for passages from "Charles Francis Adams: An Autobiography" and "A Cycle of Adams Letters"; Hamlin Garland, for chapters from "A Son of the Middle Border"; Howard W. Odum, for chapters from "Rainbow Round My Shoulder"; Michael Pupin, for pages from "From Immigrant to Inventor"; and Oswald Garrison Villard, for statements and letters from "John Brown: A Biography Fifty Years After."

Acknowledgment is also due the following publishers or holders of copyright material for permission to reprint selections from it:

The American Historical Association, for "The Autobiography of Martin Van Buren" and "The Diary and Letters of Salmon P. Chase."

D. Appleton and Company, New York, for "My Life," by George Francis Train, "Forty Years of It," by Brand Whitlock, and "Abraham Lincoln," by William H. Herndon and Jesse W. Weik.

The Bobbs-Merrill Company, for "Rainbow Round My Shoulder," by Howard W. Odum, copyright 1928.

The Cosmopolitan Book Corporation, for "Buffalo Bill's Life Story."

The Dial Press, for "The Journal of Nicholas Cresswell."

R. R. Donnelley and Sons for "A Woman's Story of Pioneer Illinois," by Christiana Holmes Tillson.

Harper and Brothers, for "Life on the Mississippi" and "Roughing It," by Mark Twain.

Houghton Mifflin Company, for "Riata and Spurs," by Charles A. Siringo, used by permission of and by arrangement with Houghton Mifflin Company.

Little, Brown and Company, for "Life in a New England Town," by John Quincy Adams.

The Macmillan Company, for "Reminiscences of Peace and War," by Mrs. Roger A Pryor, copyright by The Macmillan Company;

"The Road," by Jack London, copyright by The Macmillan Company; and "A Son of the Middle Border," by Hamlin Garland, copyright by The Macmillan Company.

Frances Low Partridge, for "Some Recollections," by Captain Charles Porter Low.

G. P. Putnam's Sons, for "John Randolph of Roanoke," by William Cabell Bruce.

Thomas C. Russell, for "The Shirley Letters," edited, revised, and privately printed by Mr. Russell.

Charles Scribner's Sons, for "From Immigrant to Inventor," by Michael Pupin.

World Book Company, for "Ox-Team Days on the Oregon Trail," by Ezra Meeker and Howard R. Driggs, copyright 1922 by World Book Company, Yonkers-on-Hudson, New York.

PREFACE

THE notion behind this book was that the history of America lay already written in pages which individual Americans had handed down about themselves, and that this history was best when the individuals were least "historical"—least conscious, in other words, that they were playing rôles or making contributions or revealing tendencies. The desire was to find men and women in significant times and significant places, from the earliest permanent settlements to the present day, who had been moved to describe their purely personal experiences in such a way that—luck being with the editor in his search—a connected and interesting narrative of American life should emerge when the whole thing got put together.

More emphasis was placed upon "interesting" than upon "connected." A completely articulated tale could not be told, of course, in any number of volumes. But if the people who talked were interesting people, and did or saw done interesting, illuminating things—then the story would be worth reading. And if the people were fairly well distributed over space and time, the story would be history too. To this end a very copious literature was ransacked, and thousands of pages were rejected for one reason or another before the sixty-four chapters which follow were admitted into the narrative.

Now there already existed a sufficient number of source books in American history, collections of documents illustrating this or that, students' guides to original materials, and so on. The aim was never to compete with those, or even to invite comparisons with them, but to go after another kind of excellence altogether. This book should be, in a word, continuously readable; as in my experience those other books had never been.

If freshness was achieved, it was achieved in three ways:

First, nothing was admitted merely because it was representative of a period, a movement, or a place. Many important themes of American history will not be found here in any form—the reason being either that the theme itself never lent itself to the purposes of personal narrative, or that it did not interest the editor, or that no piece of autobiography dealing with it happened to turn up. Politics are slighted except at moments of exceptional and exciting importance; institutional and constitutional history will have to be read in other books; there are no treaties, declarations, statutes, or the like.

Second, the appearance of documents was avoided. Headings, footnotes, summaries in fine print were dispensed with, and although in many cases condensation was necessary, asterisks were not inserted to spoil the page. Students of history who wish to see what was left out may easily do so by consulting the volumes cited in the Bibliography of Chapter Sources. The layman will not care.

Third, continuity was aimed at through the device of beginning each chapter not with the words of the person who wrote it but with a running paragraph designed to fill whatever obvious gap appeared between those words and the words of the previous writer. This was difficult, since to tell everything in between would be to concoct another history and so defeat the purpose of the book. Enough has been said in such places, I hope, to lead the reader comfortably on. Certainly my desire is that the book can be read from the first page to the last without a complaint either that I have stood in the way or that I have failed to give proper assistance.

The responsibility rests after all with the sixty-four Americans, from John Smith to John Wesley Gordon, who tell their stories here. Some of them—John Smith, William Bradford, Benjamin Franklin, Thomas Jefferson, Alexander Hamilton, John Quincy Adams, Aaron Burr, Martin Van Buren, P. T. Barnum, Daniel Boone, Mark Twain, Buffalo Bill, John Brown, U. S. Grant, Henry Adams, and Jack London—have very familiar names. Others will be known to a comparative few. Not every reader, I trust, will elsewhere have come across Samuel Sewall's account of how he paid his aged court to a Boston lady two hundred years ago, William Byrd's delightful strictures on the North Carolina frontier, Anne Grant's description of Colonel Schuyler's barn, Alexander Graydon's picture of recruiting for the Continental Army, Nicholas Cresswell's confession of his capitulation to feminine Indian charms near Pittsburgh, Charles Lee's audacious letters to and about George Washington, William Maclay's inimitable mockery of the aristocratic John Adams, Alexander Hamilton's plain story of his relations with Mrs. Reynolds, John Randolph's incredible letter to Mrs. Morris and her even more incredible reply, Peter Cartwright's proud tale of how he refused to dance, Mrs. Tillson's bitter miniature of Brice Hanna, Dame Shirley's letters from the California gold fields, Clarence King's family portrait of the Newtys, Josiah Henson's history of his trudge to Canada, Charles Francis Adams's analysis of Seward and Sumner, Henry Adams's indictment of Jim Fisk and Jay Gould,

Ward McAllister's elegant defense of the Four Hundred, Jack London's Dantesque sketch of the Erie County pen, and Black Ulysses's monologue of the endless road that stretches from now straight on —how far?

I have full faith in these and in all the other people who speak here. They seemed such as could be trusted to tell their own stories, editor or no editor, bad editor or good. And I am convinced that they have written *an* autobiography of America. *The* autobiography remains to be written; and always will.

M. V. D.

New York, 1929.

PREFACE

CONTENTS

Book I

FOOTHOLDS ON THE EASTERN SHORE

Book IV

THE GENERATION OF THE FATHERS

Book V

DEMOCRACY AND TRADE TRIUMPHANT

Book VI

BEYOND THE ALLEGHENIES

Book VII

BEYOND THE MISSISSIPPI

Book VIII

WHITE AND BLACK

Book IX

CIVIL WAR AND RECONSTRUCTION

BOOK X

THE SILVER AGE

BOOK I

FOOTHOLDS ON THE EASTERN SHORE

BOOK I.

FOOTHOLDS ON THE EASTERN SHORE.

CHAPTER I

FOR AN unknown number of centuries this continent, together with its sister continent to the south and the long neck of land between them, lay in a shadow which the eyes of Europe could not penetrate. The dark forests on the eastern and western coastal plains, the mountain ranges east and west, and the great valley of grass and sand that spread across the center—these were the silent possession of a people who in their turn did not guess that a new race would come with sails across the eastern sea and with new weapons, new tools, new ideas change everything. When this did happen it was in a sense an accident. Christopher Columbus, sailing west in 1492 with three Spanish vessels whose crews were terrified by the strange waters they traversed, thought only that he was finding a new passage to India and to all that East which was so valuable to Europe for its gold and spices. The island he landed on, probably one of the Bahamas, and the islands he next saw, Cuba and Haiti, seemed to him India indeed; and he called the inhabitants Indians. In the course of three later expeditions he explored the Caribbean, the east coast of Central America, and the north coast of South America; and died believing that India was at last somehow within the easy reach of Spain. It remained for his successors, men venturing out of Spain, Portugal, France, and England, to realize that America was a vast obstruction placed across the promised way to wealth; and to run the length of this obstruction north and south in search of passages through, finally rounding Cape Horn with proof that still another vast ocean lay between them and the wished-for world of perfume, spice, and gold. It remained for other generations to decide that America must be taken on its own terms, and worked for what it would yield. The sixteenth century went on; more expeditions came; chiefly it was adventurers hungry for gold or power who conquered to the south in the names of Portugal and Spain; then in the north, more than a century after Columbus, the English made a new and important contribution.

The first Englishmen who came, the Cabots at the close of the fifteenth century and Hawkins, Drake, and Raleigh in the sixteenth, were explorers or adventurers; but with the turn of the seventeenth

3

century the ideas of population and commerce came into play, the desire for permanent colonies was born. Companies of gentlemen and merchants were formed in England—corporations out of which came the two first colonies, with towns and plantations, that we shall see.

Toward the end of the year 1606 one hundred and twenty men, among them John Smith, sailed from London with orders for government sealed in a box. It was their destiny, as founders of Jamestown in Virginia, to found also the life in America which our narrative will follow. Captain Smith has become the spokesman for this little company through "The General History of Virginia," wherein he relates the dangers and difficulties of the settlement.

THE transportation of the company was committed to Captain Christopher Newport, a Mariner well practised for the Western parts of America. But their orders for government were put in a box, not to be opened, nor the governors known until they arrived in Virginia.

On the 19 of December, 1606, we set sail from Blackwall, but by unprosperous winds were kept six weeks in the sight of England; all which time Master Hunt, our preacher, was so weak and sick that few expected his recovery. Yet although he were but twenty miles from his habitation (the time we were in the Downs), and notwithstanding the stormy weather, nor the scandalous imputations of some few (little better then atheists, of the greatest rank amongst us) suggested against him, all this could never force from him so much as a seeming desire to leave the business, but preferred the service of God, in so good a voyage, before any affection to contest with his godless foes whose disastrous designs (could they have prevailed) had even then overthrown the business, so many discontents did then arise, had he not with the water of patience, and his godly exhortations (but chiefly by his true devoted examples), quenched those flames of envy, and dissension.

The first land they made they called Cape Henry; where thirty of them, recreating themselves on shore, were assaulted by five savages, who hurt two of the English very dangerously.

That night was the box opened, and the orders read, in which Bartholomew Gosnoll, John Smith, Edward Wingfield, Christopher Newport, John Ratliffe, John Martin, and George Kendall, were named to be the Council, and to choose a President amongst them for a year, who with the Council should govern. Matters of moment were to be examined by a jury, but determined by the major part of the Council, in which the President had two voices.

Until the 13 of May they sought a place to plant in; then the Council was sworn, Master Wingfield was chosen President, and an oration made why Captain Smith was not admitted of the Council as the rest.

Now falleth every man to work, the Council contrive the fort, the rest cut down trees to make place to pitch their tents; some provide clapboard to relade the ships, some make gardens, some nets, etc. The savages often visited us kindly. The President's overweening jealousy would admit no exercise at arms, or fortification but the boughs of trees cast together in the form of a half moon by the extraordinary pains and diligence of Captain Kendall.

Newport, Smith, and twenty others, were sent to discover the head of the river: by divers small habitations they passed, in six days they arrived at a town called Powhatan, consisting of some twelve houses, pleasantly seated on a hill; before it three fertile isles, about it many of their cornfields; the place is very pleasant, and strong by nature; of this place the Prince is called Powhatan, and his people Powhatans. To this place the river is navigable: but higher within a mile, by reason of the rocks and isles, there is not passage for a small boat; this they call the falls. The people in all parts kindly entreated them, till being returned within twenty miles of Jamestown they gave just cause of jealousy: but had God not blessed the discoverers otherwise than those at the fort, there had then been an end of that plantation; for at the fort, where they arrived the next day, they found 17 men hurt and a boy slain by the savages, and had it not chanced a cross bar shot from the ships struck down a bough from a tree amongst them, that caused them to retire, our men had all been slain, being securely all at work, and their arms in dry fats.

Hereupon the President was contented the fort should be pallisadoed, the ordnance mounted, his men armed and exercised: for many were the assaults and ambuscadoes of the savages, and our men by their disorderly straggling were often hurt, when the savages by the nimbleness of their heels well escaped.

What toil we had, with so small a power to guard our workmen adays, watch all night, resist our enemies, and effect our business, to relade the ships, cut down trees, and prepare the ground to plant our corn, etc., I refer to the reader's consideration.

Six weeks being spent in this manner, Captain Newport (who was hired only for our transportation) was to return with the ships.

Now Captain Smith, who all this time from their departure from the Canaries was restrained as a prisoner upon the scandalous suggestions of some of the chief (envying his repute), who feigned he intended to usurp the government, murder the Council, and make himself King, that his confederates were dispersed in all the three ships, and that divers of his confederates that revealed it would affirm it; for this he was committed as a prisoner.

Thirteen weeks he remained thus suspected, and by that time the ships should return they pretended out of their commiseration to refer him to the Council in England to receive a check, rather than by particulating his designs make him so odious to the world as to touch his life, or utterly overthrow his reputation. But he so much scorned their charity, and publicly defied the uttermost of their cruelty; he wisely prevented their policies, though he could not suppress their envies; yet so well he demeaned himself in this business, as all the company did see his innocency, and his adversaries' malice, and those suborned to accuse him accused his accusers of subornation; many untruths were alleged against him; but being so apparently disproved, begat a general hatred in the hearts of the company against such unjust commanders, that the President was adjudged to give him 200*l.*; so that all he had was seized upon, in part of satisfaction, which Smith presently returned to the store for the general use of the colony.

Many were the mischiefs that daily sprung from their ignorant (yet ambitious) spirits; but the good doctrine and exhortation of our Preacher Master Hunt reconciled them, and caused Captain Smith to be admitted to the Council.

The next day all received the Communion, the day following the savages voluntarily desired peace, and Captain Newport returned to England with news; leaving in Virginia 100 the 15 of June, 1607.

Being thus left to our fortunes, it fortuned that within ten days scarce ten amongst us could either go or well stand, such extreme weakness and sickness oppressed us. And thereat none need marvel if they consider the cause and reason, which was this.

Whilst the ships stayed, our allowance was somewhat bettered by a daily proportion of biscuits which the sailors would pilfer to sell, give, or exchange with us, for money, saxefras, furs, or love. But when they departed, there remained neither tavern, beer house, nor place of relief but the common kettle. Had we been as free from all sins as gluttony and drunkenness, we might have been canonized for saints; but our President would never have been admitted, for engrossing to his private, oatmeal, sack, oil, aquavitæ, beef, eggs, or what not, but the kettle; that indeed he allowed equally to be distributed, and that was half a pint of wheat, and as much barley boiled with water for a man a day, and this, having fried some

26 weeks in the ship's hold, contained as many worms as grains; so that we might truly call it rather so much bran than corn; our drink was water, our lodgings castles in the air.

From May to September, those that escaped lived upon sturgeon and sea-crabs; fifty in this time we buried; the rest seeing the President's projects to escape these miseries in our pinnace by flight (who all this time had neither felt want nor sickness), so moved our dead spirits as we deposed him; and established Ratliffe in his place, (Gosnoll being dead, Kendall deposed). Smith newly recovered, Martin and Ratliffe was by his care preserved and relieved, and the most of the soldiers recovered with the skillful diligence of Master Thomas Wotton, our surgeon general.

But now was all our provision spent, the sturgeon gone, all help abandoned, each hour expecting the fury of the savages; when God, the patron of all good endeavors, in that desperate extremity so changed the hearts of the savages that they brought such plenty of their fruit and provision as no man wanted.

Such actions have ever since the world's beginning been subject to such accidents, and everything of worth is found full of difficulties; but nothing so difficult as to establish a commonwealth so far remote from men and means, and where men's minds are so untoward as neither do well themselves, nor suffer others. But to proceed.

The new President, and Martin, being little beloved, of weak judgment in dangers and less industry in peace, committed the managing of all things abroad to Captain Smith: who by his own example, good words, and fair promises set some to mow, others to bind thatch, some to build houses, others to thatch them, himself always bearing the greatest task for his own share, so that in short time he provided most of them lodgings, neglecting any for himself.

This done, seeing the savages' superfluity begin to decrease (with some of his workmen), shipped himself in the shallop to search the country for trade. The want of the language, knowledge to manage his boat without sails, the want of a sufficient power (knowing the multitude of the savages), apparel for his men, and other necessaries, were infinite impediments; yet no discouragement.

Wingfield and Kendall living in disgrace, seeing all things at random in the absence of Smith, the company's dislike of their President's weakness, and their small love to Martin's never mending sickness, strengthened themselves with the sailors and other confederates to regain their former credit and authority, or at least such means aboard the pinnace (being fitted to sail as Smith had appointed for trade) to alter her course and to go for England.

Smith unexpectedly returning had the plot discovered to him; much trouble he had to prevent it, till with store of saber and musket shot he forced them stay or sink in the river: which action cost the life of Captain Kendall.

The President and Captain Archer not long after intended also to have abandoned the country, which project also was curbed and suppressed by Smith.

And now, the winter approaching, the rivers became so covered with swans, geese, ducks, and cranes, that we daily feasted with good bread, Virginia peas, pumpkins, and putchamins, fish, fowl, and divers sorts of wild beasts as fat as we could eat them: so that none of our tuftaffaty humorists desired to go for England.

But our comedies never endured long without a tragedy; some idle exceptions being muttered against Captain Smith for not discovering the head of Chickahamania river, and taxed by the Council to be too slow in so worthy an attempt. The next voyage he proceeded so far that with much labor by cutting of trees asunder he made his passage; but when his barge could pass no farther, he left her in a broad bay out of danger of shot, commanding none should go ashore till his return: himself with two English and two savages went up higher in a canoe; but he was not long absent but his men went ashore, whose want of government gave both occasion and opportunity to the savages to surprise one George Cassen, whom they slew, and much failed not to have cut off the boat and all the rest.

Smith, little dreaming of that accident, being got to the marshes at the river's head, twenty miles in the desert, had his two men slain (as is supposed) sleeping by the canoe, whilst himself by fowling sought them victual: who finding he was beset with 200 savages, two of them he slew, still defending himself with the aid of a savage his guide, whom he bound to his arm with his garters, and used him as a buckler, yet he was shot in his thigh a little, and had many arrows that stuck in his clothes; but no great hurt, till at last they took him prisoner.

When this news came to Jamestown, much was their sorrow for his loss, few expecting what ensued.

Six or seven weeks those barbarians kept him prisoner, many strange triumphs and conjurations they made of him, yet he so demeaned himself amongst them, as he not only diverted them from surprising the fort but procured his own liberty, and got himself and his company such estimation amongst them that those savages admired him more than their own Quiyouckosucks.

The manner how they used and delivered him is as followeth.

The savages having drawn from George Cassen whither Captain Smith was gone, prosecuting that opportunity they followed him with 300 bowmen, conducted by the King of Pamaunkee, who in divisions searching the turnings of the river found Robinson and Emry by the fireside: these they shot full of arrows and slew. Then finding the Captain, as is said, that used the savage that was his guide as his shield (three of them being slain and divers other so galled), all the rest would not come near him. Thinking thus to have returned to his boat, regarding them, as he marched, more than his way, slipped up to the middle in an oozy creek and his savage with him; yet durst they not come to him till, being near dead with cold, he threw away his arms. Then according to their composition they drew him forth and led him to the fire where his men were slain. Diligently they chafed his benumbed limbs.

He demanding for their captain, they showed him Opechan-kanough, king of Pamaunkee, to whom he gave a round ivory double compass dial. Much they marveled at the playing of the fly and needle, which they could see so plainly and yet not touch it because of the glass that covered them. But when he demonstrated by that globe-like jewel the roundness of the earth and skies, the sphere of the sun, moon, and stars, and how the sun did chase the night round about the world continually; the greatness of the land and sea, the diversity of nations, variety of complexions, and how we were to them Antipodes, and many other such like matters, they all stood as amazed with admiration.

Notwithstanding, within an hour after they tied him to a tree, and as many as could stand about him prepared to shoot him: but the King holding up the compass in his hand, they all laid down their bows and arrows, and in a triumphant manner led him to Orapaks, where he was after their manner kindly feasted, and well used.

At last they brought him to Werowocomoco, where was Powhatan their Emperor. Here more then two hundred of those grim courtiers stood wondering at him, as he had been a monster; till Powhatan and his train had put themselves in their greatest braveries. Before a fire upon a seat like a bedstead, he sat covered with a great robe, made of raccoon skins, and all the tails hanging by. On either hand did sit a young wench of 16 or 18 years, and along on each side the house, two rows of men, and behind them as many women, with all their heads and shoulders painted red; many of their heads bedecked with the white down of birds: but every one with something: and a great chain of white beads about their necks.

At his entrance before the King, all the people gave a great shout. The Queen of Appamatuck was appointed to bring him water to wash his hands, and another brought him a bunch of feathers, instead of a towel to dry them. Having feasted him after their best barbarous manner they could, a long consultation was held, but the conclusion was, two great stones were brought before Powhatan: then as many as could laid hands on him, dragged him to them, and thereon laid his head, and being ready with their clubs to beat out his brains, Pocahontas, the King's dearest daughter, when no entreaty could prevail, got his head in her arms, and laid her own upon his to save his from death: whereat the Emperor was contented he should live to make him hatchets, and her bells, beads, and copper; for they thought him as well of all occupations as themselves. For the King himself will make his own robes, shoes, bows, arrows, pots; plant, hunt, or do anything so well as the rest.

Two days after, Powhatan having disguised himself in the most fearfulest manner he could, caused Captain Smith to be brought forth to a great house in the woods, and there upon a mat by the fire to be left alone. Not long after, from behind a mat that divided the house, was made the most dolefulest noise he ever heard: then Powhatan, more like a devil than a man, with some two hundred more as black as himself, came unto him and told him now they were friends, and presently he should go to Jamestown, to send him two great guns, and a grindstone, for which he would give him the County of Capahowosick, and for ever esteem him as his son Nantaquoud.

So to Jamestown with 12 guides Powhatan sent him. That night they quartered in the woods, he still expecting (as he had done all this long time of his imprisonment) every hour to be put to one death or other for all their feasting. But almighty God by his divine providence had mollified the hearts of those stern barbarians with compassion. The next morning betimes they came to the fort, where Smith having used the savages with what kindness he could, he showed Rawhunt, Powhatan's trusty servant, two demi-culverins and a millstone to carry Powhatan: they found them somewhat too heavy; but when they did see him discharge them, being loaded with stones, among the boughs of a great tree loaded with icicles, the ice and branches came so tumbling down, that the poor savages ran away half dead with fear. But at last we regained some confidence with them, and gave them such toys: and sent to Powhatan his women, and children such presents as gave them in general full content.

Long before this, Master John Rolfe, an honest gentleman, and of good behavior, had been in love with Pocahontas, and she with him, which thing at that instant I made known to Sir Thomas Dale by a letter from him, wherein he entreated his advice, and she acquainted her brother with it, which resolution Sir Thomas Dale well approved. The bruit of this marriage came soon to the knowledge of Powhatan, a thing acceptable to him, as appeared by his sudden consent, for within ten days he sent Opachisco, an old uncle of hers, and two of his sons, to set the manner of the marriage, and to do in that behalf what they requested, for the confirmation thereof, as his deputy; which was accordingly done about the first of April. And ever since we have had friendly trade and commerce, as well with Powhatan himself, as all his subjects.

CHAPTER II

JAMESTOWN AND Virginia persisted under many hardships, physical and political, and Captain John Smith was by no means at the end of a useful career. But meanwhile another colony was preparing. The noncomformists in England, persecuted under James I, began to think of the New World as a place which could be made to conform to their religious and economic necessities. A small band of them, after ten years of exile in Holland, persuaded seventy merchants of London to finance an expedition to America; on September 6, 1620, William Bradford with a hundred other Pilgrims set sail from Plymouth for Virginia. They sighted Cape Cod in November, and after a month of vain effort to strike farther south landed at Plymouth, which Captain John Smith had marked on his map of New England. Bradford, whose narrative follows, soon became governor of Plymouth Colony. He tells of the landing, the first miserable winter, the experiment with communism that was so readily abandoned upon being found unworkable, the relations with the Indians, and the fate of a free spirit, Thomas Morton, who was among the first to discover that New England had been settled not for the sake of religious or social liberty but as a stronghold of the Puritan faith.

WEDNESDAY, the 6th of December, we set out, being very cold and hard weather. We were a long while after we launched from the ship before we could get clear of a sandy point which lay within less than a furlong of the same. At length we got clear of the sandy point and got up our sails, and within an hour or two we got under the weather shore, and then had smoother water and better sailing, but it was very cold, for the water froze on our clothes, and made them many times like coats of iron.

That night we returned again ashipboard with resolution the next morning to settle on some of those places. So, in the morning, after we had called on God for direction, we came to this resolution, to go presently ashore again, and to take a better view of two places which we thought most fitting for us; for we could not now take time for further search or consideration, our victuals being much spent, especially our beer, and it being now the 19th [new style 29th] of December. After our landing and viewing of the places so well as we could, we came to a conclusion by most voices to set on the mainland, on the first place, on an high ground where there is a great deal of land cleared and hath been planted with corn three or four years ago, and there is a very sweet brook runs under the hillside and many delicate springs of as good water as can be drunk, and where we may harbor our shallops and boats exceeding well, and in this brook much good fish in their season. On the further side of the river also much corn ground cleared. In one field is a great hill [*i.e.* Burial Hill] on which we point to make a platform and plant our ordnance which will command all round about; from thence we may see into the bay and far into the sea; and we may see thence Cape Cod. Our greatest labor will be fetching of our wood, which is half a quarter of an English mile, but there is enough so far off. What people inhabit here we yet know not, for as yet we have seen none.

Thursday the 28th of December [new style, Jan. 7th] . . . in the afternoon we went to measure out the ground, and first we took notice how many families they were, willing all single men that had no wives to join with some family as they thought fit, that so we might build fewer houses; which was done and we reduced them to nineteen families. To greater families we allotted larger plots; to every person half a pole in breadth and three in length, and so lots were cast where every man should lie; which was done and staked out. We thought this proportion was large enough at the first, for houses and gardens to impale them round, considering the weakness of our people, many of them growing ill with colds, for our former discoveries in frost and storms and the wading at Cape Cod had brought much weakness amongst us.

In these hard and difficult beginnings they found some discontents and murmurings arise amongst some, and mutinous speeches and carriages in other; but they were soon quelled, and overcome, by the wisdom, patience, and just and equal carriage of things, by the Governor and better part which clave faithfully together in the main. But that which was most sad, and lamentable, was, that in two or three months' time half of their company died, especially in January and February, being the depth of winter, and wanting houses and other comforts; being infected with scurvy and other diseases, which this long voyage and their inaccommodate condition had brought upon them; so as there died sometimes two or three of a day, in the foresaid time; that of one hundred and odd persons scarce fifty remained: and of these in the time of most distress there was but six or seven sound persons; who to their great commendations, be it spoken, spared no pains, night nor day, but with abundance of toil and hazard of their own health, fetched them wood, made them fires, drest them meat, made their beds, washed their loathsome clothes, clothed and unclothed them; in a word did all the homely, and necessary offices for them, which dainty and queasy stomachs cannot endure to hear named, and all this willingly and cheerfully, without any grudging in the least, showing herein their true love unto their friends and brethren; a rare example and worthy to be remembered. Two of these seven were Mr. William Brewster, their reverend Elder, and Myles Standish, their Captain and military commander (unto whom myself, and many others were much beholden in our low, and sick condition) and yet the Lord so upheld these persons, as in this general calamity they were not at all infected either with sickness, or lameness. And what I have said of these, I may say of many others who died in this general visitation and others yet living; that whilst they had health, yea or any strength continuing they were not wanting to any that had need of them; and I doubt not but their recompense is with the Lord.

But I may not here pass by another remarkable passage not to be forgotten. As this calamity fell among the passengers that were to be left here to plant, and were hasted ashore and made to drink water, that the seamen might have the more beer, and one in his sickness desiring but a small can of beer, it was answered, that if he were their own father he should have none; the disease began to fall amongst them also, so as almost half of their company died before they went away, and many of their officers and lustiest men, as the boatswain, gunner, three quartermasters, the cook, and others. At which the master was something struck and sent to the sick ashore and told the Governor he should send for beer for them that had need of it, though he drunk water homeward bound. But now amongst his company there was far another kind of carriage in this misery than amongst the passengers; for they that before had been boon companions in drinking and jollity in the time of their health and welfare, began now to desert one another in this calamity, saying they would not hazard their lives for them, they should be infected by coming to help them in their cabins, and so, after they came to die by it, would do little or nothing for them, but if they died let them die. But such of the passengers as were yet aboard showed them what mercy they could, which made some of their hearts relent, as the boatswain (and some others), who was a proud young man, and would often curse and scoff at the passengers: but when he grew weak, they had compassion on him and helped him; then he confessed he did not deserve it at their hands, he had abused them in word and deed. O! saith he, you, I now see, show your love like Christians indeed one to another, but we let one another lie and die like dogs. Another lay cursing his wife, saying if it had not been for her he had never come this unlucky voyage, and anon cursing his fellows, saying he had done this and that, for some of them, he had spent so much, and so much, amongst them, and they were now weary of him, and did not help him, having need. Another gave his companion all he had, if he died, to help him in his weakness: he went and got a little spice and made him a mess of meat once or twice, and because he died not so soon as he expected, he went amongst his fellows, and swore the rogue would cozen him, he would see him choked before he made him any more meat: and yet the poor fellow died before morning.

All this while the Indians came skulking about them, and would sometimes show themselves aloof of, but when any approached near them, they would run away; and once they stole away their tools where they had been at work and were gone to dinner. But about the 16th of March a certain Indian came boldly amongst them, and spoke to them in broken English, which they could well understand, but marveled at it. At length they understood by discourse with him, that he was not of these parts, but belonged to the eastern parts where some English ships came to fish, with whom he was acquainted, and could name sundry of them by their names, amongst whom he had got his language. He became profitable to them in acquainting them with many things concerning the state of the country in the East-parts where he lived, which was afterwards profitable unto them; as also of the people here, of their names, number and strength, of their situation and distance from this place, and who was chief amongst them. His name was Samasett; he told them also of another Indian whose name was Squanto, a native of this place, who had been in England and could speak better English than himself. Being after some time of entertainment, and gifts dismissed, a while after he came again, and five more with him, and they brought again all the tools that were stolen away before, and made way for the coming of their great Sachem, called Massasoyt. Who about four or five days came with the chief of his friends, and other attendance with the aforesaid Squanto. With whom after friendly entertainment, and some gifts given him, they made a peace with him (which hath now continued this twenty-four years).

On the day called Christmas-day, the Governor called them out to work (as was used), but the most of this new company excused themselves, and said it went against their consciences to work on that day. So the Governor told them that if they made it matter of conscience, he would spare them, till they were better informed; so he led away the rest and left them; but when they came home at noon, from their work, he found them in the street at play openly; some pitching the bar, and some at stool-ball, and such like sports. So he went to them, and took away their implements, and told them, that was against his conscience, that they should play, and others work; if they made the keeping of it matter of devotion, let them keep their houses, but there should be no gaming, or reveling in the streets. Since which time nothing hath been attempted that way, at least openly.

So they began to think how they might raise as much corn as they could, and obtain a better crop than they had done; that they might not still thus languish in misery. At length, after much debate of things, the Governor (with the advice of the chiefest amongst them) gave way that they should set corn every man for his own particular, and in that regard trust to themselves; in all other things to go on in the general way as before. And so assigned to every family a parcel of land, according to the proportion of their number, for that end, only for present use (but made no division for inheritance), and ranged all boys, and youth under some family. This had very good success; for it made all hands very industrious, so as much more corn was planted, than otherwise would have been; by any means the Governor or any other could use, and saved him a great deal of trouble, and gave far better content. The women now went willingly into the fields, and took their little ones with them to set corn; which before would allege weakness and inability; whom to have compelled would have been thought great tyranny, and oppression.

The experience that was had in this common course, and condition, tried sundry years, and that amongst godly, and sober men; may well evince, the vanity of that conceit of Plato's, and other ancients, applauded by some of later times. That the taking away of property, and bringing in community into a commonwealth; would make them happy and flourishing; as if they were wiser than God; for this community (for far as it was) was found to breed much confusion, and discontent, and retard much employment, that would have been to their benefit, and comfort. For the young men that were most able and fit for labor, and service, did repine that they should spend their time and strength to work for other men's wives, and children, without any recompense. The strong, or man of parts, had no more in division of victuals, and clothes, than he that was weak, and not able to do a quarter the other could, this was thought injustice. The aged and graver men to be ranked, and equalized, in labors, and victuals, clothes, etc., with the meaner, and younger sort, thought it some indignity, and disrespect unto them. And for men's wives to be commanded, to do service for other men, as dressing their meat, washing their clothes, etc., they deemed it a kind of slavery, neither could many husbands well brook it. Upon the point all being to have alike, and all to do alike, they thought themselves in the like condition, and one as good as another; and so if it did not cut off those relations, that God hath set amongst men; yet it did at least much diminish, and take off the mutual respects, that should be preserved amongst them. And would have been worse if they had been men of another condition. Let none object this is men's corruption; and nothing to the course itself; I answer, seeing all men have this corruption in them, God in his wisdom saw another course fitter for them.

But to return. After this course settled, and by that their corn was planted, all their victuals were spent, and they were only to rest on God's providence; at night not many times knowing where to have a bit of anything the next day. And so, as one well observed, had need to pray that God would give them their daily bread, above all people in the world. Yet they bore these wants with great patience and alacrity of spirit, and that for so long a time as for the most part of two years.

There came over one Captain Wollaston, and with him three or four more of some eminency, who brought with them a great many servants, with provisions and other implements for to begin a plantation; and pitched themselves in a place within the Massachusetts, which they called, after their captain's name, Mount Wollaston. Amongst whom was one Mr. Morton, who, it should seem, had some small adventure (of his own or other men's) amongst them; but had little respect amongst them, and was slighted by the meanest servants. Having continued there some time, and not finding things to answer their expectations, nor profit to arise as they looked for, Captain Wollaston takes a great part of the servants, and transports them to Virginia, where he puts them off at good rates, selling their time to other men; and writes back to one Mr. Rassdall, one of his chief partners, and accounted their merchant, to bring another part of them to Virginia likewise, intending to put them off there as he had done the rest. And he, with the consent of the said Rassdall, appointed one Fitcher to be his Lieutenant, and govern the remains of the plantation, till he or Rassdall returned to take further order thereabout. But this Morton above-said, having more craft than honesty (who had been a kind of pettifogger, of Furnefell's Inn), in the other's absence, watches an opportunity (commons being but hard amongst them), and got some strong drink and other junkets, and made them a feast; and after they were merry, he began to tell them, he would give them good counsel. "You see," saith he, "that many of your fellows are carried to Virginia; and if you stay till this Rassdall returns, you will also be carried away and sold for slaves with the rest. Therefore I would advise you to thrust out this Lieutenant Fitcher; and I, having a part in the plantation, will receive you as my partners and consociates; so may you be free from service, and we will converse, trade, plant, and live together as equals, and support and protect one another," or to like effect. This counsel was easily received; so they took opportunity, and thrust Lieutenant Fitcher out of doors, and would suffer him to come no more amongst them, but forced him to seek bread to eat, and other relief from his neighbors, till he could get passages for England. After this they fell to great licentiousness, and led a dissolute life, pouring out themselves into all profaneness. And Morton became lord of misrule, and maintained (as it were) a school of Atheism. And after they had got some goods into their hands, and got much by trading with the Indians, they spent it as vainly, in quaffing and drinking both wine and strong waters in great excess, and, as some reported, ten shillings worth in a morning. They also set up a May-pole, drinking and dancing about it many days together, inviting the Indian women, for their consorts, dancing and frisking together (like so many fairies, or furies rather), and worse practices. As if they had anew revived and celebrated the feast of the Roman goddess Flora, or the beastly practices of the mad Bacchanalians. Morton likewise (to show his poetry) composed sundry rhymes and verses, some tending to lasciviousness, and others to the detraction and scandal of some persons, which he affixed to this idle or idol May-pole.*

They changed also the name of their place, and instead of calling it Mount Wollaston, they called it Merry Mount, as if this jollity

---

* Morton's verses may be found in his own account, "The New English Canaan," Amsterdam, 1637.

> Drink and be merry, merry, merry, boys;
> Let all your delight be in Hymen's joys;
> Io to Hymen now the day is come,
> About the merry May-pole take a room.

would have lasted ever. But this continued not long, for after Morton was sent for England (as follows to be declared), shortly after came over that worthy gentleman, Mr. John Endicott, who brought over a patent under the broad seal, for the government of the Massachusetts, who visiting those parts caused that May-pole to be cut down, and rebuked them for their profaneness, and admonished them to look there should be better walking; so they now, or others, changed the name of their place again, and called it Mount Dagon.

Now, to maintain this riotous prodigality and profuse excess, Morton, thinking himself lawless, and hearing what gain the French and fishermen made by trading of pieces, powder, and shot to the Indians, he, as the head of this consortship, began the practice of the same in these parts; and first he taught them how to use them, to charge and discharge, and what proportion of powder to give the piece, according to the size or bigness of the same; and what shot to use for fowl, and what for deer. And having thus instructed them, he employed some of them to hunt and fowl for him, so as they became far more active in that employment than any of the English, by reason of their swiftness of foot, and nimbleness of body,

> Make green garlons, bring bottles out;
> And fill sweet Nectar, freely about.
> Uncover thy head, and fear no harm,
> For here's good liquor to keep it warm.
> > Then drink and be merry, etc.
> > Io to Hymen, etc.
>
> Nectar is a thing assign'd,
> By the Deity's own mind,
> To cure the heart opprest with grief,
> And of good liquors is the chief.
> > Then drink, etc.
> > Io to Hymen, etc.
>
> Give to the melancholy man
> A cup or two of 't now and then;
> This physic will soon revive his blood,
> And make him be of a merrier mood.
> > Then drink, etc.
> > Io to Hymen, etc.
>
> Give to the nymph that's free from scorn,
> No Irish stuff nor Scotch overworn.
> Lasses in beaver coats, come away;
> Ye shall be welcome to us night and day
> > To drink and be merry, etc.
> > Io to Hymen, etc.

being also quick-sighted, and by continual exercise well knowing the haunts of all sorts of game. So as when they saw the execution that a piece would do, and the benefit that might come by the same, they became mad, as it were, after them, and would not stick to give any price they could attain to for them; accounting their bows and arrows but baubles in comparison of them.

So sundry of the chief of the straggling plantations, meeting together, agreed by mutual consent to solicit those of Plymouth (who were then of more strength than them all) to join with them to prevent the further growth of this mischief, and suppress Morton and his consorts before they grew to further head and strength. Those that joined in this action (and after contributed to the charge of sending him for England) were from Pascataway, Namkeake, Winisimett, Weesagascusett, Natasco, and other places where any English were seated. Those of Plymouth being thus sought too by their messengers and letters, and weighing both their reasons, and the common danger, were willing to afford them their help; though themselves had least cause of fear or hurt. So, to be short, they first resolved jointly to write to him, and in a friendly and neighborly way to admonish him to forbear these courses, and sent a messenger with their letters to bring his answer. But he was so high as he scorned all advice, and asked who had to do with him; he had and would trade pieces with the Indians in despite of all, with many other scurrilous terms full of disdain. They sent to him a second time, and bade him be better advised, and more temperate in his terms, for the country could not bear the injury he did; it was against their common safety, and against the king's proclamation. He answered in high terms as before, and that the king's proclamation was no law; demanding what penalty was upon it. It was answered, more than he could bear, his majesty's displeasure. But insolently he persisted, and said the king was dead and his displeasure with him, and many the like things; and threatened withal that if any came to molest him, let then look to themselves, for he would prepare for them. Upon which they saw there was no way but to take him by force; and having so far proceeded, now to give over would make him far more haughty and insolent. So they mutually resolved to proceed, and obtained of the Governor of Plymouth to send Captain Standish, and some other aid with him, to take Morton by force. The which accordingly was done; but they found him to stand stiffly in his defense, having made fast his doors, armed his consorts, set divers dishes of powder and bullets ready on the table; and if they had not been overarmed with drink, more hurt might have been done.

They summoned him to yield, but he kept his house, and they could get nothing but scoffs and scorns from him; but at length, fearing they would do some violence to the house, he and some of his crew came out, but not to yield, but to shoot; but they were so steeled with drink as their pieces were too heavy for them; himself with a carbine (overcharged and almost half filled with powder and shot, as was after found) had thought to have shot Captain Standish; but he stepped to him, and put by his piece, and took him. Neither was there any hurt done to any of either side, save that one was so drunk that he ran his own nose upon the point of a sword that one held before him as he entered the house; but he lost but a little of his hot blood. Morton they brought away to Plymouth, where he was kept, till a ship went from the Isle of Shoals for England, with which he was sent to the Council of New England; and letters written to give them information of his course and carriage; and also one was sent at their common charge to inform their Honors more particularly, and to prosecute against him. But he fooled of the messenger, after he was gone from hence, and though he went for England, yet nothing was done to him, not so much as rebuked, for aught was heard; but returned the next year. Some of the worst of the company were dispersed, and some of the more modest kept the house till he should be heard from. But I have been too long about so unworthy a person, and bad a cause.

Book II

THE COLONIAL SCENE

CHAPTER III

PLYMOUTH AND Massachusetts, with the other New England colonies which succeeded them, grew slowly at first. For one thing there was the Civil War in England, during which few men emigrated from a scene where the Puritan faith was being tested on its own ground. But the colonies did maintain themselves, and eventually they grew rapidly—not only Virginia and New England now but New York, Pennsylvania, New Jersey, Delaware, Maryland, and Carolina, with their mixtures of English, Dutch, German, and Swedish blood. Before the end of the seventeenth century the settlements which strung themselves along the Atlantic coast could claim 200,000 inhabitants, most of these living on farms or in thinly scattered villages. Yet towns were growing up, social classes were distinguishing themselves, the professions and the trades were becoming established, and in general the human scene was thickening into variety and significance.

During the last decade of the century the established Congregational Church of New England, disturbed by new winds of doctrine that had long been blowing through the northern colonies, experienced a fit of reaction in the course of which an attempt was made to exterminate those children of Satan called witches. Learned and serious divines—the real rulers of the land—firmly believed that the Devil was trading for the souls of Puritans and using those souls to further the cause of a new kingdom of evil upon earth. Wars with the Indians, crop failures, and pestilences contributed to a state of panic which reached its climax in Salem, Massachusetts, when evidence was produced of the existence of witchcraft there. The Reverend Cotton Mather testified to the truth of the charge that Satan was bending human beings to his uses, and he has given accounts of the trials as a result of which some twenty men and women of Salem were hanged.

WE have been advised by some credible Christians yet alive, that a malefactor, accused of witchcraft as well as murder, and executed in this place more than forty years ago, did then give notice of an horrible plot against the country by witchcraft, and

a foundation of witchcraft then laid, which if it were not season-
ably discovered would probably blow up and pull down all the
churches in the country. And we have now with horror seen the
discovery of such a witchcraft! An army of devils is horribly broke
in upon the place which is the center, and, after a sort, the first-
born of our English settlements; and the houses of the good people
there are filled with the doleful shrieks of their children and servants, tormented by invisible hands, with tortures altogether preternatural. After the mischiefs there endeavored, and since in part
conquered, the terrible plague, of evil angels, hath made its progress
into some other places, where other persons have been in like
manner diabolically handled. These our poor afflicted neighbors,
quickly after they become infected and infested with these demons,
arrive to a capacity of discerning those which they conceive the
shapes of their troublers; and notwithstanding the great and just
suspicion, that the demons might impose the shapes of innocent
persons in their spectral exhibitions upon the sufferers (which may
perhaps prove no small part of the witch-plot in the issue), yet
many of the persons thus represented being examined, several of
them have been convicted of a very damnable witchcraft. Yea,
more than one twenty have confessed that they have signed unto
a book which the devil showed them, and engaged in his hellish
design of bewitching and ruining our land. We know not, at least
I know not, how far the delusions of Satan may be interwoven into
some circumstances of the confessions; but one would think all
the rules of understanding human affairs are at an end, if after
so many most voluntary harmonious confessions, made by intelligent persons of all ages, in sundry towns, at several times,
we must not believe the main strokes wherein those confessions all
agree; especially when we have a thousand preternatural things
every day before our eyes, wherein the confessors do acknowledge
their concernment, and give demonstration of their being so concerned. If the devils now can strike the minds of men with any
poisons of so fine a composition and operation, that scores of innocent people shall unite in confessions of a crime which we see
actually committed, it is a thing prodigious, beyond the wonders
of the former ages, and it threatens no less than a sort of dissolution
upon the world. Now, by these confessions 'tis agreed that the devil
has made a dreadful knot of witches in the country, and by the
help of witches has dreadfully increased that knot; that these
witches have driven a trade commissioning their confederate spirits,
to do all sorts of mischiefs to the neighbors, whereupon there have

ensued such mischievous consequences upon the bodies and estates of the neighborhood, as could not otherwise be accounted for. Yea, that at prodigious witch-meetings, the wretches have proceeded so far as to concert and consult the methods of rooting out the Christian religion from this country, and setting up instead of it, perhaps a more gross diabolism than ever the world saw before.

FROM THE TRIAL OF GEORGE BURROUGHS

This G. B. was indicted for witchcraft, and in the prosecution of the charge against him he was accused by five or six of the bewitched, as the author of their miseries; he was accused by eight of the confessing witches, as being a head actor at some of their hellish rendezvous, and one who had the promise of being a king in Satan's kingdom, now going to be erected. He was accused by nine persons for extraordinary lifting, and such feats of strength as could not be done without a diabolical assistance. And for other such things he was accused, until about thirty testimonies were brought in against him; nor were these judged the half of what might have been considered for his conviction. However they were enough to fix the character of a witch upon him according to the rules of reasoning, by the judicious Gaule, in that case directed.

The testimonies of the other sufferers concurred with these; and it was remarkable that, whereas biting was one of the ways which the witches used for the vexing of the sufferers, when they cried out of G. B. biting them, the print of the teeth would be seen on the flesh of the complainers, and just such a set of teeth as G. B.'s would then appear upon them, which could be distinguished from those of some other men's. Others of them testified that in their torments G. B. tempted them to go unto a sacrament, unto which they perceived him with a sound of trumpet summoning of other witches, who quickly after the sound would come from all quarters unto the rendezvous. One of them falling into a kind of trance affirmed that G. B. had carried her away into a very high mountain, where he showed her mighty and glorious kingdoms, and said, "He would give them all to her, if she would write in his book"; but she told him, "They were none of his to give"; and refused the motions; enduring of much misery for that refusal.

It cost the Court a wonderful deal of trouble, to hear the testimonies of the sufferers; for when they were going to give in their depositions, they would for a long time be taken with fits that made them uncapable of saying anything. The chief judge asked the prisoner, who he thought hindered these witnesses from giving their testimonies. And he answered, "He supposed it was the devil." That honorable person replied, "How comes the devil then to be so loath to have any testimony borne against you?" Which cast him into very great confusion.

Accordingly several of the bewitched had given in their testimony, that they had been troubled with the apparitions of two women, who said that they were G. B.'s two wives, and that he had been the death of them; and that the magistrates must be told of it, before whom if B. upon his trial denied it, that they did not know but that they should appear again in court. Now G. B. had been infamous for the barbarous usage of his two late wives, all the country over. Moreover, it was testified, the specter of G. B. threatening of the sufferers told them he had killed (besides others) Mrs. Lawson and her daughter Ann. And it was noted, that these were the virtuous wife and daughter of one at whom this G. B. might have a prejudice for his being serviceable at Salem Village, from whence himself had in ill terms removed some years before; and that when they died, which was long since, there were some odd circumstances about them, which made some of the attendants there suspect something of witchcraft, though none imagined from what quarter it should come.

Well, G. B. being now upon his trial, one of the bewitched persons was cast into horror at the ghost of B.'s two deceased wives then appearing before him, and crying for vengeance against him. Hereupon several of the bewitched persons were successively called in, who, all not knowing what the former had seen and said, concurred in their horror of the apparition, which they affirmed that he had before him. But he, though much appalled, utterly denied that he discerned anything of it; nor was it any part of his conviction.

A famous divine recites this among the convictions of a witch: "The testimony of the party bewitched, whether pining or dying; together with the joint oaths of sufficient persons that have seen certain prodigious pranks or feats wrought by the party accused." Now, God had been pleased so to leave this G. B. that he had ensnared himself by several instances, which he had formerly given of a preternatural strength, and which were now produced against him. He was a very puny man, yet he had often done things beyond the strength of a giant. A gun of about seven foot barrel, and so heavy that strong men could not steadily hold it out with both hands; there were several testimonies, given in by persons of credit and honor, that he made nothing of taking up such a gun behind the lock with but one hand, and holding it out like a pistol at arms-end. G. B. in his vindication was so foolish as to say, "That an Indian was there, and held it out at the same time." Whereas none of the spectators ever saw any such Indian; but they supposed, the "Black Man" (as the witches call the devil; and they generally say he resembles an Indian) might give him that assistance. There was evidence likewise brought in, that he made nothing of taking up whole barrels filled with molasses or cider in very disadvantageous postures and carrying of them through the difficultest places out of a canoe to the shore.

Yea, there were two testimonies, that G. B. with only putting the forefinger of his right hand into the muzzle of an heavy gun, a fowling-piece of about six or seven-foot barrel, did lift up the gun, and hold it out at arms-end; a gun which the deponents thought strong men could not with both hands lift up and hold out at the butt-end, as is usual. Indeed, one of these witnesses was overpersuaded by some persons to be out of the way upon G. B.'s trial; but he came afterwards with sorrow for his withdraw[al], and gave in his testimony. Nor were either of these witnesses made use of as evidences in the trial.

Faltering, faulty, unconstant, and contrary answers upon judicial and deliberate examination, are counted some unlucky symptoms of guilt, in all crimes, especially in witchcrafts. Now there never was a prisoner more eminent for them than G. B. both at his examination and on his trial. His tergiversations, contradictions, and falsehoods were very sensible. He had little to say, but that he had heard some things that he could not prove, reflecting upon the reputation of some of the witnesses.

Only he gave in a paper to the jury; wherein, although he had many times before granted, not only that there are witches, but also that the present sufferings of the country are the effects of horrible witchcrafts, yet he now goes to evince it, "That there neither are, nor ever were witches, that having made a compact with the devil can send a devil to torment other people at a distance." This paper was transcribed out of Ady; which the Court presently knew, as soon as they heard it. But he said, he had taken none of it out of any book; for which his evasion afterwards was, that a gentleman gave him the discourse in a manuscript, from whence he transcribed it.

The jury brought him in guilty. But when he came to die, he utterly denied the fact whereof he had been thus convicted.

FROM THE TRIAL OF MARTHA CARRIER

Martha Carrier was indicted for the bewitching certain persons, according to the form usual in such cases pleading not guilty to her indictment; there were first brought in a considerable number of the bewitched persons; who not only made the court sensible of a horrid witchcraft committed upon them, but also deposed that it was Martha Carrier or her shape that grievously tormented them by biting, pricking, pinching and choking of them. It was further deposed that while this Carrier was on her examination before the magistrates, the poor people were so tortured that every one expected their death upon the very spot, but that upon the binding of Carrier they were eased. Moreover the look of Carrier then laid the afflicted people for dead; and her touch, if her eye at the same time were off them, raised them again. Which things were also now seen upon her trial. And it was testified, that upon the mention of some having their necks twisted almost round by the shape of this Carrier, she replied, "It's no matter though their necks had been twisted quite off."

Before the trial of this prisoner several of her own children had frankly and fully confessed, not only that they were witches themselves, but that this their mother had made them so. This confession they made with great shows of repentance, and with much demonstration of truth. They related place, time, occasion; they gave an account of journeys, meetings and mischiefs by them performed, and were very credible in what they said. Nevertheless, this evidence was not produced against the prisoner at the bar, inasmuch as there was other evidence enough to proceed upon.

Allin Toothaker testified that Richard, the son of Martha Carrier, having some difference with him, pulled him down by the hair of the head. When he rose again he was going to strike at Richard Carrier; but fell down flat on his back to the ground and had not power to stir hand or foot, until he told Carrier he yielded; and then he saw the shape of Martha Carrier go off his breast.

This Toothaker had received a wound in the wars; and he now testified that Martha Carrier told him he should never be cured. Just afore the apprehending of Carrier, he could thrust a knitting needle into his wound, four inches deep; but presently after her being seized, he was thoroughly healed.

One Foster, who confessed her own share in the witchcraft for which the prisoner stood indicted, affirmed that she had seen the prisoner at some of their witch meetings, and that it was this Carrier, who persuaded her to be a witch. She confessed, that the devil carried them on a pole to a witch-meeting; but the pole broke, and she hanging about Carrier's neck, they both fell down, and she then received a hurt by the fall whereof she was not at this very time recovered.

In the time of this prisoner's trial, one Susanna Sheldon in open court had her hands unaccountably tied together with a wheel-band, so fast that without cutting it could not be loosed. It was done by a specter; and the sufferer affirmed it was the prisoner's.

Memorandum. This rampant hag, Martha Carrier, was the person, of whom the confessions of the witches, and of her own children among the rest, agreed, that the devil had promised her she should be Queen of Hell.

CHAPTER IV

JUDGE SAMUEL SEWALL GOES COURTING

THE PERSECUTION of witches ceased; and the reaction against the violence with which it had been carried on was felt in a diminution of the prestige of such theocrats as Mather. New England was taking on a more secular tone, pious and blameless as its leading citizens might still be. Boston grew into a little city of busy wharves and streets down which Americans went on a variety of worldly as well as godly errands. In 1717 Judge Samuel Sewall, an excellent man of affairs and the keeper of an inimitable diary of his daily doings, lost his wife. There followed a restless period during which the old gentleman debated with himself concerning a second marriage; contracted one; became a widower again; and launched upon the troubled waters of still further courtships. His account, taken from his diary, of the negotiations which he carried on with Madam Winthrop is also an account of Boston in the early years of the eighteenth century.

JULY 3, 1717. Last night my wife was taken very sick; this extraordinary pain and fainting was of long continuance, whereby I was obliged to abide at home and not go to the commencement. This is the second year of my absence from that solemnity.

8r. 15. My wife got some relapse by a new cold and grew very bad; sent for Mr. Oakes, and he sat up with me all night.

16. The distemper increases; yet my wife speaks to me to go to bed.

17. Thursday, I asked my wife whether 'twere best for me to go to lecture: she said, I can't tell; so I stayed at home. Put up a note. It being my son's lecture, and I absent, was taken much notice of. Major General Winthrop and his lady visit us. I thank her that she would visit my poor wife.

Friday, 8r. 18. My wife grows worse and exceedingly restless. Prayed God to look upon her. Asked not after my going to bed.

7th day, 8r. 19. Called Dr. C. Mather to pray, which he did excellently in the dining room, having suggested good thoughts to my wife before he went down. After Mr. Wadsworth prayed in the chamber when 'twas supposed my wife took little notice. About

32

a quarter of an hour past four, my dear wife expired in the afternoon, whereby the chamber was filled with a flood of tears. God
is teaching me a new lesson; to live a widower's life. Lord help me
to learn; and be a sun and shield to me, now so much of my comfort and defense are taken away.

8r. 20. I go to the public worship forenoon and afternoon. My
son has much ado to read the note I put up, being overwhelmed
with tears.

8r. 21. Monday, my dear wife is emboweled and put in a cere-
cloth, the weather being more than ordinarily hot.

Midweek, 8r. 23. My dear wife is interred. Bearers, Lieut. Gov.
Dumer, Major Gen. Winthrop; Col. Elisha Hutchinson, Col. Townsend; Andrew Belcher, Esq., and Simeon Stoddard, Esq. I intended
Col. Taylor for a bearer, but he was from home. Had very comfortable weather. Brother Gerrish prayed with us when returned
from the tomb; I went into it. Governor had a scarf and ring, and
the bearers, Governor Dudley, Brother Sewall, Hirst, Gerrish.

Nov. 7. 5. Last night died the excellent Waitstill [Wait Still]
Winthrop, Esq., for parentage, piety, prudence, philosophy, love to
New England ways and people very eminent. His son not come,
though sent for.

Dec. 1. Madam Winthrop comes not to meeting in the afternoon. I enquire of Mr. Winthrop. He saith she was not well at
noon: but was better.

Dec. 2. Serene and cold. Dr. Cotton Mather dines with us. I
visit Madam Winthrop at her own house; tell her of my sending
Hanah to Salem to-morrow; ask her advice as to selling Mr.
Hirst's goods: she advises to sell all but plate and linen. I ask her
to give and take condolence. She thanks me for my kindness; I tell
her she is beforehand with me. When I came away I prayed God
to dwell with her, counsel and comfort her. She desired my prayers.

Feb. 3. 2. I sent Madam Winthrop, Smoking Flax Inflamed, the
Jewish Children of Berlin, and my small vial of Tears, by Mr.
Gerrish with my service: she thanks me, and returns her service
to me.

Feb. 6. This morning wandering in my mind whether to live a
single or a married life; I had a sweet and very affectionate medi-
tation concerning the Lord Jesus; nothing was to be objected
against his person, parentage, relations, estate, house, home! Why
did I not resolutely, presently close with him! And I cried mightily
to God that He would help me so to do!

March 10. In the afternoon, though 'twas a very cold day, I carried Madam Usher her letter, delivered it to her with my own

hand. I was held below stairs where a fire was made. In Madam Usher's absence Madam Henchman took occasion highly to commend Madam Winthrop, the Major General's widow.

March 14. Deacon Marion comes to me, sits with me a great while in the evening; after a great deal of discourse about his courtship—he told [me] the Olivers said they wished I would court their aunt. I said little, but said 'twas not five months since I buried my dear wife. Had said before 'twas hard to know whether best to marry again or no; whom to marry. Gave him a book of the Berlin Jewish Converts.

Sept. 5. Going to son Sewall's I there meet with Madam Winthrop, told her I was glad to meet her there, had not seen her a great while; gave her Mr. Homes's sermon.

7r 30. Mr. Colman's lecture: daughter Sewall acquaints Madam Winthrop that if she pleased to be within at 3 P.M. I would wait on her. She answered she would be at home.

8r 1. Saturday, I dine at Mr. Stoddard's: from thence I went to Madam Winthrop's just at 3. Spake to her, saying, my loving wife died so soon and suddenly, 'twas hardly convenient for me to think of marrying again; however I came to this resolution, that I would not make my court to any person without first consulting with her. Had a pleasant discourse about 7 [seven] single persons sitting in the fore-seat 7r 29th, viz., Madam Rebekah Dudley, Catharine Winthrop, Bridget Usher, Deliverance Legg, Rebekah Loyd, Lydia Colman, Elizabeth Bellingham. She propounded one and another for me; but none would do, said Mrs. Loyd was about her age.

October 3. 2. Waited on Madam Winthrop again; 'twas a little while before she came in. Her daughter Noyes being there alone with me, I said, I hoped my waiting on her mother would not be disagreeable to her. She answered she should not be against that that might be for her comfort. I saluted her, and told her I perceived I must shortly wish her a good time (her mother had told me, she was with child, and within a month or two of her time). By and by in came Mr. Airs, chaplain of the castle, and hanged up his hat, which I was a little startled at, it seeming as if he was to lodge there. At last Madam Winthrop came in, too. After a considerable time, I went up to her and said, if it might not be inconvenient I desired to speak with her. She assented, and spake of going into another room; but Mr. Airs and Mrs. Noyes presently rose up, and went out, leaving us there alone. Then I ushered in discourse from the names in the foreseat; at last I prayed that Katharine [Mrs. Winthrop] might be the person assigned for me. She instantly took it up in the way of denial, as if she had catched at an opportunity to do it, saying she could not do it before she was asked. Said that was her mind unless she should change it, which she believed she should not; could not leave her children. I expressed my sorrow that she should do it so speedily, prayed her consideration, and asked her when I should wait on her again. She setting no time, I mentioned that day sennight. Gave her Mr. Willard's *Fountain* opened with the little print and verses; saying, I hoped if we did well read that book, we should meet together hereafter, if we did not now. She took the book and put it in her pocket. Took leave.

8r 5. Midweek, I dined with the court; from thence went and visited cousin Jonathan's wife, lying in with her little Betty. Gave the nurse 2s. Although I had appointed to wait upon her, Madam Winthrop, next Monday, yet I went from my cousin Sewall's thither about 3 P.M. The nurse told me Madam dined abroad at her daughter Noyes's, they were to go out together. I asked for the maid, who was not within. Gave Kate a penny and a kiss, and came away. Accompanied my son and dâter Cooper in their remove to their new house.

8r 6th. A little after 6 P.M. I went to Madam Winthrop's. She was not within. I gave Sarah Chickering, the maid, 2s, Juno, who brought in wood, 1s. Afterward the nurse came in; I gave her 18d, having no other small bill. After awhile Dr. Noyes came in with his mother; and quickly after his wife came in: they sat talking, I think, till eight o'clock. I said I feared I might be some interruption to their business: Dr. Noyes replied pleasantly he feared they might be an interruption to me, and went away. Madam seemed to harp upon the same string. Must take care of her children; could not leave that house and neighborhood where she had dwelt so long. I told her she might do her children as much or more good by bestowing what she laid out in housekeeping, upon them. Said her son would be of age the 7th of August. I said it might be inconvenient for her to dwell with her daughter-in-law, who must be mistress of the house. I gave her a piece of Mr. Belcher's cake and ginger-bread wrapped up in a clean sheet of paper; told her of her father's kindness to me when treasurer, and I constable. My daughter Judith was gone from me and I was more lonesome— might help to forward one another in our journey to Canaan.—Mr. Eyre came within the door; I saluted him, ask'd how Mr. Clark did, and he went away. I took leave about 9 o'clock. I told [her] I came now to refresh her memory as to Monday night; said she had not forgot it. In discourse with her, I asked leave to speak with her sister; I meant to gain Madam Mico's favor to persuade her sister. She seemed surprised and displeased, and said she was in the same condition!

In the evening I visited Madam Winthrop, who treated me with a great deal of courtesy; wine, marmalade. I gave her a news-letter about the Thanksgiving; proposals, for sake of the verses for David Jeffries. She tells me Dr. Increase Mather visited her this day, in Mr. Hutchinson's coach.

8r 11th. I write a few lines to Madam Winthrop to this purpose: "Madam, these wait on you with Mr. Mayhew's sermon, and ac-count of the state of the Indians on Martha's Vineyard. I thank you for your unmerited favors of yesterday; and hope to have the happiness of waiting on you to-morrow before eight o'clock after noon. I pray God to keep you, and give you a joyful entrance upon the two hundred and twenty-ninth year of Christopher Columbus his discovery; and take leave, who am, Madam, your humble servant.   "S. S."

Sent this by Deacon Green, who delivered it to Sarah Chickering, her mistress not being at home.

Mrs. Anne Cotton came to door ('twas before 8), said Madam Winthrop was within, directed me into the little room, where she was full of work behind a stand; Mrs. Cotton came in and stood. Madam Winthrop pointed to her to set me a chair. Madam Win-throp's countenance was much changed from what 'twas on Mon-day, looked dark and lowering. At last, the work (black stuff or silk) was taken away, I got my chair in place, had some converse, but very cold and indifferent to what 'twas before. Asked her to acquit me of rudeness if I drew off her glove. Inquiring the reason, I told her 'twas great odds between handling a dead goat, and a living lady. Got it off. I told her I had one petition to ask of her, that was, that she would take off the negative she laid on me the third of October; she readily answered she could not, and enlarged upon it; she told me of it so soon as she could; could not leave her house, children, neighbors, business. I told her she might do some good to help and support me. Mentioning Mrs. Gookin, Nath, the widow Weld was spoken of; said I had visited Mrs. Denison. I told her yes! Afterwards I said, if after a first and second vagary she would accept of me returning, her victorious kindness and good will would be very obliging. She thanked me for my book (Mr. Mayhew's sermon), but said not a word of the letter. When she insisted on the negative, I prayed there might be no more thunder and lightning, I should not sleep all night. I gave her Dr. Preston, the Church's Marriage and the Church's Carriage, which cost me 6s at the sale. The door standing open, Mr. Airs came in, hung up his hat, and sat down. After awhile, Madam Winthrop moving, he went out. Jno. Eyre looked in, I said, How do ye, or, your servant, Mr. Eyre: but heard no word from him. Sarah filled a glass of wine, she drank to me, I to her, she sent Juno home with me with a good lantern, I gave her 6d and bid her thank her mistress. In some of our discourse, I told her I had rather go to the stone house adjoining to her, than to come to her against her mind. Told her the reason why I came every other night was lest I should drink too deep draughts of pleasure. She had talked of canary, her kisses were to me better than the best canary. Explained the expression concerning Columbus.

8r 17. In the evening I visited Madam Winthrop, who treated me courteously, but not in clean linen as sometimes. She said she did not know whether I would come again, or no. I asked her how she could so impute inconstancy to me. (I had not visited her since Wednesday night being unable to get over the indisposition received by the treatment received that night, and I *must* in it seemed to sound like a made piece of formality.) Gave her this day's gazette.

8r 18. Visited Madam Mico, who came to me in a splendid dress. I said, It may be you have heard of my visiting Madam Winthrop, her sister. She answered, Her sister had told her of it. I asked her good will in the affair. She answered, If her sister were for it, she should not hinder it. I gave her Mr. Homes's sermon. She gave me a glass of canary, entertained me with good discourse, and a respectful remembrance of my first wife. I took leave.

8r 19. Midweek, visited Madam Winthrop; Sarah told me she was at Mr. Walley's, would not come home till late. I gave her Hanah 3 oranges with her duty, not knowing whether I should find her or no. Was ready to go home: but said if I knew she was there, I would go thither. Sarah seemed to speak with pretty good courage, she would be there. I went and found her there, with Mr. Walley and his wife in the little room below. At 7 o'clock I mentioned going home; at 8 I put on my coat, and quickly waited on her home. She found occasion to speak loud to the servant, as if she had a mind to be known. Was courteous to me; but took occasion to speak pretty earnestly about my keeping a coach: I said 'twould cost £100 per annum: she said 'twould cost but £40. Spake much against John Winthrop, his false-heartedness. Mr. Eyre came in and sat awhile; I offered him Dr. Incr. Mather's sermons, whereof Mr. Apleton's ordination sermon was one; said he had them already. I said I would give him another. Exit. Came away somewhat late.

8r 20. At Council, Col. Towsend spake to me of my hood: should get a wig. I said 'twas my chief ornament: I wore it for sake of the day. Brother Odlin, and Sam, Mary, and Jane Hirst dine with us. Promised to wait on the Governor about 7. Madam Winthrop not being at lecture, I went thither first; found her very serene with her dâter Noyes, Mrs. Dering, and the widow Shipreev sitting at a little table, she in her armchair. She drank to me, and I to Mrs. Noyes. After awhile prayed the favor to speak with her. She took one of the candles, and went into the best room, closed the shutters, sat down upon the couch. She told me Madam Usher had been there, and said the coach must be set on wheels, and not by rusting. She spake something of my needing a wig. Asked me what her sister said to me. I told her, she said, If her sister were for it, she would not hinder it. But I told her, she did say she would be glad to have me for her brother. Said, I shall keep you in the cold, and asked her if she would be within to-morrow night, for we had had but a running feat. She said she could not tell whether she should, or no. I took leave. As were drinking at the Governor's, he said: In England the ladies minded little more than that they might have money, and coaches to ride in. I said, and New England brooks its name. At which Mr. Dudley smiled. Governor said they were not quite so bad here.

8r 21. Friday, my son, the minister, came to me P.M. by appointment and we pray one for another in the old chamber; more especially respecting my courtship. About 6 o'clock I go to Madam Winthrop's; Sarah told me her mistress was gone out, but did not tell me whither she went. She presently ordered me a fire; so I went in, having Dr. Sibb's *Bowels* with me to read. I read two first sermons, still nobody came in: at last about 9 o'clock Mr. Jno. Eyre came in; I took the opportunity to say to him as I had done to Mrs. Noyes before, that I hoped my visiting his mother would not be disagreeable to him; he answered me with much respect. When 'twas after 9 o'clock he of himself said he would go and call her, she was but at one of his brothers: a while after I heard Madam Winthrop's voice, inquiring something about John. After a good while and clapping the garden door twice or thrice, she came in. I mentioned something of the lateness; she bantered me, and said I was later. She received me courteously. I asked when our proceedings should be made public: she said they were like to be no more public than they were already. Offered me no wine that I remember. I rose up at 11 o'clock to come away, saying I would put on my coat. She offered not to help me. I prayed her that Juno might light me home, she opened the shutter, and said 'twas pretty light abroad; Juno was weary and gone to bed. So I came home by starlight as well as I could. At my first coming in, I gave Sarah five shillings.

Oct. 22. Dâter Cooper visited me before my going out of town, stayed till about sunset. I brought her going near as far as the Orange Tree. Coming back, near Leg's Corner, little David Jeffries saw me, and looking upon me very lovingly, asked me if I was going to see his grandmother? I said, Not to-night. Gave him a penny, and bid him present my service to his grandmother.

Oct. 24. I went in the hackney coach through the Common, stopped at Madam Winthrop's (had told her I would take my departure from thence). Sarah came to the door with Katee in her arms: but I did not think to take notice of the child. Called her mistress. I told her, being encouraged by David Jeffries loving eyes, and sweet words, I was come to inquire whether she could find in her heart to leave that house and neighborhood, and go and dwell with me at the south end; I think she said softly, Not yet. I told her it did not lie in my lands to keep a coach. If I should, I should be in danger to be brought to keep company with her neighbor Brooker (he was a little before sent to prison for debt). Told her I had an antipathy against those who would pretend to give themselves; but nothing of their estate. I would a proportion of my estate with myself. And I supposed she would do so. As to a periwig, my best and greatest friend, I could not possibly have a greater, began to find me with hair before I was born, and had continued to do so ever since; and I could not find in my heart to go to another. She commended the book I gave her, Dr. Preston, the Church Marriage; quoted him saying 'twas inconvenient keeping out of a fashion commonly used. I said the time and tide did circumscribe my visit. She gave me a dram of black cherry brandy, and gave me a lump of sugar that was in it. She wished me a good journey. I prayed God to keep her, and came away. Had a very pleasant journey to Salem.

31. 2. She proves her husband's will. At night I visited Madam Winthrop about 6 p.m. They told me she was gone to Madam Mico's. I went thither and found she was gone; so returned to her house, read the Epistles to the Galatians, Ephesians in Mr. Eyre's Latin Bible. After the clock struck 8 I began to read the 103 Psalm. Mr. Wendell came in from his warehouse. Asked me if I were alone. Spake very kindly to me, offered me to call Madam Winthrop. I told him, She would be angry, had been at Mrs. Mico's; he helped me on with my coat and I came home: left the gazette in the Bible, which told Sarah of, bid her present my service to Mrs. Winthrop, and tell her I had been to wait on her if she had been at home.

Nov. 1. I was so taken up that I could not go if I would.

Nov. 2. Midweek, went again, and found Mrs. Alden there, who quickly went out. Gave her about one-half pound of sugar almonds, cost 3s per pound. Carried them on Monday. She seemed pleased with them, asked what they cost. Spake of giving her a hundred pounds per annum if I died before her. Asked her what sum she would give me, if she should die first? Said I would give her time to consider of it. She said she heard as if I had given all to my children by deeds of gift. I told her 'twas a mistake, Point-Judith was mine, &c. That in England, I owned, my father's desire was that it should go to my eldest son; 'twas £20 per annum; she thought 'twas forty. I think when I seemed to excuse pressing this, she seemed to think 'twas best to speak of it; a long winter was coming on. Gave me a glass or two of canary.

Nov. 4th. Friday, went again about 7 o'clock; found there Mr. John Walley and his wife: sat discoursing pleasantly. I showed them Isaac Moses's [an Indian] writing. Madam W. served comfeits to us. After awhile a table was spread, and supper was set. I urged Mr. Walley to crave a blessing; but he put it upon me. About 9 they went away. I asked Madam what fashioned necklace I should present her with. She said, None at all. I asked her whereabout we left off last time; mentioned what I had offered to give her; asked her what she would give me; she said she could not change her condition: she had said so from the beginning; could not be so far from her children, the lecture. Quoted the Apostle Paul affirming that a single life was better than a married. I answered that was for the present distress. Said she had not pleasure in things of that nature as formerly: I said, you are the fitter to make me a wife. If she held in that mind, I must go home and bewail my rashness in making more haste than good speed. However, considering the supper, I desired her to be within next Monday night, if we lived so long. Assented. She charged me with saying, that she must put away Juno, if she came to me: I utterly denied it, it never came into my heart; yet she insisted upon it; saying it came in upon discourse about the Indian woman that obtained her freedom this court. About 10 I said I would not disturb the good orders of her house, and came away. She not seeming pleased with my coming away. Spake to her about David Jeffries, had not seen him.

Monday, Nov. 7th. My son prayed in the old chamber. Our time had been taken up by son and daughter Cooper's visit; so that I only read the 130th and 143d Psalm. 'Twas on the account of my courtship. I went to Mad. Winthrop; found her rocking her little Katee in the cradle. I excused my coming so late (near eight). She set me an armchair and cushion; and so the cradle was between her armchair and mine. Gave her the remnant of my almonds; she did not eat of them as before; but laid them away; I said I came to inquire whether she had altered her mind since Friday, or remained of the same mind still. She said, Thereabouts. I told her I loved her, and was so fond as to think that she loved me: she said had a great respect for me. I told her, I had made her an offer, without asking any advice; she had so many to advise with, that 'twas a hindrance. The fire was come to one short brand besides the block, which brand was set up in end; at last it fell to pieces, and no recruit was made: she gave me a glass of wine. I think I repeated again that I would go home and bewail my rashness in making more haste than good speed. I would endeavor to contain myself, and not go on to solicit her to do that which she could not consent to. Took leave of her. As came down the steps she bid me have a care. Treated me courteously. Told her she had entered the fourth year of her widowhood. I had given her the news-letter before: I did not bid her draw off her glove as sometime I had done. Her dress was not so clean as sometime it had been. Jehovah jireh!

Midweek, 9r 9th. Dine at Brother Stoddard's: were so kind as to inquire of me if they should invite Mad. Winthrop; I answered No. Had a noble treat. At night our meeting was at the widow Belknap's. Gave each one of the meeting one of Mr. Homes's sermons, 12 in all; she sent her servant home with me with a lantern. Madam Winthrop's shutters were open as I passed by.

Nov. 11th. Went not to Mad. Winthrop's. This is the second withdraw.

Nov. 21. About the middle of December Madam Winthrop made a treat for her children; Mr. Sewall, Prince, Willoughby: I knew nothing of it; but the same day abode in the Council chamber for fear of the rain, and dined alone upon Kilby's pies and good beer.

March 5. Lord's day, serene, and good but very cold, yet had a comfortable opportunity to celebrate the Lord's Supper. Mr. Prince, P.M., preached a funeral sermon from Psal. 90, 10. Gave Capt. Hill a good character. Just as I sat down in my seat, one of my foreteeth in my under jaw came out, and I put it in my pocket. This old servant and daughter of music leaving me, does thereby give me warning that I must shortly resign my head: the Lord help me to do it cheerfully!

CHAPTER V

BENJAMIN FRANKLIN STARTS A CAREER

THE CITY of Boston had two rivals in the Middle Colonies. New York and Philadelphia, founded respectively by Dutchmen and Quakers, now flourished too. Only three years after the blasting of Judge Sewall's hopes Boston lost one of her most famous sons to Philadelphia when Benjamin Franklin, a young printer, went down through New York and made his entrance into the city where he was to conduct a great career as author, publisher, scientist, improver of public works, statesman, and diplomat. From his "Autobiography" we give Franklin's own account of his first days in the new city, of the company he formed about him there, and of the steps he soon took to make the town more habitable.

I WAS in my working dress, my best clothes being to come round by sea. I was dirty from my journey; my pockets were stuffed out with shirts and stockings, and I knew no soul nor where to look for lodging. I was fatigued with traveling, rowing, and want of rest, I was very hungry; and my whole stock of cash consisted of a Dutch dollar, and about a shilling in copper. The latter I gave the people of the boat for my passage, who at first refused it, on account of my rowing; but I insisted on their taking it. A man being sometimes more generous when he has but a little money than when he has plenty, perhaps through fear of being thought to have but little.

Then I walked up the street, gazing about till near the market-house I met a boy with bread. I had made many a meal on bread, and, inquiring where he got it, I went immediately to the baker's he directed me to, in Second Street, and asked for biscuit intending such as we had in Boston; but they, it seems, were not made in Philadelphia. Then I asked for a three-penny loaf, and was told they had none such. So not considering or knowing the difference of money, and the greater cheapness nor the names of his bread, I bade him give me three-penny worth of any sort. He gave me, accordingly, three great puffy rolls. I was surprised at the quantity, but took it, and, having no room in my pockets, walked off with a roll under each arm, and eating the other. Thus I went up Market Street as far as Fourth Street, passing by the door of

42

Mr. Read, my future wife's father; when she, standing at the door, saw me, and thought I made, as I certainly did, a most awkward, ridiculous appearance. Then I turned and went down Chestnut Street and part of Walnut Street, eating my roll all the way, and, coming round, found myself again at Market Street wharf, near the boat I came in, to which I went for a draught of the river water; and, being filled with one of my rolls, gave the other two to a woman and her child that came down the river in the boat with us, and were waiting to go farther.

Thus refreshed, I walked again up the street, which by this time had many clean-dressed people in it, who were all walking the same way. I joined them, and thereby was led into the great meeting-house of the Quakers near the market. I sat down among them, and, after looking round awhile and hearing nothing said, being very drowsy through labor and want of rest the preceding night, I fell fast asleep, and continued so till the meeting broke up, when one was kind enough to rouse me. This was, therefore, the first house I was in, or slept in, in Philadelphia.

Walking down again toward the river, and, looking in the faces of people, I met a young Quaker man, whose countenance I liked, and, accosting him, requested he would tell me where a stranger could get lodging. We were then near the sign of the Three Mariners. "Here," says he, "is one place that entertains strangers, but it is not a reputable house; if thee wilt walk with me, I'll show thee a better." He brought me to the Crooked Billet in Water Street. Here I got a dinner; and, while I was eating it, several sly questions were asked me, as it seemed to be suspected from my youth and appearance, that I might be some runaway.

After dinner, my sleepiness returned, and being shown to a bed, I lay down without undressing, and slept till six in the evening, was called to supper, went to bed again very early, and slept soundly till next morning. Then I made myself as tidy as I could, and went to Andrew Bradford the printer's. I found in the shop the old man his father, whom I had seen at New York, and who, traveling on horseback, had got to Philadelphia before me. He introduced me to his son, who received me civilly, gave me a breakfast, but told me he did not at present want a hand, being lately supplied with one; but there was another printer in town, lately set up, one Keimer, who, perhaps, might employ me; if not, I should be welcome to lodge at his house, and he would give me a little work to do now and then till fuller business should offer.

The old gentleman said he would go with me to the new printer; and when we found him, "Neighbor," says Bradford, "I have brought to see you a young man of your business; perhaps you may want such a one." He asked me a few questions, put a composing stick in my hand to see how I worked, and then said he would employ me soon, though he had just then nothing for me to do; and, taking old Bradford, whom he had never seen before, to be one of the town's people that had a good will for him, entered into a conversation on his present undertaking and prospects; while Bradford, not discovering that he was the other printer's father, on Keimer's saying he expected soon to get the greatest part of the business into his own hands, drew him on by artful questions, and starting little doubts, to explain all his views, what interest he relied on, and in what manner he intended to proceed. I, who stood by and heard all, saw immediately that one of them was a crafty old sophister, and the other a mere novice. Bradford left me with Keimer, who was greatly surprised when I told him who the old man was.

Keimer's printing-house, I found, consisted of an old shattered press, and one small, worn-out font of English, which he was then using himself, composing an Elegy on Aquila Rose, before-mentioned, an ingenious young man, of excellent character, much respected in the town, clerk of the Assembly, and a pretty poet. Keimer made verses too, but very indifferently. He could not be said to write them, for his manner was to compose them in the types directly out of his head. So there being no copy, but one pair of cases, and the Elegy likely to require all the letters, no one could help him. I endeavored to put his press (which he had not yet used, and of which he understood nothing) into order fit to be worked with; and, promising to come and print off his Elegy as soon as he should have got it ready, I returned to Bradford's, who gave me a little job to do for the present, and there I lodged and dieted. A few days after, Keimer sent for me to print off the Elegy. And now he had got another pair of cases, and a pamphlet to reprint, on which he set me to work.

These two printers I found poorly qualified for their business. Bradford had not been bred to it, and was very illiterate; and Keimer, though something of a scholar, was a mere compositor, knowing nothing of presswork. He had been one of the French prophets, and could act their enthusiastic agitations. At this time he did not profess any particular religion, but something of all on occasion; was very ignorant of the world, and had, as I afterward found, a good deal of the knave in his composition. He did not like my lodging at Bradford's while I worked with him. He had a house, indeed, but without furniture, so he could not lodge me;

but he got me a lodging at Mr. Read's, before mentioned, who was the owner of his house; and, my chest and clothes being come by this time, I made rather a more respectable appearance in the eyes of Miss Read than I had done when she first happened to see me eating my roll in the street.

I began now to have some acquaintance among the young people of the town, that were lovers of reading, with whom I spent my evenings very pleasantly; and gaining money by my industry and frugality, I lived very agreeably, forgetting Boston as much as I could, and not desiring that any there should know where I resided, except my friend Collins, who was in my secret, and kept it when I wrote him.

Keimer and I lived on a pretty good familiar footing, and agreed tolerably well, for he suspected nothing of my setting up. He retained a great deal of his old enthusiasms and loved argumentation. We therefore had many disputations. I used to work him so with my Socratic method, and had trepanned him so often by questions apparently so distant from any point we had in hand, and yet by degrees lead to the point, and brought him into difficulties and contradictions, that at last he grew ridiculously cautious, and would hardly answer me the most common question, without asking first, *"What do you intend to infer from that?"* However, it gave him so high an opinion of my abilities in the confuting way, that he seriously proposed my being his colleague in a project he had of setting up a new sect. He was to preach the doctrines, and I was to confound all opponents. When he came to explain with me upon the doctrines, I found several conundrums which I objected to, unless I might have my way a little to, and introduce some of mine.

Keimer wore his beard at full length, because somewhere in the Mosaic law it is said, *"Thou shalt not mar the corners of thy beard."* He likewise kept the Seventh day, Sabbath; and these two points were essentials with him. I disliked both; but agreed to admit them upon condition of his adopting the doctrine of using no animal food. "I doubt," said he, "my constitution will not bear that." I assured him it would, and that he would be the better for it. He was usually a great glutton, and I promised myself some diversion in half starving him. He agreed to try the practice, if I would keep him company. I did so, and we held it for three months. We had our victuals dressed, and brought to us regularly by a woman in the neighborhood, who had from me a list of forty dishes, to be prepared for us at different times, in all which there was neither fish, flesh, nor fowl, and the whim suited me the better at this time from the cheapness of it, not costing us above eighteenpence sterling each per week. I have since kept several Lents most strictly, leaving the common diet for that, and that for the common, abruptly, without the least inconvenience, so that I think there is little in the advice of making those changes by easy gradations. I went on pleasantly, but poor Keimer suffered grievously, tired of the project, longed for the flesh-pots of Egypt, and ordered a roast pig. He invited me and two women friends to dine with him; but, it being brought too soon upon table, he could not resist the temptation, and ate the whole before we came.

I had made some courtship during this time to Miss Read. I had a great a great respect and affecton for her, and had some reason to believe she had the same for me; but, as I was about to take a long voyage, and we were both very young, only a little above eighteen, it was thought most prudent by her mother to prevent our going too far at present, as a marriage, if it was to take place, would be more convenient after my return, when I should be, as I expected, set up in my business. Perhaps, too, she thought my expectations not so well founded as I imagined them to be.

My chief acquaintances at this time were Charles Osborne, Joseph Watson, and James Ralph, all lovers of reading. The two first were clerks to an eminent scrivener or conveyancer in the town, Charles Brogden; the other was clerk to a merchant. Watson was a pious, sensible young man, of great integrity; the others rather more lax in their principles of religion, particularly Ralph, who, as well as Collins, had been unsettled by me, for which they both made me suffer. Osborne was sensible, candid, frank; sincere and affectionate to his friends; but, in literary matters, too fond of criticizing. Ralph was ingenious, genteel in his manners, and extremely eloquent; I think I never knew a prettier talker. Both of them great admirers of poetry, and began to try their hands in little pieces. Many pleasant walks we four had together on Sundays into the woods, near Schuylkill, where we read to one another, and conferred on what we read.

Ralph was inclined to pursue the study of poetry, not doubting but he might become eminent in it, and make his fortune by it, alleging that the best poets must, when they first began to write, make as many faults as he did. Osborne dissuaded him, assured him he had no genius for poetry, and advised him to think of nothing beyond the business he was bred to; that, in the mercantile way, though he had no stock, he might, by his diligence and punctuality, recommend himself to employment as a factor, and in time acquire wherewith to trade on his own account. I approved the amusing one's self with poetry now and then, so far as to improve one's language, but no farther.

On this it was proposed that we should each of us, at our next meeting, produce a piece of our own composing, in order to improve by our mutual observations, criticisms, and corrections. As language and expression were what we had in view, we excluded all considerations of invention by agreeing that the task should be a version of the eighteenth Psalm, which describes the descent of a Deity. When the time of our meeting drew nigh, Ralph called on me first, and let me know his piece was ready. I told him I had been busy, and, having little inclination, had done nothing. He then showed me his piece for my opinion, and I much approved it, as it appeared to me to have great merit. "Now," says he, "Osborne never will allow the least merit in anything of mine, but makes 1000 criticisms out of mere envy. He is not so jealous of you; I wish, therefore, you would take this piece, and produce it as yours; I will pretend not to have had time, and so produce nothing. We shall then see what he will say to it." It was agreed, and I immediately transcribed it, that it might appear in my own hand.

We met; Watson's performance was read; there were some beauties in it, but many defects. Osborne's was read; it was much better; Ralph did it justice; remarked some faults, but applauded the beauties. He himself had nothing to produce. I was backward; seemed desirous of being excused; had not had sufficient time to correct, etc.; but no excuse could be admitted; produce I must. It was read and repeated; Watson and Osborne gave up the contest, and joined in applauding it. Ralph only made some criticisms, and proposed some amendments; but I defended my text. Osborne was against Ralph, and told him he was no better a critic than poet, so he dropped the argument. As they two went home together, Osborne expressed himself still more strongly in favor of what he thought my production; having restrained himself before, as he said, lest I should think it flattery. "But who would have imagined," said he, "that Franklin had been capable of such a performance; such painting, such force, such fire! He has even improved the original. In his common conversation he seems to have no choice of words; he hesitates and blunders; and yet, good God! how he writes!" When we next met, Ralph discovered the trick we had played him, and Osborne was a little laughed at.

This transaction fixed Ralph in his resolution of becoming a poet. I did all I could to dissuade him from it, but he continued scribbling verses till *Pope* cured him. He became, however, a pretty good prose writer. More of him hereafter. But, as I may not have occasion again to mention the other two, I shall just remark here, that Watson died in my arms a few years after, much lamented, being the best of our set. Osborne went to the West Indies, where he became an eminent lawyer and made money, but died young. He and I had made a serious agreement, that the one who happened first to die should, if possible, make a friendly visit to the other, and acquaint him how he found things in that separate state. But he never fulfilled his promise.

I should have mentioned before, that, in the autumn of the preceding year, I had formed most of my ingenious acquaintance into a club of mutual improvement, which we called the JUNTO; we met on Friday evenings. The rules that I drew up required that every member, in his turn, should produce one or more queries on any point of Morals, Politics, or Natural Philosophy, to be discussed by the company; and once in three months produce and read an essay of his own writing, on any subject he pleased. Our debates were to be under the direction of a president, and to be conducted in the sincere spirit of inquiry after truth, without fondness for dispute, or desire of victory; and, to prevent warmth, all expressions of positiveness in opinions, or direct contradiction were after some time made contraband, and prohibited under small pecuniary penalties.

George Webb, who had found a female friend that lent him wherewith to purchase his time of Keimer, now came to offer himself as a journeyman to us. We could not then employ him; but I foolishly let him know as a secret that I soon intended to begin a newspaper, and might then have work for him. My hopes of success, as I told him, were founded on this, that the then only newspaper, printed by Bradford, was a paltry thing, wretchedly managed, no way entertaining, and yet was profitable to him; I therefore thought a good paper would scarcely fail of good encouragement. I requested Webb not to mention it; but he told it to Keimer, who immediately, to be beforehand with me, published proposals for printing one himself, on which Webb was to be employed. I resented this; and, to counteract them, as I could not yet begin our paper, I wrote several pieces of entertainment for Bradford's paper, under the title of the BUSY BODY, which Breintnal continued some months. By this means the attention of the public was fixed on that paper, and Keimer's proposals, which we burlesqued and ridiculed, were disregarded. He began his paper, however, and, after carrying it on three quarters of a year, with at most only ninety subscribers, he offered it to me for a trifle; and I, having been ready some time to go on with it, took it in hand directly; and it proved in a few years extremely profitable to me.

Our first papers made a quite different appearance from any before in the province; a better type, and better printed; but some spirited remarks of my writing, on the dispute then going on between Governor Burnet and the Massachusetts Assembly, struck the principal people, occasioned the paper and the manager of it to be much talked of, and in a few weeks brought them all to be our subscribers.

Their example was followed by many, and our number went on growing continually. This was one of the first good effects of my having learnt a little to scribble; another was, that the leading men, seeing a newspaper now in the hands of one who could also handle a pen, thought it convenient to oblige and encourage me. Bradford still printed the votes, and laws, and other public business. He had printed an address of the House to the governor, in a coarse, blundering manner; we reprinted it elegantly and correctly, and sent one to every member. They were sensible of the difference: it strengthened the hands of our friends in the House, and they voted us their printers for the year ensuing.

About this time, our club meeting, not at a tavern, but in a little room of Mr. Grace's, set apart for that purpose, a proposition was made by me, that, since our books were often referred to in our disquisitions upon the queries, it might be convenient to us to have them altogether where we met, that upon occasion they might be consulted; and by thus clubbing our books to a common library, we should, while we liked to keep them together, have each of us the advantage of using the books of all the other members, which would be nearly as beneficial as if each owned the whole. It was liked and agreed to, and we filled one end of the room with such books as we could best spare. The number was not so great as we expected; and though they had been of great use, yet some inconveniences occurring for want of due care of them, the collection, after about a year, was separated, and each took his books home again.

And now I set on foot my first project of a public nature, that for a subscription library. I drew up the proposals, got them put into form by our great scrivener, Brockden, and, by the help of my friends in the Junto, procured fifty subscribers of forty shillings each to begin with, and ten shillings a year for fifty years, the term our company was to continue. We afterwards obtained a charter, the company being increased to one hundred: this was the mother of all the North American subscription libraries, now so numerous. It is become a great thing itself, and continually increasing. These libraries have improved the general conversation of the Americans, made the common tradesmen and farmers as intelligent as most gentlemen from other countries, and perhaps have contributed in some degree to the stand so generally made throughout the colonies in defense of their privileges.

I began now to turn my thoughts a little to public affairs, beginning, however, with small matters. The city watch was one of the first things that I conceived to want regulation. It was managed by the constables of the respective wards in turn; the constable warned a number of housekeepers to attend him for the night. Those who chose never to attend, paid him six shillings a year to be excused, which was supposed to be for hiring substitutes, but was, in reality, much more than was necessary for that purpose, and made the constableship a place of profit; and the constable, for a little drink, often got such ragamuffins about him as a watch, that respectable housekeepers did not choose to mix with. Walking the rounds, too, was often neglected, and most of the nights spent in tippling. I thereupon wrote a paper to be read in Junto, representing these irregularities, but insisting more particularly on the inequality of this six-shilling tax of the constables, respecting the circumstances of those who paid it, since a poor widow housekeeper, all whose property to be guarded by the watch did not perhaps exceed the value of fifty pounds, paid as much as the wealthiest merchant, who had thousands of pounds' worth of goods in his stores.

On the whole, I proposed as a more effectual watch, the hiring of proper men to serve constantly in that business; and as a more equitable way of supporting the charge, the levying a tax that should be proportioned to the property. This idea, being approved by the Junto, was communicated to the other clubs, but as arising in each of them; and though the plan was not immediately carried into execution, yet, by preparing the minds of people for the change, it paved the way for the law obtained a few years after, when the members of our clubs were grown into more influence.

About this time I wrote a paper (first to be read in Junto, but it was afterward published) on the different accidents and carelessnesses by which houses were set on fire, with cautions against them, and means proposed of avoiding them. This was much spoken of as a useful piece, and gave rise to a project, which soon followed it, of forming a company for the more ready extinguishing of fires, and mutual assistance in removing and securing of goods when in danger. Associates in this scheme were presently found, amounting to thirty. Our articles of agreement obliged every member to keep always in good order, and fit for use, a certain number of leather buckets, with strong bags and baskets (for packing and transporting of goods), which were to be brought to every fire; and we agreed to meet once a month and spend a social evening together, in discoursing and communicating such ideas as occurred to us upon the subject of fires, as might be useful in our conduct on such occasions.

The utility of this institution soon appeared, and many more desiring to be admitted than we thought convenient for one company, they were advised to form another, which was accordingly done; and this went on, one new company being formed after another, till they became so numerous as to include most of the inhabitants who were men of property; and now, at the time of my writing this, though upward of fifty years since its establishment, that which I first formed, called the Union Fire Company, still subsists and flourishes, though the first members are all deceased but myself and one, who is older by a year than I am. The small fines that have been paid by members for absence at the monthly meetings have been applied to the purchase of fire engines, ladders, fire-hooks, and other useful implements for each company, so that I question whether there is a city in the world better provided with the means of putting a stop to beginning conflagrations; and, in fact, since these institutions, the city has never lost by fire more than one or two houses at a time, and the flames have often been extinguished before the house in which they began has been half consumed.

CHAPTER VI

FRANKLIN'S PHILADELPHIA was a thriving town of opportunity for such gifted youths as came to make their way. Virginia,
however, with its great estates and tobacco plantations, had along
with its small farmers a well-defined aristocracy. To this class belonged William Byrd of Westover, the richest and best-educated
man of his colony, and the possessor of a tongue unique in its time
for its tartness. When in 1728, a few years after Franklin had
walked into the northern town of trade, Byrd went to assist in
running a boundary line between Virginia and North Carolina
through the Dismal Swamp, he traversed a raw frontier which it
was amusing for him to observe and describe. His account of this
experience, which is taken from his "History of the Dividing Line,"
reflects the sharp contrast between gentleman and settler in the
South.

MARCH 5th. The day being now come, on which we had agreed
to meet the commissioners of North Carolina, we embarked
very early, which we could the easier do, having no temptation to
stay where we were. We shaped our course along the south end of
Knot's island, there being no passage open on the north. Further
still to the southward of us, we discovered two smaller islands,
that go by the names of Bell's and Church's isles. We also saw a
small New England sloop riding in the sound, a little to the south
of our course. She had come in at the new inlet, as all other vessels
have done since the opening of it. This navigation is a little difficult,
and fit only for vessels that draw no more than ten feet of water.
The trade hither is engrossed by the saints of New England, who
carry off a great deal of tobacco, without troubling themselves with
paying that impertinent duty of a penny a pound.

About two o'clock in the afternoon we were joined by two of
the Carolina commissioners, attended by Mr. Swan, their surveyor. The other two were not quite so punctual, which was the
more unlucky for us, because there could be no sport till they
came. These gentlemen, it seems, had the Carolina commission in

their keeping, notwithstanding which, they could not forbear paying too much regard to a proverb—fashionable in their country—not to make more haste than good speed.

While we continued here, we were told that on the south shore, not far from the inlet, dwelt a marooner, that modestly called himself a hermit, though he forfeited that name by suffering a wanton female to cohabit with him. His habitation was a bower, covered with bark after the Indian fashion, which in that mild situation protected him pretty well from the weather. Like the ravens, he neither plowed nor sowed, but subsisted chiefly upon oysters, which his handmaid made a shift to gather from the adjacent rocks. Sometimes, too, for change of diet, he sent her to drive up the neighbor's cows, to moisten their mouths with a little milk. But as for raiment, he depended mostly upon his length of beard, and she upon her length of hair, part of which she brought decently forward, and the rest dangled behind quite down to her rump, like one of Herodotus' East Indian pigmies. Thus did these wretches live in a dirty state of nature, and were mere Adamites, innocence only excepted.

10th. The sabbath happened very opportunely to give some ease to our jaded people, who rested religiously from every work, but that of cooking the kettle. We observed very few cornfields in our walks, and those very small, which seemed the stranger to us, because we could see no other tokens of husbandry or improvement. But, upon further inquiry, we were given to understand people only made corn for themselves and not for their stocks, which know very well how to get their own living. Both cattle and hogs ramble into the neighboring marshes and swamps, where they maintain themselves the whole winter long, and are not fetched home till the spring. Thus these indolent wretches, during one-half of the year, lose the advantage of the milk of their cattle, as well as their dung, and many of the poor creatures perish in the mire, into the bargain, by this ill-management. Some, who pique themselves more upon industry than their neighbors, will, now and then, in compliment to their cattle, cut down a tree whose limbs are loaded with the moss aforementioned. The trouble would be too great to climb the tree in order to gather this provender, but the shortest way (which in this country is always counted the best) is to fell it, just like the lazy Indians, who do the same by such trees as bear fruit, and so make one harvest for all. By this bad husbandry milk is so scarce, in the winter season, that were a big-bellied woman to long for it, she would lose her longing. And, in truth, I believe this is often the case, and at the same time a

very good reason why so many people in this province are marked
with a custard complexion.

The only business here is raising of hogs, which is managed
with the least trouble, and affords the diet they are most fond of.
The truth of it is, the inhabitants of North Carolina devour so
much swine's flesh, that it fills them full of gross humors. For
want too of a constant supply of salt, they are commonly obliged
to eat it fresh, and that begets the highest taint of scurvy. Thus,
whenever a severe cold happens to constitutions thus vitiated, it is
apt to improve into the yaws, called there very justly the country
distemper. This has all the symptoms of *syphilis,* with this aggra-
vation, that no preparation of mercury will touch it. First it seizes
the throat, next the palate, and lastly shows its spite to the poor
nose, of which it is apt in a small time treacherously to undermine
the foundation. This calamity is so common and familiar here, that
it ceases to be a scandal, and in the disputes that happen about
beauty, the noses have in some companies much ado to carry it.
Nay, it is said that once, after three good pork years, a motion
had like to have been made in the house of burgesses, that a man
with a nose should be incapable of holding any place of profit in
the province; which extraordinary motion could never have been
intended without some hopes of a majority.

Thus, considering the foul and pernicious effects of eating swine's
flesh in a hot country, it was wisely forbidden and made an
abomination to the Jews, who lived much in the same latitude
with Carolina.

11th. We ordered the surveyors early to their business, who
were blessed with pretty dry grounds for three miles together.
But they paid dear for it in the next two, consisting of one continued frightful pocoson, which no creatures but those of the
amphibious kind ever had ventured into before. This filthy quagmire did in earnest put the men's courage to a trial, and though I
cannot say it made them lose their patience, yet they lost their
humor for joking. They kept their gravity like so many Spaniards,
so that a man might then have taken his opportunity to plunge up
to the chin, without danger of being laughed at. However, this
unusual composure of countenance could not fairly be called complaining. Their day's work ended at the mouth of Northern's creek,
which empties itself into Northwest river; though we chose to
quarter a little higher up the river, near Mossy point. This we did
for the convenience of an old house to shelter our persons and
baggage from the rain, which threatened us hard. We judged the
thing right, for there fell a heavy shower in the night, that drove

the most hardy of us into the house. Though, indeed, our case was not much mended by retreating thither, because that tenement having not long before been used as a pork store, the moisture of the air dissolved the salt that lay scattered on the floor, and made it as wet within doors as without. However, the swamps and marshes we were lately accustomed to had made such beavers and otters of us that nobody caught the least cold. We had encamped so early, that we found time in the evening to walk near half a mile into the woods. There we came upon a family of mulattoes that called themselves free, though by the shyness of the master of the house, who took care to keep least in sight, their freedom seemed a little doubtful. It is certain many slaves shelter themselves in this obscure part of the world, nor will any of their righteous neighbors discover them. On the contrary, they find their account in settling such fugitives on some out-of-the-way corner of their land, to raise stocks for a mean and inconsiderable share, well knowing their condition makes it necessary for them to submit to any terms. Nor were these worthy borderers content to shelter runaway slaves, but debtors and criminals have often met with the like indulgence. But if the government of North Carolina has encouraged this unneighborly policy in order to increase their people, it is no more than what ancient Rome did before them, which was made a city of refuge for all debtors and fugitives, and from that wretched beginning grew up in time to be mistress of a great part of the world. And, considering how fortune delights in bringing great things out of small, who knows but Carolina may, one time or other, come to be the seat of some other great empire?

14th. Before nine of the clock this morning, the provisions, bedding and other necessaries, were made up into packs for the men to carry on their shoulders into the Dismal. They were victualed for eight days at full allowance, nobody doubting but that would be abundantly sufficient to carry them through that inhospitable place; nor indeed was it possible for the poor fellows to stagger under more. As it was, their loads weighed from 60 to 70 pounds, in just proportion to the strength of those who were to bear them. It would have been unconscionable to have saddled them with burthens heavier than that, when they were to lug them through a filthy bog, which was hardly practicable with no burthen at all. Besides this luggage at their backs, they were obliged to measure the distance, mark the trees, and clear the way for the surveyors every step they went. It was really a pleasure to see with how much cheerfulness they undertook, and with how much spirit they went through all this drudgery. For their greater safety, the commissioners took care to furnish them with Peruvian bark, rhubarb and hipocoacanah, in case they might happen, in that wet journey, to be taken with fevers or fluxes. Although there was no need of example to inflame persons already so cheerful, yet to enter the people with the better grace, the author and two more of the commissioners accompanied them half a mile into the Dismal. The skirts of it were thinly planted with dwarf reeds and gall bushes, but when we got into the Dismal itself, we found the reeds grew there much taller and closer, and, to mend the matter, were so interlaced with bamboo-briers, that there was no scuffling through them without the help of pioneers. At the same time, we found the ground moist and trembling under our feet like a quagmire, insomuch that it was an easy matter to run a ten-foot pole up to the head in it, without exerting any uncommon strength to do it. Two of the men, whose burthens were the least cumbersome, had orders to march before, with their tomahawks, and clear the way in order to make an opening for the surveyors. By their assistance we made a shift to push the line half a mile in three hours, and then reached a small piece of firm land, about 100 yards wide, standing up above the rest like an island. Here the people were glad to lay down their loads and take a little refreshment, while the happy man, whose lot it was to carry the jug of rum, began already, like Æsop's bread-carriers, to find it grew a good deal lighter.

In the meantime the three commissioners returned out of the Dismal the same way they went in, and, having joined their brethren, proceeded that night as far as Mr. Wilson's. This worthy person lives within sight of the Dismal, in the skirts whereof his stock range and maintain themselves all the winter, and yet he knew as little of it as he did of Terra Australis Incognita. He told us a Canterbury tale of a North Briton, whose curiosity spurred him a long way into this great desert, as he called it, near twenty years ago, but he having no compass, nor seeing the sun for several days together, wandered about till he was almost famished; but at last he bethought himself of a secret his countrymen make use of to pilot themselves in a dark day. He took a fat louse out of his collar, and exposed it to the open day on a piece of white paper, which he brought along with him for his journal. The poor insect, having no eyelids, turned himself about till he found the darkest part of the heavens, and so made the best of his way towards the north. By this direction he steered himself safe out, and gave such a frightful account of the monsters he saw, and the distresses he underwent, that no mortal since has been hardy enough to go upon the like dangerous discovery.

At the end of 18 miles we reached Timothy Ivy's plantation, where we pitched our tent for the first time, and were furnished with everything the place afforded. We perceived the happy effects of industry in this family, in which every one looked tidy and clean, and carried in their countenances the cheerful marks of plenty. We saw no drones there, which are but too common, alas, in that part of the world. Though, in truth, the distemper of laziness seizes the men oftener much than the women. These last spin, weave and knit, all with their own hands, while their husbands, depending on the bounty of the climate, are slothful in everything but getting of children, and in that only instance make themselves useful members of an infant colony.

Since the surveyors had entered the Dismal, they had laid eyes on no living creature: neither bird nor beast, insect nor reptile came in view. Doubtless, the eternal shade that broods over this mighty bog, and hinders the sunbeams from blessing the ground, makes it an uncomfortable habitation for anything that has life. Not so much as a Zealand frog could endure so aguish a situation. It had one beauty, however, that delighted the eye, though at the expense of all the other senses: the moisture of the soil preserves a continual verdure, and makes every plant an evergreen, but at the same time the foul damps ascend without ceasing, corrupt the air, and render it unfit for respiration. Not even a turkey buzzard will venture to fly over it, no more than the Italian vultures will over the filthy lake Avernus, or the birds in the Holy Land, over the Salt sea, where Sodom and Gomorrah formerly stood.

In these sad circumstances, the kindest thing we could do for our suffering friends was to give them a place in the Litany. Our chaplain, for his part, did his office, and rubbed us up with a seasonable sermon. This was quite a new thing to our brethren of North Carolina, who live in a climate where no clergyman can breathe, any more than spiders in Ireland.

For want of men in holy orders, both the members of the council and justices of the peace are empowered by the laws of that country to marry all those who will not take one another's word; but for the ceremony of christening their children, they trust that to chance. If a parson come in their way, they will crave a cast of his office, as they call it, else they are content their offspring should remain as arrant pagans as themselves. They account it among their greatest advantages that they are not priest-ridden, not remembering that the clergy is rarely guilty of bestriding such as have the misfortune to be poor. One thing may be said for the inhabitants of that province, that they are not troubled with any religious fumes, and have the least superstition of any people living. They do not know Sunday from any other day, any more than Robinson Crusoe did, which would give them a great advantage were they given to be industrious. But they keep so many sabbaths every week, that their disregard of the seventh day has no manner of cruelty in it, either to servants or cattle.

We ordered several men to patrol on the edge of the Dismal, both towards the north and towards the south, and to fire guns at proper distances. This they performed very punctually, but could hear nothing in return, nor gain any sort of intelligence. In the meantime whole flocks of women and children flew hither to stare at us, with as much curiosity as if we had lately landed from Bantam or Morocco. Some borderers, too, had a great mind to know where the line would come out, being for the most part apprehensive lest their lands should be taken into Virginia. In that case they must have submitted to some sort of order and government; whereas, in North Carolina, every one does what seems best in his own eyes. There were some good women that brought their children to be baptized, but brought no capons along with them to make the solemnity cheerful. In the meantime it was strange that none came to be married in such a multitude, if it had only been for the novelty of having their hands joined by one in holy orders. Yet so it was, that though our chaplain christened above a hundred, he did not marry so much as one couple during the whole expedition. But marriage is reckoned a lay contract in Carolina, as I said before, and a country justice can tie the fatal knot there, as fast as an archbishop. None of our visitors could, however, tell us any news of the surveyors, nor indeed was it possible any of them should at that time, they being still laboring in the midst of the Dismal. It seems they were able to carry the link this day no further than one mile and sixty-one poles, and that whole distance was through a miry cedar bog, where the ground trembled under their feet most frightfully. In many places too their passage was retarded by a great number of fallen trees, that lay horsing upon one another. Though many circumstances concurred to make this an unwholesome situation, yet the poor men had no time to be sick, nor can one conceive a more calamitous case than it would have been to be laid up in that uncomfortable quagmire. Never were patients more tractable, or willing to take physic, than these honest fellows; but it was from a dread of laying their bones in a bog that would soon spew them up again. That consideration also put them upon more caution about their lodging. They first covered the ground with square pieces of cypress bark, which now, in the spring, they could easily slip off the tree for that purpose. On this they spread their bedding; but unhappily the weight and warmth of their bodies made the water rise up betwixt the joints of the bark, to their great inconvenience. Thus they lay not only moist, but also exceedingly cold, because their fires were continually going out. For no sooner was the trash upon the surface burnt away, but immediately the fire was extinguished by the moisture of the soil, insomuch that it was great part of the sentinel's business to rekindle it again in a fresh place, every quarter of an hour. Nor could they indeed do their duty better, because cold was the only enemy they had to guard against in a miserable morass, where nothing can inhabit.

20th. We could get no tidings yet of our brave adventurers, notwithstanding we despatched men to the likeliest stations to inquire after them. They were still scuffling in the mire, and could not possibly forward the line this whole day more than one mile and sixty-four chains. Every step of this day's work was through a cedar bog, where the trees were somewhat smaller and grew more into a thicket. It was now a great misfortune to the men to find their provisions grow less as their labor grew greater; they were all forced to come to short allowance, and consequently to work hard without filling their bellies. Though this was very severe upon English stomachs, yet the people were so far from being discomfited at it, that they still kept up their good humor, and merrily told a young fellow in the company, who looked very plump and wholesome, that he must expect to go first to pot, if matters should come to extremity. This was only said by way of jest, yet it made him thoughtful in earnest. However, for the present he returned them a very civil answer, letting them know that, dead or alive, he should be glad to be useful to such worthy good friends. But, after all, this humorous saying had one very good effect, for that younker, who before was a little inclined by his constitution to be lazy, grew on a sudden extremely industrious, that so there might be less occasion to carbonade him for the good of his fellow travelers.

21st. The surveyors and their attendants began now in good earnest to be alarmed with apprehensions of famine, nor could they forbear looking with some sort of appetite upon a dog which had been the faithful companion of their travels. Their provisions were now near exhausted. They had this morning made the last distribution, that so each might husband his small pittance as he pleased. Now it was that the fresh colored young man began to tremble every joint of him, having dreamed, the night before, that the Indians were about to barbecue him over live coals. The prospect of famine determined the people, at last, with one consent, to abandon the line for the present, which advanced but slowly, and make the best of their way to firm land. Accordingly they set off very early, and, by the help of the compass which they carried along with them, steered a direct westwardly course. They marched from morning till night, and computed their journey to amount to about four miles, which was a great way, considering the difficulties of the ground. It was all along a cedar swamp, so dirty and perplexed, that if they had not traveled for their lives, they could not have reached so far. On their way they espied a turkey buzzard, that flew prodigiously high to get above the noisome exhalations that ascend from that filthy place. This they were willing to understand as a good omen, according to the superstition of the ancients, who had great faith in the flight of vultures. However, after all this tedious journey, they could yet discover no end of their toil, which made them very pensive, especially after they had eaten the last morsel of their provisions. But to their unspeakable comfort, when all was hushed in the evening, they heard the cattle low, and the dogs bark, very distinctly, which, to men in that distress, was more delightful music than Faustina or Farinelli could have made. In the meantime the commissioners could get no news of them from any of their visitors, who assembled from every point of the compass.

However long we might think the time, yet we were cautious of showing our uneasiness, for fear of mortifying our landlord. He had done his best for us, and therefore we were unwilling he should think us dissatisfied with our entertainment. In the midst of our concern, we were most agreeably surprised, just after dinner, with the news that the Dismalites were all safe. These blessed tidings were brought to us by Mr. Swan, the Carolina surveyor, who came to us in a very tattered condition. After very short salutations, we got about him as if he had been a Hottentot, and began to inquire into his adventures. He gave us a detail of their uncomfortable voyage through the Dismal, and told us, particularly, they had pursued their journey early that morning, encouraged by the good omen of seeing the crows fly over their heads; that, after an hour's march over very rotten ground, they, on a sudden, began to find themselves among tall pines, that grew in the water, which in many places was knee deep. This pine swamp, into which that of Coropeak drained itself, extended near a mile in breadth; and though it was exceedingly wet, yet it was much harder at bottom than the rest of the swamp; that about ten in the morning they recovered firm land, which they embraced with as much pleasure as shipwrecked wretches do the shore. After these honest adventurers had congratulated each other's deliverance, their first inquiry was for a good house, where they might satisfy the importunity of their stomachs. Their good genius directed them to Mr. Brinkley's, who dwells a little to the southward of the line. This man began immediately to be very inquisitive, but they declared they had no spirits to answer questions, till after dinner. "But pray, gentlemen," said he, "answer me one question at least: what shall we get for your dinner?" To which they replied, "No matter what, so it be but enough." He kindly supplied their wants as soon as possible, and by the strength of that refreshment they made a shift to come to us in the evening, to tell their own story. They all looked very thin, and as ragged as the Gibeonite ambassadors did in the days of yore.

Our surveyors told us they had measured ten miles in the Dismal, and computed the distance they had marched since to amount to about five more, so they made the whole breadth to be fifteen miles in all.

Surely there is no place in the world where the inhabitants live with less labor than in North Carolina. It approaches nearer to the description of Lubberland than any other, by the great felicity of the climate, the easiness of raising provisions, and the slothfulness of the people. Indian corn is of so great increase, that a little pains will subsist a very large family with bread, and then they may have meat without any pains at all, by the help of the low grounds, and the great variety of mast that grows on the high land. The men, for their parts, just like the Indians, impose all the work upon the poor women. They make their wives rise out of their beds early in the morning, at the same time that they lie and snore, till the sun has risen one-third of his course, and dispersed all the unwholesome damps. Then, after stretching and yawning for half an hour, they light their pipes, and, under the protection of a cloud of smoke, venture out into the open air; though, if it happens to be never so little cold, they quickly return shivering into the chimney corner. When the weather is mild, they stand leaning with both their arms upon the cornfield fence, and gravely consider whether they had best go and take a small heat at the hoe: but generally find reasons to put it off till another time. Thus they loiter away their lives, like Solomon's sluggard, with their arms across, and at the winding up of the year scarcely have bread to eat. To speak the truth, it is a thorough aversion to labor that makes people file off to North Carolina, where plenty and a warm sun confirm them in their disposition to laziness for their whole lives.

26th. Since we were like to be confined to this place, till the people returned out of the Dismal, it was agreed that our chaplain might safely take a turn to Edenton, to preach the Gospel to the infidels there, and christen their children. He was accompanied thither by Mr. Little, one of the Carolina commissioners, who, to show his regard for the church, offered to treat him on the road with a fricassee of rum. They fried half a dozen rashers of very fat bacon in a pint of rum, both which being dished up together, served the company at once both for meat and drink. Most of the rum they get in this country comes from New England, and is so bad and unwholesome, that it is not improperly called "kill-devil." It is distilled there from foreign molasses, which, if skillfully managed, yields near gallon for gallon. Their molasses comes from the same country, and has the name of "long sugar" in Carolina, I suppose from the ropiness of it, and serves all the purposes of sugar, both in their eating and drinking. When they entertain their friends bountifully, they fail not to set before them a capacious bowl of Bombo, so called from the admiral of that name. This is a compound of rum and water in equal parts, made palatable with the said long sugar. As good humor begins to flow, and the bowl to ebb, they take care to replenish it with sheer rum, of which there always is a reserve under the table. But such generous doings happen only when that balsam of life is plenty.

7th. The next day being Sunday, we ordered notice to be sent to all the neighborhood that there would be a sermon at this place, and an opportunity of christening their children. But the likelihood of rain got the better of their devotion, and what, perhaps, might still be a stronger motive of their curiosity. In the morning we despatched a runner to the Nottoway town, to let the Indians know we intended them a visit that evening, and our honest landlord was so kind as to be our pilot thither, being about four miles from his house. Accordingly in the afternoon we marched in good order to the town, where the female scouts, stationed on an eminence for that purpose, had no sooner spied us, but they gave notice of our approach to their fellow citizens by continual whoops and cries, which could not possibly have been more dismal at the sight of their most implacable enemies. This signal assembled all their great men, who received us in a body, and conducted us into the fort.

The women wear necklaces and bracelets of these precious materials, when they have a mind to appear lovely. Though their complexions be a little sad-colored, yet their shapes are very straight and well proportioned. Their faces are seldom handsome, yet they have an air of innocence and bashfulness, that with a little less dirt would not fail to make them desirable. Such charms might have had their full effect upon men who had been so long deprived of female conversation, but that the whole winter's soil was so crusted on the skins of those dark angels, that it required a very strong appetite to approach them. The bear's oil, with which they anoint their persons all over, makes their skins soft, and at the same time protects them from every species of vermin that use to be troublesome to other uncleanly people. We were unluckily so many, that they could not well make us the compliment of bed-fellows, according to the Indian rules of hospitality, though a grave matron whispered one of the commissioners very civilly in the ear, that if her daughter had been but one year older, she should have been at his devotion.

It is by no means a loss of reputation among the Indians, for damsels that are single to have intrigues with the men; on the contrary, they account it an argument of superior merit to be liked by a great number of gallants. However, like the ladies that game, they are a little mercenary in their amours, and seldom bestow their favors out of stark love and kindness. But after these women have once appropriated their charms by marriage, they are from thenceforth faithful to their vows, and will hardly ever be tempted by an agreeable gallant, or be provoked by a brutal or even by a careless husband to go astray. The little work that is done among the Indians is done by the poor women, while the men are quite idle, or at most employed only in the gentlemanly diversions of hunting and fishing. In this, as well as in their wars, they use nothing but firearms, which they purchase of the English for skins. Bows and arrows are grown into disuse, except only amongst their boys. Nor is it ill policy, but on the contrary very prudent, thus to furnish the Indians with firearms, because it makes them depend entirely upon the English, not only for their trade, but even for their subsistence. Besides, they were really able to do more mischief, while they made use of arrows, of which they would let silently fly several in a minute with wonderful dexterity, whereas now they hardly ever discharge their firelocks more than once, which they insidiously do from behind a tree, and then retire as nimbly as the Dutch horse used to do now and then formerly in Flanders. We put the Indians to no expense, but only of a little corn for our horses, for which in gratitude we cheered their hearts with what rum we had left, which they love better than they do their wives and children. Though these Indians dwell among the English, and see in what plenty a little industry enables them to live, yet they choose to continue in their stupid idleness, and to suffer all the inconveniences of dirt, cold and want, rather than to disturb their heads with care, or defile their hands with labor.

CHAPTER VII

OCCUPATIONS MULTIPLIED both north and south, and as the eighteenth century brought the English colonies nearer to their maturity no occupation seemed more interesting than whale-fishing. Off the New England coast the cod had long been taken in great numbers; off the island of Nantucket whales abounded, and an impressive race of men grew up to hunt them in hazardous boats. Then it became necessary to cruise farther for the creatures, until eventually the life of a Nantucket whaling-man was not to be confined to any single sea. Hector St.-John de Crèvecoeur, an "American Farmer" who had come from France to enjoy the liberties and the philosophical pleasures which the New World was supposed by so many Europeans to afford, traveled among other places to the whale fisheries of Nantucket and Martha's Vineyard, and wrote an enthusiastic account of the unspoiled people whom he seemed to see there.

THE first proprietors of this island,* or rather the first founders of this town, began their careers of industry with a single whaleboat, with which they went to fish for cod; the small distance from their shores at which they caught it, enabled them soon to increase their business, and those early successes first led them to conceive that they might likewise catch the whales, which hitherto sported undisturbed on their banks. After many trials and several miscarriages, they succeeded; thus they proceeded, step by step; the profits of one successful enterprise helped them to purchase and prepare better materials for a more extensive one: as these were attended with little costs, their profits grew greater. The south sides of the island from east to west were divided into four equal parts, and each part was assigned to a company of six, which though thus separated, still carried on their business in common. In the middle of this distance, they erected a mast, provided with a sufficient number of rounds, and near it they built a temporary hut,

* Nantucket.

where five of the associates lived, whilst the sixth from his high station carefully looked toward the sea, in order to observe the spouting of the whales. As soon as any were discovered, the sentinel descended, the whale-boat was launched, and the company went forth in quest of their game. It may appear strange to you, that so slender a vessel as an *American whale-boat*, containing six diminutive beings, should dare to pursue and to attack, in its native element, the largest and strongest fish that nature has created. Yet by the exertions of an admirable dexterity, improved by a long practice, in which these people are become superior to any other whalemen; by knowing the temper of the whale after her first movement, and by many other useful observations; they seldom failed to harpoon it, and to bring the huge leviathan on the shores. Thus they went on until the profits they made enabled them to purchase larger vessels, and to pursue them farther, when the whales quitted their coasts; those who failed in their enterprises, returned to the cod fisheries, which had been their first school, and their first resource; they even began to visit the banks of Cape Breton, the isle of Sable, and all the other fishing places with which this coast of America abounds. By degrees they went a-whaling to Newfoundland, to the Gulf of St. Lawrence, to the Straits of Belleisle, the coast of Labrador, Davis's Straits, even to Cape Desolation, in 70° of latitude; where the Danes carry on some fisheries in spite of the perpetual severities of the inhospitable climate. In process of time they visited the western islands, the latitude of 34° famous for that fish, the Brazils, the coast of Guinea. Would you believe that they have already gone to the Falkland Islands, and that I have heard several of them talk of going to the South Sea! Their confidence is so great, and their knowledge of this branch of business so superior to that of any other people, that they have acquired a monopoly of this commodity. Such were their feeble beginnings, such the infancy and the progress of their maritime schemes; such is now the degree of boldness and activity to which they are arrived in their manhood. After their examples several companies have been formed in many of our capitals, where every necessary article of provisions, implements, and timber are to be found. But the industry exerted by the people of Nantucket hath hitherto enabled them to rival all their competitors; consequently this is the greatest mart for oil, whalebone, and spermaceti on the continent. It does not follow, however, that they are always successful, this would be an extraordinary field indeed, where the crops should never fail; many voyages do not repay the original cost of fitting out: they bear such misfortunes like true merchants, and as they never venture their all like gamesters, they try their fortunes again; the latter hope to win by chance alone, the former by industry, well judged speculation, and some hazard. I was there when Mr. —— had missed one of his vessels; she had been given over for lost by everybody, but happily arrived before I came away, after an absence of thirteen months. She had met with a variety of disappointments on the station she was ordered to, and rather than return empty, the people steered for the coast of Guinea, where they fortunately fell in with several whales, and brought home upward of 600 barrels of oil, beside bone. Those returns are sometimes disposed of in the towns on the continent, where they are exchanged for such commodities as are wanted; but they are most commonly sent to England, where they always sell for cash. When this is intended, a vessel larger than the rest is fitted out to be filled with oil on the spot where it is found and made, and thence she sails immediately for London.

This island * therefore, like Nantucket, is become a great nursery which supplies with pilots and seamen the numerous coasters with which this extended part of America abounds. Go where you will from Nova Scotia to the Mississippi, you will find almost everywhere some natives of these two islands employed in seafaring occupations. Their climate is so favorable to population, that marriage is the object of every man's earliest wish; and it is a blessing so easily obtained, that great numbers are obliged to quit their native land and go to some other countries in quest of subsistence. Here are to be found the most expert pilots, either for the great bay, their sound, Nantucket shoals, or the different ports in their neighborhood. In stormy weather they are always at sea, looking out for vessels, which they board with singular dexterity, and hardly ever fail to bring safe to their intended harbor. Gay-Head, the western point of this island, abounds with a variety of ochres of different colors, with which the inhabitants paint their houses.

The vessels most proper for whale fishing are brigs of about 150 tons burthen, particularly when they are intended for distant latitudes; they always man them with thirteen hands, in order that they may row two whale-boats; the crews of which must necessarily consist of six, four at the oars, one standing on the bows with the harpoon, and the other at the helm. It is also necessary that there should be two of these boats, that if one should be destroyed in attacking the whale, the other, which is never engaged at the same time, may be ready to save the hands. Five of the thir-

* Martha's Vineyard.

teen are always Indians; the last of the complement remains on board to steer the vessel during the action. They have no wages; each draws a certain established share in partnership with the proprietor of the vessel; by which economy they are all proportionately concerned in the success of the enterprise, and all equally alert and vigilant. None of these whalemen ever exceed the age of forty: they look on those who are past that period not to be possessed of all that vigor and agility which so adventurous a business requires. Indeed if you attentively consider the immense disproportion between the object assailed and the assailants; if you think on the diminutive size and weakness of their frail vehicle; if you recollect the treachery of the element on which this scene is transacted; the sudden and unforeseen accidents of winds, etc., you will readily acknowledge that it must require the most consummate exertion of all the strength, agility and judgment of which the bodies and minds of men are capable, to undertake these adventurous encounters.

As soon as they arrive in those latitudes where they expect to meet with whales, a man is sent up to the mast head; if he sees one, he immediately cries out AWAITE PAWANA, *here is a whale;* they all remain still and silent until he repeats PAWANA, *a whale,* when in less than six minutes the two boats are launched, filled with every implement necessary for the attack. They row toward the whale with astonishing velocity; and as the Indians early became their fellow-laborers in this new warfare, you can easily conceive how the Nattick expressions became familiar on board the whaleboats. Formerly it often happened that whale vessels were manned with none but Indians and the master; recollect also that the Nantucket people understand the Nattick, and that there are always five of these people on board. There are various ways of approaching the whale, according to their peculiar species; and this previous knowledge is of the utmost consequence. When these boats are arrived at a reasonable distance, one of them rests on its oars and stands off, as a witness of the approaching engagement; near the bows of the other the harpooner stands up, and on him principally depends the success of the enterprise. He wears a jacket closely buttoned, and round his head a handkerchief tightly bound: in his hands he holds the dreadful weapon, made of the best steel, marked sometimes with the name of their town, and sometimes with that of their vessels; to the shaft of which the end of a cord of due length, coiled up with the utmost care in the middle of the boat, is firmly tied; the other end is fastened to the bottom of the boat. Thus prepared they row in profound silence, leaving the whole conduct of the enterprise to the harpooner and to the steersman, attentively following their directions. When the former judges himself to be near enough to the whale, that is, at the distance of about fifteen feet, he bids them stop; perhaps she has a calf, whose safety attracts all the attention of the dam, which is a favorable circumstance; perhaps she is of a dangerous species, and it is safest to retire, though their ardor will seldom permit them; perhaps she is asleep, in that case he balances high the harpoon, trying in this important moment to collect all the energy of which he is capable. He launches it forth—she is struck: from her first movements they judge of her temper, as well as of their future success. Sometimes in the immediate impulse of rage, she will attack the boat and demolish it with one stroke of her tail; in an instant the frail vehicle disappears and the assailants are immersed in the dreadful element. Were the whale armed with the jaws of a shark, and as voracious, they never would return home to amuse their listening wives with the interesting tale of the adventure. At other times she will dive and disappear from human sight; and everything must give way to her velocity, or else all is lost. Sometimes she will swim away as if untouched, and draw the cord with such swiftness that it will set the edge of the boat on fire by the friction. If she rises before she has run out the whole length, she is looked upon as a sure prey. The blood she has lost in her flight weakens her so much, that if she sinks again, it is but for a short time; the boat follows her course with almost equal speed. She soon reappears; tired at last with convulsing the element, which she tinges with her blood, she dies, and floats on the surface. At other times it may happen that she is not dangerously wounded, though she carries the harpoon fast in her body; when she will alternately dive and rise, and swim on with unabated vigor. She then soon reaches beyond the length of the cord, and carries the boat along with amazing velocity: this sudden impediment sometimes will retard her speed, at other times it only serves to rouse her anger, and to accelerate her progress. The harpooner, with the ax in his hands, stands ready. When he observes that the bows of the boat are greatly pulled down by the diving whale, and that it begins to sink deep and to take much water, he brings the ax almost in contact with the cord; he pauses, still flattering himself that she will relax; but the moment grows critical, unavoidable danger approaches: sometimes men more intent on gain than on the preservation of their lives will run great risks; and it is wonderful how far these people have carried their daring courage at this awful moment! But it is vain to hope, their lives must be saved, the cord is cut, the boat rises again. If after thus getting loose, she re-appears, they will attack and wound her a second time. She soon dies, and when dead she is towed alongside of their vessel, where she is fastened.

The next operation is to cut with axes and spades, every part of her body which yields oil; the kettles are set a boiling, they fill their barrels as fast as it is made; but as this operation is much slower than that of *cutting up*, they fill the hold of their ship with those fragments, lest a storm should arise and oblige them to abandon their prize. It is astonishing what a quantity of oil some of these fish will yield, and what profit it affords to those who are fortunate enough to overtake them. The river St. Lawrence whale, which is the only one I am well acquainted with, is seventy-five feet long, sixteen deep, twelve in the length of its bone, which commonly weighs 3000 pounds, twenty in the breadth of their tails and pro-duces 180 barrels of oil: I once saw 16 boiled out of the tongue only. After having once vanquished this leviathan, there are two enemies to be dreaded beside the wind; the first of which is the shark: that fierce voracious fish, to which nature has given such dreadful of-fensive weapons, often comes alongside, and in spite of the people's endeavors, will share with them their prey; at night particularly. They are very mischievous, but the second enemy is much more terrible and irresistible; it is the killer, sometimes called the thrasher, a species of whales about thirty feet long. They are possessed of such a degree of agility and fierceness, as often to at-tack the largest spermaceti whales, and not seldom to rob the fisher-men of they prey; nor is there any means of defense against so potent an adversary. When all their barrels are full, for everything is done at sea, or when their limited time is expired and their stores almost expended, they return home, freighted with their valuable cargo; unless they have put it on board a vessel for the European market. Such are, as briefly as I can relate them, the different branches of the economy practiced by these bold navigators, and the method with which they go such distances from their island to catch this huge game.

The following are the names and principal characteristics of the various species of whales known to these people:

The St. Lawrence whale, just described.

The disko, or Greenland ditto.

The right whale, or seven feet bone, common on the coasts of this country, about sixty feet long.

The spermaceti whale, found all over the world, and of all sizes; the longest are sixty feet, and yield about 100 barrels of oil.

The hump-backs, on the coast of Newfoundland, from forty to seventy feet in length.

The finn-back, an American whale, never killed, as being too swift.

The sulphur-bottom, river St. Lawrence, ninety feet long; they are but seldom killed, as being extremely swift.

The grampus, thirty feet long, never killed on the same account.

The killer or thrasher, about thirty feet; they often kill the other whales with which they are at perpetual war.

The black fish whale, twenty feet, yields from eight to ten barrels.

The porpoise, weighing about 160 pounds.

In 1769 they fitted out 125 whalemen; the first fifty that returned brought with them 11,000 barrels of oil. In 1770 they fitted out 135 vessels for the fisheries, at thirteen hands each; four West-Indiamen, twelve hands; twenty-five wood vessels, four hands; eighteen coasters, five hands; fifteen London traders, eleven hands. All these amount to 2158 hands, employed in 197 vessels. Trace their progressive steps between the possession of a few whale-boats, and that of such a fleet!

The moral conduct, prejudices, and customs of a people who live two-thirds of their time at sea, must naturally be very different from those of their neighbors, who live by cultivating the earth. That long abstemiousness to which the former are exposed, the breathing of saline air, the frequent repetitions of danger, the boldness acquired in surmounting them, the very impulse of the winds, to which they are exposed; all these, one would imagine must lead them, when on shore, to no small desire of inebriation, and a more eager pursuit of those pleasures, of which they have been so long deprived, and which they must soon forego. There are many appetites that may be gratified on shore, even by the poorest man, but which must remain unsatisfied at sea. Yet notwithstanding the powerful effects of all these causes, I observed here, at the return of their fleets, no material irregularities; no tumultuous drinking assemblies: whereas in our continental towns, the thoughtless seaman indulges himself in the coarsest pleasures; and vainly thinking that a week of debauchery can compensate for months of abstinence, foolishly lavishes in a few days of intoxication, the fruits of half a year's labor. On the contrary all was peace here, and a general decency prevailed throughout; the reason I believe is, that almost everybody here is married, for they get wives very young; and the pleasure of returning to their families absorbs every other desire. The motives that lead them to the sea are very different from those of most other sea-faring men; it is neither idleness nor profligacy that sends them to that element; it is a settled plan of life, a well founded hope of earning a livelihood; it is because their soil is bad, that they are early initiated to this profession, and were they to stay at home, what could they do? The sea therefore becomes to them a kind of patrimony; they go to whaling with as much pleasure and tranquil indifference, with as strong an expectation of success, as a landsman undertakes to clear a piece of swamp. The first is obliged to advance his time, and labor, to procure oil on the surface of the sea; the second advances the same to procure himself grass from grounds that produced nothing before but hassocks and bogs. Among those who do not use the sea, I observed the same calm appearance as among the inhabitants on the continent; here I found, without gloom, a decorum and reserve, so natural to them, that I thought myself in Philadelphia. At my landing I was cordially received by those to whom I was recommended, and treated with unaffected hospitality by such others with whom I became acquainted; and I can tell you, that it is impossible for any traveler to dwell here one month without knowing the heads of the principal families. Wherever I went I found a simplicity of diction and manners, rather more primitive and rigid than I expected; and I soon perceived that it proceeded from their secluded situation, which has prevented them from mixing with others. It is therefore easy to conceive how they have retained every degree of peculiarity for which this sect was formerly distinguished. Never was a bee-hive more faithfully employed in gathering wax, bee-bread, and honey, from all the neighboring fields, than are the members of this society; every one in the town follows some particular occupation with great diligence, but without that servility of labor which I am informed prevails in Europe. The mechanic seemed to be descended from as good parentage, was as well dressed and fed, and held in as much estimation as those who employed him; they were once nearly related; their different degrees of prosperity is what has caused the various shades of their community. But this accidental difference has introduced, as yet, neither arrogance nor pride on the one part, nor meanness and servility on the other. All their houses are neat, convenient, and comfortable; some of them are filled with two families, for when the husbands are at sea, the wives require less house-room. They all abound with the most substantial furniture, more valuable from its usefulness than from any ornamental appearance. Wherever I went, I found good cheer, a welcome reception; and after the second visit I felt myself as much at my ease as if I had been an old acquaintance of the family. They had as great plenty of everything as if their island had been part of the golden quarter of Virginia (a valuable tract of land on Cape

Charles): I could hardly persuade myself that I had quitted the adjacent continent, where everything abounds, and that I was on a barren sandbank, fertilized with whale oil only. As their rural improvements are but trifling, and only of the useful kind, and as the best of them are at a considerable distance from the town, I amused myself for several days in conversing with the most intelligent of the inhabitants of both sexes, and making myself acquainted with the various branches of their industry; the different objects of their trade; the nature of that sagacity which, deprived as they are of every necessary material, produce, etc., yet enables them to flourish, to live well, and sometimes to make considerable fortunes. The whole is an enigma to be solved only by coming to the spot and observing the national genius which the original founders brought with them, as well as their unwearied patience and perseverance. They have all, from the highest to the lowest, a singular keenness of judgment, unassisted by any academical light; they all possess a large share of good sense, improved upon the experience of their fathers; and this is the surest and best guide to lead us through the path of life, because it approaches nearest to the infallibility of instinct. Shining talents and University knowledge, would be entirely useless here, nay, would be dangerous; it would pervert their plain judgment, it would lead them out of that useful path which is so well adapted to their situation; it would make them more adventurous, more presumptuous, much less cautious, and therefore less successful. It is pleasing to hear some of them tracing a father's progress and their own, through the different vicissitudes of good and adverse fortune. I have often, by their firesides, traveled with them the whole length of their career, from their earliest steps, from their first commercial adventure, from the possession of a single whale-boat, up to that of a dozen large vessels! This does not imply, however, that every one who began with a whale-boat, has ascended to a like pitch of fortune; by no means, the same casualty, the same combination of good and evil which attend human affairs in every other part of the globe, prevail here: a great prosperity is not the lot of every man, but there are many and various gradations; if they all do not attain riches, they all attain an easy subsistence. After all, is it not better to be possessed of a single whale-boat, or a few sheep pastures; to live free and independent under the mildest governments, in a healthy climate, in a land of charity and benevolence; than to be wretched as so many are in Europe, possessing nothing but their industry: tossed from one rough wave to another; engaged either in the most servile labors for the smallest pittance, or fettered with the links of the most irksome dependence, even without the hopes of rising?

CHAPTER VIII

ANNE GRANT LIVES AMONG THE ALBANIANS

UP ALONG the Hudson from New York extended a society which, though now part of the British system, had much about it still that was Dutch. The old families of New York, the Schuylers, for instance, held vast proprietary estates, and on one of these Mrs. Anne Grant of Loggan spent some of her youthful years. Her picture of the Schuylers and their world is heightened, like Crèvecoeur's, by eighteenth-century sentiments about the perfect society; yet almost nowhere else in that time does so clear a vision emerge of life as one city and one family lived it.

THE city of Albany stretched along the banks of the Hudson: one very wide and long street lay parallel to the river, the intermediate space between it and the shore being occupied by gardens. The town, in proportion to its population, occupied a great space of ground. This city, in short, was a kind of semi-rural establishment. Every house had its garden, well, and a little green behind: before every door, a tree was planted, rendered interesting by being coeval with some beloved member of the family. Many of their trees were of a prodigious size and extraordinary beauty, but without regularity, every one planting the kind that best pleased him, or which he thought would afford the most agreeable shade to the open portico at his door, which was surrounded by seats, and ascended by a few steps. It was in these that each domestic group was seated in summer evenings to enjoy the balmy twilight or the serenely clear moonlight. Each family had a cow, fed in a common pasture at the end of the town. In the evening the herd returned all together, of their own accord, with their tinkling bells hung at their necks, along the wide and grassy street, to their wonted sheltering trees, to be milked at their masters' doors.

The foundations both of friendship and still tenderer attachments were here laid very early by an institution which I always thought had been peculiar to Albany till I found, in Dr. Moore's "View of Society on the Continent," an account of a similar custom subsisting in Geneva. The children of the town were all divided into companies,

as they called them, from five or six years of age, till they became
marriageable. How those companies first originated, or what were
their exact regulations, I cannot say; though I, belonging to none,
occasionally mixed with several, yet always as a stranger, notwithstanding that I spoke their current language fluently. Every company contained as many boys as girls. But I do not know that there
was any limited number: only this I recollect, that a boy and girl
of each company, who were older, cleverer, or had some other pre-
eminence above the rest, were called heads of the company, and as
such were obeyed by the others. Whether they were voted in, or
attained their preëminence by a tacit acknowledgment of their
superiority, I know not; but, however it was attained, it was never
disputed. The company of little children had also their heads. All
the children of the same age were not in one company. There were
at least three or four of equal ages, who had a strong rivalry with
each other; and children of different ages, in the same family, belonged to different companies. Wherever there is human nature,
there will be a degree of emulation, strife, and a desire to lower
others, that we may exalt ourselves. Dispassionate as my friends
comparatively were, and bred up in the highest attainable candor
and innocence, they regarded the company most in competition with
their own with a degree of jealous animosity. Each company, at
a certain time of the year, went in a body to gather a particular kind
of berries, to the hill. It was a sort of annual festival, attended with
religious punctuality. Every company had a uniform for this purpose; that is to say, very pretty light baskets made by the Indians,
with lids and handles, which hung over the arm, and were adorned
with various colors. One company would never allow the least degree of taste to the other in this instance, and was sure to vent its
whole stock of spleen in decrying the rival baskets. Nor would they
ever admit that the rival company gathered near so much fruit on
these excursions as they did. The parents of these children seemed
very much to encourage this manner of marshaling and dividing
themselves. Every child was permitted to entertain the whole company on its birthday, and once besides, during winter and spring.
The master and mistress of the family always were bound to go
from home on these occasions; while some old domestic was left to
attend and watch over them, with an ample provision of tea, chocolate, preserved and dried fruits, nuts, and cakes of various kinds, to
which was added cider, or a sillabub; for these young friends met at
four, and did not part till nine or ten, and amused themselves with
the utmost gayety and freedom in any way their fancy dictated. I
speak from hearsay; for no person that does not belong to the

company is ever admitted to these meetings. Other children or young people visit occasionally, and are civilly treated; but they admit of no intimacies beyond their company. The consequence of these exclusive and early intimacies was, that grown up, it was reckoned a sort of apostasy to marry out of one's company, and, indeed, it did not often happen. The girls, from the example of their mothers, rather than any compulsion, very early became notable and industrious, being constantly employed in knitting stockings, and making clothes for the family and slaves: they even made all the boys' clothes. This was the more necessary, as all articles of clothing were extremely dear. Though all the necessaries of life, and some luxuries, abounded, money, as yet, was a scarce commodity. This industry was the more to be admired, as children were here indulged to a degree, that, in our vitiated state of society, would have rendered them good for nothing.

The children returned the fondness of their parents with such tender affection, that they feared giving them pain as much as ours do punishment, and very rarely wounded their feelings by neglect or rude answers. Yet the boys were often willful and giddy at a certain age, the girls being sooner tamed and domesticated.

These youths were apt, whenever they could carry a gun (which they did at a very early period), to follow some favorite negro to the woods, and, while he was employed in felling trees, to range the whole day in search of game, to the neglect of all intellectual improvement; and they thus contracted a love of savage liberty which might, and in some instances did, degenerate into licentious and idle habits. Indeed, there were three stated periods in the year, when for a few days young and old, masters and slaves, were abandoned to unruly enjoyment, and neglected every serious occupation for pursuits of this nature.

Col. Schuyler had many relations in New York; and the governor and other ruling characters there carefully cultivated the acquaintance of a person so well qualified to instruct and inform them on certain points. Having considerable dealings in the fur-trade, too, he went every winter to the capital for a short time, to adjust his commercial concerns, and often took his favorite niece along with him, who, being of an uncommon quick growth and tall stature, soon attracted attention by her personal graces, as well as by the charms of her conversation.

Miss Schuyler had the happiness to captivate her cousin Philip, eldest son of her uncle, who was ten years older than herself, and was in all respects to be accounted a suitable, and, in the worldly sense, an advantageous match for her. His father was highly satisfied to have the two objects on whom he had bestowed so much care and culture united. They were married in the year 1719, when she was in the eighteenth year of her age. When the old colonel died, he left considerable possessions to be divided among his children; and from the quantity of plate, paintings, etc., which they shared, there is reason to believe he must have brought some of his wealth from Holland, as in those days people had little means of enriching themselves in new settlements. He had, also, considerable possessions in a place near the town, now called Fishkill, about twenty miles below Albany. His family residence, however, was at the Flats, a fertile and beautiful plain on the banks of the river. He possessed about two miles on a stretch of that rich and level champaign. This possession was bounded on the east by the River Hudson, whose high banks overhung the stream and its pebbly strand, and were both adorned and defended by elms (larger than ever I have seen in any other place), decked with natural festoons of wild grapes, which abound along the banks of this noble stream. These lofty elms were left, when the country was cleared, to fortify the banks against the masses of thick ice which make war upon them in spring, when the melting snows burst this glassy pavement, and raise the waters many feet above their usual level. This precaution not only answers that purpose, but gratifies the mind by presenting to the eye a remnant of the wild magnificence of Nature amidst the smiling scenes produced by varied and successful cultivation. As you came along by the north end of the town, where the *Patroon* had his seat, you afterwards passed by the enclosures of the citizens, where they planted their corn, and arrived at the Flats, Col. Schuyler's possession.

Be it known that the house I had so much delight in recollecting had no pretension to grandeur, and very little to elegance. It was a large brick house of two, or rather three stories (for there were excellent attics), besides a sunk story, finished with the exactest neatness. The lower floor had two spacious rooms, with large light closets: on the first there were three rooms, and in the upper one four. Through the middle of the house was a very wide passage, with opposite front and back doors, which in summer admitted a stream of air peculiarly grateful to the languid senses. It was furnished with chairs and pictures like a summer-parlor. Here the family usually sat in hot weather, when there were no ceremonious strangers.

Valuable furniture (though perhaps not very well chosen or assorted) was the favorite luxury of these people; and in all the houses I remember, except those of the brothers, who were every way more liberal, the mirrors, the paintings, the china, but above all the state-bed, were considered as the family teraphim, secretly worshiped, and only exhibited on very rare occasions. But in Col. Schuyler's family, the rooms were merely shut up to keep the flies, which in that country are an absolute nuisance, from spoiling the furniture. Another motive was, that they might be pleasantly cool when opened for company. This house had, also, two appendages common to all those belonging to persons in easy circumstances there. One was a large portico at the door, with a few steps leading up to it, and floored like a room: it was open at the sides, and had seats all round. Above was either a slight wooden roof, painted like an awning, or a covering of lattice-work, over which a transplanted wild vine spread its luxuriant leaves and numerous clusters. The grapes, though small, and rather too acid till sweetened by the frost, had a beautiful appearance. What gave an air of liberty and safety to these rustic porticos, which always produced in my mind a sensation of pleasure that I know not how to define, was the number of little birds domesticated there. For their accommodation, there was a small shelf built within the portico where they nestled safely from the touch of slaves and children, who were taught to regard them as the good genii of the place, not to be disturbed with impunity.

At the back of the large house was a smaller and lower one, so joined to it as to make the form of a cross. There one or two lower and smaller rooms below, and the same number above, afforded a refuge to the family during the rigors of winter, when the spacious summer-rooms would have been intolerably cold, and the smoke of prodigious wood-fires would have sullied the elegantly clean furniture. Here, too, was a sunk story, where the kitchen was immediately below the eating-parlor, and increased the general warmth of the house. In summer the negroes inhabited slight outer kitchens, in which food was dressed for the family. Those who wrought in the fields often had their simple dinner cooked without, and ate it under the shade of a great tree. One room, I should have said, in the greater house only, was opened for the reception of company: all the rest were bed-chambers for their accommodation; the domestic friends of the family occupying neat little bedrooms in the attics, or in the winter-house. This house contained no drawing-room: that was an unheard-of luxury. The winter-rooms had carpets: the lobby had oilcloth painted in lozenges, to imitate blue and white marble. The best bedroom was hung with family portraits, some of which were admirably executed; and in the eating-room, which, by the by, was rarely used for that purpose, were some fine Scripture paintings. That which made the greatest impression on my imagination, and seemed to be universally admired, was one of Esau coming to demand the anticipated blessing: the noble, manly figure of the luckless hunter, and the anguish expressed in his comely though strong-featured countenance, I shall never forget. The house fronted the river, on the brink of which, under shades of elm and sycamore, ran the great road toward Saratoga, Stillwater, and the Northern Lakes. A little simple avenue of morello cherry-trees, enclosed with a white rail, led to the road and river, not three hundred yards distant. Adjoining to this, on the south side, was an enclosure subdivided into three parts, of which the first was a small hayfield, opposite the south end of the house; the next, not so long, a garden; and the third, by far the largest, an orchard. These were surrounded by simple deal fences. Now, let not the Genius that presides over pleasure-grounds, nor any of his elegant votaries, revolt with disgust while I mention the unseemly ornaments which were exhibited on the stakes to which the deals of these same fences were bound. Truly they consisted of the skeleton heads of horses and cattle, in as great numbers as could be procured, stuck upon the abovesaid poles. This was not mere ornament either, but a most hospitable arrangement for the accommodation of the small familiar birds before described. The jaws are fixed on the pole, and the skull uppermost. The wren, on seeing a skull thus placed, never fails to enter by the orifice, which is too small to admit the hand of an infant, lines the pericranium with small twigs and horsehair, and there lays her eggs in full security. It is very amusing to see the little creature carelessly go out and in at this aperture, though you should be standing immediately beside it. Not satisfied with providing these singular asylums for their feathered friends, the negroes never fail to make a small round hole in the crown of every old hat they can lay their hands on, and nail it to the end of the kitchen for the same purpose. You often see in such a one, at once, thirty or forty of these odd little domiciles, with the inhabitants busily going out and in.

Adjoining to the orchard was the most spacious barn I ever beheld, which I shall describe for the benefit of such of my readers as have never seen a building constructed on a plan so comprehensive. This barn, which, as will hereafter appear, answered many beneficial purposes besides those usually allotted for such edifices, was of a vast size, at least a hundred feet long, and sixty wide. The roof rose to a very great height in the midst, and sloped down till it came within ten feet of the ground, when the walls commenced, which, like the whole of this vast fabric, were formed of wood. It was raised three feet from the ground by beams resting on stone; and on these beams was laid, in the middle of the buildings, a very massive oak floor. Before the door was a large sill, sloping downwards, of the same materials. A breadth of about twelve feet on each side of this capacious building was divided off for cattle. On one side ran a manger, at the above-mentioned distance from the wall, the whole length of the building, with a rack above it: on the other were stalls for the other cattle, running, also, the whole length of the building. The cattle and horses stood with their hinder parts to the wall, and their heads toward the thrashing-floor. There was a prodigious large box, or open chest, in one side, built up for holding the corn after it was thrashed; and the roof, which was very lofty and spacious, was supported by large cross-beams. From one to the other of these was stretched a great number of long poles, so as to form a sort of open loft, on which the whole rich crop was laid up. The floor of those parts of the barn which answered the purposes of a stable and cow-house was made of thick slab-deals, laid loosely over the supporting beams. And the mode of cleaning those places was by turning the boards, and permitting the dung and litter to fall into the receptacles left open below for the purpose; thence, in spring, they were often driven down to the river, the soil in its original state not requiring the aid of manure. In the front of this vast edifice there were prodigious folding-doors, and two others that opened behind.

Certainly never did cheerful rural toils wear a more exhilarating aspect than while the domestics were lodging the luxuriant harvest in this capacious repository. When speaking of the doors, I should have mentioned that they were made in the gable-ends; those in the back equally large to correspond with those in the front, while on each side of the great doors were smaller ones for the cattle and horses to enter. Whenever the corn or hay was reaped or cut, and ready for carrying home, which in that dry and warm climate happened in a very few days, a wagon loaded with hay, for instance, was driven into the midst of this great barn; loaded, also, with numberless large grasshoppers, butterflies, and cicadas, who came along with the hay. From the top of the wagon, this was immediately forked up into the loft of the barn, in the midst of which was an open space left for the purpose; and then the unloaded wagon drove in rustic state out of the great door at the other end. In the meantime, every member of the family witnessed or assisted in this summary process, by which the building and thatching of stacks was at once saved; and the whole crop and cattle were thus compendiously lodged under one roof.

Aunt * was a great manager of her time, and always contrived to create leisure hours for reading: for that kind of conversation which is properly styled gossiping, she had the utmost contempt. Light, superficial reading, such as merely fills a blank in time, and glides over the mind without leaving an impression, was little known there; for few books crossed the Atlantic but such as were worth carrying so far for their intrinsic value. She was too much accustomed to have her mind occupied with objects of real weight and importance to give it up to frivolous pursuits of any kind. She began the morning with reading the Scriptures. They always breakfasted early, and dined two hours later than the primitive inhabitants, who always took that meal at twelve. This departure from the ancient customs was necessary in this family, to accommodate the great numbers of British, as well as strangers from New York, who were daily entertained at her liberal table. This arrangement gave her the advantage of a longer forenoon to dispose of. After breakfast she gave orders for the family details of the day, which, without a scrupulous attention to those minutiæ which fell more properly under the notice of her young friends, she always regulated in the most judicious manner, so as to prevent all appearance of hurry and confusion. There was such a rivalry among domestics, whose sole ambition was her favor, and who had been trained up from infancy, each to their several duties, that excellence in each department was the result both of habit and emulation; while her young *protégées* were early taught the value and importance of good housewifery, and were sedulous in their attention to little matters of decoration and elegance, which her mind was too much engrossed to attend to; so that her household affairs, ever well regulated, went on in a mechanical kind of progress that seemed to engage little of her attention, though her vigilant and over-ruling mind set every spring of action in motion.

Having thus easily and speedily arranged the details of the day, she retired to read in her closet, where she generally remained till about eleven; when, being unequal to distant walks, the colonel and she, and some of her elder guests, passed some of the hotter hours among those embowering shades of her garden in which she took great pleasure. Here was their lyceum: here questions in religion and morality, too weighty for table-talk, were leisurely and coolly discussed, and plans of policy and various utility arranged. From this retreat they sojourned to the portico; and while the colonel either retired to write, or went to give directions to his servants,

* "Aunt" was the familiar title of Mrs. Schuyler.

she sat in this little tribunal, giving audience to new settlers, followers of the army left in hapless dependence, and others who wanted assistance or advice, or hoped she would intercede with the colonel for something more peculiarly in his way, he having great influence with the colonial government. At the usual hour her dinner-party assembled, which was generally a large one: it commonly consisted of some of her intimate friends or near relations; her adopted children, who were inmates for the time being; and strangers, sometimes invited merely as friendless travelers, on the score of hospitality, but often welcomed for sometime as stationary visitors, on account of worth or talents that gave value to their society; and, lastly, military guests, selected with some discrimination on account of the young friends, whom they wished not only to protect, but cultivate by an improving association. Conversation here was always rational, generally instructive, and often cheerful. The afternoon frequently brought with it a new set of guests. Tea was always drunk early here, and, as I have formerly observed, was attended with so many petty luxuries of pastry, confectionery, etc., that it might well be accounted a meal by those whose early and frugal dinners had so long gone by. In Albany it was customary, after the heat of the day was past, for the young people to go in parties of three or four, in open carriages, to drink tea at an hour or two's drive from home. The receiving and entertaining this sort of company generally was the province of the younger part of the family; and of those many came, in summer evenings, to the Flats, when tea, which was very early, was over. The young people, and those who were older, took their different walks while madame sat in her portico, engaged in what might comparatively be called light reading,—essays, biography, poetry, etc.,—till the younger party set out on their return home, and her domestic friends rejoined her in her portico, where, in warm evenings, a slight repast was sometimes brought; but they more frequently shared the last and most truly social meal within.

Winter made little difference in her mode of occupying her time. She then always retired to her closet to read at stated periods.

The hospitalities of this family were so far beyond their apparent income, that all strangers were astonished at them. To account for this, it must be observed, that, in the first place, there was, perhaps, scarce an instance of a family possessing such uncommonly well-trained, active, and diligent slaves as that which I describe. The set that were staid servants when they married had some of them died off by the time I knew the family; but the principal roots from whence the many branches then flourishing sprung yet remained.

These were two women, who had come originally from Africa while very young: they were most excellent servants, and the mothers or grandmothers of the whole set, except one white-woolled negro-man, who in my time sat by the chimney, and made shoes for all the rest.

It may appear extraordinary, with so moderate an income as could in those days be derived even from a considerable estate in that country, how madame found means to support that liberal hospitality which they constantly exercised. I know the utmost they could derive from their lands, and it was not much: some money they had, but nothing adequate to the dignity, simple as it was, of their style of living, and the very large family they always drew around them. But with regard to the plenty, one might almost call it luxury, of their table, it was supplied from a variety of sources, that rendered it less expensive than could be imagined. Indians, grateful for the numerous benefits they were daily receiving from them, were constantly bringing the smaller game, and, in winter and spring, loads of venison. Little money passed from one hand to another in the country; but there was constantly, as there always is in primitive abodes before the age of calculation begins, a kindly commerce of presents. The people of New York and Rhode Island, several of whom were wont to pass a part of the summer with the colonel's family, were loaded with all the productions of the farm and river. When they went home, they again never failed, at the season, to send a large supply of oysters, and all other shellfish, which at New York abounded, besides great quantities of tropical fruit, which, from the short run between Jamaica and New York, were there almost as plenty and cheap as in their native soil. Their farm yielded them abundantly all that, in general, agriculture can supply; and the young relatives who grew up about the house were rarely a day without bringing some provision from the wood or the stream. The negroes, whose business lay frequently in the woods, never willingly went there, or anywhere else, without a gun, and rarely came back empty handed. Presents of wine, then a very usual thing to send to friends to whom you wished to show a mark of gratitude, came very often, possibly from the friends of the young people who were reared and instructed in that house of benediction. As there were no duties paid for the entrance of any commodity there, wine, rum, and sugar were cheaper than can easily be imagined; and in cider they abounded.

The negroes of the three truly united brothers, not having home employment in winter, after preparing fuel, used to cut down trees, and carry them to an adjoining sawmill, where, in a very short time, they made great quantities of planks, staves, etc., which is usually styled lumber, for the West India market. And when a shipload of their flour, lumber, and salted provisions, was accumulated, some relative, for their behoof, freighted a vessel, and went out to the West Indies with it. In this Stygian schooner, the departure of which was always looked forward to with unspeakable horror, all the stubborn or otherwise unmanageable slaves were embarked, to be sold by way of punishment. This produced such salutary terror, that preparing the lading of this fatal vessel generally operated as a temporary reform, at least. When its cargo was discharged in the West Indies, it took in a lading of wine, rum, sugar, coffee, chocolate, and all other West India productions, paying for whatever fell short of the value, and, returning to Albany, sold the surplus to their friends, after reserving to themselves a most liberal supply of all the articles so imported. Thus they had not only a profusion of all the requisites for good housekeeping, but had it in their power to do what was not unusual there in wealthy families, though none carried it so far as these worthies.

CHAPTER IX

EVIDENCE ACCUMULATED during the eighteenth century concerning a curious custom called tarrying, or bundling. The custom was no doubt of very long standing in both Europe and America, but only in the second half of this century did travelers begin to observe and describe its attendant rites. The precise nature of these rites will be disclosed by two witnesses, one of whom speaks for a nineteenth-century generation.

1. THOMAS ANBUREY

Lieutenant Thomas Anburey of the British Army wrote a letter from America in 1777 which said:

THE night before we came to this town [Williamstown, Mass.], being quartered at a small log hut, I was convinced in how innocent a view the Americans look upon that indelicate custom they call *bundling*. Though they have remarkable good feather beds, and are extremely neat and clean, still I preferred my hard mattress, as being accustomed to it; this evening, however, owing to the badness of the roads, and the weakness of my mare, my servant had not arrived with my baggage at the time for retiring to rest. There being only two beds in the house, I inquired which I was to sleep in, when the old woman replied, "Mr. Ensign," here I should observe to you, that the New England people are very inquisitive as to the rank you have in the army; "Mr. Ensign," says she, "our Jonathan and I will sleep in this, and our Jemima and you shall sleep in that." I was much astonished at such a proposal, and offered to sit up all night, when Jonathan immediately replied, "Oh, la! Mr. Ensign, you won't be the first man our Jemima has bundled with, will it, Jemima?" when little Jemima, who, by the bye, was a very pretty, black-eyed girl, of about sixteen or seventeen, archly replied, "No, father, not by many, but it will be with the first Britainer" (the name they give to Englishmen). In this dilemma what could I do? The smiling invitation of pretty

Jemima—the eye, the lip, the—Lord ha' mercy, where am I going to? But wherever I may be going now, I did not go to bundle with her—in the same room with her father and mother, my kind *host* and *hostess* too! I thought of that—I thought of more besides—to struggle with the passions of nature; to clasp Jemima in my arms —to—do what? you'll ask—why, to do—nothing! for if amid all these temptations, the lovely Jemima had melted into kindness, she had been an outcast from the world—treated with contempt, abused by violence, and left perhaps to perish! No, Jemima; I could have endured all this to have been blessed with you, but it was too vast a sacrifice, when you was to be the victim! Suppose how great the test of virtue must be, or how cold the American constitution, when this unaccountable custom is in hospitable repute, and perpetual practice.

2. PORTLAND, MAINE

John Neal, editing *The Yankee* at Portland, Maine, printed this communication from a contributor in the issue of August 13, 1828:

MR. NEAL—If you wish to know the truth about bundling, I think your correspondent V. could tell you all about it—it seems by his confession that he had practiced it on a large scale. I never heard of the thing till about three years ago; an acquaintance of mine had gone to spend the summer with an aunt, who lived somewhere near Sandy river. The following is a copy of one of her letters while there:

"I should have written sooner, so don't think me unkind, for I have been waiting for something to write about. You requested me to give you a faithful description of the country, the manners and customs of the inhabitants, etc. I have not been here quite three months, but I have been everywhere, seen everything, and got acquainted with everybody. I shall certainly inform you of everything I have seen or heard that is worth relating.

"You remember how you told me, before I left home, that I was so well looking that if I went so far back in the country I should be very much admired and flattered, and have as many lovers as I could wish for. I find it all true. The people here are remarkably kind and attentive to me; they seem to think that I must be something more than common because I have always lived so near Portland.

"But I must tell you that since I have been here I have had a beau. You must know that the young men, *in particular*, are very attentive to me. Well, among these is *one* who is considered the finest young man in the place, and well he may be—he owns a good farm, which has a large barn upon it, and a neat two-story house, all finished. These are the fruits of his own industry; besides he is remarkably good-looking, is very large but well-proportioned, and has a good share of what I call real manly beauty. Soon after my arrival here I was introduced to this man—no, not *introduced* neither, for they never think of such a thing here. They all know me of course, because I am a *stranger*. Some days, three, four, or half a dozen, call to see me, whom I never before saw or heard of; they come and speak to me as if I were an old acquaintance, and I converse with them as freely as if I had always known them from childhood. In this kind of a way I got acquainted with my beau, that *was;* he was very attentive to me from our first meeting. If we happened to be going anywhere in company he was sure to offer me his arm—no, I am wrong again, he never offered me his arm in his life. If you go to walk with a young man here, instead of offering you his arm as the young men do up our way, he either takes your hand in his, or passes one arm around your waist; and this he does with such a provoking, careless honesty, that you cannot for your life be offended with him. Well, I had walked with my Jonathan several times in this kind of style. I confess there was something in him I could not but like—he does not lack for wit, and has a good share of common sense; his language is never studied—he always seems to speak from the heart. So when he asked what sort of a companion he would make, I very candidly answered, that I thought he would make a very agreeable one. 'I think just so of you,' said he, 'and it shall not be my fault,' he continued, 'if we are not companions for life.' 'We shall surely make a bargain,' said he, after sitting silent a few moments, 'so we'll *bundle* to-night.' '*Bundle* what?' I asked. '*We* will bundle together,' said he; 'you surely know what I mean.' I know that our farmers bundle *wheat, cornstalks* and *hay;* do you mean that you want me to help you bundle any of these?' inquired I. 'I mean that I want you to stay with me to-night! It is the custom in this place, when a man stays with a girl, if it is warm weather, for them to throw themselves on the bed, outside the bed clothes; if the weather is cold, they crawl under the clothes, then if they have anything to *say,* they say it—when they get tired of talking they go to sleep; this is what we call bundling—now what do you call it in your part of the world?' 'We have no such works,' answered I; 'not amongst respectable people, nor do I think that any people would, that either thought themselves respectable, or wished to be thought so.'

"Don't be too severe upon us, Miss ——, I have always observed that those who *make believe* so much modesty, have in reality but little. I always act as I feel, and speak as I think. I wish you to do the same, but have none of your make-believes with me—you smile —you begin to think you have been a little too scrupulous—you have no objection to bundling *now*, have you?' 'Indeed I have.' 'I am not to be trifled with; so, if you refuse, I have done with you forever.' 'Then be done as quick as you please, for I'll not bundle with you nor with any other man.' 'Then farewell, proud girl,' said he. 'Farewell, honest man,' said I, and off he went, sure enough.

"I have since made inquiries about *bundling,* and find that it is *really* the custom here, and that they think no more harm of it, than we do our way of a young couple sitting up together. I have known an instance, since I have been here, of a girl's taking her sweetheart to a neighbor's house and asking for a bed or two to lodge in, or rather to *bundle* in. They had company at her father's, so that their beds were occupied; she thought no harm of it. She and her family are respectable.

"Grandmother says bundling was a very common thing in our part of the country, in old times; that most of the first settlers lived in log houses, which seldom had more than one room with a fireplace; in this room the old people slept, so if one of their girls had a sweetheart in the winter she must either sit with him in the room where her father and mother slept, or take him into her sleeping room. She would choose the latter for the sake of being alone with him; but sometimes when the cold was very severe, rather than freeze to death, they would crawl under the bed-clothes; and this, after a while, became a habit, a custom, or a fashion. The man that I am going to send this by, is just ready to start, so I cannot stop to write more now. In my next I'll give you a more particular account of the people here. Adieu."

Mr. Editor, you may be sure that what is related in the foregoing letter is the truth. I know that there is considerable *other* information in it, mixed up with *that* about which you wished to be informed, but I could not very well separate it.

Book III
REVOLUTION

CHAPTER X

THE THIRD quarter of the eighteenth century found 1,500,000 people in the colonies, and saw their slow but steady movement in the direction of independence from England, whose king and ministers persisted too long in prescribing that America contribute to the commercial support of the mother country. The king's prerogative was more and more questioned; the presence of an army of 10,000 men, presumably sent over to protect the colonies from foreign attack, was particularly galling in view of the fact that the colonies were expected to pay a portion of its expense; and taxation by parliament became increasingly unwelcome. Then the possibility of self-government began in some quarters to be apparent; and there developed schools of revolutionaries who agitated the new cause. Yet the Americans, even in 1775 when the first fighting was done at Lexington and Concord, and in 1776 when the Declaration of Independence was adopted by the Continental Congress, were far from united in spirit and purpose. Many were loyal to the king; many were indifferent; only the rabble, it was charged by men of property and weight, were hot for change.

Alexander Graydon's recollections of his life at Philadelphia in the days before the war, and his narrative of his experiences with the Continental army as it was being organized, is a calm observer's report of the time in its several tempers of loyalty, intolerance, and revolt.

AT the corner of Norris's Alley was a singular old-fashioned structure, laid out in the style of a fortification, with abundance of angles, both salient and reëntering. Its two wings projected to the street, in the manner of bastions; to which the main building, retreating from sixteen to eighteen feet, served for a curtain. Within it was cut up into a number of apartments, and, on that account, was exceedingly well adapted to the purpose of a lodging-house; to which use it had been long appropriated. An additional convenience was a spacious yard on the back of it, extending half way to Front Street, enclosed by a high wall, and ornamented with a double row of venerable lofty pines, which afforded a very agreeable *rus in urbe,* or rural scene, in the heart of the city. The lady who had resided here, and given some celebrity to the stand by the style of her accommodations, either dying or declining business, my mother was persuaded by her friends to become her successor; and, accordingly, obtained a lease of the premises, and took possession of them, to the best of my recollection, in the year 1764 or 1765. While in this residence, and in a still more commodious one in the upper part of Front Street, to which she, some years afterwards, removed, she had the honor, if so it might be called, of entertaining strangers of the first rank who visited the city.

A biographical sketch of the various personages, who, in the course of eight or nine years, became inmates of this house, might, from the hand of a good delineator, be both curious and amusing. Among these were persons of distinction, and some of no distinction; many real gentlemen, and some, no doubt, who were merely pretenders to the appellation. Some attended by servants in gay liveries; some with servants in plain coats, and some with no servants at all. It was rarely without officers of the British army. It was, at different times, nearly filled by those of the forty-second or Highland regiment, as also by those of the Royal Irish. Besides these, it sometimes accommodated officers of other armies and other uniforms. Of this description was the Baron de Kalb, who visited this country, probably about the year 1768 or 1769; and who fell a major-general in the army of the United States, at the battle of Cambden. Though a German by birth, he had belonged to the French service, and had returned to France, after the visit just mentioned. During our revolutionary contest, he came to tender us his services, and returned no more. The steady and composed demeanor of the Baron bespoke the soldier and philosopher; the man who had calmly estimated life and death; and who, though not prodigal of the one, had no unmanly dread of the other. He was not, indeed, a young man; and his behavior at the time of his death, as I have heard it described by Mons. Dubuisson, his aid-de-camp, was exactly conformable to what might have been supposed from his character.

Another of our foreign guests was one Badourin, who wore a white cockade, and gave himself out for a general in the Austrian service; but, whether general or not, he, one night, very unexpectedly, left his quarters, making a masterly retreat, with the loss of no other baggage than that of an old trunk, which, when opened, was found to contain only a few old Latin and German books. Among the former was a folio, bound in parchment, which I have now before me. It is a ponderous tract of the mystical Robert Fludd, *alias* De Fluctibus, printed at Oppenheim, in the year 1618, and, in part, dedicated to the Duke of Guise, whom, the author informs us, he had instructed in the art of war. It is to this writer, probably, that Butler thus alludes in his Hudibras:—

> He, Anthroposophus and *Floud,*
> And Jacob Behman understood.

From this work of Mr. Fludd, which, among a fund of other important matter, treats of astrology and divination, it is not improbable that its quondam possessor, Mr. Badourin, might have been a mountebank conjurer, instead of a general.

Among those of rank from Great Britain with whose residence we were honored, I recollect Lady Moore and her daughter, a sprightly miss, not far advanced in her teens, and who having apparently no dislike to be seen, had more than once attracted my attention; for I was just touching that age when such objects begin to be interesting, and excite feelings which disdain the invidious barriers with which the pride of condition would surround itself. Not that the young lady was stately; my vanity rather hinted, she was condescendingly courteous; and I had, no doubt, read of women of quality falling in love with their inferiors. Nevertheless, the extent of my presumption was a look or a bow, as she now and then tripped along through the entry. Another was Lady Susan Obrien, not more distinguished by her title than by her husband, who accompanied her, and had figured as a comedian on the London stage, in the time of Garrick, Mossop, and Barry. Although Churchhill charges him with being an imitator of Woodward, he yet admits him to be a man of parts; and he has been said to have surpassed all his contemporaries in the character of the fine gentleman; in his easy manner of treading the stage, and particularly of drawing his sword; to which action he communicated a swiftness and a grace which Garrick imitated, but could not equal. Obrien is presented to my recollection as a man of the middle height, with a symmetrical form, rather light than athletic. Employed by the father to instruct Lady Susan in elocution, he taught her, it seems, that it was no sin to love; for she became his wife; and, as I have seen it mentioned in the Theatrical Mirror, obtained for him, through the interest of her family, a post in America. But what this post was, or where it located him, I never heard.

A third person of celebrity and title was Sir William Draper, who made a tour to this country a short time after his newspaper encounter with Junius. It has even been suggested that this very incident sent the knight on his travels. Whether or not it had so important a consequence, it cannot be denied that Sir William *caught a tartar* in Junius; and that, when he commenced his attack, he had evidently underrated his adversary.

During his stay in Philadelphia, no one was so assiduous in his attentions to him as Mr. Richardson, better known at that time by the name of Frank Richardson, then from England on a visit to his friends. This gentleman was one of the most singular and successful of American adventurers. The son of one of our plainest Quakers, he gave early indications of that cast of character which has raised him to his present station, that of a colonel in the British Guards. At a time, when such attainments formed no part of education in Pennsylvania, he sedulously employed himself in acquiring skill in the use of the small sword and the pistol, as if to shine as a duellist had been the first object of his ambition. Either from a contempt for the dull pursuits of the "home-keeping youth" of his day, or from the singularity of his propensities repelling association, he was solitary and rarely with companions. Fair and delicate to effeminacy, he paid great attention to his person, which he had the courage to invest in scarlet, in defiance of the society to which he belonged, in whose mind's eye, perhaps as to that of the blind man of Locke, this color from their marked aversion to it, resembles the sound of a trumpet; and no less in defiance of the plain manners of a city, in which, except on the back of a soldier, a red coat was a phenomenon, and always indicated a Creole, a Carolinian, or a dancing-master. With these qualifications, and these alone perhaps, Mr. Richardson, at an early age, shipped himself for England, where soon, having the good fortune to establish a reputation for courage by drawing his sword in behalf of a young man of rank, in a broil at the theater, he was received into the best company, and thence laid the foundation of his preferment. Such, at least, was the generally received account of his rise. But whether accurate or not, his intimate footing with Sir William is an evidence of the style of his company whilst abroad, as well as of the propriety of his conclusion, that his native land was not his sphere.

From Philadelphia, Sir William passed on to New York, where, if I mistake not, he married. During his residence in that city, he frequently amused himself with a game of rackets, which he played with some address; and he set no small value on the talent. There was a mechanic in the place, the hero of the tennis court, who was so astonishingly superior to other men, that there were few whom he could not beat with one hand attached to the handle of a wheel-barrow. Sir William wished to play with him, and was gratified; the New Yorker having urbanity enough to cede the splendid stranger some advantages, and even in conquering, to put on the appearance of doing it with difficulty. Yet, apart, he declared that he could have done the same with the incumbrance of the wheel-barrow. These are hearsay facts. They come, however, from persons of credit, in the way of being acquainted with them.

Major George Etherington, of the Royal Americans, was an occasional inmate of our house, from its first establishment on the large scale, until the time of its being laid down, about the year 1774. He seemed to be always employed in the recruiting service, in the performance of which he had a snug economical method of his own. He generally dispensed with the noisy ceremony of a recruiting coterie; for having, as it was said, and I believe truly, passed through the principal grades in its composition, namely, those of drummer and sergeant, he was a perfect master of the inveigling arts which are practiced on the occasion, and could fulfill, at a pinch, all the duties himself. The major's *forte* was a knowledge of mankind, of low life especially; and he seldom scented a subject that he did not, in the end, make his prey. He knew his man, and could immediately discover a fish that would bite. Hence he wasted no time in angling in wrong waters. His superior height, expansive frame, and muscular limbs, gave him a commanding air among the vulgar; and, while enforcing his suit with all the flippancy of halbert elocution, he familiarly held his booby by the button, his small, black, piercing eyes, which derived additonal animation from the intervention of a sarcastic, upturned nose, penetrated to the fellow's soul, and gave him distinct intelligence of what was passing there. In fact, I have never seen a man with a cast of countenance so extremely subtile and investigating. I have myself, more than once, undergone its scrutiny; for he took a very friendly interest in my welfare, evinced by an occasional superintendence of my education, in so far, at least, as respects the exterior accomplishments. Above all things, he enjoined upon me the cultivation of the French language, of which he had himself acquired a smattering from a temporary residence in Canada; and he gave me a pretty sharp lecture upon a resolution I had absurdly taken up, not to learn dancing, from an idea of its being an effeminate and unmanly recreation. He combated my folly with arguments, of which I have since felt the full force; but which, as they turned upon interests, I was then too young to form conceptions of, they produced neither conviction nor effect. Fortunately for me, I had to deal with a man who was not thus to be baffled. He very properly assumed the rights of mature age and experience, and, accordingly, one day, on my return from school, he accosted me with, "Come here, young man, I have something to say to you," and with a mysterious air conducted me to his chamber. Here I found myself entrapped. Godwin, the assistant of Tioli the dancing-master, was prepared to give me a lesson. Etherington introduced me to him as the pupil he had been speaking of, and saying, he would leave us to ourselves, he politely retired. The arrangement with Tioli was, that I should be attended in the major's room until I was sufficiently drilled for the public school; and the ice thus broken, I went on, and, instead of standing in a corner, like a goose on one leg (the major's comparison), "while music softens, and while dancing fires," I became qualified for the enjoyment of female society, in one of its most captivating forms.

From these gentlemen of the army, I pass to one of the navy, rude and boisterous as the element to which he belonged. His name I think was Wallace, the commander of a ship of war on the American station, and full fraught, perhaps, with the ill-humor of the mother country toward her colonies, which she was already beginning to goad to independence. His character upon the coast was that of being insolent and brutal beyond his peers; and his deportment as a lodger was altogether of a piece with it. Being asked by my mother, who, by the desire of the gentlemen, was in the custom of taking the head of her table, if he would be helped to a dish that was near her, "Damme, madam," replied the ruffian, "it is to be supposed that at a public table every man has a right to help himself, and this I mean to do." With a tear in her eye, she besought him to pardon her, assuring him that, in future, he should not be offended by her officiousness.

At another time, when Joseph Church of Bristol, who has already been mentioned as a friend of the family, was in town and at our house, which, in his visits to the city, he always made his home, my mother mentioned to the gentlemen, who were about sitting down to supper, but three or four in number, of whom Captain Wallace was one, that there was a friend of hers in the house, a very honest, plain man, of the society of Friends, and begged to know if it would be agreeable to them that he should be brought into supper. They all readily assented, and none with more alacrity than Wallace. Accordingly Mr. Church was introduced, and sat down. During supper, the captain directed his chief discourse to him, interlarded with a deal of very coarse and insolent raillery on his broad brim, etc. Church bore it all very patiently until after supper, when he at length ventured to say—"Captain, thou hast made very free with me, and asked me a great many questions, which I have endeavored to answer to thy satisfaction: Wilt thou now permit me to ask thee one in my turn?"—"Oh by all means," exclaimed the captain, "anything that you please, friend—what is it?"—"Why then, I wish to be informed, what makes thee drink so often; art thou really dry every time thou carriest the liquor to thy mouth?" This was a home thrust at the seaman, whose frequent potations had already produced a degree of intoxication. At once, forgetting the liberties he had taken, and the promise he had given of equal freedom in return, he broke out into a violent rage, venting himself in the most indecent and illiberal language, and vociferating, with an unlucky logic which recoiled upon himself—"What! do you think I am like a hog, only to drink when I am dry?" But matters had gone too far for a reply, and the object of his wrath very prudently left the table and the room as expeditiously as possible. It cannot be denied, that there was some provocation in the question proposed; but he knows little of the Quaker character who does not know that the non-resisting tenet does not prohibit the use of dry sarcasm, which here was unquestionably in its place.

Yet another, of some eminence, though not exactly in the same kind, whom I ought not to omit, was Rivington the printer, of New York. This gentleman's manners and appearance were sufficiently dignified, and he kept the best company. He was an everlasting dabbler in theatrical heroics. Othello was the character in which he liked best to appear; and converting his auditory into the "Most potent, grave, and reverend signiors" of Venice, he would deliver his unvarnished tale:

"Her father lov'd me, oft invited me," etc.

With the same magic by which the listening gentlemen were turned into senators, my mother was transformed into Desdemona; and from the frequent spoutings of Rivington, the officers of the 42d regiment, and others, who were then in the house, became familiarized to the appellation, and appropriated it. Thus, Desdemona, or rather Desdy, for shortness, was the name she generally afterwards went by among that set of lodgers; and I recollect the concluding line of a poetical effusion of Lieutenant Rumsey of the 42d, on occasion of some trifling *fracas,* to have been—

For Desdy, believe me, you don't become airs!

In the daily intercourse with her boarders which my mother's custom of sitting at the head of her table induced, such familiarities might be excused. They were only to be repelled, at least, by a formal austerity of manner, which was neither natural to her, nor for her interest to assume. The cause of umbrage was a midnight riot, perpetrated by Rumsey, Rivington, and Dr. Kearsley, in which the Doctor, mounted on horseback, rode into the back parlor, and even upstairs, to the great disturbance and terror of the family; for, as it may well be supposed, there was a direful clatter. *Quadrupedante sonitu quatit ungula domum.*

If want of occupation, as we are told, is the root of all evil, my youth was exposed to very great dangers. The interval between my leaving the academy, and being put to the study of the law at about the age of sixteen, was not less than eighteen months; an invaluable period, lost in idleness and unprofitable amusement. It had the effect to estrange me for a time from my school- companions, and, in their stead, to bring me acquainted with a set of young men, whose education and habits had been wholly different from my own. They were chiefly designed for the sea, or engaged in the less humiliating mechanical employments; and were but the more to my taste for affecting a sort of rough independence of manners, which appeared to me manly. They were not, however, worthless; and such of them as were destined to become men and citizens have, with few exceptions, filled their parts in society with reputation and respectability. As I had now attained that stage in the progress of the mind, in which

> Neglected Tray and Pointer lie,
> And covies unmolested fly,

the void was supplied by an introduction into the fair society, with which these young men were in the habit of associating. It consisted generally of Quakers; and there was a witching one among them, with whom, at a first interview in a party on the water, I became so violently enamored, as to have been up, perhaps, to the part of a Romeo or a Pyramus, had the requisite train of untoward circumstances ensued. But as there were no feuds between our houses, nor unnatural parents to "forbid what they could not prohibit," the matter in due time passed off without any dolorous catastrophe. Nor was it long before I was translated into a new set of female acquaintance, in which I found new objects to sigh for. Such, indeed, I was seldom, if ever, without, during the rest of my nonage; and with as little reason, perhaps, as any one, to complain of adverse stars. Nevertheless, I should hesitate in pronouncing this season of life happy. If its enjoyments are great, so are its solicitudes; and although it should escape the pangs of "slighted vows and cold disdain," it yet is racked by a host of inquietudes, doubt, distrust, jealousy, hope deferred by the frustration of promised interviews, and wishes sickening under the weight of obstacles too mighty to be surmounted.

But the peril of fine eyes was not the only one which beset me. During my residence in the Slate-house, I had contracted an intimacy with the second son of Dr. Thomas Bond, who lived next door; a connection which continued for several years. He was perhaps a year older than myself, and had, in like manner, abandoned his studies, and prematurely bidden adieu to the College of Princeton. Handsome in his person, in his manner confident and assured, he had the most lordly contempt for the opinion of the world, that is the sober world, of any young man I have known; as well as a precocity in fashionable vices, equaled by few, and certainly exceeded by none. Admiring his talents and accomplishments, I willingly yielded him the lead in our amusements, happy in emulating his *degagée* air and rakish appearance. He it was who first introduced me to the fascination of a billiard-table, and initiated me into the other seductive arcana of city dissipation. He also showed me where beardless youth might find a Lethe for its timidity, in the form of an execrable potion called wine, on the very moderate terms of two and sixpence a quart. At an obscure inn in Race Street, dropping in about dark, we were led by a steep and narrow staircase to a chamber in the third story, so lumbered with beds as scarcely to leave room for a table and one chair, the beds superseding the necessity of more. Here we poured down the fiery beverage; and valiant in the novel feeling of intoxication, sallied forth in quest of adventures. Under the auspices of such a leader, I could not fail to improve; nor was his progress less promoted by so able a second. In a word, we aspired to be rakes, and were gratified. Mr. Richard Bond was the favorite of his father, studied physic under him, and, notwithstanding his addiction to pleasure, would probably have made a respectable figure in his profession: for he had genius, no fondness for liquor, no unusual want of application to business, and vanity, perhaps, more than real propensity, had prompted his juvenile excesses. But he was destined to finish his career at an early age, by that fatal disease to youth, a pulmonary consumption. He had a presentiment of this, and frequently said when in health, it would be his mortal distemper. Yet his frame seemed not to indicate it: he had a prominent chest, with a habit inclined to fullness. Our intimacy had ceased for some time before his death: I know not why, unless he had been alienated by a latent spark of jealousy, in relation to a young lady, for whom we both had a partiality; mine, indeed, slight and evanescent; his deep and more lasting, and which, I have understood, only ended with his life.

But a period was now approaching which tended equally to interrupt the pursuits of pleasure and of business; and, inasmuch as it did the latter, to lessen my chagrin at being disqualified for engaging in it. Pennsylvania, hitherto so tranquil and so happy, was, in common with her sister provinces, about to experience the calamities, which, sooner or later, seem the inevitable destiny of every region inhabited by man. Her golden age was at its close; and that iron era which was to sever the ties of friendship and of blood; to set father against son, and brother against brother, with many other frightful evils in its train, was about to supervene.

In preparing for the scene of war that was approaching, no martial employment was neglected. It was even deemed of consequence to be a marksman with a pistol; and connected with this object, I recollect an unpleasant incident, which might also have proved a serious one. Captain Biddle and myself, having gone out to take a shot, and posted ourselves in a situation thought convenient and safe, we marked our target on a board fence, in a cross street, between Arch and Race Streets. We had fired several times, and were loading again, when a man suddenly coming upon us, out of breath, pale as ashes, without his hat, and his hair standing on end, exclaimed that we had killed his child. This information, as may be supposed, put a stop to our amusement; and we immediately accompanied him to his house with feelings not to be envied. When we arrived, however, we found matters not so bad as had been anticipated. The child was crying in its mother's arms: it had been struck upon the body; but the force of the blow had been broken by a loose linsey petticoat. The ball had passed through a pane of glass; and, from the appearance of the hole, exactly corresponding to its size, without diverging cracks, it must have had considerable force, though discharged at a distance which we thought greater than our pistols would carry. By expressions of concern for the accident, and the accompaniment of a few dollars, our transgression was overlooked, and all perturbation composed.

The daily, unremitted course of exercise which my military duties and my fencing at this time imposed, had thoroughly established my health. The serious aspect of the times had also brought temperance into fashion; and, instead of tavern suppers, I generally passed my evenings with my female acquaintances, among whom there was one to whom my affections were deeply and permanently engaged. The attachment was reciprocal; and the din of arms which threatened us with a separation, involving a cruel uncertainty in respect to the destiny of our love, but served to render it more ardent and more tender. Vows of constancy were mutually plighted;

and we gave so much of our time to each other, that I had little to spare to my quondam companions, whom I was really desirous of shaking off, and who, on their part, complained that I had turned dangler, and become good for nothing. There was a time when their raillery might have had some effect, but now it was entirely thrown away, and, like a true knight, I wholly devoted myself to my mistress and my country.

The object now was to raise my company, and as the streets of the city had been pretty well swept by the preceding and contemporary levies, it was necessary to have recourse to the country. My recruiting party was therefore sent out in various directions; and each of my officers, as well as myself, exerted himself in the business. Among the many unpleasant peculiarities of the American service, it was not the least that the drudgery, which in old military establishments belongs to sergeants and corporals, here devolved on the commissioned officers; and that the whole business of recruiting, drilling, etc., required their unremitted personal attention. This was more emphatically the case in recruiting, since the common opinion was, that the men and the officers were never to be separated, and hence, to see the persons who were to command them, and, above all, the captain, was deemed of vast importance by those inclining to enlist; for this reason I found it necessary, in common with my brother officers, to put my feelings most cruelly to the rack; and in an excursion I once made to Frankford, they were tried to the utmost. A number of fellows at the tavern, at which my party rendezvoused, indicated a desire to enlist, but although they drank freely of our liquor, they still held off. I soon perceived that the object was to amuse themselves at our expense, and that, if there might be one or two among them really disposed to engage, the others would prevent them. One fellow in particular, who had made the greatest show of taking the bounty, presuming on the weakness of our party, consisting only of a drummer, corporal, my second lieutenant, and myself, began to grow insolent, and manifested an intention to begin a quarrel, in the issue of which, he, no doubt, calculated on giving us a drubbing. The disgrace of such a circumstance presented itself to my mind in colors the most dismal, and I resolved, that, if a scuffle should be unavoidable, it should, at least, be as serious as the hangers, which my lieutenant and myself carried by our sides, could make it. Our endeavor, however, was to guard against a contest; but the moderation we testified was attributed to fear. At length the arrogance of the principal ruffian rose to such a height, that he squared himself for battle, and advanced toward me in an attitude of defiance. I put him by with an admonition to be quiet, though with a secret determination, that, if he repeated the insult, to begin the war, whatever might be the consequence. The occasion was soon presented; when, taking excellent aim, I struck him with my utmost force between the eyes, and sent him staggering to the other end of the room. Then instantly drawing our hangers, and receiving the manful coöperation of the corporal and drummer, we were fortunate enough to put a stop to any further hostilities. It was sometime before the fellow I had struck recovered from the blow, but when he did, he was quite an altered man. He was submissive as could be wished, begging my pardon for what he had done, and although he would not enlist, he hired himself to me for a few weeks as a fifer, in which capacity he had acted in the militia; and during the time he was in this employ, he bore about the effects of his insolence, in a pair of black eyes. This incident would be little worthy of relating, did it not serve in some degree to correct the error of those who seem to conceive the year 1776 to have been a season of almost universal patriotic enthusiasm. It was far from prevalent, in my opinion, among the lower ranks of the people, at least in Pennsylvania. At all times, indeed, licentious leveling principles are much to the general taste, and were, of course, popular with us; but the true merits of the contest were little understood or regarded. The opposition to the claims of Britain originated with the better sort: it was truly aristocratic in its commencement; and as the oppression to be apprehended had not been felt, no grounds existed for general enthusiasm. The cause of liberty, it is true, was fashionable, and there were great preparations to fight for it; but zeal, proportioned to the magnitude of the question, was only to be looked for in the minds of those sagacious politicians, who inferred effects from causes, and who, as Mr. Burke expresses it, "snuffed the approach of tyranny in every tainted breeze."

Certain it was, at least, that recruiting went on but heavily. Some officers had been more successful than others, but none of the companies were complete: mine, perhaps, contained about half its complement of men, and these had been obtained by dint of great exertion. In this situation, Captain Lenox of Shee's regiment also, suggested the trying our luck on the Eastern shore of Maryland, particularly at Chester, situated on the river of that name. It having been a place of some trade, it was supposed there might be seamen or longshoremen there, out of employ. We accordingly set out on the expedition, making our first effort at Warwick, an inconsiderable village, a few miles within the boundaries of Maryland. Here we remained a day or two, our stay having been prolonged by bad weather. At the tavern we put up at, we made acquaintance with a gentleman of note, who resided in the neighborhood, and pretty generally known by the familiar name of Dan Heath. He seemed to like our company, as he was continually with us while we stayed. Mr. Health was a sportsman, and apparently too little interested in political concerns, to be either much of a Whig or a Tory, though, from the indifference he evinced, we rather concluded him the latter. He helped us, however, to a recruit, a fellow, he said, who would do to stop a bullet as well as a better man, and, as he was a truly worthless dog, he held, that the neighborhood would be much indebted to us for taking him away. When we left Warwick, he fulfilled his promise of accompanying us some miles under pretense of aiding us in getting men, but as he showed us none, we were convinced that he attended us more for his own sake than ours, and that, having nothing to do, probably, he had availed himself of the opportunity to kill a little time. He gave the tone to the conversation on the road, which generally turned on the sports of the turf and the cockpit; but he never spoke with so much animation, as when expatiating on those feats of human prowess, wherein victory is achieved by *tooth and nail*, in modern phrase, by biting and gouging: and pointing out to us one of the heroes of these direful conflicts, "There," says he, "is a fellow that has not his match in the country: see what a set of teeth he has, a man's thumb would be nothing to them."

On bidding good morning to Mr. Heath, with whose vivacity we were amused, we pursued our course to Chester, and as soon as we arrived there, delivered our letters of introduction. The gentlemen to whom they were addressed received us with the utmost politeness, and declared their warmest wishes for the success of our errand, though accompanied with expressions of regret that they could not give us encouragement to beat up in their town, as well because there were few, if any, in it, that were likely to enlist, as that their own province was about raising troops; and as that was the case, it would not be taken well should they assist in transferring any of their men to the line of Pennsylvania. With such unfavorable prospects in Maryland, it would have been folly to have proceeded further: we, therefore, set off on our way home the next morning, declining several invitations to dinner. We found this country well deserving of its reputation for hospitality. Between Warwick and Georgetown, we were taken home to lodge by a gentleman of the name of Wilmer, whom we had never seen before: We were warmly pressed by Mr. Harry Pierce, with whom we met by accident on the road, to spend some time with him at his residence in the neighborhood, and met with no less cordiality from Mr. Thomas Ringold, of Chester, who had once, when very young, lodged at my mother's. Returning by Warwick, we sent forward our solitary recruit, for whom we tossed up; and in winning, I was, in fact, but a very small gainer, since his merits had been set at their full value by Mr. Heath; and he was never fit for anything better than the inglorious post of camp color man.

After this unsuccessful jaunt I bent my course to the Four-lane-ends, Newtown, and Corryell's Ferry; thence passing into Jersey, I proceeded to the Hickory tavern, to Pittstown, Baptisttown, Flemmingtown, and other towns, whose names I do not remember. As Captain Stewart (the late General Walter Stewart) of our regiment had recently reaped this field, I was only a gleaner: In the whole of my tour, therefore, I picked up but three or four men: and could most sincerely have said:

> That the recruiting trade, with all its train
> Of endless cure, fatigue, and endless pain,

I could most gladly have renounced, even without the very preferable alternative of Captain Plume. My number of privates might now have amounted to about forty, but these were soon augmented by the noble addition of one and twenty stout native Americans, brought by Lieutenants Edwards and Forrest from Egg Harbor.

Towards spring our battalion was complete; and already, from the unremitted attention that had been paid to it by the officers of every grade, it had made, for so short a time, a very laudable progress in discipline. Besides partial drillings, it was exercised every morning and evening; and what was of still more importance, habits of obedience and subordination were strictly inculcated and maintained. We were comparatively well armed, uniformed, and equipped; and it is but justice to say, that, in point of all the exteriors, by which military corps are tested, ours was on a footing with the most promising on the continent. We were quartered in the barracks, together with the other battalions that were raising; and by way of counteracting the general gloom, not diminished by the practice of fast days and sermons, borrowed from New England, we promoted balls and other amusements. Had the contest been a religious one, and our people been inflamed by a zeal on points of faith like the Crusaders, or the army of Cromwell, this might have been the proper method of exciting them to acts of heroism; but they were to be taken as they were, and as this was not the case, it was certainly not the mode to make soldiers in Pennsylvania. The puritanical spirit was unknown among us.

The Declaration of Independence, whose date will never be forgotten so long as liberty remains the fashion, and demagogues continue to thrive upon it, was, with the utmost speed, transmitted to the armies; and, when received, read to the respective regiments. If it was not embraced with all the enthusiasm that has been ascribed to the event, it was, at least, hailed with acclamations, as, no doubt, any other act of congress, not flagrantly improper, would at that time have been. The propriety of the measure had been little canvassed among us; and perhaps it was to our honor, considered merely as soldiers, that we were so little of politicians. A predilection for republicanism, it is true, had not reached the army, at least the Pennsylvania line; but as an attempt to negotiate, in our unorganized situation, would probably have divided and ruined us, the step was considered wise, although a passage of the Rubicon, and calculated to close the door to accommodation. Being looked upon as unavoidable, if resistance was to be persisted in, it was approved; and produced no resignations among the officers that I am aware of, except that of Lieutenant-Colonel William Allen, already mentioned, who was with his regiment in Canada. He called at our camp on his way to Philadelphia, where he appeared somewhat surprised and mortified, that his example had no followers.

Being now independent, we had no further use for a king, or even the semblance of one; for which reason, the equestrian statue of George the Third in New York was thrown down and demolished. The head of the king was cut off by way of inflaming the public valor: but so little was the spirit of seventy-six like the spirit of subsequent eras, that the act was received with extreme coldness and indifference. Had even George himself been among us, he would have been in no great danger of personal injury, at least from the army.

Among the disaffected in Philadelphia, Dr. Kearsley was pre-eminently ardent and rash. An extremely zealous loyalist, and impetuous in his temper, he had given much umbrage to the Whigs; and, if I am not mistaken, he had been detected in some hostile machinations. Hence he was deemed a proper subject for the fashionable punishment of tarring, feathering, and carting. He was seized at his own door by a party of the militia, and, in the attempt to resist them, received a wound in his hand from a bayonet. Being overpowered, he was placed in a cart provided for the purpose, and, amidst a multitude of boys and idlers, paraded through the streets to the tune of the rogues' march. I happened to be at the coffee-house when the concourse arrived there. They made a halt, while the Doctor, foaming with rage and indignation, without his hat, his wig disheveled and bloody from his wounded hand, stood up in the cart and called for a bowl of punch. It was quickly handed to him; when, so vehement was his thirst, that he drained it of its contents before he took it from his lips. What were the feelings of others on this lawless proceeding I know not, but mine, I must confess, revolted at the spectacle. I was shocked at seeing a lately respected citizen so cruelly vilified, and was imprudent enough to say, that, had I been a magistrate, I would, at every hazard, have interposed my authority in suppression of the outrage. But this was not the only instance which convinced me that I wanted nerves for a revolutionist. It must be admitted, however, that the conduct of the populace was marked by a lenity which peculiarly distinguished the cradle of our republicanism. Tar and feathers had been dispensed with, and, excepting the injury he had received in his hand, no sort of violence was offered by the mob to their victim. But to a man of high spirit, as the Doctor was, the indignity in its lightest form was sufficient to madden him: it probably had this effect, since his conduct became so extremely outrageous, that it was thought necessary to confine him. From the city he was soon after removed to Carlisle, where he died during the war.

A few days after the carting of Mr. Kearsley, Mr. Isaac Hunt, the attorney, was treated in the same manner, but he managed the matter much better than his precursor. Instead of braving his conductors like the Doctor, Mr. Hunt was a pattern of meekness and humility; and at every halt that was made, he rose and expressed his acknowledgments to the crowd for their forbearance and civility. After a parade of an hour or two, he was set down at his own door, as uninjured in body as in mind. He soon after removed to one of the islands, if I mistake not, to Barbados, where, it was understood, he took orders.

Not long after these occurrences, Major Skene, of the British army, ventured to show himself in Philadelphia. Whatever might have been his inducement to the measure, it was deemed expedient by the newly constituted authorities to have him arrested and secured. A guard was accordingly placed over him at his lodgings, at the city tavern. The officer to whose charge he was especially committed was Mr. Francis Wade, the brewer, an Irishman of distinguished zeal in the cause, and one who was supposed to possess talents peculiarly befitting him for the task of curbing the spirit of a haughty Briton, which Skene undoubtedly was. I well recollect the day that the guard was paraded to escort him out of the city on his way to some other station. An immense crowd of spectators stood before the door of his quarters, and lined the street through which he was to pass. The weather being warm, the window sashes of his apartment were raised, and Skene, with his bottle of wine upon the table, having just finished his dinner, roared out, in the voice of a Stentor, *God save great George our King.* Had the spirit of seventy-five, in any degree, resembled the spirit of Jacobinism, to which it has been unjustly compared, this bravado would unquestionably have brought the major to the *lamp post,* and set his head upon a pike; but as, fortunately for him, it did not, he was suffered to proceed with his song, and the auditory seemed more generally amused than offended.

Perhaps I may be excused for these trifling details, when it is considered that they serve to mark the temper of the times, and to show that they were not all fire and fury, as certain modern pretenders, to the spirit of *seventy-six,* have almost persuaded us they were. It ought to be granted, indeed, that an equal degree of toleration was not everywhere to be met with. It would scarcely have been found in that description of persons, which soon arrogated, and have since voted, themselves the exclusive possession of all the patriotism in the nation. Even that small portion of the monopolists which resided at Reading, revolted at a moderation they did not understand; and all who were less violent and bigoted than themselves were branded as Tories. All the families which had removed from Philadelphia were involved in this reproach; and, in their avoidance of the enemy, to the manifest injury of their affairs, they were supposed to exhibit proofs of disaffection. Nor was I much better off: my having risked myself in the field was nothing: I should have stayed at home, talked big, been a militia-man, and hunted Tories,

CHAPTER XI

NICHOLAS CRESSWELL SHUNS THE WAR

GRAYDON IN Philadelphia was sufficiently disapproving of the harsh measures taken by the patriots against the loyalists. But what of a loyalist himself? In Alexandria, Virginia, a young Englishman who had come over in 1774 to make his fortune as a colonial farmer found himself in decidedly hot water. To him all was confusion and nonsense—an uprising of beggars and knaves. Nicholas Cresswell kept a diary in which he recorded his first shock of dismay, his journey into the back country along the Ohio River where he met with interesting adventures among the Indians, and at length his escape through New York from a situation wherein he also might have suffered the fate of the untimely faithful.

E VERYTHING here * is in the utmost confusion. Committees are appointed to inspect into the characters and conduct of every tradesman, to prevent them selling tea or buying British manufactures. Some of them have been tarred and feathered, others had their property burnt and destroyed by the populace. Independent companies are raising in every county on the continent, appointed adjutants and train their men as if they were on the eve of a war. A General Congress of the different colonies met at Philadelphia on the 5th of last month are still sitting, but their business is a profound secret. Subscription is raising in every colony on the continent for the relief of the people of Boston. The King is openly cursed, and his authority set at defiance. In short, everything is ripe for rebellion. The New Englanders by their canting, whining, insinuating tricks have persuaded the rest of the colonies that the government is going to make absolute slaves of them. This I believe never was intended, but the Presbyterian rascals have had address sufficient to make the other colonies come into their scheme. By everything that I can understand, in the different company I have been in, independence is what the Massachusetts people aim at, but am not in the least doubt but the government will take such salutary and speedy measure, as will

* Alexandria, Virginia, October, 1774.

entirely frustrate their abominable intentions. I am afraid it will be some time before this hubbub is settled and there is nothing to be done now. All trade is almost at a stand, every one seems to be at a loss in what manner to proceed. For my own part, did I not think this affair would be over in the spring, I would immediately return home. But I am very unwilling to return in a worse condition than I was when I came out and be laughed at by all my friends. If I return now and matters are settled they will never consent to my leaving England again, and I am very sensible from what I have already seen of the country, that I can with a small sum make a very pretty fortune here, in a little time if I am anyways fortunate, as a farmer. Mr. Kirk advises me to stay till spring and take a tour in the back country, gives me every possible encouragement, and offers me every assistance in his power. I will take his advice. Am determined not to return till I can do it with credit, without those rascals do persuade the colonies into a rebellion.

Friday, August 4th, 1775. Agreed to go with Major Crawford to Mr. John Gibson's, an Indian trader, about 12 miles below Fort Pitt.* He is a man that has great interest amongst the Indians, consequently the best person to direct me how to dispose of my goods to the best advantage. *Monday, August 7th, 1775.* At Mr. Crawford's waiting for Major Crawford. I believe he is a dilatory man and little dependence to be put in him. *Tuesday, August 8th, 1775.* Very uneasy to wait here, doing nothing. Am afraid I shall be too late to return home this fall. Went with Miss Crawford and Miss Grimes to John Minton's. When we came to a small creek we had to cross the girls tucked up their petticoats above their knees and forded it with the greatest indifference. Nothing unusual here, though these are the first people in the country.

Wednesday, August 9th, 1775. Mr. Berwick and I set out this morning to Major Crawford's, but met him at his mistress's. This woman is common to him, his brother, half brother, and his own son, and is his wife's sister's daughter at the same time. A set of vile brutes. He informs me the Congress have discarded all the governors on the continent and taken all affairs civil and military into their management. Independence is what these scoundrels aim at. Confusion to their schemes. *Thursday, August 10th, 1775.* At Capt. Stephenson's. Instructed his people to make a stack of wheat. Farming in a poor uncultivated state here. Capt. Stephenson an honest, worthy man. Went to V. Crawford's in the evening. No

* Pittsburgh. Cresswell is now concluding his tour of the back country.

prospect of Major Crawford going to Gibson's soon. Determined
to set out for Fort Pitt on Monday next. *Friday, August 11th, 1775.*
Last night Miss G. came. A fine blooming Irish girl. The flesh overcame the spirit.

Sunday, August 13th, 1775. Mr. Berwick was kind enough to
let me ride his horse to Fort Pitt, where I am to deliver him to a
certain Mr. John Meddison. Left Mr. V. Crawford's and with him
I left my watch, buckles, breast buckles, stock buckle and silver
buttons, with a paper directing how I would have them disposed
of if death should happen to my lot, as every one tells me that I
am running a great risk of being killed by the Indians. I am not
afraid of meeting with bad usage from them. Got to Mr. John De
Camp's at night.

Fort Pitt—Monday, August 14th, 1775. Left Mr. De Camp's
Dined at Turtle Creek. Arrived at Fort Pitt in the evening with
only two dollars in my pocket and very shabby dress.

Monday, August 21st, 1775. Mr. Anderson informs me that the
Indians are not well pleased at any one going into their country
dressed in a hunting shirt. Got a calico shirt made in the Indian
fashion, trimmed up with silver brooches and armplates so that I
scarcely know myself. Crossed the Allegheny River and went about
two miles and camped at a small run to be ready to start early
in the morning. We had forgotten a tin kettle in town. I went back
for it while Mr. Anderson made a fire, returning in the dark lost
my way and got to an Indian camp, where I found two squaws,
but they could not speak English. By signs made them understand what I wanted and they put me right.

Indian Country—Tuesday, August 22nd, 1775. A very heavy fog
this morning. We had got two bottles of rum, two loaves of bread,
and a bacon ham along with us. Agreed to take a dram to prevent us catching the fever and ague, but drank rather too much
and most stupidly forgot our provisions. Got to Logg's Town about
noon, crossed the river and went to Mr. John Gibson's. Lodged
there, but would not make our wants known for fear of being
laughed at. We crossed the river in a canoe made of hickory bark,
stretched open with sticks. *Wednesday, August 23rd, 1775.* Proceeded on our journey, but not one morsel of provision. Crossed
Great Beaver Creek at Capt. White-Eye's house. This is an Indian
warrior of the Delaware's nation. Camped at Little Beaver Creek
with three Indian squaws and a man. Nothing to eat but berries
such as we found in the woods. Find Mr. Anderson a good hearty
companion. One of the Indian squaws invited me to sleep with her,

but I pretended to be sick. She was very kind and brought me some plums she got in the woods.

Saturday, August 26th, 1775. Set out early this morning, traveled very hard till noon, when we passed through the largest plum tree thicket I ever saw. I believe it was a mile long, nothing but the plum and cherry trees. Killed a rattlesnake. Just as the sun went down we stopped to get our supper on some dewberries (a small berry something like a gooseberry). Mr. Anderson had gone before me and said he would ride on about two miles to a small run where he intended to camp, as soon as I had got sufficient. I mounted my horse and followed him till I came to a place where the road forked. I took the path that I supposed he had gone and rode till it began to be dark, when I imagined myself to be wrong, and there was not a possibility of me finding my way back in the night. Determined to stay where I was till morning, I had no sooner alighted from my horse, but I discovered the glimmering of a fire about four hundred yards from me. This rejoiced me exceedingly, supposing it was Mr. Anderson. When I got there, to my great disappointment and surprise found three Indian women and a little boy. I believe they were as much surprised as I was. None of them could speak English and I could not speak Indian. I alighted and marked the path I had come and that I had left, on the ground with the end of my stick, made a small channel in the earth which I poured full of water, laid some fire by the side of it, and then laid myself down by the side of the fire, repeating the name of Anderson which I soon understood they knew.

The youngest girl immediately unsaddled my horse, unstrapped the belt, hoppled him, and turned him out, then spread my blankets at the fire and made signs for me to sit down. The oldest made me a little hash of dried venison and bear's oil, which eat very well, but neither bread or salt. After supper they made signs I must go to sleep. Then they held a consultation for some time which made me very uneasy, the two eldest women and the boy laid down on the opposite side of the fire and some distance away. The youngest (she had taken so much pains with my horse) came and placed herself very near me. I began to think she had some amorous design upon me. In about half an hour she began to creep nearer me and pulled my blanket. I found what she wanted and lifted it up. She immediately came to me and made me as happy as it was in her power to do. She was young, handsome, and healthy. Fine regular features and fine eyes; had she not painted them with red before she came to bed!—and I suppose answers as well as My Lady in the dark.

Sunday, August 27th, 1775. This morning my bedfellow went into the woods and caught her horse and mine, saddled them, put my blanket on the saddle, and prepared everything ready, seemingly with a great deal of good nature. Absolutely refused my assistance. The old woman got me some dried venison for breakfast. When I took my leave returned the thanks as well as I could by signs. My bedfellow was my guide and conducted me through the woods, where there were no signs of a road or without my knowing with certainty whither I was going. She often mentioned John Anderson and talked a great deal in Indian. I attempted to speak Indian, which diverted her exceedingly. In about an hour she brought me to Mr. Anderson's camp, who had been very uneasy at my absence and employed an Indian to seek me. I gave my Dulcinea a match coat, with which she seemed very well pleased.

Tuesday, August 29th, 1775. Left White-Eye's town. Saw the bones of one Mr. Cammel, a white man, that had been killed by the Indians. Got to Co-a-shoking about noon. It is at the forks of the Muskingham. The Indians have removed from Newcomer Town to this place. King Newcomer lives here. Sold part of my goods here to good advantage. Crossed a branch of Muskingham and went to Old Hundy, this is a scattering Indian settlement. Lodged at a Mohawk Indian's house, who offered me his sister and Mr. Anderson his daughter to sleep with us, which we were obliged to accept.

Wednesday, August 30th, 1775. My bedfellow very fond of me this morning and wants to go with me. Find I must often meet with such encounters as these if I do not take a squaw to myself. She is young and sprightly, tolerably handsome, and can speak a little English. Agreed to take her. She saddled her horse and went with us to New Hundy about 3 miles off, where she had several relations who made me very welcome to such as they had. From there to Coashoskis, where we lodged in my squaw's brother's, made me a compliment of a young wolf but I could not take it with me. *Thursday, August 31st, 1775.* At Coashoskis. Mr. Anderson could not find his horse. Sold all my goods for furs. In the afternoon rambled about the town, smoking tobacco with the Indians and did everything in my power to make myself agreeable to them. Went to see the King. He lives in a poor house, and he is as poor in dress as any of them, no emblem of royalty or majesty about him. He is an old man, treated me very kindly, called me his good friend, and hoped I would be kind to my squaw. Gave me a small string of wampum as a token of friendship. My squaw uneasy to see me write so much.

Saturday, September 9th, 1775. Left the town. Mr. Anderson, N. and I went to the Tuscarora town. Then got lost in the woods and rambled till dark, when we camped by the side of a little run. Very merry this afternoon with our misfortune. *Sunday, September 10th, 1775.* Rambled till noon when we found ourselves at Bouquet's old fort, now demolished. Went to an Indian camp, where Mr. Anderson met with an old wife of his, who would go with him, which he agreed to. We have each of us a girl. It is an odd way of traveling, but we are obliged to submit to it. Met with Mr. Anderson's people in the evening, camped by the side of Tuscarora Creek. Saw the vestige, the Tuscarora old town, but now deserted. *Tuesday, Sept. 12th, 1775.* Our squaws are very necessary, fetching our horses to the camp and saddling them, making our fire at night and cooking our victuals, and every other thing they think will please us. Traveled over several barren mountains, some of them produce great plenty of wild grapes. Lodged in an old Indian camp. Bad water.

Saturday, September 30th, 1775. Went over the river and bought a porcupine skin of an Indian. It is something like our hedgehog at home, only the quills are longer. The Indians dye them of various colors and work them on their trinkets. Mr. Edward Rice promised me his horse to carry me to V. Crawford's on Monday. Sold my gun to Mr. James Berwick, who gave me a copy of the Indian speech. Saw the Indians dance in the council house. N. very uneasy, she weeps plentifully. I am unhappy that this honest creature has taken such a fancy to me.

Sunday, October 1st, 1775. Took leave of most of my acquaintances in town. Mr. Douglas gave me an Indian tobacco pouch made of a mink skin adorned with porcupine quills. Determined to go to New York and make my escape to the English army. Marchington will send the horse to Leesburg. In short, I have no other alternative, if I stay among the *Sleber,* I must go to *Liaj.* Great numbers—I believe half the people in town—are *Sgnik Sdneirf.* Some of the people have hung Washington, Putnam, and Mifflin on their sign post in public.

Monday, October 21st, 1776. This morning I am told that the committee of this town* will not permit me to depart this colony as they look upon me to be a spy and that I must be obliged to give security or go to jail. Whether this is done to get me to enlist into their service or some rascal has informed against me I cannot tell.

* Alexandria, Virginia.

Saturday, Oct. 26th, 1776. These three days I have spent most disagreeably—nothing to do and all alone. When I reflect on my present situation it makes me miserable. I am now in an enemy's country, forbidden to depart. Little to subsist upon and dare not do anything to get a living, for fear of getting myself ranked as an inhabitant and be obliged to carry arms against my native country. My interest and inclination, unhappy alternative indeed, to turn parricide or starve. Am determined to go amongst the Indians. I look upon them to be the more humane people of the two.

Wednesday, November 27th, 1776. The committee met to-day. Am informed it is to search my papers, if not to take me up and imprison me, but will be prepared for them. *Thursday, Nov. 28, 1776.* This morning three of the committee men waited on me and informed me that the committee did not think it prudent to let me go out of the country at this time and hoped that I would give my word of honor not to depart this colony for three months. Otherwise they would confine me. I was obliged to do the first as the lesser evil of the two. They were polite enough not to search my chest. Spent the evening at Mr. Kirk's, who seemed very glad that I was obliged to stay. This affronted me, we both got drunk and quarreled about state affairs.

Alexandria, Virginia—Friday, November 29, 1776. Very sick with my last night's debauch, and very sorry for my last night's conduct. My present disagreeable confinement, the loss of three years of the most valuable part of life, the disappointments and misfortunes I have met with since I left my native country, and what is worst of all, the certainty of being reproached with obstinacy and extravagancy on my return. These bitter reflections will intrude themselves involuntarily, and create a lowness of spirit which too often is the cause of me drinking more than is of service. I must and will call my resolution and fortitude to my aid, or I shall insensibly sink into the sot or the drunkard. A character so despicable ought to be avoided with the greatest care. Mr. Kirk and I made up the quarrel this morning. Must not quarrel with him. He confesses that he did everything in his power to intoxicate me, on purpose to raise my spirits. I will not borrow my spirits in that manner for the future. Left Leesburg. Dined at Mosse's Ordinary. Got to Alexandria. Spent the evening with Mr. McCrey.

Monday, Dec. 9th, 1776. This morning I was remarkably low-spirited. About three o'clock in the afternoon Mr. Hugh Neilson came and insisted on my spending the evening at *The Billet*. I have spent it with a vengeance with Flemming, Patterson, Cleone More, Capt. Wm. Johnston and H. Neilson. Sent them all to bed drunk and I am now going to bed myself at 9 in the morning as drunk as an honest man could wish. *Tuesday, December 10th, 1776.* Got up at 2 in the afternoon. Got drunk before 10, with the same company I was with yesterday and am now going to bed at 2 in the morning, most princely drunk indeed. I saw all my companions in bed before I left them, but most damnable drunk. A fine course of life truly, drunk every night, this is tampering with the devil to it. *Wednesday, Dec. 11th, 1776.* Much indisposed this morning. I hear my pet companions and brothers in iniquity coming upstairs, but am determined to keep sober to-day. *Thursday, Dec. 12th, 1776.* Last night was the worst we have had since we first commenced the trade of drunkards. Mr. Kirk and P. Cavan joined us. We instituted a foolish society by the name of the Black-eyed Club. I was President and Mr. More Secretary. All of us got most intolerably drunk. This is the first day that I have had any time for reflection this week. Uneasiness of mind first engaged me in this last debauch. Good company induced me to continue it and now a bitter reflection, an aching head, a sick stomach, a trembling hand and a number of disagreeable concomitants that are annexed to this detestable vice cause me to quit the pursuit. Drunkenness is certainly one of the most odious vices that mankind can possibly be guilty of, the consequences are so exceedingly pernicious to our health, our happiness and interest. It is astonishing that any being endued with the faculty of thinking, should take such pains to divest himself of reason, that knowingly and willingly he will destroy his constitution and sink himself below the level of a brute. Mr. Kirk came and spent the evening at my lodgings.

Saturday, December 14th, 1776. News that General Howe is at Trenton in the Jerseys, from Philadelphia. It is certain the Congress has left Philadelphia and are now at Baltimore. Great numbers of recruiting parties are out to raise men, but can scarcely get a man by any means, though their bounty is 12£. None will enlist that can avoid it. They get some servants and convicts which are purchased from their masters, these will desert the first opportunity. The violent *Slebers* are much dispirited. The politicians (or rather timid Whigs) give all up for lost. And the Tories begin to exult. The time is out that the flying camp was enlisted for, and it is said that they refuse to serve any longer, though they have been solicited in the strongest terms. This will make a great deficiency in their army, the loss of ten thousand men. I am convinced that if General Howe will push to Philadelphia the day is his own. Find it will be best for me to remove out of town for a little while or I may stand a chance of going to jail as I am too often abusing these rascals. Am determined to go into Berkley.

Piedmont, Berkley County, Virginia—Tuesday, December 17th, 1776. Went to Mr. Nourse's. He was much surprised to see me, supposed that I had been gone. Insists on me spending the Christmas with him. *Wednesday, Dec. 18th, 1776.* Exceedingly unhappy, every one here is industriously employed, and I am living for no use in creation, except it be to eat and drink. The pleasure that this numerous family enjoys and the company and conversation of each other, the apparent harmony, peace and quietness that subsist amongst them, call thoughts of a very unpleasing nature to my mind, and make me miserable. Every one does the utmost to keep up my spirits and make the time pass agreeable. Miss Kitty Nourse is not the most backward in this particular. She is one of the most sensible, agreeable and well-bred girls that I have seen since I left England. Added to these, industry, economy (which by the by, is a virtue very seldom to be met with in either male or female in this country), wit, good nature, and a handsome person altogether renders her a reliable and agreeable companion. Was I fixed in my place of life and nothing at home, should think myself happy. To prevent any disagreeable passion intruding, am determined to leave the house to-morrow

On Board the "Bell and Mary," New York Harbor—Wednesday, May 14th, 1777. This morning the wind came round to south, weighed and got up to the town about noon. Moored our ship opposite the navy brewhouse which is on Long Island. Mr. Robinson went ashore, but won't permit Mr. Keir and me to go until he has seen the Admiral. I must now determine what to do, whether to enter into the army or return home. If I was at liberty to follow my own inclination I would enter into the army, but the solemn promise I made Mr. Mason on the 14th of April utterly forbids it, which was not to enter into any army for 12 months from that day. To this gentleman I am under very great and many obligations. Had it not been for his kind interposition on the 20th of October, 1775, and his offering to be bound in a very large sum, that I should not depart the colony of six months from that time, I must have been dragged to prison or have entered into their army. What stamps the greater value upon the obligation, he did it unsolicited and unknown to me. He also gave me letters of recommendation to the members of Congress and the Governor Council of Virginia. Nay, I believe he extorted this promise from me out of a principle of humanity extended to my parents, who, he understood from my accounts, are much averse to me entering into the army. I am certain Mr. Mason can have no view of interest in what he did for me, it is impossible that he should have any, only that arising from a generous mind, helping a stranger in distress. Should I let my inclination or my necessity get the better of my honour, I shall forever detest myself, as a mean, dirty rascal. No, forbid it honor, forbid it Heaven, be the consequence what it will, I will not enter into the army till the expiration of my promised time. But the thought of returning home a beggar is worse than death. I can bear to write upon this subject no longer.

Friday, May 16th, 1777. This morning waited upon General Howe, and was introduced to him by Major Cuzler. His Excellency asked me about the affairs in Virginia and whether I thought there was a great many friends to government there. To both questions I answered him with truth to the best of my knowledge. But I think his information has been bad and his expectations too sanguine. I told him my own situation very candidly, gave him my real reasons why I could not enter into the army. He behaved to me with the greatest politeness, seemed to approve of my honorable resolution as he was pleased to call it, and promised to do anything for me that lay in his power in repect to my getting home. That is, if I meet with a ship to my mind that is bound home he will give me a permit to go in her. I believe Mr. Keir will enter into the army and have some prospect of getting a lieutenancy in Major Holland's Guides. He is referred to Sir Wm. Erskine, his countryman, therefore he needs not fear, for the Scotch will hang together. Lodged at one Capt. Millar's, a Scotch refugee from Norfolk in Virginia. It is a mean, dirty, nasty hole; I am determined to leave it to-morrow.

Sunday, June 1st, 1777. My present situation is far from being agreeable, though much better than it was a month ago. I now breathe the air of liberty and freedom, which I have been a stranger to since October 20th, 1775. For very substantial reasons, I have never mentioned this in my journal before, as I have always carried it about with me, and have always had a notion that I should be obliged to make my escape, something in the manner I at last effected it. If my own handwriting had been produced as a witness against me (supposing I had been taken in attempting to make my escape by the people who did not personally know me) I might have had some small chance of regaining my liberty, but had I always carried such a capital witness against me, in my pocket, and have been taken before I had time to destroy it, my life must undoubtedly have paid the forfeiture of my folly and imprudence.

Instead of going to church I will rectify that mysterious part of my journal, while it is fresh in my memory. Probably at some future period, when I have less time (for I have absolutely too much at present to do anything as it ought to be done), but more inclination and my mind more at ease than it is at the present, I may revise and correct the many errors that frequently occur in it. I think I shall defer it till I am an old man, for at present I have no thoughts of turning author.

In the month of March, 1775, I wrote to all my friends in England and freely declared my sentiments upon the present rebellion. Indeed, I then called it by no other name to my friends. My letters I sent by a friend bound to Leghorn, but the council of safety's boat boarded him in the Bay and he was obliged to give up all the letters he had on board, mine amongst the rest, which were read before the council of safety and sent express to the committee at Alexandria, with orders to secure my person as one inimical to the rights and liberties of America. But I was gone into the back country before the express arrived at Alexandria. However, the letters were lodged with the chairman of the committee till my return in October, 1775, when a meeting of the committee was immediately called and they thought proper in their great wisdom and prudence to make a resolve that the body of Nicholas Cresswell should be committed to the care of the jail keeper until he, the said Nicholas Cresswell, was fully convinced of his political errors.

In short, I was arraigned, tried, condemned, and the sentence nearly put in execution before I knew anything about it, but by the kind interposition of Mr. Thomson Mason immediately reprieved, by his offering to be bound in any sum they chose to mention that I should not depart the colony of six months without their consent. I was utterly unacquainted with the whole proceeding till the day after the committee had agreed to send me to jail. When Mr. Mason in a very polite letter let me know what he had done for me, hoping that I would make myself as easy as possible in the colony during the limited time, as he did not doubt but matters would be accommodated before the expiration of six months, as he trusted implicitly to my honor, the fulfilling the contract he had made in my favor, at the same time made me an offer of his house and assistance in anything that lay in his power. I then removed to Leesburg and before the expiration of the six months was taken sick and continued so till the latter end of July, 1776. In this time I was not disturbed by the committee. I thought it a proper time to get away. Accordingly, I got letters of recommendation to some members of the Congress from my friend Mr. Mason, by which means I got a pass from the Congress, dated August 29th, 1776.

By virtue of this pass I was permitted to go to New York, from which place I intended to make my escape to our army then on Long Island. I got to New York on the 7th of September, 1776, and had laid the plan for my escape to our fleet or Long Island whichever I could get to, by means of a floating stage that was moored in the old ship. No other thing, either boat or canoe, was to be found. Just as I had found this out I unfortunately met with Mr. Thomson, a Presbyterian parson and chaplain to one of the Virginia regiments then at New York. With this gentleman I had quarreled about politics in November, 1774. I believe he remembered it and suspected my design, but for that evening behaved with the greatest politeness, only took care to put a guard over me. On the next morning he told me he knew my sentiments and if I did not choose to return to Virginia with Lieutenant Noland I would be put in the provo immediately. I assured him curiosity was my only motive for coming there. I had no intention of going to the enemy. This would not satisfy the Rev. Sir, I must either return to Virginia or go to the provo. I had no other alternative, and to convince him that I had no intention of making my escape I would cheerfully return with Mr. Noland, but hoped he would not send me in the character of a prisoner. He assured me Mr. Noland would go with me in the character of a companion. I was under the necessity of submitting to this puritanic priest for fear of worse consequences. Mr. Noland behaved very well to me all the way, always willing to do as I did and had it not been for the thoughts of him being as a guard over me, would have been an excellent companion.

Mr. Thomson had wrote to the committee of Leesburg concerning me by Mr. Noland, who accordingly met and was for committing me to prison. But by the interest of Mr. Mason I was a second time reprieved and they agreed to take my own parole for four months from the 20th of September, 1776, to the 20th of January, 1777. In that time they used many threats and persuasions to get me into their army. I had got Muller's Treatise upon Fortification and Gunnery, which some of their military officers had seen in my lodgings. I had got some of the technical terms belonging to the profession by heart, which I always took care to use before the most vain part of them, especially if I knew them to be ignorant. Such as those are always the best puffs with the vulgar herd. When I happened into company with those who understood it I always took care to give them evasive and ambiguous answers. By these means I became consequential amongst them, and I believe it was the chief reason why they treated me with so much civility as they were pleased to call it.

My first parole was no sooner expired but I was obliged to give a second for three months from the 5th of February to the 5th of May, which I broke with great reluctance only one day. But if such a breach of honor can be excused I certainly may, in justice, claim some title to it, because I suffered in consequence of a law made after the offense was committed. When I wrote my letters, which were the original cause of my confinement, there was no act or resolve made by the Colonial Convention or the Congress to imprison any one merely for his sentiments. The act, resolve, edict or whatever name it has for imprisonment and confiscation of the efforts of friends to government, was made by the Congress in March, 1776, after I had had a *Ne Exit Colonia* upon me for near six months. I think this is a sufficient and ample excuse for my breaking my parole a single day. I am weary with scribbling, therefore will give over.

Wednesday, July 9th, 1777. Went to New York in the boat with Col. Cotton to purchase stores for the voyage. Dined with Capt. Scott on board the Brig *Harriet*. Drunk tea at Mrs. Bennett's with Major L.'s lady and several other ladies. After tea I waited upon Mrs. L. to her lodgings. She insisted upon me staying to sup and spend the evening with her and I did not need much solicitation to spend an evening with a handsome and polite young lady. After supper and a cheerful glass of good wine we entered into a very agreeable *tête-à-tête* and then oh, matrimony, matrimony, thou coverest more female frailties than charity does sins! Nicholas, if ever thou sinned religiously in thy life, it has been this time. This kind, affable, and most obliging lady in public was most rigidly religious. At Mrs. Bennett's she had treated the character of a poor lady in the neighborhood, who had made a slip and unfortunately been caught in the fact, in a most barbarous and cruel manner. She ran over the Scriptures from Genesis to Revelations, for sentences to prove the heinous crime of fornication. In that strain she continued till after supper and then I soon found she was made of warm flesh and blood. In short, she is the greatest medley I ever knew. In public she has all the apparent religion of the most rigid and hypocritical Presbyterian parson, the neatness and temperance of a Quaker with the modesty of a vestal. In private, the air and behavior of a professed courtesan, and in bed the lechery of a guinea pig,—(Nicholas, Nicholas if ever human being). Such a one, I think, would make me very happy, but rather than I would marry one who overacts the part of religion, pretends to so much chastity and is in appearances a stiff, prudish, formal lump of mortality, I would go into Lapland and be dry nurse to a bear. But stop, Nicholas, don't treat the lady so unmercifully. Her husband is gone to the war. She remembers the saying that all cuckolds go to heaven, therefore if he should happen to die in the bed of honor and not have time to prepare himself properly for a future state. . . . *On Board the Brig, Thursday, July 10, 1777.* This morning returned to the ship. Ruminating upon my last night's adventure most of this day, it will not bear reflection. Understand we are to have the *Niger* frigate for our convoy. Went ashore with Cols. Reid and Cotton, but returned on board in the evening. This has been one of the hottest days we have had this summer. *Friday, July 11, 1777.* A note, or rather billet-doux from Mrs. L. I am convinced that women, as well as ships, birds and fish, are steered by the tail. Can the poor girl get no one in town to relieve her concupiscence, but she must be under the necessity of sending for me? I am determined to go, at all events. It would be ungrateful to refuse so kind an offer. My shipmates begin to smell a rat, I am rated by them confoundedly, but let them go on. While I fare well at no expense to myself I care not. Should like her better if she were not so religious.

Saturday, July 12th, 1777. I think I have taken my farewell of New York, though I promised to pay one visit more, but never intend to perform. Cannot bear the abominable hypocrite. I wish to be at sea but hear nothing of our sailing this week. I wish to be at home and yet dread the thought of returning to my native country a beggar. The word sounds disagreeable in my ears, but yet it is more pleasing and creditable than the epithet of rascal and villain, even if a large and opulent fortune was annexed to them, though one of the latter sort is in general better received, than an indigent honest man. I am poor as Job, but not quite so patient. Will hope for better days. If I am at present plagued with poverty, my conscience does not accuse me of any extravagance or neglect of sufficient magnitude to bring me into such indigent circumstances. However, I have credit, health, friends and good spirits, which is some consolation in the midst of all my distresses. Better days may come.

CHAPTER XII

THE WAR went on with General George Washington in chief command of the American forces, and it went on badly at first, for although Boston was evacuated by the British troops the cities of New York and Philadelphia were lost in 1776 and 1777 respectively. Washington achieved brilliant successes at Trenton and Princeton, however; and in 1777 an extensive British campaign along the Hudson, designed to cut the country in two, failed when General Burgoyne surrendered to General Gates at Saratoga. In that campaign the British were reënforced by Germans from Brunswick, with Baron Riedesel as their commander. Sailing for America in 1776, Riedesel had expressed the hope that his wife might follow him in due season. This she did, with the result that her bearing behind the British lines gained her the affection and respect of Americans as well as British. Her journal gives the situation at Saratoga.

WHEN the army again moved, on the 11th of September, 1777, it was at first intended to leave me behind; but upon my urgent entreaties, and as other ladies were to follow the army, I received, finally, the same permission. We made only small day's marches, and were very often sick; yet always contented at being allowed to follow. I had still the satisfaction of daily seeing my husband. A great part of my baggage I had sent back, and had kept only a small summer wardrobe. In the beginning all went well. We cherished the sweet hope of a sure victory, and of coming into the "promised land"; and when we passed the Hudson river, and General Burgoyne said, "The English never lose ground," our spirits were greatly exhilarated. But that which displeased me was, that the wives of all the officers belonging to the expedition, knew beforehand everything that was to happen; and this seemed the more singular to me, as I had observed, when in the armies of the Duke Ferdinand, during the Seven Years' war, with how much secrecy everything was conducted. But here, on the contrary, the Americans were apprised beforehand of all our intentions; so that at every place where we came they already awaited us; a circumstance which hurt us exceedingly. On the 19th of September, there was an affair between the two armies, which, it is true, ended to our advantage; although we were, nevertheless, obliged to make a halt at a place called Freeman's farm. I was an eyewitness of the whole affair; and as I knew that my husband was in the midst of it, I was full of care and anguish, and shivered at every shot, for I could hear everything. I saw a great number of wounded, and what was still more harrowing, they even brought three of them into the house where I was. One of these was Major Harnage, the husband of a lady of our company; another, a lieutenant, whose wife, also, was of our acquaintance; and the third, a young English officer of the name of Young.

I lived in a pretty well built house, in which I had a large room. The doors and the wainscot were of solid cedar, a wood that is very common in this vicinity. They burn it frequently, especially when there are many midges around, as these insects cannot stand the odor of it. It is said, however, that its smoke is very injurious to the nerves, so much so, indeed, as to cause women with child to bring forth prematurely. As we were to march farther, I had a large calash made for me, in which I, my children, and both my women servants had seats; and in this manner I followed the army, in the midst of the soldiers, who were merry, singing songs, and burning with a desire for victory. We passed through boundless forests and magnificent tracts of country, which, however, were abandoned by all the inhabitants, who fled before us, and reënforced the army of the American general, Gates. In the sequel this cost us dearly, for every one of them was a soldier by nature, and could shoot very well; besides, the thought of fighting for their fatherland and their freedom, inspired them with still greater courage. During this time, my husband was obliged to encamp with the main body of the army. I remained about an hour's march behind the army, and visited my husband every morning in the camp. Very often I took my noon meal with him, but most of the time he came over to my quarters and ate with me. The army were engaged daily in small skirmishes, but all of them of little consequence. My poor husband, however, during the whole time, could not get a chance either to go to bed or undress. As the season had now become more inclement, a Colonel Williams of the artillery, observing that our mutual visits were very fatiguing, offered to have a house built for me, with a chimney, that should not cost more than five or six guineas, and which I could steadily occupy. I took him up, and the house, which was twenty feet square, and had a good fireplace, was begun. They called it the block-house. For such a structure, large trees of equal thickness are selected, which are joined together, making it very durable and warm, especially if covered with clay. I was to remove into it the following day, and was the more rejoiced at it, as the nights were already damp and cold, and my husband could live in it with me, as he would then be very near his camp. Suddenly, however, on the 7th of October, my husband, with the whole general staff, decamped. Our misfortunes may be said to date from this moment. I had just sat down with my husband at his quarters to breakfast. General Frazer, and, I believe, Generals Burgoyne and Phillips, also, were to have dined with me on that same day. I observed considerable movement among the troops. My husband thereupon informed me, that there was to be a reconnaissance, which, however, did not surprise me, as this often happened. On my way homeward, I met many savages in their war-dress, armed with guns. To my question where they were going, they cried out to me, "War! war!" which meant that they were going to fight. This completely overwhelmed me, and I had scarcely got back to my quarters, when I heard skirmishing, and firing, which by degrees, became constantly heavier, until, finally, the noises became frightful. It was a terrible cannonade, and I was more dead than alive. About three o'clock in the afternoon, in place of the guests who were to have dined with me, they brought in to me, upon a litter, poor General Frazer (one of my expected guests), mortally wounded. Our dining table, which was already spread, was taken away, and in its place they fixed up a bed for the general. I sat in a corner of the room trembling and quaking. The noises grew continually louder. The thought that they might bring in my husband in the same manner was to me dreadful, and tormented me incessantly. The general said to the surgeon, "Do not conceal anything from me. Must I die?" The ball had gone through his bowels, precisely as in the case of Major Harnage. Unfortunately, however, the general had eaten a hearty breakfast, by reason of which the intestines were distended, and the ball, so the surgeon said, had not gone, as in the case of Major Harnage, between the intestines, but through them. I heard him often, amidst his groans, exclaim, "Oh, fatal ambition! Poor General Burgoyne! My poor wife!" Prayers were read to him. He then sent a message to General Burgoyne, begging that he would have him buried the following day at six o'clock in the evening, on the top of a hill, which was a sort of a redoubt. I knew no longer which way to turn. The whole entry and the other rooms were filled with the sick, who were suffering with the camp-sickness, a kind of dysentery. Finally, toward evening, I saw my husband coming, upon which I forgot all my sufferings, and thanked God that he had spared him to me. He ate in great haste with me and his adjutant, behind the house. We had been told that we had gained an advantage over the enemy, but the sorrowful and downcast faces which I beheld, bore witness to the contrary, and before my husband again went away, he drew me to one side and told me that everything might go very badly, and that I must keep myself in constant readiness for departure, but by no means to give any one the least inkling of what I was doing. I therefore pretended that I wished to move into my new house the next morning, and had everything packed up. My lady Ackland occupied a tent not far from our house. In this she slept, but during the day was in the camp. Suddenly one came to tell her that her husband was mortally wounded, and had been taken prisoner. At this she became very wretched. We comforted her by saying that it was only a slight wound, but as no one could nurse him as well as herself, we counseled her to go at once to him, to do which she could certainly obtain permission. She loved him very much, although he was a plain, rough man, and was almost daily intoxicated; with this exception, however, he was an excellent officer. She was the loveliest of women. I spent the night in this manner—at one time comforting her, and at another looking after my children, whom I had put to bed. As for myself, I could not go to sleep, as I had General Frazer and all the other gentlemen in my room, and was constantly afraid that my children would wake up and cry, and thus disturb the poor dying man, who often sent to beg my pardon for making me so much trouble. About three o'clock in the morning, they told me that he could not last much longer. I had desired to be apprised of the approach of this moment. I, accordingly, wrapped up the children in the bed coverings, and went with them into the entry. Early in the morning, at eight o'clock, he expired. After they had washed the corpse, they wrapped it in a sheet, and laid it on a bedstead. We then again came into the room, and had this sad sight before us the whole day. At every instant, also, wounded officers of my acquaintance arrived, and the cannonade again began. A retreat was spoken of, but there was not the least movement made toward it. About four o'clock in the afternoon, I saw the new house which had been built for me, in flames: the enemy, therefore, were not far from us. We learned that General Burgoyne intended to fulfill the last wish of General Frazer, and to have him buried at six o'clock, in the place designated by him. This occasioned an unnecessary delay, to which a part of the misfortunes of the army was owing. Precisely at six o'clock the corpse was brought out, and we saw the entire body of generals with their retinues on the hill assisting at the obsequies. The English chaplain, Mr. Brudenel, performed the funeral services. The cannon balls flew continually around and over the party. The

American general, Gates, afterward said, that if he had known that it was a burial he would not have allowed any firing in that direction. Many cannon balls also flew not far from me, but I had my eyes fixed upon the hill, where I distinctly saw my husband in the midst of the enemy's fire, and therefore I could not think of my own danger.

The order had gone forth that the army should break up after the burial, and the horses were already harnessed to our calashes. I did not wish to set out before the troops. The wounded Major Harnage, although he was so ill, dragged himself out of bed, that he might not remain in the hospital, which was left behind protected by a flag of truce. As soon as he observed me in the midst of the danger, he had my children and maid servants put into the calashes, and intimated to me that I must immediately depart. As I still begged to be allowed to remain, he said to me, "Well, then your children at least must go, that I may save them from the slightest danger." He understood how to take advantage of my weak side. I gave it up, seated myself inside with them, and we drove off at eight o'clock in the evening.

The greatest silence had been enjoined; fires had been kindled in every direction; and many tents left standing, to make the enemy believe that the camp was still there. We traveled continually the whole night. Little Frederica was afraid, and would often begin to cry. I was, therefore, obliged to hold a pocket handkerchief over her mouth, lest our whereabouts should be discovered.

At six o'clock in the morning a halt was made, at which every one wondered. General Burgoyne had all the cannon ranged and counted, which worried all of us, as a few more good marches would have placed us in security. My husband was completely exhausted, and seated himself during this delay, in my calash, where my maid servants were obliged to make room for him; and where he slept nearly three hours with his head upon my shoulder. In the meantime, Captain Willoe brought me his pocketbook containing bank bills, and Captain Geismar, his beautiful watch, a ring, and a well filled purse, and begged me to keep all these for them. I promised them to do my utmost. At last, the army again began its march, but scarcely had we proceeded an hour on the way, when a fresh halt was made, in consequence of the enemy being in sight. They were about two hundred men who came to reconnoiter, and who might easily have been taken prisoners by our troops, had not General Burgoyne lost his head. It rained in torrents. My lady Ackland had her tent set up. I advised her once more to betake herself to her husband, as she could be so useful to him in his present situation.

Finally, she yielded to my solicitations, and sent a message to General Burgoyne, through his adjutant, my Lord Patterson, begging permission to leave the camp. I told her that she should insist on it; which she did, and finally obtained his consent. The English chaplain, Mr. Brudenel, accompanied her; and, bearing a flag of truce, they went together in a boat over to the enemy. There is a familiar and beautiful engraving of this event in existence. I saw her again afterward in Albany, at which time her husband was almost entirely recovered, and both thanked me heartily for my advice.

On the 9th, we spent the whole day in a pouring rain, ready to march at a moment's warning. The savages had lost their courage, and they were seen in all directions going home. The slightest reverse of fortune discouraged them, especially if there was nothing to plunder. My chambermaid did nothing, cursed her situation, and tore out her hair. I entreated her to compose herself, or else she would be taken for a savage. Upon this she became still more frantic, and asked, "whether that would trouble me?" And when I answered "yes" she tore her bonnet off her head, letting her hair hang down over her face, and said, "You talk well! You have your husband! But we have nothing to look forward to, except dying miserably on the one hand, or losing all we possess on the other!" Respecting this last complaint, I promised, in order to quiet her, that I would make good all the losses of herself and the other maid. The latter, my good Lena, although also very much frightened, said nothing.

Toward evening, we at last came to Saratoga, which was only half an hour's march from the place where we had spent the whole day. I was wet through and through by the frequent rains, and was obliged to remain in this condition the entire night, as I had no place whatever where I could change my linen. I, therefore, seated myself before a good fire, and undressed my children; after which, we laid ourselves down together upon some straw. I asked General Phillips, who came up to where we were, why we did not continue our retreat while there was yet time, as my husband had pledged himself to cover it, and bring the army through? "Poor woman," answered he, "I am amazed at you! completely wet through, have you still the courage to wish to go further in this weather! Would that you were only our commanding general! He halts because he is tired, and intends to spend the night here and give us a supper." In this latter achievement, especially, General Burgoyne was very fond of indulging. He spent half the nights in singing and drinking, and amusing himself with the wife of a commissary, who was his mistress, and who, as well as he, loved champagne.

On the 10th, at seven o'clock in the morning, I drank some tea by way of refreshment; and we now hoped from one moment to another, that at last we would again get under way. General Burgoyne, in order to cover our retreat, caused the beautiful houses and mills at Saratoga, belonging to General Schuyler, to be burned. An English officer brought some excellent broth, which he shared with me, as I was not able to refuse his urgent entreaties. Thereupon we set out upon our march, but only as far as another place not far from where we had started. The greatest misery and the utmost disorder prevailed in the army. The commissaries had forgotten to distribute provisions among the troops. There were cattle enough, but not one had been killed. More than thirty officers came to me, who could endure hunger no longer. I had coffee and tea made for them, and divided among them all the provisions with which my carriage was constantly filled; for we had a cook who, although an arrant knave, was fruitful in all expedients, and often in the night crossed small rivers, in order to steal from the country people, sheep, poultry and pigs. He would then charge us a high price for them—a circumstance, however, that we only learned a long time afterward. At last my provisions were exhausted, and in despair at not being able to be of any further help, I called to me Adjutant General Patterson, who happened at that moment to be passing by, and said to him passionately: "Come and see for yourself these officers, who have been wounded in the common cause, and who now are in want of everything, because they do not receive that which is due them. It is, therefore, your duty to make a representation of this to the general." At this he was deeply moved, and the result was, that, a quarter of an hour afterward, General Burgoyne came to me himself and thanked me very pathetically for having reminded him of his duty. He added, moreover, that a general was much to be pitied when he was not properly served nor his commands obeyed. I replied, that I begged his pardon for having meddled with things which, I well knew, a woman had no business with, but that it was impossible to keep silent, when I saw so many brave men in want of everything, and had nothing more to give them. Thereupon he thanked me once more (although I believe that in his heart he has never forgiven me this lashing), and went from me to the officers, and said to them, that he was very sorry for what had happened, but he had now through an order remedied everything, but why had they not come to him as his cook stood always at their service. They answered that English officers were not accustomed to visit the kitchen of their general, and that they had received any morsel from me with pleasure, as they were convinced I had given it to them directly from my heart. He then gave the most express orders that the provisions should be properly distributed. This only hindered us anew, besides not in the least bettering our situation. The general seated himself at table, and the horses were harnessed to our calashes ready for departure. The whole army clamored for a retreat, and my husband promised to make it possible, provided only that no time was lost. But General Burgoyne, to whom an order had been promised if he brought about a junction with the army of General Howe, could not determine upon this course, and lost everything by his loitering. About two o'clock in the afternoon, the firing of cannon and small arms was again heard, and all was alarm and confusion. My husband sent me a message telling me to betake myself forthwith into a house which was not far from there. I seated myself in the calash with my children, and had scarcely driven up to the house, when I saw on the opposite side of the Hudson river, five or six men with guns, which were aimed at us. Almost involuntarily I threw the children on the bottom of the calash and myself over them. At the same instant the churls fired, and shattered the arm of a poor English soldier behind us, who was already wounded, and was also on the point of retreating into the house. Immediately after our arrival a frightful cannonade began, principally directed against the house in which we had sought shelter, probably because the enemy believed, from seeing so many people flocking around it, that all the generals made it their headquarters. Alas! it harbored none but wounded soldiers, or women! We were finally obliged to take refuge in a cellar, in which I laid myself down in a corner not far from the door. My children laid down on the earth with their heads upon my lap, and in this manner we passed the entire night. A horrible stench, the cries of the children, and yet more than all this, my own anguish, prevented me from closing my eyes. On the following morning the cannonade again began, but from a different side. I advised all to go out of the cellar for a little while, during which time I would have it cleaned, as otherwise we would all be sick. They followed my suggestion, and I at once set many hands to work, which was in the highest degree necessary; for the women and children being afraid to venture forth, had soiled the whole cellar. After they had all gone out and left me alone, I for the first time surveyed our place of refuge. It consisted of three beautiful cellars, splendidly arched. I proposed that the most dangerously wounded of the officers should be brought into one of them; that the women should remain in another; and that all the rest should stay in the third, which was nearest the entrance. I had just given the cellars a good sweeping, and had fumigated them by sprinkling vinegar on burning coals, and each one had found his place prepared for him—when a fresh and terrible cannonade threw us all once more into alarm. Many persons, who had no right to come in, threw themselves against the door. My children were already under the cellar steps, and we would all have been crushed, if God had not given me strength to place myself before the door, and with extended arms prevent all from coming in; otherwise every one of us would have been severely injured. Eleven cannon balls went through the house, and we could plainly hear them rolling over our heads. One poor soldier, whose leg they were about to amputate, having been laid upon a table for this purpose, had the other leg taken off by another cannon ball, in the very middle of the operation. His comrades all ran off, and when they again came back they found him in one corner of the room, where he had rolled in his anguish, scarcely breathing. I was more dead than alive, though not so much on account of our own danger, as for that which enveloped my husband, who, however, frequently sent to see how I was getting along, and to tell me that he was still safe.

The wife of Major Harnage, a Madame Reynels, the wife of the good lieutenant who the day previous had so kindly shared his broth with me, the wife of the commissary, and myself, were the only ladies who were with the army. We sat together bewailing our fate, when one came in, upon which they all began whispering, looking at the same time exceedingly sad. I noticed this, and also that they cast silent glances toward me. This awakened in my mind the dreadful thought that my husband had been killed. I shrieked aloud, but they assured me that this was not so, at the same time intimating to me by signs, that it was the lieutenant—the husband of our companion—who had met with misfortune. A moment after she was called out. Her husband was not yet dead, but a cannon ball had taken off his arm close to the shoulder. During the whole night we heard his moans, which resounded fearfully through the vaulted cellars. The poor man died toward morning. We spent the remainder of this night in the same way as the former ones. In the meantime my husband came to visit me, which lightened my anxiety and gave me fresh courage. On the following morning, however, we got things better regulated. Major Harnage, his wife, and Mrs. Reynels, made a little room in a corner, by hanging curtains from the ceiling. They wished to fix up for me another corner in the same manner, but I preferred to remain near the door, so that in case of fire I could rush out from the room. I had some straw brought in and laid my bed upon it, where I slept with my children—my maids sleeping not far from us. Directly opposite us three English officers were quartered—wounded, it is true, but, nevertheless, resolved not to be left behind in case of retreat. One of these was a Captain Green, aid-de-camp of General Phillips, a very valuable and agreeable man. All three assured me, upon their oaths, that in case of hasty retreat, they would not leave me, but would each take one of my children upon his horse. For myself, one of my husband's horses constantly stood saddled and in readiness. Often my husband wished to withdraw me from danger by sending me to the Americans; but I remonstrated with him on the ground, that to be with people whom I would be obliged to treat with courtesy, while, perhaps, my husband was being killed by them, would be even yet more painful than all I was now forced to suffer. He promised me, therefore, that I should henceforward follow the army. Nevertheless, I was often in the night filled with anxiety lest he should march away. At such times, I have crept out of my cellar to reassure myself, and if I saw the troops lying around the fires (for the nights were already cold), I would return and sleep quietly. The articles which had been intrusted to me caused me much uneasiness. I had fastened them inside of my corset, as I was in constant terror lest I should lose some of them, and I resolved in future never to undertake such a commission again. On the third day, I found an opportunity for the first time to change my linen, as my companions had the courtesy to give up to me a little corner—the three wounded officers, meanwhile, standing guard not far off. One of these gentlemen could imitate very naturally the bellowing of a cow, and the bleating of a calf; and if my little daughter Frederica cried during the night, he would mimic these animals, and she would at once become still, at which we all laughed heartily.

Our cook saw to our meals, but we were in want of water; and in order to quench thirst, I was often obliged to drink wine, and give it, also, to the children. It was, moreover, the only thing that my husband could take, which fact so worked upon our faithful Rockel, that he said to me one day, "I fear that the general drinks so much wine, because he dreads falling into captivity, and is therefore weary of life." The continual danger in which my husband was encompassed, was a constant source of anxiety to me. I was the only one of all the women, whose husband had not been killed or wounded, and I often said to myself—especially since my husband was placed in such great danger day and night—"Shall I be the only fortunate one?" He never came into the tent at night; but lay outside by the watch-fires. This alone was sufficient to have caused his death, as the nights were damp and cold.

As the great scarcity of water continued, we at last found a soldier's wife who had the courage to bring water from the river, for no one else would undertake it, as the enemy shot at the head of every man who approached the river. This woman, however, they never molested; and they told us afterward, that they spared her on account of her sex.

I endeavored to divert my mind from my troubles by constantly busying myself with the wounded. I made them tea and coffee, and received in return a thousand benedictions. Often, also, I shared my noonday meal with them. One day a Canadian officer came into our cellar, who could scarcely stand up. We at last got it out of him, that he was almost dead with hunger. I considered myself very fortunate to have it in my power to offer him my mess. This gave him renewed strength, and gained for me his friendship. Afterward, upon our return to Canada, I learned to know his family. One of our greatest annoyances was the stench of the wounds when they began to suppurate.

One day I undertook the care of Major Plumpfield, adjutant of General Phillips, through both of whose cheeks a small musket ball had passed, shattering his teeth and grazing his tongue. He could hold nothing whatever in his mouth. The matter from the wound almost choked him, and he was unable to take any other nourishment, except a little broth, or something liquid. We had Rhine wine. I gave him a bottle of it, in hopes that the acidity of the wine would cleanse his wound. He kept some continually in his mouth; and that alone acted so beneficially that he became cured, and I again acquired one more friend. Thus, in the midst of my hours of care and suffering, I derived a joyful satisfaction, which made me very happy.

On one of these sorrowful days, General Phillips, having expressed a desire to visit me, accompanied my husband, who, at the risk of his own life, came once or twice daily to see me. He saw our situation, and heard me earnestly beg my husband not to leave me behind in case of a hasty retreat. Then, as he marked my great reluctance to fall into the hands of the Americans, he spoke in my behalf; and as he was going away he said to my husband, "No! not for ten thousand guineas would I come here again, for my heart is entirely, entirely broken!"

Not all of those, however, who were with us deserved our compassion. There were, also, poltroons in our little company, who ought not to have remained in the cellar, and who afterwards, when we became prisoners, took their places in the ranks and could parade perfectly well. In this horrible situation we remained six days. Finally, they spoke of capitulating, as by temporizing for so long a time, our retreat had been cut off. A cessation of hostilities took place, and my husband, who was thoroughly worn out, was able, for the first time in a long while, to lie down upon a bed. In order that his rest might not be in the least disturbed, I had a good bed made up for him in a little room; while I, with my children and both my maids, laid down in a little parlor close by. But about one o'clock in the night, some one came and asked to speak to him. It was with the greatest reluctance that I found myself obliged to awaken him. I observed that the message did not please him, as he immediately sent the man back to headquarters, and laid himself down again considerably out of humor. Soon after this, General Burgoyne requested the presence of all the generals and staff officers at a council-of-war, which was to be held early the next morning; in which he proposed to break the capitulation, already made with the enemy, in consequence of some false information just received. It was, however, finally decided, that this was neither practicable nor advisable; and this was fortunate for us, as the Americans said to us afterwards, that had the capitulation been broken we all would have been massacred; which they could have done the more easily, as we were not over four or five thousand men strong, and had given them time to bring together more than twenty thousand.

On the morning of the 16th of October, my husband was again obliged to go to his post, and I once more into my cellar.

On this day, a large amount of fresh meat was distributed among the officers, who, up to this time, had received only salted provisions, which had exceedingly aggravated the wounds of the men. The good woman who constantly supplied us with water, made us capital soup from the fresh meat. I had lost all appetite, and had the whole time taken nothing but crusts of bread dipped in wine. The wounded officers, my companions in misfortune, cut off the best piece of the beef and presented it to me, with a plate of soup. I said to them that I was not able to eat anything, but as they saw that it was absolutely necessary I should take some nourishment, they declared that they themselves would not touch a morsel until I had given them the satisfaction of taking some. I could not longer withstand their friendly entreaties, upon which they assured me that it made them very happy to be able to offer me the first good thing which they themselves enjoyed.

On the 17th of October the capitulation was consummated. The generals waited upon the American general-in-chief Gates, and the troops laid down their arms, and surrendered themselves prisoners of war. Now the good woman, who had brought us water at the risk of her life, received the reward of her services. Every one threw a whole handful of money into her apron, and she received altogether over twenty guineas. At such a moment, the heart seems to be specially susceptible to feelings of gratitude.

At last, my husband sent to me a groom with a message that I should come to him with our children. I, therefore, again seated myself in my dear calash; and, in the passage through the American camp, I observed, with great satisfaction, that no one cast at us scornful glances. On the contrary, they all greeted me, even showing compassion on their countenances at seeing a mother with her little children in such a situation. I confess that I feared to come into the enemy's camp, as the thing was so entirely new to me. When I approached the tents, a noble looking man came toward me, took the children out of the wagon, embraced and kissed them, and then with tears in his eyes helped me also to alight. "You tremble," said he to me, "fear nothing." "No," replied I, "for you are so kind, and have been so tender toward my children, that it has inspired me with courage." He then led me to the tent of General Gates, with whom I found Generals Burgoyne and Phillips, who were upon an extremely friendly footing with him. Burgoyne said to me, "You may now dismiss all your apprehensions, for your sufferings are at an end." I answered him, that I should certainly be acting very wrongly to have any more anxiety, when our chief had none, and especially when I saw him on such a friendly footing with General Gates. All the generals remained to dine with General Gates. The man, who had received me so kindly, came up and said to me, "It may be embarrassing to you to dine with all these gentlemen; come now with your children into my tent, where I will give you, it is true, a frugal meal, but one that will be accompanied by the best of wishes." "You are certainly," answered I, "a husband and a father, since you show me so much kindness." I then learned that he was the American General Schuyler. He entertained me with excellent smoked tongue, beefsteak, potatoes, good butter and bread. Never have I eaten a better meal. I was content. I saw that all around me were so likewise; but that which rejoiced me more than everything else was, that my husband was out of all danger. As soon as we had finished dinner, he invited me to take up my residence at his house, which was situated in Albany, and told me that General Burgoyne would, also, be there. I sent and asked my husband what I should do. He sent me word to accept the invitation; and as it was two days' journey from where we were, and already five o'clock in the afternoon, he advised me to set out in advance, and to stay overnight at a place distant about three hours' ride. General Schuyler was so obliging as to send with me a French officer, who was a very agreeable man, and commanded those troops who composed the reconnoitering party of which I have before made mention. As soon as he had escorted me to the house where we were to remain, he went back. I found in this house a French physician, and a mortally wounded Brunswick officer, who was under his care, and who died a few days afterward. The wounded man extolled highly the good nursing of the doctor, who may have been a very skillful surgeon, but was a young coxcomb. He rejoiced greatly when he heard that I could speak his language, and began to entertain me with all kinds of sweet speeches and impertinences; among other things, that he could not believe it possible that I was a general's wife, because a woman of such rank would not certainly follow her husband into the camp. I ought, therefore, to stay with him, for it was better to be with the conquerors than the conquered. I was beside myself with his insolence, but dared not let him see the contempt with which he inspired me, because I had no protector. When night came on he offered to share his room with me; but I answered, that I should remain in the apartment of the wounded officers, whereupon he distressed me still more with all kinds of foolish flatteries, until, suddenly, the door opened and my husband and his adjutant entered. "Here, sir, is my husband," said I to him, with a glance meant to annihilate him. Upon this he withdrew looking very sheepish. Yet, afterward, he was so polite as to give up his room to us. The day after this, we arrived at Albany, where we had so often longed to be. But we came not, as we supposed we should, as victors! We were, nevertheless, received in the most friendly manner by the good General Schuyler, and by his wife and daughters, who showed us the most marked courtesy, as, also, General Burgoyne, although he had—without any necessity it was said—caused their magnificently built houses to be burned. But they treated us as people who knew how to forget their own losses in the misfortunes of others. Even General Burgoyne was deeply moved at their magnanimity, and said to General Schuyler, "Is it to *me,* who have done you so much injury, that you show so much kindness!" "That is the fate of war," replied the brave man, "let us say no more about it." We remained three days with them, and they acted as if they were very reluctant to let us go. Our cook had remained in the city with the camp equipage of my husband, but the second night after our arrival, the whole of it was stolen from us, notwithstanding an American guard of ten or twenty men had been deputed for its protection. Nothing remained to us except the beds of myself and children, and a few trifles that I had kept by me for my own use—and this too, in a land where one could get nothing for money, and at a time when we were in want of many things; consequently, my husband was obliged to board his adjutant, quartermaster, etc., and find them in everything. The English officers—our friends, as I am justified in calling them, for during the whole of my sojourn in America they always acted as such—each one gave us something. One gave a pair of spoons, another some plates, all of which we were obliged to use for a long time, as it was not until three years afterward, in New York, that we found an opportunity, although at great cost, to replace a few of the things we had lost. Fortunately, I had kept by me my little carriage, which carried my baggage. As it was already very late in the season, and the weather raw, I had my calash covered with coarse linen, which in turn was varnished over with oil; and in this manner we set out on our journey to Boston, which was very tedious, besides being attended with considerable hardships.

I know not whether it was my carriage that attracted the curiosity of the people to it—for it certainly had the appearance of a wagon in which they carry around rare animals—but often I was obliged to halt, because the people insisted upon seeing the wife of the German general with her children. For fear that they would tear off the linen covering from the wagon in their eagerness to see me, I very often alighted, and by this means got away more quickly.

CHAPTER XIII

GENERAL GEORGE WASHINGTON had other difficulties than those of insufficient funds and temporary defeat. One which is now amusing grew out of the character of his second in command, Charles Lee, who once had been an officer in the British army but who at the outbreak of hostilities in America had declared himself a friend of liberty and been made Major General. He was a witty adventurer who is said to have declared that the more he saw of men the better he liked his dogs. Captured by the British in 1776, he had not been released long before he fell a victim—as he always insisted— of Washington's tyrannical rage. On a hot summer's day at the battle of Monmouth, where he had been given command in place of the Marquis de Lafayette, he happened to be withdrawing his men at the moment of Washington's arrival on the scene. To Washington and others it looked like retreat. Washington spoke sharply to Lee—some say he swore—and Lee never forgave or forgot. A nettled correspondence began between the two next day, and when this ended with Lee's court-martial and dismissal from the army he spent the rest of his days in an attempt to get even with his tongue and pen. He retired at last to a farm in Virginia and died there in 1782, still wicked and still witty.

To GENERAL WASHINGTON

Camp, English Town, July 1st [30th June] 1778.

SIR,
From the knowledge I have of your Excellency's character, I must conclude, that nothing but the misinformation of some very stupid, or misrepresentation of some very wicked person, could have occasioned your making use of such very singular expressions as you did, on my coming up to the ground where you had taken post: they implied, that I was guilty either of disobedience of orders, of want of conduct, or want of courage. Your Excellency will therefore infinitely oblige me, by letting me know, on which of these three articles you ground your charge, that I may prepare for my justifi-

cation; which I have the happiness to be confident I can do, to the Army, to the Congress, to America, and to the World in general. Your Excellency must give me leave to observe, that neither yourself, nor those about your person, cou'd, from your situation, be in the least judges of the merits or demerits of our maneuvers; and, to speak with a becoming pride, I can assert, that to these maneuvers the success of the day was entirely owing. I can boldly say, that had we remained on the first ground, or had we advanced, or had the retreat been conducted in a manner different from what it was, this whole army, and the interest of America, would have risked being sacrificed. I ever had (and I hope ever shall have) the greatest respect and veneration for General Washington; I think him endowed with many great and good qualities; but in this instance, I must pronounce, that he has been guilty of an act of cruel injustice towards a man who certainly has some pretentions to the regard of every servant of this country; and, I think, Sir, I have a right to demand some reparation for the injury committed; and unless I can obtain it, I must, in justice to myself, when this campaign is closed (which I believe will close the war), retire from a service, at the head of which is placed a man capable of offering such injuries: —but, at this same time, in justice to you, I must repeat that I from my soul believe, that it was not a motion of your own breast, but instigated by some of those dirty earwigs who will forever insinuate themselves near persons in high office; for I really am convinced, that when General Washington acts from himself, no man in his army will have reason to complain of injustice or indecorum.

I am, Sir, and hope I ever shall have reason to continue, your most sincerely devoted humble Servant,

CHARLES LEE.

FROM GENERAL WASHINGTON

Headquarters, English Town, June 30th, 1778.

SIR:

I received your letter (dated, through mistake, the 1st of July) expressed, as I conceive, in terms highly improper. I am not conscious of having made use of any very singular expressions at the time of my meeting you, as you intimate. What I recollect to have said, was dictated by duty, and warranted by the occasion. As soon as circumstances will permit, you shall have an opportunity either of justifying yourself to the army, to Congress, to America, and to the world in general; or of convincing them that you were guilty of a breach of orders, and of misbehavior before the enemy, on the 28th inst., in not attacking them as you had been directed, and in making an unnecessary, disorderly, and shameful retreat.

I am Sir, your most obedient Servant,

Go. WASHINGTON.

To GENERAL WASHINGTON

Camp, June 28th [30th], 1778.

SIR,

I beg your Excellency's pardon for the inaccuracy in misdating my letter. You cannot afford me greater pleasure than in giving me the opportunity of showing to America, the sufficiency of her respective servants. I trust, that the temporary power of office, and the tinsel dignity attending it, will not be able, by all the mists they can raise, to offiscate the bright rays of truth. In the meantime, your Excellency can have no objection to my retiring from the army. I am, Sir,

Your most obedient Humble Servant,

CHARLES LEE.

To GEN. WASHINGTON

Camp, June 30th, 1778.

SIR,

Since I had the honor of addressing my letter by Colonel Fitzgerald to your Excellency, I have reflected on both your situation and mine; and beg leave to observe, that it will be for our mutual convenience, that a Court of Inquiry should be immediately ordered; but I could wish it might be a court-martial: for, if the affair is drawn into length, it may be difficult to collect the necessary evidences, and perhaps might bring on a paper war betwixt the adherents to both parties, which may occasion some disagreeable feuds on the Continent; for all are not my friends, nor all your admirers. I must entreat, therefore, from your love of justice, that you will immediately exhibit your charge; and that on the first halt, I may be brought to a trial, and am, Sir,

Your Most obedient Humble Servant,

CHARLES LEE.

While Lee was waiting for the result of his trial he relieved himself in a letter to Robert Morris.

To Robert Morris

Brunswick, July 3rd, 1778.

My Dear Sir,

To use the words of my Lord Chatham, have we not a gracious Prince on the throne? Is he not still the same? I trust he is; but there is something rotten betwixt him and his people—not content with robbing me and the brave men under my command of the honor due to us—a most hellish plan has been formed (and I may say at least not discouraged by headquarters) to destroy forever my honor and reputation—I have demanded a court-martial which has fortunately been granted—if I had been let alone, I should with patience have suffered 'em to pick up the laurels which I had shaken down and laid at their feet; but the outrageous attacks made are enough to drive patience itself to madness—I shall not trouble you at present with a detail of the action, but by all that's sacred, Gen. Washington had scarcely any more to do in it than to strip the dead—by want of proper intelligence we were ordered to attack the covering party supposed to consist only of fifteen hundred men—our intelligence as usual was false—it proved to be the whole flower of the British army, grenadiers, light infantry, cavalry and artillery, amounting in the whole to seven thousand men—by the temerity, folly and contempt of orders of General Wain we found ourselves engaged in the most extensive plain in America—separated from our main body the distance of eight miles—the force we could bring to action not more than three thousand men—in danger every moment of having our flanks turned by their cavalry—it required the utmost presence of mind and courage to extricate ourselves out of this dangerous situation, and on this occasion it is no crime to do justice to myself. Upon my soul I feel I know the whole army saw and must acknowledge that I did exhibit great presence of mind and not less address—although my orders were perpetually counteracted, I maneuvered my antagonists from their advantageous ground into as disadvantageous a one—no confusion was seen, the battalions and artillery supported and were supported by each other through a plain of four miles, without losing a single gun, a single color, or sacrificing a single battalion until I led 'em totally exhausted into the ground where the general was posted, who had, as I observed before, nothing to do but to strip their dead—it is true they cannonaded each other for some time but the enemy were so completely worn down that they could never attempt the least impression—the General has the madness to charge me with making a shameful retreat—I never retreated in fact (for till I joined him it was not a retreat but a necessary and I may say in my own defense masterly maneuver) I say I never retreated but by his positive order who invidiously sent me out of the field when the victory was assured—such is my recompense for having sacrificed my friends, my connections, and perhaps my fortune for having twice extricated this man and his whole army out of perdition, and now having given him the only victory he ever tasted. Do not, my dear friend, imagine I talk in this heated manner to every man—to you I venture to pour out my indignation—but I give you my word I am so sensible of my ticklish situation that I am with others perfectly moderate and guarded—the cool parts of this letter I wish you would read to Richard Henry Lee and Duar, to what others you think prudent.

I am most sincerely and affectionately yours,

C. LEE.

This was the unfavorable finding of the court-martial on August 12, 1778.

The Court met according to adjournment.

The Court having considered the first charge against Major-General Lee, the evidence and his defense, are of opinion, that he is guilty of disobedience of orders, in not attacking the enemy on the 28th of June, agreeable to repeated instructions; being a breach of the latter part of article 5th, section 2d of the Articles of War. The Court having considered the second charge aganist Major-General Lee, the evidence and his defense, are of opinion, he is guilty of misbehavior before the enemy on the 28th of June, by making an unnecessary, and in some few instances, a disorderly retreat; being a breach of the 13th article of the 13th section of the Articles of War. The Court having considered the third charge against Major-General Lee, are of opinion, that he is guilty of disrespect to the Commander-in-Chief in two letters dated the 1st of July and the 28th of June; being a breach of the 2d article, section 2d of the Articles of War. The Court do sentence Major-General Lee to be suspended from any command in the armies of the United States of North America, for the term of twelve months.

The Court adjourn without day.

STIRLING, *M. G.* and *President.*

And this was Lee's opinion of it.

To Col. Aaron Burr

October   , 1778.

Dear Sir,

As you are so kind as to interest yourself so warmly in my favor, I cannot resist the temptation of writing you a few lines. Till these two days, I was convinced the Congress would unanimously have rescinded the absurd, shameful sentence of the court-martial; but, within these two days, I am taught to think that equity is to be put out of the question, and the decision of the affair to be put entirely on the strength of party; and, for my own part, I do not see how it is possible, if the least decency or regard for national dignity has place, that it can be called a party business. I wish I could send you the trial, and will the moment I can obtain one. I think myself, and I dare say you will think on the perusal, that the affair redounds more to my honor, and the disgrace of my persecutors, than, in the warmth of indignation, either I or my aide-de-camps have represented it. As I have no idea that a proper reparation will be made to my injured reputation, it is my intent, whether the sentence is reversed or not reversed, to resign my commission, retire to Virginia, and learn to hoe tobacco, which I find is the best school to form a consummate *general*. This is a discovery I have lately made. Adieu.

Dear Sir, believe me to be your most

Sincerely obliged Servant,

C. Lee.

While waiting for the redress which never came Lee amused himself by a correspondence with a young heiress of Philadelphia. But she evidently did not understand his wit.

To Miss Rebecca Franks

Philadelphia, Dec. 20th, 1778.

Madam,

When an officer of the respectable rank which I bear is grossly traduced and caluminated, it is incumbent on him to clear up the affair to the world, with as little delay as possible. The spirit of defamation and calumny (I am sorry to say it) is grown to a prodigious and intolerable height on this continent. If you had accused me of a design to procrastinate the war, or of holding a treasonable correspondence with the enemy, I could have borne it: this I am used to; and this happened to the great Fabius Maximus. If you had accused me of getting drunk as often as I could get liquor, as *two Alexanders the Great* have been charged with this vice, I should, perhaps, have sat patient under the imputation; or, even if you had given the plainest hints, that I had stolen the soldiers' shirts, this I could have put up with, as the great Duke of Marlborough would have been an example; or if you had contented yourself with asserting that I was so abominable a sloven as never to part with my shirt, until my shirt parted with me, the anecdotes of my illustrious namesake of Sweden would have administered some comfort to me. But the calumny you have, in the fertility of your malicious wit, chosen to invent, is of so new, so unprecedented, and so hellish a kind, as would make Job himself swear like a Virginia Colonel.

Is it possible that the celebrated Miss Franks, a lady who has had every human and divine advantage, who has read (or, at least, might have read), in the *originals*, the New and Old Testaments (though I am afraid she too seldom looks even into the translations); I say, is it possible that Miss Franks, with every human and divine advantage, who might, and ought to have read these two good books, which (an old Welsh nurse, whose uncle was reckoned the best preacher in Merionethshire, assured me) enjoin charity, and denounce vengeance against slander and evil speaking; is it possible, I again repeat it, that Miss Franks should, in the face of the day, carry her malignity so far, in the presence of three most respectable personages (one of the oldest religion in the world, one of the newest; for he is a new-light man; and the other, most probably, of no religion at all, as he is an English sailor); but I demand it again and again, is it possible, that Miss Franks should assert it, in the presence of these respectable personages, "That I wore green breeches patched with leather"? To convict you, therefore, of the falsehood of this most diabolical slander; to put you to eternal silence (if you are not past all grace), and to cover you with a much larger patch of infamy than you have wantonly endeavored to fix on my breeches, I have thought proper, by the advice of three very grave friends (lawyers and members of Congress, of course excellent judges in delicate points of honor), to send you the said breeches, and, with the consciousness of truth on my side, to submit them to the most severe inspection and scrutiny of you and all those who may have entered into this wicked cabal against my honor and reputation. I say, I dare you, and your whole junto, to your worst: turn them, examine them, inside and outside, and if you find them to be green breeches patched with leather, and not actually legitimate *sherry vallies*,* such as his

* A kind of long breeches reaching to the ankle, with a broad stripe of leather on the inside of the thigh, for the convenience of riding.

Majesty of Poland wears (who, let me tell you, is a man that has made more fashions than all your knights of the Meschianza* put together, notwithstanding their beauties) ; I repeat it (though I am almost out of breath with repetitions and parentheses), that if these are proved to be patched green breeches, and not real legitimate *sherry vallies* (which a man of the first *bon ton* might be proud of), I will submit in silence to all the scurrility which, I have no doubt, you and your abettors are prepared to pour out against me, in the public papers, on this important and interesting occasion. But, Madam! Madam! reputation (as "Common Sense," very sensibly, though not very uncommonly observes), is a serious thing. You have already injured me in the tenderest part, and I demand satisfaction; and as you cannot be ignorant of the laws of dueling, having conversed with so many Irish officers, whose favorite topic it is, particularly in the company of ladies, I insist on the privilege of the injured party, which is, to name his hour and weapons; and as I intend it to be a very serious affair, I will not admit of any seconds; and you may depend upon it, Miss Franks, that whatever may be your spirit on the occasion, the world shall never accuse General Lee with having turned his back upon you. In the meantime,

I am, &c., Yours,

CHARLES LEE.

Miss Franks, Philadelphia.

P. S. I have communicated the affair only to my confidential friend ———, who has mentioned it to no more than seven members of Congress and nineteen women, six of whom are old maids; so that there is no danger of its taking wind on my side; and, I hope, you will be equally guarded on your part.

TO MISS REBECCA FRANKS

Philadelphia, Jan. 28th, 1779.

MADAM,

Nothing has happened to me of late, that has given me more concern than the serious light in which I am told you are persuaded to consider the harmless jocular letter I wrote to you; I say, persuaded to consider; because on the first receipt of it, when you were directed by your own excellent understanding alone, you conceived it as it was meant, an innocent *jeu d'esprit*.

---

* An entertainment given by General Howe just before the evacuation of Philadelphia, at which were introduced tilts and tournaments in favor of the ladies, of whom Miss Franks was one.

I do not mean to compliment, when I assure you, upon my honor, that it was the good opinion I had of your understanding which encouraged me to indulge myself in this piece of raillery, which in effect, is not in the least directed against you, but against myself and a few others; if it contains any satire, you are obviously the vehicle, not the object.

My acquaintance with you is too slender to admit of my taking any liberties which border on familiarity; and unless I had been taught to believe, that the liberality of your mind and cheerfulness of your disposition were such that you would be pleased with any effort to make you laugh for a moment in these melancholy times, I declare upon the word of an honest man, if I had thought a single sentence of this trash could have given you uneasiness, I would sooner have put my hand into the fire than have written it. Thank God, I have not that petulant itch for scribbling, or vain ambition of passing for a wit, as to

> Give virtue scandal, innocence a fear,
> Or from the soft-eyed virgin steal a tear.

And, to speak my real thoughts, I am thoroughly persuaded, that you must suffer yourself to be biased by people infinitely your inferiors in capacity; and if you really are offended by what nobody, who is not below mediocrity in understanding, can mistake for anything but an harmless joke, founded on the good opinion of the person to whom it is addressed, I confess I have been much deceived in you. I must, therefore, think that by consulting yourself alone, you will consider it in its proper light, and believe me to be, with the greatest respect,

Madam, your most obedient,

And very humble servant,

CHARLES LEE.

Spring came, and Lee still was delivering himself of tirades against "His Excellency," this time in letters to General Gates.

To MAJOR GENERAL HORATIO GATES

Philadelphia, March 29th, 1779.

MY DEAR GATES,

I should in propriety have answered the last letter (indeed the only letter) I have received from you—but was prevented by imaginary business and a resolution when I did write to write to you in the most ample manner on a variety of subjects—concerning your interests and my own—but as I had reason to believe one or two of your letters had been intercepted, I did not choose to communicate my sentiments by the Common Post—I have waited therefore for some other means—and I should wait longer, but as I shall set out for Virginia in a few days; as no other means do present themselves, and above all as there is such a visible revolution in the minds of men on certain subjects—I am determined to delay it no longer—by a revolution in the minds of men, I mean that our Great Gargantua, or Lama Babak (for I know not which title is the properest) begins to be no longer considered as an infallible Divinity—and that those who have been sacrificed or near sacrificed on his altar, begin to be esteemed as wantonly and foolishly offered up—so that in fact it matters not much (nay I could almost wish that it should happen) if what I now throw upon paper should be read by all the Sergeants, Corporals, Committee Men and Wagoners betwixt this place and Boston. I shall begin by confessing that I live (and wish to live) on good terms with two men with whom you (my dearest friend) are at daggers drawn—Arnold, and Wilkinson—the former has been so cruelly, wantonly and I think wickedly persecuted by the President of this abominable State and a Banditti of ignorant of obsequious mercenary Clowns his Satellites called the Council of State, that although I am totally unacquainted with Mr. Arnold's merits or demerits I could not help pitying him, and pity, as you know, melts the mind to love—on this principle, and on this principle only, I am Arnold's friend and I persuade myself, not incompatibly, with the sincere love and regard I have for you—With respect to the latter, Wilkinson; I really think that he has been a man, more sinned against than sinning. I think (at least from all I have been able to gather) that he as well as your honor, has been made a most egregious dupe in the affair betwixt you— it is a dark, black piece of business and I have no doubt will one day be developed to the world. He was put on a wrong scent when he aimed his pistol at your head, and when you aimed at his— Alexander (pas le Grand, mais le Gros) and his Hephestion McWilliams were the proper objects of your respective resentments— but of this more hereafter—Now quantum ad me attinet—You know how I have been persecuted and unjustly dealt with both by bodies corporate and individuals—the latter I have the pleasure to assure you I have completely got the better of—some I have shamed and others put to flight—the bodies corporate begin (from many visible signs) to be quite ashamed themselves of the injustice done me—to speak plain, the Members of the Congress are become extremely civil in their words and actions to the man whom they so lately affected to shun as the plague—indeed I do not find that there is a single member so devoid of grace as to insinuate that the charges brought against me had the shadow of support—two notorious idiots perhaps excepted—one Penn of North Carolina, a broken attorney, and a Scudder of the Jerseys, a gossiping pragmatical Presbyterian Doctor or apothecary, to both which worthies I have given a very dowsing slap on the face in a letter, which I make no doubt you will soon see, addressed to the Divine W. H. Drayton—nunc ad te, et eas res quæ te attinent—I hope you are in earnest when you talk of resigning—You cannot serve with safety —a mine is under your feet—the materials for your destruction are heaped up and prepared, and the least error (such as are incident to humanity) blows you up—for my own part I would have sent my commission to the devil long ago, but was prevented by the advice of, I believe, the devil's eldest brother, who had assumed the form and really persuaded me that he was my warmest friend— but no art, no artifice shall (you may depend upon it) prevail upon me to draw my sword again at least whilst Gargantua or Lama Babak is at the head of our Armies. I am sorry for the poor American soldiers, who have certainly merit, virtue and courage—but they must inevitably be beat or rather drowned if they depend on such a bladder of emptiness and pride—nunc iterum ad me. Have you got my fine mare from Mr. Hastings? If you have not, I beg you will, and send her up to our horses' heaven by the first fair occasion. I beg Mrs. Gates' pardon, but I think you ought to send her up likewise—for I am told your farm from want of her superintendence is in a damnable condition—My love to her and Bob, who, upon my soul is a fine boy—a clap and a duel in the same year for one of his age indicate a great man. I send you (though I suppose you have seen 'em) some strictures on the affair of Monmouth, or perhaps it might more properly he called a supplement to my defense —the soldiers here (Baron de Kalb in particular) are pleased to say it has merit—read it, and give me your opinion—I have some queries political and military ready for the press, which are whacking ones, and which I believe will hurt Gargantua's digestion. Adieu —God bless you

My Dear Friend,

C. L.

Philadelphia, April 4th, 1779.

My Dear Gates,

A Captain Taylor will deliver you this. He has suffered much in the cause (as he you and I thought) of liberty and the rights of mankind, but whether we have not been dupes to this righteous

fanaticism begins with me to be a doubt—it is certain at least that
in this state a most odious tryanny is established—but be this as
it may, his intentions were honest, and his sufferings have been
great—He has been manacled, endungeoned, and tried for his life—
I knew him when I was on my parole last spring in this place
and I can assert that his zeal was unbounded—I therefore recommend him most earnestly to your patronage and protection—I entreat that you will do him every service in your power which
Adams and Lovell, two staunch Republicans and honest men (if I
do not mistake them), assure me is considerable in that district
which for your happiness is consigned to you—for from these Middle States, libera Nos, Domine—by the Middle States, I mean
Pennsylvania and the Jerseys—which are inhabited by the refuse
of the Irish, the descendants of the worst part of the Germans and
by the first hypocrites of the most hypocritical sects—stiff necked
Presbyterians, Quakers, New Light Men and the whole family of
the devil. They have the gasconade, thievery and lying of the Irish—
the stupidity, avarice and sordid disposition of the lower Germans—
to sum up the whole, Washington is their God, Joe Reed their dic-
tator, or rather despotic prince, and Roberdeau is a Saint amongst
them—but damn 'em—let's talk no more about 'em. I have been
amusing myself here in writing or rather throwing on paper several
crude reveries, which you shall one day see. My chief performance
is a plan for the establishment of a Military Colony in some happy
climate of America, perhaps as wild, though not quite so poetical,
as Horace's schemes for all the Romans to transplant themselves
to the fortunate islands, for the amelioration of their morals. I send
you inclosed the extract of a letter from a gentleman in South
Carolina which I request you will take care shall be published in
the Boston papers; I am much pleased with its appearance, as it
prepares the road for my (as I told you in my last letter) whacking
queries, which are to spoil Gargantua's digestion. There is likewise
a letter from Mr. North to Mr. Tudor respecting the recovery of
my fine mare, which I beg when she is recovered you will take into
your care and protection and when you have a fair opportunity send
up to our ἵππων παραδίζων or, in English, Horses Paradise. My
love as usual to Mrs. Gates, Bob, and to that excellent young man,
Major Armstrong, whose father the General, I am sorry to say it,
I saw him the other night with a Mulatto girl in the streets.

                           Yours, Dear Gates—
                                    CHARLES LEE.

We leave him on his land in Virginia writing to his sister back in
England.

To Miss Sidney Lee

Virginia, Dec. 11th, 1781.

My Dearest Sister,

The last year I wrote you many letters by different hands, but God knows whether a single one has reached you—Your last letter made me extremely happy; or more properly doubly happy; as it assured me of your health and spirits, and of the reception which my Court Martial met with in England, indeed it made its own comments. I remember it was once asked, I think it was Mrs. Hinks asked me, when I intended to put a period to my peregrinations? My answer, was, that whenever I could find a country where power was in righteous hands—on this principle, I now find, I may be a pilgrim to all eternity. Great God, what a dupe and a victim have I been to the talismanic name of Liberty! for I now have reason to believe (from the materials of the Modern World) that this bright Goddess is a Chimera—but I must not warm on this subject, but stop before I run into leze Majeste. I shall therefore confine myself to a few comfortable facts, firstly, that I am much rejoiced that you are in health and spirits; secondly, that I am well not only in these two points, but that I am sound in honor; that is to say the whole Continent cries out loudly against the iniquitous tribunals before which my affair was brought. I can now say no more; my love to all our friends and relations; and be assured, there is not on earth a more affectionate brother than yours,

CHARLES LEE.

CHAPTER XIV

SAMUEL CURWEN, LOYALIST, RETURNS FROM EXILE

THE WAR, continuing in the north, in the west, and on the sea, entered its crucial phase in the south, being determined as to its outcome by the surrender of Cornwallis to Washington at Yorktown, Virginia, in 1781. Peace was not fully made until 1783; it was only then that the loyalists who had suffered exile, and who now wished to return, could think of doing so. Among those excellent gentlemen who, finding the zeal of the American patriots unpleasing at the commencement of the war, were punished for refusing to share it was Judge Samuel Curwen of Boston. He had been one of several hundred merchants and lawyers who addressed resolutions of sympathy and approbation to Governor Hutchinson of Massachusetts when in 1774, after a trying term of office, he sailed for relief to England. When the crisis arrived these resolutions were remembered by the zealots, who endeavored to compel the signers to recant through the newspapers. Judge Curwen, unwilling to unbend so far, preferred rather to leave the country. His correspondence in 1784 shows the temper of his return after eight years in England, and the state in which he found his property and affairs.

FEB. 17, 1784. London. Received several letters from Salem, encouraging me to hope I may be permitted to return to my native country.

FROM WILLIAM PYNCHON, ESQ.

Salem, Jan. 2, 1784.

DEAR SIR:

I have made inquiry amongst your friends, and all agree that although there seems to be no prospect of a repeal of the laws against absentees, yet the inhabitants of this town, the committees, and all orders, seem very desirous of your returning in the spring. As Mr. Cabot, by whom I shall send this, is urgent for it, and can inform you of the present temper and disposition of the people towards you, it will be needless for me to give you particulars. Assurances from hence as to security, etc., while the laws remain unrepealed, we cannot give you, other than private opinion only. Mr. Cabot will acquaint you, and, by what Mr. Vans says, you will have it in letters from several, that there is little or no danger of any prosecutions on the laws but from the respective towns, committees, etc., where the absentee belonged; and all seem to agree there can be, from present appearances, no danger from any of this town. Mr. Cabot will acquaint you as to the successes of all who have returned hither, and as to such as have returned to other states. At Providence, and in some parts of Connecticut, those who returned have been more cordially received and treated, and we hope a like temper will take place in Massachusetts in the spring and summer. Alcock *evasit et abdicavit* with bag and baggage, and Whitaker seems to be hastening after him. These two politicians seem to have been the authors and promoters of more mischief than it is possible that any two who are left behind them either should or would effect, or even attempt. They resembled Swift's committee of ways and means for continuing the war and promoting malevolence and contention as long as possible; but at length they became contemned and deserted by all, and I cannot recollect any better proof or assurance you can have than the fate of these two persons as to the temper of the people of this town, and as to their disposition for peace and benevolence. However, you will doubtless attend to what you see in the public prints, as the resolves of assemblies in this and the other states, and judge for yourself. Mr. Dana has returned from Russia, and if you return here, during his continuance among us, it may prove a fortunate circumstance to you, as I have heard him repeatedly say much in favor of your attachments, connections, etc.

I remain, dear sir, most respectfully, your friend,

WILLIAM PYNCHON.

FROM WILLIAM PYNCHON, ESQ.

Salem, March 2, 1784.

I have advised Mr. Oliver to seek you out and inform you about us all, who wish and expect your return in the summer; as he is young, and a stranger, I doubt not you will notice him and render him all the kind offices which you may observe him to need. I have desired Mr. Bartlet to advise with you as to some of the latest and best plays, farces, etc., which we wish much to see.

March 4. The *Pilgrim* not sailing this morning, I find time to recollect an omission I made last night. Some Americans have lately returned *via* Philadelphia to Boston, among them William

McNeal, who went off with the troops from thence, and E. Williams, who was an officer in the British service at New York, and now receives half pay. McNeal, by means of the Committee of Safety, was taken up and used roughly on account of his conduct, as it is said, during the blockade at Boston; but Williams met with no insult or obstruction there or at Salem, but is gone into the country to settle his affairs and then return to Nova Scotia. It is true he did not choose needlessly to go to the parade, or insurance offices, etc., but went about Salem visiting his particular friends, and met with no indecency in the streets or elsewhere. Many have urged me heretofore to write, that you might return and reside here without the least danger or insult; but while such as Alcock and Whitaker had the lead, I could not think nor say so. Now I may safely tell you what I have heard heretofore in the market-place, from some that are most desirous now for your return:—"Oh, let them return, by all means; but they must remember, that they are to go down on their knees to the General Court in the first place, to the committee in the next, and to their townsmen too, and ask pardon, and then we may even let them stay among us, provided they behave as they ought; even your Col. Browne himself must submit to this."

Your own and your friends' feelings require no observation on such insolence. This cannot now tend in the least to discourage your return; lest it should heretofore, I thought best not to mention it. Farewell.

Yours truly,
WILLIAM PYNCHON.

To WILLIAM VANS, ESQ., SALEM

London, May 21, 1784.

DEAR SIR:

Your favor of 2d January, was, I acknowledge, unexpected; but did not surprise me, though at this late day. *The difference of your sentiments from mine and those of my mistaken friends,* needed not to have caused the destruction of your former letter; for how wide soever our political notions have been, or perhaps now are, that letter, I dare say, conceived in purity of intention, and brought forth in decency of expression, could not have failed to prove informative and amusing; and on that score a welcome present. Besides, I sit in judgment on no man; wishing for candor towards myself, I think it my duty to practice it in my turn to all; referring it to God alone to approve or condemn, who alone has the right; and to knaves and fools who have none, to usurp that right.

The doubts that have hitherto discouraged my attempting to trust the faithless waves again, are derived from more than one source. However wanting in respect the appellation, I had rather be accounted a timid friend, a light you say I am viewed in, than an enemy; a reproach I am not conscious to have deserved.

Your report of the returned penitents to their former habitations, strengthens my belief of lenity towards myself, should I ever be in a condition to stand in need of such *lenity*. However, if I rightly understand the meaning of your caution to address to the care of a friend, you yourself, sanguine and positive as you are of the safety of my person and property, think it a proper precaution to slip behind the curtain for a while after entering on the territories of the United States; a part, Mr. Vans, I shall on no account stoop to act, dissimulation being no part of my character, and I am too late in life to assume new habits.

I am well pleased to hear of the singular moderation of the town of Salem; if other towns have been violent in words only, as your letter intimates, their character is greatly injured and the public abused.

Having answered your letter, I now take leave, after subscribing myself with due regards.

Your friend,
S. CURWEN.

FROM JONATHAN SEWALL

Bristol June 28, 1784.

You have not told me when you intend to embark; if you think proper to give me seasonable notice of the time, perhaps I may trouble you with the care of one or two letters, provided you dare be the bearer of them from an *alien—traitor* by law, *vide Act of* 1779. If you have any qualms, as I don't know but you may, upon good grounds, give me but a hint of your fears or wishes, and I shall conform to either, as my letters will be of no importance to myself or my correspondents—no treason, no politics, I assure you. If you go, as I with twenty-eight others still remain exiles, it is not probable we shall ever see each other again, in this world. God only knows what kind of one the next will be, whether more or less dirty—be it what it may, if we meet I shall most joyfully take you by the hand. Indeed I don't absolutely despair of seeing you again in this strange world, for upon my soul, though I was born and bred yet I am a stranger in it; but my design is to go out to Nova Scotia this autumn or early in the spring—there, if you wish, you may see me, but while the unjust, illiberal, lying act of 1779 remains unrepealed, never will I set foot on the territories of the thirteen United Independent States. I feel no resentment against them. I wish them more happiness in their unnatural independence than my judgment allows me to hope for them—but I have been mistaken throughout the whole voyage; yet, however I may have been out in my former opinions, I wish my judgment may still be erroneous—I wish, most sincerely, my native country may meet all the happiness she has sought, *per fas et nefas*—she thinks she has obtained it—I wish she may not be mistaken; but I have my doubts.

Mrs. Sewall accepts with thanks your compliments, and returns them most cordially; my sister, whom you kindly remember, died, poor girl, on the 17th of May last, after a paralytic stroke about three months before; I think I may say, she has gone with as few faults on her head as any of us can expect to go with. I miss her greatly,—but why should we complain?

I am your humble servant and sincere friend,

JONA. SEWALL.

To Hon. Judge Sewall, Bristol

London, June 29, 1784.

Dear Sir:

On some accounts I shall return to America with reluctance, having many doubts on my mind of meeting such a reception as will encourage my continued abode in that land of purity, sanctity and liberty. I feel too independent a spirit within to apprehend or regard any danger from republican licentiousness, which ever has been my contempt and abhorrence.

The following *inter nos*. The success of my application to the commissioners, now sitting in the Treasury, I am as yet ignorant of; my memorial or petition was this day delivered in, and is to be considered to-morrow. Whatever shall be the event I shall endeavor to support the same spirit, though a success equal to my supposed just expectations would serve as pillars or buttresses in an old tottering edifice, to add strength and support thereto.

Please make my compliments to your family, and to Mr. Samuel Sewall if in your neighborhood.

Dear sir, your affectionate friend, etc.,

S. CURWEN.

Sept. 25. Arrived at Boston, and at half past three o'clock landed at the end of Long-wharf, after an absence of nine years and five months, occasioned by a lamented civil war, excited by ambitious, selfish men here and in England, to the disgrace, dishonor, distress, and disparagement of these extensive territories. By plunder and rapine some few have accumulated wealth, but many more are greatly injured in their circumstances; some have to lament over the wreck of their departed wealth and estates, of which pitiable number I am; my affairs having sunk into irretrievable ruin.

To Capt. Michael Coombs, London

Salem, Mass., Oct. 9, 1784.

DEAR SIR:

This day fortnight, at half past three P.M., I landed on the head of the Long-wharf, in Boston, being the first American ground I had touched since May 12, 1775, when I departed from Philadelphia. It is no less strange than unaccountable, how low, mean and diminutive everything on shore appeared to me. On Sunday, being the day following, I left for this place, where I alighted at the house of my former residence, and not a man, woman, or child, but expressed a satisfaction at seeing me, and welcomed me back. Thus much for myself.

The few things for your *widow* I have delivered into her hands, and I find her a woman of uncommon vigor and equanimity, nor do I think one to be met with who has better acquitted herself in the late trying times. By her resolution she has preserved the household furniture from confiscation and waste, and your account-books from inspection, though menaced and flattered by the state agents. The melancholy derangement of my own affairs has so entirely unsettled me, that I can scarce attend to anything. I think it very unlikely my house can be saved. It shall be among my first engagements to attend to your affairs.

With real regard, your friend,

S. CURWEN.

To Jonathan Smith, Esq., Philadelphia

Salem, Oct. 9, 1784.

DEAR SIR:

A few days since I returned to the place of my nativity, after an absence of more than nine years, in which interval I find great revolutions to have taken place, not only with regard to the civil and political state of America in general, but also with respect to the property of individuals. Whilst some from the narrowest and basest condition have arisen to high honors and great wealth, others from comfortable, reputable, and even respectable and affluent, have fallen into indigent and distressed circumstances; and although the latter is not exactly my case, I confess myself verging to that point; my affairs are sadly deranged, but I hope time and application will cure the disorder. For that purpose, I beg you will forward to me a box containing my account-books left in your father's hands for security during my absence.

Your most obedient servant,
S. Curwen.

To Capt. Michael Coombs, London

Salem, Nov. 15, 1784.

Dear Sir:

I have waited on Mr. Sewall, a lawyer of your town; from him I learn he has undertaken to procure the necessary papers, and will, at my pressing instance, set about it immediately; my argument being constantly, *delay is almost as fatal to my friend as total neglect.*

I am now to congratulate you on the salvation of your wharf and warehouse from the villainous hands of the rapacious harpies, the commissioners; that part of your real estate, by great luck was neglected in the libel by which your other was seized and confiscated, and therefore it still remains your property. What debts are claimed and proved, must, by the law that confiscates, be levied on and taken out of the estate sold, the remainder escheats to the public treasury. But so infamously knavish has been the conduct of the commissioners, that though frequent attempts have been made to bring them to justice, and respond for the produce of the funds resting in their hands, so numerous are the defaulters in *that august body,* the General Court, that all efforts have hitherto proved vain. Not twopence in the pound have arrived to the public treasury of all the confiscations!

Mr. Sewall says, were you disposed, he would advise you not to come here, until the act respecting refugees or absentees be passed, which will be, it is thought, this session.

The triumphant here look down with contempt on the vanquished; their little minds are not equal to the astonishing success of their feeble arms. God bless the worthy and blast the villainous of every party.

Very truly yours,
S. Curwen.

To Hon. Judge Sewall, Bristol, England

Salem, Nov. 22, 1784.

Dear Sir:

I find myself completely ruined. I confess I cannot bear to stay and perish under the ruins of my late ample property, and shall, therefore, as soon as I can recover my account-books, left in Philadelphia on my departure from America, and settle my deranged affairs, retreat to Nova Scotia, unless my allowance shall be taken from me. I am ignorant whether it may be prudent to make application to the commissioners on American refugees' affairs; but being here by their indulgence, I wish my allowance may continue. And if in this representation you can afford me any assistance by yourself, or in concert with Mr. Danforth, to whom I have also written, I shall thankfully acknowledge your counsel and aid, as a kind endeavor to rescue from want your old and faithful friend,

S. Curwen.

Book IV
THE GENERATION OF THE FATHERS

CHAPTER XV

THE NEW nation whose existence had been determined by the victory and the peace had still to prove that it could survive as a separate society. Industry and trade were in need of reorganization; the government was crippled by inexperience and by financial embarrassments; and the population north and south was far from homogeneous. Soon the west was to be opened for settlement, thus adding still another ingredient to the mixture. It was a time of chaos; yet it was also a time favored by the presence of remarkable men who through ambition and ability wrought the new country into some kind of unity.

In the two years immediately following the peace a landed gentleman of Virginia happened to write letters to his daughters in which he gave them instructions expressive not merely of his own disposition but of a time and place as well. Thomas Jefferson, addressing Martha and Mary Jefferson, disclosed his idea of what a civilized young lady should be in the years 1783 and 1784.

To Martha Jefferson

Annapolis, Nov. 28th, 1783.

MY dear Patsy—After four days' journey, I arrived here without any accident, and in as good health as when I left Philadelphia. The conviction that you would be more improved in the situation I have placed you than if still with me, has solaced me on my parting with you, which my love for you has rendered a difficult thing. The acquirements which I hope you will make under the tutors I have provided for you will render you more worthy of my love; and if they cannot increase it, they will prevent its diminution. Consider the good lady who has taken you under her roof, who has undertaken to see that you perform all your exercises, and to admonish you in all those wanderings from what is right or what is clever, to which your inexperience would expose you: consider her, I say, as your mother, as the only person to whom, since the loss with which Heaven has pleased to afflict you, you can now look up; and that her displeasure or disapprobation, on any occasion, will be an immense misfortune, which should you be so unhappy as to incur by any unguarded act, think no concession too much to regain her good-will. With respect to the distribution of your time, the following is what I should approve:

From 8 to 10, practice music.

From 10 to 1, dance one day and draw another.

From 1 to 2, draw on the day you dance, and write a letter next day.

From 3 to 4, read French.

From 4 to 5, exercise yourself in music.

From 5 till bedtime, read English, write, etc.

Communicate this plan to Mrs. Hopkinson, and if she approves of it, pursue it. As long as Mrs. Trist remains in Philadelphia, cultivate her affection. She has been a valuable friend to you, and her good sense and good heart make her valued by all who know her, and by nobody on earth more than me. I expect you will write me by every post. Inform me what books you read, what tunes you learn, and inclose me your best copy of every lesson in drawing. Write also one letter a week either to your Aunt Eppes, your Aunt Skipwith, your Aunt Carr, or the little lady from whom I now inclose a letter, and always put the letter you so write under cover to me. Take care that you never spell a word wrong. Always before you write a word, consider how it is spelt, and, if you do not remember it, turn to a dictionary. It produces great praise to a lady to spell well. I have placed my happiness on seeing you good and accomplished; and no distress which this world can now bring on me would equal that of your disappointing my hopes. If you love me, then strive to be good under every situation and to all living creatures, and to acquire those accomplishments which I have put in your power, and which will go far towards ensuring you the warmest love of your affectionate father,

Th. Jefferson.

P.S.—Keep my letters and read them at times, that you may always have present in your mind those things which will endear you to me.

Annapolis, Dec. 11th, 1783.

I hope you will have good sense enough to disregard those foolish predictions that the world is to be at an end soon. The Almighty has never made known to anybody at what time he created it; nor will he tell anybody when he will put an end to it, if he ever means to do it. As to preparations for that event, the best way is for you always to be prepared for it. The only way to be so is, never to say or do a bad thing. If ever you are about to say anything amiss, or to do anything wrong, consider beforehand you will feel something within you which will tell you it is wrong, and ought not to be said or done. This is your conscience, and be sure and obey it. Our Maker has given us all this faithful internal monitor, and if you always obey it you will always be prepared for the end of the world; or for a much more certain event, which is death. This must happen to all; it puts an end to the world as to us; and the way to be ready for it is never to do a wrong act.

Annapolis, Dec. 22d, 1783.

I omitted in that letter to advise you on the subject of dress, which I know you are a little apt to neglect. I do not wish you to be gayly clothed at this time of life, but that your wear should be fine of its kind. But above all things and at all times let your clothes be neat, whole, and properly put on. Do not fancy you must wear them till the dirt is visible to the eye. You will be the last one who is sensible of this. Some ladies think they may, under the privileges of the *déshabillé*, be loose and negligent of their dress in the morning. But be you, from the moment you rise till you go to bed, as cleanly and properly dressed as at the hours of dinner or tea. A lady who has been seen as a sloven or a slut in the morning, will never efface the impression she has made, with all the dress and pageantry she can afterwards involve herself in. Nothing is so disgusting to our sex as a want of cleanliness and delicacy in yours. I hope, therefore, the moment you rise from bed, your first work will be to dress yourself in such style, as that you may be seen by any gentleman without his being able to discover a pin amiss, or any other circumstance of neatness wanting.

Annapolis, Jan. 15th, 1783.

My dear Martha—I am anxious to know what books you read, what tunes you play, and to receive specimens of your drawing. With respect to your meeting M. Simitière at Mr. Rittenhouse's, nothing could give me more pleasure than your being much with that worthy family, wherein you will see the best examples of rational life, and learn to esteem and copy them. But I should be very tender of intruding you on the family; as it might, perhaps, be not always convenient for you to be there at your hours of attending M. Simitière. I can only say, then, that if it has been desired by Mr. and Mrs. Rittenhouse, in such a manner as that Mrs. Hopkinson shall be satisfied that they will not think it inconvenient, I would have you thankfully accept it; and conduct yourself with so much attention to the family as that they may never feel themselves incommoded by it. I hope Mrs. Hopkinson will be so good as to act for you in this matter with that delicacy and prudence of which she is so capable. I have much at heart your learning to draw, and should be uneasy at your losing this opportunity, which probably is your last.

Annapolis, February 18th, 1784.

I am sorry M. Simitière cannot attend you, because it is probable you will never have another opportunity of learning to draw, and it is a pretty and pleasing accomplishment. With respect to the payment of the guinea, I would wish him to receive it; because if there is to be a doubt between him and me which of us acts rightly, I would wish to remove it clearly off my own shoulders. You must thank Mrs. Hopkinson for me for the trouble she gave herself in this matter; from which she will be relieved by paying M. Simitière his demand.

To Mary Jefferson

Paris, Sept. 20th, 1785.

My dear Polly—I have not received a letter from you since I came to France. If you knew how much I love you and what pleasure the receipt of your letters gave me at Philadelphia, you would have written to me, or at least have told your aunt what to write, and her goodness would have induced her to take the trouble of writing it. I wish so much to see you, that I have desired your uncle and aunt to send you to me. I know, my dear Polly, how sorry you will be, and ought to be, to leave them and your cousins; but your sister and myself cannot live without you, and after a while we will carry you back again to see your friends in Virginia. In the meantime you shall be taught here to play on the harpsichord, to draw, to dance, to read and talk French, and such other things as will make you more worthy of the love of your friends; but above all things, by our care and love of you, we will teach you to love us more than you will do if you stay so far from us. I have had no opportunity since Colonel Le Maire went, to send you anything; but when you come here you shall have as many dolls and playthings as you want for yourself, or to send to your cousins whenever you shall have opportunities. I hope you are a very good girl, that you love your uncle and aunt very much, and are very thankful to them for all their goodness to you; that you never suffer yourself to be angry with anybody, that you give your playthings to those who want them, that you do whatever anybody desires of you that is right, that you never tell stories, never beg for anything, mind your books and your work when your aunt tells you, never play but when she permits you, nor go where she forbids you; remember, too, as a constant charge, not to go out without your bonnet, because it will make you very ugly, and then we shall not love you so much. If you always practice these lessons we shall continue to love you as we do now, and it is impossible to love you any more. We shall hope to have you with us next summer, to find you a very good girl, and to assure you of the truth of our affection for you. Adieu, my dear child. Yours affectionately,

Th. Jefferson.

CHAPTER XVI

FOUR YEARS later in the north, after a stormy political period during which a constitution for the new government was being drafted, the young representative of a great New England family, John Quincy Adams, son of John and Abigail Adams and destined himself to be president, read law in an office at Newburyport, Massachusetts. An exceedingly conscientious student and on the whole a sober youth, he yet found time to disport himself at evening parties; and it is our good fortune that he sat down at night in his diary an account of the men, and particularly of the young ladies, whom he had met.

JANUARY 6th, 1788. Heard Mr. Carey preach two sermons this day; but the weather was very cold. In the afternoon the Parson was extremely vehement; in an occasional discourse upon the renewal of the year, he complained exceedingly that the language of the people was "the time is not come," and with all his powers of eloquence and of reasoning, he exerted to prove that the time is come. He was rather too violent: his zeal was so animated that he almost had the appearance of being vexed and chagrined. But he said he was not aiming at popularity. Passed the evening with Dr. Kilham at Mr. Carter's, where we had a whole magazine of antiquity. Miss Sally Jenkins was there. I was pleased with her manners. She is of the middling female size and has a fine form, the features of her face are regular, and were not the nose too much inclined to the aquiline, would be very handsome. Twenty-two, I should think her age; but perhaps she is two or three years younger. She conversed not much, and indeed in the state of female education here there are very few young ladies who talk and yet preserve our admiration. For my own part, the most difficult task that could be assigned me would be to carry on a conversation with one of our fine ladies; the topics upon which they are able to be fluent are so totally different from any of those with which I have ever been conversant, that I feel the same embarrassment that I should with one whose language I should be wholly unacquainted with. This is not meant however to apply to Miss Jenkins, who is, I hope, of a different cast; perhaps I shall discover on a better acquaintance attractions in her besides those of person, and they will appear the more amiable as they are the more rare.

9th. This day our State Convention is to meet in Boston for the purpose of assenting to and ratifying the Federal Constitution. The members from this town went for Boston yesterday, except Mr. Parsons, who will go to-morrow. The conjectures concerning the issue of their debates are different, according to the dispositions of the speculators. Some think there will be a great majority for adopting the Constitution, while others hope the opposite party will greatly preponderate. In the evening I played with Mr. Parsons at back-gammon, and was beat by him. After leaving the office, I pass'd the remainder of the evening with Townsend at Mrs. Hooper's.

13th. This morning Townsend called on me, and invited me to go and hear Parson Tucker. We met Little in the street, who turned about, and walked that way with us. When we got to the meeting-house we found there was to be no service there in the forenoon, and as it was then too late to go anywhere else we turned back and went home. Dined with Dr. Kilham at Dr. Sweet's, and Little dined with us. We spent the afternoon and drank tea there. Mrs. Swett is handsome, and, like most of our ladies, is perfectly acquainted with the various forms of propriety in company which have been established here. She has too much good breeding to know anything upon speculative subjects, and she has a proper aversion to politics. She has, however, I believe, a good understanding, and is infinitely superior to many of our female beauties who flutter in all the pride of variegated colors. After I returned home, Thompson called and delivered me a letter from W. Cranch. I went with the Dr. to see Mr. Jackson, but he was not at home, and we called in at Mrs. Emery's. This lady and her daughter converse more to my satisfaction than the generality of my female acquaintance. In their company my time passes away fast; and I am not often able to say as much.

16th. It snowed all the forenoon; but the weather continued moderating, and in the afternoon a steady rain took place of the snow; and when I came this evening from the office, the ground was covered all the way with one continual glare of ice. It was dangerous walking, and I came as much as half the way without lifting my feet. I spent the evening at home, writing to make good the time which I have lately lost; but I accomplished my purpose only in part. It may be observed that I say of late little but of what I do in the evening; and the reason is, that the only varieties of any

kind that take place are in that part of the day. At about nine in
the morning I regularly go to the office, and when I do not lose my
time in chat with Amory or Townsend, I take up my Lord Coke,
and blunder along a few pages with him. At two I return to dinner;
at three again attend at the office, and again consult my old author.
There I remain till dark, and as Mr. Parsons for special reasons, to
him best known, objects to our having a fire in the office in the evening while he is absent, as soon as daylight begins to fail we put up
our books, and then employ the remainder of the day as best suits
our convenience and the feelings of the moment. I go but little into
company, and yet I am not industrious. I am recluse, without being
studious; and I find myself equally deprived of the pleasures of
society, and of the sweet communion with the mighty dead. I am
no stranger to the midnight lamp; yet I observe not that I make a
rapid progress in any laudable pursuit. I begin seriously to doubt
of the goodness of my understanding, and am not without my fears
that as I increase in years the dullness of my apprehension likewise
increases. But we are all mortal.

18th. This afternoon I wrote a couple of letters to send by Mr.
Atkins, who goes to Boston to-morrow. One for N. Freeman, and
the other from [for?] Wm. Cranch; and as I could not finish
before dark I ventured to stay in the office till seven o'clock. I then
went with Townsend to Mr. Atkins's, to give him the letters. Miss
Dashwood was there, a young lady from Boston. She speaks thick
and quick, which is at present all I have to say of her, except that
by candlelight she looks handsome. I came home; and then went
with the Doctor to Mrs. Emery's. There we found Mrs. Jackson and
Miss Fletcher. Mrs. Jackson looks better than I ever saw her, and
was in high spirits. She talked almost all the time, and would have
talked well, had she not appeared rather too fond, in repeating some
gentlemen's speeches, to render every word, even those which are
most superfluous, words which if used before women, even by a
man, at least argue ill-breeding, but which the lips of every woman
ought to be ignorant of pronouncing. Miss Fletcher sat two hours,
and scarcely opened her mouth. The poor girl is in love, and when
her friend is absent she can utter nothing but sighs. This evening,
it is true, she had no chance to speak, but she was not only silent
but absent. She did not appear to enjoy the conversation, and all
Mrs. Jackson's wit could scarcely soften her features to a smile.
After they were gone, we sat there about half an hour in chat with
Miss Emery. She is Thompson's favorite, and in this as in many
other instances he shows the goodness of his taste.

22d. This afternoon, Leonard White called on me, and sat about half an hour. He came from Haverhill this morning, and returns to-night. Between four and five I received an invitation from Put, nam and F. Bradbury to join them for a party at sleighing. Though not peculiarly desirous to go I did not refuse; and at about six o'clock we started. We went to Sawyer's tavern, about three miles off, and there danced till between twelve and one. The company was rather curiously sorted, but the party was agreeable. I danced with the eldest Miss Frazier, with Miss Fletcher, and with Miss Coats. Miss Fletcher appears to be about twenty. She is not tall, but has what is called a very genteel shape. Her complexion is fair, and her eye is sometimes animated with a very pleasing expression; but unfortunately she is in love, and unless the object of her affections is present she loses all her spirits, grows dull and unsociable, and can be pleased with nothing. This evening she was obliged to dispense with his company; and the usual effect took place. I endeavored as much as possible to bring on a conversation; but all to no purpose.

> "She sat like Patience on a monument,
> Smiling at grief."

And, as I found she could talk only in monosyllables, I was glad to change my partner. Miss Coats is not in love, and is quite sociable. Her manners are not exactly what I should wish for a friend of mine; yet she is agreeable. I am not obliged with her both to make and support the conversation; and moreover, what is very much in her favor, she is an only daughter and her father has money. We returned to town a little after twelve; but the weather was not very agreeable, as it snowed violently. After we had carried home the ladies, Putnam came to lodge with me. We sat and chatted about an hour, and then retired to bed.

23d. ...I passed the evening at Dr. Swett's. Mrs. and Miss Cazneau were there. We had some agreeable and entertaining conversation, but singing soon came on to the carpet, and then the usual nonsense succeeded. I believe I will try one of these days and see if I cannot stop the career of this same singing, at least for one evening. I even got quit this time with singing once. In order not to appear singular, I was in the common way urging Miss Cazneau to sing; she told me she would upon condition that I should sing first. I hummed over a tune; but avoided claiming the fulfillment of Miss C's promise, and so she would not sing, which happened very much to my satisfaction. A short time before nine I left them.

30th. I went up to the office in the morning, and sat a couple of hours; but I felt restless and dissipated. I could not study, and therefore walked down in town and sauntered about. Dined with G. Bradbury and Charles at Mr. Hooper's. He is very sanguine in his hopes for the adoption of the Constitution. Passed the evening at Mr. Bradbury's. Dr. Smith and all his family were there. We had some music in the beginning of the evening, and afterwards played a number of very amusing sports, such as start; what is it like? cross questions; I love my love with an A; and a number more. My opinion of such diversions I have already given, when it was confined to a number of young persons; but that the most inexcusable levities of youth should appear in the garb of old-age is something that calls for more than disapprobation, nor will a gray-haired trifler excite our pity merely, but must raise our indignation and contempt. Mr. Bradbury, however, is a very respectable man; and, as this conduct has here the sanction of custom, it is not him but the manners of the times that I blame.

5th. The weather this day has been extreme cold. I have not experienced the severity of the season so much since the winter I passed in Sweden. I passed the evening with Townsend and Amory at Dr. Smith's. The old man is very fond of telling long stories, and indeed it is quite necessary to attend to him. There are, however, two young ladies in the house, to whom we attend with much more pleasure. Miss Smith may be twenty years old; she is not handsome, but has a great degree of animation in her eye, and, as the want of it appears conspicuous in every other feature, the mixture of opposites has a singular effect upon her countenance. Her person is not elegant, nor is her taste in dress such as suits my mind. She has a satirical turn, and is fond of being esteemed witty. So much, I think, I can judge from the short acquaintance I have with her; perhaps at some future period I may be able to say more. Miss Putnam I will mention the next time I fall in company with her. We played at whist about a couple of hours; after which we sung or attempted to sing; for, of all the company, Amory was the only one that could sing so as to give any kind of entertainment.

7th. This day, at about noon, the news arrived in this town that the Federal Constitution was yesterday adopted and ratified by a majority of nineteen members in our State Convention. In this town the satisfaction is almost universal; for my own part, I have not been pleased with this system, and my acquaintance have long-since branded me with the name of an *anti-federalist*. But I am now converted, though not convinced. My feelings upon the occasion have not been passionate nor violent; and, as upon the decision of this question I find myself on the weaker side, I think it my duty to submit without murmuring against what is not to be helped. In our government, opposition to the acts of a majority of the people is rebellion to all intents and purposes; and I should view a man who would now endeavor to excite commotions against this plan, as no better than an insurgent who took arms last winter against the Courts of Justice. This afternoon I went, in company with a number of young ladies and gentlemen of this town, upon a sleighing party. We rode about eight miles into Newbury, and by dark returned to Sawyer's tavern. After drinking tea we went to dancing, and, excepting supper, continued so till about midnight. I danced with Miss Coats and Miss Smith, both of whom were very agreeable partners. At twelve we broke up, and returned home. Thompson came and lodged with me. Mr. S. Cutler came and sat about half an hour with me; he was exceedingly mortified at having overset his sleigh. Some of the ladies were affronted, and some affrighted; so that, in returning, he had somewhat of an uncomfortable time, sweating between two fires. In the company was an Irish gentleman by the name of Hutchinson, a man of genuine wit and humor, and a person of much reading and information. He has a vessel here loading, and expects to sail for Ireland in a week or ten days.

8th. This afternoon the delegates from Newbury and from this town returned home from Convention. A number of very respectable citizens, and a number who were not very respectable, went out on horseback to meet the members and escort them into town; as they came along the bells at the different churches were set to ringing, and this noisy expression of joy was continued with some intermissions till eight o'clock in the evening. The mob huzzaed, and one would have thought that every man from the adoption of the Constitution had acquired a sure expectancy of an independent fortune. I passed the evening at home in reading and writing.

9th. Mr. Parsons gave me this morning a packet of letters which I have been expecting these five weeks. There was, however, but one short letter from Europe. In the afternoon Amory went for Salem. I took a ride with Townsend, S. Cutler, J. Greenleaf, Prout, Thompson, and three or four ladies in a sleigh. We rode out as far as Mr. Dalton's farm; and, after taking something of a circuitous route, returned and took tea at Sawyer's. After passing an hour we all returned to town. I spent the evening at Mrs. Hooper's. It was the first time I had been there since her misfortune. She bears it well, though frequent sighs rise deep from her breast. Mr. L. Jenkins was there, a good, honest, simple soul, without the least kind of harm in him. Miss Lucy Knight was there too. She has a very amiable countenance, a fine form and a benevolent disposition. Townsend says she has no sensibility, and I think her countenance wants some of that expression which communicates the charm of sympathy to our souls. She may be possessed of many virtues, and if so will attract my esteem and respect; but she is incapable of loving, and therefore could never be an object of love to me. A young fellow by the name of Rogers for a year and a half paid the closest attention to her; and when it was daily expected that they would be published he suddenly left her, and neglected her entirely. She wrote him a letter containing a dismission, and appears not to have had a disagreeable sensation upon the subject ever since. A disposition like this certainly smooths the path of life; but at the same time it certainly serves to make 'it narrow and contracted.

14th. I attended at the office only in the forenoon; the after part of the day being employed in rigging for the ball. I had sent a billet to Miss H. Greenleaf requesting the honor of waiting upon her. She was not engaged and I was taken at my word, which will teach me to be sincere. It was late before I could get a carriage, and, when I went for my lady, I found all the rest of the family were gone, which was against me again. The ballrooms were too small,—not one-quarter of the ladies could dance at a time. I danced enough myself, and made out to affront three or four ladies; which is much in my favor. Townsend took cold in making the preparations for this ball, and was so unwell that at about eleven o'clock he went home, and consigned his lady, Miss L. Knight, to me. She being very agreeable was, upon the whole, I believe, more the object of my attentions than another lady. This cannot now be helped, and whatever is, is right. Between three and four in the morning the remainder of the company retired. Putnam lodged with me. The party was perfectly agreeable.

15th. We indulged ourselves this morning till almost twelve o'clock before we rose. I called at the office, and passed about half an hour there. I felt rather dissipated, and somewhat indisposed for study. In the afternoon, when I called at the office I found Mr. Wendell there,—a singular eccentric character with whom I was acquainted while I was in College, and whom I have probably mentioned before now. He still persists in his singularities, and in walking from Boston the day before yesterday froze one of his feet. Townsend is quite unwell; has an uncomfortable cough and sore throat. But he went with me to visit several of the ladies who were of the company last evening. We first called at Captain Coombs's, where we only found Miss Nancy Jenkins. She holds her head too stiff for elegance and has read too many novels, which render her manners rather fantastical and affected. We stopped a few moments to see Miss Coats, who was well, and we then went to Judge Greenleaf's, where we drank tea. Here were young ladies, I had almost said, innumerable; a choice of every complexion, and probably of every disposition. Among them all Miss Derby has the most promising appearance; but she in company is reserved. The Judge talked about religion and politics, and Mrs. Greenleaf passed encomiums upon the British Constitution; but the young ladies were all silent. We took our departure quite early, and I passed the remainder of the evening at Mrs. Hooper's where I found Miss Knight and Mr. Cutler. Learned to play quadrille.

16th. The most violent snowstorm that has appeared in the course of the winter; it began in the night, and continued all this day. In the evening it cleared up. Townsend was not out. Amory and I dined with Mr. Parsons. Captain Hodge likewise was of the company. I wrote a letter in the afternoon, or rather part of a letter, to W. Cranch. From the office we went and passed an hour with Mrs. Jackson, where we found Mr. Wendell, feasting upon his apples and nuts. He slept last night in Mr. J. Tracey's green house, which is entirely unprotected from the inclemency of the season; and, the better to enjoy the benefits of the open air, he stripped himself entirely naked. He converses in the same style that he did a year ago; and appears to me too consistent for a distracted person, as many suppose him to be. We spent the remainder of the evening at Dr. Smith's. I made an apology to Miss Smith for a blunder which took place at the ball. She appeared plainly to be offended, but was satisfied after I had made my explanation. I know not whether to like or to dislike this girl, but perhaps time will supply me with the means of information. At supper Amory was excessively diverted with the appearance of a Bologna sausage, which the Doctor introduced, and which Mr. Cutler observed would be ripe in June. After supper I got seated next to Miss Putnam, and entered into conversation with her. I found her inclined to flattery, a defect not uncommon among our young ladies; and I answered her in her own way, as I always do. When a lady pays me a compliment I always consider myself indebted to her until I return one at least of equal value; and I am generally so good a creditor that I pay with large interest. I have even once or twice in my life so far surpassed a lady in that way as to silence her, and make her ashamed of attacking me with those weapons; but I never flatter a lady that I esteem.

CHAPTER XVII

YOUNG ADAMS had spoken with some irony of the expectations which certain citizens of Newburyport entertained of the time when the Constitution should be ratified and the new government installed. Ratification proceeded with much debate, and not without signs of animosity between the sections. Then on April 6th, 1789, the chosen representatives met in New York to count electoral votes and notify the first president and vice president of their new dignities. The president was George Washington and the vice president was John Adams of Massachusetts—both of them members of a group which another group labeled as aristocratic, even monarchical. Certainly to such ardent republicans as William Maclay, senator from Pennsylvania, the sessions in New York were mingled comedy and tragedy, since Adams and his kind seemed bent upon constructing a little kingdom, not a great democracy. Maclay recorded with amused disgust the hankerings of the vice president and his followers—even, Maclay insinuated, of His Excellency George Washington himself.

APRIL 25th, Saturday.—Attended the House Ceremonies, endless ceremonies, the whole business of the day. I did not embark warmly this day. Otis, our Secretary, makes a most miserable hand at it. The grossest mistakes made on our minutes, and it cost us an hour or two to rectify them. I was up as often I believe as was necessary, and certainly threw so much light on two subjects that the debate ended on each.

The Vice-President, as usual, made us two or three speeches from the Chair. I will endeavor to recollect one of them. It was on the reading of a report which mentioned that the President should be received in the Senate chamber and proceed thence to the House of Representatives to be sworn: "Gentlemen, I do not know whether the framers of the Constitution had in view the two kings of Sparta or the two consuls of Rome when they formed it; one to have all the power while he held it, and the other to be nothing. Nor do I know whether the architect that formed our room and the wide chair in it (to hold two, I suppose), had the Constitution before him. Gentlemen, I feel great difficulty how to act. I am possessed of two separate powers; the one in *esse* and the other in *posse*. I am Vice-President. In this I am nothing, but I may be everything. But I am president also of the Senate. When the President comes into the Senate, what shall I be? I can not be [president] then. No, gentlemen, I cannot, I cannot. I wish gentlemen to think what I shall be."

Here, as if oppressed with a sense of his distressed situation, he threw himself back in his chair. A solemn silence ensued. God forgive me, for it was involuntary, but the profane muscles of my face were in tune for laughter in spite of my indisposition. Elsworth thumbed over the sheet Constitution and turned it for some time. At length he rose and addressed the Chair with the umost gravity: "Mr. President, I have looked over the Constitution (pause), and I find, sir, it is evident and clear, sir, that wherever the Senate are to be, there, sir, you must be at the head of them. But further, sir (here he looked aghast, as if some tremendous gulf had yawned before him), I shall not pretend to say."

Thursday next is appointed for swearing in the President.

30th April, Thursday.—This is a great, important day. Goddess of etiquette, assist me while I describe it. The Senate stood adjourned to half after eleven o'clock. About ten dressed in my best clothes; went for Mr. Morris' lodgings, but met his son, who told me that his father would not be in town until Saturday. Turned into the Hall. The crowd already great. The Senate met. The Vice-President rose in the most solemn manner. This son of *Adam* seemed impressed with deeper gravity, yet what shall I think of him? He often, in the midst of his most important airs—I believe when he is at loss for expressions (and this he often is, wrapped up, I suppose, in the contemplation of his own importance)—suffers an unmeaning kind of vacant laugh to escape him. This was the case to-day, and really to me bore the air of ridiculing the farce he was acting. "Gentlemen, I wish for the direction of the Senate. The President will, I suppose, address the Congress. How shall I behave? How shall we receive it? Shall it be standing or sitting?"

Here followed a considerable deal of talk from him which I could make nothing of. Mr. Lee began with the House of Commons (as is usual with him), then the House of Lords, then the King, and then back again. The result of his information was, that the Lords sat and the Commons stood on the delivery of the King's speech. Mr. Izard got up and told how often he had been in the Houses of Parliament. He said a great deal of what he had seen there. [He] made, however, this sagacious discovery, that the Commons stood because they had no seats to sit on, being arrived at the bar of the House of Lords. It was discovered after some time that the King sat, too, and had his robes and crown on.

Mr. Adams got up again and said he had been very often indeed at the Parliament on those occasions, but there always was such a crowd, and *ladies along,* that for his part he could not say how it was. Mr. Carrol got up to declare that he thought it of no consequence how it was in Great Britain; they were no rule to us, etc. But all at once the Secretary, who had been out, whispered to the Chair that the Clerk from the Representatives was at the door with a communication. Gentlemen of the Senate, how shall he be received? A silly kind of resolution of the committee on that business had been laid on the table some days ago. The amount of it was that each House should communicate to the other what and how they chose; it concluded, however, something in this way: That everything should be done with all the *propriety* that was *proper.* The question was, Shall this be adopted, that we may know how to receive the Clerk? It was objected [that] this will throw no light on the subject; it will leave you where you are. Mr. Lee brought the House of Commons before us again. He reprobated the rule; declared that the Clerk should not come within the bar of the House; that the proper mode was for the Sergeant-at-Arms, with the mace on his shoulder, to meet the Clerk at the door and receive his communication; we are not, however, provided for this ceremonious way of doing business, having neither mace nor sergeant nor Masters in Chancery, who carry down bills from the English Lords.

Mr. Izard got up and labored unintelligibly to show the great distinction between a communication and a delivery of a thing, but he was not minded. Mr. Elsworth showed plainly enough that if the Clerk was not permitted to deliver the communication, the Speaker might as well send it inclosed. Repeated accounts came [that] the Speaker and Representatives were at the door. Confusion ensued; the members left their seats. Mr. Read rose and called attention of the Senate to the neglect that had been shown Mr. Thompson, late Secretary. Mr. Lee rose to answer him, but I could not hear one word he said. The Speaker was introduced, followed by the Representatives. Here we sat an hour and ten minutes before the President arrived—this delay was owing to Lee, Izard, and Dalton, who had stayed with us while the Speaker came in, instead of going to attend the President. The President advanced between the Senate and Representatives, bowing to each. He was placed in the chair by the Vice-President; the Senate with their President on the right, the Speaker and the Representatives on his left. The Vice-President rose and addressed a short sentence to him. The import of it was that he should now take the oath of office as President. He seemed to have forgot half what he was to say, for he made a dead pause and stood for some time, to appearance, in a vacant mood. He finished with a formal bow, and the President was conducted out of the middle window into the gallery, and the oath was administered by the Chancellor. Notice that the business done was communicated to the crowd by proclamation, etc., who gave three cheers, and repeated it on the President's bowing to them.

As the company returned into the Senate chamber, the President took the chair and the Senators and Representatives their seats. He rose, and all arose also, and addressed them (see the address). This great man was agitated and embarrassed more than ever he was by the leveled cannon or pointed musket. He trembled, and several times could scarce make out to read, though it must be supposed he had often read it before. He put part of the fingers of his left hand into the side of what I think the tailors call the fall of the breeches [corresponding to the modern side-pocket], changing the paper into his left [right] hand. After some time he then did the same with some of the fingers of his right hand. When he came to the words *all the world*, he made a flourish with his right hand, which left rather an ungainly impression. I sincerely, for my part, wished all set ceremony in the hands of the dancing-masters, and that this first of men had read off his address in the plainest manner, without ever taking his eyes from the paper, for I felt hurt that he was not first in everything. He was dressed in deep brown, with metal buttons, with an eagle on them, white stockings, a bag, and sword.

4th May, Monday.—Went pretty early to the post-office to deliver letters. As I came back, met General St. Clair. He seemed desirous of speaking with me; said he had been at my lodgings, and asked me what I thought of the President's new arrangements. It was the first I had heard of them. The President is neither to entertain nor receive invitations. He is to have levee days on Tuesdays and Fridays, when only he is to be seen. I told the General that General Washington stood on as difficult ground as he ever had done in his life: that to suffer himself to be run down, on the one hand, by a crowd of visitants so as to engross his time, would never do, as it would render the doing of business impracticable; but, on the other hand, for him to be seen only in public on stated times, like an Eastern Lama, would be equally offensive. If he was not to be seen but in public, where nothing confidential could pass between him and any individual, the business would, to all appearance, be done without him, and he could not escape the charge of favoritism. All court would be paid to the supposed favorite; weakness and insignificance would be considered as characteristic of the President, and he would not escape contempt; that it was not thus the General gained the universal plaudits of his admiring fellow-citizens. I reiterated these ideas in every shape and in every different light I could place them for near half an hour that we walked in front of St. Paul's Church. The General said he wished to collect men's sentiments, and the design was to communicate them to the General [Washington]. I told him my late conduct in the Senate had been such as would render any opinion of mine very ungracious at court, and perhaps he had best never make any mention of my name. Much more was said, but not worth committing to paper.

Now the Vice-President rose to draw the attention of the Senate to the manner of delivering the answer to the President. A committee was appointed to confer on this and other subjects with a committee of Representatives. "There are three ways, gentlemen" (said our Vice-President), "by which the President may communicate with us. One is personally. If he comes here, we must have a seat for him. In England it is called a *throne*. To be sure, it is behind that seat we must seek for shelter and protection. The second is by a minister of state. The third is by his chamberlain or one of his aides-de-camp, I had almost said, but that is a military phrase. It may become a great constitutional question." Seeing the House look blank, he said, "I throw these things out for gentlemen to think of." Mr. Lee got up and said something on the propriety of having a seat with a canopy for the President. Mr. Langdon said something, but did not seem well collected, and spoke so low I did not hear him.

The time was trifled till near three o'clock. The day was cold, and the members collected near the fire, leaving their seats. The committee returned with the message, and it really read vastly better, and was altered in the exceptional phrases. In one place, speaking of the Government, it mentioned "dignity and *splendor*." I submitted it to the gentlemen who had the amending of it whether "respectability" was not better than *splendor*. Mr. Carrol, of the committee, did not defend the word "splendor," but said "respectability" had been used before, if he recollected right. Mr. Patterson said it sounded much better than "respectability," and rounded the period. Dr. Johnson said "splendor" signified in this place the highest perfection of government. These were the three members of the committee. I mentioned that, if the word *respectabil-*

ity had been used immediately before, it would be improper; that *dignity* alone I thought expressed all that was wanted. As to the seeking of sounding names and pompous expressions, I thought them exceptionable on that very account, and that no argument was necessary to show it; that different men had a train of different ideas raised by the same word; that "splendor," when applied to government, brought into my mind, instead of the highest perfection, all the faulty finery, brilliant scenes, and expensive trappings of royal government, and impressed my mind with an idea quite the reverse of republican respectability, which I thought consisted in firm and prudent councils, frugality, and economy.

I found I was not seconded, and concluded that my motion went to recommend a reconsideration of the word "splendor" to the committee. They did not alter it, and the answer was agreed to. The Vice-President rose in the chair and repeated twice, with more joy in his face than I had ever seen him assume before, he hoped the Government would be supported with *dignity and splendor*. I thought he did it by way of triumph over me for a former defeat I gave him, but maybe I was mistaken.

May 8th.—Attended a joint committee on the papers of the old Congress. Made progress in the business. Agreed to meet at half-past ten on Monday and report. Senate formed. The Secretary, as usual, had made some mistakes, which were rectified, and now Mr. Elsworth moved for the report of the Joint Committee to be taken up on the subject of titles. It was accordingly done. Mr. Lee led the business. He took his old ground—all the world, civilized and savage, called for titles; that there must be something in human nature that occasioned this general consent; that, therefore, he conceived it was right. Here he began to enumerate many nations who gave titles—such as Venice, Genoa, and others. The Greeks and Romans, it was said, had no titles, "but" (making a profound bow to the Chair) "you were pleased to set us right in this with respect to the Conscript Fathers the other day." Here he repeated the Vice-President's speech of the 23d ultimo [April], almost verbatim all over.

Mr. Elsworth rose. He had a paper in his hat, which he looked constantly at. He repeated almost all that Mr. Lee had said, but got on the subject of kings—declared that the sentence in the primer of *fear God and honor the king* was of great importance; that kings were of divine appointment; that Saul, the head and shoulders taller than the rest of the people, was elected by God and anointed by his appointment.

I sat, after he had done, for a considerable time, to see if anybody would rise. At last I got up and first answered Lee as well as I could with nearly the same arguments, drawn from the Constitution, as I had used on the 23d ult. I mentioned that within the space of twenty years back more light had been thrown on the subject of governments and on human affairs in general than for several generations before; that this light of knowledge had diminished the veneration for titles, and that mankind now considered themselves as little bound to imitate the follies of civilized nations as the brutalities of savages; that the abuse of power and the fear of bloody masters had extorted titles as well as adoration, in some instances from the trembling crowd; that the impression now on the minds of the citizens of these States was that of horror for kingly authority.

Izard got up. He dwelt almost entirely on the antiquity of kingly government. He could not, however, well get further back than Philip of Macedon. He seemed to have forgot both Homer and the Bible. He urged for something equivalent to nobility having been common among the Romans, for they had three names that seemed to answer to honorable, or something like it, before and something behind. He did not say Esquire. Mr. Carrol rose and took my side of the question. He followed nearly the track I had been in, and dwelt much on the information that was now abroad in the world. He spoke against kings. Mr. Lee and Mr. Izard were both up again. Elsworth was up again. Langdon was up several times, but spoke short each time. Patterson was up, but there was no knowing which side he was of. Mr. Lee considered him as against him and answered him, but Patterson finally voted with Lee. The Vice-President repeatedly helped the speakers for titles. Elsworth was enumerating how common the appellation of President was. The Vice-President put him in mind that there were presidents of fire companies and of a cricket club. Mr. Lee at another time was saying he believed some of the states authorized titles by their Constitutions. The Vice-President, from the chair, told him that Connecticut did it. At sundry other times he interfered in a like manner. I had been frequently up to answer new points during the debate.

I collected myself for a last effort. I read the clause in the Constitution against titles of nobility; showed that the spirit of it was against not only granting titles by Congress, but against the permission of foreign potentates granting *any titles whatever;* that as to kingly government, it was equally out of the question, as a republican government was guaranteed to every State in the Union; that they were both equally forbidden fruit of the Constitution. I called the attention of the House to the consequences that were like to follow; that gentlemen seemed to court a rupture with the other House. The Representatives had adopted the report, and were this day acting on it, or according to the spirit of the report. We were proposing a title. Our conduct would mark us to the world as actuated by the spirit of dissension, and the characters of the Houses would be as aristocratic and democratical.

The report [of the Committee on Titles] was, however, rejected. "Excellency" was moved for as a title by Mr. Izard. It was withdrawn by Mr. Izard, and "highness" with some prefatory word, proposed by Mr. Lee. Now long harangues were made in favor of this title. "Elective" was placed before. It was insisted that such a dignified title would add greatly to the weight and authority of the Government both at home and abroad. I declared myself totally of a different opinion; that at present it was impossible to add to the respect entertained for General Washington; that if you gave him the title of any foreign prince or potentate, a belief would follow that the manners of that prince and his modes of government would be adopted by the President. (Mr. Lee had, just before I got up, read over a list of the titles of all the princes and potentates of the earth, marking where the word "highness" occurred. The Grand Turk had it, all the princes of Germany had [it], sons and daughters of crown heads, etc.) That particularly "elective highness," which sounded nearly like "electoral highness," would have a most ungrateful sound to many thousands of industrious citizens who had fled from German oppression; that "highness" was part of the title of a prince or princes of the blood, and was often given to dukes; that it was degrading our President to place him on a par with any prince of any blood in Europe, nor was there one of them that could enter the list of true glory with him.

But I will minute no more. The debate lasted till half after three o'clock, and it ended in appointing a committee to consider of a title to be given to the President. This whole silly business is the work of Mr. Adams and Mr. Lee; Izard follows Lee, and the New England men, who always herd together, follow Mr. Adams. Mr. Thompson says this used to be the case in the old Congress. I had, to be sure, the greatest share in this debate, and must now have completely sold (no, sold is a bad word, for I have got nothing for it) every particle of court favor, for a court our House seems determined on, and to run into all the fooleries, fopperies, fineries, and pomp of royal etiquette; and all this for Mr. Adams.

May 9th.—Attended the Hall at ten o'clock to go on the Judicial Committee. Met many of the members. I know not the motive, but I never was received with more familiarity, nor quite so much, before by the members. Elsworth in particular seemed to show a kind of fondness. The Judicial Committee did no business. Senate formed. It took a long time to correct the minutes. Otis keeps them miserably. At length the committee came in and reported a title— *His Highness the President of the United States of America and Protector of the Rights of the Same.* Mr. Few had spoken a word or two with me, and signified his unwillingness to do anything hastily. He got up and spoke a great deal against hasty measures. He did not pointedly move for postponement, but it amounted nearly to it. The Clerk of the other House in the meantime appeared at the bar and announced the adoption of the report of the Joint Committee (rejecting titles).

Up now got the Vice-President, and for forty minutes did he harangue us from the chair. He began first on the subject of order, and found fault with everything almost, but down he came to particulars, and pointedly blamed a member for disorderly behavior. The member had mentioned the appearance of a captious disposition in the other House. This was disorderly and spoke with asperity. The member meant was Mr. Izard. All this was only prefatory. On he got to his favorite topic of titles, and over the old ground of the immense advantage of, the absolute necessity of them. When he had exhausted this subject he turned a new leaf, I believe, on the conviction that the postponement would be carried and perhaps the business lost by an attention to the other House.

"Gentlemen, I must tell you that it is you and the President that have the making of titles. Suppose the President to have the appointment of Mr. Jefferson at the court of France. Mr. Jefferson is, in virtue of that appointment, the most illustrious, the most powerful, and what not. But the President must be himself something that includes all the dignities of the diplomatic corps and something greater still. What will the common people of foreign countries, what will the sailors and the soldiers say, 'George Washington, President of the United States'? They will despise him *to all eternity.* This is all nonsense to the philosopher, but so is all government whatever."

The above I recollect with great precision, but he said fifty more things, equally injudicious, which I do not think worth minuting. It is evident that he begins to despair of getting the article of titles through the House of Representatives, and has turned his eye to get it done solely by the Senate.

Having experienced relief by the interference of sundry members, I had determined not to say another word, but his new leaf appeared so absurd I could not help some animadversions on it. I rose. Mr. President, the Constitution of the United States has designated our Chief Magistrate by the appellation of the *President of the United States of America*. This is his title of office, nor can we alter, add to, or diminish it without infringing the Constitution. In like manner persons authorized to transact business with foreign powers are styled *Ambassadors, Public Ministers,* etc. To give them any other appellation would be an equal infringement. As to grades of orders or titles of nobility, nothing of the kind can be established by Congress.

Can, then, the President and Senate do that which is prohibited to the United States at large? Certainly not. Let us read the Constitution: *No title of nobility shall be granted by the United States*. The Constitution goes further. The servants of the public are prohibited from accepting them from any foreign state, king, or prince. So that the appellations and terms given to nobility in the Old World are contraband language in the United States, nor can we apply them to our citizens consistent with the Constitution. As to what the common people, soldiers, and sailors of foreign countries may think of us, I do not think it imports us much. Perhaps the less they think, or have occasion to think of us, the better.

But suppose this a desirable point, how is it to be gained? The English excepted, foreigners do not understand our language. We must use Hohen Mogende to a Dutchman, Beylerbey to a Turk or Algerine, and so of the rest. From the English indeed we may borrow terms that would not be wholly unintelligible to our own citizens. But will they thank us for the compliment? Would not the plagiarism be more likely to be attended with contempt than respect among all of them? It has been admitted that all this is nonsense to the philosopher. I am ready to admit that every high-sounding, pompous appellation, descriptive of qualities which the object does not possess, must appear bombastic nonsense in the eye of every wise man. But I can not admit such an idea with respect to government itself. Philosophers have admitted not the utility but the necessity of it [government], and their labors have been directed to correct the vices and expose the follies which have been ingrafted upon it, and to reduce the practice of it to the principles of common sense, such as we see exemplified by the merchant, the mechanic, and the farmer, whose every act or operation tends to a productive or beneficial effect, and, above all, to illustrate this fact, that government was instituted for the benefit of the people, and that no act of government is justifiable that has not this for its object. Such has been the labor of philosophers with respect to government, and sorry indeed would I be if their labors should be in vain.

After all this he had to put the question, and the postponement was carried.

May 11th.—I have actually delayed making up my journal for this day until the morning of the 12th. I feel how very wrong it is. There is a bluntness over my memory already. The first thing I did in the morning was delivering my letters at the post-office. Called to see if Mr. Morris was come to town. He was not. Met two committees at the hall: first on the affairs of the Old Congress Papers. This business disposed of, the second on the judiciary department. Senate met. Mr. Lee moved to put off the order of the day, on the subject of titles, until to-morrow. Agreed to. He then moved to consider the appointing of a Sergeant-at-Arms. This lost, Mr. Izard and sundry gentlemen of the Senate [were] dissatisfied with our Vice-President. He takes on him to school the members from the chair. His grasping after titles had been observed by everybody. Mr. Izard, after describing his air, manner, deportment, and personal figure in the chair, concluded with applying the title of *Rotundity* to him. I have really often looked at him with surprise mingled with contempt when he is in the chair and no business before the Senate. Instead of that sedate, easy air which I would have him possess, he will look on one side, then on the other, then ·down on the knees of his breeches, then dimple his visage with the most silly kind of half smile which I can not well express in English. The Scotch-Irish have a word that hits it exactly—*smudging*. God forgive me for the vile thought, but I can not help thinking of a monkey just put into breeches when I saw him betray such evident marks of self-conceit. He made us a speech this day also, but, as I did not minute the heads of it when he spoke, I will not attempt to recollect it.

Through the whole of this base business I have endeavored to mark the conduct of General Washington. I have no clew that will lead me fairly to any just conclusion as to his sentiments. I think it scarce possible, but he must have dropped something on the subject which has excited so much warmth. If he did, it was not on our side, or I would have heard it. But no matter. I have, by plowing with the heifer of the other House, completely defeated them.

The committee was now ordered to wait on the President to know the time when he will be pleased to receive the address of the Senate. The report of the joint committee on the enrollment of papers was read, and the House adjourned.

And now I hope we have disposed of a business [relating to titles] which in one shape or other has engaged almost the whole time of the Senate from the 23d of April, the day that our Vice-President began it.

Senate met. The address [to the President] was read over, and we proceeded in carriages to the President's to present it. Having no part to act but that of a mute, I had nothing to embarrass me. We were received in an antechamber. Had some little difficulty about seats, as there were several wanting, from whence may be inferred that the President's major-domo is not the most provident, as our numbers were well enough known. We had not been seated more than three minutes when it was signified to us to wait on the President in his levee-room. The Vice-President went foremost, and the Senators followed without any particular order. We made our bows as we entered, and the Vice-President, having made a bow, began to read an address. He was much confused. The paper trembled in his hand, though he had the aid of both by resting it on his hat, which he held in his left hand. He read very badly all that was on the front pages. The turning of the page seemed to restore him, and he read the rest with more propriety. This agitation was the more remarkable, as there were but twenty-two persons present and none of them strangers.

The President took his reply out of his coat pocket. He had his spectacles in his jacket pocket, having his hat in his left hand and the paper in his right. He had too many objects for his hands. He shifted his hat between his forearm and the left side of his breast. But taking his spectacles from the case embarrassed him. He got rid of this small distress by laying the spectacle-case on the chimney-piece. Colonel Humphreys stood on his right, Mr. Lear on his left. Having adjusted his spectacles, which was not very easy, considering the engagements on his hands, he read the reply with tolerable exactness and without much emotion. I thought he should have received us with his spectacles on, which would have saved the making of some uncouth motions. Yet, on the whole, he did nearly as well as anybody could have done the same motions. Could the laws of etiquette have permitted him to have been disencumbered of his hat, it would have relieved him much.

After having read his reply, he delivered the paper to the Vice-President with an easy inclination, bowed around to the company, and desired them to be seated. This politeness seems founded on reason, for men, after standing quite still some time, want to sit, if it were for only a minute or two. The Vice-President did not comply, nor did he refuse, but stood so long that the President repeated the request. He declined it by making a low bow, and retired. We made our bows, came out to the door, and waited till our carriages took us up. Colonel Humphreys waited on us to the door.

Had agreed with sundry of our Pennsylvania friends to go to the levee. General Muhlenberg came to me and told me they would meet me in the committee-room. We did so, and went to the levee. I went foremost, and left them to follow and do as well as they could. Indeed, they had no great thing of a pattern, for I am but a poor courtier. The company was large for the room. The foreign Ministers were there, Van Berkel, the Dutch Minister (for the first time, I suppose), gaudy as a peacock. Our Pennsylvanians withdrew before me. The President honored me with a particular *tête-à-tête*. "How will this weather suit your farming?" "Poorly, sir; the season is the most backward I have ever known. It is remarkably so here, but by letters from Pennsylvania vegetation is slow in proportion there." "The fruit, it is to be expected, will be safe; backward seasons are in favor of it, but in Virginia it was lost before I left that place." "Much depends on the exposure of the orchard. Those with a northern aspect have been found by us [in Pennsylvania] to be the most certain in producing fruit." "Yes, that is a good observation and should be attended to." Made my bow and retired.

Senate adjourned early. At a little after four I called on Mr. Bassett, of the Delaware State. We went to the President's to dinner. The company were: President and Mrs. Washington, Vice-President and Mrs. Adams, the Governor and his wife, Mr. Jay and wife, Mr. Langdon and wife, Mr. Dalton and a lady (perhaps his wife), and a Mr. Smith, Mr. Bassett, myself, Lear, Lewis, the President's two secretaries. The President and Mrs. Washington sat opposite each other in the middle of the table; the two secretaries, one at each end. It was a great dinner, and the best of the kind I ever was at. The room, however, was disagreeably warm.

First was the soup; fish roasted and boiled; meats, gammon, fowls, etc. This was the dinner. The middle of the table was garnished in the usual tasty way, with small images, flowers (artificial), etc. The dessert was, first apple pies, pudding, etc.; then iced creams, jellies, etc.; then watermelons, muskmelons, apples, peaches, nuts.

It was the most solemn dinner ever I sat at. Not a health drank; scarce a word said until the cloth was taken away. Then the President, filling a glass of wine, with great formality drank to the health of every individual by name round the table. Everybody imitated him, charged glasses, and such a buzz of "health, sir," and "health, madam," and "thank you, sir," and "thank you, madam," never had I heard before. Indeed, I had liked to have been thrown out in the hurry; but I got a little wine in my glass, and passed the ceremony. The ladies sat a good while, and the bottles passed about; but there was a dead silence almost. Mrs. Washington at last withdrew with the ladies.

I expected the men would now begin, but the same stillness remained. The President told of a New England clergyman who had lost a hat and wig in passing a river called the Brunks. He smiled, and everybody else laughed. He now and then said a sentence or two on some common subject, and what he said was not amiss. Mr. Jay tried to make a laugh by mentioning the circumstance of the Duchess of Devonshire leaving no stone unturned to carry Fox's election. There was a Mr. Smith, who mentioned how *Homer* described *Æneas* leaving his wife and carrying his father out of flaming Troy. He had heard somebody (I suppose) witty on the occasion; but if he had ever read it he would have said *Virgil*. The President kept a fork in his hand, when the cloth was taken away, I thought for the purpose of picking nuts. He ate no nuts, however, but played with the fork, striking on the edge of the table with it. We did not sit long after the ladies retired. The President rose, went upstairs to drink coffee; the company followed. I took my hat and came home.

CHAPTER XVIII

ABIGAIL ADAMS ADMIRES THE SOCIETY OF PHILADELPHIA

THE NEXT year, in 1790, the capital was moved from New York to Philadelphia, where it was to remain ten years before the establishment of Washington on the Potomac. Philadelphia was now a rich and cultivated city, and somewhat to the discomfiture of the purest republicans it proceeded to provide the atmosphere of a court. Salons like those of the brilliant Mrs. William Bingham became centers of political as well as social activity; and the aristocrats were eminently satisfied. In 1790-1 Abigail Adams, wife of John, wrote letters to her relatives and friends in which she celebrated the elegance of that "republican court."

Philadelphia, 21 November, 1790.

MRS. BINGHAM has been twice to see me. I think she is more amiable and beautiful than ever. I have seen many very fine women since I have been here. Our Nancy Hamilton is the same unaffected, affable girl we formerly knew her. She made many kind inquiries after you; so did Mrs. Bingham. I have not yet begun to return visits, as the ladies expect to find me at home, and I have not been in a state of health to do it; nor am yet in a very eligible state to receive their visits. I, however, endeavored to have one room decent to receive them, which, with my own chamber, is as much as I can boast of, at present, being in tolerable order. The difficulty of getting workmen, Mr. Hamilton pleads as an excuse for the house not being ready. Mrs. Lear was in to see me yesterday, and assures me that I am much better off than Mrs. Washington will be when she arrives, for that their house is not likely to be completed this year. And, when all is done, it will not be Broadway. If New York wanted any revenge for the removal, the citizens might be glutted if they would come here, where every article has become almost double in price, and where it is not possible for Congress, and the appendages, to be half as well accommodated for a long time. One would suppose that the people thought Mexico was before them, and that Congress were the possessors.

I would tell you that I had an ague in my face, and a violent toothache, which has prevented my writing to you all day; but I am determined to brave it out this evening, and inquire how you do. Without further complaint, I have become so tender, from keeping so much in a warm chamber, that, as soon as I set my foot out, I am sure to come home with some new pain or ache.

On Friday evening last, I went with Charles to the drawing-room, being the first of my appearance in public. The room became full before I left it, and the circle very brilliant. How could it be otherwise, when the dazzling Mrs. Bingham and her beautiful sisters were there; the Misses Allen, and Misses Chew; in short, a constellation of beauties! I am serious when I say so, for I really think them what I describe them. Mrs. Bingham has certainly given laws to the ladies here, in fashion and elegance; their manners and appearance are superior to what I have seen. I have been employed, for several days last week, in returning visits. Mrs. Powell, I join the general voice in pronouncing a very interesting woman. She is aunt to Mrs. Bingham, and is one of the ladies you would be pleased with. She looks turned of fifty, is polite and fluent as you please, motherly and friendly.

I have received many invitations to tea and cards, in the European style, but have hitherto declined them, on account of my health and the sickness of your brother. I should like to be acquainted with these people, and there is no other way of coming at many of them, but by joining in their parties; but the roads to and from Bush Hill are all clay, and, in open weather, up to the horses' knees; so you may suppose that much of my time must be spent at home; but this, you know, I do not regret, nor is it any mortification to me. If I could send for you, as usual, and my dear boys, it would add greatly to my pleasure and happiness. Mrs. Otis comes frequently, and passes the day with me, and yesterday I had the whole family to keep Christmas with me.

The weather is winter in all respects, and such a plain of snow puts out my eyes. We have a warm side, as well as a cold one, to our house. If there is anything we can do for you, let me know.

I should spend a very dissipated winter, if I were to accept of one-half the invitations I receive, particularly to the routes, or tea and cards. Even Saturday evening is not excepted, and I refused an invitation of that kind for this evening. I have been to one assembly. The dancing was very good; the company of the best kind. The President and Madam, the Vice-President and Madam, Ministers of State, and their Madams, &c.; but the room despicable;

the etiquette,—it was difficult to say where it was to be found. Indeed, it was not New York; but you must not report this from me. The managers have been very polite to me and my family. I have been to one play, and here again we have been treated with much politeness. The actors came and informed us that a box was prepared for us. The Vice-President thanked them for their civility, and told them that he would attend whenever the President did. And last Wednesday we were all there. The house is equal to most of the theaters we meet with out of France. It is very neat, and prettily fitted up; the actors did their best; "The School for Scandal" was the play. I missed the divine Farren; but upon the whole it was very well performed. On Tuesday next I go to a dance at Mr. Chew's, and on Friday sup at Mr. Clymer's; so you see I am likely to be amused.

Present me kindly to all my New York friends. That I was attached to that place is most true, and I shall always remember with pleasure the fifteen months passed there; but, if I had you and your family, I could be very well pleased here, for there is an agreeable society and friendliness kept up with all the principal families, who appear to live in great harmony, and we meet at all the parties nearly the same company. To-morrow the President dines with us, the Governor, the Ministers of State, and some Senators. Of all the ladies I have seen and conversed with here, Mrs. Powell is the best informed. She is a friendly, affable, good woman, sprightly, full of conversation. There is a Mrs. Allen, who is as well-bred a woman as I have seen in any country, and has three daughters, who may be styled the three Graces.

I received yours of February 13th, and was happy to learn that you and your little ones were well. I wrote to you by the Chief Justice, and sent your silk by him. He promised me to visit you, and from him you will learn how we all are. We have had, ever since this month began, a succession of bad weather, and, for this week past, the coldest weather that I have experienced this winter. The ground is now covered with snow. This, if it would last, would let me out of my cage, and enable me to go to the assembly on the birthday of the President, which will be on Tuesday next. On Thursday last I dined with the President, in company with the ministers and ladies of the court. He was more than usually social. I asked him after Humphreys, from whom I knew he had received despatches a few days before. He said that he was well, and at Lisbon. When I returned home, I told your father that I conjectured Mr. Humphreys would be nominated for Lisbon, and the next day the Senate received a message, with his nomination, as resident minister at the Court of Portugal; the President having received official information that a minister was appointed here, Mr. Friere, as I before informed you. He asked very affectionately after you and the children, and at table picked the sugar-plums from a cake, and requested me to take them for master John. Some suppose, that, if your husband was here, he would have the command of the troops which are to be raised and sent against the Indians. If such an idea as that is in his mind, I am happy that your friend is three thousand miles distant. I have no fancy that a man, who has already hazarded his life in defense of his country, should risk a tomahawk and scalping-knife, where, though a conqueror, no glory is to be obtained, though much may be lost. I most sincerely hope he may be successful in his private enterprise; for the way to command Fortune is to be as independent of her as possible.

The equanimity of your disposition will lead you to a patient submission to the allotments of Providence. The education of your children will occupy much of your time, and you will always keep in mind the great importance of first principles, and the necessity of instilling the precepts of morality very early into their minds. Youth is so imitative, that it catches at everything. I have a great opinion of Dr. Watts's "Moral Songs for Children." They are adapted to the capacities, and they comprehend all the social and relative duties of life. They impress the young mind with the ideas of the Supreme Being, as their creator, benefactor, and preserver. They teach brotherly love, sisterly affection, and filial respect and reverence. I do not know any book so well calculated for the early period of life; and they may be made as pleasant to them, by the method of instructing, as a hundred little stories, which are taught them, containing neither a rule of life, nor a sentiment worth retaining, such as little John will now run over, of "Jack and Jill," and "Little Jack Horner." As a trial of their memory, and a practice for their tongues, these may be useful, but no other way.

CHAPTER XIX

THOMAS JEFFERSON ON THE HAMILTONIANS

THE TEN years at Philadelphia saw the issue which Maclay had tentatively defined in New York sharpened into an important political conflict between federalists, or supporters of a strong central government with all favors going to men of wealth and power, and republicans, or supporters of a government definitely democratic in its administration. The conflict was enriched—some said degraded— by personalities; the result being a cleavage between men like Alexander Hamilton, federalist from New York, and men like Thomas Jefferson, republican from Virginia. Jefferson, returning at the dawn of the new government from his service as diplomat in France, soon made himself the center around which the radical forces swirled; and in notes which have come down under the title "The Anas" he delivered himself of a judgment against what he considered the powers not only of centralization but of corruption.

A SHORT review of facts will show, that the contests of that day were contests of principle, between the advocates of republican, and those of kingly government, and that had not the former made the efforts they did, our government would have been, even at this early day, a very different thing from what the successful issue of those efforts have made it.

The alliance between the States under the old Articles of Confederation, for the purpose of joint defense against the aggression of Great Britain, was found insufficient, as treaties of alliance generally are, to enforce compliance with their mutual stipulations; and these, once fulfilled, that bond was to expire of itself, and each State to become sovereign and independent in all things. Yet it could not but occur to every one, that these separate independencies, like the petty States of Greece, would be eternally at war with each other, and would become at length the mere partisans and satellites of the leading powers of Europe. All men must have looked forward to some further bond of union, which would insure eternal peace, and a political system of our own, independent of that of Europe. Whether all should be consolidated into a single government, or each remain independent as to internal matters, and the whole form a single nation as to what was foreign only, and whether that national government should be a monarchy or republic, would of course divide opinions, according to the constitutions, the habits, and the circumstances of each individual. Some officers of the army, as it has always been said and believed (and Steuben and Knox have ever been named as the leading agents), trained to monarchy by military habits, are understood to have proposed to General Washington to decide this great question by the army before its disbandment, and to assume himself the crown on the assurance of their support. The indignation with which he is said to have scouted this parricide proposition was equally worthy of his virtue and wisdom. The next effort was (on suggestion of the same individuals, in the moment of their separation) the establishment of an hereditary order under the name of the Cincinnati, ready prepared by that distinction to be ingrafted into the future frame of government, and placing General Washington still at their head. The General wrote to me on this subject, while I was in Congress at Annapolis, and an extract from my letter is inserted in 5th Marshall's history, page 28. He afterwards called on me at that place on his way to a meeting of the society, and after a whole evening of consultation, he left that place fully determined to use all his endeavors for its total suppression. But he found it so firmly riveted in the affections of the members, that, strengthened as they happened to be by an adventitious occurrence of the moment, he could effect no more than the abolition of its hereditary principle. He called again on his return, and explained to me fully the opposition which had been made, the effect of the occurrence from France, and the difficulty with which its duration had been limited to the lives of the present members.

The want of some authority which should procure justice to the public creditors, and an observance of treaties with foreign nations, produced, some time after, the call of a convention of the States at Annapolis. Although, at this meeting, a difference of opinion was evident on the question of a republican or kingly government, yet, so general through the States was the sentiment in favor of the former, that the friends of the latter confined themselves to a course of obstruction only, and delay, to everything proposed; they hoped, that nothing being done, and all things going from bad to worse, a kingly government might be usurped, and submitted to by the people, as better than anarchy and wars internal and external, the certain consequences of the present want of a general government. The effect of their maneuvers, with the defective attendance of

Deputies from the States, resulted in the measure of calling a more general convention, to be held at Philadelphia. At this, the same party exhibited the same practices, and with the same views of preventing a government of concord, which they foresaw would be republican, and of forcing through anarchy their way to monarchy. But the mass of that convention was too honest, too wise, and too steady, to be baffled and misled by their maneuvers. One of these was a form of government proposed by Colonel Hamilton, which would have been in fact a compromise between the two parties of royalism and republicanism. According to this, the executive and one branch of the legislature were to be during good behavior, *i.e.*, for life, and the governors of the States were to be named by these two permanent organs. This, however, was rejected; on which Hamilton left the convention, as desperate, and never returned again until near its final conclusion. These opinions and efforts, secret or avowed, of the advocates for monarchy, had begotten great jealousy through the States generally; and this jealousy it was which excited the strong opposition to the conventional constitution; a jealousy which yielded at last only to a general determination to establish certain amendments as barriers against a government either monarchical or consolidated. In what passed through the whole period of these conventions, I have gone on the information of those who were members of them, being absent myself on my mission to France.

I returned from that mission in the first year of the new government, having landed in Virginia in December, 1789, and proceeded to New York in March, 1790, to enter on the office of Secretary of State. Here, certainly, I found a state of things which, of all I had ever contemplated, I the least expected. I had left France in the first year of her revolution, in the fervor of natural rights, and zeal for reformation. My conscientious devotion to these rights could not be heightened, but it had been aroused and excited by daily exercise. The President received me cordially, and my colleagues and the circle of principal citizens apparently with welcome. The courtesies of dinner parties given me, as a stranger newly arrived among them, placed me at once in their familiar society. But I cannot describe the wonder and mortification with which the table conversations filled me. Politics were the chief topic, and a preference of kingly over republican government was evidently the favorite sentiment. An apostate I could not be, nor yet a hypocrite; and I found myself for the most part, the only advocate on the republican side of the question, unless among the guests there chanced to be some member of that party from the legislative Houses. Hamilton's financial system had then passed. It had two objects; 1st, as a puzzle, to exclude popular understanding and inquiry; 2d, as a machine for the corruption of the legislature; for he avowed the opinion, that man could be governed by one of two motives only, force or interest; force, he observed, in this country was out of the question, and the interests, therefore, of the members must be laid hold of, to keep the legislative in unison with the executive. And with grief and shame it must be acknowledged that his machine was not without effect; that even in this, the birth of our government, some members were found sordid enough to bend their duty to their interests, and to look after personal rather than public good.

It is well known that during the war the greatest difficulty we encountered was the want of money or means to pay our soldiers who fought, or our farmers, manufacturers and merchants, who furnished the necessary supplies of food and clothing for them. After the expedient of paper money had exhausted itself, certificates of debt were given to the individual creditors, with assurance of payment so soon as the United States should be able. But the distresses of these people often obliged them to part with these for the half, the fifth, and even a tenth of their value; and speculators had made a trade of cozening them from the holders by the most fraudulent practices, and persuasions that they would never be paid. In the bill for funding and paying these, Hamilton made no difference between the original holders and the fraudulent purchasers of this paper. Great and just repugnance arose at putting these two classes of creditors on the same footing, and great exertions were used to pay the former the full value, and to the latter, the price only which they had paid, with interest. But this would have prevented the game which was to be played, and for which the minds of greedy members were already tutored and prepared. When the trial of strength on these several efforts had indicated the form in which the bill would finally pass, this being known within doors sooner than without, and especially, than to those who were in distant parts of the Union, the base scramble began. Couriers and relay horses by land, and swift sailing pilot boats by sea, were flying in all directions. Active partners and agents were associated and employed in every State, town, and country neighborhood, and this paper was bought up at five shillings, and even as low as two shillings in the pound, before the holder knew that Congress had already provided for its redemption at par. Immense sums were thus filched from the poor and ignorant, and fortunes accumulated by those who had themselves been poor enough before. Men thus enriched by the dexterity of a leader, would follow of course the chief who was leading them to fortune, and become the zealous instruments of all his enterprises.

This game was over, and another was on the carpet at the moment of my arrival; and to this I was most ignorantly and innocently made to hold the candle. This fiscal maneuver is well known by the name of the Assumption. Independently of the debts of Congress, the States had during the war contracted separate and heavy debts; and Massachusetts particularly, in an absurd attempt, absurdly conducted, on the British post of Penobscott: and the more debt Hamilton could rake up, the more plunder for his mercenaries. This money, whether wisely or foolishly spent, was pretended to have been spent for general purposes, and ought, therefore, to be paid from the general purse. But it was objected, that nobody knew what these debts were, what their amount, or what their proofs. No matter; we will guess them to be twenty millions. But of these twenty millions, we do not know how much should be reimbursed to one State, or how much to another. No matter; we will guess. And so another scramble was set on foot among the several States, and some got much, some little, some nothing. But the main object was obtained, the phalanax of the Treasury was reënforced by additional recruits. This measure produced the most bitter and angry contest ever known in Congress, before or since the Union of the States. I arrived in the midst of it. But a stranger to the ground, a stranger to the actors on it, so long absent as to have lost all familiarity with the subject, and as yet unaware of its object, I took no concern in it. The great and trying question, however, was lost in the House of Representatives. So high were the feuds excited by this subject, that on its rejection business was suspended. Congress met and adjourned from day to day without doing anything, the parties being too much out of temper to do business together. The eastern members particularly, who, with Smith from South Carolina, were the principal gamblers in these scenes, threatened a secession and dissolution. Hamilton was in despair. As I was going to the President's one day, I met him in the street. He walked me backwards and forwards before the President's door for half an hour. He painted pathetically the temper into which the legislature had been wrought; the disgust of those who were called the creditor States; the danger of the *secession* of their members, and the separation of the States. He observed that the members of the administration ought to act in concert; that though this question was not of my department, yet a common duty should make it a common concern; that the President was the center on which all administrative questions ultimately rested, and that all of us should rally around him, and support, with joint efforts, measures approved by him; and that the question having been lost by a small majority only, it was probable that an appeal from me to the judgment and discretion of some of my friends, might effect a change in the vote, and the machine of government, now suspended, might be again set into motion. I told him that I was really a stranger to the whole subject; that not having yet informed myself of the system of finances adopted, I knew not how far this was a necessary sequence; that undoubtedly, if its rejection endangered a dissolution of our Union at this incipient stage, I should deem that the most unfortunate of all consequences, to avert which all partial and temporary evils should be yielded. I proposed to him, however, to dine with me the next day, and I would invite another friend or two, bring them into conference together, and I thought it impossible that reasonable men, consulting together coolly, could fail, by some mutual sacrifices of opinion, to form a compromise which was to save the Union. The discussion took place. I could take no part in it but an exhortatory one, because I was a stranger to the circumstances which should govern it. But it was finally agreed, that whatever importance had been attached to the rejection of this proposition, the preservation of the Union and of concord among the States was more important, and that therefore it would be better that the vote of rejection should be rescinded, to effect which, some members should change their votes. But it was observed that this pill would be peculiarly bitter to the southern States, and that some concomitant measure should be adopted, to sweeten it a little to them. There had before been propositions to fix the seat of government either at Philadelphia, or at Georgetown on the Potomac; and it was thought that by giving it to Philadelphia for ten years and to Georgetown permanently afterwards, this might, as an anodyne, calm in some degree the ferment which might be excited by the other measure alone. So two of the Potomac members (White and Lee, but White with a revulsion of stomach almost convulsive) agreed to change their votes, and Hamilton undertook to carry the other point. In doing this, the influence he had established over the eastern members, with the agency of Robert Morris with those of the middle States, effected his side of the engagement; and so the Assumption was passed, and twenty millions of stock divided among favored States, and thrown in as a pabulum to the stock-jobbing herd. This added to the number of votaries to the Treasury, and made its chief the master of every vote in the legislature, which might give to the government the direction suited to his political views.

I know well, and so must be understood, that nothing like a majority in Congress had yielded to this corruption. Far from it. But a division, not very unequal, had already taken place in the honest part of that body, between the parties styled republican and federal. The latter being monarchists in principle, adhered to Hamilton of course, as their leader in that principle, and this mercenary phalanx added to them, insured him always a majority in both Houses: so that the whole action of legislature was now under the direction of the Treasury. Still the machine was not complete. The effect of the funding system, and of the Assumption, would be temporary; it would be lost with the loss of the individual members whom it has enriched, and some engine of influence more permanent must be contrived, while these myrmidons were yet in place to carry it through all opposition. This engine was the Bank of the United States. All that history is known, so I shall say nothing about it. While the government remained at Philadelphia, a selection of members of both Houses were constantly kept as directors who, on every question interesting to that institution, or to the views of the federal head, voted at the will of that head; and, together with the stock-holding members, could always make the federal vote that of the majority. By this combination, legislative expositions were given to the constitution, and all the administrative laws were shaped on the model of England, and so passed. And from this influence we were not relieved, until the removal from the precincts of the bank, to Washington.

Here then was the real ground of the opposition which was made to the course of administration. Its object was to preserve the legislature pure and independent of the executive, to restrain the administration to republican forms and principles, and not permit the constitution to be construed into a monarchy, and to be warped, in practice, into all the principles and pollutions of their favorite English model. Nor was this an opposition to General Washington. He was true to the republican charge confided to him; and has solemnly and repeatedly protested to me, in our conversations, that he would lose the last drop of his blood in support of it; and he did this the oftener and with the more earnestness, because he knew my suspicions of Hamilton's designs against it, and wished to quiet them. For he was not aware of the drift, or of the effect of Hamilton's schemes. Unversed in financial projects and calculations and budgets, his approbation of them was bottomed on his confidence in the man.

But Hamilton was not only a monarchist, but for a monarchy bottomed on corruption. In proof of this, I will relate an anecdote, for the truth of which I attest the God who made me. Before the President set out on his southern tour in April, 1791, he addressed a letter of the fourth of that month, from Mount Vernon, to the

Secretaries of State, Treasury and War, desiring that if any serious and important cases should arise during his absence, they would consult and act on them. And he requested that the Vice President should also be consulted. This was the only occasion on which that officer was ever requested to take part in a cabinet question. Some occasion for consultation arising, I invited those gentlemen (and the Attorney General, as well as I remember) to dine with me, in order to confer on the subject. After the cloth was removed, and our question agreed and dismissed, conversation began on other matters, and by some circumstance, was led to the British constitution, on which Mr. Adams observed, 'Purge that constitution of its corruption, and give to its popular branch equality of representation, and it would be the most perfect constitution ever devised by the wit of man." Hamilton paused and said, "Purge it of its corruption, and give to its popular branch equality of representation, and it would become an *impracticable* government: as it stands at present, with all its supposed defects, it is the most perfect government which ever existed." And this was assuredly the exact line which separated the political creeds of these two gentlemen. The one was for two hereditary branches and an honest elective one: the other, for an hereditary King, with a House of Lords and Commons corrupted to his will, and standing between him and the people. Hamilton was, indeed, a singular character. Of acute understanding, disinterested, honest, and honorable in all private transactions, amiable in society, and duly valuing virtue in private life, yet so bewitched and perverted by the British example, as to be under thorough conviction that corruption was essential to the government of a nation. Mr. Adams had originally been a republican. The glare of royalty and nobility, during his mission to England, had made him believe their fascination a necessary ingredient in government; and Shay's rebellion, not sufficiently understood where he then was, seemed to prove that the absence of want and oppression, was not a sufficient guarantee of order. His book on the American constitutions having made known his political bias, he was taken up by the monarchical federalists in his absence, and on his return to the United States, he was by them made to believe that the general disposition of our citizens was favorable to monarchy. He here wrote his Davila, as a supplement to a former work, and his election to the Presidency confirmed him in his errors. Innumerable addresses too, artfully and industriously poured in upon him, deceived him into a confidence that he was on the pinnacle of popularity, when the gulf was yawning at his feet, which was to swallow up him and his deceivers. For when General Washington was withdrawn, these *energumeni* of royalism, kept in check hitherto by the dread of his honesty, his firmness, his patriotism, and the authority of his name, now mounted on the car of State and free from control, like Phaëton on that of the sun, drove headlong and wild, looking neither to right nor left, nor regarding anything but the objects they were driving at; until, displaying these fully, the eyes of the nation were opened, and a general disbandment of them from the public councils took place.

Mr. Adams, I am sure, has been long since convinced of the treacheries with which he was surrounded during his administration. He has since thoroughly seen, that his constituents were devoted to republican government, and whether his judgment is resettled on its ancient basis, or not, he is conformed as a good citizen to the will of the majority, and would now, I am persuaded, maintain its republican structure with the zeal and fidelity belonging to his character. For even an enemy has said, "he is always an honest man, and often a great one." But in the fervor of the fury and follies of those who made him their stalking horse, no man who did not witness it can form an idea of their unbridled madness, and the terrorism with which they surrounded themselves. The horrors of the French revolution, then raging, aided them mainly, and using that as a raw head and bloody bones, they were enabled by their stratagems of X. Y. Z. in which —— was a leading mountebank, their tales of tub-plots, ocean massacres, bloody buoys, and pulpit lyings and slanderings, and maniacal ravings of their Gardeners, their Osgoods and parishes, to spread alarm into all but the firmest breasts. Their Attorney General had the impudence to say to a republican member, that deportation must be resorted to, of which, said he, "You republicans have set the example"; thus daring to identify us with the murderous Jacobins of France. These transactions, now recollected but as dreams of the night, were then sad realities; and nothing rescued us from their liberticide effect, but the unyielding opposition of those firm spirits who sternly maintained their post in defiance of terror, until their fellow citizens could be aroused to their own dangers, and rally and rescue the standard of the constitution. This has been happily done. Federalism and monarchism have languished from that moment, until their treasonable combinations with the enemies of their country during the late war, their plots of dismembering the Union, and their Hartford convention, have consigned them to the tomb of the dead; and I fondly hope, "we may now truly say, we are all republicans, all federalists," and that the motto of the standard to which our country will forever rally, will be, "federal union, and republican government"; and sure I am we may say, that we are indebted for the preservation of this point of ralliance, to that opposition of which so injurious an idea is so artfully insinuated and excited in this history.

Much of this relation is notorious to the world; and many intimate proofs of it will be found in these notes. From the moment where they end, of my retiring from the administration, the federalists got unchecked hold of General Washington. His memory was already sensibly impaired by age, the firm tone of mind for which he had been remarkable, was beginning to relax, its energy was abated, a listlessness of labor, a desire for tranquillity had crept on him, and a willingness to let others act, and even think for him. Like the rest of mankind, he was disgusted with atrocities of the French revolution, and was not sufficiently aware of the difference between the rabble who were used as instruments of their perpetration, and the steady and rational character of the American people, in which he had not sufficient confidence. The opposition too of the republicans to the British treaty, and the zealous support of the federalists in that unpopular but favorite measure of theirs, had made him all their own. Understanding, moreover, that I disapproved of that treaty, and copiously nourished with falsehoods by a malignant neighbor of mine, who ambitioned to be his correspondent, he had become alienated from myself personally, as from the republican body generally of his fellow-citizens; and he wrote the letters to Mr. Adams and Mr. Carroll, over which, in devotion to his imperishable fame, we must forever weep as monuments of mortal decay.

CHAPTER XX

THE BRILLIANT Hamilton, Secretary of the Treasury and organizer of the nation's finances, had been cited by Jefferson as being in favor of corruption—a necessary element, so to speak, in efficient government by intelligent and energetic men. And the first scandal of the new administration, speculation by office-holders in government claims, did not spare his name. In 1792 he was forced to extricate himself from a predicament in that connection, a predicament which was not lessened by the fact that a woman was involved. In 1797, after the scandal had become public, he published in "The Reynolds Pamphlet" a complete confession of his entanglement with the wife of James Reynolds, blackmailer—defending himself, however, against the charge of corruption, which he met by a counter-charge of Jacobinism, or extreme and bigoted republicanism on the part of his calumniating enemies.

O F all the vile attempts which have been made to injure my character, that which has been lately revived in Nos. V and VI of the "History of the United States for 1796," is the most vile. This it will be impossible for any *intelligent*, I will not say *candid*, man to doubt, when he shall have accompanied me through the examination.

I owe perhaps to my friends an apology for condescending to give a public explanation. A just pride with reluctance stoops to a formal vindication against so despicable a contrivance, and is inclined rather to oppose to it the uniform evidence of an upright character. This would be my conduct on the present occasion, did not the tale seem to derive a sanction from the names of three men of some weight and consequence in the society; a circumstance which I trust will excuse me for paying attention to a slander that, without this prop, would defeat itself by intrinsic circumstances of absurdity and malice.

The charge against me is a connection with one James Reynolds for purposes of improper pecuniary speculation. My real crime is an amorous connection with his wife for a considerable time, with his privity and connivance, if not originally brought on by a combination between the husband and wife with the design to extort money from me.

This confession is not made without a blush. I cannot be the apologist of any vice because the ardor of passion may have made it mine. I can never cease to condemn myself for the pang which it may inflict in a bosom eminently entitled to all my gratitude, fidelity, and love. But that bosom will approve, that, even at so great an expense, I should effectually wipe away a more serious stain from a name which it cherishes with no less elevation than tenderness. The public, too, will, I trust, excuse the confession. The necessity of it to my defense against a more heinous charge could alone have extorted from me so painful an indecorum.

The first reflection which occurs on a perusal of the documents is that it is morally impossible I should have been foolish as well as depraved enough to employ so vile an instrument as Reynolds for such *insignificant ends,* as are indicated by different parts of the story itself. My enemies, to be sure, have kindly portrayed me as another Chartres on the score of moral principle. But they have been ever bountiful in ascribing talents. It has suited their purpose to exaggerate such as I may possess, and to attribute to them an influence to which they are not entitled. But the present accusation imputes to me as much folly as wickedness. All the documents show, and it is otherwise matter of notoriety, that Reynolds was an obscure, unimportant, and profligate man. Nothing could be more weak, because nothing could be more unsafe than to make use of such an instrument; to use him, too, without any intermediate agent more worthy of confidence who might keep me out of sight; to write him numerous letters recording the objects of the improper connection (for this is pretended and that the letters were afterwards burnt at my request) ; to unbosom myself to him with a prodigality of confidence, by very unnecessarily telling him, as he alleges, of a connection in speculation between myself and Mr. Duer. It is very extraordinary, if the head of the money department of a country, being unprincipled enough to sacrifice his trust and his integrity, could not have contrived objects of profit sufficiently large to have engaged the coöperation of men of far greater importance than Reynolds, and with whom there could have been due safety, and should have been driven to the necessity of unkenneling such a reptile to be the instrument of his cupidity.

But, moreover, the scale of the concern with Reynolds, such as it is presented, is contemptibly narrow for a rapacious speculating Secretary of the Treasury. Clingman, Reynolds, and his wife were manifestly in very close confidence with each other. It seems there was a free communication of secrets. Yet in clubbing their different items of information as to the supplies of money which Reynolds received from me, what do they amount to? Clingman states that Mrs. Reynolds told him, that at a certain time her husband had received from me upwards of eleven hundred dollars. A note is produced which shows that at one time fifty dollars were sent to him, and another note is produced, by which and the information of Reynolds himself through Clingman, it appears that at another time three hundred dollars were asked and refused. Another sum of two hundred dollars is spoken of by Clingman as having been furnished to Reynolds at some other time. What a scale of speculation is this for the head of a public treasury, for one who, in the very publication that brings forward the charge, is represented as having procured to be funded at forty millions a debt which ought to have been discharged at ten or fifteen millions for the criminal purpose of enriching himself and his friends? He must have been a clumsy knave, if he did not secure enough of this excess of twenty-five or thirty millions, to have taken away all inducement to risk his character in such bad hands and in so huckstering a way—or to have enabled him, if he did employ such an agent, to do it with more means and to better purpose. It is curious that this rapacious Secretary should at one time have furnished his speculating agent with the paltry sum of fifty dollars; at another, have refused him the inconsiderable sum of three hundred dollars, declaring upon his honor that it was not in his power to furnish it. This declaration was true or not: if the last, the refusal ill comports with the idea of a speculating connection; if the first, it is very singular that the head of the treasury, engaged without scruple in schemes of profit, should be destitute of so small a sum. But if we suppose this officer to be living upon an inadequate salary, without any collateral pursuits of gain, the appearances then are simple and intelligible enough, applying to them the true key.

It appears that Reynolds and Clingman were detected by the then Comptroller of the Treasury, in the odious crime of suborning a witness to commit perjury, for the purpose of obtaining letters of administration on the estate of a person who was living, in order to receive a small sum of money due to him from the Treasury. It is certainly extraordinary that the confidential agent of the head of that department should have been in circumstances to induce a resort to so miserable an expedient. It is odd, if there was a speculating connection, that it was not more profitable both to the Secretary and to his agent than are indicated by the circumstances disclosed.

It is also a remarkable and very instructive fact that, notwithstanding the great confidence and intimacy which subsisted between Clingman, Reynolds, and his wife, and which continued till after the period of the liberation of the two former from the prosecution against them, neither of them has ever specified the objects of the pretended connection in speculation between Reynolds and me. The pretext that the letters which contained the evidence were destroyed is no answer. They could not have been forgotten, and might have been disclosed from memory. The total omission of this could only have proceeded from the consideration that detail might have led to detection. The destruction of letters besides is a fiction, which is refuted not only by the general improbability that I should put myself upon paper with so despicable a person on a subject which might expose me to infamy, but by the evidence of extreme caution on my part in this particular, resulting from the laconic and disguised form of the notes which are produced; they prove incontestibly that there was an unwillingness to trust Reynolds with my handwriting. The true reason was that I apprehended he might make use of it to impress upon others the belief of some pecuniary connection with me, and besides implicating my character, might render it the engine of a false credit, or turn it to some other sinister use. Hence the disguise; for my conduct in admitting at once and without hesitation that the notes were from me proves that it was never my intention by the expedient of disguising my hand to shelter myself from any serious inquiry.

I proceed in the next place to offer a frank and plain solution of the enigma, by giving a history of the origin and progress of my connection with Mrs. Reynolds, of its discovery, real and pretended, by the husband, and of the disagreeable embarrassments to which it exposed me.

Some time in the summer of the year 1791, a woman called at my house in the city of Philadelphia, and asked to speak with me in private. I attended her into a room apart from my family. With a seeming air of affliction she informed me that she was a daughter of a Mr. Lewis, sister to a Mr. G. Livingston of the State of New York, and wife to a Mr. Reynolds, whose father was in the Commissary Department during the war with Great Britain; that her husband, who for a long time had treated her very cruelly, had lately left her to live with another woman, and in so destitute a condition that, though desirous of returning to her friends, she had not the means; that knowing I was a citizen of New York, she had taken the liberty to apply to my humanity for assistance.

I replied, that her situation was a very interesting one—that I was disposed to afford her assistance to convey her to her friends, but this at the moment not being convenient to me (which was the fact), I must request the place of her residence, to which I should bring or send a small supply of money. She told me the street and the number of the house where she lodged. In the evening I put a bank-bill in my pocket and went to the house. I inquired for Mrs. Reynolds and was shown upstairs, at the head of which she met me and conducted me into a bedroom. I took the bill out of my pocket and gave it to her. Some conversation ensued, from which it was quickly apparent that other than pecuniary consolation would be acceptable.

After this I had frequent meetings with her, most of them at my own house; Mrs. Hamilton with her children being absent on a visit to her father. In the course of a short time, she mentioned to me that her husband had solicited a reconciliation, and affected to consult me about it. I advised to it, and was soon after informed by her that it had taken place. She told me besides that her husband had been engaged in speculation, and she believed could give information respecting the conduct of some persons in the department which would be useful. I sent for Reynolds who came to me accordingly.

In the course of our interview, he confessed that he had obtained a list of claims from a person in my department which he had made use of in his speculations. I invited him, by the expectation of my friendship and good offices, to disclose the person. After some affectation of scruple, he pretended to yield, and ascribed the infidelity to Mr. Duer, from whom he said he had obtained the list in New York, while he (Duer) was in the department.

As Mr. Duer had resigned his office some time before the seat of government was removed to Philadelphia, this discovery, if it had been true, was not very important—yet it was the interest of my passions to appear to set value upon it, and to continue the expectation of friendship and good offices. Mr. Reynolds told me he was going to Virginia, and on his return would point out something in which I could serve him. I do not know but he said something about employment in a public office.

On his return he asked employment as a clerk in the Treasury Department. The knowledge I had acquired of him was decisive against such a request. I parried it by telling him, what was true, that there was no vacancy in my immediate office, and that the appointment of clerks in the other branches of the department was left to the chiefs of the respective branches. Reynolds alleged, as

Clingman relates, as a topic of complaint against me, that I had promised him *employment* and had *disappointed* him. The situation of the wife would naturally incline me to conciliate this man. It is possible I may have used vague expressions which raised expectation; but the more I learned of the person, the more inadmissible his employment in a public office became. Some material reflections will occur here to a discerning mind. Could I have preferred my private gratification to the public interest, should I not have found the employment he desired for a man whom it was so convenient to me, on my own statement, to lay under obligations? Had I had any such connection with him, as he has since pretended, is it likely that he would have wanted other employment? Or is it likely that, wanting it, I should have hazarded his resentment by a persevering refusal? This little circumstance shows at once the delicacy of my conduct, in its public relations, and the impossibility of my having had the connection pretended with Reynolds.

The intercourse with Mrs. Reynolds, in the meantime continued; and though various reflections (in which a further knowledge of Reynolds' character and the suspicion of some concert between the husband and wife bore a part) induced me to wish a cessation of it; yet, her conduct made it extremely difficult to disentangle myself. All the appearances of violent attachment, and of agonizing distress at the idea of a relinquishment, were played with a most imposing art. This, though it did not make me entirely the dupe of the plot, yet kept me in a state of irresolution. My sensibility, perhaps my vanity, admitted the possibility of a real fondness; and led me to adopt the plan of a gradual discontinuance rather than of a sudden interruption, as least calculated to give pain, if a real partiality existed.

Mrs. Reynolds, on the other hand, employed every effort to keep up my attention and visits. Her pen was freely employed, and her letters were filled with those tender and pathetic effusions which would have been natural to a woman truly fond and neglected.

One day, I received a letter from her, intimating a discovery by her husband. It was a matter of doubt with me whether there had been really a discovery by accident, or whether the time for the catastrophe of the plot was arrived.

The same day, being the 15th of December, 1791, I received from Mr. Reynolds the letter by which he informs me of the detection of his wife in the act of writing a letter to me, and that he had obtained from her a discovery of her connection with me, suggesting that it was the consequence of an undue advantage taken of her distress.

On answer to this I sent him a note, or message, desiring him to call upon me at my office, which I think he did the same day.

He in substance repeated the topics contained in his letter, and concluded, as he had done there, that he was resolved to have satisfaction.

I replied that he knew best what evidence he had of the alleged connection between me and his wife, that I neither admitted nor denied it; that if he knew of any injury I had done him, entitling him to satisfaction, it lay with him to name it.

He traveled over the same ground as before, and again concluded with the same vague claim of satisfaction, but without specifying the kind which would content him. It was easy to understand that he wanted money, and, to prevent an explosion, I resolved to gratify him. But willing to manage his delicacy, if he had any, I reminded him that I had at our first interview, made him a promise of service, that I was disposed to do it as far as might be proper, and in my power, and requested him to consider in what manner I could do it, and to write to me. He withdrew with a promise of compliance.

Two days after, the 17th of December, he wrote me the letter. The evident drift of this letter is to exaggerate the injury done by me, to make a display of sensibility, and to magnify the atonement which was to be required. It, however, comes to no conclusion, but proposes a meeting at the *George Tavern,* or at some other place more agreeable to me, which I should name.

On receipt of this letter, I called upon Reynolds, and, assuming a decisive tone, told him that I was tired of his indecision, and insisted upon his declaring to me explicitly what it was he aimed at. He again promised to explain by letter.

On the 19th, I received the promised letter, the essence of which is that he was willing to take a thousand dollars as a plaister for his wounded honor.

I determined to give it to him, and did so in two payments, as per receipts dated the 22d of December and 3d of January. It is a little remarkable that an avaricious speculating Secretary of the Treasury should have been so straitened for money as to be obliged to satisfy an engagement of this sort by two different payments!

On the 17th of January, I received the letter by which Reynolds writes me to *renew my visits to his wife.* He had before requested that I would see her no more. The motive to this step appears in the conclusion of the letter: "*I rely* upon your befriending me, *if there should anything offer that should be to my advantage,* as you *express a wish to befriend me.*" Is the preëxistence of a speculating connection reconcilable with this mode of expression?

If I recollect rightly, I did not immediately accept the invitation, nor till after I had received several very importunate letters from Mrs. Reynolds.

On the 24th of March following I received a letter from Reynolds, and on the same day one from his wife. These letters will further illustrate the obliging coöperation of the husband with his wife to aliment and keep alive my connection with her.

These letters, collectively, furnish a complete elucidation of the nature of my transactions with Reynolds. They resolve them into an amorous connection with his wife, detected, or pretended to be detected by the husband, imposing on me the necessity of a pecuniary composition with him, and leaving me afterwards under a duress for fear of disclosure, which was the instrument of levying upon me from time to time *forced loans*. They apply directly to this state of things, the notes which Reynolds was so careful to preserve, and which had been employed to excite suspicion.

The variety of shapes which this woman could assume was endless. In a conversation between her and a gentleman whom I am not at liberty publicly to name, she made a voluntary confession of her belief and even knowledge, that I was innocent of all that had been laid to my charge by Reynolds or any other person of her acquaintance, spoke of me in exalted terms of esteem and respect, declared in the most solemn manner her extreme unhappiness lest I should suppose her accessory to the trouble which had been given me on that account, and expressed her fear that the resentment of Mr. Reynolds on *a particular score* might have urged him to improper lengths of revenge—appearing at the same time extremely agitated and unhappy.

Thus has my desire to destroy this slander completely led me to a more copious and particular examination of it, than I am sure was necessary. The bare perusal of the letters from Reynolds and his wife is sufficient to convince my greatest enemy that there is nothing worse in the affair than an irregular and indelicate amor. For this, I bow to the just censure which it merits. I have paid pretty severely for the folly, and can never recollect it without disgust and self-condemnation. It might seem affectation to say more.

ALEXANDER HAMILTON.

PHILADELPHIA, *July*, 1797.

CHAPTER XXI

AARON BURR, DUELLIST AND CONSPIRATOR

HAMILTON MADE an especially dangerous enemy as the decade drew to its close. The career of Aaron Burr was a lurid episode in public life at the turn of the century. Clever, ambitious, reckless, philandering, and—so his enemies said—thoroughly unprincipled, Burr rose out of New York politics to be vice president in 1801, and by a certain irony was only prevented from being president, when the tie between his votes and Jefferson's had to be resolved, through the influence of Hamilton, who preferred a philosopher to an adventurer. In 1804, stung by the criticism of Hamilton, Burr challenged his old enemy and rival to a duel, and killed him. Two years later, still more or less in disgrace for this, Burr started West on a mysterious mission which never has been perfectly understood. Some said he was only speculating in Louisiana lands, others that he had in mind an expedition to take Mexico away from Spain, and others that he plotted the separation of the West from the union—the new country between the Alleghenies and the Mississippi that had been officially opened up in 1787, and that already was filling with farms and towns, was to have been his kingdom. He enlisted the help of Harman Blennerhassett, an interesting and philosophical Irishman who had retired to America and built a house on Blennerhasset's Island opposite Marietta, Ohio, where he dabbled in chemistry and reflected upon the nature of man. The plan, whatever it was, failed; Blennerhassett was ruined; and the two were imprisoned and tried for treason. Though they were acquitted by John Marshall, Burr was now definitely destroyed as a public personage, and retreated to Europe for an exile of four years.

Judge William P. Van Ness, Burr's second at the duel, has left a memorandum of the affair. It is followed here by Hamilton's statement before he went to his death and by Burr's letter to his beloved daughter Theodosia, written on the eve of the meeting.

Statement of Judge Van Ness

ON the afternoon of the 17th of June last (1804), I received a note from Colonel Burr requesting me to call on him the following morning. Upon my arrival he alleged that it had, of late, been frequently stated to him that General Hamilton had, at different times and upon various occasions, used language and expressed opinions highly injurious to his reputation; that he had for some time felt the necessity of calling on General Hamilton for an explanation of his conduct, but that the statements which had been made to him did not appear sufficiently authentic to justify the measure; that a newspaper had, however, been recently put into his hands, in which he perceived a letter signed Charles D. Cooper, containing something which he thought demanded immediate investigation. Urged by these circumstances, and justified by the evident opinion of his friends, he had determined to write General Hamilton a note upon the subject, which he requested me to deliver. I assented to this request, and, on my return to the city, which was at eleven o'clock the same morning, I delivered to General Hamilton the note which I received from Colonel Burr for that purpose, and of which the following is a copy:

No. I

New York, June 18, 1804.

SIR,

I send for your perusal a letter signed Charles D. Cooper, which, though apparently published some time ago, has but very recently come to my knowledge. Mr. Van Ness, who does me the favor to deliver this, will point out to you that clause of the letter to which I particularly request your attention.

You must perceive, sir, the necessity of a prompt and unqualified acknowledgment or denial of the use of any expression which would warrant the assertions of Mr. Cooper. I have the honor to be

Your obedient servant,

A. BURR.

General HAMILTON.

General Hamilton read the note of Mr. Burr and the printed letter of Mr. Cooper to which it refers, and remarked that they required some consideration, and that in the course of the day he would send an answer to my office. At half past ten o'clock General Hamilton called at my house, and said that a variety of engagements would demand his attention during the whole of that day and the next; but that on Wednesday, the 20th inst., he would furnish me with such an answer to Colonel Burr's letter as he should deem most suitable and compatible with his feelings. In the evening of Wednesday, the 20th, while I was from home, the following letter, addressed to Colonel Burr, was left at my house, under cover to me.

No. II

New York, June 20, 1804.

Sir,

I have maturely reflected on the subject of your letter of the 18th inst., and the more I have reflected the more I have become convinced that I could not, without manifest impropriety, make the avowal or disavowal which you seem to think necessary. The clause pointed out by Mr. Van Ness is in these terms: "I could detail to you *a still more despicable* opinion which General Hamilton *has expressed* of Mr. Burr." To endeavor to discover the meaning of this declaration, I was obliged to seek in the antecedent part of this letter for the opinion to which it referred as having been already disclosed. I found it in these words: "General Hamilton and Judge Kent have declared, in *substance,* that they looked upon Mr. Burr to be a *dangerous man,* and one *who ought not to be trusted with the reins of government."*

The language of Doctor Cooper plainly implies that *he* considered this opinion of you, which he attributes to me, as a *despicable* one; but he affirms that I have expressed some other *more despicable,* without, however, mentioning to whom, when or where. 'Tis evident that the phrase "still more despicable" admits of infinite shades, from very light to very dark. How am I to judge of the degree intended? Or how shall I annex any precise idea to language so indefinite?

Between gentlemen, *despicable* and *more despicable* are not worth the pains of distinction; when, therefore, you do not interrogate me as to the opinion which is specifically ascribed to me, I must conclude that you view it as within the limits to which the animadversions of political opponents upon each other may justifiably extend, and, consequently, as not warranting the idea which Doctor Cooper appears to entertain. If so, what precise inference could you draw as a guide for your conduct, were I to acknowledge that I had expressed an opinion of you *still more despicable* than the one which is particularized? How could you be sure that even this opinion had exceeded the bounds which you would yourself deem admissible between political opponents?

But I forbear further comment on the embarrassment to which the requisition you have made naturally leads. The occasion forbids a more ample illustration, though nothing could be more easy than to pursue it.

Repeating that I cannot reconcile it with propriety to make the acknowledgment or denial you desire, I will add, that I deem it inadmissible, on principle, to consent to be interrogated as to the justice of the *inferences* which may be drawn by others from whatever I have said of a political opponent in the course of fifteen years competition. If there were no other objection to it, this is sufficient, that it would tend to expose my sincerity and delicacy to injurious imputations from every person who may at any time have conceived the *import* of my expressions differently from what I may then have intended or may afterward recollect. I stand ready to avow or disavow promptly and explicitly any precise or definite opinion which I may be charged with having declared of any gentleman. More than this cannot fitly be expected from me; and, especially, it cannot be reasonably expected that I shall enter into any explanation upon a basis so vague as that you have adopted. I trust, on more reflection, you will see the matter in the same light with me. If not, I can only regret the circumstance, and must abide the consequences.

The publication of Doctor Cooper was never seen by me till after the receipt of your letter. I have the honor to be, &c.,

A. HAMILTON.

Colonel BURR.

On the morning of Thursday, the 21st, I delivered to Colonel Burr the above letter, and, in the evening, was furnished with the following letter for General Hamilton, which I delivered to him at 12 o'clock on Friday, the 22d inst.:

No. III

New York, June 21, 1804.

SIR,

Your letter of the 20th inst. has been this day received. Having considered it attentively, I regret to find in it nothing of that sincerity and delicacy which you profess to value.

Political opposition can never absolve gentlemen from the necessity of a rigid adherence to the laws of honor and the rules of decorum. I neither claim such privilege nor indulge it in others.

The common sense of mankind affixes to the epithet adopted by Doctor Cooper the idea of dishonor. It has been publicly applied to me under the sanction of your name. The question is not whether he has understood the meaning of the word, or has used it according to syntax and with grammatical accuracy, but whether you have authorized this application, either directly or by uttering expressions or opinions derogatory to my honor. The time "when" is in your own knowledge, but no way material to me, as the calumny has now first been disclosed so as to become the subject of my notice, and as the effect is present and palpable.

Your letter has furnished me with new reasons for requiring a definite reply.

I have the honor to be,
Sir, your obedient
A. BURR.

General HAMILTON.

General Hamilton perused it, and said it was such a letter as he had hoped not to have received; that it contained several offensive expressions, and seemed to close the door to all further reply; that he had hoped the answer he had returned to Colonel Burr's first letter would have given a different direction to the controversy; that he thought Mr. Burr would have perceived that there was a difficulty in his making a more specific reply, and would have desired him to state what had fallen from him that might have given rise to the inference of Doctor Cooper. He would have done this frankly; and he believed it would not have been found to exceed the limits justifiable among political opponents. If Mr. Burr should be disposed to give a different complexion to the discussion, he was willing to consider the last letter not delivered; but if that communication was not withdrawn, he could make no reply, and Mr. Burr must pursue such course as he should deem most proper.

At the request of General Hamilton, I replied that I would detail these ideas to Colonel Burr; but added, that if in his first letter he had introduced the idea (if it was a correct one) that he could recollect of no terms that would justify the construction made by Dr. Cooper, it would, in my opinion, have opened a door for accommodation. General Hamilton then repeated the same objections to this measure which were stated in substance in his first letter to Colonel Burr.

When I was about leaving him he observed, that if I preferred it, he would commit his refusal to writing. I replied, that if he had resolved not to answer Colonel Burr's letter, that I could report that to him verbally, without giving him the trouble of writing it. He again repeated his determination not to answer; and that Colonel Burr must pursue such course as he should deem most proper.

In the afternoon of this day I reported to Colonel Burr, at his house out of town, the answer and the determination of General Hamilton, and promised to call on him again in the evening to learn his further wishes. I was detained in town, however, this evening, by some private business, and did not call on Colonel Burr until the following morning, Saturday, the 23d June. I then received from him a letter for General Hamilton, which is numbered IV; but, as will presently be explained, never was delivered. The substance of it will be found in Number XII.

When I returned with this letter to the city, which was about two o'clock in the afternoon of the same day, I sent a note to General Hamilton's office, and also to his house, desiring to know when it would be convenient to him to receive a communication. The servant, as he informed me, received for answer at both places that General Hamilton had gone to his country seat. I then wrote the note of which No. V is a copy, and sent it out to him in the country.

No. V

June 23, 1804.

SIR,

In the afternoon of yesterday I reported to Colonel Burr the result of my last interview with you, and appointed the evening to receive his further instructions. Some private engagements, however, prevented me from calling on him till this morning. On my return to the city, I found, upon inquiry, both at your office and house, that you had returned to your residence in the country. Lest an interview there might be less agreeable to you than elsewhere, I have taken the liberty of addressing you this note, to inquire when and where it will be most convenient to you to receive a communication.

Your most obedient and very humble servant,

W. P. VAN NESS.

General HAMILTON.

To this I received for answer No. VI, which follows:

No. VI

Grange, June 23, 1804.

SIR,

I was in town to-day till half past one. I thank you for the delicacy which dictated your note to me. If it is indispensable the communication should be made before Monday morning, I must receive it here; but I should think this cannot be important. On Monday, by nine o'clock, I shall be in town at my house in Cedar street, No. 52, where I should be glad to see you. An additional reason for preferring this is, that I am unwilling to occasion you trouble.

With esteem I am your obedient servant,

A. HAMILTON.

At nine o'clock on Monday, the 25th of June, I called on General Hamilton, at his house in Cedar street, to present the letter No. IV already alluded to, and with instructions for a verbal communication, of which the following notes, No. VII, handed me by Mr. Burr, were to be the basis. The substance of which, though in terms as much softened as my injunctions would permit, was accordingly communicated to General Hamilton.

No. VII

A. Burr, far from conceiving that rivalship authorizes a latitude not otherwise justifiable, always feels greater delicacy in such cases, and would think it meanness to speak of a rival but in terms of respect; to do justice to his merits; to be silent of his foibles. Such has invariably been his conduct towards Jay, Adams, and Hamilton; the only three who can be supposed to have stood in that relation to him.

That he has too much reason to believe that, in regard to Mr. Hamilton, there has been no reciprocity. For several years his name has been lent to the support of base slanders. He has never had the generosity, the magnanimity, or the candor to contradict or disavow. Burr forbears to particularize, as it could only tend to produce new irritations; but, having made great sacrifices for the sake of harmony; having exercised forbearance until it approached to humiliation, he has seen no effect produced by such conduct but a repetition of injury. He is obliged to conclude that there is, on the part of Mr. Hamilton, a settled and implacable malevolence; that he will never cease, in his conduct towards Mr. Burr, to violate those courtesies of life; and that, hence, he has no alternative but to announce these things to the world; which, consistently with Mr. Burr's ideas of propriety, can be done in no way but that which he had adopted. He is incapable of revenge, still less is he capable of imitating the conduct of Mr. Hamilton, by committing secret depredations on his fame and character. But these things must have an end.

Before I delivered the written communication with which I was charged, General Hamilton said that he had prepared a written reply to Colonel Burr's letter of the 21st, which he had left with Mr. Pendleton, and wished me to receive. I answered, that the communication I had to make to him was predicated upon the idea that he would make no reply to Mr. Burr's letter of the 21st of June, and that I had so understood him in our conversation of the 22d. General Hamilton said that he believed, before I left him, he had proffered a written reply. I observed that, when he answered verbally, he had offered to put that *refusal* in writing; but that, if he had now prepared a written reply, I would receive it with pleasure. I accordingly called on Mr. Pendleton on the same day (Monday, June 25th), between *one* and *two* o'clock P.M., and stated to him the result of my recent interview with General Hamilton, and the reference he had made to him.

I then received from Mr. Pendleton No. VIII, which follows:

No. VIII

New York, June 22, 1804.

SIR,

Your first letter, in a style too peremptory, made a demand, in my opinion, unprecedented and unwarrantable. My answer, pointing out the embarrassment, gave you an opportunity to take a less exceptionable course. You have not chosen to do it; but, by your last letter, received this day, containing expressions *indecorous* and improper, you have increased the difficulties to explanation intrinsically incident to the nature of your application.

If by a "definite reply" you mean the direct avowal or disavowal required in your first letter, I have no other answer to give than that which has already been given. If you mean anything different, admitting of greater latitude, it is requisite you should explain.

I have the honor to be, sir, your obedient servant,

ALEX. HAMILTON.

A. BURR, Esq.

This letter was unsealed, but I did not read it in his presence. After some conversation relative to what General Hamilton would say on the subject of the present controversy, during which Mr. Pendleton read from a paper his ideas on the subject, he left me for the purpose of seeing and consulting Mr. Hamilton, taking the paper with him. In about an hour he called at my house. I informed him that I had shown to Colonel Burr the letter he had given me from

General Hamilton; that, in his opinion, it amounted to nothing more than the verbal reply I had already reported; that it left the business precisely where it then was; that Mr. Burr had very explicitly stated the injuries he had received and the reparation he demanded, and that he did not think it proper to be asked now for further explanation. Towards the conclusion of the conversation I informed him that Colonel Burr required a general disavowal of any intention, on the part of General Hamilton, in his various conversations, to convey expressions derogatory to the honor of Mr. Burr. Mr. Pendleton replied that he believed General Hamilton would have no objections to make such declarations, and left me for the purpose of consulting him, requesting me to call in the course of the afternoon for an answer. I called on him, accordingly, about six o'clock. He then observed that General Hamilton declined making such a disavowal as I had stated in our last conversation; that he, Mr. Pendleton, did not then perceive the whole force and extent of it; and presented me with the following paper, No. IX, which I transmitted in the evening to Mr. Burr.

No. IX

In answer to a letter properly adapted to obtain from General Hamilton a declaration whether he had charged Colonel Burr with any particular instance of dishonorable conduct, or had impeached his private character either in the conversation alluded to by Doctor Cooper, or in any other particular instance to be specified, he would be able to answer consistently with his honor and the truth, in substance, that the conversation to which Doctor Cooper alluded turned wholly on political topics, and did not attribute to Colonel Burr any instance of dishonorable conduct, nor relate to his private character; and in relation to any other language or conversation of General Hamilton which Colonel Burr will specify, a prompt and frank avowal or denial will be given.

The following day (Tuesday, 26th June), as early as was convenient, I had an interview with Colonel Burr, who informed me that he considered General Hamilton's proposition a mere evasion, that evinced a desire to leave the injurious impressions which had arisen from the conversations of General Hamilton in full force; that when he had undertaken to investigate an injury his honor had sustained, it would be unworthy of him not to make that investigation complete. He gave me further instructions, which are substantially contained in the following letter to Mr. Pendleton, No. X.

No. X

June 26, 1804.

SIR,

The letter which you yesterday delivered to me, and your subsequent communication, in Colonel Burr's opinion, evince no disposition, on the part of General Hamilton, to come to a satisfactory accommodation. The injury complained of and the reparation expected are so definitely expressed in Colonel Burr's letter of the 21st instant, that there is not perceived a necessity for further explanation on his part. The difficulty that would result from confining the inquiry to any particular times and occasions must be manifest. The denial of a specified conversation only would leave strong implication that on other occasions improper language had been used. When and where injurious opinions and expressions had been uttered by General Hamilton must be best known to him, and of him only will Colonel Burr inquire. No denial or declaration will be satisfactory unless it be general, so as wholly to exclude the idea that rumors derogatory to Colonel Burr's honor have originated with General Hamilton, or have been fairly inferred from anything he has said. A definite reply to a requisition of this nature was demanded by Colonel Burr's letter of the 21st instant. This being refused, invites the alternative alluded to in General Hamilton's letter of the 20th.

It was required by the position in which the controversy was placed by General Hamilton on Friday (June 22d) last, and I was immediately furnished with a communication demanding a personal interview. The necessity of this measure has not, in the opinion of Colonel Burr, been diminished by the general's last letter, or any communication which has since been received. I am, consequently, again instructed to deliver you a message as soon as it may be convenient for you to receive it. I beg, therefore, you will be so good as to inform me at what hour I can have the pleasure of seeing you.

Your most obedient and humble servant,

W. P. VAN NESS.

NATHANIEL PENDLETON, Esq.

In the evening of the same day I received from him the following answer:

No. XI

June 26, 1804.

Sir,

I have communicated the letter which you did me the honor to write to me of this date, to General Hamilton. The expectations now disclosed on the part of Colonel Burr appear to him to have greatly extended the original ground of inquiry, and, instead of presenting a particular and definite case for explanation, seem to aim at nothing less than an inquisition into his most confidential conversations, as well as others, through the whole period of his acquaintance with Colonel Burr.

While he was prepared to meet the particular case fairly and fully, he thinks it inadmissible that he should be expected to answer at large as to everything that he may possibly have said in relation to the character of Colonel Burr at any time or upon any occasion. Though he is not conscious that any charges which are in circulation to the prejudice of Colonel Burr have originated with him, except one which may have been so considered, and which has long since been fully explained between Colonel Burr and himself, yet he cannot consent to be questioned generally as to any rumors which may be afloat derogatory to the character of Colonel Burr, without specification of the several rumors, many of them, probably, unknown to him. He does not, however, mean to authorize any conclusion as to the real nature of his conduct in relation to Colonel Burr by his declining so loose and vague a basis of explanation, and he disavows an unwillingness to come to a satisfactory, provided it be an honorable, accommodation. His objection is the very indefinite ground which Colonel Burr has assumed, in which he is sorry to be able to discern nothing short of predetermined hostility. Presuming, therefore, that it will be adhered to, he has instructed me to receive the message which you have it in charge to deliver. For this purpose I shall be at home and at your command to-morrow morning from eight to ten o'clock.

I have the honor to be respectfully,

Your obedient servant,

Nathaniel Pendleton.

Wm. P. Van Ness, Esq.

I transmitted this to Colonel Burr; and, after a conference with him, in which I received his further instructions, and that no misunderstanding might arise from verbal communication, I committed to writing the remarks contained in No. XII, which follows:

No. XII

Wednesday morning, June 27, 1804.

SIR,

The letter which I had the honor to receive from you, under date of yesterday, states, among other things, that, in General Hamilton's opinion, Colonel Burr has taken a very indefinite ground, in which he evinces nothing short of predetermined hostility, and General Hamilton thinks it inadmissible that the inquiry should extend to his confidential as well as other conversations. To this Colonel Burr can only reply, that secret whispers traducing his fame and impeaching his honor are at least equally injurious with slanders publicly uttered; that General Hamilton had, at no time and in no place, a right to use any such injurious expressions; and that the partial negative he is disposed to give, with the reservations he wishes to make, are proofs that he has done the injury specified.

Colonel Burr's request was, in the first instance, proposed in a form the most simple, in order that General Hamilton might give to the affair that course to which he might be induced by his temper and his knowledge of facts. Colonel Burr trusted with confidence, that, from the frankness of a soldier and the candor of a gentleman, he might expect an ingenuous declaration. That if, as he had reason to believe, General Hamilton had used expressions derogatory to his honor, he would have had the magnanimity to retract them; and that if, from his language, injurious inferences had been improperly drawn, he would have perceived the propriety of correcting errors which might thus have been widely diffused. With these impressions Colonel Burr was greatly surprised at receiving a letter which he considered as evasive, and which, in manner, he deemed not altogether decorous. In one expectation, however, he was not wholly deceived; for the close of General Hamilton's letter contained an intimation that, if Colonel Burr should dislike his refusal to acknowledge or deny, he was ready to meet the consequences. This Colonel Burr deemed a sort of defiance, and would have felt justified in making it the basis of an immediate message; but, as the communication contained something concerning the indefiniteness of the request; as he believed it rather the offspring of false pride than of reflection; and as he felt the utmost reluctance to proceed to extremities while any other hope remained, his request was repeated in terms more explicit. The replies and propositions on the part of General Hamilton have, in Colonel's Burr's opinion, been constantly, in substance, the same.

Colonel Burr disavows all motives of predetermined hostility, a charge by which he thinks insult added to injury. He feels as a gentleman should when his honor is impeached or assailed; and, without sensations of hostility or wishes of revenge, he is determined to vindicate that honor at such hazard as the nature of the case demands.

The length to which this correspondence has extended only tending to prove that the satisfactory redress, earnestly desired, cannot be attained, he deems it useless to offer any proposition except the single message which I shall now have the honor to deliver.

With great respect, your obedient servant,

W. P. VAN NESS.

NATHANIEL PENDLETON, Esq.

I handed this to Mr. Pendleton at twelve o'clock on Wednesday the 27th. After he had perused it, agreeable to my instructions, I delivered the message which it is unnecessary to repeat. The request it contained was acceded to. After which Mr. Pendleton remarked that a court was then sitting in which General Hamilton had much business to transact, and that he had also some private arrangements to make, which would render some delay unavoidable. I acceded to his wish, and Mr. Pendleton said he would call on me again in the course of the day or the following morning, to confer further relative to time and place.

Thursday, June 28th, ten o'clock P.M., Mr. Pendleton called on me with a paper which he said contained some views of General Hamilton, and which he had received from him. I replied, that if the paper contained a definite and specific proposition for an accommodation, I would with pleasure receive it, and submit it to the consideration of my principal; if not, that I must decline taking it, as Mr. Burr conceived the correspondence completely terminated by the acceptance of the invitation contained in the message I had yesterday delivered. Mr. Pendleton replied that the paper did not contain any proposition of the kind I alluded to, but remarks on my last letter. I, of course, declined receiving it. Mr. Pendleton then took leave, and said that he would call again in a day or two to arrange time and place.

Tuesday, July 3d, I again saw Mr. Pendleton; and, after a few subsequent interviews, the time when the parties were to meet was ultimately fixed for the morning of the 11th of July instant. The occurrences of that interview will appear from the following statement, No. XIII, which has been drawn up and mutually agreed to by the seconds of the parties.

No. XIII

Colonel Burr arrived first on the ground, as had been previously agreed. When General Hamilton arrived, the parties exchanged salutations, and the seconds proceeded to make their arrangements. They measured the distance, ten full paces, and cast lots for the choice of position, as also to determine by whom the word should be given, both of which fell to the second of General Hamilton. They then proceeded to load the pistols in each other's presence, after which the parties took their stations. The gentleman who was to give the word then explained to the parties the rules which were to govern them in firing, which were as follows: "The parties being placed at their stations, the second who gives the word shall ask them whether they are ready; being answered in the affirmative, he shall say—*present!* After this the parties shall present and fire *when they please.* If one fires before the other, the opposite second shall say *one, two, three, fire,* and he shall then fire or lose his fire. He then asked if they were prepared; being answered in the affirmative, he gave the word *present,* as had been agreed on, and both parties presented and fired in succession. The intervening time is not expressed, as the seconds do not precisely agree on that point. The fire of Colonel Burr took effect, and General Hamilton almost instantly fell. Colonel Burr advanced towards General Hamilton with a manner and gesture that appeared to General Hamilton's friend to be expressive of regret; but, without speaking, turned about and withdrew, being urged from the field by his friend, as has been subsequently stated, with a view to prevent his being recognized by the surgeon and bargemen who were then approaching. No further communication took place between the principals, and the barge that carried Colonel Burr immediately returned to the city. We conceive it proper to add, that the conduct of the parties in this interview was perfectly proper, as suited the occasion.

Statement of Hamilton

On my expected interview with Colonel Burr, I think it proper to make some remarks explanatory of my conduct, motives and views.

I was certainly desirous of avoiding this interview for the most cogent reasons.

1. My religious and moral principles are strongly opposed to the practice of dueling, and it would ever give me pain to be obliged to shed the blood of a fellow-creature in a private combat forbidden by the laws.

2. My wife and children are extremely dear to me, and my life is of the utmost importance to them in various views.

3. I feel a sense of obligation toward my creditors; who, in case of accident to me, by the forced sale of my property, may be in some degree sufferers. I did not think myself at liberty, as a man of probity, lightly to expose them to this hazard.

4. I am conscious of no *ill will* to Colonel Burr distinct from political opposition which, as I trust, has proceeded from pure and upright motives.

Lastly, I shall hazard much, and can possibly gain nothing by the issue of the interview.

But it was, as I conceive, impossible for me to avoid it. There were *intrinsic* difficulties in the thing, and *artificial* embarrassments from the manner of proceeding on the part of Colonel Burr.

Intrinsic, because it is not to be denied that my animadversions on the political principles, character, and views of Colonel Burr have been extremely severe; and, on different occasions, I, in common with many others, have made very unfavorable criticisms on particular instances of the private conduct of this gentleman.

In proportion as these impressions were entertained with sincerity, and uttered with motives and for purposes which might appear to me commendable, would be the difficulty (until they could be removed by evidence of their being erroneous) of explanation or apology. The disavowal required of me by Colonel Burr, in a general and definite form, was out of my power, if it had really been proper for me to submit to be so questioned; but I was sincerely of the opinion that this could not be; and in this opinion I was confirmed by that of a very moderate and judicious friend whom I consulted. Besides that, Colonel Burr appeared to me to assume, in the first instance, a tone unnecessarily peremptory and menacing, and, in the second, positively offensive. Yet I wished, as far as might be practicable, to leave a door open for accommodation. This, I think, will be inferred from the written communications made by me and by my direction, and would be confirmed by the conversations between Mr. Van Ness and myself which arose out of the subject.

I am not sure whether, under all the circumstances, I did not go further in the attempt to accommodate than a punctilious delicacy will justify. If so, I hope the motives I have stated will excuse me.

It is not my design, by what I have said, to affix any odium on the character of Colonel Burr in this case. He doubtless has heard of animadversions of mine which bore very hard upon him; and it is probable that, as usual, they were accompanied with some falsehoods. He may have supposed himself under a necessity of acting as he has done. I hope the grounds of his proceeding have been such as ought to satisfy his own conscience.

I trust, at the same time, that the world will do me the justice to believe that I have not censured him on light grounds nor from unworthy inducements. I certainly have had strong reasons for what I have said, though it is possible that in some particulars I have been influenced by misconstruction or misinformation. It is also my ardent wish that I may have been more mistaken than I think I have been, and that he, by his future conduct, may show himself worthy of all confidence and esteem, and prove an ornament and blessing to the country.

As well, because it is possible that I may have injured Colonel Burr, however convinced myself that my opinions and declarations have been well founded, as from my general principles and temper in relation to similar affairs, I have resolved, if our interview is conducted in the usual manner, and it pleases God to give me the opportunity, to reserve and throw away my first fire, and I have thoughts even of reserving my second fire, and thus giving a double opportunity to Colonel Burr to pause and to reflect.

It is not, however, my intention to enter into any explanations on the ground—apology from principle, I hope, rather than pride, is out of the question.

To those who, with me, abhorring the practice of dueling, may think that I ought on no account to add to the number of bad examples, I answer, that my *relative* situation, as well in public as private, enforcing all the considerations which men of the world denominate honor, imposed on me (as I thought) a peculiar necessity not to decline the call. The ability to be in future useful, whether in resisting mischief or effecting good, in those crises of our public affairs which seem likely to happen, would probably be inseparable from a conformity with prejudice in this particular.

A. H.

Burr to Theodosia

New York, July 10, 1804.

Having lately written my will, and given my private letters and papers in charge to you, I have no other direction to give you on the subject but to request you to burn all such as, if by accident made public, would injure any person. This is more particularly applicable to the letters of my female correspondents. All my letters, and copies of letters, of which I have retained copies, are in the six blue boxes. If your husband or any one else (no one, however, could do it so well as he) should think it worth while to write a sketch of my life, some materials will be found among these letters.

Tell my dear Natalie that I have not left her anything, for the very good reason that I had nothing to leave to any one. My estate will just about pay my debts and no more—I mean, if I should die this year. If I live a few years, it is probable things may be better. Give Natalie one of the pictures of me. There are three in this house; that of Stewart, and two by Vanderlyn. Give her any other little tokens she may desire. One of those pictures, also, I pray you to give to Doctor Eustis. To Bartow something—what you please.

I pray you and your husband to convey to Peggy the small lot, not numbered, which is the fourth article mentioned in my list of property. It is worth about two hundred and fifty dollars. Give her also fifty dollars in cash as a reward for her fidelity. Dispose of Nancy as you please. She is honest, robust, and good-tempered. Peter is the most intelligent and best-disposed black I have ever known. (I mean the black boy I bought last fall from Mr. Turnbull.) I advise you, by all means, to keep him as the valet of your son. Persuade Peggy to live with you if you can.

I have desired that my wearing apparel be given to Frederic. Give him also a sword or pair of pistols.

Burn immediately a small bundle, tied with a red string which you will find in the little flat writing-case—that which we used with the curricle. The bundle is marked *"Put."*

The letters of *Clara* (the greater part of them) are tied up in a white handkerchief, which you will find in the blue box No. 5. You may hand them to Mari, if you please. My letters to Clara are in the same bundle. You, and by-and-by Aaron Burr Alston, may laugh at *gamp* when you look over this nonsense.

Many of the letters of *Clara* will be found among my ordinary letters, filed and marked, sometimes *"Clara,"* sometimes "L."

I am indebted to you, my dearest Theodosia, for a very great portion of the happiness which I have enjoyed in this life. You have completely satisfied all that my heart and affections had hoped or even wished. With a little more perseverance, determination, and industry, you will obtain all that my ambition or vanity had fondly imagined. Let your son have occasion to be proud that he had a mother. Adieu. Adieu.

A. BURR.

I have directed that the flat writing-case and the blue box No. 5, both in the library, be opened only by you. There are six of these blue boxes, which contain my letters and copies of letters, except those two clumsy quarto volumes, in which letter-press copies are pasted. They are somewhere in the library. The keys of the other five boxes are in No. 5.

It just now occurs to me to give poor dear Frederic my watch. I have already directed my executors here to give him my wearing apparel. When you come hither you must send for Frederic, and open your whole heart to him. He loves *me* almost as much as Theodosia does; and he does love *you* to adoration.

I have just now found four packets of letters between *Clara and Mentor* besides those in the handkerchief. I have thrown them loose into box No. 5. What a medley you will find in that box!

The seal of the late General Washington, which you will find in the blue box No. 5, was given to me by Mr. and Mrs. Law. You may keep it for your son, or give it to whom you please.

Assure Mrs. Law of my latest recollection. Adieu. Adieu.

A. BURR.

CHAPTER XXII

THE NEW century was to bring new manners and a new, more intensely democratic world. But the old world died slowly, still managing the grand style and still peopling America with amazing characters. Perhaps the most picturesque gentleman of that old régime was John Randolph of Roanoke, representative of a great Virginia family and for many years Republican house leader in Congress. Benjamin Perley Poore, who as a clerk of long standing in Washington had excellent opportunities for observing the heroes in action, has left a description of Randolph on the floor of the Senate, and with that our record begins. But the most striking act of his life was the writing of a letter in 1814 to his cousin Nancy Randolph, recently become the wife of Gouverneur Morris. Randolph had always hated Nancy, and now after a visit to her at Morrisania returned to an old charge that years ago in Virginia she had under particularly scandalous circumstances made away with her newborn illegitimate child. His letter, and the even mightier reply of Mrs. Morris, circulated widely at the time in manuscript. With this Homeric touch and to the sound of this ample rhetoric the great generation may be allowed to march off the scene.

Poore's Sketch of Randolph

SENATOR RANDOLPH, of Virginia, attracted the most attention on the part of strangers. He was at least six feet in height, with long limbs, an ill-proportioned body, and a small, round head. Claiming descent from Pocahontas, he wore his coarse, black hair long, parted in the middle, and combed down on either side of his sallow face. His small, black eyes were expressive in their glances, especially when he was engaged in debate, and his high-toned and thin voice would ring through the Senate Chamber like the shrill scream of an angry vixen. He generally wore a full suit of heavy, drab-colored English broadcloth, the high, rolling collar of his surtout coat almost concealing his head, while the skirts hung in voluminous folds about his knee-breeches and the white leather tops of his boots. He used to enter the Senate Chamber wearing a pair of silver spurs, carrying a heavy riding-whip, and followed by a favorite hound, which crouched beneath his desk. He wrote, and occasionally spoke, in riding-gloves, and it was his favorite gesture to point the long index finger of his right hand at his opponent as he hurled forth tropes and figures of speech at him. Every ten or fifteen minutes, while he occupied the floor, he would exclaim in a low tone, "Tims, more porter!" and the assistant doorkeeper would hand him a foaming tumbler of potent malt liquor, which he would hurriedly drink, and then proceed with his remarks, often thus drinking three or four quarts in an afternoon. He was not choice in his selection of epithets, and as Mr. Calhoun took the ground that he did not have the power to call a Senator to order, the irate Virginian pronounced President Adams "a traitor," Daniel Webster "a vile slanderer," John Holmes "a dangerous fool," and Edward Livingston "the most contemptible and degraded of beings, whom no man ought to touch, unless with a pair of tongs." One day, while he was speaking with great freedom of abuse of Mr. Webster, then a member of the House, a Senator informed him in an undertone that Mrs. Webster was in the gallery. He had not the delicacy to desist, however, until he had fully emptied the vials of his wrath. Then he set upon Mr. Speaker Taylor, and after abusing him soundly he turned sarcastically to the gentleman who had informed him of Mrs. Webster's presence, and asked, "Is Mrs. Taylor present also?"

Correspondence of Randolph and Mrs. Morris

Greenwich Street, Oct. 31, 1814.

MADAM:

When, at my departure from Morrisania, in your sister's presence, I bade you remember the past, I was not apprised of the whole extent of your guilty machinations. I had nevertheless seen and heard enough in the course of my short visit to satisfy me that your own dear experience had availed nothing toward the amendment of your life. My object was to let you know that the eye of man as well as of that God, of whom you seek not, was upon you—to impress upon your mind some of your duty toward your husband, and, if possible, to rouse some dormant spark of virtue, if haply any such should slumber in your bosom. The conscience of the most hardened criminal has, by a sudden stroke, been alarmed into repentance and contrition. Yours, I perceive, is not made of penetrable stuff. Unhappy woman, why will you tempt the forbearance of that Maker who has, perhaps, permitted you to run your course

of vice and sin that you might feel it to be a life of wretchedness,
alarm and suspicion? You now live in the daily and nightly dread
of discovery. Detection itself can hardly be worse. Some of the
proofs of your guilt (you know to which of them I allude) ; those
which in despair you sent me through Dr. Meade on your leaving
Virginia; those proofs, I say, had not been produced against you
had you not falsely used my name in imposing upon the generous
man to whose arms you have brought pollution! to whom next to
my unfortunate brother you were most indebted, and whom next to
him you have most deeply injured. You told Mr. Morris that I had
offered you marriage subsequent to your arraignment for the most
horrible of crimes, when you were conscious that I never at any
time made such proposals. You have, therefore, released me from
any implied obligation (with me it would have been sacred; notwithstanding you laid no injunction of the sort upon me, provided
you had respected my name and decently discharged your duties to
your husband), to withhold the papers from the inspection of all
except my own family.

I laid them before Tudor soon after they came into my hands
with the whole story of his father's wrongs and your crime. But
to return:

You represented to Mr. Morris that I had offered you marriage.
Your inveterate disregard of truth has been too well known to me
for many years to cause any surprise on my part at this or any other
falsehood that you may coin to serve a turn. In like manner, you
instigated Mr. Morris against the Chief Justice whom you knew to
have been misled with respect to the transactions at R. Harrison's,
and who knew no more of your general or subsequent life than the
Archbishop of Canterbury. Cunning and guilt are no match for
wisdom and truth, yet you persevere in your wicked course. Your
apprehensions for the life of your child first flashed conviction on
my mind that your hands had deprived of life that of which you
were delivered in October, 1792, at R. Harrison's. The child, to
interest his feelings in its behalf, you told my brother Richard
(when you entrusted to him the secret of your pregnancy and implored him to hide your shame) was begotten by my brother,
Theodorick, who died at Bizarre of a long decline the preceding
February. You knew long before his death (nearly a year) he was
reduced to a mere skeleton; that he was unable to walk; and that
his bones had worn through the skin. Such was the inviting object
whose bed (agreeably to your own account) you sought, and with
whom, to use your own paraphrase, you played 'Alonzo and Cora,'
and, to screen the character of such a creature, was the life and

fame of this most gallant of men put in jeopardy. He passed his word, and the pledge was redeemed at the hazard of all that man can hold dear. Domestic peace, reputation and life, all suffered but the last. His hands received the burthen, bloody from the womb, and already lifeless. Who stifled its cries, God only knows and you. His hands consigned it to an uncoffined grave. To the prudence of R. Harrison, who disqualified himself from giving testimony by refraining from a search under the pile of shingles, some of which were marked with blood—to this cautious conduct it is owing that my brother Richard did not perish on the same gibbet by your side, and that the foul stain of incest and murder is not indelibly stamped on his memory and associated with the idea of his offspring. Your alleged reason for not declaring the truth (fear of your brothers) does not hold against a disclosure to his wife, your sister, to whom he was not allowed to impart the secret.

But her own observation supplied all defect of positive information and, had you been first proceeded against at law, your sister being a competent witness, you must have been convicted, and the conviction of her husband would have followed as a necessary consequence; for who would have believed your sister to have been sincere in her declaration that she suspected no criminal intercourse between her husband and yourself?

When, some years ago, I imparted to her the facts (she had a right to know them), she expressed no surprise but only said, she was always satisfied in her own mind that it was so. My brother died *suddenly* in June, 1790, only three years after his trial. I was from home. Tudor, because he believes you capable of anything, imparted to me the morning I left Morrisania his misgivings that you had been the perpetrator of that act, and, when I found your mind running upon poisonings and murders, I too had my former suspicions strengthened. If I am wrong, I ask forgiveness of God and even of you. A dose of medicine was the avowed cause of his death. Mrs. Dudley, to whom my brother had offered an asylum in his house, who descended from our mother's sister, you drove away. Your quarrels with your own sister, before fierce and angry, now knew no remission. You tried to force her to turn you out of doors that you might have some plausible reason to assign for quitting Bizarre. But, after what my poor brother had been made to suffer, in mind, body and estate, after her own suffering as wife and widow from your machinations, it was not worth while to try to save anything from the wreck of her happiness, and she endured you as well as she could, and you poured on. But your intimacy with one of the slaves, *your 'dear* Billy Ellis,' thus you commenced your epistles to this Othello! attracted notice. You could stay no longer at Bizarre, you abandoned it under the plea of ill usage and, after various shiftings of your quarters, you threw yourself on the humanity of Capt. and Mrs. Murray (never appealed to in vain), and here you made a bold stroke for a husband—Dr. Meade. Foiled in this game, your advances became so immodest you had to leave Grovebrook. You, afterwards, took lodgings at Prior's (a public garden), whither I sent by your sister's request, and in her name $100. You returned them by the bearer, Tudor, then a schoolboy, because sent in her name which you covered with obloquy. But to S. G. Tucker, Esq., you represented that I had sent the money, suppressing your sister's name, and he asked me if I was not going to see 'poor Nancy'? You sent this, a direct message, and I went. You were at that time fastidiously neat, and so was the apartment. I *now* see *why* the bank note was returned—but the bait did not take—I left the apartment and never beheld you more until in Washington as the wife of Mr. Morris. Your subsequent association with the players—your decline into a very *drab*—I was informed of by a friend in Richmond. You left Virginia—whether made a condition of your——or not, I know not, but the Grantor would not, as I heard, suffer you to associate with his wife. From Rhode Island, you wrote to me, begging for money. I did not answer your letter. Mr. Sturgis, of Connecticut, with whom you had formed an acquaintance, and with whom you corresponded! often brought me messages from you. He knows how coolly they were received. When Mr. Morris brought you to Washington, he knew that I held aloof from you. At his instance, who asked me if I intended to mortify his wife by not visiting her, I went. I repeated my visit to ascertain whether change of circumstances had made any change in your conduct. I was led to hope you had seen your errors and was smoothing his passage through life. A knowledge that he held the staff in his own hands and a mistaken idea of his character (for I had not done justice to the kindness of his nature) fortified this hope. Let me say that, when I heard of your living with Mr. Morris as his *housekeeper,* I was glad of it as a means of keeping you from worse company and courses. Considering him as a perfect man of the world, who, in courts and cities at home and abroad, had in vain been assailed by female blandishments, the idea of his marrying you never entered my head. Another connection did. My first intimation of the marriage was its announcement in the newspapers. I then thought, Mr. Morris being a traveled man, might have formed his taste on a foreign model. Silence was my only course. Chance has again thrown you under my eye. What do I see? A vampire that, after sucking the best blood of my race, has flitted off to the North, and struck her harpy fangs into an infirm old man. To what condition of being have you reduced him? Have you made him a prisoner in his own house that there may be no witness of your lewd amours, or have you driven away his friends and old domestics that there may be no witnesses of his death? Or do you mean to force him to Europe where he will be more at your mercy, and, dropping the boy on the highway, rid yourself of all incumbrances at once? 'Uncle,' said Tudor, 'if ever Mr. Morris' eyes are opened, it will be through this child whom, with all her grimaces in her husband's presence, 'tis easy to see she cares nothing for except as an instrument of power. How shocking she looks! I have not met her eyes three times since I have been in the house. My first impression of her character, as far back as I can remember, is that she was an unchaste woman. My brother knew her even better than I. She could never do anything with him.'

I have done. Before this reaches your eye, it will have been perused by him, to whom, next to my brother, you are most deeply indebted, and whom, next to him, you have most deeply wronged. If he be not both blind and deaf, he must sooner or later unmask you unless *he too die of cramps* in his *stomach*. You understand me. If I were persuaded that his life is safe in your custody, I might forbear from making this communication to him. Repent before it is too late. May I hear of that repentance and never see you more.

JOHN RANDOLPH OF ROANOKE.

Morrisania, January 16th, 1815.

SIR:

My husband yesterday communicated to me for the first time your letter of the last of October, together with that which accompanied it, directed to him.

In your letter to my husband, you say, 'I wish I could withhold the blow but I must in your case do what under a change of circumstances I would have you do unto me.' This, Sir, seems fair and friendly. It seems, Sir, as if you wished to apprise Mr. Morris and him only of circumstances important to his happiness and honor, though fatal to my reputation, leaving it in his power to cover them in oblivion or display them to the world as the means of freeing him from a monster unfit to live. But this was mere seeming. Your real object was widely different. Under the pretext of consulting Com. Decatur and Mr. Bleecker, you communicated your slanders to them, and then to Mr. Ogden. You afterwards displayed them to Mr. Wilkins, who having heard them spoken of in the city, called on you to know on what foundation they stood. How many others you may have consulted, to how many others you may have published your malicious tale, I know not, but I venture to ask whether this be conduct under a change of circumstances you would have others pursue toward you? You have professed a sense of gratitude for obligations you suppose my husband to have laid you under. Was the attempt to blacken my character and destroy his peace of mind a fair return? There are many other questions which will occur to candid minds on the perusal of your letter. For instance, did *you* believe these slanders? If you did, why did you permit your nephew to be fed from my bounty and nursed by my care during nearly three months? Could you suppose him safe in the power of a wretch who had murdered his father? Does it consist with the dignified pride of family you affect to have him, whom you announce as your heir, and destined to support your name, dependent on the charity of a negro's concubine? You say I confine my husband a prisoner in his house that there may be no witnesses of my lewd amours, and have driven away his friends and old domestics that there may be no witnesses of his death. If I wished to indulge in amours, the natural course would be to mingle in the pleasures and amusements of the city, or at least to induce my husband to go abroad and leave me a clear stage for such misdeeds. Was it with a view to multiply witnesses of my ill conduct that you published tales tending as far as they are believed to make his house a solitude? It cannot escape your observation that you take on you to assert things which, had they existed, you could not know. Thus you say your brother 'passed his word and the pledge was redeemed at the hazard of all that a man can hold dear'! Pray, Sir, admitting (though it is not true) that I had exacted from your brother a promise of secrecy, how could you have known it unless he betrayed it? and, if he betrayed it, how was the pledge redeemed? Again you say that 'I instigated Mr. Morris to write to the Chief Justice whom I knew to have been misled.' Had the instigation been a fact, how could you come by the knowledge of it? Like many other things in your letter, it happens to be a downright falsehood, and is, therefore, a just standard for him to estimate the rest of your assertions. Permit me to observe also that it is an additional proof of your intention to spread your slander abroad; for, had you meant to communicate information to Mr. Morris, you would not have hazarded such a charge. People of proper feelings require that the evidence of accusation be strong in proportion as the guilt is enormous; but those, who feel themselves capable of committing the blackest crimes, will readily suspect others, and condemn without proof on a mere hearsay, on the suggestion of a disturbed fancy or instigation of a malevolent heart. Those who possess a clear conscience and sound mind, will look through your letter for some *proof* of my guilt. They will look in vain. They will find, indeed, that you have thought proper to found suspicions on suspicions of your nephew, and, with no better evidence, you have the insolence to impute crime at which nature revolts. You will perhaps say that you mention a piece of evidence in your possession—a letter which I wrote on leaving Virginia. As far as that goes, it must be admitted, but permit me to tell you that the very mention of it destroys your credibility with honorable minds. To say, as you do, that I laid no injunction of secrecy will strike such minds as a pitiful evasion. If you had the feelings of a man of honor, you would have known that there are things the communication of which involves that injunction. You have heard of principle and pretend to justify the breach of confidence by my want of respect for your name. But you acknowledge that you communicated the information to my sister and her son Tudor (this a boy of eleven years old) shortly after you became possessed of it. Thus was my reputation, as far as it lay in your power, committed to the discretion of a woman and a child many years before the imputed want of respect for your name! Formerly Jack Randolph—now, 'John Randolph of Roanoke.' It was then a want of respect to the great John Randolph of Roanoke to say he had done the honor of offering his hand to his poor cousin Nancy. I shall take more notice of this in its proper place, and only add here that among the respectable people of Virginia the affectation of greatness must cover you with ridicule.

But, to return to this breach of confidence, without which you have not the shadow of evidence to support your slanders. While on the chapter of self-contradictions (which, with all due respect to 'John Randolph of Roanoke,' make up the history of his life), I must notice a piece of evidence not indeed contained in your letter, but written by your hand. I have already hinted at the indelicacy of leaving your nephew so long in my care with the view of meeting observations which no person can fail to make on a conduct so extraordinary in itself and inconsistent with your charges against me. You pretend to have discovered, all at once in this house, the confirmation of your suspicions, but surely the suspicion was sufficient to prevent a person having a pretense to delicacy from subjecting himself to such obligations. One word, however, as to this sudden discovery made by your great sagacity. Recollect, Sir, when you rose from table to leave Morrisania, you put in my husband's hand a note to my sister expressing your willingness that she and her son should pass the winter in his house. Surely, the discovery must have been made at that time, if at all. You will recollect, too, some other marks of confidence and affection, let me add of respect also, which I forbear to mention because you would no doubt deny them, and it would be invidious to ask the testimony of those who were present. One act, however, must not be unnoticed. It speaks too plain a language to be misunderstood, and was too notorious to be denied. When you entered this house, and when you left it, you took me in your arms, you pressed me to your bosom, you impressed upon my lips a kiss which I received as a token of friendship from a near relation. Did you then believe that you held in your arms, that you pressed to your bosom, that you kissed the lips of, a common prostitute, the murderess of her own child and of your brother? Go, tell this to the world that scorn may be at no loss for an object. If you did not believe it, make out a certificate that 'John Randolph of Roanoke' is a base calumniator. But no, you may spare yourself this trouble. It is already written. It lies before me, and I proceed to notice what it contains in a more particular manner.

And first, Sir, as to the fact communicated shortly before I left Virginia. That your brother Theodoric paid his addresses to me, you knew and attempted to supplant him by calumny. Be pleased to remember that, in my sister Mary's house, you led me to the portico, and, leaning against one of the pillars, expressed your surprise at having heard from your brother Richard that I was engaged to marry his brother, Theodoric. That you hoped it was not true, for he was unworthy of me. To establish this opinion, you made many assertions derogatory to his reputation—some of which I knew to be false. Recollect that, afterwards, on one of those occasions (not infrequent), when your violence of temper had led you into an unpleasant situation, you, in a letter to your brother, Richard, declared you were unconscious of ever having done anything in all your life which could offend me, unless it was that conversation, excusing it as an act of heroism, like the sacrifice of his own son by Brutus, for which I ought to applaud you. The defamation of your brother whom I loved, your stormy passions, your mean selfishness, your wretched appearance, rendered your attentions disagreeable. Your brother, Richard, a model of truth and honor, knew how much I was annoyed by them. He knew of the letters with which you pestered me from Philadelphia till one of them was returned in a blank cover, when I was absent from home. By whom it was done, I knew not; for I never considered it of importance enough to inquire. It was your troublesome attentions which induced Richard to inform you of my engagement. At that time, my father had other views. Your property, as well as that of your brothers, was hampered by a British debt. My father, therefore, preferred for my husband a person of clear and considerable estate. The sentiment of my heart did not accord with his intentions. Under these circumstances, I was left at Bizarre, a girl, not seventeen, with the man she loved. I was betrothed to him, and considered him as my husband in the presence of that God whose name you presume to invoke on occasions the most trivial and for purposes the most malevolent. We should have been married, if Death had not snatched him away a few days after the scene which began the history of my sorrows. Your brother, Richard, knew every circumstance, but you are mistaken in supposing I exacted from him a promise of secrecy. He was a man of honor. Neither the foul imputations against us both, circulated by that kind of friendship which you have shown to my husband, nor the awful scene, to which he was afterwards called as an accomplice in the horrible crime, with which you attempt to blacken his memory, could induce him to betray the sister of his wife, the wife of his brother; I repeat it, Sir, the crime with which you now attempt to blacken his memory. You say that, to screen the character of such a creature as I am, the life and the fame of that most generous and gallant of men was put in jeopardy. His life alas! is now beyond the reach of your malice, but his fame, which should be dear to a brother's heart, is stabbed by the hand of his brother. You not only charge me with the heinous crime of infanticide, placing him in the condition of an accomplice, but you proceed to say that 'had it not been for the prudence of Mr. Harrison, or the mismanagement of not putting *me* first on my trial, we should both have swung on the same gibbet and the foul stain of incest and murder been stamped on his memory and associated with the idea of his offspring.' This, Sir, is the language you presume to write and address to me, enclosed in a cover to my husband for his inspection, after having been already communicated to other people. I will, for a moment, put myself out of question, and suppose the charge to be true. What must be the indignation of a feeling heart to behold a wretch rake up the ashes of his deceased brother to blast his fame? Who is there of nerve so strong as not to shudder at your savage regret that we did not swing on the same gibbet? I well remember, and you cannot have forgotten that, when sitting at the hospitable home of your venerable father-in-law, you threw a knife at that brother's head, and, if passion had not diverted the aim, he would much earlier have been consigned to the grave, and you much earlier have met the doom which awaits your murderous disposition. It was, indeed, hoped that age and reflection had subdued your native barbarity. But, setting aside the evidence which your letter contains, the earnestness with which you disclosed in the presence of Col. Morris and his brother the Commodore [your desire?] to shoot a British soldier, to bear off his scalp and hang it up as an ornament in your house at Roanoke, shows that you have still the heart of a savage. I ask not of you but of a candid world whether a man like you is worthy of belief. On the melancholy occasion you have thought proper to bring forward there was the strictest examination. Neither your brother or myself had done anything to excite enmity, yet we were subjected to an unpitying persecution. The severest scrutiny took place; you know it. He was acquitted to the joy of numerous spectators, expressed in shouts of exultation. This, Sir, passed in a remote county of Virginia more than twenty years ago. You have revived the slanderous tale in the most populous city in the United States. For what? To repay my kindness to your nephew by tearing me from the arms of my husband and blasting the prospects of my child! Poor innocent babe, now playing at my feet, unconscious of his mother's wrongs. But it seems that on my apprehensions for his life first flashed convictions on your mind that my own hand had deprived in October, 1792, that of which I was delivered. You ought to have said, the last of September.

You must, Mr. Randolph, have a most extraordinary kind of apprehension; for one child can induce you to believe in the destruction of another. But, waiving this absurdity, you acknowledge that every fact, which had come to your knowledge, every circumstance you had either heard or dreamt of in the long period of more than twenty years, had never imparted to you a belief, which nevertheless you expect to imprint on the minds of others. You thus pay to the rest of mankind the wretched compliment of supposing them more ready to believe the greatest crimes than 'John Randolph of Roanoke.' Doubtless there may be some, who are worthy of this odious distinction; I hope not many. I hope too that, in justice to the more rational part of the community, you will wait (before you require their faith) until some such flash shall have enlightened their minds. Mark here, for your future government, the absurdity to which falsehood and malice inevitably lead a calumniator. They have driven you, while you endeavored to palliate inconsistency of conduct, into palpable self contradiction. Sensible as you must be that no respectable person can overlook the baseness of leaving your nephew so long, or even permitting him to come, under the roof of the wretch you describe me to be, you are compelled to acknowledge that you did not believe in the enormities you charge, until yourself had paid a visit to Morrisania. Thus you not only invalidate everything like evidence to support your criminations but found them on circumstances which produce an effect (if they operate at all) directly opposite to that for which they are cited.

You have, Sir, on this subject presumed to use my sister's name. Permit me to tell you, I do not believe one word of what you say. Were it true, it is wholly immaterial. But that it is not true, I have perfect conviction.

The assertion rests only on your testimony, the weight and value of which has been already examined. The contradiction is contained in her last letter to me, dated Dec. 17th, of which I enclose a copy. You will observe she cautions me against believing anything inconsistent with her gratitude for my kindness, and assures me that, although prevented from spending the winter with us, she is proud of the honor done her by the invitation. With this letter before me, I should feel it an insult to her as well as an indignity to myself if I made any observations on your conduct at Bizarre. No one can think so meanly of a woman who moves in the sphere of a lady as to suppose she could be proud of the honor of being invited to spend a winter with the concubine of one of her slaves. Nevertheless, though I disdain an answer to such imputations, I am determined they shall appear in the neighborhood under your hand; so that your character may be fully known and your signature forever hereafter be not only what it has hitherto been, the appendage of vainglorious boasting, but the designation of malicious baseness. You say I drove Mrs. Dudley from my sister's house. A falsehood more absurd could hardly have been invented. She left the house the day before your brother was buried. I shall not enter into a detail of the circumstances, but this assertion also shall be communicated to the neighborhood. It is well that your former constituents should know the creature in whom they put their trust. Virginians, in general, whatever may be their defects, have a high sense of honor. You speak with affected sensibility of my sister's domestic bliss, and you assume an air of indignation at the violence of my temper. Be pleased to recollect that, returning from a morning ride with your brother, you told me you found it would not do to interfere between man and wife; that you had recommended to him a journey to Connecticut to obtain a divorce; that he made no reply, nor spoke a single word afterwards. Recollect, too, how often, and before how many persons, and in how many ways, you have declared your detestation of her conduct as a wife and her angry passions. One form of expression occurs which is remarkable: 'I have heard,' said you, 'that Mrs. Randolph was handsome, and, perhaps, had I ever seen her in a good humor, I might have thought so; but her features are so distorted by constant wrath that she has to me the air of a fury.' And now, as to my disposition and conduct, be pleased not to forget (for people of a certain sort should have good memories) that, during full five years after your brother's death, and how much longer, I know not, I was the constant theme of your praise and, though you wearied every one else, you seemed on that subject to be yourself indefatigable. I should not say these things, if they rested merely on my own knowledge, for you would not hesitate to deny them, and I should be very sorry that my credibility were placed on the same level with yours. You have addressed me as a notorious liar, to which I make no other answer than that the answer, like your other charges, shall be communicated to those who know us both. You will easily anticipate their decision. In the meantime, it may not be amiss to refresh your memory with one sample of your veracity. There are many who remember, while your slaves were under mortgage for the British debt, your philanthropic assertion that you would make them free and provide tutors for them. With this project, you wearied all who would listen. When, by the sale of some of them, a part of the debt was discharged, and an agreement made to pay the rest by installments, you changed your mind. This was not inexcusable, but when you set up for representation in Congress, and the plan to liberate your slaves was objected to in your District, you published, to the astonishment of numbers, who had heard you descant on your liberal intentions, that you *never* had any such idea. Thus your first step in public life was marked with falsehood. On entering the door of Congress, you became an outrageous patriot. Nothing in the French Revolution was too immoral or too impious for your taste and applause. Washington and Britain were the objects of your obloquy. This patriotic fever lasted till the conclusion of Mr. Chase's trial, from which you returned, complaining of the fatigue of your public labors, but elated with the prospect of a foreign mission. As usual, you rode your new Hobby to the annoyance of all who like me were obliged to listen. Your expected voyage enchanted you so much that you could not help talking of it even to your deaf nephew: '*Soon, my boy, we shall be sailing over the Atlantic.*' But, all at once, you became silent and seemed in deep melancholy. It appeared soon after that Mr. Jefferson and Mr. Madison, knowing your character, had prudently declined a compliance with your wishes. A new scene now opened; you became a patriot, double distilled, and founded your claim to the confidence of new friends on the breach of that which had been reposed by your old ones. I know not what others may think as to your treacherous disclosure of Mr. Madison's declaration, 'that the French want money and must have it,' but it is no slight evidence of his correct conduct, in general, that *you* had nothing else to betray.

With the same insensibility to shame, which marks your allegations, you have denied the fact of turning me out of doors. This also shall be made known in the neighborhood where it must be well remembered. I take the liberty again to refresh your memory. Shortly after your nephew (whom I had nursed several weeks in a dangerous illness at the hazard of my life) had left home to take the benefit of a change of air, you came into the room one evening, after you had been a long time in your chamber with my sister, and said, addressing yourself to me, 'Nancy, when do you leave this house? The sooner the better for you take as many liberties as if you were in a tavern.' On this occasion as on others, my course was silent submission. I was poor, I was dependent. I knew the house was kept in part at your expense. I could not therefore appeal to my sister. I replied with the humility, suitable to my forlorn condition, 'I will go as soon as I can.' You stalked haughtily about the room, and poor, unprotected 'Nancy' retired to seek the relief of tears. Every assertion of yours respecting my visit to Grovebrook is false. Mr. Murray cannot but acknowledge that I went there with Judge Johnston in his carriage, on my way to Hanover, after repeated invitations from his family, conveyed in letters from his daughters; that I left there in the chariot of my friend, Mr. Swan; that they pressed me not only to prolong my stay but to repeat my visit. Of this, Mr. Curd, a gentleman sent by Mr. Swan to escort me, was a witness.

You are unfortunate in what passed two years after when I saw you at Richmond, but, before I refresh your memory on this subject, I must notice another malicious falsehood respecting my residence, while in Richmond. You say I took lodgings at Prior's, a public garden. It is true Mr. Prior owned a large lot in Richmond, and that there was a pubilc building on it, in which public balls and entertainments were given, and this lot a public garden, but it is equally true that Mr. Prior's dwelling and the enclosure round it were wholly distinct from that garden. In that house, I lodged. My chamber was directly over Mrs. Prior's, a lady of as good birth as Mr. John Randolph and of far more correct principles. All this, Sir, you perfectly well know. From that chamber, I wrote you a note, complaining that your nephew, then a school boy in Richmond, was not permitted to see me. You sent [it] back, after writing on the same sheet, 'I return your note that you may compare it with my answer, and ask yourself, if you are not unjust to one who through life has been your friend.' This, with the recital of your professions of regard, made to my friend Lucy Randolph and her husband and her husband's brother Ryland, led me to suppose you had, in the last scene at Bizarre, acted only as my sister's agent. I, therefore, wrote to you, remonstrating against the reason you assigned for turning me out of doors, which you yourself knew to be unfounded, for you had often observed that I was 'Epicene, the Silent Woman.' You knew that I was continually occupied at my needle or other work for the house, obeying, to the best of my knowledge, the orders I received, differing from any other servant only in this: I received no wages, but was permitted to sit at table, where I did not presume to enter into conversation or taste of wine, and very seldom of tea or coffee. I gave my letter open into the hands of Ryland Randolph, to be put by him into your hands. I pause here, Sir, to ask, whether, on the receipt of this letter, you pretended to deny having turned me out of doors? You dare not say so. You shortly after paid me a visit, the only one during your stay. You sat on my bedstead, I cannot say my bed, for I had none, I was too poor. When weary, my limbs were rested on a blanket, spread over the sacking. Your visit was long, and I never saw you from that day until we met in Washington. Some days after, you sent your nephew to offer me $100 on the part of his mother. I supposed this to be a turn of delicacy, for, had you been the bearer of money from her, you would have delivered it, when you were in my chamber, and given me every needful assurance of the quarter from which it came. But, let it have come from whom it might, my feelings were too indignant to receive a boon at the hands of those by whom I had been so grievously wounded. I readily conceive, Sir, that this must have appeared to you inexplicable, for it must be very difficult for you to conceive how a person in my condition would refuse money from any quarter. It is true that, afterwards, when in Newport, suffering from want, and borne down by a severe ague and fever, I was so far humbled as to request not the gift (I would sooner have perished) but the loan of half that sum. My petition struck on a cold heart that emitted no sound. You did not deign to reply. You even made a boast of your silence. I was then so far off my groans could not be heard in Virginia. You no longer apprehended the [reproaches] which prompted your ostentatious offer at Richmond. Yes, Sir, you were silent. You then possessed the letter on which you grounded your calumnies. You supposed me so much in your power that I should not dare to complain of your unkindness. Yes, Sir, you were silent, and you left your nephew nearly three months dependent on the charity of her, to whom in the extreme of wretchedness you had refused the loan of fifty dollars. Yes, Sir, you were silent. Perhaps, you hoped that the poor forlorn creature you had turned out of doors would, under the pressure of want, and far removed from every friend, be driven to a vicious course, and enable you to justify your barbarity by charges such as you have now invented.

You say you were informed of my associating with the players and my decline into a very drab by a friend in Richmond. Your letter shall be read in Richmond. You must produce that friend, unless you are willing yourself to father the falsehood which in Richmond will be notorious.

I defy you, Mr. Randolph, to substantiate by the testimony of any credible witness a single fact injurious to my reputation from the time you turned me out of doors until the present hour; and God knows that, if suffering could have driven me to vice, there was no want of suffering. My husband, in permitting me to write this letter, has enjoined me not to mention his kindness, otherwise I could give a detail of circumstances which, as they would not involve any pecuniary claim, might touch even *your* heart. You speak of him as an infirm old man, into whom I have struck the fangs of a harpy, after having acted in your family the part of a vampire. I pray you, Mr. 'John Randolph of Roanoke,' to be persuaded that such idle declamation, though it might become a school boy to his aunt and cousins, is misplaced on the present occasion. You know as little of the manner in which my present connection began as of other things with which you pretend to be acquainted. I loved my husband before he made me his wife. I love him still more now that he has made me mother of one of the finest boys I ever saw; now that his kindness soothes the anguish which I cannot but feel from your unmanly attack. I am very sorry I am obliged to speak of your nephew. I would fain impute to his youth, or to some other excusable cause, his unnatural, and I must say, criminal, conduct. I hope the strength of my constitution, the consolation I derive from the few friends who are left and the caresses of my beloved babe will enable me to resist the measures taken for my destruction by him and his uncle. Had his relations rested only on your testimony, I should not have hesitated to have acquitted him of the charge; but a part of them at least, not fully detailed in your letter, was made in Mr. Ogden's presence. This young man received several small sums of money which I sent him unasked, while he remained at Cambridge. Early in April, by a letter, which he addressed to me as his 'Dear good Aunt,' he requested the loan of thirty or forty dollars. I did not imitate the example you had set but immediately enclosed a check payable to his order for thirty dollars. I heard no more of him until the end of July, when a letter, dated in Providence, announced his intention of seeing me soon at Morrisania. At the same time, letters to my husband mentioned the dangerous condition of his health. On the 4th of August, a phaeton drove to the door with a led horse, and a person, appearing to be a servant, stepped out and inquired for Mr. Randolph. He was directed to the stable, and shortly after Mr. Randolph landed from the boat of a Packet. His appearance bespoke severe illness. I showed him to his chamber, and venture to say from that time to the moment of his departure he was treated by me with the tenderness and kindness of a mother. The injunction I have already mentioned restrains me from going into particulars. My health was injured by the fatigue to which I was exposed, the burthen of which I could not diminish without neglecting him; for I could not procure good nurses or servants. My husband's health, too, was, I believe, injured by the confinement which this youth occasioned; for he was prevented from taking a journey we were about to make for air and exercise among the mountains of New Jersey. We were also under the disagreeable necessity of keeping a servant whom our friends had denounced as a thief. By the bye, I have reason to believe he is one of those 'ancient domestics' you have taken under your protection. If so, I must in justice to myself inform you that your friend, Geo. Bevens, dismissed only two days before your arrival, was shortly after admitted to a lodging in the Bridewell of New York for theft. I had an opportunity, indeed I was made by my laundress, to observe that your nephew (though driving his phaeton with a servant on horseback) had not a pair of stockings fit to wear; his man, Jonathan, dunning him in my presence for his wages. At one time, in particular, passing by his door, I heard Jonathan ask for money. My heart prompted me to offer relief. As I entered his room for that purpose (it was two days after a violent hemorrhage which threatened his life), he was rising feebly from his bed, and, when I mentioned my object, said in a tremulous voice, 'My dear Aunt, I was coming to ask you.' I bade his servant follow me and gave him $5.00. Tudor had returned the $30 first borrowed but, shortly afterwards, increased the debt $10 to furnish as I supposed, his traveling companion, Mr. Bruce [of Rhode Island], with the means of returning home. A few days after that, I supplied him with an additional $20. I gave stockings and, before his departure, sent $30 to one of Mr. Morris' nieces to purchase handkerchiefs which he wanted and which his mother said he could not afford to buy. The evening you left Morrisania, I received a note from this lady excusing herself for not executing my commission by reason of the death of a cousin and returning the money because she understood that my sister was to go the next Tuesday. You witnessed my surprise at receiving such information in such a way. You will recollect what followed. After your departure, I communicated the note to your nephew, and told him, as he was going to town, he could purchase the handkerchiefs for himself. I gave him thirty dollars which he put in his pocket and thanked me. Two days after, when in town, he said to me, 'Aunt, I wish you would choose the handkerchiefs yourself; I should value them more.' He forgot, however, to return the money. I purchased the Hdkffs, together with a merino tippet to protect his chest, and received again his thanks which were reiterated the same day by his mother at Mr. Ogden's. The debt, amounting to $65, she paid at Morrisania. The $30 were enclosed in her note, dated Saturday morning, of which I send you herewith [a] copy together with that of the 3rd November from Philadelphia.

And now, Sir, put the actual parties out of the question, and say what credit can be due to the calumnies of a person in your nephew's situation, soliciting and receiving favors to the very last moment. Let me add, after he had poured his slanders into your ear or repeated them from your dictation, he left me to discharge one of his doctor's bills, which he said I offered to pay, and receive his thanks in advance. Is it proper, or is it decent to found such calumnies on the suspicions of such a creature? even supposing them to have originated in his mind, and not been, as is too probable, instigated by you? Could anything but the most determined and inveterate malice induce any one above the level of an idiot to believe the only fact he pretended to articulate? Who can believe me cruel to my child? When it is notorious my fault is too great indulgence; that my weakness is too great solicitude, and that I have been laughed at for instances of maternal care by which my health was impaired. You cite as from him these words, 'How shocking she looks. I have not met her eyes three times since I have been in the house.' Can you believe this? Can you believe others to believe it? How happens it you did not cry out as any one else would have done? 'Why did you stay in that house? Why did you submit to her kindness? Why did you accept her presents? Why did you pocket her money?' To such an apostrophe he might have replied perhaps, 'Uncle, I could not help it. I was penniless, in daily expectation that you or my mother would bring relief. When at last she came, I found her almost as ill-off as myself. We were both detained till you arrived.' To this excuse, which is a very lame one for a person who had a phaeton to sell or pledge, any one who feels a spark of generosity in his bosom would reply, 'Why, then, wretch, having from necessity or choice laid yourself under such a load of obligations, do you become the calumniator of your benefactress? Are you yet to learn what is due to the rites of hospitality, or have you, at the early age of nineteen, been taught to combine profound hypocrisy with deadly hate and assume the mask of love that you may more surely plant the assassin's dagger? Where did you learn these horrible lessons?' This last, Sir, would have been a dangerous question on your part. He might have replied and may yet reply, 'Uncle, I learned this from you.'

But, to return to the wonderful circumstance that this young man had not met my eyes above once a month, though he saw me frequently every day. That he met them seldomer than I wished is true. I was sorry to observe what others had remarked, that he rarely looked any one in the face. I excused this sinister air to myself, and tried to excuse it to others as a proof of uncommon modesty, of which nevertheless he gave no other proof. I sometimes succeeded in my endeavors to make people believe that this gloomy, guilty look proceeded from bashfulness. I know not, and shall not pretend to guess, what heavy matter pressed on his conscience; perhaps it was only the disposition to be criminal. At present [now] that he has an opportunity (with your assistance) to gratify that disposition, he will, I presume, be less capable of assuming the air of an honest man [and] he will probably find himself frequently on leaving good company in condition to repeat the same sentence of self-condemnation: 'Uncle, I have not met their eyes three times since I have been in the house.'

You make him say, 'my first impression as far back as I can remember is that she was an unchaste woman—my brother knew her better than I—she never could do anything with him'—This too is admirable testimony to support your filthy accusations.

Pray, Mr. John Randolph of Roanoke, why did you not inform your audience that, when you turned me out of doors, this Mr. Tudor Randolph was but nine years old, and his brother, poor deaf and dumb Saint George, just thirteen— Can it be necessary to add to your confusion by a single remark? It seems to me, if any one present at your wild declamation, had noticed this fact, you would have been hissed even by a sisterhood of old maids. Unluckily for you, I have letters from poor Saint George, one of which, written shortly before his late malady, is filled with assurances of attachment. In that which I received, while I was in Washington, he makes particular and affectionate inquiries respecting Col. [Monroe's] family. These show that he does not participate in your ingratitude, but feels as he ought the kindness of that gentleman, who, at your instance, took him into his family in London and watched over him with parental care. You repay this favor by slanders which I have the charity to believe you are too polite to pronounce in the Col's presence. I have a letter from my sister telling me the pleasure St. George manifested at the present of my portrait I made him. I have a letter also from her, shortly after her house was burnt, in which she tells me among the few things saved she was rejoiced to find my portrait which you brought out with your own. By this act, you have some right to it, and, should my present ill health lead me shortly to the grave, you may hang it up in your castle at Roanoke next to the Englishman's scalp—a trophy of the family prowess. I observe, Sir, in the course of your letter allusion to one of Shakespeare's best tragedies. I trust you are by this time convinced that you have clumsily performed the part of 'honest Iago.' Happily for my life, and for my husband's peace, you did not find in him a headlong, rash Othello. For a full and proper description of what you have written and spoken on this occasion, I refer you to the same admirable author. He will tell you it is a tale told by an idiot, full of sound and fury, signifying nothing.

ANN C. MORRIS.

Book V

DEMOCRACY AND TRADE TRIUMPHANT

CHAPTER XXIII

JOHN BERNARD MEETS THE YANKEE PEDDLER

THE FEDERALISTS fell from power. The republicans under Jefferson and his successors inaugurated a new simplicity in government which matched the temper of a swiftly expanding democracy. The west and southwest opened themselves more widely to emigration and settlement, and the purchase of Louisiana enormously extended the national boundaries, which by the treaty of 1783 already reached as far as the Mississippi. Another war with England, the War of 1812, confirmed the United States in its own confidence. From every section of the country, new as well as old, came signs of a time triumphant for democracy and the self-made American, bred in no tradition but grasping at circumstance in order to mold it into the forms of new and picturesque careers.

Up in New England the Yankee flourished on shrewd virtues which won the contempt—or the envy—of other sections. John Bernard, an English actor who trouped with signal success through the States in the early years of the nineteenth century, has left an unsurpassed portrait of the New England gentlemen of trade, the Yankee peddler.

THE Yankee is the Yorkshireman of America; the same cunning, calculating, persevering personage, with an infusion of Scotch hardiness and love of wandering. Like him, he goes upon the principle that all men are rogues, and like him he is instanced by his customers as the best illustration of the doctrine. He has the same talent for expedients; the same keen eye to character and to expedite a sale; the same want of nicety in regard to means, so long as they are not legally offensive (going to jail he considers not so much a disgrace as a waste of time), so that it would be just as appropriate to call the refined gentry and enlightened manufacturers of the County of York "regular Yorkshiremen," as to cite any man who moves in the respectable circle of Boston as "a regular Yankee."

This curious class of mammalia, the "Down-Easter" as it is often called, is divisible into three species—the swapper, the jobber, and the peddler, all agreeing in one grand characteristic—love of prey—

but varying in many striking particulars. The swapper claims precedence in point of antiquity, his character and name being a direct importation from Yorkshire. The word to "swap," meaning to exchange, is still current there and possesses a high historic interest, some local historians having proved, I believe, that it was this peculiarity in the Northern Saxons which for so many years drove the hordes of inv ders to the South. The swapper is the only division of the tribe that may be called stationary, though he is not more peculiar in this respect than in the mode he adopts to make a fortune. He thinks neither of buying, nor selling, nor growing, nor manufacturing; the key to his El Dorado is—exchange. With most this practice is a passion, with many a disease; some are inoculated with the virus, but the majority have it in the natural way, and it has then all the precocity of genius, with the tenacity of faith. It shows itself in childhood, when the infant swaps its milk for marbles; and at school, when the boy swaps everything but floggings. As his possessions increase he puts all he owns into a state of transition; house, land, and cattle are drawn into the whirlpool; even coat, hat, and boots. He soon loves swapping for its own sake; the means becomes the end; the mere act and business of exchanging seems essential to his existence. If now analyzed the feeling would be found pure; if it is no love of lucre, it is much less envy of his fellow-creatures' possessions; it is neither desire of profit nor of accumulation; it is simply the love of novelty.

I made these discoveries principally during my residence at a country-box near Boston, where my nearest neighbor was a specimen of this class, in the last stage of the disorder. Every morning that he heard I was at home he was sure to pay me a visit in order, as he termed it, to "make a trade." Whatever object his eye rolled upon it roused "that one dear thought"—to barter; my plow for his cart, my horse for his cow, or my dog for his cat. If I proved obdurate to the advantages proposed on one point, he attacked me on another. Not an inch of my property but suggested some article of exchange on his own premises. Would I swap my peaches for plums? my carrots for cabbages? I verily believe, had I not agreed to gratify him on some occasions, he would have proposed to swap the rats in our barns, or the snails in our orchards. At times I endeavored to soften my refusal by inviting him to dinner, but the mania still clung to him as his real hunger and thirst. On pouring out some brandy he remembered that he had a keg at home, he should like to trade away; and the sight of my mutton suggested the idea of a score of sheep which he would make over to me for two oxen.

The appearance of my friend was in strict keeping with his ruling propensity. His dress was constantly undergoing mutations in which the variety of colors and textures precluded the monotonous impression of a suit. He was half nankeen one day, half leather the next. Every market morning furnished some novelty, particularly in his hats, which were enthroned and deposed with all the despatch of Grand Turks.

The second species of "Down-Easter," a jobber, is a man of genius, mechanical it may be, but still a genius. He has probably been taught a trade, shoemaking for instance, which, being conducive to reflection, leads him into a view of the varied wants of man from the foot upwards, from the bed he requires to rest upon, to the roof that must cover him. All arts agree in requiring certain qualities, such as solidity, convenience, proportion, and durability, whence it is obvious if a man thoroughly understands the craft of shoemaking (to say nothing of its philosophy, the giving neatness to an ugly foot, which will restore enjoyment to a sensitive mind), he has a guide and handmaid to the sister arts, a pass-key to the cells of mechanism, in whose works practice will give proficiency. Thus he superadds to his original vocation carpentry, cabinet and coffin making, bricklaying, and farriery; and as soon as his mind is sufficiently stored he collects his tools (for knowledge, with him, is action), crams them into a basket, and strides off to the Western States, where in every new-formed settlement he proves a welcome visitor, supplying to each house that slight assistance which their comfort may require. Joking apart, there is not a doubt that this class of men are among the most useful in the Union. They unite to a rough expertness, in all they undertake, the temperance and industry demanded by the state of things about them, and virtue, in this case, meets with its reward. The man that can turn his hand to anything, generally turns everything into his hand; his leather pouch soon exhibits the appearance of a tumor, till he is at length enabled to eschew vagrancy, buy a plot of ground, and build a shop in some fast-rising settlement, which he opens in "the general line"; when, as the increasing wants of the community call for the introduction of regular trades, they also introduce customers to consume his cheese and bacon.

A jobber is generally a red-faced, yellow-haired man, with light-blue eyes and a capacious mouth, dressed in a nankeen suit which was made for him when a lad, and from whose expressive restrictions his republican frame is now freeing itself at back, elbows, and waistband.

But the grand division of the tribe is the New England peddler, who, unlike the last described, has no inventive ingenuity, save in the art of puffing, and still less like the first, not the slightest taste for swapping. He considers his own goods so much superior to his customers' that nothing but hard cash can represent their value. To buy cheap and sell high comprehends for him the whole cycle of human knowledge; the supreme excellence of north-country stuffs is his religion; and science has taught him to believe that the world itself would not go round but to the tick of a New England clock. The same spirit which carried his ancestors into the backwoods with their train of teams and children sends him every spring on a voyage of discovery to the South. This visit is regarded by the Southern trader in the light of a visitation; he may be truly said to have Yankee-phobia, and to look upon a "Connecticut chap" as a commercial Scythian, a Tartar of the North whose sole business in life is to make inroads on his peace and profit. He ranks him in the list of plagues next to the yellow fever, and before locusts, taxation, and a wet spring; indeed, some go so far as to suppose that a shower of Yankees was the crowning pestilence which made Pharaoh give up the Israelites.

The panic they occasion is not more from a terror of their cleverness than of their singularly indomitable spirit. There is no getting rid of them. None of the usual similes of a burr, or sticking-plaster, give any idea of a peddler's tenacity; he has the grip of a crab with the suction of a mosquito; you can't deny, you can't insult, you can't fatigue him; you can only dismiss him by a purchase. Such a character must be particularly obnoxious to an indolent and relaxed community. A tornado could not create greater havoc in the ease and enjoyment of a Carolinian evening than the buzzing and humming of such a wasp. In some places his mere appearance is the sounding of a tocsin to bar doors and windows, while many even double lock drawers, to prevent a conjuration over the counter by which the money seems to leap out of the till into the peddler's pocket. It may be amusing to pause for an instant on such a scene.

Suppose a village in one of the rich Virginia or Carolinian valleys, clustering round a road that climbs up a hill so almost perpendicular that it seems to realize the idea of Jacob's ladder. From the gate of the planter's lawn run, or, rather, stagger off, the sheds of the butcher, the baker, and the blacksmith, terminated by that arena for cock-fighting and politics, a tavern. About sunset labor has ceased and the inhabitants are leaning or lying out of their doors, the cows are wandering home, the children are playing about, and the "niggers" are laughing loud in the distant sugar-houses. In this sweet hour of calm all hearts are disposed to indulge in Christian emotions. Look at the group and you'd take them for a colony of Moravians, with all enemies pardoned and all cares forgotten; when suddenly a pedestrian is seen wending down the hill, his legs, in the slanting sunbeams, sending their shadows half a mile before him. By this length of staff he might be taken for a pilgrim, but the sprawl of his walk awakens anything but sacred associations. Gradually his hull looms into distinctness, they perceive he is a long-backed man, with a crouching head and loaded shoulders; suspicions are excited; and at length one who may have suffered more than the rest, perhaps, from the endemic, recognizes its symptoms and exclaims, "I'll be shot if it ain't a Yankee!" At these words if there is not a general rout, or springing up, and banging-to of doors, it must be because their faculties are prostrated by the surprise, and they lie spellbound, as cattle are said to do on the approach of the anaconda. As the enemy advances at a swinging pace among them, his keen gray eye rolling round in selection of a victim, they remember the strange man who first found out their quiet hiding-place, and the wonder and contempt this curious species of fellow-creature at first excited—a fellow who would neither drink, bet, nor talk politics, but kept prying into holes and corners to prove the extent of their needs, and who ultimately walked away with all the silver of the settlement. Whatever may have been their former experience, one of the number is a doomed man. If he doesn't want a clock which ticks loud enough to scare away the rats, or a razor so keen that if you but strop it overnight and put it under your pillow you'll wake up clean shaved in the morning, yet—"Sure alive, missis wants a new cap," and he's got a small stock, "jest such as the squires' wives wear at the camp-meetin's"; or, "The young gals need some gowns," and he has "all kinds of cotton that are all the better for bein' turned—for the inside gets fresh as t'other's wearin' out."

The "Down-Easter's" system of attacking a stubborn antagonist displays great generalship. He begins by resting his pack upon the half-hatch of the door; its numerous contents presently require a field of display; nowhere so fitting as on the counter within, if it be a shop; he begs leave but to show them; "Look at them, mister, they won't sting you." The outworks once carried, his shot (caps and combs, "hankychers," etc.) fly about in all directions and take deadly effect on some of the family. By a singular fatality everything that is tried on seems to be made expressly for the wearer; she never looked so well in anything before. And equally strange is the discovery that, up to that moment, they had been living without a solitary convenience. Every one but the father perceives the necessity of Sally having a pair of shoes, Enoch a jack-knife, and the parlor a timepiece. From the shop Jonathan fights his way into the backroom, and there his victim, driven into a corner, is beaten into an acknowledgment of his wants and deficiencies, and the capitulation that ensues is a discussion of their number and the expense of supplying them. When the campaign is over in one house he proceeds to another, and so on to all in succession, till he arrives at the tavern, where he usually succeeds in trading the landlord out of bed and breakfast.

Smarting under this infliction, it can be no wonder that the Virginians indulge in occasional vituperations, insist that the Yankee cheats them in every transaction, and that, however he may vary his commodities from the traditionary wooden nutmegs and red-flannel sausages, swindling is still his talent, his stimulus, and local distinction. In proof of this they point to the fact that there are no Jews in New England, the competition being too great for them to exist.

CHAPTER XXIV

THE SPEECH and spirit of democracy had still to invade the capital at Washington. They seemed to do so on March 4, 1829, when Andrew Jackson, "Old Hickory," "The People's Champion," the hero of New Orleans, and a seasoned politician from Tennessee beyond the mountains, walked bareheaded to the capital and before an enormous crowd received the oath of presidency from John Marshall. The reception which he gave at the White House following this ceremony was a riot; the rabble pressed upon him, broke dishes and tables, pushed forward to grasp his hand. Democracy had mounted the throne.

Yet its reign was a stormy one, and Jackson, master of politics, was called upon to master many gales—not the least of which was that which blew through Washington society when he appointed Major Eaton Secretary of War. The trouble was over Mrs. Eaton, whom that society could not accept. Jackson's defense of Mrs. Eaton has been described at length by Martin Van Buren, another member of the new Cabinet, and later president himself.

THE Eaton-imbroglio, though in no proper sense political, exerted perhaps a more injurious influence upon the management of public affairs than could be ascribed to any of the disturbing questions of the excited period of which I write. Breaking out at the very commencement of the administration, kept alive by feelings of the bitterest character and soon directed to the accomplishment of political as well as personal objects it maintained for two years a foothold at the seat of the Federal Government, a plague to social intercourse, destructive in many instances of private friendship, deranging public business and for a season, at least, disparaging the character of the Government. Except perhaps the disreputable scenes that were witnessed in England, occasioned by the quarrel between George IV and his unfortunate Queen, there has not been seen in modern times so relentless and so reckless a foray upon all those interests as that to which I refer.

The dissatisfaction caused by Gen. Jackson's Cabinet arrangements was not confined to a particular class, neither was it in all cases, occasioned by precisely the same causes. Major Eaton was the son of a highly respectable lady of Tennessee, a widow at the time of which I write, much esteemed by Gen. Jackson, and her son also had strongly ingratiated himself in his regard and was the author, I think, of the first formal history of the General's life. Major Lewis, Eaton's brother-in-law, had long been an intimate personal friend of the General, came with him to Washington and was for many years an inmate of his family. The cast of the Cabinet carried a suspicion to the minds of many of General Jackson's Tennessee friends, including a majority of the representatives of that State in Congress, that Eaton and Lewis had exerted a preponderating influence in its construction. Their *amor proprius* was offended by this as they thought it evinced an undeserved preference, and jealousies and enmities accordingly sprang up among his supporters in Tennessee many of which were never healed. Major Donelson, a nephew of Mrs. Jackson, whose wife was also her neice, and who had been from his infancy a member of the General's family—a man moreover of much more ability than he had credit for—partook largely of this feeling. The seeds of dissatisfaction with and opposition to the first act of the President were thus extensively and deeply sown not only in his own State but in his immediate household.

The hostile feelings towards the new Cabinet, at its start, entertained by these branches of malcontents were, in variously modified forms, extended to the President himself and, in the sequel, especially to the individual whose advancement was supposed—how correctly will be hereafter seen—to have been the main object in its formation. It was not long before they found vent and through the same channel. Major Eaton, the new Secretary of War, had married a young widow of much beauty and considerable smartness in respect to whose relations with himself before marriage, and whilst she was the wife of another, there had been unfavorable reports. A question was on that account raised as to her fitness for the social position otherwise due to the wife of a member of the Cabinet, her unworthiness alleged, with various degrees of publicity, and her exclusion from fashionable society insisted on. The President, whilst willing and at all times avowedly ready to open the door to the severest scrutiny as to the facts, but confiding in her innocence with a sincerity that no man doubted, resented these doings, with the spirit and resolution natural to him on all occasions, but especially when feeling called upon to defend his friends. An issue was in this way and thus early formed between him and respectable, numerous and very powerful portions of his supporters which, independently of any question as to the wisdom, justice, or propriety of the ground assumed on either side, could not possibly fail to generate ill-will and speedily to sever the amicable relations which had until that time existed between them.

Congress was fortunately upon the eve of its adjournment when this struggle commenced, and the President, the new Cabinet, the officers of Government and the good people of Washington, or, perhaps more correctly speaking, the fashionable society of Washington, with temporary visitors to the seat of Government,—not an inconsiderable number at the commencement of a new administration— were the principal persons, before whom and by whom the question of Mrs. Eaton's eligibility was in the first instance discussed and acted upon. Reaching Washington some two months after the controversy had commenced, and my appointment having in no degree contributed to its occurrence, I was entirely uncommitted on my arrival, but finding the traces of the feud too plain not to be intelligible, in walks which it was my duty to frequent, and too disturbing in their character to be disregarded, I felt the necessity of deciding upon the course I ought to take in respect to it without unnecessary delay. After looking at the matter in every aspect in which I thought it deserved to be considered I decided, for reasons not now necessary to assign, to make no distinction in my demeanor towards, or in my intercourse with the families of the gentlemen whom the President had, with the approbation of the Senate, selected as my Cabinet associates, but to treat all with respect and kindness and not to allow myself, by my own acts, to be mixed up in such a quarrel.

The female members of the President's family were Mrs. Donelson, the wife of his private Secretary, and her cousin, Miss Easton, both nieces of Mrs. Jackson and both excellent and highly esteemed ladies. Unaffected and graceful in manners, amiable and purely feminine in disposition and character, and bright and self-possessed in conversation, they were fair representatives of the ladies of Kentucky and Tennessee. On an occasion when the name of Mrs. Eaton was accidentally and harmlessly introduced, and which was shortly after my interview above described, Mrs. Donelson, in the presence of her cousin, expressed her surprise that whilst almost every tongue in the city was canvassing that lady's merits and demerits she had never heard me say anything upon the subject, a remark the tone of which rather than the substance conveyed, though gently, a complaint of my reserve. I was under an engagement which called me away and had only time to assure her that my silence had not arisen from an unwillingness to talk with them upon the subject and that with her permission I would do so upon the first favorable occasion.

She took me at my word and we fixed the time when I was to call upon them for that purpose. When we met I was happy to be immediately relieved from the embarrassment that seemed inseparable from the parties to and the nature of our discussion, by a statement from Mrs. Donelson of the grounds on which she justified the course she was pursuing, which was a marked one and decidedly adverse to the lady in question. She spoke of her as possessing a bad temper and a meddlesome disposition and said that the latter had been so much increased by her husband's elevation as to make her society too disagreeable to be endured. She did not allude to any rumored imputations upon her fame; she might not have believed them, she might have omitted to notice them from motives of delicacy, or she might have thought allusion to them unnecessary on account of the sufficiency of those which she frankly acknowledged. Whether influenced by the one or the other motive I had no desire to inquire but took the matter up on the grounds on which she had placed it. For the sake of the discussion only, I agreed, after a moment's reflection, to admit that she was right in her views of Mrs. Eaton's character and disposition and proceeded to impress upon her that although her reasons would excuse her from cultivating a close intimacy with that lady they neither required nor would justify her, having regard to her position as the female head of her Uncle's family, to decline her society to the extent to which she had gone, and to caution her against being controlled in her course by persons whom she esteemed, and who were entitled to her respect and regard, but whose opinions upon that particular subject as I thought—indeed, as I was certain—were unduly influenced. It is unnecessary to recapitulate my arguments; they were, in some respects, to her at least, of a more serious character than any that she had previously allowed to be taken into her consideration; they related to the situation of her Uncle, whom she dearly loved, to the difficulties he had to contend with in the performance of his public duties, to the value he placed upon the peace and harmony of his family and the misery he suffered in seeing them destroyed by an affair in respect to which she certainly knew that he acted a sincere part, and to the extent to which her course sanctioned imputations of a graver character both upon the lady in question and upon himself for sustaining her, which were used by his enemies to injure him; &c. &c. Before I had concluded Miss Easton who had sought to hide her emotions by gradually withdrawing herself from sight in the embrasure of the window, sobbed aloud, and I perceived that Mrs. Donelson besides being deeply agitated was also offended by my allusions to the probability that she had been unduly influenced by others upon such a subject. I rose from my seat, begging her to excuse whatever I might, under the excitement of the moment, have said to hurt her feelings, but perfectly satisfied that they were too far committed to be reached by anything I could urge, and I asked her permission to drop the subject. To this she assented, acknowledging that she had been momentarily ruffled by some of my remarks but assuring me that she was not offended with me.

The nature of the personal feelings which the state of things I have described was calculated to engender among those connected with the Government and residing at Washington may be easily inferred. All were more or less affected by it and it was under its adverse influences that we worked through the spring, summer and the first months of the autumn. Those feelings grew every day more and more bitter because they were to a great degree smothered as no opportunity was presented for their open indulgence on the part of the leading officials. The entertainment given to the Diplomatic Corps in the spring was a dinner party of gentlemen only and passed off without embarrassment. A Cabinet dinner, to which the ladies of the families of the members who composed it would have to be invited was not even spoken of in my hearing before the month of November. That subject was then introduced by the President in one of our rides, which, when the weather permitted, were almost of daily occurrence and gradually lengthened as presenting the best opportunities for consultation left to us by the press of visitors and other preoccupations. He had, he said, been led to postpone his Cabinet dinners to so late a period by an undefined apprehension that the violent feelings of the members on both sides of the social problem out of which our difficulties had arisen, and of which he had not been suffered to remain ignorant, might lead to unavoidable acts on his part with which he thought it would be more difficult for an Administration to deal in its infancy, than after it had been some time under way and been allowed opportunities to advance itself in the favor of the people. Public business, he remarked, must always be attended to when the occasion for its performance arises, but with matters of ceremony, like that under consideration, he thought a greater latitude was allowable. As the session of Congress was, however, near at hand, when this matter should not rest undisposed of he thought the sooner it was entered upon the better.

I had entertained similar apprehensions and had therefore omitted to allude to the subject in our familiar conversations—embracing, from time to time, almost every other subject. But I never expected an outbreak upon the President's invitation, believing rather that the public explanations of the stand which I did not doubt was contemplated by a portion of the Cabinet would be reserved for mine, which would naturally follow. I expressed that opinion to him with much confidence and it was decided that his invitations should be forthwith sent out.

There were no absentees at the President's Cabinet dinner, and no very marked exhibitions of bad feeling in any quarter, but there were nevertheless sufficient indications of its existence to destroy the festive character of the occasion and to make it transparently a formal and hollow ceremony. The President escorted the wife of the Secretary of the Treasury to the table and I gave my arm to Mrs. Donelson. The disposition of the others I have forgotten, but I well remember the care with which the arrangement of the parties was made. The general was, as usual, courteous and affable although suffering much from bad health and more from mortification at what was passing before his eyes. My young friend and partner for the entertainment summoned up spirits enough to call my attention, chiefly by glances, to the signs of the hour and following the movements of our host, we left the table with the ladies after which the company dispersed sooner than usual. I had intended to spend a few moments with the President after they were gone but soon perceived that the return he had received for all his sacrifices of old friendships and his unhesitating confrontal of enemies in the formation of the Cabinet which had just left him had overcome his feelings, and commending him to his pillow I also took my leave.

The display I had witnessed would have been sufficient to put me on my guard in respect to my own contemplated entertainment if that had been needed. But without such warning I understood too well the motives which pointed to that occasion as one best adapted for a kind of semi-official notification of the rule by which some of my associates intended to be governed, to fail of circumspection in my movements. That they would decline my invitation I had no doubt, but whether in so doing, they would only assert and exercise their own rights without offense to me, or whether they would go farther could only be known by the sequel. It was my business to be prepared for either contingency.

According to the established forms of society in Washington it would have been my office as host to give the highest position and the most marked attention to the wife of the Secretary of the Treasury, if no ladies were present except those of members of the Cabinet. Mrs. Ingham was an excellent and estimable person, but excitable and especially stirred up upon the vexed question which agitated the official and social circles of the Federal Capital. I was entirely willing to pay all the honors due to herself and to her position. [I was nevertheless quite confident that she would decline, and I was not disposed to make the vacancy occasioned by that event conspicuous by filling it with a lady of inferior rank.] But Mrs. Randolph, the widow of Gov. Thomas Mann Randolph, of Virginia, and the only surviving child of President Jefferson, in all respects one of the worthiest women of America, was then residing at Washington, a lady with whom and with her family consisting of an unmarried daughter and of Mr. and Mrs. N. P. Trist, the latter also her daughter, my relations were cordial and intimate. I waited upon her in person, informed her of my intention to invite the Cabinet to dine with me and of my desire to combine with that official ceremony an act of respect towards her which had been already too long delayed and requested her to name the day if she was willing to do me the honor to attend.

She cheerfully agreed to my proposition, the day was fixed and the invitation extended to all the members of her family. I need scarcely say, at least to those acquainted with the ways of Washington, that it would have been quite impossible to prevent this proceeding on my part from becoming known without any agency of hers to the other invited guests who were thus apprised of my intention to give the precedence to Mrs. Randolph. As my dinner party was to be what in common parlance is called a ladies' dinner I was desirous that there should be no lack of ladies and anticipating further declensions I invited several military gentlemen and their wives, who all attended. I was obliged to omit my highly esteemed and amiable friend the Commander in Chief, because Mrs. M. (who was his second wife) had made herself—more to his amusement than annyoance, for he took such things lightly—a conspicuous party to the war which raged around us; but I remember well the presence of the veterans, Hull and Chauncey and of Commodore Warrington and of the wives of all three who were among the most agreeable as they were also the leading members of the society of Washington.

Mr. Branch writes that he "will avail himself of the honor of dining with Mr. Van Buren" on &c. but that he is requested to say in behalf of Mrs. Branch and the young ladies that "circumstances unnecessary to detail will deprive them of the pleasure," &c. Mr. Berrien presents his respects but pleads a "conditional engagement to leave the city" for his own declension and "her state of health" for that of his daughter. According to the best of my recollection Mr. Ingham accepted for himself, and Mrs. Ingham certainly declined. The other two members of the Cabinet, Major Eaton and Mr. Barry, brought apologies from their wives, who were faithful allies and who it appeared had also resolved to remain behind their batteries. Thus it resulted that at the second Cabinet dinner of the season to which all the ladies of the family of its members were invited not one of them "assisted", and the party being freed from any kind of embarrassment their joy was unconfined. Mrs. Randolph especially manifested the greatest gratification to the satisfaction of all my guests who reverenced her almost as much as I did; to come quite up to that mark required a more intimate knowledge of her admirable qualities than they had enjoyed opportunities to acquire.

Determined to go through with the matter in hand, so far as I was myself concerned, and to have done with it, I sent out invitations shortly after my Cabinet dinner and after Congress had assembled, for a large evening party. With some modifications my official associates held to their previous course, and to add fuel to the flame a communication appeared in the *Washington Journal* newspaper, over the signature of "Tarquin," (!) charging me with an attempt, in conjunction with Sir Charles Vaughan, the British Minister, to force a person upon the society of Washington who was not entitled to its privileges and calling upon those who had been invited to resent the outrage by refusing to be present. The circles of Washington however quite naturally declined to be instructed in the proprieties and moralities of social intercourse by a "Tarquin" and no party of the season was attended more numerously or enjoyed more hilariously.

Suffering at the time from ill-health and much exhausted by the reception I availed myself of the moment when the attention of my guests was attracted by the commencement of dancing to retire to a sofa in a lower room for rest. I had not been there long before a friend entered and said, in a jocular tone, "Are you here, Sir!—You ought to be above if you wish to prevent a fight!" and answered my look of inquiry by the information that Mrs. Eaton and Mrs. M. had jostled each other, doubtless accidentally, in the crowd, and that the collision had provoked manifestations of mutual resentment sufficiently marked to attract attention and to excite general remark. I received his story as a jest, which it probably was in a measure, and begged him to see fair play in my behalf and to leave me to my repose.

I have described more particularly than they would appear to deserve these two entertainments, but for a brief season they obtained much consequence as incidents of a campaign in which social, political and personal feuds were so mixed up that all of them were more or less affected by every movement, and the gossips had looked forward to the arrangement of my parties as the occasion and the field for a general engagement. When they were over it was found that they had not materially contributed to the development of hostilities, and I confess that I experienced all the complacency naturally inspired by the consciousness of having passed unscathed through an ordeal as difficult and as severe as could be devised by a conspiracy of excited women and infuriated partisans. But the outbreak was not long delayed. At a ball given by the Russian Minister, Baron Krudener, in the absence of Mrs. Ingham, led Mrs. Eaton to supper, as ranking next to her, and Madame Huygens, the wife of the Dutch Envoy, was assigned to the Secretary of War. Madame Huygens was reported to have been highly offended by the arrangement and to have declared that she would retaliate by giving a party to which Mrs. Eaton should not be invited and that her example would be followed by Messrs. Ingham, Branch and Berrien. Major Eaton was a man of moderate intellectual capacities, but justly distinguished for the kindness, generosity and unobtrusiveness of his disposition and demeanor. If he had done the wrong before his marriage which was imputed to him, as to which I knew and sought to know nothing, he had also done all that a man could do to remedy the evil and there was no reason even to suspect that the life of the lady after marriage was not, in that respect at least, free from reproach. A reverend gentleman had indeed carried rumors to the President to the effect that her conduct had been exceptionable on a visit to the Northern cities. The General insisted that his informer should go immediately and sift the stories thoroughly, assuring him that if his report sustained them by reliable facts no one would have reason to complain of his own course in the matter. The mission was accepted, the Cabinet, except Major Eaton, was called together in the evening to hear the report but it was found to amount to nothing.

A man of the temperament I have ascribed to Eaton was likely, under any circumstances, to have warm and sympathizing friends. The number in his case, was of course greatly increased by the patronage at his disposal and by the favor with which he was regarded by the President. These pressed upon the latter the Major's grievances with much earnestness and their appeals found favorable responses in his own breast. The alleged threat of Madame Huygens and the three parties which certainly followed—whether she actually threatened them or not—supplied ample and stirring materials for such complaints. The President sent for me at an early hour one morning and I went to him before breakfast. I found him deeply moved by communications that had been made to him on the previous evening. His eyes were blood-shot and his appearance in other respects indicated that he had passed a sleepless night, as he indeed admitted had been literally the case. He was however unexcited in manner. The stories so often told of his violent and furious style on occasions of great anger or deep feeling, so far as my observation extended, had no other foundation than this that when he thought he could in that way best influence anybody to do his duty—of which I have given some instances and shall give others —he would assume an earnestness and an emphasis much beyond what he really felt. To me he always appeared most calm when he felt most intensely. On the occasion of his very narrow escape from assassination, at the funeral of Warren R. Davis, I followed him to the White House, immediately after the rites of burial were concluded, and found him sitting with one of Major Donelson's children on his lap and conversing with General Scott, himself apparently the least disturbed person in the room.

He presented, with deliberation and clearness, the reasons which led him to regard the proceedings to which I have referred as an attack upon himself designed to be made effectual through a combination between members of his Cabinet and the wife of one of the Foreign Ministers, and stated, in the same manner, the course which he thought it would become him to pursue, which was—if his views should prove to be well founded to dismiss his own Ministers and to send Mr. Huygens his passports.

His immediate object was to attend to the latter, and to that end he had sent for me to obtain my counsel and coöperation. My personal relations with Chevalier and Madame Huygens were of a friendly and indeed intimate character. I had no reason to doubt that she felt hurt as was represented, by the occurrences at Baron Krudener's, but deemed it quite unlikely that she would have given expression to her feelings in the way which had been reported to the President. If, however, the information of the latter was correct, I could not for a moment doubt the propriety of the course he suggested, in that direction, and declared this opinion to him without hesitation.

As soon as I reached my office I informed Chevalier Huygens by note that I desired to see him on business, and that as it would also be necessary to communicate with Madame Huygens I would call at his house at a named hour. For reasons, not necessary to be stated, they anticipated the object of my visit and received me with their usual kindness. After declining their invitation to the pipe and schiedam, notwithstanding the appropriateness of these preliminaries to a Dutch negotiation, I stated explicitly that the President disclaimed all right or desire to meddle with their social relations or with the question of whom they invited or whom they omitted to invite to their houses, but that declarations had been attributed to Madame Huygens and communicated to the President which went beyond the exercise of the rights which belonged to them, and I described the impressions which the possibility of the correctness of his information had made upon his mind. Madame Huygens assured me solemnly that she had never used the expressions attributed to her or any of similar import—that she had been too long connected with diplomatic life, and understood too well what belonged to her position, to meddle in such matters and that she had only pursued the path I conceded to her without advising with others or troubling herself about their course. The Chevalier united earnestly in the views she expressed, and avowed his conviction of the accuracy of her recollections, and my mission was thus satisfactorily concluded. As we had no desire to pursue the inquiry further I reported the result to the President who received the information with unaffected pleasure for he sympathized heartily with the respect and regard I entertained for the Dutch Minister and his estimable family.

CHAPTER XXV

HALF A dozen years later, while Jackson still was president, the most sublimely vulgar of all Americans was to commence a great career as showman, wizard of publicity, and genius of humbug. P. T. Barnum's "Autobiography" recalls some of the startling methods by which this prince of dollars conquered the American mind in the eighteen thirties, and by which he made himself master of the art of fooling fifteen million people.

THE least deserving of all my efforts in the show line was the one which introduced me to the business; a scheme in no sense of my own devising; one which had been some time before the public and which had so many vouchers for its genuineness that at the time of taking possession of it I honestly believed it to be genuine; something, too, which, as I have said, I did not seek, but which by accident came in my way and seemed almost to compel my agency— such was the "Joice Heth" exhibition which first brought me forward as a showman.

In the latter part of July, 1835, Mr. Coley Bartram, of Reading, Connecticut, called at our store. He was acquainted with Mr. Moody and myself. He informed us that he had owned an interest in an extraordinary negro woman, named Joice Heth, whom he believed to be one hundred and sixty-one years of age, and whom he also believed to have been the nurse of General Washington. He had sold out his interest to his partner, R. W. Lindsay, of Jefferson County, Kentucky, who was now exhibiting her in Philadelphia, but not having much tact as a showman, he was anxious to sell out and return home. Mr. Bartram also handed me a copy of *The Pennsylvania Inquirer,* of July 15, 1835, and directed my attention to the following advertisement, which I here transcribe *verbatim :*

CURIOSITY.—The citizens of Philadelphia and its vicinity have an opportunity of witnessing at the MASONIC HALL, one of the greatest natural curiosities ever witnessed, viz., JOICE HETH, a negress aged 161 years, who formerly belonged to the father of Gen. Washington. She has been a member of the Baptist Church one hundred and sixteen years, and can rehearse many hymns, and sing them according to former custom. She was born near the old Potomac River in

Virginia, and has for ninety or one hundred years lived in Paris, Kentucky, with the Bowling family.

All who have seen this extraordinary woman are satisfied of the truth of the account of her age. The evidence of the Bowling family, which is respectable, is strong, but the original bill of sale of Augustine Washington, in his own handwriting, and other evidence which the proprietor has in his possession, will satisfy even the most incredulous.

A lady will attend at the hall during the afternoon and evening for the accommodation of those ladies who may call.

The New York newspapers had already furnished descriptions of this wonderful personage, and becoming considerably excited upon the subject, I proceeded at once to Philadelphia and had an interview with Lindsay at the Masonic Hall. I was favorably struck with the appearance of the old woman. So far as outward indications were concerned, she might almost as well have been called a thousand years old as any other age. She was lying upon a high lounge in the middle of the room; her lower extremities were drawn up, with her knees elevated some two feet above the top of the lounge. She was apparently in good health and spirits, but former disease or old age, or perhaps both combined, had rendered her unable to change her position; in fact, although she could move one of her arms at will, her lower limbs were fixed in their position, and could not be straightened. She was totally blind, and her eyes were so deeply sunken in their sockets that the eyeballs seemed to have disappeared altogether. She had no teeth, but possessed a head of thick bushy gray hair. Her left arm lay across her breast, and she had no power to remove it. The fingers of her left hand were drawn down so as nearly to close it, and remained fixed and immovable. The nails upon that hand were about four inches in length, and extended above her wrist. The nails upon her large toes also had grown to the thickness of nearly a quarter of an inch.

She was very sociable, and would talk almost incessantly so long as visitors would converse with her. She sang a variety of ancient hymns, and was very garrulous when speaking of her protégé "dear little George," as she termed the great father of our country. She declared that she was present at his birth, that she was formerly the slave of Augustine Washington, the father of George, and that she was the first person who put clothes upon him. "In fact," said Joice, and it was a favorite expression of hers, "I raised him." She related many interesting anecdotes of "her dear little George," and this, mixed with her conversations upon religious subjects, for she claimed to be a member of the Baptist Church, rendered her exhibition an extremely interesting one.

I asked Mr. Lindsay for the proofs of her extraordinary age, and he exhibited what purported to be a bill of sale from Augustine Washington, of the county of Westmoreland, Virginia, to "Elizabeth Atwood," of "one negro woman, named Joice Heth, aged fifty-four years, for and in consideration of the sum of thirty-three pounds lawful money of Virginia." The document bore the date "fifth day of February, one thousand seven hundred and twenty-seven," and was "sealed and delivered in presence of Richard Buckner and William Washington."

The story told by Lindsay and "Aunt Joice" was, that Mrs. Elizabeth Atwood was a sister-in-law of Augustine Washington, that the husband of Joice was a slave of Mrs. Atwood, and for that reason the above sale was made. As Mrs. Atwood was a near neighbor of Mr. Washington, Aunt Joice was present at the birth of "little George," and she having long been the old family nurse, was the first person called upon to clothe the new-born infant.

The story seemed plausible, and the "bill of sale" had every appearance of antiquity. It was exhibited in a glass frame, was very sallow in appearance, and seemed to have been folded for such a great length of time that the folds were worn nearly through, and in some parts entirely so.

I inquired why the existence of such an extraordinary old woman had not been discovered and made known long ago. The reply was that she had been lying in an outhouse of John S. Bowling of Kentucky for many years, that no one knew or seemed to care how old she was, that she had been brought thither from Virginia a long time ago, and that the fact of her extreme age had been but recently brought to light by the discovery of this old bill of sale in the Record office in Virginia, by the son of Mr. Bowling, who, while looking over the ancient papers in that office, happened to notice the paper endorsed Joice Heth, that his curiosity was excited, and from inquiries made in that neighborhood he was convinced that the document applied to his father's old slave then living, and who was therefore really one hundred and sixty-one years of age; that he thereupon took the paper home, and became confirmed in regard to the identity of Joice with the slave described in that paper.

This whole account appeared to me satisfactory, and I inquired the price of the negress. Three thousand dollars was the sum named, but before leaving Philadelphia I received from Mr. Lindsay a writing, stipulating that I should have the right at any time within ten days to become her owner upon paying to him the sum of one thousand dollars.

With this paper I started for New York, determined if possible to purchase Joice Heth. I did not possess more than five hundred dollars in cash, but my glowing representations to a friend, of the golden harvest which I was sure the exhibition must produce, induced him to loan me the other five hundred dollars, and after a few days, during which time I sold my interest in the grocery store to my partner, Moody, I returned to Philadelphia with the money, and became the proprietor of the negress.

I engaged Lindsay to continue the exhibition in Philadelphia for a week, in order to allow me time to make the necessary arrangements for her reception in New York.

I applied to Mr. William Niblo, who, I believe, had seen the old negress in Philadelphia. He did not recognize me as the person who a few months previously had applied to him for the situation of bar-keeper. We soon made a bargain for the exhibition of Aunt Joice in one of the large apartments in his dwelling-house in the vicinity of his saloon, which was at that time a large, open and airy establishment where musical and light entertainments were given, the guests during the intermission, as well as at other times, being supplied with ice-cream and other refreshments, in little alcove-boxes fitted up with tables, and running nearly all the distance around his garden.

These alcoves were tastefully decorated on the outside with festoons of lamps of variegated colors, and the grand walk through the middle of the garden was illuminated on each side by chaste and pretty transparencies, about seven feet high and two feet wide, each surmounted with a large globular lamp. These transparencies were then new in the city of New York, and were very attractive. They were gotten up by W. J. and H. Hannington, who have since become so celebrated for glass-staining and decorative painting. Mr. H. Hannington prepared me several transparencies, two feet by three in size, which I had placed upon a hollow frame and lighted from the inside. It was painted in colors with white letters, and read:

JOICE HETH

161

YEARS OLD

The terms of my engagement with Mr. Niblo were these: He was to furnish the room and lights, pay the expense of printing, advertising, and a ticket-seller, and retain therefor one-half of the gross receipts. The result proved an average of about $1,500 per week.

I engaged as an assistant in exhibiting "Aunt Joice" Mr. Levi Lyman. He was a lawyer by profession, and had been practicing in Penn Yan, N. Y. He was a shrewd, sociable, and somewhat indolent

Yankee; possessed a good knowledge of human nature; was polite, agreeable, could converse on most subjects, and was admirably calculated to fill the position for which I engaged him.

Of course, in carrying out my new vocation of showman, I spared no reasonable efforts to make it successful. I was aware of the great power of the public press, and I used it to the extent of my ability. Lyman wrote a brief memoir of Joice, and putting it into a pamphlet form, illustrated with her portrait, sold it to visitors on his own account, at six cents per copy. I had the same portrait printed on innumerable small bills, and also flooded the city with "posters," setting forth the peculiar attraction which "the nurse of Washington" presented.

Our exhibition usually opened with a statement of the manner in which the age of Joice Heth was discovered, as well as the account of her antecedents in Virginia, and a reading of the bill of sale. We would then question her in relation to the birth and youth of General Washington, and she always gave satisfactory answers in every particular. Individuals among the audience would also frequently ask her questions, and put her to the severest cross-examinations, without ever finding her to deviate from what had every evidence of being a plain unvarnished statement of facts.

Later, I took Joice Heth on tour through New England. In Boston we opened our exhibition in the small ballroom of Concert Hall, at the corner of Court and Hanover streets. The fame of Joice had preceded her, the city was well posted with large bills announcing her coming, and the newspapers had heralded her anticipated arrival in such a multiplicity of styles, that the public curiosity was on tip-toe. I remember that one of the papers, after giving a description of Joice Heth, and the great satisfaction which her exhibition had given in New York, added, "It *rejoice-heth* us exceedingly to know that we shall be permitted to look upon the old patriarch."

The celebrated Maelzel was exhibiting his equally celebrated "automaton chess-player" in the large ballroom of Concert Hall; but the crowd of visitors to see Aunt Joice was so great that our room could not accommodate them, and Mr. Maelzel was induced to close his exhibition, and give us his large room. I had frequent interviews and long conversations with Mr. Maelzel. I looked upon him as the great father of caterers for public amusement, and was pleased with his assurance that I would certainly make a successful showman.

"I see," said he, in broken English, "that you understand the value of the press, and that is the great thing. Nothing helps the showman like the types and the ink. When your old woman dies," he added, "you come to me, and I will make your fortune. I will let you have my 'carousal,' my automaton trumpet-player, and many curious things which will make plenty of money." I thanked him for his generous proposals, and assured him that should circumstances render it feasible, I should apply to him.

Our exhibition room continued to attract large numbers of visitors for several weeks before there was any visible falling off. I kept up a constant succession of novel advertisements and unique notices in the newspapers, which tended to keep old Joice fresh in the minds of the public, and served to sharpen the curiosity of the people.

When the audiences began to decrease in numbers, a short communication appeared in one of the newspapers, signed *"A Visitor,"* in which the writer claimed to have made an important discovery. He stated that Joice Heth, as at present exhibited, was a humbug, whereas if the simple truth was told in regard to the exhibition, it was really vastly curious and interesting. "The fact is," said the communication, "Joice Heth is not a human being. What purports to be a remarkably old woman is simply a curiously constructed automaton, made up of whalebone, india-rubber, and numberless springs ingeniously put together, and made to move at the slightest touch, according to the will of the operator. The exhibitor is a ventriloquist, and all the conversations apparently held with the ancient lady are purely imaginary, so far as she is concerned, for the answers and incidents purporting to be given and related by her, are merely the ventriloquial voice of the exhibitor."

Maelzel's ingenious mechanism somewhat prepared the way for this announcement, and hundreds who had not visited Joice Heth were now anxious to see the curious automaton; while many who had seen her were equally desirous of a second look, in order to determine whether or not they had been deceived. The consequence was, our audiences again largely increased.

From Boston we went to Hingham, and thence in succession to Lowell, Worcester, Springfield, and Hartford, meeting with most satisfactory success. Everywhere there appeared to be conviction of the extreme longevity of Joice.

We hastened our return to New York to fill a second engagement I had made with Mr. Niblo. The American Institute held its annual Fair at his garden, and my engagement was to commence at the same time. The great influx of visitors to the Fair caused our room to be continually crowded, insomuch that we were frequently compelled to announce to applicants that the hall was full, and no more could be admitted for the present. In those cases we would hurry up the exhibition, cut short a hymn or two, answer questions with great rapidity, and politely open the front door as an egress to visitors, at the same time opening the entrance from the garden for the ingress of fresh customers.

From Niblo's we went to New Haven for three days, where the crowds were as large as usual. We then returned to New York and proceeded to Newark, where I met with the usual success. From Newark we returned to New York and went to Albany for one week to fill an engagement made with Mr. Meech, the proprietor of the Museum.

While exhibiting there, light evening entertainments were given in the theater of the Museum, one part of which consisted of remarkable feats of balancing, plate spinning, stilt walking, etc., by "Signor Antonio." The balancing and spinning of crockery was nearly or quite new in this country—to me it was entirely so. It was also as surprising as it was novel. The daring feats of Antonio upon stilts, his balancing guns with the bayonets resting on his nose, and various other performances which I had never seen before, attracted my attention. I inquired of Mr. Meech where Antonio came from. He informed me that he was an Italian—had sailed from England to Canada, whence he had proceeded to Albany, and had never exhibited in any other American city. Learning that Mr. Meech did not desire his services after that week, I sought an interview with Antonio, and in ten minutes engaged him to perform for me in any portion of the United States for one year from date, at the salary of $12 per week, besides board and traveling expenses. I did not know exactly where I should use my protégé, but I was certain that there was money in him, and thus I became interested in my second show.

Antonio, Joice Heth, Lyman and myself, left Albany for New York, stopping at the private boarding house in Frankfort street which I had taken the spring previous, but had sold out soon after engaging Aunt Joice. I left my two shows in Frankfort street while I went to join my wife and daughter, who were boarding with a Mr. Knapp, in Cherry street.

The first favor which I asked of Antonio was, that he should submit to be thoroughly washed—an operation to which he had apparently been a stranger for several years; and the second, that he should change his name. I did not think "Antonio" sufficiently "foreign," hence I named him Signor Vivalla, to both which propositions he consented. I immediately wrote a notice announcing the extraordinary qualities of Signor Vivalla, who had just arrived from

Italy, elaborately setting forth the wonders of his performances. This was published as an article of news in one of the city papers, and I forwarded a dozen copies to the several theatrical managers in New York, and elsewhere.

I first called upon William Dinneford, Esq., manager of the Franklin Theatre, but he declined engaging the "eminent Italian artist." He had seen so many performances of that kind which were vastly more extraordinary than anything which Vivalla could do, he would not think of engaging him.

"Now," says I, "Mr. Dinneford, I beg your pardon, but I must be permitted to say that you are mistaken. You have no doubt seen strange things in your life, but, my dear sir, I should never have imported Signor Vivalla from Italy, unless I had authentic evidence that he was the only artist of the kind who ever left that country." "What are your terms?" asked Dinneford, who (like many worthy young ladies, and many other republicans of the first water) was evidently beginning to melt under the magic influence of a foreign importation. "You shall have him one night for nothing," I replied. "If you like him after one trial, you shall have him the remainder of the week for fifty dollars—but, understand me, this is only that the public may be able to see what he is. After that, my terms are $50 per night."

My proposition for the one night was accepted. I invoked the powers of "printer's ink" and woodcuts for three days and nights previous to the first appearance of "the renowned and extraordinary Italian artist, Signor Vivalla," and they were potent for my purpose. The house was crammed. I marched upon the stage as a supernumerary to assist Vivalla in arranging his plates and other "crockery ware," to hand him the gun to fire when he had divested himself of one of his stilts, and was hopping across the stage on one stilt ten feet high, and to aid him in handling his muskets, etc. This was my "first appearance on any stage."

The applause which followed each of the Italian's feats was tremendous. It was such as only a Chatham or a Bowery audience could give. Manager Dinneford was delighted, and before we left the stage he engaged Vivalla for the week. At the termination of the performances Vivalla was called before the curtain, and as I did not consider it policy for him to be able to speak English (although he could do so very well, having traveled several years in England), I went out with him and addressed the audience in his name, thanking them for their generosity, and announcing him for the remainder of the week.

In the meantime I had opened the exhibition of Joice Heth in the large hall at the junction of the Bowery and Division street, but as I saw that Vivalla's prospects were bright, and that his success would depend in a great measure upon management, I left Lyman to exhibit Joice. After she had remained in that location for several weeks, he took her to several towns in Connecticut and elsewhere. Vivalla remained a second week at the Franklin Theater, for which I received $150—immediately after which, I realized the same sum for his services one week in Boston; and then we proceeded to Washington city to fulfill an engagement I had made with Wemyss, my profits depending on the receipts. The theater in Washington was a small out-of-the-way-place, and we opened, Jan. 16, 1836, to a house not exceeding $30. It was a hard beginning, for the stipulations required $50 more before I was entitled to a penny!

As this was my first visit to Washington I was much interested in visiting the capitol and other public buildings. I also satisfied my curiosity in seeing Clay, Calhoun, Benton, John Quincy Adams, Richard M. Johnson, Polk, and other leading statesmen of the time. I was also greatly gratified in calling upon Anne Royall, author of the Black Book, publisher of a little paper called "Paul Pry," and quite a celebrated personage in her day. I had exchanged *The Herald of Freedom* with her journal and she strongly sympathized with me in my persecutions. She was delighted to see me and although she was the most garrulous old woman I ever saw, I passed a very amusing and pleasant time with her. Before leaving her, I manifested my showman propensity by trying to hire her to give a dozen or more lectures on "Government" in the Atlantic cities, but I could not engage her at any price, although I am sure the speculation would have been a very profitable one. I never saw this eccentric woman again; she died at a very advanced age, October 1, 1854, at her residence in Washington.

There was incessant snow in Washington during Vivalla's engagement, and I was so unexpectedly a loser by the operation that I had not sufficient funds to return to Philadelphia. After much hesitation, and with a deep feeling of sadness and humiliation, I pawned my watch and chain for thirty-five dollars, promising to redeem it within a month. Fortunately, however, Mr. Wemyss arrived on Saturday morning, bringing with him Lucius Junius Booth and Miss Waring, afterwards Mrs. Sefton. Mr. Wemyss loaned me thirty-five dollars, and I redeemed my watch, paying a dollar for the use of the money a few hours.

Vivalla and myself proceeded to Philadelphia, and opened at the Walnut Street, on the 26th, to a slim house. "Signor Vivalla's" performances were well received. On the second night, however, I heard two or three distinct hisses from the pit. It was the first time that my protégé had received the slightest mark of disapprobation since I had engaged him, and I was surprised. Vivalla, who, under my management, had become proud of his profession, was excessively annoyed. I proceeded, therefore, to that portion of the house whence the hissing emanated, and found that it came from a circus performer named Roberts and his friends. It seems that Roberts was a balancer and juggler, and he declared he could do all that Vivalla could. I was certain he could *not,* and told him so. Some hard words ensued. I then proceeded to the ticket-office, where I wrote several copies of a "card," and proceeding to the printing-offices of various newspapers, climbing up narrow stairs and threading dark alleys for the purpose, I secured its appearance in the papers of the next morning. The card was headed *"One Thousand Dollars Reward!"* and then proceeded to state that Signor Vivalla would pay the foregoing sum to any man who would publicly accomplish his (Vivalla's) feats, at such public place as Vivalla should designate.

Roberts came out with a card the next day, accepting Vivalla's offer, calling on him to put up the thousand dollars, to name the time and place of trial, and stating that he could be found at a certain hotel near Green's Circus, of which he was a member. I borrowed a thousand dollars of my friend Oliver Taylor—went to Mr. Warren, treasurer of the Walnut, and asked him what share of the house he would give me if I would get up an excitement that should bring in four or five hundred dollars a night. (The entire receipts the night previous were but seventy-five dollars.) He replied that he would give me one-third of the gross receipts. I told him I had a crotchet in my head, and would inform him within an hour whether it would work. I then called upon Roberts and showed him my thousand dollars. "Now," says I, "I am ready to put up this money in responsible hands, to be forfeited and paid to you if you accomplish Signor Vivalla's feats."

"Very well," said Roberts, with considerable bravado; "put the money into the hands of Mr. Green, the proprietor of the circus"— to which I assented.

"Now," said I, "I wish you to sign this card, to be published in handbills and in to-morrow's newspapers." He read it. It stated that Signor Vivalla having placed one thousand dollars in hands satisfactory to himself, to be forfeited to him if he succeeded in performing the various feats of the said Vivalla, he (Roberts) would make the public trial to do so on the stage of the Walnut street Theater, on the night of the 30th inst. "You don't expect me to perform *all* of Vivalla's feats, do you?" said Roberts, after reading the card. "No, I don't *expect* you *can*, but if you do *not*, of course you will not win the thousand dollars," I replied. "Why, I know nothing about walking on stilts, and am not fool enough to risk my neck in that way," said Roberts.

Several persons, circus-riders and others, had crowded around us, and exhibited some degree of excitement. My thousand dollars was still openly displayed in my hand. I saw that Roberts was determined to back out, and as that would not be consistent with my plans, I remarked that he and I could do our own business without the intermeddling of third parties, and I would like to see him alone. He took me upstairs to his room, and bolting the door, I thus addressed him:

"Now, Roberts, you said to the public in your card that you accepted Vivalla's offer. What was that offer? Why, that he would give a thousand dollars to the man who could accomplish his feats. Now, you may spin a plate or two as well as Vivalla, but Vivalla spins ten plates at once, and I doubt whether you can do it—if not, you lose the reward. Again, you confess that you cannot perform on stilts. Of course, then, you don't accomplish 'his feats,' and therefore you could not receive the thousand dollars." "But I can toss balls and do tricks which Vivalla can't accomplish," said Roberts. "I have no doubt of that," I replied, "but that has nothing to do with Vivalla's offer." "Oh, I see," said Roberts, in a huff, "you have fixed up a Yankee card to suit yourself, and left a hole to sneak out of." "Not at all, Mr. Roberts. I have made a specific offer, and am ready to fulfill it. Do not fret nor be angry, for you shall find me your friend instead of an enemy." I then inquired whether he was engaged to Mr. Green. "Not at present," he replied, "as the circus is closed." "Well," I responded, "it is evident you cannot gain the thousand dollars. I did not intend you should, but I will give you $30 if you will perform under my directions one night at the Walnut street Theater, and will keep your own counsel."

He consented to this, and I then asked him to sign the card, and give himself no uneasiness. He signed, and I had it thoroughly published, first closing my bargain with the treasurer of the Walnut for one-third of the gross receipts on the trial night, provided there was $400 in the house.

The next day I brought Roberts and Vivalla privately together, and by practicing they soon discovered what tricks each could accomplish, and we then proceeded to arrange the manner in which the trial should come off, and how it should terminate.

In the meantime the excitement about the coming trial of skill was fast increasing. Suitable "notices" were inserted in the papers, bragging that Roberts was an American, and could beat the foreigner all hollow. Roberts in the meantime announced in the papers that if, as he expected, he should obtain the thousand dollars, a portion of it should be disbursed for charitable purposes. I set the Press at work lustily, in the shape of handbills, squibs, etc. Before the night of trial arrived, the excitement had reached fever heat. I knew that a crowded house was *un fait accompli.*

I was not disappointed. The pit and upper boxes were crowded to suffocation. In fact, the sales of tickets to these localities were stopped because no more persons could possibly gain admittance. The dress circle was not so full, though even that contained many more persons than had been in it at one time during the previous two or three months.

The contest was a very interesting one. Roberts of course was to be beaten, and it was agreed that Vivalla should at first perform his *easiest* feats, in order that the battle should be kept up as long as possible. Roberts successively performed the same feats that Vivalla did. Each party was continually cheered by his friends and hissed by his opponents. Occasionally some of Roberts's friends from the pit would call out, "Roberts, beat the little Frenchman," "One Yankee is too much for two Frenchmen any time," etc. The contest lasted about forty minutes, when Roberts came forward and acknowledged himself defeated. He was obliged to give up on the feat of spinning two plates at once, one in each hand. His friends urged him to try again, but on his declining, they requested him to perform his own peculiar feats (juggling, tossing the balls, etc.). This he did, and his performances, which continued for twenty minutes, were highly applauded.

As soon as the curtain fell, the two contestants were called for. Before they went out I had concluded a private arrangement with Roberts for a month—he to perform solely as I directed. When he went before the curtain, therefore, he informed the audience that he had a lame wrist, which was indeed the fact. He further informed them that he could do more feats of various kinds than Vivalla could, and he would challenge Vivalla to such a trial at any time and place he pleased, for a wager of five hundred dollars. "I accept that challenge," said Vivalla, who stood at Roberts's side, "and I name next Tuesday night in this theater." "Bravo," cried Vivalla's friends, as vigorously as "bravo" had been shouted by the friends of Roberts.

Three hearty cheers were given by the enthusiastic audience, and the antagonists, looking daggers at each other, withdrew at opposite sides of the curtain. Before the uproar of applause had ceased,

Roberts and Vivalla had met upon the stage, shaken hands, and were enjoying a hearty laugh, while little Vivalla, with thumb to his nose, was making curious gyrations to an imaginary picture on the back of the screen, or possibly to a real *tableau vivant* in front of the curtain. The receipts of the theater on that night were $593.25, of which I received one-third—$197.75.

The contest on the Tuesday night following was nearly as profitable to me as the first one, as so indeed were several similar trials of skill brought forward in Dinneford's Franklin Theater, New York, and various other places, during the month of Roberts's engagement.

These details serve to show (though it may be revealing some of the "tricks of the trade") how such matters are frequently managed in theaters and other places of amusement. The people are repeatedly wrought to excitement and take sides most enthusiastically in trials of skill, when, if the truth were known, the whole affair is a piece of management between the prominent parties. The entertainment of the time may be an offset to the "humbug" of the transaction, and it may be doubted whether managers of theaters will be losers by these revelations of mine, for the public appears disposed to be amused even when they are conscious of being deceived.

Meanwhile poor old Joice had sickened, and with her attendant, a faithful colored woman whom I hired in Boston, had gone to my brother's house in Bethel, where she was provided with warm apartments and the best medical and other assistance.

On the 21st of February, 1836, my brother's horses and sleigh stopped at the door of my boarding-house, in New York. The driver handed me a letter from my brother Philo, stating that Aunt Joice was no more. She died at his house on Friday night, the 19th, and her body was then in the sleigh, having been conveyed to New York for me to dispose of as I thought proper. I at once determined to have it returned to Bethel and interred in our village burial-ground, though for the present it was placed in a small room of which I had the key.

The next morning I called on an eminent surgeon who, upon visiting Joice at Niblo's, had expressed a desire to institute a post-mortem examination if she should die in this country. I agreed that he should have the opportunity, if unfortunately it should occur while she was under my protection. I now informed him that Aunt Joice was dead, and he reminded me of my promise. I admitted it, and immediately proceeded to arrange for the examination to take place on the following day.

In the meantime a mahogany coffin and plate were procured and taken to the hall where the examination was to take place. A large number of physicians, students, and several clergymen and editors were present. Among the last named class was Richard Adams Locke, author of the celebrated "Moon Hoax," who was at that time editor of the New York *Sun*. An absence of ossification of the arteries in the immediate region of the heart was deemed by the dissector and most of the gentlemen present as evidence against the assumed age of Joice.

When all had withdrawn excepting the surgeon, his particular friend Locke, Lyman, and myself, the surgeon remarked, addressing me, that there was surely some mistake in regard to the alleged age of Joice; that instead of being 161 years old, she was probably not over eighty. I stated to him, in reply, what was strictly true, that I had hired Joice in perfect good faith, and relied upon her appearance and the documents as evidence of the truth of her story. The same gentleman had examined her when alive on exhibition at Niblo's. He rejoined that he had no doubt I had been deceived in the matter, that her personal appearance really did indicate extreme longevity, but that the documents must either have been forged, or else they applied to some other individual. Lyman, who was always ready for a joke, no matter what the cost nor at whose expense, here made a remark regarding the inability of the faculty to decide with much precision in regard to a case of this kind. His observations wounded the feelings of the surgeon, and taking the arm of his friend Locke, they left the hall—I fear in not very good humor.

The *Sun* of the next day (February 25, 1836) contained an editorial, written of course by Locke, commencing as follows:

"DISSECTION OF JOICE HETH.—PRECIOUS HUMBUG EXPOSED.—The anatomical examination of the body of Joice Heth yesterday, resulted in the exposure of one of the most precious humbugs that ever was imposed upon a credulous community."

Mr. Locke then proceeded to give a scientific account of the dissection, and the reasons he had for doubting her story.

Here let me say a word in reply to the captious who may claim that I was overcredulous in accepting the story of Joice and her exhibitor, as a matter of fact. I assert, then, that when Joice Heth was living, I never met with six persons out of the many thousands who visited her, who seemed to doubt the claim of her age and history. Hundreds of medical men assured me that they thought the statement of her age was correct, and Dr. Rogers himself, in his parting conversation above noted, remarked to me that he expected to have spoiled half a dozen knives in severing the ossification in the arteries around the region of the heart and chest.

I will only add, that the remains of Joice were removed to Bethel, and buried respectably. . . .

In 1865 the space occupied for my Museum purposes was more than double what it was in 1842. The Lecture Room, originally narrow, ill-contrived and inconvenient, was so enlarged and improved that it became one of the most commodious and beautiful amusement halls in the City of New York. At first, my attractions and inducements were merely the collection of curiosities by day, and an evening entertainment consisting of such variety performances as were current in ordinary shows. Then Saturday afternoons, and, soon afterwards, Wednesday afternoons, were devoted to entertainments and the popularity of the Museum grew so rapidly that I presently found it expedient and profitable to open the great Lecture Room every afternoon, as well as every evening, on every week-day in the year. The first experiments in this direction more than justified my expectations, for the day exhibitions were always more thronged than those of the evening. Of course, I made the most of the holidays, advertising extensively and presenting extra inducements; nor did attractions elsewhere seem to keep the crowd from coming to the Museum. On great holidays, I gave as many as twelve performances to as many different audiences.

By degrees the character of the stage performances was changed. The transient attractions of the Museum were constantly diversified, and educated dogs, industrious fleas, automatons, jugglers, ventriloquists, living statuary, tableaux, gypsies, Albinos, fat boys, giants, dwarfs, rope-dancers, live "Yankees," pantomime, instrumental music, singing and dancing in great variety, dioramas, panoramas, models of Niagara, Dublin, Paris, and Jerusalem; Hannington's dioramas of the Creation, the Deluge, Fairy Grotto, Storm at Sea; the first English Punch and Judy in this country, Italian Fantoccini, mechanical figures, fancy glass-blowing, knitting machines and other triumphs in the mechanical arts; dissolving views, American Indians, who enacted their warlike and religious ceremonies on the stage—these, among others, were all exceedingly successful.

Apart from the merit and interest of these performances, and apart from everything connected with the stage, my permanent collec   of curiosities is, without doubt, abundantly worth the uni-
    rge of admission to all the entertainments of the establish-
    I can therefore afford to be accused of "humbug" when
    transient novelties as increase its attractions. If I have
    estionable dead mermaid in my Museum, it should
    ed that I have also exhibited cameleopards, a rhi-
    ears, orang-outangs, great serpents, etc., about

which there could be no mistake because they were alive; and I should hope that a little "clap-trap" occasionally, in the way of transparencies, flags, exaggerated pictures, and puffing advertisements, might find an offset in a wilderness of wonderful, instructive, and amusing realities. Indeed, I cannot doubt that the sort of "clap-trap" here referred to, is allowable, and that the public like a little of it mixed up with the great realities which I provide. The titles of "humbug," and the "prince of humbugs," were first applied to me by myself. I made these titles a part of my "stock in trade," and may here quote a passage from the "Fortunes of the Scattergood Family," a work by the popular English writer, Albert Smith:

"'It's a great thing to be a humbug,' said Mr. Rossett. 'I've been called so often. It means hitting the public in reality. Anybody who can do so, is sure to be called a humbug by somebody who can't.'"

I thoroughly understood the art of advertising, not merely by means of printer's ink, which I have always used freely, and to which I confess myself so much indebted for my success, but by turning every possible circumstance to my account. It was my monomania to make the Museum the town wonder and town talk. I often seized upon an opportunity by instinct, even before I had a very definite conception as to how it should be used, and it seemed, somehow, to mature itself and serve my purpose. As an illustration, one morning a stout, hearty-looking man came into my ticket-office and begged some money. I asked him why he did not work and earn his living? He replied that he could get nothing to do and that he would be glad of any job at a dollar a day. I handed him a quarter of a dollar, told him to go and get his breakfast and return, and I would employ him at light labor at a dollar and a half a day. When he returned I gave him five common bricks.

"Now," said I, "go and lay a brick on the sidewalk at the corner of Broadway and Ann Street; another close by the Museum; a third diagonally across the way at the corner of Broadway and Vesey Street, by the Astor House; put down the fourth on the sidewalk in front of St. Paul's Church, opposite; then, with the fifth brick in hand, take up a rapid march from one point to the other, making the circuit, exchanging your brick at every point, and say nothing to any one."

"What is the object of this?" inquired the man.

"No matter," I replied; "all you need to know is that it brings you fifteen cents wages per hour. It is a bit of my fun, and to assist me properly you must seem to be as deaf as a post; wear a serious countenance; answer no questions; pay no attention to any one; but attend faithfully to the work and at the end of every hour by

St. Paul's clock show this ticket at the Museum door; enter, walking solemnly through every hall in the building; pass out, and resume your work."

With the remark that it was "all one to him, so long as he could earn his living," the man placed his bricks and began his round. Half an hour afterwards, at least five hundred people were watching his mysterious movements. He had assumed a military step and bearing, and looking as sober as a judge, he made no response whatever to the constant inquiries as to the object of his singular conduct. At the end of the first hour, the sidewalks in the vicinity were packed with people all anxious to solve the mystery. The man, as directed then went into the Museum, devoting fifteen minutes to a solemn survey of the halls, and afterwards returning to his round. This was repeated every hour till sundown, and whenever the man went into the Museum a dozen or more persons would buy tickets and follow him, hoping to gratify their curiosity in regard to the purpose of his movements. This was continued for several days—the curious people who followed the man into the Museum considerably more than paying his wages—till finally the policeman, to whom I had imparted my object, complained that the obstruction of the sidewalks by crowds had become so serious that I must call in my "brick man." This trivial incident excited considerable talk and amusement; it advertised me; and it materially advanced my purpose of making a lively corner near the Museum.

CHAPTER XXVI

AMERICA WAS proud of its peddlers, its politicians, its showmen. It was to become proud of its ships upon the sea, and of the wealth they carried around the world. Crèvecœur has spoken of the Nantucket whalers who in the eighteenth century extended the domain of American experience across difficult waters where waves and whales were equal hazards. Their trade flourished on halfway through the century which followed, with New Bedford the great port of embarkation and the port of entry for marvelous merchandise brought back from all the countries of the globe. These years saw other exciting maritime developments as well, with the result that American shipping became synonymous over the world for speed and daring. The privateers and frigates of 1812 had struck terror into an enemy who had felt only contempt hitherto for the American navy. But now the most beautiful and spectacular of all vessels were the clipper ships, which grew in number and fame as the century wore on until steam drove them off the seas. They carried tremendous sail and made remarkable speed, scouring between west and east, around South America and Africa, carrying oftentimes cargoes of peculiar interest. Such names as the *Flying Cloud,* the *Sovereign of the Seas,* and the *Staffordshire* were famous names in the Fifties.

Charles Porter Low, member of a family noted for its lines of clipper ships, remembers how he took the *N. B. Palmer* on far voyages, and how on one voyage he beat the *Flying Cloud.*

ON the sixth of May (1851) we left New York for San Francisco with light winds from the southwest. In latitude 82° north, longitude 51° 34′ west we passed the Brig *Emblem* of Halifax, water-logged and abandoned, mainmast gone a few feet above the deck, foremast and fore-topmast and bowsprit and jib-boom standing. It had evidently been abandoned for some time and we did not stop as there was nothing to be gained. We crossed the line twenty-eight days from New York. It was no fault of the ship, but of the weather, that the passage was so much longer than my two previous voyages, for the ship was all I could wish for, and much faster than any ship I had ever sailed in, and a splendid sea boat in heavy weather.

On the sixth of June we passed the Island of Fernando Noronha off the coast of Brazil, a Portuguese convict settlement in 5° south latitude. On the ninth passed Pernambuco; about ten miles off the town looked very pretty with its white houses. With moderate breezes along the South American coast we made Staten Land on the third of July, and on the sixth passed Cape Horn, sixty-one days from New York. We crossed the line in the Pacific in eighty-eight days and on the twenty-first of August entered San Francisco Bay, one hundred and seven days from New York, two days shorter time than my passage in the *Samuel Russell*. The pilot came to an anchor some three miles from the wharf, refusing to take the ship any further till next day. I had my boat lowered and manned, and rowed to the city, where I met Mr. Sanford, the agent for A. A. Low & Bros. He was a regular driver, a Nantucket man, and he wanted to know why I had not brought the ship up near the wharf. I told him "The pilot refused to bring her any nearer," and he said, "The ship must come up to the wharf," and I said, "If she must come up, she must," and having found the wharf we were to tie up to, I went back on board and told the pilot, "The ship *must* go to the wharf at once." He said he would not take her. I told him then that I would, and I ordered up all hands and set all the sails, skysail and all. There was an ebb tide, and the wind light abeam and I knew I could take the ship right alongside of the wharf. We got under weigh and went along finely. I knew that sails would stop a ship, as well as send her ahead, and I kept every stitch of canvas on her, so that if I missed the wharf I could still keep command of her and try again, but there was no occasion, for as soon as I got near enough I backed the main-yard and went alongside the wharf so easily that there was hardly a jar. The steamer *Senator* was lying alongside of the next wharf and my flying-jib-boom just lifted two of her planks off the wheel-box. A great crowd on the wharf cheered me most heartily. Mr. Sanford cried out, "Well done!" As soon as we were made fast I took in the sails and furled them. It was the prettiest piece of seamanship ever done in San Francisco and I received lots of compliments. The pilot felt very mean about it; he stayed down below till we got near the wharf, but said nothing.

We had no trouble this time; the crew were paid off and left, only the ordinary seamen and boys stayed by. The stevedores under Commodore Allen took charge and the cargo was discharged in a short time. Mr. Sanford saved me a great deal of trouble.

San Francisco was filled with smart men, and in a year the place had greatly improved. Wharves had been built, and many fine stores had replaced the wooden shanties. But there were a great many bad men in the place and they had committed so many robberies and murders that it became necessary to have a Vigilance Committee to root them out. One Sunday at noon I saw three men taken from the jail and hanged somewhere near Market Street, before a great crowd. Many more were hanged and many sent out of the city and warned that if they returned they would be strung up. Exciting times then, but the city was saved, and it became very safe for men and women to go around the streets day or night.

After discharging the cargo we took in some three hundred tons of ballast and seventy-five Chinese dead bodies in wooden boxes as freight. At that time captains received an eighth of money paid for passage, but dead bodies were considered freight. So one smart captain, to secure this passage money, loaded his cabin with corpses and called them passengers. This is a fact. He was paid seventy-five dollars for each one, and as he had some hundred dead Chinamen in his cabin, he pocketed a very nice little sum.

After getting our ballast in, we hauled out into the stream to save wharfage, as we had to wait nearly a fortnight to get a crew. Sailors were very scare and wages twenty-five dollars a month; but by the seventh of October we had enough men to handle the ship and we sailed for Shanghai. I had for passengers Mr. Harry Burdett who had been with me on the *Samuel Russell,* and came from New York with me, Stephen S. Smith, a lumber merchant in San Francisco, and a Mr. Keeler, who had once been a schoolmate of mine. In 1849, at the beginning of the gold fever, he and three hundred others bought an old whaling bark and loaded her with lumber and stores of all kinds, and chose an old whaling Captain to take her to San Francisco. He had not been to sea for some years and he thought this was a good chance to see the old places where he had been so many times. The first place he stopped at was Fayal, one of the Azores. Then he brought up at the Cape de Verde Islands; from there he went to Rio Janeiro and Montevideo; also stopped at the Falkland Islands to shoot geese and other game. After rounding the Horn he put into Talcahuano, and then went to Valparaiso. Here the passengers kicked when he said the *next* place he would stop at was the Society Islands! It had been very pleasant during the first part of the voyage to see strange places, but so long a voyage began to be rather tedious. They had been out six months already, and wanted to get to their destination. So they turned him out and secured another Captain, but the old bark was a slow sailor and it was very nearly a year from the time they left the United States before they arrived at San Francisco. It was very amusing to hear the old Captain tell of his experience. He had been very successful after his arrival and made quite a little "pile," and now was going home by the way of China on business.

After getting to sea we had one good day's work of two hundred and eighty miles, then calms and then three days' good run, then many days of calm. On the tenth of November at two P.M. we made out a vessel dismasted, eight miles to windward. We hauled on a wind and beat up to her, and found her to be the American ship *Austerlitz,* a Boston ship in ballast, bound from San Francisco to China, Captain Day. She had been dismasted in a cyclone four days previously. I lowered a boat and went on board to see what could be done. There was nothing but her foremast standing and her mizzen-mast with a cross-jack set. She had four hundred tons of stone ballast in her lower hold and she rolled terribly, with a quick, jerky roll, so that it was almost impossible to stand on your feet. She was a rotten old tub, not fit to be sent to sea. The Captain had his wife and a little girl of about three years old with him. The ship was a long way from China, and it being hurricane season, it was useless to try to save her, and after a talk with the Captain I told him he was justified in abandoning her and that I would take all hands on board my ship and land them in China. I then returned to my ship; shortened sail to her three topsails, and hove to as close to the *Austerlitz* as it was safe, and with two of my boats and one of the other ship's, went to work to save some stores, canvas, paints, rope and other things easily transported. It was slow work, and it was twelve o'clock at night before we had the Captain, wife and child safely on board. I told the Captain he must set fire to the ship as she would be dangerous for another vessel to run into. The crew with their dunnage, and the Captain with all his personal property, being safely on board, the wind quite fresh, I filled away. Captain Day felt very badly to see the flames as they rose high in the air, consuming his home in which he had lived for a number of years. The worst of it was that at daylight the wind died away to a calm. If it had only done that six hours sooner, I could have saved a great deal more of provisions and other stores, but she was gone and that was the end of her. The *Austerlitz* had two good officers and fourteen good sailors, so that I was well manned even in case I met with a hurricane. Captain Day and Mrs. Burdett and a gang of men went to work and painted the between-decks and the upper works, and my ship looked finely to go into Shanghai.

On the fifteenth of November we were running with a fresh breeze from the east, when I noticed the weather ahead looked very squally and the sky very black and threatening. The barometer was falling and I felt sure I was running into a cyclone. My passenger, Mr. Smith, said he would like to see a typhoon. I told him I would show him all *I* wanted to see of one. At four P.M. the wind came in heavy gusts and I shortened sail to three close-reefed topsails, but still kept on my course; at six P.M. there was no doubt that I was running right into a hurricane. Mr. Smith said he had seen enough, and went below, drenched to the skin from a sea that toppled over the quarter deck. I knew that the hurricane was traveling west and that by heaving to I could get out of it, so I called all hands and took in fore and mizzen-topsails, and hove ship with her head to the eastward. It blew a furious gale all night and it was nearly twenty-four hours before the barometer had risen enough and the weather settled enough for me to make sail and proceed on my voyage. That I was wise in heaving to when I did was shown soon after I arrived in Shanghai, for the report came from there that the ship *Witchcraft*, Captain Rogers, had put into Hong Kong dismasted in a typhoon in the Pacific. Sometime after I reached Hong Kong and saw Captain Rogers, who was an old friend of mine, I compared logs with him and found I was only twenty-five miles to the eastward of him when he was dismasted, and that if I had stood on for two hours longer, I might have been in the same fix.

After the typhoon we had good weather and brisk winds from northeast to east northeast, and I arrived in Shanghai on the twenty-fourth day of November, 1851. After lying there for some two weeks I was ordered to proceed to Whampoa, and on December eighth I left Shanghai and proceeded down the river, passed Gulataff Island, and in seventy-five hours anchored in Hong Kong. I had sailed a distance of eight hundred and forty-six miles, an average of eleven miles an hour; it was about as short a passage as was ever made. December fifteenth I left for Whampoa to take in a cargo of teas and silks for New York.

Nothing of moment happened that I remember, and we took in our cargo and on the ninth of January set sail for home. At nine A.M. on the tenth we passed the Great Ladrone Islands near Macao, and with fresh northeast monsoon and rainy weather sailed rapidly down the China Sea. Five days out we passed the Great Natuna. In ten days from Macao we passed out of Sunda Strait into the Indian Ocean. February nineteenth passed Cape of

Good Hope, forty-four days from Macao. April second took a pilot and steamboat and at four P.M. hauled alongside the wharf eighty-four days from Macao to New York.

On the twenty-third of May the ship was ready for sea and was towed down the Bay with a large number of friends to see us off. The weather was fine and at two P.M. we cast off from the steamer, made sail and soon left the shore far astern. We had some twenty passengers on board, some four or five ladies among them. The next morning at breakfast my wife was the only one who joined me at that meal; all the rest were seasick. Now it is a great lottery for a shipmaster in taking a wife, and one who has never been on the water. A wife may be seasick all the voyage, or she may be very timid and afraid of a squall or a breeze of wind, which makes it very uncomfortable for the husband as well as herself. My first fear, of her being seasick, was now put at rest, and I was soon to know that there was nothing to fear as far as being timid was concerned, for on the third day out we had a strong breeze from the southwest and I was carrying sail as much as the spars would allow, and the ship careened over so that the water rushed past the port holes of the cabin with a great rush. About ten P.M. the ladies, being scared, went to my wife's room and asked her if there was any danger. She replied, "I don't know, my husband is on deck." They received no other comfort from her, but when I heard of it, it was a great comfort to me. During the twenty-four hours that followed, the ship made three hundred and ninety-six miles, a big day's run. After this the wind died down and we had pleasant weather, and nothing of interest happened until the seventh of June, when we came up with the clipper ship *Gazelle,* which left New York six days before us. The next day she was twelve miles astern of us, but we were now in the Doldrums, and for four days we were in company with the *Gazelle.* Some days she would get a breeze and come up to us and again we would run away from her. On the thirteenth of June we took the southeast trades and crossed the equator twenty-four days from New York, the *Gazelle* a long way astern. We had light trades from the equator to the latitude of 32° south. At noon of the first of July, after taking the sun for my latitude, a ship was sighted dead to windward, and I took the spy glass and went up to the mizzen-top, and after a good look at her I made up my mind it was the *Flying Cloud,* that left New York ten days before us. This ship on her first voyage made the passage to San Francisco in eighty-nine days, and was considered the fastest vessel ever built. She was commanded by Captain Creesy, an old friend of mine, but I left San Francisco ten days after she did and beat her to China. She left China for New York about the same time as the *N. B. Palmer* and I beat her ten days on the passage, and now I had come up with her, beating her ten days thus far and only forty days out. I felt very proud of it. We were both running before the wind and I was confident that I could outsail her, so I hauled up close to the wind with my studding-sails shaking and waited for her to come up with me; I wanted to be certain that it was the *Flying Cloud;* and sure enough, she ran alongside of me and Captain Creesy hailed me and wanted to know when I left New York. I replied, "Ten days after you." He was so mad he would have nothing more to say. My ship was now at a standstill, and he was going ahead at full speed, and he ran ahead of me. Shortly after I filled away, the wind hauled ahead, and we had to haul in the studding-sails and brace sharp on a wind, and he got quite a start of me. I expected that on a wind he would beat me at least a mile an hour, but next day, just twenty-four hours after he passed me, he was but twelve miles ahead. The weather now changed, and for eight days we had heavy gales with snow and hail. In latitude forty-eight south, at midnight, while making sail, a man by the name of Lemons shot the mate through the leg, and another man by the name of Dublin Jack knocked the second mate down with a handspike. I was just getting my boots on to go on deck, when the mate called to the steward to give him a musket. I jumped out of my room and inquired what the matter was, and the mate told me he was shot and that I must not go on deck. I took the musket in my hand, but he said it was not loaded. I replied that it did not matter, and bade him tell the steward to call the carpenter and sailmaker and get a lantern and come on deck. The crew were hoisting up the mizzen-topsail, and as soon as the sail was set I ordered all hands to pass before the mate and myself, and told the mate to pick out the man who shot him. He said Dublin Jack was the one. I had him put in irons, and then the man Lemons came up and said *he* was the man who had shot the mate. I started to raise the musket to knock him down, but as I had seen nothing of the row, and my blood was cool, I dropped it and asked him where the pistol was. He said he had thrown it overboard. I asked him if it was a revolver. He said "No, and that if it had been, neither I nor my mate would be alive now." I only replied, "You are mighty cool about it," and ordered the irons to be put on him and placed him in the after hatch. I took the irons off of Dublin Jack and told him to keep a good lookout for himself, as I should keep my eye on him. He replied, "All right, keep it on me." And I meant to, for I knew he was a big rascal. I then sent the watch below. Fortunately we had two English surgeons on board, and I sent the mate down to have his leg looked at. As it was my watch on deck I stayed there till I saw the second mate with his arm in a sling and asked what the matter was. He said that when the mate was shot, Dublin Jack knocked him down with a handspike. I told him he should have let me know before I let Jack out of irons, and that would have saved a good deal of trouble. However, the men had gone below and I could do nothing before morning. Mr. Mowbray and Mr. Colby reported to me that the ball had gone through the left leg about a foot above the knee; it had not touched the bone and there was no danger of the wound proving serious, but they said that the mate must keep quiet for some time.

The next morning I called all hands to witness punishment. I had for a crew thirty able seamen, six ordinary and four boys, and placed as I was, with my mate laid up, my second and third mates incompetent, I felt that I must not show the least fear, but must show that I was able to take care of my ship. I had a rope stretched across the ship, and told the men that if any of them stepped across it I would shoot them. I had my pistol ready, and Dublin Jack, for whom I was on the watch, stepped one leg over the rope. I went for him at once, caught him by the throat, carried him nearly fifty feet and landed him on the quarter deck, put the irons on him quick as a flash and lashed him to the mizzen-mast. Then I had Lemons taken out of the after hatch and triced up to the mizzen-rigging, and told the second mate to give him four dozen lashes with a piece of ratline stuff. He refused, saying he had never done such a thing. Neither had I, but it was no time to falter, and I told him to give me the rope, and I thrashed Lemons well, for I was angry at him and angry at the second mate for not supporting me. He was then taken down and put in the after hatch, and then Dublin Jack had his turn. He wanted to know what I was flogging him for. I told him for knocking the second mate down, and because I wanted to. After the thrashing was over I went forward and told the men if they were not satisfied with the morning's work, to step out one by one and I would thrash the whole of them. Fortunately for me, none of them wanted to try it, but there is nothing like a show of strength. I then sent them to breakfast. After they had eaten their breakfast I turned all hands to and worked them till I found there was no more mischief in them, when I let them have their watch and watch, and everything was quiet. But I had a hard time of it. Mr. Haines, the mate, was laid up for eighteen days, and the second and third mates were of little account, so that I had to keep the deck almost constantly. The weather was fearful; storm after storm with high seas and snow, rain and hail, kept me on deck, and for eighteen days I did not sleep below, but tumbled down in the corner of the house on deck in my wet clothes, and got only a few hours' sleep during the twenty-four. I only went to my room to wind my chronometers and take the time, and yet my wife in all these troublous times never gave a sign of fear, but was braver than any man in the cabin. Fifty-seven days out we passed Cape Horn, but the gales continued. On the twenty-sixth of July Mr. Haines returned to duty and I had a little rest, but for twelve days or a fortnight the stormy weather continued, the wind being ahead most of the time. We were twenty-eight days from Cape Horn when we sighted the Andes Mountains near Valparaiso. On the sixteenth of August we anchored in Valparaiso harbor in thirty-five fathoms of water. In stowing the cargo in New York the stevedores had stowed the beef and bread and coal under many tons of cargo, so I put into Valparaiso to get beef, bread and coal, and also to send the two mutineers home to be tried for attempted murder on the high seas.

Book VI

BEYOND THE ALLEGHENIES

CHAPTER XXVII

MEANWHILE A NEW world had opened up beyond the blue mountains which so long had confined the population of America within a coastal plain. Not many openings offered through this barrier, and even they were difficult. The Northern passage by way of the Mohawk Valley was held by the Iroquois Indians. Further down it was possible, but laborious, to travel across Pennsylvania by wagon as far as the Ohio River at Pittsburgh. There were Southern passes from Virginia and the Carolinas to Kentucky; but the interior everywhere bristled with threats of Indian hostility. As early as 1740 traders had picked their way into the interior, but not until a generation later did men like Daniel Boone—some were more important than he, but none is so famous —attempt the conquest of that dark and bloody ground. Boone himself has told the things he did.

IT was on the first of May, 1769, that I resigned my domestic happiness, and left my family and peaceable habitation on the Yadkin river, in North Carolina, to wander through the wilderness of America, in quest of the country of Kentucky, in company with John Finley, John Stuart, Joseph Holden, James Money, and William Cool.

On the 7th of June, after traveling through a mountainous wilderness, in a western direction, we found ourselves on Red River, where John Finley had formerly been trading with the Indians, and, from the top of an eminence, saw with pleasure the beautiful level of Kentucky. For sometime we had experienced the most uncomfortable weather. We now encamped, made a shelter to defend us from the inclement season, and began to hunt and reconnoiter the country. We found abundance of wild beasts in this vast forest.... The buffaloes were more numerous than cattle on other settlements, browsing on the leaves of the cane, or cropping the herbage on those extensive plains. We saw hundreds in a drove; and the numbers about the salt springs were amazing. In the forest, the habitation of beasts of every American kind, we hunted with great success until December.

On the 22d of December, John Stuart and I had a pleasing ramble; but fortune changed the day at the close of it. We had passed through a great forest, in which stood myriads of trees, some gay with blossoms, others rich with fruits. Nature was here a series of wonders and a fund of delight. Here she displayed her ingenuity and industry in a variety of flowers and fruits, beautifully colored, elegantly shaped, and charmingly flavored; and we were diverted with numberless animals, presenting themselves perpetually to our view. In the decline of the day, near Kentucky river, as we ascended the brow of a small hill, a number of Indians rushed out of a thick cane brake, and made us prisoners. The Indians plundered us, and kept us in confinement seven days. . . . During this, we discovered no uneasiness or desire to escape, which made them less suspicious; but in the dead of night, as we lay by a large fire, in a thick cane brake, when sleep had locked up their senses, my situation not disposing me to rest, I gently awoke my companion. We seized this favorable opportunity, and departed, directing our course toward our old camp, but found it plundered, and our company dispersed or gone home.

About this time my brother, Squire Boon, with another adventurer, who came to explore the country shortly after us, was wandering through the forest, and accidentally found our camp. Notwithstanding our unfortunate circumstances, and our dangerous situation, surrounded with hostile savages, our meeting fortunately in the wilderness, gave us the most sensible satisfaction.

Soon after this, my companion in captivity, John Stuart, was killed by the savages; and the man that came with my brother returned home by himself. We were then in a dangerous, helpless situation, exposed daily to perils and death, among savages and wild beasts, not a white man in the country but ourselves.

Thus many hundred miles from our families in the howling wilderness, we did not continue in a state of indolence, but hunted every day, and prepared a little cottage to defend us from the winter storms. We met with no disturbance through the winter.

On the first of May, 1770, my brother returned home by himself, for a new recruit of horses and ammunition, leaving me alone, without bread, salt, or sugar, or even a horse or dog. I passed a few days uncomfortably. The idea of a beloved wife and family, and their anxiety on my account, would have disposed me to melancholy, if I had further indulged the thought.

Until the 27th of July, I spent the time in an uninterrupted scene of sylvan pleasures, when my brother, to my great felicity, met me according to appointment, at our old camp. Soon after we left the place, and proceeded to Cumberland river, reconnoitering that part of the country, and giving names to the different rivers.

In March, 1771, I returned home to my family, being determined to bring them as soon as possible, at the risk of my life and fortune, to reside in Kentucky, which I esteemed a second paradise.

On my return I found my family in happy circumstances. I sold my farm at Yadkin, and what goods we could not carry with us; and,

On the 25th of September, 1773, we bade farewell to our friends, and proceeded on our journey to Kentucky, in company with five more families, and forty men that joined us in Powell's Valley, which is 150 miles from the now settled parts of Kentucky, but this promising beginning was soon overcast with a cloud of adversity.

On the 10th of October, the rear of our company was attacked by a number of Indians, who killed six and wounded one man. Of these my eldest son was one that fell in the action. Though we repulsed the enemy, yet this unhappy affair scattered our cattle, brought us into extreme difficulty, and so discouraged the whole company, that we retreated forty miles to Clench river. We had passed over two mountains, Powell's and Walden's, and were approaching Cumberland mountain, when this adverse fortune overtook us. These mountains are in the wilderness, in passing from the old settlements in Virginia to Kentucky, are ranged in a southwest and northeast direction, are of great length and breadth, and not far distant from each other. Over them nature hath formed passes less difficult than might be expected from the view of such huge piles. The aspect of these cliffs is so wild and horrid, that it is impossible to behold them without terror.

Until the sixth of June, 1774, I remained with my family on the Clench when I and Michael Stoner were solicited by Governor Dunmore, of Virginia, to conduct a number of surveyors to the falls of Ohio. This was a tour of near eight hundred miles, and took us sixty-two days.

On my return, Governor Dunmore gave me the command of three garrisons, during the campaign against the Shawanese.

In March, 1775, at the solicitation of a number of gentlemen of North Carolina, I attended their treaty at Wataga, with the Cherokee Indians, to purchase the lands on the south side of Kentucky river. After this, I undertook to mark out a road in the best passage from the settlements, through the wilderness to Kentucky.

Having collected a number of enterprising men, well armed, I soon began this work. We proceeded until we came within fifteen miles of where Boonsborough now stands, where the Indians attacked us, and killed two, and wounded two more.

This was the 20th of March, 1775. Three days after, they attacked us again; we had two killed and three wounded. After this we proceeded on to Kentucky river without opposition.

On the 1st of April, we began to erect the fort of Boonsborough, at a salt-lick, sixty yards from the river, on the south side.

On the 4th, they killed one of our men.

On the 14th of June, having finished the fort, I returned to my family, on the Clench. Soon after I removed my family to the fort; we arrived safe; my wife and daughter being the first white women that stood on the banks of Kentucky river.

December 24th. The Indians killed one man, and wounded another, seeming determined to persecute us for erecting this fort.

July 14, 1776. Two of Col. Calway's daughters, and one of mine, were taken prisoners near the fort. I immediately pursued the Indians, with only eighteen men.

On the 16th, I overtook them, killed two of them, and recovered the girls.

The Indians had divided themselves into several parties, and attacked, on the same day, all our settlements and forts, doing a great deal of mischief. The husbandman was shot dead in the field, and most of the cattle were destroyed. They continued their hostilities until

The 15th of April, 1777, when a party of 100 of them attacked Boonsborough and killed one man, and wounded four.

July 4th, they attacked it again with 200 men, and killed one and wounded two. They remained forty-eight hours, during which we killed seven of them. All the settlements were attacked at the same time.

July 19th. Col. Logan's fort was besieged by 200 Indians: they did much mischief; there were only fifteen men in the fort; they killed two, and wounded four of them. Indians' loss unknown.

July 25th. Twenty-five men came from Carolina. About

August 20th, Colonel Bowman arrived with 100 men from Virginia. Now we began to strengthen, and had skirmishes with the Indians almost every day. The savages now learned the superiority of the LONG KNIFE, as they call the Virginians; being outgeneraled in almost every battle. Our affairs began to wear a new aspect; the enemy did not now venture open war, but practiced secret mischief.

January 1, 1778. I went with thirty men to the Blue Licks, on Licking river, to make salt for the different garrisons.

February 7th. Hunting by myself, to procure meat for the company, I met a party of 102 Indians and two Frenchmen, marching against Boonsborough. They pursued and took me; and next day I capitulated for my men, knowing they could not escape. They were twenty-seven in number, three having gone home with salt. The Indians, according to the capitulation, used us generously. They carried us to Old Chelicothe, the principal Indian town on Little Miami.

On the 18th of February we arrived there, after an uncomfortable journey, in very severe weather.

On the 10th of March, I and ten of my men were conducted to Detroit.

On the 30th, we arrived there, and were treated by Governor Hamilton, the British commander at that post, with great humanity.

The Indians had such an affection for me, that they refused £100 sterling offered them by the governor, if they would leave me with the others, on purpose that he might send me home on my parole. Several English gentlemen there, sensible of my adverse fortune, and touched with sympathy, generously offered to supply my wants, which I declined with many thanks, adding that I never expected it would be in my power to recompense such unmerited generosity. The Indians left my men in captivity with the British at Detroit.

On the 10th of April, they brought me towards Old Chelicothe, where we arrived on the 25th day of the same month. This was a long and fatiguing march, through an exceeding fertile country, remarkable for fine springs and streams of water. At Chelicothe, I spent my time as comfortable as I could expect; was adopted, according to their customs, into a family, where I became a son, and had a great share in the affection of my new parents, brothers, sisters, and friends. I was exceedingly familiar and friendly with them, always appearing as cheerful and satisfied as possible, and they put great confidence in me. I often went a-hunting with them, and frequently gained their applause for my activity at our shooting matches. I was careful not to exceed many of them in shooting; for no people are more envious than they in this sport. I could observe in their countenance and gestures the greatest expressions of joy when they exceeded me; and, when the reverse happened, of envy. The Shawanese king took great notice of me, and treated me with profound respect, and entire friendship, often entrusting me to hunt at my liberty. I frequently returned with the spoils of the woods, and as often presented some of what I had taken to him, expressive of duty to my sovereign. My food and lodging was in common with them, not so good indeed as I could desire; but necessity made everything acceptable.

I now began to meditate an escape, but carefully avoided giving suspicion.

Until the 1st day of June I continued at Old Chelicothe, and then was taken to the salt springs on Sciota, and kept there ten days making salt. During this time, I had hunted with them, and found the land, for a great extent above this river, to exceed the soil of Kentucky, if possible, and remarkably well watered.

On my return to Chelicothe, four hundred and fifty of the choicest Indian warriors were ready to march against Boonsborough, painted and armed in a fearful manner. This alarmed me, and I determined to escape.

On the 16th of June, before sunrise, I went off secretly, and reached Boonsborough on the 20th, a journey of one hundred and sixty miles, during which I had only one meal. I found our fortress in a bad state, but we immediately repaired our flanks, gates, posterns, and formed double bastions, which we completed in ten days. One of my fellow prisoners escaping after me, brought advice, that on account of my flight, the Indians had put off their expedition for three weeks.

About August 1st, I set out with nineteen men to surprise Point Creek Town on Sciota. Within four miles we fell in with thirty Indians going against Boonsborough. We fought, and the enemy gave way. We suffered no loss. The enemy had one killed, and two wounded. We took three horses and all their baggage. The Indians having evacuated their town and gone all together against Boonsborough, we returned, passed them on the 6th day, and on the 7th arrived safe at Boonsborough.

On the 8th, the Indian army, 444 in number, commanded by Capt. Duquesne, and eleven other Frenchmen, and their own chiefs, came and summoned the fort. I requested two days consideration, which they granted. During this, we brought in through the posterns all the horses and other cattle we could collect.

On the 9th, in the evening, I informed their commander, that we were determined to defend the fort, while a man was living. They then proposed a treaty, and said if we sent out nine men to conclude it, they would withdraw. The treaty was held within sixty yards of the fort, as we suspected the savages. The articles were agreed to and signed; when the Indians told us, it was their custom for two Indians to shake hands with every white man in the treaty, as an evidence of friendship. We agreed to this also. They immediately grappled us to take us prisoners, but we cleared ourselves of them, though surrounded by hundreds, and gained the fort safe, except one that was wounded by a heavy fire from their army. On this they began to undermine the fort, beginning at the water-mark of Kentucky river, which is sixty yards from the fort. We discovered this by the water being made muddy with the clay and countermined them by cutting a trench across their subterranean passage. The enemy discovering this, by the clay we threw out of the fort, desisted.

On the 20th of August, they raised the siege.

Two darling sons, and a brother I have lost by savage hands, which have also taken forty valuable horses, and an abundance of cattle. Many dark and sleepless nights have I spent, separated from the cheerful society of men, scorched by the summer's sun, and pinched by the winter's cold, an instrument ordained to settle the wilderness. But now the scene is changed: peace crowns the sylvan shade.

CHAPTER XXVIII

PETER CARTWRIGHT GOES WEST AND BECOMES A MUSCULAR CHRISTIAN

BOONE HAD been an explorer and adventurer, and had expended most of his energies upon hostile Indians. The lands that had been conquered became very soon, however, habitations for industrious and peaceful men; Kentucky and Tennessee began to produce a civilization. Only a few years after the Revolution a child of Virginia, Peter Cartwright, was taken by his family over a now familiar route into the frontier world of Kentucky. His "Autobiography" tells of that early journey; and goes on to celebrate Cartwright's exploits as a circuit-riding preacher. The religion which went with the western settlers was vigorous if grotesque; Cartwright gives a taste of the muscularity with which he and his kind defended the faith.

I WAS born September 1st, 1785, in Amherst County, on James River, in the State of Virginia. My parents were poor. My father was a soldier in the great struggle for liberty, in the Revolutionary war with Great Britain. He served over two years. My mother was an orphan. Shortly after the united colonies gained their independence, my parents moved to Kentucky, which was a new country. It was an almost unbroken wilderness from Virginia to Kentucky at that early day, and this wilderness was filled with thousands of hostile Indians, and many thousands of the emigrants to Kentucky lost their lives by these savages. There were no roads for carriages at that time, and although the emigrants moved by thousands, they had to move on pack horses. Many adventurous young men went to this new country. The fall my father moved, there were a great many families who joined together for mutual safety, and started for Kentucky. Besides the two hundred families thus united, there were one hundred young men, well armed, who agreed to guard these families through, and, as a compensation, they were to be supported for their services. After we struck the wilderness we rarely traveled a day but we passed some white persons, murdered and scalped by the Indians while going to or returning from Kentucky. We traveled on till Sunday, and, instead of resting that day, the voice of the company was to move on.

It was a dark, cloudy day, misty with rain. Many Indians were seen through the day skulking round by our guards. Late in the evening we came to what was called "Camp Defeat," where a number of emigrant families had been all murdered by the savages a short time before. Here the company called a halt to camp for the night. It was a solemn, gloomy time; every heart quaked with fear.

Soon the captain of our young men's company placed his men as sentinels all round the encampment. The stock and the women and children were placed in the center of the encampment. Most of the men that were heads of families, were placed around outside of the women and children. Those who were not placed in this position, were ordered to take their stand outside still, in the edge of the brush. It was a dark, dismal night, and all expected an attack from the Indians.

That night my father was placed as a sentinel, with a good rifle, in the edge of the brush. Shortly after he took his stand, and all was quiet in the camp, he thought he heard something moving toward him, and grunting like a swine. He knew there was no swine with the moving company, but it was so dark he could not see what it was. Presently he perceived a dark object in the distance, but nearer him than at first, and believing it to be an Indian, aiming to spring upon him and murder him in the dark, he leveled his rifle, and aimed at the dark lump as well as he could, and fired. He soon found he had hit the object, for it flounced about at a terrible rate, and my father gathered himself up and ran into camp.

When his gun fired, there was an awful screaming throughout the encampment by the women and children. My father was soon inquired of as to what was the matter. He told them the circumstances of the case, but some said he was scared and wanted an excuse to come in; but he affirmed that there was no mistake, that there was something, and he had shot it; and if they would get a light and go with him, if he did not show them something, then they might call him a coward forever. They got a light and went to the place, and there they found an Indian, with a rifle in one hand and a tomahawk in the other, dead. My father's rifle-ball had struck the Indian nearly central in the head.

There was but little sleeping in the camp that night. However, the night passed away without any further alarms, and many glad hearts hailed the dawn of a new day. The next morning, as soon as the company could pack up, they started on their journey.

In a few days after this, we met a lone man, who said his name was Baker, with his mouth bleeding at a desperate rate, having been shot by an Indian. Several of his teeth and his jaw bone were broken by a ball from the Indian's gun. His account of a battle with the Indians was substantially as follows:

There were seven young white men returning to Virginia from Kentucky, all well armed; one of them, a Frenchman, had a considerable sum of money with him. All seven were mounted on fine horses, and they were waylaid by seven Indians.

When the white men approached near the ambush, they were fired on by the Indians, and three shot down; the other four dismounted and shot down three of the Indians. At the second fire of the Indians, two more of the white men fell, and at the second fire of the white men, two more of the Indians fell. Then there were two and two. At the third fire of the Indians, Baker's only remaining companion fell, and he received the wound in the mouth. Thinking his chance a bad one, he wheeled and ran, loading his gun as he went. Finding a large, hollow tree, he crept into it, feet foremost, holding his rifle ready cocked, expecting them to look in, when he intended to fire. He heard the Indians cross and recross the log twice, but they did not look in.

At this perilous moment, he heard the large cowbell that was on one of the drove of cattle of our company, and shortly after he crawled out of the log, and made his way to us, the happiest man I think I ever saw. Our company of young men rushed to the battleground, and found the dead white men and Indians, and dug two separate graves, and buried them where they fell. They got all the horses and clothes of the white men slain, and the Frenchman's money, for the surviving Indians had not time to scalp or strip them.

When we came within seven miles of the Crab Orchard, where there was a fort and the first white settlement, it was nearly night. We halted, and a vote was taken whether we should go on to the fort, or camp there for the night. Indians had been seen in our rear through the day. All wanted to go through except seven families, who refused to go any further that night. The main body went on, but they, the seven families, carelessly striped off their clothes, laid down without any guards, and went to sleep.

Some time in the night, about twenty-five Indians rushed on them, and every one, men, women, and children was slain, except one man, who sprang from his bed and ran into the fort, barefooted and in his night clothes. He brought the melancholy news of the slaughter.

The captain of the fort was an old, experienced ranger and Indian warrior. These murderous bands of savages lived north of the Ohio River, and would cross over into Kentucky, kill and steal, and then recross the Ohio into their own country. The old captain knew the country well, and the places of their crossing the river. Early next morning he called for volunteers, mounted men, and said he could get ahead of them. A goodly company turned out, and, sure enough, they got ahead of the Indians, and formed an ambush for them. Soon they saw the Indians coming, and, at a given signal, the whites fired on them. At the first shot all were killed but three; these were pursued, two of them killed, and but one made his escape to tell the sad news. All the plunder of the murdered families was retaken.

Kentucky was claimed by no particular tribe of Indians, but was regarded as a common hunting ground by the various tribes, east, west, north, and south. It abounded in various valuable game, such as buffalo, elk, bear, deer, turkeys, and many other smaller game, and hence the Indians struggled hard to keep the white people from taking possession of it. Many hard and bloody battles were fought, and thousands killed on both sides; and rightly was it named the "land of blood." But finally the Indians were overpowered and driven off, and the white man obtained a peaceful and quiet possession.

The Kentuckians labored under many, very many, disadvantages and privations; and had it not been for the fertility of the soil and the abundance of wild meat, they must have suffered beyond endurance. But the country soon filled up, and entered into the enjoyment of improved and civilized life.

Young Cartwright, growing up, entered the strenuous service of a backwoods church. Here he may be viewed in characteristic poses.

Our last quarterly-meeting was a camp-meeting. We had a great many tents, and a large turnout for a new country, and, perhaps, there never was a greater collection of rabble and rowdies. They came drunk, and armed with dirks, clubs, knives, and horse-whips, and swore they would break up the meeting. After interrupting us very much on Saturday night, they collected early on Sunday morning, determined on a general riot. At eight o'clock I was appointed to preach. About the time I was half through my discourse, two very fine-dressed young men marched into the congregation with loaded whips, and hats on, and rose up and stood in the midst of the ladies, and began to laugh and talk. They were near the stand, and I requested them to desist and get off the seats; but they cursed me, and told me to mind my own business, and said they would not get down. I stopped trying to preach, and called for a magistrate. There were two at hand, but I saw they were both afraid. I ordered them to take these men into custody, but they said they could not do it. I told them, as I left the stand, to command me to take them, and I would do it at the risk of my life. I advanced toward them. They ordered me to stand off, but I advanced. One of them made a pass at my head with his whip, but I closed in with him, and jerked him off the seat. A regular scuffle ensued. The congregation by this time were all in commotion. I heard the magistrate give general orders, commanding all friends of order to aid in suppressing the riot. In the scuffle I threw my prisoner down, and held him fast; he tried his best to get loose; I told him to be quiet, or I would pound his chest well. The mob rose, and rushed to the rescue of the two prisoners, for they had taken the other young man also. An old and drunken magistrate came up to me, and ordered me to let my prisoner go. I told him I should not. He swore if I did not, he would knock me down. I told him to crack away. Then one of my friends, at my request, took hold of my prisoner, and the drunken justice made a pass at me; but I parried the stroke, and seized him by the collar and the hair of the head, and fetching him a sudden jerk forward, brought him to the ground, and jumped on him. I told him to be quiet, or I would pound him well. The mob then rushed to the scene; they knocked down seven magistrates, and several preachers and others. I gave up my drunken prisoner to another, and threw myself in front of the friends of order. Just at this moment the ringleader of the mob and I met; he made three passes at me, intending to knock me down. The last time he struck at me, by the force of his own effort he threw the side of his face toward me. It seemed at that moment I had not power to resist temptation, and I struck a sudden blow in the burr of the ear and dropped him to the earth. Just at that moment the friends of order rushed by hundreds on the mob, knocking them down in every direction. In a few minutes, the place became too strait for the mob, and they wheeled and fled in every direction; but we secured about thirty prisoners, marched them off to a vacant tent, and put them under guard till Monday morning, when they were tried, and every man was fined to the utmost limits of the law. The aggregate amount of fines and costs was near three hundred dollars. They fined my old drunken magistrate twenty dollars, and returned him to court, and he was cashiered of his office. On Sunday, when we had vanquished the mob, the whole encampment was filled with mourning; and although there was no attempt to resume preaching till evening, yet, such was our confused state, that there was not then a single preacher on the ground willing to preach, from the presiding elder, John Sale, down. Seeing we had fallen on evil times, my spirit was stirred within me. I said to the elder, "I feel a clear conscience, for under the necessity of the circumstances we have done right, and now I ask to let me preach."

"Do," said the elder, "for there is no other man on the ground can do it."

The encampment was lighted up, the trumpet blown, I rose in the stand, and required every soul to leave the tents and come into the congregation. There was a general rush to the stand. I requested the brethren, if ever they prayed in all their lives, to pray now. My voice was strong and clear, and my preaching was more of an exhortation and encouragement than anything else. My text was, "The gates of hell shall not prevail." In about thirty minutes the power of God fell on the congregation in such a manner as is seldom seen; the people fell in every direction, right and left, front and rear. It was supposed that not less than three hundred fell like dead men in mighty battle; and there was no need of calling mourners, for they were strewed all over the camp-ground; loud wailings went up to heaven from sinners for mercy, and a general shout from Christians, so that the noise was heard afar off. Our meeting lasted all night, and Monday and Monday night; and when we closed on Tuesday, there were two hundred who had professed religion, and about that number joined the Church. . . .

Shortly after this I journeyed on toward my home in Christian County, Kentucky. Saturday night came on, and found me in a strange region of country, and in the hills, knobs, and spurs of the Cumberland Mountains. I greatly desired to stop on the approaching Sabbath and spend it with a Christian people; but I was now in a region of country where there was no Gospel minister for many miles around, and where, as I learned, many of the scattered population had never heard a Gospel sermon in all their lives, and where the inhabitants knew no Sabbath only to hunt and visit, drink and dance. Thus lonesome and pensive, late in the evening, I hailed at a tolerably decent house, and the landlord kept entertainment. I rode up and asked for quarters. The gentleman said I could stay, but he was afraid I would not enjoy myself very much as a traveler, inasmuch as they had a party meeting there that night to have a little dance. I inquired how far it was to a decent house of entertainment on the road; he said seven miles. I told him if he would treat me civilly and feed my horse well, by his leave I would stay. He assured me I should be treated civilly. I dismounted and went in. The people collected, a large company. I saw there was not much drinking going on.

I quietly took my seat in one corner of the house, and the dance commenced. I sat quietly musing, a total stranger, and greatly desired to preach to this people. Finally, I concluded to spend the next day (Sabbath) there, and ask the privilege to preach to them.

I had hardly settled this point in my mind, when a beautiful, ruddy young lady walked very gracefully up to me, dropped a handsome courtesy, and pleasantly, with winning smiles, invited me out to take a dance with her. I can hardly describe my thoughts or feelings on that occasion. However, in a moment I resolved on a desperate experiment. I rose as gracefully as I could; I will not say with some emotion, but with many emotions. The young lady moved to my right side; I grasped her right hand with my right hand, while she leaned her left arm on mine. In this position we walked on the floor. The whole company seemed pleased at this act of politeness in the young lady, shown to a stranger. The colored man, who was the fiddler, began to put his fiddle in the best order. I then spoke to the fiddler to hold a moment, and added that for several years I had not undertaken any matter of importance without first asking the blessing of God upon it, and I desired now to ask the blessing of God upon this beautiful young lady and the whole company, that had shown such an act of politeness to a total stranger.

Here I grasped the young lady's hand tightly and said, "Let us all kneel down and pray," and then instantly dropped on my knees, and commenced praying with all the power of soul and body that I could command. The young lady tried to get loose from me, but I held her tight. Presently she fell on her knees. Some of the company kneeled, some stood, some fled, some sat still, all looked curious. The fiddler ran off into the kitchen, saying, "Lord a marcy, what de matter? what is dat mean?"

While I prayed some wept, and wept out aloud, and some cried for mercy. I rose from my knees and commenced an exhortation, after which I sang a hymn. The young lady who invited me on the floor lay prostrate, crying earnestly for mercy. I exhorted again, I sang and prayed nearly all night. About fifteen of that company professed religion, and our meeting lasted next day and next night, and as many more were powerfully converted. I organized a society, took thirty-two into the Church, and sent them a preacher. My landlord was appointed leader, which post he held for many years. This was the commencement of a great and glorious revival of religion in that region of country, and several of the young men converted at this Methodist preacher dance became useful ministers of Jesus Christ.

CHAPTER XXIX

CARTWRIGHT WAS no more uncouth than Davy Crockett, child of Tennessee at the end of the century. In him we find a purely native product—born in the backwoods, working and hunting and marrying there, and issuing thence to cut a figure in public affairs. His account of two courtships is an account of a man and of a generation.

I WENT to the house of an honest old Quaker, by the name of John Kennedy, who had removed from North Carolina, and proposed to hire myself to him, at two shillings a day. He agreed to take me a week on trial; at the end of which he appeared pleased with my work, and informed me that he held a note on my father for forty dollars, and that he would give me that note if I worked for him six months. I was certain enough that I should never get any part of the note; but then I remembered it was my father that owed it, and I concluded it was my duty as a child to help him along, and ease his lot as much as I could. I told the Quaker I would take him up at his offer, and immediately went to work. I never visited my father's house during the whole time of this engagement, though he lived only fifteen miles off. But when it was finished, and I had got the note, I borrowed one of my employer's horses, and, on a Sunday evening, went to pay my parents a visit. Some time after I got there, I pulled out the note and handed it to my father, who supposed Mr. Kennedy had sent it for collection. The old man looked mighty sorry, and said to me he had not the money to pay it, and didn't know what he should do. I then told him I had paid it for him, and it was then his own; that it was not presented for collection, but as a present from me. At this, he shed a heap of tears; and as soon as he got a little over it, he said he was sorry he couldn't give me anything, but he was not able, he was too poor.

The next day, I went back to my old friend, the Quaker, and set in to work for him for some clothes; for I had now worked a year without getting any money at all, and my clothes were nearly all worn out, and what few I had left were mighty indifferent. I worked in this way for about two months; and in that time a young woman from North Carolina, who was the Quaker's niece, came on a visit to his house. And now I am just getting on a part of my history that I know I never can forget. For though I have heard people talk about hard loving, yet I reckon no poor devil in this world was ever cursed with such hard love as mine has always been, when it came on me. I soon found myself head over heels in love with this girl, whose name the public could make no use of; and I thought that if all the hills about there were pure chink, and all belonged to me, I would give them if I could just talk to her as I wanted to; but I was afraid to begin, for when I would think of saying anything to her, my heart would begin to flutter like a duck in a puddle; and if I tried to outdo it and speak, would get right smack up in my throat, and choak me like a cold potato. It bore on my mind in this way, till at last I concluded I must die if I didn't broach the subject; and so I determined to begin and hang on a-trying to speak, till my heart would get out of my throat one way or t'other. And so one day at it I went, and after several trials I could say a little. I told her how well I loved her; that she was the darling object of my soul and body; and I must have her, or else I should pine down to nothing, and just die away with the consumption.

I found my talk was not disagreeable to her; but she was an honest girl, and didn't want to deceive nobody. She told me she was engaged to her cousin, a son of the old Quaker. This news was worse to me than war, pestilence, or famine; but still I knowed I could not help myself. I saw quick enough my cake was dough, and I tried to cool off as fast as possible; but I had hardly safety pipes enough, as my love was so hot as mighty nigh to burst my boilers. But I didn't press my claims any more, seeing there was no chance to do anything.

I began now to think, that all my misfortunes growed out of my want of learning. I had never been to school but four days, as the reader has already seen, and did not yet know a letter.

I thought I would try to go to school some; and as the Quaker had a married son, who was living about a mile and a half from him, and keeping a school, I proposed to him that I would go to school four days in the week, and work for him the other two, to pay my board and schooling. He agreed I might come on those terms; and so at it I went, learning and working back and forwards, until I had been with him nigh on to six months. In this time I learned to read a little in my primer, to write my own name, and to cipher some in the three first rules in figures. And this was all the schooling I ever had in my life, up to this day. I should have continued longer, if it hadn't been that I concluded I couldn't do any longer without a wife; and so I cut out to hunt me one.

I found a family of very pretty little girls that I had known when very young. They had lived in the same neighborhood with me, and I had thought very well of them. I made an offer to one of them, whose name is nobody's business, no more than the Quaker girl's was, and I found she took it very well. I still continued paying my respects to her, until I got to love her as bad as I had the Quaker's niece; and I would have agreed to fight a whole regiment of wild cats if she would only have said she would have me. Several months passed in this way, during all of which time she continued very kind and friendly. At last, the son of the old Quaker and my first girl had concluded to bring their matter to a close, and my own little queen and myself were called on to wait on them. We went on the day, and performed our duty as attendants. This made me worse than ever; and after it was over, I pressed my claim very hard on her, but she would still give me a sort of evasive answer. However, I gave her mighty little peace, till she told me at last she would have me. I thought this was glorification enough, even without spectacles. I was then about eighteen years old. We fixed the time to be married; and I thought if that day come, I should be the happiest man in the created world, or in the moon, or anywhere else.

I had by this time got to be mighty fond of the rifle, and had bought a capital one. I most generally carried her with me wherever I went, and though I had got back to the old Quaker's to live, who was a very particular man, I would sometimes slip out and attend the shooting matches, where they shot for beef; I always tried, though, to keep it a secret from him. He had at the same time a bound boy living with him, who I had gotten into almost as great a notion of the girls as myself. He was about my own age, and was deeply smitten with the sister to my intended wife. I knowed it was in vain to try to get the leave of the old man for my young associate to go with me on any of my courting frolics; but I thought I could fix a plan to have him along, which would not injure the Quaker, as we had no notion that he should ever know it. We commonly slept upstairs, and at the gable end of the house there was a window. So one Sunday, when the old man and his family were all gone to meeting, we went out and cut a long pole, and, taking it to the house, we set it up on one end in the corner, reaching up the chimney as high as the window. After this we would go upstairs to bed, and then putting on our Sunday clothes, would go out at the window, and climb down the pole, take a horse apiece, and ride about ten miles to where his sweetheart lived, and the girl I claimed as my wife. I was always mighty careful to be back before day, so as to escape being found out; and in this way I continued my attentions very closely until a few days before I was to be married, or at least thought I was, for I had no fear that anything was about to go wrong.

Just now I heard of a shooting-match in the neighborhood, right between where I lived and my girl's house; and I determined to kill two birds with one stone,—to go to the shooting match first, and then to see her. I therefore made the Quaker believe I was going to hunt for deer, as they were pretty plenty about in those parts; but, instead of hunting them, I went straight on to the shooting-match, where I joined in with a partner, and we put in several shots for the beef. I was mighty lucky, and when the match was over I had won the whole beef. This was on a Saturday, and my success had put me in the finest humor in the world. So I sold my part of the beef for five dollars in the real grit, for I believe that was before banknotes was invented; at least I had never heard of any. I now started on to ask for my wife; for, though the next Thursday was our wedding day, I had never said a word to her parents about it. I had always dreaded the undertaking so bad, that I had put the evil hour off as long as possible; and, indeed, I calculated they knowed me so well, they wouldn't raise any objections to having me for their son-in-law. I had a great deal better opinion of myself, I found, than other people had of me; but I moved on with a light heart, and my five dollars jingling in my pocket, thinking all the time there was but few greater men in the world than myself.

In this flow of good humor I went ahead, till I got within about two miles of the place, when I concluded I would stop awhile at the house of the girl's uncle; where I might inquire about the family, and so forth, and so on. I was indeed just about ready to consider her uncle, my uncle; and her affairs, my affairs. When I went in, though, I found her sister there. I asked how all was at home? In a minute I found from her countenance something was wrong. She looked mortified, and didn't answer as quick as I thought she ought, being it was her *brother-in-law* talking to her. However, I asked her again. She then burst into tears, and told me her sister was going to deceive me; and that she was to be married to another man the next day. This was as sudden to me as a clap of thunder of a bright sunshiny day. It was the capstone of all the afflictions I had ever met with; and it seemed to me, that it was more than any human creature could endure. It struck me perfectly speechless for some time, and made me feel so weak, that I thought I should sink down. I however recovered from my shock after a little, and rose and started without any ceremony, or even bidding anybody good-by. The young woman followed me out to the gate, and entreated me to go on to her father's, and said she would go with me. She said the young man, who was going to marry her sister, had got the license, and had asked for her; but she assured me her father and mother both preferred me to him; and that she had no doubt but that, if I would go on, I could break off the match. But I found I could go no further. My heart was bruised, and my spirits were broken down; so I bid her farewell, and turned my lonesome and miserable steps back again homeward, concluding that I was only born for hardship, misery, and disappointment. I now began to think, that in making me, it was entirely forgotten to make my mate; that I was born odd, and should always remain so, and that nobody would have me.

I continued in this down-spirited situation for a good long time, until one day I took my rifle and started hunting. While out, I made a call at the house of a Dutch widow, who had a daughter that was well enough as to smartness, but she was as ugly as a stone fence. She was, however, quite talkative, and soon begun to laugh at me about my disappointment.

She seemed disposed, though, to comfort me as much as she could; and, for that purpose, told me to keep in good-heart, that "there was as good fish in the sea as had ever been caught out of it." I doubted this very much; but whether or not, I was certain that she was not one of them, for she was so homely that it almost give me a pain in the eyes to look at her.

But I couldn't help thinking, that she had intended what she had said as a banter for me to court her ! ! !—the last thing in creation I could have thought of doing. I felt little inclined to talk on the subject, it is true; but, to pass off the time, I told her I thought I was born odd, and that no fellow to me could be found. She protested against this, and said if I would come to their reaping, which was not far off, she would show me one of the prettiest little girls there I had ever seen. She added that the one who had deceived me was nothing to be compared with her. I didn't believe a word of all this, for I had thought that such a piece of flesh and blood as she was had never been manufactured, and never would again. I agreed with her, though, that the little varmint had treated me so bad, that I ought to forget her, and yet I couldn't do it. I concluded the best way to accomplish it was to cut out again, and see if I could find any other that would answer me; and so I told the Dutch girl I would be at the reaping, and would bring as many as I could with me.

I employed my time pretty generally in giving information of it, as far as I could, until the day came; and I then offered to work for my old friend, the Quaker, two days, if he would let his bound boy go with me one to the reaping. He refused, and reproved me pretty considerable roughly for my proposition; and said, if he was in my place he wouldn't go; that there would be a great deal of bad company there; and that I had been so good a boy, he would be sorry for me to get a bad name. But I knowed my promise to the Dutch girl, and I was resolved to fulfill it; so I shouldered my rife, and started by myself. When I got to the place, I found a large company of men and women, and among them an old Irish woman, who had a great deal to say. I soon found out from my Dutch girl, that this old lady was the mother of the little girl she had promised me, though I had not yet seen her. She was in an outhouse with some other youngsters, and had not yet made her appearance. Her mamma, however, was no way bashful. She came up to me, and began to praise my red cheeks, and said she had a sweetheart for me. I had no doubt she had been told what I come for, and all about it. In the evening I was introduced to her daughter, and I must confess, I was plaguy well pleased with her from the word go. She had a good countenance, and was very pretty, and I was full bent on making up an acquaintance with her.

It was not long before the dancing commenced, and I asked her to join me in a reel. She very readily consented to do so; and after we had finished our dance, I took a seat alongside of her, and entered into a talk. I found her very interesting; while I was setting by her, making as good a use of my time as I could, her mother came to us, and very jocularly called me her son-in-law. This rather confused me, but I looked on it as a joke of the old lady, and tried to turn it off as well as I could; but I took care to pay as much attention to her through the evening as I could. I went on the old saying, of salting the cow to catch the calf. I soon become so much pleased with this little girl, that I began to think the Dutch girl had told me the truth, when she said there was still good fish in the sea.

We continued our frolic till near day, when we joined in some plays, calculated to amuse youngsters. I had not often spent a more agreeable night. In the morning, however, we all had to part; and I found my mind had become much better reconciled than it had been for a long time. I went home to the Quaker's, and made a bargain to work with his son for a low-priced horse. He was the first one I had ever owned, and I was to work six months for him. I had been engaged very closely five or six weeks, when this little girl run in my mind so, that I concluded I must go and see her, and find out what sort of people they were at home. I mounted my horse and away I went to where she lived, and when I got there I found her father a very clever old man, and the old woman as talkative as ever. She wanted badly to find out all about me, and as I thought to see how I would do for her girl. I had not yet seen her about, and I began to feel some anxiety to know where she was.

In a short time, however, my impatience was relieved, as she arrived at home from a meeting to which she had been. There was a young man with her, who I soon found was disposed to set up claims to her, as he was so attentive to her that I could hardly get to slip in a word edgeways. I began to think I was barking up the wrong tree again; but I was determined to stand up to my rack, fodder or no fodder. And so, to know her mind a little on the subject, I began to talk about starting, as I knowed she would then show some sign, from which I could understand which way the wind blowed. It was then near night, and my distance was fifteen miles home. At this my little girl soon began to indicate to the other gentleman that his room would be the better part of his company. At length she left him, and came to me, and insisted mighty hard that I should not go that evening; and, indeed, from all her actions and the attempts she made to get rid of him, I saw that she preferred me all holler. But it wasn't long before I found trouble enough in another quarter. Her mother was deeply enlisted for my rival, and I had to fight against her influence as well as his. But the girl herself was the prize I was fighting for; and as she welcomed me, I was determined to lay siege to her, let what would happen. I commenced a close courtship, having cornered her from her old beau; while he set off, looking on, like a poor man at a country frolic, and all the time almost gritting his teeth with pure disappointment. But he didn't dare to attempt anything more, for now I had gotten a start, and I looked at him every once in a while as fierce as a wild-cat. I stayed with her until Monday morning, and then I put out for home.

It was about two weeks after this that I was sent for to engage in a wolf hunt, where a great number of men were to meet, with their dogs and guns, and where the best sort of sport was expected. I went as large as life, but I had to hunt in strange woods, and in a part of the country which was very thinly inhabited. While I was out it clouded up, and I began to get scared; and in a little while I was so much so, that I didn't know which way home was, nor anything about it. I set out the way I thought it was, but it turned out with me, as it always does with a lost man, I was wrong, and took exactly the contrary direction from the right one. And for the information of young hunters, I will just say, in this place, that whenever a fellow gets bad lost, the way home is just the way he don't think it is. This rule will hit nine times out of ten. I went ahead, though, about six or seven miles, when I found night was coming on fast; but at this distressing time I saw a little woman streaking it along through the woods like all wrath, and so I cut on too, for I was determined I wouldn't lose sight of her that night any more. I run on till she saw me, and she stopped; for she was as glad to see me as I was to see her, as she was lost as well as me. When I came up to her, who should she be but my little girl, that I had been paying my respects to. She had been out hunting her father's horses, and had missed her way, and had no knowledge where she was, or how far it was to any house, or what way would take us there. She have been traveling all day, and was mighty tired; and I would have taken her up, and toated her, if it hadn't been that I wanted her just where I could see her all the time, for I thought she looked sweeter than sugar; and by this time I loved her almost well enough to eat her.

At last I came to a path, that I knowed must go somewhere, and so we followed it, till we came to a house, at about dark. Here we stayed all night. I set up all night courting; and in the morning we parted. She went to her home, from which we were distant about seven miles, and I to mine, which was ten miles off.

I now turned in to work again; and it was about four weeks before I went back to see her. I continued to go occasionally, until I had worked long enough to pay for my horse, by putting in my gun with my work, to the man I had purchased from; and then I began to count whether I was to be deceived again or not. At our next meeting we set the day for our wedding; and I went to my father's, and made arrangements for an infair, and returned to ask her parents for her. When I got there, the old lady appeared to be mighty wrathy; and when I broached the subject, she looked at me as savage as a meat ax. The old man appeared quite willing, and treated me very clever. But I hadn't been there long before the old woman as good as ordered me out of her house. I thought I would put her in mind of old times, and see how that would go with her. I told her she had called me her son-in-law before I had attempted to call her my mother-in-law, and I thought she ought to cool off. But her Irish was up too high to do anything with her, and so I quit trying. All I cared for was, to have her daughter on my side, which I knowed was the case then; but how soon some other fellow might knock my nose out of joint again, I couldn't tell. I, however, felt rather insulted at the old lady, and I thought I wouldn't get married in her house. And so I told her girl, that I would come the next Thursday, and bring a horse, a bridle, and saddle for her, and she must be ready to go. Her mother declared I shouldn't have her; but I knowed I should, if somebody else didn't get her before Thursday. I then started, bidding them good-day, and went by the house of a justice of the peace, who lived on the way to my father's and made a bargain with him to marry me.

When Thursday came, all necessary arrangements were made at my father's to receive my wife; and so I took my eldest brother and his wife, and another brother, and a single sister that I had, and two other young men with me, and cut out to her father's house to get her. We went on, until we got within two miles of the place, where we met a large company that had heard of the wedding, and were waiting. Some of that company went on with my brother and sister, and the young man I had picked out to wait on me. When they got there, they found the old lady as wrathy as ever. However, the old man filled their bottle, and the young men returned in a hurry. I then went on with my company, and when I arrived I never pretended to dismount from my horse, but rode up to the door, and asked the girl if she was ready; and she said she was. I then told her to light on the horse I was leading; and she did so. Her father, though, had gone out to the gate, and when I started he commenced persuading me to stay and marry there; that he was entirely willing to the match, and that his wife, like most women, had entirely too much tongue; but that I oughtn't to mind her. I told him if she would ask me to stay and marry at her house, I would do so. With that he sent for her, and after they had talked for some time out by themselves, she came to me and looked at me mighty good, and asked my pardon for what she had said, and invited me stay. She said it was the first child she had ever had to marry; and she couldn't bear to see her go off in that way; that if I would light, she would do the best she could for us. I couldn't stand everything, and so I agreed, and we got down, and went in. I sent off then for my parson, and got married in a short time; for I was afraid to wait long, for fear of another defeat. We had as good treatment as could be expected; and that night all went on well. The next day we cut out for my father's, where we met a large company of people, that had been waiting a day and a night for our arrival. We passed the time quite merrily, until the company broke up; and having gotten my wife, I thought I was completely made up, and needed nothing more in the whole world. But I soon found this was all a mistake—for now having a wife, I wanted everything else; and, worse than all, I had nothing to give for it.

I remained a few days at my father's, and then went back to my new father-in-law's; where, to my surprise I found my old Irish mother in the finest humor in the world.

She gave us two likely cows and calves, which though it was a small marriage-portion, was still better than I had expected, and indeed, it was about all I ever got. I rented a small farm and cabin, and went to work; but I had much trouble to find out a plan to get anything to put in my house. At this time, my good friend the Quaker came forward to my assistance, and gave me an order to a store for fifteen dollars' worth of such things as my little wife might choose. With this, we fixed up pretty grand, as we thought, and allowed to get on very well. My wife had a good wheel, and knowed exactly how to use it. She was also a good weaver, as most of the Irish are, whether men or women; and being very industrious with her wheel, she had, in little or no time, a fine web of cloth, ready to make up; and she was good at that too, and at almost anything else that a woman could do.

We worked on for some years, renting ground, and paying high rent, until I found it wasn't the thing it was cracked up to be; and that I couldn't make a fortune at it just at all. So I concluded to quit it, and cut out for some new country. In this time we had two sons, and I found I was better at increasing my family than my fortune. It was therefore the more necessary that I should hunt some better place to get along; and as I knowed I would have to move at some time, I thought it was better to do it before my family got too large, that I might have less to carry.

The Duck and Elk river country was just beginning to settle, and I determined to try that. I had now one old horse, and a couple of two-year-old colts. They were both broke to the halter, and my father-in-law proposed, that, if I went, he would go with me, and take one horse to help me move. So we all fixed up, and I packed my two colts with as many of my things as they could bear; and away we went across the mountains. We got on well enough, and arrived safely in Lincoln county, on the head of the Mulberry fork of Elk river. I found this a very rich country, and so new, that game, of different sorts, was very plenty. It was here that I began to distinguish myself as a hunter, and to lay the foundation for all my future greatness; but mighty little did I know of what sort it was going to be. Of deer and smaller game I killed an abundance;

but the bear had been much hunted in those parts before, and were not so plenty as I could have wished. I lived here in the years 1809 and '10, to the best of my recollection, and then I moved to Franklin county, and settled on Bean creek, where I remained till after the close of the last war.

CHAPTER XXX

TIMOTHY FLINT FLOATS DOWN THE OHIO

THERE WAS also new country north of the Ohio. It had been formally opened in 1787, and people had been steadily drifting into it from the east. But the great migration began in the first decade of the nineteenth century, when a veritable flood of human beings—it has been estimated at a million—poured through the passes of the Alleghenies, embarked upon the Ohio at Pittsburgh or points further down, and floated lazily on into the heart of a continent only now beginning to be appreciated for its extent and richness of promise. In 1815 a New England clergyman, Timothy Flint, took the journey with his family. The banks of La Belle Rivière were already lined with cabins and villages; yet much was still there of the original Eden which the imagination of men had found the interior of America to be.

WITH many prayers on my own part, and that of my friends, that these evils might not follow me, my family left the land of their fathers the fourth of October, 1815. Toward the latter part of the month, we began to ascend the Allegany hills. In our slow mode of traveling, we had had them in view several days. With their interminable blue outline, stretching hill beyond hill, and interposing to the imagination of such travelers as we were, a barrier to return almost as impassable as the grave, it may easily be imagined with what interest we contemplated them. It is, I believe, generally conceded to the inhabitants of New England, that, perhaps, with the exception of the Scotch, they have more national feeling than any other people. We had broken all the ties that render the place, where we first drew breath, so dear. Occasional samples of the people and the country beyond these hills, not at all calculated to sooth our feelings, or to throw pleasing associations over our contemplated residence beyond them, had frequently met us. The people on our route constantly designated them by the appellation of "back-woodsmen," and we heard these men themselves uniformly calling their baggage "plunder." The wolf, the bear, and the bald eagle, were the most frequent emblems in the tavern-signs,

322

near the acclivities of these mountains. The bald eagle itself was soaring in the blue of the atmosphere, high above the summits of the first ridge, and its shrill and savage cries were sufficiently loud to reach our ears.

We had, too, many "compagnons de voyage," exact samples of the general character of New England emigrants; poor, active, parsi-monious, inquisitive, and fully impressed that no country, in moral advantages, could equal the country which they had left. They felt, in common with us, their love for the dear homes they had left increasing as they receded from them. In common with us, too, they calculated to have taken a final farewell of those homes. When we had at last reached the highest point of the first of the three parallel ridges, before we began to descend a declivity, which we expected would forever shield the Atlantic country from our view; before we went "over the hills and far away," it will readily be conceived, that a family which had been reared in seclusion, such as ours, would be likely to drop "some natural tears," and to take a long and anxious look at the land, which contained all their ties and charities.

We passed hundreds of Pittsburgh wagons, in the crossing. Many of them had broken axles and wheels, and in more than one place it was pointed out to us, that teams had plunged down the precipices and had perished. In descending the ridges, a winding road, just wide enough to admit one carriage, was carried round the verge of the declivity, perhaps for more than a mile. In this case, if two carriages met, there would be no alternative but to retreat to the commencement of the narrow way. To prevent this, it is necessary that the carriage, which is commencing the ascent or descent, give notice by blowing a horn, or sending a messenger in advance.

These people, who drive teams between Philadelphia and Pitts-burgh, were to me, in their manners and way of living, a new species, perfectly unique in their appearance, language, and habits. They devote themselves to this mode of subsistence for years, and spend their time continually on the road. They seemed to me to be more rude, profane, and selfish, than either sailors, boatmen, or hunters, to whose modes of living theirs is the most assimilated. We found them addicted to drunkenness, and very little disposed to assist each other. Such was the aspect they presented to us. We were told, there were honorable exceptions, and even associations, who, like the sacred band of Thebes, took a kind of oath to stand by, and befriend each other. I often dropped among them, as by accident, that impressive tract, the "Swearer's Prayer." I was pleased to re-mark the result of their reflections, as they read the tract, apart on their window-seats. In some it seemed to produce a momentary thoughtfulness; in others a smile; and again in others, a deep growl of acquiescence, very like that which every one has heard, who has attended a council of Indians, and heard them express a kind of reluctant assent to terms proposed to them.

In the valley, between the middle and the last of the parallel ridges, we encountered a drove of more than a thousand cattle and swine, from the interior of Ohio; a name which yet sounded in our ears like the land of savages. The appearance of the swine and cattle, in our eyes, had an unnatural shagginess, and roughness, like wolves; and such, you know, even yet, are the impressions of multitudes of the Atlantic people, with respect to that beautiful country. The name of the country from which this drove came, added something, no doubt, to these associations. They were from "Mad River." We were told that the chief drover, a man as untamed and wild in appearance, as Robinson's man, Friday, was taking them on to Pennsylvania to fatten, previous to their being sold in the Philadelphia market.

There is a considerable tract of table-land, before you descend the last hill, and on this there was a public house. Here we encountered a stage broken down. The passengers had been drenched in rain. They were a company of tinners, going to establish themselves somewhere in the West, and a printer from Connecticut, with his young and beautiful wife, about to commence a printing-office for a gazette in Kentucky. This fine young woman, who had suffered her share with the rest, gave us an example of natural equanimity and philosophy. She was cheerful and conversable, while the other women were querulous, in tears, and out of temper with everything about them, and full of all the tedious complaints with which inexperienced travelers meet the incidental disasters of their way.

Our journey from the beautiful Moravian settlements in Pennsylvania had been rendered sometimes tedious, and sometimes amusing, by the company of a German Lutheran minister and his family, who had been sent out to some Lutheran settlements on the Big Miami. He was recommended to us as an amiable and exemplary man, and had been reared, I believe, in Germany. A more singular specimen of a clergyman could not well be presented to a New England minister. He was a short, robust man, with a round and ruddy face, with a singular expression, between cheerfulness and apathy. When traveling, he had constantly in his mouth a pipe, in form much like that musical instrument called a serpent, in which the smoke circulated through many circumvolutions, and finally reached his mouth through a silver mouthpiece. He rode a huge

Pennsylvania horse, apparently with no consciousness of want of feeling for his wife and children, who, for the most part, trudged along beside their wagon on foot. When we arrived at the public house, and were seated to the substantial and sumptuous fare that is furnished at the good houses in these regions, and this family at the same time ordered their national diet, boiled potatoes, sour milk, and mush, we could easily discover by the longing looks of the children, that, all national preferences to the contrary, it would have been easy to persuade them to exchange their diet for ours.

I can scarcely hope to give you any impression of our feelings when we began to descend the last ridge, and the boundless valley of the Ohio began to open upon our view. The finishing of the superb national road from Baltimore to Wheeling, and the present ease and frequency of crossing the mountains, will soon render it difficult to conceive what a new and strange world opened at that time and place before the imagination of an unpracticed Atlantic traveler. In such an unexplored and unlimited view of a country to be our resting-place, and the field of our labors, where there was no fixed point, no shelter for our hopes and expectations, where all must necessarily be strange, a country to which, in approaching, we had constantly heard the term "back woods" applied, melancholy thoughts and painful remembrances would naturally arise in our minds. I fear that my family and myself feel more bitterly and painfully than is the common lot to feel, the gloomy and depressing sensation of experiencing ourselves strangers in a strange land.

Many travelers and emigrants to this region, view the first samples of the modes of traveling in the western world, on the Allegany at Oleanne point, or the Monongahela at Brownsville. These are but the retail specimens. At Pittsburgh, where these rivers unite, you have the thing in gross, and by wholesale. The first thing that strikes a stranger from the Atlantic, arrived at the boat-landing, is the singular, whimsical, and amusing spectacle, of the varieties of water-craft of all shapes and structures. There is the stately barge, of the size of a large Atlantic schooner, with its raised and outlandish looking deck. This kind of craft, however, which required twenty-five hands to work it up stream, is almost gone into disuse, and though so common ten years ago, is now scarcely seen. Next there is the keel-boat, of a long, slender, and elegant form, and generally carrying from fifteen to thirty tons. This boat is formed to be easily propelled over shallow waters in the summer season, and in low stages of the water is still much used, and runs on waters not yet frequented by steamboats. Next in order are the Kentucky flats, or in the vernacular phrase, "broadhorns," a species of ark, very nearly resembling a New England pig-stye. They are fifteen feet wide, and from forty to one hundred feet in length, and carry from twenty to seventy tons. Some of them, that are called family-boats, and used by families in descending the river, are very large and roomy, and have comfortable and separate apartments, fitted up with chairs, beds, tables and stoves. It is no uncommon spectacle to see a large family, old and young, servants, cattle, hogs, horses, sheep, fowls, and animals of all kinds, bringing to recollection the cargo of the ancient ark, all embarked, and floating down on the same bottom. Then there are what the people call "covered sleds," or ferryflats, and Allegany-skiffs, carrying from eight to twelve tons. In another place are pirogues of from two to four tons burden, hollowed sometimes from one prodigious tree, or from the trunks of two trees united, and a plank rim fitted to the upper part. There are common skiffs, and other small craft, named, from the manner of making them, "dugouts," and canoes hollowed from smaller trees. These boats are in great numbers, and these names are specific, and clearly define the boats to which they belong. But besides these, in this land of freedom and invention, with a little aid, perhaps, from the influence of the moon, there are monstrous anomalies, reducible to no specific class of boats, and only illustrating the whimsical archetypes of things that have previously existed in the brain of inventive men, who reject the slavery of being obliged to build in any received form. You can scarcely imagine an abstract form in which a boat can be built, that in some part of the Ohio or Mississippi you will not see, actually in motion. The New York canal is beginning, indeed, to bring samples of this infinite variety of water-craft nearer to the inspection of the Atlantic people.

This variety of boats, so singular in form, and most of them apparently so frail, is destined in many instances to voyages of from twelve hundred to three thousand miles. Keel-boats, built at this place, start on hunting expeditions for points on the Missouri, Arkansas, and Red River, at such distances from Pittsburgh as these. Such are the inland voyages on these long streams, and the terms of the navigation are as novel as are the forms of the boats. You hear of the danger of "riffles," meaning probably, ripples, and planters, and sawyers, and points, and bends, and shoots, a corruption, I suppose, of the French "chute." You hear the boatmen extolling their prowess in pushing a pole, and you learn the received opinion, that a "Kentuck" is the best man at a pole, and a Frenchman at the oar. A firm push of the iron-pointed pole on a fixed log, is termed a "reverend" set. You are told when you embark, to bring your "plunder" aboard, and you hear about moving "fernenst" the stream; and you gradually become acquainted with a copious vocabulary of this sort. The manners of the boatmen are as strange as their language. Their peculiar way of life has given origin not only to an appropriate dialect, but to new modes of enjoyment, riot, and fighting. Almost every boat, while it lies in the harbor has one or more fiddles scraping continually aboard, to which you often see the boatmen dancing. There is no wonder that the way of life which the boatmen lead, in turn extremely indolent, and extremely laborious; for days together requiring little or no effort, and attended with no danger, and then on a sudden, laborious and hazardous, beyond Atlantic navigation; generally plentiful as it respects food, and always so as it regards whisky, should always have seductions that prove irresistible to the young people that live near the banks of the river. The boats float by their dwellings on beautiful spring mornings, when the verdant forest, the mild and delicious temperature of the air, the delightful azure of the sky of this country, the fine bottom on the one hand, and the romantic bluff on the other, the broad and smooth stream rolling calmly down the forest, and floating the boat gently forward,—all these circumstances harmonize in the excited youthful imagination. The boatmen are dancing to the violin on the deck of their boat. They scatter their wit among the girls on the shore who come down to the water's edge to see the pageant pass. The boat glides on until it disappears behind a point of wood. At this moment, perhaps, the bugle, with which all the boats are provided, strikes up its note in the distance over the water. These scenes, and these notes, echoing from the bluffs of the beautiful Ohio, have a charm for the imagination, which, although I have heard a thousand times repeated, and at all hours, and in all positions, is even to me always new, and always delightful. No wonder that the young, who are reared in these remote regions, with that restless curiosity which is fostered by solitude and silence, who witness scenes like this so frequently, no wonder that the severe and unremitting labors of agriculture, performed directly in the view of such scenes, should become tasteless and irksome. No wonder that the young along the banks of the great streams, should detest the labors of the field, and embrace every opportunity, either openly, or, if minors, covertly, to escape and devote themselves to the pernicious employment of boating. And in this view we may account for the detestation of the inhabitants along these great streams towards steamboats, which are every day diminishing the number of small boats and boatmen, and which have already withdrawn from the western waters, probably ten thousand from that employment. And yet with all these seductions for the eye and the imagination, no life is so slavish, none so precarious and dangerous. In no employment do the hands so wear out. After the lapse of so very short a period since these waters have been navigated in this way, at every bend, and every high point of the river, you are almost sure to see, as you stop for a moment, indications of the "narrow house"; the rude monument, the coarse memorial, carved on an adjoining tree by a brother boatman, which marks that an exhausted boatman there yielded his breath, and was buried.

Our first river voyage commenced in the early part of November, on a beautiful autumnal afternoon. We had waited a considerable time for the rising of the river, for as yet no boat of any considerable draught of water was able to descend. We had become impatient of remaining here, and embarked in a very small flat-boat, laden with factory cottons and cutlery. The owner was from Dorchester in Massachusetts, and probably his whole capital was embarked on this bottom. He was as little experienced in this mode of navigation as we were. Our notions of what we had to expect on this voyage were formed from contemplating the gentle and equable current of this beautiful river, and resulted in the persuasion, that the whole trip would be an excursion of pleasure and entire safety. Hundreds of emigrants from the eastern country commence this descent equally inexperienced.

About one o'clock in the afternoon we began to float down the Allegany and in a few moments we were moving on the broad bosom of the Ohio, at the point of junction nearly a mile in width. The autumns of every part of our country are beautiful, but those of the western country are preëminently so. Nothing resulting from beauty of sky, temperature of air, and charm of scenery, can surpass what was now above us and around us. The bright sun, the mild blue sky, a bland feeling of the atmosphere, the variegated foliage of the huge sycamores which line the banks of the Ohio, their leaves turning red and yellow, and finely contrasting with the brilliant white of their branches, the unruffled stream, which reflected in its bosom the beautiful surrounding nature,—all things conspired to give us very high anticipations from being wafted down "la belle rivière." We were congratulating each other, that this was indeed worth all the toils and privations we had endured in arriving at the Ohio. But, alas, for human calculations! While we were noticing every object on the banks with such intense interest, while the owner was seated amidst his goods and wares, indulging probably in golden dreams of easy, certain, and great profits, while one of the company that you know of, was completely given up to reverie, at which you have so often smiled,—on a sudden the roar of the river admonished us that we were near a ripple. We had with us that famous book "The Navigator," as it is called. The boat began to exchange its gentle and imperceptible advance for a furious progress. Soon after, it gave a violent bounce against a rock on one side, which threatened to capsize it. On recovering her level, she immediately bounced on the opposite side, and that in its turn was keeled up. Instead of running to the oar, we ran to look in the "Navigator." The owner was pale. The children shrieked. The hardware came tumbling upon us from the shelves, and Mrs. F. was almost literally buried amidst locks, latches, knives, and pieces of domestic cotton. The gentle river had not intended in this first alarm to swallow us up, but only to give us timely warning, that too much tranquillity and enjoyment are not to be expected here. We floated off from this ripple, which bore the ominous name of "Dead Man's," into the smooth water, with no other injury than the chaotic state of our lading. But from that moment, adieu to our poetic dreams of floating down the beautiful river in such perfect safety. We were continually running to the "Navigator," astonished to find how full the river was of chutes and ripples.

At Beaver in Pennsylvania we exchanged this dangerous and tedious mode of conveyance, for one more suited to the present stage of the water. We purchased a large skiff. It has the advantage of being able to run in any stage of the water, without grounding, and is perfectly safe. In fine weather it furnishes a very pleasant way of descending the river. But we soon found that we had exchanged one inconvenience for another. We could look round us indeed; we went forward securely. But at one time the sun beat intensely upon us. At another we suffered from fogs and rains. At every landing, too, where we stopped to spend the night, and find lodging, we were obliged to remove every article of lading from the boat, and not too well assured, that some of the numerous adventurers would not take away our boat during the night.

In this manner we floated by many thriving villages, that had just risen in the wilderness, and many indications of commencing settlements. The Ohio broadened evidently at every advancing bend. The bottoms diverged farther from the shores, and the fertility of the soil increased. We remarked a curious but uniform circumstance, which applies equally to the Mississippi, and all its tributaries. It is, that with few exceptions, where the bluffs of the river rise immediately from the shore on the one hand, the bottoms broaden on the other; and when the bluff commences at the termination of the bottom, that commences on the opposite shore. Thus they regularly alternate with each other.

At Steubenville, in Ohio, we remarked that the river seemed to develop its character for broadness and fertility. Here we first began to notice the pawpaw, the persimmon, and other new and beautiful shrubs and plants, peculiar to this climate. Here, too, we saw the most obvious proofs of the advance of this most flourishing country, in population and improvement, the more entire development of which has been so astonishing within the last ten years. Where we now saw a large village, with the spires of churches, an entire street of large brick buildings, manufactories, a market-house, and the bustle of a busy town, only eighteen years before, there had been a solid and compact forest of vast sycamores and beeches. They numbered already in this town four thousand inhabitants.

We found a new source of amusement in contemplating a set of twelve or fourteen hands, walking slowly forward, and half bent, with the shoulder firmly fixed against the knob of a long pole, whose iron point was set in the bottom, and thus apparently with great labor propelling the boat against the stream. As soon as they have walked the length of the boat, they raise their pole, walk forward in Indian file, and renew their "set," as the phrase is, again. I shall, however, more naturally remark upon the mode of pushing a boat against the stream in another place. It is a very laborious and slow process, very expensive and troublesome. Steamboats, save one, were not in use at this time. I was obliged to move in my excursions, in a keelboat. I was compelled to know, to my cost, all about pushing a boat up stream with a pole. "Quæque ipse miserrima vidi." Justly to appreciate the value of steamboats on these waters, one must have moved up them, as long, as dangerously, and as laboriously, as I have done.

We landed at Marietta, just above the mouth of the Muskingum. It is a considerable village. In the forms of the houses and the arrangements about them, you discover that this is an establishment from New England. A number of well-informed and respectable emigrants from that country had preceded us, and had just arrived in the village. Mr. R., a pious and amiable man, who has since deceased, was minister there. I had letters to the venerable General Putnam, the patriarch of this colony.

Though this is in some sense a Yankee region, and Ohio is called, on the opposite shore, the Yankee state, you do not the less hear at all these towns, and everywhere in this state, fine stories about Yankee tricks, and Yankee finesse, and wooden nutmegs, and pitcoal indigo, and gin made by putting pinetops in the whisky. The poor Irish have not had more stories invented and put into their mouths. I might relate a score of Yankee tricks, that different people assured us had been played off upon them. I will only remark, that wherever we stopped at night and requested lodgings, we were constantly asked if we were Yankees; and when we answered that we were, we constantly saw a lengthening of visage ensue, but were generally complimented in the end with granting our request, and assurances that our appearance and my profession answered for us. We were then compelled to hear of impositions and pretty tricks, and small thefts, and more than all, departure without paying off bills, which, they alleged, had been practiced upon them by Yankees. The emigrants upon whom these charges are fixed, which are probably magnified, both in number and enormity, are as often other people, as Yankees. But as these last eminently possess the power of talking, and inspire a sort of terror by their superior acuteness, and as that terror procures a certain degree of respect, many a blockhead from the southern and middle states has wished to shine his hour, as a wise man, and has assumed this terrific name; and thus the impression has finally been established, that almost all the emigrants who pass down the river, are Yankees. The common reply of the boatmen to those who ask them what is their lading, is, "Pit-coal indigo, wooden nutmegs, straw baskets, and Yankee notions."

To return to Marietta. General Putnam was a veteran of the revolution, an inhabitant of Marietta, one of the first purchasers and settlers in the country. He had moved here, when it was one compact and boundless forest, vocal only with the cry of owls, the growl of bears, and the death-song of the savages. He had seen that forest fall under the ax,—had seen commodious, and after that, splendid dwellings, rise round him. He had seen the settlement sustain an inundation, which wafted away the dwellings, and in some instances the inhabitants in them. The cattle and all the improvements of cultivation were swept away. He had seen the country suffer all the accumulated horrors of an Indian war. He had seen its exhaustless fertility and its natural advantages triumph over all. He had seen Marietta make advances toward acquainting itself with the Gulf of Mexico, by floating off from its banks a number of sea vessels built there. He had seen the prodigious invention of steamboats experimented on the Ohio, and heard their first thunder, as they swept by his dwelling. He had survived to see them become so common, as to be no more objects of curiosity. He had witnessed a hundred boats, laden for New Orleans, pass by in the compass of a few hours. He had surrounded his modest, but commodious dwelling with fruit trees of his own planting; and finer, or more loaded orchards than his, no country could offer. In the midst of rural plenty, and endeared friends, who had grown up around him,—far from the display of wealth, the bustle of ambition and intrigue, the father of the colony, hospitable and kind without ostentation and without effort, he displayed in these remote regions, the grandeur, real and intrinsic, of those immortal men, who achieved our revolution. Of these great men, most of whom, and General Putnam among the rest, have passed away, there seems to have arisen a more just and a more respectful estimate. Greater and more unambitious men, no age or country has reared. Cato's seems to have been their motto —"esse quam videri."

At the close of November we departed from Marietta. The days were still delightful. But the earth in the morning was whitened with frost. The advanced season admonished us, that we could no longer go on safely or commodiously, in an open boat. We purchased a Kentucky flat, of forty tons burden, subject however to the incumbrance of a family, who had been already insured a passage in it. A few hours before sunset we went on board with a number of passengers, beside my family, and I introduced my family to the one that was already on board. He proved to be a fine, healthy-looking Kentuckian, with a young and pretty wife, two or three negro servants, and two small children. He was a fair specimen of the rough and frank Kentucky character of men of his class; an independent farmer, who had swarmed from the old homestead hive in Kentucky. Land, there, he said, had already become too scarce and dear. He wanted elbow-room, did not wish to have a neighbor within three miles of him, and was moving to the upper Mississippi, for range. It had become too dark on board for him to distinguish my family or profession. "So," said he, "I find I am chartered on a rail-splitting Yankee," adding an epithet that I omit. Some one politely mentioned to him my profession. His wife observed in the phrase of the country, "My husband swears hard. His father and mine are both religious. I should be forever thankful to you, if you would cure him of the habit of swearing." I remarked, that since we were thrown together, and were under the necessity of occupying the same boat for some days, it would be extremely gratifying to me if he would desist from the habit, at least while we were together. The usual remarks were added, on the folly and vulgarity of swearing, and its utter want of temptation. He replied, that it was not his habit to swear in the presence of ministers, or gentlemen, to whom he knew it was offensive. He continued, in an earnest tone, to state that all his relatives were religious, and that he was almost the single stray sheep from the flock; he had often tried to "get religion," as the phrase is here; he had labored as hard for it, as he ever had at rolling logs, and that whatever was the reason, do all he could, to him it would never come; and now, if it would come to him of itself, good; but if not, that he meant to try for it no more. He pledged himself, in conclusion, that he would abstain from swearing while with me, as far as he could remember to abstain, and he faithfully redeemed his pledge. He proved an excellent steersman for the boat, and a kind and friendly, if not a pleasant companion. He had been many years a boatman on the Ohio, the Mississippi, and its waters; and had a great fund of interesting narrative appertaining to his numerous voyages. . . .

The twenty-eighth of April, 1816, we came in sight of what had long been the subject of our conversations, our inquiries, and curiosity, the far-famed Mississippi. It is a view, which has left on my mind a most deep and durable impression, marking a period, from which commenced a new era in my existence. We had been looking forward to this place as the pillars of Hercules. The country on this side had still some unbroken associations with our native land. This magnificent river, almost dividing the continent, completely severed this chain. We were now, also, to experience the novelty of propelling a boat against the current of one of the mightiest and most rapid rivers in the world. The junction of the Ohio and Mississippi does not impress that idea of physical grandeur, which fills up your anticipations. But allow the fancy to range the boundless forests and prairies, through which it brings down the sweeping tribute, which it has collected from distant and nameless mountains, and from a hundred shores, and you will not contemplate this mighty stream without an intense interest. A sharp point, almost at right angles with either river, mingles their waters in the midst of deep and ancient forests, where the eye expatiates over vast and swampy woods, perhaps fifty miles in extent. Turn the point, and your eye catches the vast Mississippi, rolling down his mass of turbid waters, which seem, compared with the limpid and greenish-colored waters of the Ohio, to be of almost a milky whiteness. They exactly resemble waters in which white ashes have been mixed and remain suspended. A speculation was got up, to form a great city at the delta, and in fact they raised a few houses upon piles of wood. The houses were inundated, and when we were there, "they kept the town," as the boatmen phrased it, in a vast flat boat, a hundred feet in length, in which there were families, liquor-shops, drunken men and women, and all the miserable appendages to such a place. To render the solitude of the pathless forest on the opposite shore more dismal, there is one gloomy-looking house there.

CHAPTER XXXI

THE WESTERN population, confined at first to the banks of the Ohio and the Mississippi and their many tributaries, spread slowly in across the prairies. Ohio, Indiana, and Illinois filled up as Kentucky and Tennessee were filling up below La Belle Rivière. Emigration went from the Carolinas and Virginia; it went also with increasing vigor from New England. The two streams mingled in states like Illinois, producing a race of men and women apart. Or so at any rate it seemed to Christiana Holmes Tillson, who, joining the movement from New England in 1822, settled in Illinois among curious yet likable people. She has described them, along with the details of her own home-making, in letters to her family. The story begins with a night spent on the way to her new home.

BRICE HANNA was a tall, well-formed man with good features, and but for his surly expression might have been called handsome. When we arrived at his house he dismounted, came up to the carriage, and told us there was another house on the other side of the swamp where we could stay; that he had been from home all the week; that his wife was sick, and that we could not be accommodated *anyhow*. Your father told him that it was nearly sunset, and that he should not attempt to go through a five-mile swamp until he could do it by daylight, so we unpacked ourselves and moved toward the house, and with much fear and trembling I set my foot on the threshold of Brice Hanna's cabin. There was but one room in the main cabin, which I at once perceived was unusually clean for an establishment of that kind. There were two beds nicely made, with clean pillows and handsome bedquilts, the floor clean, and the coarse chairs looking as if they had just been scrubbed. In a large, open fireplace was a cheerful fire of oak logs, which were supported by one old iron andiron and a stone on the other side. But what most puzzled me was a pretty woman—who did not seem to be more than twenty—sitting with her feet on a chair, and with pillows around her, and holding her infant in her lap. Her skin was very fair, and she had an abundance of jet black, curly hair, and

334

bright, black eyes. She had on a pretty pink calico dress, which with her baby's gear had the appearance of thorough cleanliness. She looked a little annoyed when we first went in, but politely asked us to be seated, and by her manner we concluded that she was mistress of the mansion.

Brice had not made his appearance, but he finally came in, bringing a stone, which he threw down with an oath, saying he had had his eye on that rock for some time, and thought it would be a match for the one in the fireplace. He commenced pulling out the andiron, swearing at the fire for being too hot. His wife looked on tremblingly, and asked why he was not willing to have the andiron remain, as it was "a heap handier than the stone." With another string of oaths he jerked out the poor andiron, and taking it to the door he threw it as far as he could into the yard. Such things might do for the broadcloth gentry, but he did not belong to the gentry; at the same time giving one of his menacing glances at us. He went out, but returned in a few minutes to say to his wife that the woman she had there—who, with her husband and boy, occupied a little cabin in the yard—"should not stay in his diggings another night," and with another oath said, "clare them out." "Well, what is the matter?" asked the trembling wife. "Matter! why the cursed——" a list of epithets too fearful to repeat; "infernal fool has let the hogs and cows get into my cornfield and destroy more corn and potatoes than thar eternally cursed necks are worth; so I'll clare them out," finishing off his sentence with another string of oaths not to be outdone by Sancho Panza's proverbs.

The poor wife would shrink down when the blast was heaviest, but after he had gone would brighten up again. When one of the storms had subsided and he had gone on to anathematize the man and boy with curses loud and heavy, I ventured to ask her how long she had been a cripple. She said only a few months; that just before her baby was born she fell into the well and broke some of her bones, and was so hurt all over that she had not been able to walk since, and if it had been God's will she should have wished never to have come out alive. She was ignorant, but pretty, and with a sweet expression; so much truthfulness was manifested in all she said that my heart went out to her with a compassion that I cannot express.

After a while the fiend again made his appearance with a large slice of bacon and corn bread in his hand, and with his foot he kicked along a chair until he reached his wife, and seating himself by her side he took out a long bowie knife and commenced eating. Looking at her with something of a subdued tone, he said: "This is the first corn bread and bacon I have tasted since I went from here." "Too bad," she remarked, pleasantly; "and what did you eat all the week?" "Why, you see, I was hauling for Marshall; Marshall is building a big house; and I have been hauling brick and timber. When I gits to the house Marshall will call to that infernal old black cook of his'n to get my supper, and the ——" usual list of expletives, "fool goes and makes me some coffee as black as her derned old face, and some of them 'are cussed light Yankee biscuits, and some beef that was just warmed through as the old bull was when he was running alive and bellering, and when you put your knife inter hit, by thunder, the blood would run. Haven't had a bite of pone, or corn-dodger, or hog meat, not any since last Monday morning." "Too bad; didn't they give you any milk?" "Jest so; axed for milk, and the old black devil brought me some jest from the cow; haven't seen a sip of buttermilk or clabber." "Too bad." She looked pleased that he had become sufficiently subdued to bear soothing.

We had previously called for supper, and were summoned into the cabin in the yard, which was used for a kitchen and dining-room. The woman of all work—the wife of the man who didn't keep the hogs out of the cornfield—was standing at a side table where we were to be seated for our evening repast. I have forgotten what we had for food, but remember the cleanliness of the rough furnishing, and that a saucer standing on the table, filled with lard, with a strip of white cloth laid in it and one end raised up at the side of the saucer, burning, served to light the table and the whole room. We went back from our supper to where the happy pair were still seated, he looking as if he had blown another blast and had settled down to sulk, and the wife trying to look happy, and smiling through her tears. He sat awhile as if trying to think of something disagreeable to say or do. All at once a happy thought seemed to occur to him, and looking at us with malicious satisfaction he commenced a furious rubbing and scratching, pushing up his sleeves and looking at his wrists. He turned suddenly around and asked us if we had any beds of our own to stretch on for the night. He had seen all we took from the carriage, and knew that we had no beds along, and looked satanically happy when he announced that we would all get the itch, as all in the house had it, and swore that the cursed old fellow who couldn't keep the cows out of the cornfield had brought the itch to them. Such startling information would have been fearful had I not looked at the honest face of the poor wife, who, without uttering a word, showed plainly that it was news to her, and I felt sure it was only a scheme of his own to make us uncomfortable. He seemed disappointed that he had not made a greater sensation, and as no one replied to his last effort he settled himself to think of something else disagreeable.

At last, with a more extended swear than before, he said he was tired, and was going to bed; it would do for gentry, who could stay in bed as long as they pleased, to sit up late, "but I'm no gentry, and I'm going to bed." There were two beds in the room, standing foot to foot, on the side opposite the fireplace. One was for us, the other for Brice, wife and baby, your Uncle Robert making his bed on the floor with the carriage cushions and a buffalo robe which had been purchased at Shawneetown. He evidently felt relieved that he was not under the necessity of getting into the infected beds. Although I did not believe there was any danger, I took the precaution to spread some pocket handkerchiefs over the pillows, and by only removing my outside garments and putting on gloves, a thing I could not induce your father to do, felt pretty secure as to infection, but not quite comfortable as respected the mood of mine host. Being very tired I thought I would lie down, but not allow myself to sleep. Our trunks were deposited in the same room where we were, and I imagined that there had been a suspicious eyeing throughout the evening, and that the inside as well as the out might prove attractive; as we were so evidently in close quarters with a madman, was not altogether at ease about our personal safety. I was very tired, and Morpheus finally overcame all my resolutions and made me forgetful of danger.

I do not know how long I had slept, when aroused by the crying of baby and the coarse swearing of the father. He scolded his wife for letting it cry, and then cursed the "little imp; imp of the devil." The wife said the child needed caring for, and would not go to sleep without it; that it must be taken to the fire and made dry and comfortable, but he swore he would gag the squalling brat. After a while he sprang out of bed and pulling the child from under the bed clothes, declared he would roast it. There was in the fireplace a large fire, made of oak logs, which were all aglow and gave light to the whole room. He took the baby under one arm, and with two or three bounds was at the fireplace. He commenced raking open the coals, still holding baby under his arm, swearing he would make a back-log; "yes, I'll brile ye." I kept both eyes open and trembled for the fate of the baby, when, to my surprise, he seated himself, carefully warmed the dry linen that was hanging by the fire, and in the most handy manner performed all that a good nurse or mother could have done. And now that baby was dry and there was no good reason for crying, and swearing did not soothe, he pressed "the brat, imp of the devil," to his breast, and commenced singing a good Methodist hymn in a soft, subdued voice, and had it been my first impression I should have supposed him a most devout Christian. A more sudden change from the profane to the devotional could not be imagined.

This scene occurred forty-eight years ago, and now it is as fresh to my mind as at that time, but perfectly to describe it would be impossible. The most provoking part of the last performance was that I had to enjoy it alone; no one to share with me the ludicrous climax of the closing hymn, your father and Uncle Robert being asleep. As soon as it was light we were up and ready for a leave-taking. At the five-mile house on the other side of the swamp we found a plain, decent family, who gave us a breakfast of "common doings," corn bread and bacon, without any attempt at "wheat bread and chicken fixings," and from them we heard more of Brice Hanna. The man told us that Brice had a good farm and in his way kept his family comfortable, took pride in having the best wagon and horses in the county. He had always been proud of his wives, the one we saw being his third, but his greatest pride was in his peculiar capacity for swearing. He once took an oath that he would not swear again for two years, from the fact that he had found a man down in "Shawnee" who could out-swear him, and he said he felt mean ever after. He was true to his vow, but when the two years had expired commenced with renewed vigor. The gossip of the settlement was that his first wife died of a broken heart, that he had poisoned the second, and that the poor young creature whom we saw had jumped into the well to drown herself, but the water not being deep, was pulled out with nothing but bruises for her effort. The man did not believe the story of his having poisoned his second wife, but thought what was reported of the last might be true.

Arrived in Illinois, Mrs. Tillson found what it was like to grow up with a new country.

The first few months' housekeeping was made uncomfortable by the Sunday visiting. We had no regular preaching, and with my new beginnings in domestic duties and the evenings—two in each week —which I devoted to copying letters for your father, I found but little time for reading. The eastern mail came in once in two weeks, and your father being postmaster he usually had papers in every mail from all directions, and although they would be weeks in reaching us they brought the latest intelligence from the civilized world and were about all I could find time to read during the week. I tried to have Sunday for books, when I did not go to "preaching," which time, I felt, was spent without profit and instruction, and but for example's sake would have preferred a quiet day at home.

But there were no such Sundays for me. By the time our breakfast was over and our morning work disposed of there would be a tremendous knocking at the door, accompanied by sonorous demands of "who keeps the house?" Sometimes with the knocking would come, "housekeepers within?" sometimes nothing but a loud, drawling, "h-o-u-s-e-k-e-e-p-e-r-s!" and when the door was opened a backwoodsman would walk in with a big baby on his arm, followd by his wife with the youngest in both her arms, would introduce his lady, and let us know they had come for a day's visit; thinking I was "strange ones 'ere," they reckoned they ought to get acquainted. Being few—either male or female—who wore any outdoor garments, the women wore their bonnets in the house and added nothing on going out but a little shawl that came about to the bottom of the waist, said waist being a very short one. I suppose, living as they did in cabins without windows and keeping both doors open for the admittance of light—windows and out of doors was all the same to them in respect to warmth—and having come from a more southern climate, they had never learned the necessity of protection from the cold.

I think during the first three months there was rarely a Sunday when we were not called on to entertain some of these families, who came as if to a show, and would go about the house taking up things and ask, "whart's this 'ere fixin'?" open the closet and ask how we sold plates. When informed they were not for sale, could not see why we "wanted such a mighty lot," "never seed so many together, reckoned they cost a heap." The most amusing thing would be their remarks at the table, and their petting the children before coming to the table. "Hush up, honey, and be good; see thar, Auntee Tillson is gwine to have dinner right sure. Reckon she'll have some sweetened bread, cake, and all them pretty dishes." When they had satisfied their appetites and taken a final smoke they would make a move to depart, and invite us to go and spend Sunday with them. We would thank them, and say we would go to see them some week day, we did not visit on the Sabbath. We felt we were very fortunate in breaking up the practice without offending them. Of all our Sunday visitors, I think but one ever repeated the visit on that day, and though they were very jealous and suspicious I never knew of any offense being given.

Our dear Charley opened his eyes upon the rough cabin walls, and with his chubby fists in his mouth he looked—as Mother Kilpatrick declared—as if he was two months old and knew us all.

We felt we had a precious gift, but the way to take care of it was the puzzle. It was the fifteenth of September, the nights cool and chilly, and the days too cool to expose a thing so tender to the rough blasts. We had a sheet-iron stove set in the wall between the bedrooms; when the wind favored, we could kindle a fire to dress the baby, but when adverse winds prevailed we had him rolled in a blanket and taken to the kitchen to be dressed. The toilet was soon made, as the western women felt that water was a deadly application for babies. They kept their babies' heads covered with a thick calico cap until they were several months old, in which time a black surface would form and cover the scalp. They would then commence a season of cleaning by saturating the head with either hog or "bar's" (bear) grease, and then as it would come loose, pick off the black coating. As it would usually come off in large blotches, it gave a sad, leopard-like appearance to the little "honey."

Mrs. Kilpatrick offered her services as nurse and stayed with me two weeks, and rendered all the assistance that she knew and felt to be necessary, and did many things that I have no doubt she deemed unnecessary. She asked me the first morning, after I had taken a cup of coffee with some light bread crumbled into it, what she should get for my dinner; had heard the Yankee women dieted at such times; for herself, she always took pork and cabbage for her first meal. I mention this to show her ideas of nursing the sick, which extended into all her other ways of management; yet she was kind, and probably exercised much forbearance in gratifying the notions of a Yankee.

Jesse Buzan—who rented our bottom-field—had a wife whose great enjoyment seemed to consist in coming every day to inspect. She was taken quite by surprise when one day I offered her a piece of what I told her was Yankee pie. She looked blank and said, "I didn't think you would say the like of that; I allus knowed youens were all Yankees, but Billy said 'don't let on that we know it, kase it'll jest make them mad.'" I told her I was proud to be called a Yankee, and that she need never fear to speak of it. She looked incredulous, and then said, "Billy and I have always found you jess so, but some folks say they have been here when Yankees come in, and you talk a heap of things that you don't say to us." "Do they say I talk against any one?" "O no, not that; but you use a heap of words to Yankees that you don't when you talk to us. They say, too, you put a lot of nasty truck in your bread. It is what you keep in a bottle, purlass, I believe, is the name, and they say it is full of dead flies, and bugs, and cricket legs." I brought forward my little bottle of dissolved pearl ash, looking so clear and pure, and showed it to her, but it seemed hard to give up her old prejudice. . . .

Besides the burden of cooking, there were many others. Every Monday morning, instead of pumping out a boiler of soft water, the kettle had to be suspended over the fire by means of pot-hooks fastened to a trammel that was suspended from a bar in the chimney. The getting the kettle hung was too severe for a woman's muscle, and a man had to be called in to the performance. Then a small kettle containing ashes and water must also be put on the fire; when the small kettle boiled and the water became lye, it was taken off and settled as you would a pot of coffee; not with egg, but with cold water. When the large kettle of water boiled, the water from the small kettle must be dipped into it and stirred until flakes like snowflakes came up, and then, as Mother Seward—who instructed me in the process—would say, "the water was broke." The scum was then taken off from the top and the water dipped into tubs to cool, a thick sediment would fall to the bottom of the tubs, leaving the water clean and pure, ready for use. As several kettles full had to pass through this process, it would occupy the first half of washing day, thereby bringing everything wrong. When the clothes were washed I, contrary to all rule among my neighbors, hung them on a line instead of the fence, but as clothespins were not known there, had to wait until I could find Loomis in the right mood to whittle some out, which, after about three months, he accomplished. The first time they were used I was attracted to the window to see what was the source of such jollification as was being shown by two of our backwoods neighbors. They were looking at the clothes yard, and calling to the third, who was on his way to join them, "See here, ain't that jest the last Yankee fixin'? jest see them ar little boys ridin' on a rope."

We had no market and must live as did our neighbors on cornbread and "flitch." "Flitch" was the fat portion of the hog, which would be laid on the floor in one corner of their smoke-house, and salt sprinkled over it; it was a filthy process, and when cooked (fried) was a disgusting food; so in order to have more comfortable fare ourselves, and to have something in readiness for the visitors that so unceremoniously came upon us, I had recourse to all the poor wits I possessed. We usually had a quarter of beef—nothing less—brought at a time; sometimes a whole animal. Your father knew nothing about cutting and dividing meat, so by the help of directions laid down in a cookery book and a little saw I attempted this art. When I could not manage among the big bones I would enlist your Uncle Robert, and we performed wonderfully. A part would be salted down to be used for cornbeef when the fresh had been eaten; the pieces for roast and steak set apart; the fat about the kidneys carefully picked out and put to dry for suet, and the remainder of the fat melted, strained, and put away for candles; a part made into "collared" or "pressed beef"; the round made into "hunter's beef," and the shins hung up in a cool place for soup; so in attending to the different ways of disposing of these things I had plenty to do, to say nothing of the care required in warm weather to keep the flies from leaving a deposit whereby animal life was engendered.

But the most tedious thing was candle-making. Each desk in the office must be supplied with two candles, and with what was necessary for other parts of the house not less than three dozen would suffice for a week. Unfortunately for my own comfort I had experimented and made improvements in dipped candles until I had succeeded in getting them of such brilliancy that no others were to be used in the office. I used to dip sixteen dozen in the fall and twenty dozen in the spring. For the spring candles I boiled the tallow in alum water to harden it for summer use. Were I to attempt to tell you the process, or the labor bestowed on these "nocturnal luminaries," you would not comprehend it, and as the day is past for making them, being a part of housekeeping, it will not be worth while to expatiate further on their merits. But oh! I can fancy my poor, tired shoulder and strained arm are now in sympathy with the toil of tallow. Not like practicing two hours on the piano, which when you are tired you can stop, but from three to four mortal hours the right arm must be in constant movement. If a rest is given to the arm the candles become too hard and break, and the tallow in the pot gets too cool, so dip, dip, dip, six candles at a time; each time the candles grow heavier and heavier, and the shoulder more rebellious. Besides the dipped candles I had molds in which I could mold two dozen at once, and all the accumulations from the beef that we weekly cooked was turned into molded candles, which your father said looked well, but did not give as clear a light as his office candles. I sometimes bought a cake of deer's tallow; it was harder than beef, but not as white; the natives used to put beeswax in their tallow. I tried it, but found they emitted an unpleasant smoke.

CHAPTER XXXII

THE CHARACTER of the new country grew more interesting and complicated with the passage of each decade. Only two decades, indeed, after Mrs. Tillson's arrival in Illinois there thrived at the capital, Springfield, a country lawyer whose education was what might have been expected in the case of a poor boy set down in an unfinished society, but whose personality was evidence that this society already possessed flavor. Abraham Lincoln, born in Kentucky, crossed into the newer north and came by way of Indiana to Illinois, where he developed into the most conspicuous of all the human products of the great region this side the Mississippi. Railsplitter, storekeeper, surveyor, and story-teller, he turned toward the law, which then furnished the best intellectual opening for any man. His partner at Springfield, William Herndon, has recalled the days of their reading and talking together—days which, according to Herndon, Lincoln was more than willing to spend away from home because Mary Todd his wife was none too easy to live with.

A MAN once called at the house to learn why Mrs. Lincoln had so unceremoniously discharged his niece from her employ. Mrs. Lincoln met him at the door, and being somewhat wrought up, gave vent to her feelings, resorting to such violent gestures and emphatic language that the man was glad to beat a hasty retreat. He at once started out to find Lincoln, determined to exact from him proper satisfaction for his wife's action. Lincoln was entertaining a crowd in a store at the time. The man, still laboring under some agitation, called him to the door and made the demand. Lincoln listened for a moment to his story. "My friend," he interrupted, "I regret to hear this, but let me ask you in all candor, can't you endure for a few moments what I have had as my daily portion for the last fifteen years?" These words were spoken so mournfully and with such a look of distress that the man was completely disarmed. It was a case that appealed to his feelings. Grasping the unfortunate husband's hand, he expressed in no uncertain terms his sympathy, and even apologized for having approached him. He said no more about the infuriated wife, and Lincoln afterward had no better friend in Springfield.

Mr. Lincoln never had a confidant, and therefore never unbosomed himself to others. He never spoke of his trials to me or, so far as I knew, to any of his friends. It was a great burden to carry, but he bore it sadly enough and without a murmur. I could always realize when he was in distress, without being told. He was not exactly an early riser, that is, he never usually appeared at the office till about nine o'clock in the morning. I usually preceded him an hour. Sometimes, however, he would come down as early as seven o'clock—in fact, on one occasion I remember he came down before daylight. If, on arriving at the office, I found him in, I knew instantly that a breeze had sprung up over the domestic sea, and that the waters were troubled. He would either be lying on the lounge looking skyward, or doubled up in a chair with his feet resting on the sill of a back window. He would not look up on my entering, and only answered my "Good morning" with a grunt. I at once busied myself with pen and paper, or ran through the leaves of some book; but the evidence of his melancholy and distress was so plain, and his silence so significant, that I would grow restless myself, and finding some excuse to go to the courthouse or elsewhere, would leave the room.

The door of the office opening into a narrow hallway was half glass, with a curtain on it working on brass rings strung on wire. As I passed out on these occasions I would draw the curtain across the glass, and before I reached the bottom of the stairs I could hear the key turn in the lock, and Lincoln was alone in his gloom. An hour in the clerk's office at the courthouse, an hour longer in a neighboring store having passed, I would return. By that time either a client had dropped in and Lincoln was propounding the law, or else the cloud of despondency had passed away, and he was busy in the recital of an Indiana story to whistle off the recollections of the morning's gloom. Noon having arrived I would depart homeward for my dinner. Returning within an hour, I would find him still in the office,—although his house stood but a few squares away,—lunching on a slice of cheese and a handful of crackers which, in my absence, he had brought up from a store below. Separating for the day at five or six o'clock in the evening, I would still leave him behind, either sitting on a box at the foot of the stairway, entertaining a few loungers, or killing time in the same way on the courthouse steps. A light in the office after dark attested his presence there till late along in the night, when, after all the world had gone to sleep, the tall form of the man destined to be the nation's President could have been seen strolling along in the shadows of trees and buildings, and quietly slipping in through the door of a modest frame house, which it pleased the world, in a conventional way, to call his home.

One of his warmest and closest friends, who still survives, maintains the theory that, after all, Lincoln's political ascendancy and final elevation to the Presidency were due more to the influence of his wife than to any other person or cause. "The fact," insists this friend, "that Mary Todd, by her turbulent nature and unfortunate manner, prevented her husband from becoming a domestic man, operated largely in his favor; for he was thereby kept out in the world of business and politics. Instead of spending his evenings at home, reading the papers and warming his toes at his own fireside, he was constantly out wth the common people, was mingling with the politicians, discussing public questions with the farmers who thronged the offices in the courthouse and state house, and exchanging views with the loungers who surrounded the stove of winter evenings in the village store. The result of this continuous contact with the world was, that he was more thoroughly known than any other man in his community. His wife, therefore, was one of the unintentional means of his promotion. If, on the other hand, he had married some less ambitious but more domestic woman, some honest farmer's quiet daughter,—one who would have looked up to and worshiped him because he uplifted her,—the result might have been different. For, although it doubtless would have been her pride to see that he had clean clothes whenever he needed them; that his slippers were always in their place; that he was warmly clad and had plenty to eat; and, although the privilege of ministering to his every wish and whim might have been to her a pleasure rather than a duty; yet I fear he would have been buried in the pleasures of a loving home, and the country would never have had Abraham Lincoln for its President."

And now he began to make up for time lost in politics by studying the law in earnest. No man had greater power of application than he. Once fixing his mind on any subject, nothing could interfere with or disturb him. Frequently I would go out on the circuit with him. We, usually, at the little country inns occupied the same bed. In most cases the beds were too short for him, and his feet would hang over the foot-board, thus exposing a limited expanse of shin bone. Placing a candle on a chair at the head of the bed, he would read and study for hours. I have known him to study in this position till two o'clock in the morning. Meanwhile, I and others who chanced to occupy the same room would be safely and soundly asleep. On the circuit in this way he studied Euclid until he could with ease demonstrate all the propositions in the six books. How he could maintain his mental equilibrium or concentrate his thoughts on an abstract mathematical proposition, while Davis, Logan, Swett, Edwards, and I so industriously and volubly filled the air with our interminable snoring was a problem none of us could ever solve. I was on the circuit with Lincoln probably one-fourth of the time. The remainder of my time was spent in Springfield looking after the business there, but I know that life on the circuit was a gay one. It was rich with incidents, and afforded the nomadic lawyers ample relaxation from all the irksome toil that fell to their lot. Lincoln loved it. I suppose it would be a fair estimate to state that he spent over half the year following Judges Treat and Davis around on the circuit. On Saturdays the court and attorneys, if within a reasonable distance, would usually start for their homes. Some went for a fresh supply of clothing, but the greater number went simply to spend a day of rest with their families. The only exception was Lincoln, who usually spent his Sundays with the loungers at the country tavern, and only went home at the end of the circuit or term of court. "At first," relates one of his colleagues on the circuit, "we wondered at it, but soon learned to account for his strange disinclination to go home. Lincoln himself never had much to say about home, and we never felt free to comment on it. Most of us had pleasant, inviting homes, and as we struck out for them I'm sure each one of us down in our hearts had a mingled feeling of pity and sympathy for him." If the day was long and he was oppressed, the feeling was soon relieved by the narration of a story. The tavern loungers enjoyed it, and his melancholy, taking to itself wings, seemed to fly away. In the rôle of a story-teller I am prone to regard Mr. Lincoln as without an equal. I have seen him surrounded by a crowd numbering as many as two and in some cases three hundred persons, all deeply interested in the outcome of a story which, when he had finished it, speedily found repetition in every grocery and lounging place within reach. His power of mimicry, as I have before noted, and his manner of recital, were in many respects unique, if not remarkable. His countenance and all his features seemed to take part in the performance. As he neared the pith or point of the joke or story every vestige of seriousness disappeared from his face. His little gray eyes sparkled; a smile seemed to gather up, curtainlike, the corners of his mouth; his frame quivered with suppressed excitement; and when the point— or "nub" of the story, as he called it—came, no one's laugh was heartier than his. These backwoods allegories are out of date now, and any lawyer, ambitious to gain prominence, would hardly dare thus to entertain a crowd, except at the risk of his reputation; but with Lincoln it gave him, in some mysterious way, a singularly firm hold on the people.

Lincoln was particularly strong in Menard county, and while on the circuit there he met with William Engle and James Murray, two men who were noted also for their story-telling proclivities. I am not now asserting for the country and the period what would at a later day be considered a very high standard of taste. Art had not such patrons as to-day, but the people loved the beautiful as Nature furnished it, and the good as they found it, with as much devotion as the more refined classes now are joined to their idols. Newspapers were scarce, and the court-house, with its cluster of itinerant lawyers, disseminated much of the information that was afterwards broken up into smaller bits at the pioneer's fireside. A curious civilization indeed, but one through which every Western State distant from the great arterial river or seaboard has had to pass.

When Lincoln, Murray, and Engle met, there was sure to be a crowd. All were more or less masters in their art. I have seen the little country tavern where these three were wont to meet after an adjournment of court, crowded almost to suffocation with an audience of men who had gathered to witness the contest among the members of the strange triumvirate. The physician of the town, all the lawyers, and not unfrequently a preacher could be found in the crowd that filled the doors and windows. The yarns they spun and the stories they told would not bear repetition here, but many of them had morals which, while exposing the weaknesses of mankind, stung like a whip-lash. Some were no doubt a thousand years old, with just enough "verbal varnish" and alterations of names and dates to make them new and crisp. By virtue of the last-named application, Lincoln was enabled to draw from Balzac a "droll story," and locating it in "Egypt" * or in Indiana, pass it off for a purely original conception. Every recital was followed by its "storm of laughter and chorus of cheers." After this had all died down, some unfortunate creature, through whose thickened skull the point had just penetrated, would break out in a guffaw, starting another wave of laughter which, growing to the proportions of a billow, would come rolling in like a veritable breaker. I have known these story-telling jousts to continue long after midnight—in some cases till the very small hours of the morning. I have seen Judge Treat, who was the very impersonation of gravity itself, sit up till the

---

* The word Egypt refers to that portion of Illinois which lies south of the famous National Road.

last and laugh until, as he often expressed it, "he almost shook his ribs loose." The next day he would ascend the bench and listen to Lincoln in a murder trial, with all the seeming severity of an English judge in wig and gown. Amid such surroundings, a leading figure in such society, alternately reciting the latest effusion of the bar-room or mimicking the clownish antics of the negro minstrel, he who was destined to be an immortal emancipator, was steadily and unconsciously nearing the great trial of his life. We shall see further on how this rude civilization crystallized both his logic and his wit for use in another day.

How Lincoln appeared and acted in the law office has been graphically and, I must confess, truthfully told by a gentleman now in New York, who was for several years a student in our office. I beg to quote a few lines from him: "My brother met Mr. Lincoln in Ottawa, Ill., one day, and said to him: 'I have a brother whom I would very much like to have enter your office as a student.' 'All right!' was his reply; 'send him down and we will take a look at him.' I was then studying law at Grand Rapids, Mich., and on hearing from my brother I immediately packed up and started for Springfield. I arrived there on Saturday night. On Sunday Mr. Lincoln was pointed out to me. I well remember this first sight of him. He was striding along, holding little Tad, then about six years old, by the hand, who could with the greatest difficulty keep up with his father. In the morning I applied at the office of Lincoln and Herndon for admission as a student. The office was on the second floor of a brick building on the public square, opposite the court-house. You went up one flight of stairs and then passed along a hallway to the rear office, which was a medium-sized room. There was one long table in the center of the room, and a shorter one running in the opposite direction, forming a T, and both were covered with green baize. There were two windows which looked into the back yard. In one corner was an old-fashioned secretary with pigeon-holes and a drawer, and here Mr. Lincoln and his partner kept their law papers. There was also a book-case containing about 200 volumes of law as well as miscellaneous books. The morning I entered the office Mr. Lincoln and his partner, Mr. Herndon, were both present. Mr. Lincoln addressed his partner thus: 'Billy, this is the young man of whom I spoke to you. Whatever arrangement you make with him will be satisfactory to me.' Then, turning to me, he said, 'I hope you will not become so enthusiastic in your studies of Blackstone and Kent as did two young men whom we had here. Do you see that spot over there?' pointing to a large ink stain on the wall. 'Well, one of these young men got so enthusiastic in his pursuit of legal lore that he fired an inkstand at the other one's head, and that is the mark he made.' I immediately began to clean up about the office a little. Mr. Lincoln had been in Congress and had the usual amount of seeds to distribute to the farmers. These were sent out with Free Soil and Republican documents. In my efforts to clean up, I found that some of the seeds had sprouted in the dirt that had collected in the office. Judge Logan and Milton Hay occupied the front offices on the same floor with Lincoln and Herndon, and one day Mr. Hay came in and said with apparent astonishment: 'What's happened here?' 'Oh, nothing,' replied Lincoln, pointing to me, 'only this young man has been cleaning up a little.' One of Lincoln's striking characteristics was his simplicity, and nowhere was this trait more strikingly exhibited than in his willingness to receive instruction from anybody and everybody. One day he came into the office and addressing his partner, said: 'Billy, what's the meaning of antithesis?' Mr. Herndon gave him the definition of the word, and I said: 'Mr. Lincoln, if you will allow me, I will give you an example.' 'All right, John, go ahead,' said Mr. Lincoln in his hearty manner. 'Phillips says, in his essay on Napoleon, "A pretended patriot, he impoverished the country; a professed Catholic, he imprisoned the Pope," ' etc. Mr. Lincoln thanked me and seemed very much pleased. Returning from off the circuit once he said to Mr. Herndon: 'Billy, I heard a good story while I was up in the country. Judge D—— was complimenting the landlord on the excellence of his beef. "I am surprised," he said, "that you have such good beef. You must have to kill a whole critter when you want any." "Yes," said the landlord, "we never kill less than a whole critter." '

"Lincoln's favorite position when unraveling some knotty law point was to stretch both of his legs at full length upon a chair in front of him. In this position, with books on the table near by and in his lap, he worked up his case. No matter how deeply interested in his work, if any one came in he had something humorous and pleasant to say, and usually wound up by telling a joke or an anecdote. I have heard him relate the same story three times within as many hours to persons who came in at different periods, and every time he laughed as heartily and enjoyed it as if it were a new story. His humor was infectious. I had to laugh because I thought it funny that Mr. Lincoln enjoyed a story so repeatedly told.

"There was no order in the office at all. The firm of Lincoln and Herndon kept no books. They divided their fees without taking any receipts or making any entries on books. One day Mr. Lincoln received $5,000 as a fee in a railroad case. He came in and said: 'Well, Billy,' addressing his partner, Mr. Herndon, 'here is our fee; sit down and let me divide.' He counted out $2,500 to his partner, and gave it to him with as much nonchalance as he would have given a few cents for a paper. Cupidity had no abiding place in his nature."

When he reached the office, about nine o'clock in the morning, the first thing he did was to pick up a newspaper, spread himself out on an old sofa, one leg on a chair, and read aloud, much to my discomfort. Singularly enough Lincoln never read any other way but aloud. This habit used to annoy me almost beyond the point of endurance. I once asked him why he did so. This was his explanation: "When I read aloud two senses catch the idea: first, I see what I read; second, I hear it, and therefore I can remember it better." He never studied law books unless a case was on hand for consideration—never followed up the decisions of the supreme courts, as other lawyers did. It seemed as if he depended for his effectiveness in managing a lawsuit entirely on the stimulus and inspiration of the final hour. He paid but little attention to the fees and money matters of the firm—usually leaving all such to me. He never entered an item in the account book. If any one paid money to him which belonged to the firm, on arriving at the office he divided it with me. If I was not there, he would wrap up my share in a piece of paper and place it in my drawer—marking it with a pencil, "Case of Roe *vs*. Doe.—Herndon's half."

On many topics he was not a good conversationalist, because he felt that he was not learned enough. Neither was he a good listener. Putting it a little strongly, he was often not even polite. If present with others, or participating in a conversation, he was rather abrupt, and in his anxiety to say something apt or to illustrate the subject under discussion, would burst in with a story. In our office I have known him to consume the whole forenoon relating stories. If a man came to see him for the purpose of finding out something which he did not care to let him know and at the same time did not want to refuse him, he was very adroit. In such cases Lincoln would do most of the talking, swinging around what he suspected was the vital point, but never nearing it, interlarding his answers with a seemingly endless supply of stories and jokes. The interview being both interesting and pleasant, the man would depart in good humor, believing he had accomplished his mission.

While Mr. Lincoln was no financier and had no propensity to acquire property,—no avarice of the get,—yet he had the capacity of retention, or the avarice of the keep. He never speculated in lands or anything else. In the days of land offices and "choice lots in a growing town" he had many opportunities to make safe ventures promising good returns, but he never availed himself of them.

His brother lawyers were making good investments and lucky turns, some of them, Davis, for example, were rapidly becoming wealthy; but Lincoln cared nothing for speculation; in fact, there was no venturesome spirit in him. His habits were very simple. He was not fastidious as to food or dress. His hat was brown, faded, and the nap usually worn or rubbed off. He wore a short cloak and sometimes a shawl. His coat and vest hung loosely on his gaunt frame, and his trousers were invariably too short. On the circuit he carried in one hand a faded green umbrella, with "A. Lincoln" in large white cotton or muslin letters sewed on the inside. The knob was gone from the handle, and when closed a piece of cord was usually tied around it in the middle to keep it from flying open. In the other hand he carried a literal carpet-bag, in which were stored the few papers to be used in court, and underclothing enough to last till his return to Springfield. He slept in a long, coarse, yellow flannel shirt, which reached half-way between his knees and ankles. It probably was not made to fit his bony figure as completely as Beau Brummel's shirt, and hence we can somewhat appreciate the sensation of a young lawyer who, on seeing him thus arrayed for the first time, observed afterwards that, "He was the ungodliest figure I ever saw."

"He never complained of the food, bed, or lodgings. If every other fellow grumbled at the bill-of-fare which greeted us at many of the dingy taverns," says David Davis, "Lincoln said nothing." He was once presiding as judge in the absence of Davis, and the case before him was an action brought by a merchant against the father of a minor son for a suit of clothes sold to the son without parental authority. The real question was whether the clothes were necessary, and suited to the condition of the son's life. The father was a wealthy farmer; the bill for the clothing was twenty-eight dollars. I happened in court just as Lincoln was rendering his decision. He ruled against the plea of necessity. "I have rarely in my life," said he, "worn a suit of clothes costing twenty-eight dollars."

"In October, 1854, Abraham Lincoln," relates a colleague, "drove into our town (Urbana) to attend court. He had the appearance of a rough, intelligent farmer, and his rude, home-made buggy and raw-boned horse inforced this belief. I had met him for the first time in June of the same year. David Davis and Leonard Swett had just preceded him. The next morning he started North, on the Illinois Central Railroad, and as he went in an old omnibus he played on a boy's harp all the way to the depot. I used to attend the Danville court, and while there, usually roomed with Lincoln and Davis. We stopped at McCormick's hotel, an old-fashioned frame country tavern. Jurors, counsel, prisoners, everybody ate at a long table. The judge, Lincoln, and I had the ladies' parlor fitted up with two beds. Lincoln, Swett, McWilliams, of Bloomington, Voorhees, of Covington, Ind., O. L. Davis, Drake, Ward Lamon, Lawrence, Beckwith, and O. F. Harmon, of Danville, Whiteman, of Iroquois County, and Chandler, of Williamsport, Ind., constituted the bar. Lincoln, Davis, Swett, I, and others who came from the western part of the state would drive from Urbana. The distance was thirty-six miles. We sang and exchanged stories all the way. We had no hesitation in stopping at a farm-house and ordering them to kill and cook a chicken for dinner. By dark we reached Danville. Lamon would have whisky in his office for the drinking ones, and those who indulged in petty gambling would get by themselves and play till late in the night. Lincoln, Davis, and a few local wits would spend the evening in Davis's room, talking politics, wisdom, and fun. Lincoln and Swett were the great lawyers, and Lincoln always wanted Swett in jury cases. We who stopped at the hotel would all breakfast together and frequently go out into the woods and hold court. We were of more consequence than a court and bar is now. The feelings were those of great fraternity in the bar, and if we desired to restrict our circle it was no trouble for Davis to freeze out any disagreeable persons. Lincoln was fond of going all by himself to any little show or concert. I have known him to slip away and spend the entire evening at a little magic lantern show intended for children. A traveling concert company, calling themselves the 'Newhall Family,' were sure of drawing Lincoln. One of their number, Mrs. Hillis, a good singer, he used to tell us was the only woman who ever seemed to exhibit any liking for him. I attended a negro-minstrel show in Chicago, where we heard Dixie sung. It was entirely new, and pleased him greatly. In court he was irrepressible and apparently inexhaustible in his fund of stories. Where in the world a man who had traveled so little and struggled amid the restrictions of such limited surroundings could gather up such apt and unique yarns we never could guess. Davis appreciated Lincoln's talent in this direction, and was always ready to stop business to hear one of his stories. Lincoln was very bashful when in the presence of ladies. I remember once we were invited to take tea at a friend's house, and while in the parlor I was called to the front gate to see a client. When I returned, Lincoln, who had undertaken to entertain the ladies, was twisting and squirming in his chair, and as bashful as a schoolboy. Everywhere, though we met a hard crowd at every court, and though things were free and easy, we were treated with great respect."

CHAPTER XXXIII

YOUTHFUL AMBITION in the Mississippi Valley had other directions in which to gaze than law and politics. While Lincoln was preparing for public life in the town of Springfield, a boy in another state across a great river dreamed of the day when he might be allowed to pilot a boat up and down the Mississippi. Samuel Clemens of Hannibal, Missouri, was captivated like other boys by the river life of his young days. The Mississippi trade was a thriving one; steamboats puffed from landing to landing, loading and unloading at towns and cities, and carrying passengers from New Orleans to Keokuk. It was a rich life, the river life; and the art of piloting one of these proud boats was so difficult as to offer an irresistible challenge. Mark Twain's "Life on the Mississippi" tells how the boy learned to respect his chosen profession.

WHEN I was a boy, there was but one permanent ambition among my comrades in our village on the west bank of the Mississippi River. That was, to be a steamboatman. We had transient ambitions of other sorts, but they were only transient. When a circus came and went, it left us all burning to become clowns; the first negro minstrel show that ever came to our section left us all suffering to try that kind of life; now and then we had a hope that, if we lived and were good, God would permit us to be pirates. These ambitions faded out, each in its turn; but the ambition to be a steamboatman always remained.

Once a day a cheap, gaudy packet arrived upward from St. Louis, and another downward from Keokuk. Before these events, the day was glorious with expectancy; after them, the day was a dead and empty thing. Not only the boys, but the whole village, felt this. After all these years I can picture that old time to myself now, just as it was then: the white town drowsing in the sunshine of a summer's morning; the streets empty, or pretty nearly so; one or two clerks sitting in front of the Water Street stores, with their splint-bottomed chairs tilted back against the walls, chins on breasts, hats slouched over their faces, asleep—with shingle-shavings enough around to show what broke them down; a sow and a litter of pigs loafing along the sidewalk, doing a good business in watermelon rinds and seeds; two or three lonely little freight piles scattered about the "levee"; a pile of "skids" on the slope of the stone-paved wharf, and the fragrant town drunkard asleep in the shadow of them; two or three wood flats at the head of the wharf, but nobody to listen to the peaceful lapping of the wavelets against them; the great Mississippi, the majestic, the magnificent Mississippi, rolling its mile-wide tide along, shining in the sun; the dense forest away on the other side; the "point" above the town, and the "point" below, bounding the river-glimpse and turning it into a sort of sea, and withal a very still and brilliant and lonely one. Presently a film of dark smoke appears above one of those remote "points"; instantly a negro drayman, famous for his quick eye and prodigious voice, lifts up the cry, "S-t-e-a-m-boat a-comin'!" and the scene changes! The town drunkard stirs, the clerks wake up, a furious clatter of drays follows, every house and store pours out a human contribution, and all in a twinkling the dead town is alive and moving. Drays, carts, men, boys, all go hurrying from many quarters to a common center, the wharf. Assembled there, the people fasten their eyes upon the coming boat as upon a wonder they are seeing for the first time. And the boat *is* rather a handsome sight, too. She is long and sharp and trim and pretty; she has two tall, fancy-topped chimneys, with a gilded device of some kind swung between them; a fanciful pilot-house, all glass and "gingerbread," perched on top of the "texas" deck behind them; the paddle-boxes are gorgeous with a picture or with gilded rays above the boat's name; the boiler-deck, the hurricane-deck, and the texas deck are fenced and ornamented with clean white railings; there is a flag gallantly flying from the jack-staff; the furnace doors are open and the fires glaring bravely; the upper decks are black with passengers; the captain stands by the big bell, calm, imposing, the envy of all; great volumes of the blackest smoke are rolling and tumbling out of the chimneys—a husbanded grandeur created with a bit of pitch-pine just before arriving at a town; the crew are grouped on the forecastle; the broad stage is run far out over the port bow, and an envied deck-hand stands picturesquely on the end of it with a coil of rope in his hand; the pent steam is screaming through the gauge-cocks; the captain lifts his hand, a bell rings, the wheels stop; then they turn back, churning the water to foam, and the steamer is at rest. Then such a scramble as there is to get aboard, and to get ashore, and to take in freight and to discharge freight, all at one and the same time; and such a yelling and cursing as the mates facilitate it all with! Ten minutes later the steamer is under way again, with no flag on the jack-staff and no black smoke issuing from the chimneys. After ten more minutes the town is dead again, and the town drunkard asleep by the skids once more.

My father was a justice of the peace, and I supposed he possessed the power of life and death over all men, and could hang anybody that offended him. This was distinction enough for me as a general thing; but the desire to be a steamboatman kept intruding, nevertheless. I first wanted to be a cabin-boy, so that I could come out with a white apron on and shake a tablecloth over the side, where all my old comrades could see me; later I thought I would rather be the deckhand who stood on the end of the stage-plank with the coil of rope in his hand, because he was particularly conspicuous. But these were only day-dreams—they were too heavenly to be contemplated as real possibilities. By and by one of our boys went away. He was not heard of for a long time. At last he turned up as apprentice engineer or "striker" on a steamboat. This thing shook the bottom out of all my Sunday-school teachings. That boy had been notoriously worldly, and I just the reverse; yet he was exalted to this eminence, and I left in obscurity and misery. There was nothing generous about this fellow in his greatness. He would always manage to have a rusty bolt to scrub while his boat tarried at our town, and he would sit on the inside guard and scrub it, where we all could see him and envy and loathe him. And whenever his boat was laid up he would come home and swell around the town in his blackest and greasiest clothes, so that nobody could help remembering that he was a steamboatman; and he used all sorts of steamboat technicalities in his talk, as if he were so used to them that he forgot common people could not understand them. He would speak of the "labboard" side of a horse in an easy, natural way that would make one wish he was dead. And he was always talking about "St. Looy" like an old citizen; he would refer casually to occasions when he was "coming down Fourth Street," or when he was "passing by the Planter's House," or when there was a fire and he took a turn on the brakes of "the old Big Missouri"; and then he would go on and lie about how many towns the size of ours were burned down there that day. Two or three of the boys had long been persons of consideration among us because they had been to St. Louis once and had a vague general knowledge of its wonders, but the day of their glory was over now. They lapsed into a humble silence, and learned to disappear when the ruthless "cub"-engineer approached. This fellow had money, too, and hair-oil. Also an ignorant silver watch and a showy brass watch-chain. He wore a leather belt and used no suspenders. If ever a youth was cordially admired and hated by his comrades, this one was. No girl could withstand his charms. He "cut out" every boy in the village. When his boat blew up at last, it diffused a tranquil contentment among us such as we had not known for months. But when he came home the next week, alive, renowned, and appeared in church all battered up and bandaged, a shining hero, stared at and wondered over by everybody, it seemed to us that the partiality of Providence for an undeserving reptile had reached a point where it was open to criticism.

This creature's career could produce but one result, and it speedily followed. Boy after boy managed to get on the river. The minister's son became an engineer. The doctor's and the postmaster's sons became "mud clerks"; the wholesale liquor dealer's son became a barkeeper on a boat; four sons of the chief merchant, and two sons of the county judge, became pilots. Pilot was the grandest position of all. The pilot, even in those days of trivial wages, had a princely salary—from a hundred and fifty to two hundred and fifty dollars a month, and no board to pay. Two months of his wages would pay a preacher's salary for a year. Now some of us were left disconsolate. We could not get on the river—at least our parents would not let us.

So, by and by, I ran away. I said I would never come home again till I was a pilot and could come in glory. But somehow I could not manage it. I went meekly aboard a few of the boats that lay packed together like sardines at the long St. Louis wharf, and humbly inquired for the pilots, but got only a cold shoulder and short words from mates and clerks. I had to make the best of this sort of treatment for the time being, but I had comforting daydreams of a future when I should be a great and honored pilot, with plenty of money, and could kill some of these mates and clerks and pay for them.

What with lying on the rocks four days at Louisville, and some other delays, the poor old *Paul Jones* fooled away about two weeks in making the voyage from Cincinnati to New Orleans. This gave me a chance to get acquainted with one of the pilots, and he taught me how to steer the boat, and thus made the fascination of river life more potent than ever for me.

It also gave me a chance to get acquainted with a youth who had taken deck passage—more's the pity; for he easily borrowed six dollars of me on a promise to return to the boat and pay it back to me the day after we should arrive. But he probably died or forgot, for he never came. It was doubtless the former, since he had said his parents were wealthy, and he only traveled deck passage because it was cooler.*

I soon discovered two things. One was that a vessel would not be likely to sail for the mouth of the Amazon under ten or twelve years; and the other was that the nine or ten dollars still left in my pocket would not suffice for so impossible an exploration as I had planned, even if I could afford to wait for a ship. Therefore it followed that I must contrive a new career. The *Paul Jones* was now bound for St. Louis. I planned a siege against my pilot, and at the end of three hard days he surrendered. He agreed to teach me the Mississippi River from New Orleans to St. Louis for five hundred dollars, payable out of the first wages I should receive after graduating. I entered upon the small enterprise of "learning" twelve or thirteen hundred miles of the great Mississippi River with the easy confidence of my time of life. If I had really known what I was about to require of my faculties, I should not have had the courage to begin. I supposed that all a pilot had to do was to keep his boat in the river, and I did not consider that that could be much of a trick, since it was so wide.

The boat backed out from New Orleans at four in the afternoon, and it was "our watch" until eight. Mr. Bixby, my chief, "straightened her up," plowed her along past the sterns of the other boats that lay at the Levee, and then said, "Here, take her; shave those steamships as close as you'd peel an apple." I took the wheel, and my heartbeat fluttered up into the hundreds; for it seemed to me that we were about to scrape the side off every ship in the line, we were so close. I held my breath and began to claw the boat away from the danger; and I had my own opinion of the pilot who had known no better than to get us into such peril, but I was too wise to express it. In half a minute I had a wide margin of safety intervening between the *Paul Jones* and the ships; and within ten seconds more I was set aside in disgrace, and Mr. Bixby was going into danger again and flaying me alive with abuse of my cowardice. I was stung, but I was obliged to admire the easy confidence with which my chief loafed from side to side of his wheel, and trimmed the ships so closely that disaster seemed ceaselessly imminent. When he had cooled a little he told me that the easy water was close ashore and the current outside, and therefore we must hug the bank, upstream, to get the benefit of the former, and stay well out, downstream, to take advantage of the latter. In my own mind I resolved to be a downstream pilot and leave the upstreaming to people dead to prudence.

* "Deck" passage—*i.e.*, steerage passage.

Now and then Mr. Bixby called my attention to certain things. Said he, "This is Six-Mile Point." I assented. It was pleasant enough information, but I could not see the bearing of it. I was not conscious that it was a matter of any interest to me. Another time he said, "This is Nine-Mile Point." Later he said, "This is Twelve-Mile Point." They were all about level with the water's edge; they all looked about alike to me; they were monotonously unpicturesque. I hoped Mr. Bixby would change the subject. But no; he would crowd up around a point, hugging the shore with affection, and then say: "The slack water ends here, abreast this bunch of China trees; now we cross over." So he crossed over. He gave me the wheel once or twice, but I had no luck. I either came near chipping off the edge of a sugar-plantation, or I yawed too far from shore, and so dropped back into disgrace again and got abused.

The watch was ended at last, and we took supper and went to bed. At midnight the glare of a lantern shone in my eyes, and the night watchman said:

"Come, turn out!"

And then he left. I could not understand this extraordinary procedure; so I presently gave up trying to, and dozed off to sleep. Pretty soon the watchman was back again, and this time he was gruff. I was annoyed. I said:

"What do you want to come bothering around here in the middle of the night for? Now, as like as not, I'll not get to sleep again to-night."

The watchman said:

"Well, if this ain't good, I'm blessed."

The "off-watch" was just turning in, and I heard some brutal laughter from them, and such remarks as "Hello, watchman! ain't the new cub turned out yet? He's delicate, likely. Give him some sugar in a rag, and send for the chambermaid to sing 'Rock-a-by Baby' to him."

About this time Mr. Bixby appeared on the scene. Something like a minute later I was climbing the pilot-house steps with some of my clothes on and the rest in my arms. Mr. Bixby was close behind, commenting. Here was something fresh—this thing of getting up in the middle of the night to go to work. It was a detail in piloting that had never occurred to me at all. I knew that boats ran all night, but somehow I had never happened to reflect that somebody had to get up out of a warm bed to run them. I began to fear that piloting was not quite so romantic as I had imagined it was; there was something very real and worklike about this new phase of it.

It was a rather dingy night, although a fair number of stars were out. The big mate was at the wheel, and he had the old tub pointed at a star and was holding her straight up the middle of the river. The shores on either hand were not much more than half a mile apart, but they seemed wonderfully far away and ever so vague and indistinct. The mate said:

"We've got to land at Jones's plantation, sir."

The vengeful spirit in me exulted. I said to myself, "I wish you joy of your job, Mr. Bixby; you'll have a good time finding Mr. Jones's plantation such a night as this; and I hope you never *will* find it as long as you live."

Mr. Bixby said to the mate:

"Upper end of the plantation, or the lower?"

"Upper."

"I can't do it. The stumps there are out of water at this stage. It's no great distance to the lower, and you'll have to get along with that."

"All right, sir. If Jones don't like it, he'll have to lump it, I reckon."

And then the mate left. My exultation began to cool and my wonder to come up. Here was a man who not only proposed to find this plantation on such a night, but to find either end of it you preferred. I dreadfully wanted to ask a question, but I was carrying about as many short answers as my cargo-room would admit of, so I held my peace. All I desired to ask Mr. Bixby was the simple question whether he was ass enough to really imagine he was going to find that plantation on a night when all plantations were exactly alike and all of the same color. But I held in. I used to have fine inspirations of prudence in those days.

Mr. Bixby made for the shore and soon was scraping it, just the same as if it had been daylight. And not only that, but singing:

"Father in heaven, the day is declining," etc.

It seemed to me that I had put my life in the keeping of a peculiarly reckless outcast. Presently he turned on me and said:

"What's the name of the first point above New Orleans?"

I was gratified to be able to answer promptly, and I did. I said I didn't know.

"Don't *know?*"

This manner jolted me. I was down at the foot again, in a moment. But I had to say just what I had said before.

"Well, you're a smart one!" said Mr. Bixby. "What's the name of the *next* point?"

Once more I didn't know.

"Well, this beats anything. Tell me the name of *any* point or place I told you."

I studied awhile and decided that I couldn't.

"Look here! What do you start out from, above Twelve-Mile Point, to cross over?"

"I—I—don't know."

"You—you—don't know?" mimicking my drawling manner of speech. "What *do* you know?"

"I—I—nothing, for certain."

"By the great Cæsar's ghost, I believe you! You're the stupidest dunderhead I ever saw or ever heard of, so help me Moses! The idea of *you* being a pilot—*you!* Why, you don't know enough to pilot a cow down a lane."

Oh, but his wrath was up! He was a nervous man, and he shuffled from one side of his wheel to the other as if the floor was hot. He would boil awhile to himself, and then overflow and scald me again.

"Look here! What do you suppose I told you the names of those points for?"

I tremblingly considered a moment, and then the devil of temptation provoked me to say:

"Well to—to—be entertaining, I thought."

This was a red rag to the bull. He raged and stormed so (he was crossing the river at the time) that I judged it made him blind, because he ran over the steering-oar of a trading-scow. Of course the traders sent up a volley of red-hot profanity. Never was a man so grateful as Mr. Bixby was; because he was brimful, and here were subjects who could *talk back*. He threw open a window, thrust his head out, and such an irruption followed as I never had heard before. The fainter and farther away the scowmen's curses drifted, the higher Mr. Bixby lifted his voice and the weighter his adjectives grew. When he closed the window he was empty. You could have drawn a seine through his system and not caught curses enough to disturb your mother with. Presently he said to me in the gentlest way:

"My boy, you must get a little memorandum-book; and every time I tell you a thing, put it down right away. There's only one way to be a pilot, and that is to get this entire river by heart. You have to know it just like A B C."

That was a dismal revelation to me; for my memory was never loaded with anything but blank cartridges. However, I did not feel discouraged long. I judged that it was best to make some allowances, for doubtless Mr. Bixby was "stretching." Presently he pulled a rope and struck a few strokes on the big bell. The stars were all gone now, and the night was as black as ink. I could hear the wheels churn along the bank, but I was not entirely certain that I could see the shore. The voice of the invisible watchman called up from the hurricane-deck:

"What's this, sir?"

"Jones's plantation."

I said to myself, "I wish I might venture to offer a small bet that it isn't." But I did not chirp. I only waited to see. Mr. Bixby handled the engine-bells, and in due time the boat's nose came to the land, a torch glowed from the forecastle, a man skipped ashore, a darky's voice on the bank said: "Gimme de k'yarpet-bag, Mass' Jones," and the next moment we were standing up the river again, all serene. I reflected deeply awhile, and then said—but not aloud— "Well, the finding of that plantation was the luckiest accident that ever happened; but it couldn't happen again in a hundred years." And I fully believed it *was* an accident, too.

By the time we had gone seven or eight hundred miles up the river, I had learned to be a tolerably plucky upstream steersman, in daylight; and before we reached St. Louis I had made a trifle of progress in night work, but only a trifle. I had a notebook that fairly bristled with the names of towns, "points," bars, islands, bends, reaches, etc.; but the information was to be found only in the notebook—none of it was in my head. It made my heart ache to think I had only got half of the river set down; for as our watch was four hours off and four hours on, day and night, there was a long four-hour gap in my book for every time I had slept since the voyage began.

My chief was presently hired to go on a big New Orleans boat, and I packed my satchel and went with him. She was a grand affair. When I stood in her pilot-house I was so far above the water that I seemed perched on a mountain; and her decks stretched so far away, fore and aft, below me, that I wondered how I could ever have considered the little *Paul Jones* a large craft. There were other differences, too. The *Paul Jones's* pilot-house was a cheap, dingy, battered rattletrap, cramped for room; but here was a sumptuous glass temple; room enough to have a dance in; showy red and gold window-curtains; an imposing sofa; leather cushions and a back to the high bench where visiting pilots sit, to spin yarns and "look at the river"; bright, fanciful "cuspidores," instead of a broad wooden box filled with sawdust; nice new oilcloth on the floor; a hospitable big stove for winter; a wheel as high as my head, costly with inlaid work; a wire tiller-rope; bright brass knobs for the bells; and a tidy, white-aproned, black "texas-tender," to bring up tarts and ices and coffee during mid-watch, day and night. Now this was "something like"; and so I began to take heart once more to believe that piloting was a romantic sort of occupation after all. The moment we were under way I began to prowl about the great steamer and fill myself with joy. She was as clean and as dainty as a drawing-room; when I looked down her long, gilded saloon, it was like gazing through a splendid tunnel; she had an oil-picture, by some gifted sign-painter, on every stateroom door; she glittered with no end of prism-fringed chandeliers; the clerk's office was elegant, the bar was marvelous, and the barkeeper had been barbered and upholstered at incredible cost. The boiler-deck (*i.e.*, the second story of the boat, so to speak) was as spacious as a church, it seemed to me; so with the forecastle; and there was no pitiful handful of deck-hands, firemen, and roustabouts down there, but a whole battalion of men. The fires were fiercely glaring from a long row of furnaces, and over them were eight huge boilers! This was unutterable pomp. The mighty engines—but enough of this. I had never felt so fine before. And when I found that the regiment of natty servants respectfully "sir'd" me, my satisfaction was complete.

At the end of what seemed a tedious while, I had managed to pack my head full of islands, towns, bars, "points," and bends; and a curiously inanimate mass of lumber it was, too. However, inasmuch as I could shut my eyes and reel off a good long string of these names without leaving out more than ten miles of river in every fifty, I began to feel that I could take a boat down to New Orleans if I could make her skip those little gaps. But of course my complacency could hardly get start enough to lift my nose a trifle into the air, before Mr. Bixby would think of something to fetch it down again. One day he turned on me suddenly with this settler:

"What is the shape of Walnut Bend?"

He might as well have asked me my grandfather's opinion of protoplasm. I reflected respectfully, and then said I didn't know it had any particular shape. My gunpowdery chief went off with a bang, of course, and then went on loading and firing until he was out of adjectives.

I had learned long ago that he only carried just so many rounds of ammunition, and was sure to subside into a very placable and even remorseful old smooth-bore as soon as they were all gone. That word "old" is merely affectionate; he was not more than thirty-four. I waited. By and by he said:

"My boy, you've got to know the *shape* of the river perfectly. It is all there is left to steer by on a very dark night. Everything else is blotted out and gone. But mind you, it hasn't the same shape in the night that it has in the daytime.

"How on earth am I ever going to learn it, then?"

"How do you follow a hall at home in the dark? Because you know the shape of it. You can't see it."

"Do you mean to say that I've got to know all the million trifling variations of shape in the banks of this interminable river as well as I know the shape of the front hall at home?"

"On my honor, you've got to know them *better* than any man ever did know the shapes of the halls in his own house."

"I wish I was dead!"

"Now I don't want to discourage you, but—"

"Well, pile it on me; I might as well have it now as another time."

"You see, this has got to be learned; there isn't any getting around it. A clear starlight night throws such heavy shadows that, if you didn't know the shape of a shore perfectly, you would claw away from every bunch of timber, because you would take the black shadow of it for a solid cape; and you see you would be getting scared to death every fifteen minutes by the watch. You would be fifty yards from shore all the time when you ought to be within fifty feet of it. You can't see a snag in one of those shadows, but you know exactly where it is, and the shape of the river tells you when you are coming to it. Then there's your pitch-dark night; the river is a very different shape on a pitch-dark night from what it is on a starlight night. All shores seem to be straight lines, then, and mighty dim ones, too; and you'd *run* them for straight lines, only you know better. You boldly drive your boat right into what seems to be a solid, straight wall (you knowing very well that in reality there is a curve there), and that wall falls back and makes way for you. Then there's your gray mist. You take a night when there's one of these grisly, drizzly, gray mists, and then there isn't *any* particular shape to a shore. A gray mist would tangle the head of the oldest man that ever lived. Well, then, different kinds of *moonlight* change the shape of the river in different ways. You see—"

"Oh, don't say any more, please! Have I got to learn the shape of the river according to all these five hundred thousand different ways? If I tried to carry all that cargo in my head it would make me stoop-shouldered."

"*No!* you only learn *the* shape of the river; and you learn it with such absolute certainty that you can always steer by the shape that's *in your head*, and never mind the one that's before your eyes."

"Very well, I'll try it; but, after I have learned it, can I depend on it? Will it keep the same form and not go fooling around?"

Before Mr. Bixby could answer, Mr. W. came in to take the watch, and he said:

"Bixby, you'll have to look out for President's Island, and all that country clear away up above the Old Hen and Chickens. The banks are caving and the shape of the shores changing like everything. Why, you wouldn't know the point above 40. You can go up inside the old sycamore snag, now." *

So that question was answered. Here were leagues of shore changing shape. My spirits were down in the mud again. Two things seemed pretty apparent to me. One was, that in order to be a pilot a man had got to learn more than any one man ought to be allowed to know; and the other was, that he must learn it all over again in a different way every twenty-four hours.

That night we had the watch until twelve. Now it was an ancient river custom for the two pilots to chat a bit when the watch changed. While the relieving pilot put on his gloves and lit his cigar, his partner, the retiring pilot, would say something like this:

"I judge the upper bar is making down a little at Hale's Point; had quarter twain with the lower lead and mark twain † with the other."

"Yes, I thought it was making down a little, last trip. Meet any boats?"

"Met one abreast the head of 21, but she was away over hugging the bar, and I couldn't make her out entirely. I took her for the *Sunny South*—hadn't any skylights forward of the chimneys."

And so on. And as the relieving pilot took the wheel his partner ‡ would mention that we were in such-and-such a bend, and say we were abreast of such-and-such a man's woodyard or plantation. This was courtesy; I supposed it was *necessity*. But Mr. W. came on watch full twelve minutes late on this particular night—a tremendous breach of etiquette; in fact, it is the unpardonable sin among pilots. So Mr. Bixby gave him no greeting whatever, but simply surrendered the wheel and marched out of the pilot-house without a word. I was appalled; it was a villainous night for blackness, we were in a particularly wide and blind part of the river, where there was no shape or substance to anything, and it seemed incredible that Mr. Bixby should have left that poor fellow to kill

<hr/>

* It may not be necessary, but still it can do no harm to explain that "inside" means between the snag and the shore.—M. T.

† Two fathoms. Quarter twain is 2¼ fathoms, 13½ feet. Mark three is three fathoms.

‡ "Partner" is technical for "the other pilot."

the boat, trying to find out where he was. But I resolved that I would stand by him anyway. He should find that he was not wholly friendless. So I stood around, and waited to be asked where we were. But Mr. W. plunged on serenely through the solid firmament of black cats that stood for an atmosphere, and never opened his mouth. "Here is a proud devil!" thought I; "here is a limb of Satan that would rather send us all to destruction than put himself under obligations to me, because I am not yet one of the salt of the earth and privileged to snub captains and lord it over everything dead and alive in a steamboat." I presently climbed up on the bench; I did not think it was safe to go to sleep while this lunatic was on watch.

However, I must have gone to sleep in the course of time, because the next thing I was aware of was the fact that day was breaking, Mr. W. gone, and Mr. Bixby at the wheel again. So it was four o'clock and all well—but me; I felt like a skinful of dry bones, and all of them trying to ache at once.

Mr. Bixby asked me what I had stayed up there for. I confessed that it was to do Mr. W. a benevolence—tell him where he was. It took five minutes for the entire preposterousness of the thing to filter into Mr. Bixby's system, and then I judge it filled him nearly up to the chin; because he paid me a compliment—and not much of a one either. He said:

"Well, taking you by and large, you do seem to be more different kinds of an ass than any creature I ever saw before. What did you suppose he wanted to know for?"

I said I thought it might be a convenience to him.

"Convenience! D——nation! Didn't I tell you that a man's got to know the river in the night the same as he'd know his own front hall?"

"Well, I can follow the front hall in the dark if I know it *is* the front hall; but suppose you set me down in the middle of it in the dark and not tell me which hall it is; how am *I* to know?"

"Well, you've *got* to, on the river!"

"All right. Then I'm glad I never said anything to Mr. W."

"I should say so! Why, he'd have slammed you through the window and utterly ruined a hundred dollars' worth of window-sash and stuff."

I was glad this damage had been saved, for it would have made me unpopular with the owners. They always hated anybody who had the name of being careless and injuring things.

I went to work now to learn the shape of the river; and of all the eluding and ungraspable objects that ever I tried to get mind or hands on, that was the chief. I would fasten my eyes upon a sharp, wooded point that projected far into the river some miles ahead of me, and go to laboriously photographing its shape upon my brain; and just as I was beginning to succeed to my satisfaction, we would draw up toward it and the exasperating thing would begin to melt away and fold back into the bank! If there had been a conspicuous dead tree standing upon the very point of the cape, I would find that tree inconspicuously merged into the general forest, and occupying the middle of a straight shore, when I got abreast of it! No prominent hill would stick to its shape long enough for me to make up my mind what its form really was, but it was as dissolving and changeful as if it had been a mountain of butter in the hottest corner of the tropics. Nothing every had the same shape when I was coming downstream that it had borne when I went up. I mentioned these little difficulties to Mr. Bixby. He said:

"That's the very main virtue of the thing. If the shapes didn't change every three seconds they wouldn't be of any use. Take this place where we are now, for instance. As long as that hill over yonder is only one hill, I can boom right along the way I'm going; but the moment it splits at the top and forms a V, I know I've got to scratch to starboard in a hurry, or I'll bang this boat's brains out against a rock; and then the moment one of the prongs of the V swings behind the other, I've got to waltz to larboard again, or I'll have a misunderstanding with a snag that would snatch the keelson out of this steamboat as neatly as if it were a sliver in your hand. If that hill didn't change its shape on bad nights there would be an awful steamboat graveyard around here inside of a year."

It was plain that I had got to learn the shape of the river in all the different ways that could be thought of—upside down, wrong end first, inside out, fore-and-aft, and "thort-ships"—and then know what to do on gray nights when it hadn't any shape at all. So I set about it. In the course of time I began to get the best of this knotty lesson, and my self-complacency moved to the front once more. Mr. Bixby was all fixed, and ready to start it to the rear again. He opened on me after this fashion:

"How much water did we have in the middle crossing at Hole-in-the-Wall, trip before last?"

I considered this an outrage. I said:

"Every trip, down and up, the leadsmen are singing through that tangled place for three-quarters of an hour on a stretch. How do you reckon I can remember such a mess as that?"

"My boy, you've got to remember it. You've got to remember

the exact spot and the exact marks the boat lay in when we had the shoalest water, in every one of the five hundred shoal places between St. Louis and New Orleans; and you mustn't get the shoal soundings and marks of one trip mixed up with the shoal soundings and marks of another, either, for they're not often twice alike. You must keep them separate."

When I came to myself again, I said:

"When I get so that I can do that, I'll be able to raise the dead, and then I won't have to pilot a steamboat to make a living. I want to retire from this business. I want a slush-bucket and a brush; I'm only fit for a roustabout. I haven't got brains enough to be a pilot; and if I had I wouldn't have strength enough to carry them around, unless I went on crutches."

"Now drop that! When I say I'll learn * a man the river, I mean it. And you can depend on it, I'll learn him or kill him."

* "Teach" is not in the river vocabulary.

Book VII

BEYOND THE MISSISSIPPI

CHAPTER XXXIV

THE VAST West beyond the great river was tracked and explored long before lines of people started moving across it in search of homes, but even this search began early. Restless America was looking now for more and more empty worlds to fill with its feet. As early as 1800 there were youths who itched for a sight of the Spanish country west of the lower Mississippi—the country of Texas which was to be a battle ground in several senses during decades to come. Ellis P. Bean of Tennessee struck off down to Mexico in this first year of the century and had adventures, recorded by him in his memoirs, which were to be only the type of many others in subsequent years of a bloody place and time.

I WAS born in the state of Tennessee, in the year 1783. I had a common education given me, and such as a frontier country could afford. At the age of seventeen years, I had a great desire to travel, and see other parts of the world. To see some foreign country was all my desire. My father said I was too young, and would not consent. But as the town of Natchez had fallen to the United States, and was a good market for the produce of Tennessee, he consented that I might bring to that country a boat-load of whisky and flour; all of which being made ready in a few days, I started in company with a young man from the same place, by the name of John Word, who had some lading with me. About three hundred miles below Knoxville, in a place called the Muscle-shoals, I broke my boat in pieces on a rock, and lost all my cargo. I only saved a small trunk of clothes. My companion concluded then that he would return; but I would not, for I wished to see that country.

I knew that I had some relations in Natchez, and, although I had lost my cargo, I could get some money from them to return to my country again. So I resolved to continue my journey. Having at that time but five dollars in my pocket, I bid adieu to my companion, and got into a family boat that was coming to Natchez. After some days' travel, I landed at Natchez.

I got acquainted with a man by the name of Nolan, that had been for some years before trading with the Spaniards in San Antonio. He told me that he was going to make another voyage to that country in October, and entreated me to go along with him. I readily agreed to go. We crossed the Mississippi at a place called the Walnut Hills, taking a west course for the Washita.

Steering a west course, through the Mississippi swamp, for the Washita, we were about forty miles from the river, when we met about fifty Spaniards, mounted on horseback, and well armed. They had been sent by the commandant at Washita to stop us; but, though our number was only twenty-one, they were afraid to attack us. We asked them their business. They told us they were in pursuit of some Choctaw Indians, that had stolen some horses. This was false, for they were hunting for our party, though they were afraid to own it. They then passed us, and in a short time returned and passed us again, and went back to Washita, where they put themselves on guard that night, thinking we would go by that place. They had their cannons mounted to receive us; but we left the town to the south of us, and continued our journey still westwardly for the Red river, through a fine country. But there were no roads or inhabitants. Crossing the Washita river the next morning and finding a large piece of rising ground, we encamped to kill some provisions, as deer were very plenty.

In about six days' journey we came to Trinity river, and, crossing it, we found the big, open prairies of that country. We passed through the plains till we reached a spring, which we called the *Painted spring,* because a rock at the head of it was painted by the Comanche and Pawnee nations in a peace that was made there by these two nations. In the vast prairie there was no wood, or any other fuel than buffalo-dung, which lay dry in great quantities. But we found that the buffalo had removed, and were getting so scarce, that, in three days after passing the spring, we were forced, in order to sustain life, to eat the flesh of wild horses, which we found in great quantities. For about nine days we were compelled to eat horseflesh, when we arrived at a river called the Brasos. Here we found elk and deer plenty, some buffalo, and wild horses by thousands.

We built a pen, and caught about three hundred of those wild horses. After some days, the Comanche nation came to see us. They were a party of about two hundred men, women, and children. We went with them to the south fork of Red river, to see their chief, by the name of Nicoroco, where we stayed with them a month. A number of them had arrows pointed, some with stone, and others with copper.

In four days more it was our misfortune to be attacked by a hundred and fifty Spaniards sent by the commandant at Chihuahua. He was general-commandant of the five northeastern internal provinces, and called Don Nimesio de Salcedo. The troops that came were piloted by Indians from Nacogdoches that came with them. They surrounded our camp about one o'clock in the morning, on the 22d of March, 1801. They took the five Spaniards and one American that were guarding our horses, leaving but twelve of us, including Cæsar. We were all alarmed by the tramping of their horses; and, as day broke, without speaking a word, they commenced their fire. After about ten minutes, our gallant leader Nolan was slain by a musket-ball which hit him in the head. In a few minutes after they began to fire grape-shot at us: they had brought a small swivel on a mule. We had a pen that we had built of logs, to prevent the Indians from stealing from us. From this pen we returned their fire until about nine o'clock. We then had two men wounded and one killed. I told my companion we ought to charge on the cannon and take it. Two or three of them agreed to it, but the rest appeared unwilling. I told them it was at most but death; and if we stood still, all would doubtless be killed; that we must take the cannon, or retreat. It was agreed that we should retreat.

In our march we came to a deep ravine. Here we took refuge, and stopped some time. They then began to come too close to us, when we commenced firing afresh. They then retreated; and about three o'clock in the afternoon they hoisted a white flag, and (through an American that was with them) told us that the commander wanted us to return to our own country, and not remain there with the Indians. We quickly agreed to go as companions with them, but not to give up our guns. It was granted, and we went back and buried our gallant leader Nolan.

The next day we started in company with the Spanish soldiers for Nacogdoches. In our journey we had to cross the Trinity which we found running over its banks. My companions and I, in a short time, made a small canoe out of a dry cottonwood, which answered very well to carry the soldiers all over. Their arms and their commander were still on the west side. I told my companions that we had it in our power to throw all their guns in the river, take what ammunition we wanted, and return. Some of them were willing; others said it would be very wrong now we were to be sent home. These last were unfortunate men who put confidence in Spanish promises. These are a people in whom you should put no trust or confidence whatever.

In some days after we arrived at Nacogdoches, the commandant told us he was waiting for orders from Chihuahua to set us at liberty and send us home. We waited in this hope for about a month, when, instead of our liberty, we were seized and put in irons, and sent off under a strong guard to San Antonio. Here we lay in prison three months. Then we were started to Mexico, but were stopped at San Luis Potosi, where we were confined in prison one year and four months. By this time we were getting bare of clothes. I told them I was a shoemaker, and would be very thankful if they would permit me, in the daytime, to sit at the door of my prison, and work at my trade. This was granted to me, and also to young Charles King. We made some money; but, in a short time afterward, orders came that we should be sent to Chihuahua. This order was quickly obeyed; and we started on horseback, with heavy irons. Yet it was cheering to think that we were going to change our prisons, hoping that in some change we might be able, some day or other, to escape.

We came to a town called Saltillo, where we were delivered over to another officer, whose duty it was to conduct us to Chihuahua. This man treated us with more humanity than had been shown us before. He took off our irons, and let us ride all the way footloose, a distance of four hundred miles. And along the road, and at all the towns, we could look at places, and walk about and see the inhabitants. And we noticed that everywhere they were mixed with Indian, but of a kind and friendly disposition. They were all exceedingly kind to us, presenting us with fruits, clothes, and money; so that, by the time we reached Chihuahua, we began to think we would soon regain our liberty.

On our arrival in town we were put in prison, and, in five or six days, were tried. Then our irons were taken off, and we had the limits of the town to walk in during the day, and at night we had to come and sleep in the soldiers' barracks. During this time we received a quarter of a dollar a day for our provisions; but, as for clothing, there was no way provided to get any. Some of my companions got leave of the general to go to other towns to live, but I thought I would find out some way of making something. I gave myself out as a hatter. There was a gentleman who trusted me for whatever was necessary to carry on that business. I employed two Spanish hatters to work with me, for, in fact, I was no hatter at all. In about six months I had so raised my name, that no one would purchase hats except of the American. By this means I got a number of journeymen to work with me. I was clear of debt, and making from fifty to sixty dollars per week. I began to lay up money, with which to try to make my escape at a future day. I had gained the

good will of all the principal men in that town, as well as the surrounding villages. I continued in this situation about four years,
when I thought it was time to try to reach my native country.

I left my shop in the hands of a foreman, and obtained leave to
visit another town forty miles distant, that I might better make my
arrangements. When I arrived there, I purchased, through others,
four horses, three guns, and as many braces of pistols. Here I was
advised by my friends to join the Catholic church, and to marry in
the country—as they did not expect the general would ever agree
to send us home, as we had come so far into the country. I put
them off by promises, but was still making my arrangements to
start for the United States: for it was not possible that I should
forget my country, or resign myself to live under a tyranny after
having enjoyed the liberty of my native land. My companions appeared to me to be reconciled and happy; excepting, however, one
of them, by the name of Thomas House. He, like myself, was determined to see his native country, if possible. As I thought he
was the only one I could get to go with me, I wrote to him. He
answered me, saying he would meet me when called on, at any
place appointed. A week after, having all things ready, and two
Spanish soldiers, who agreed to desert and go with me, I wrote to
my friend a second letter, to meet me on a certain day at an old
church, from which we would set out on our journey for the United
States. But, to my misfortune, my letter fell into the hands of
another companion of mine, named Tony Waters, who was from
Winchester, Virginia.

As soon as he got it, he broke it open and read it, and immediately reported it to the commanding officer of Chihuahua; thinking
thus to ingratiate himself by selling his countrymen and companions.
This was no sooner known, than orders came to the town where I
was to put me in close confinement, which was done without any
delay. After I was in the dungeon, I was put in the stocks for that
day. The next day I was ironed with two pairs of strong irons. The
third day I was taken out of my prison, and led to the governor,
who asked me if I knew why I was imprisoned. I told him I did not.
He then showed me my letter, and asked me if I had written it.
I told him I had. He asked me if any of my companions were going.
I said, no. He asked if the one to whom I had wrote had agreed to
go. I said no; but I wrote to invite him, and had received no answer,
nor did I expect any, as the letter did not reach him. He asked me
if I had arms. I told him that I had none—for my horses, arms, and
other things, were kept at a different place from where I lived, and

search had been made, and nothing found, as I had previously been informed.

I was returned to prison, and next morning orders came that I should not talk with any one. I then thought that my undertaking was at an end, inasmuch as I was forbidden to see or talk to any one. But, about twelve o'clock the next day, they brought into my prison one of my companions, who was at the point of death. As I before remarked, my companions had gone to different towns. He was taken sick at a place some distance off, and requested that he might see me before he died. As the Catholic religion obliges them to comply in such cases, he was brought to me. But my poor, unfortunate countryman did not expect to find me ironed and in close confinement. When the prison-door was opened, he saw me, came in and sat down, and said to me: "I never thought to see you in this place; but, though it is a prison, I shall not leave you until I die, which I expect will be in a few days. Yet I shall die in the company of a countryman." He then laid himself down. The distress of my friend afflicted me more than ever, but I could not help either him or myself. I had yet a little money; with it I sent and got some wine; and, after a little while, a lady sent me some dinner, and I got him up, and he ate some.

This young man was named Joel Pearce, from North Carolina. Some time after, I asked him if he had not been told, before he came, that I was in prison. He said he knew nothing about it until he came to the town; and that the commandant told him I was a bad man, and was going to run away, for which reason I was put in prison. He said also that it was better for my companion to go to some house in the town, and not come to stay with me; for, as he had done nothing, he could stay where he pleased. My companion said, "No, I will go and stay with him." I told him also it would be better to go to a house of some of my friends, where he would be well treated, and, I hoped, recover. He said, no, he would die there, for he had no hope of recovering. He continued with me for five or six days in this situation, and, I perceived, was daily growing weaker. During this time, I forgot my prison, and thought only of my sick friend. By this time he was able to converse with me but little. In the height of our affliction, the justice of the town sent into our jail a big Indian, charged with murder. He brought with him a jew's-harp, and played on it all the time. This so distracted the head of my poor countryman, that I requested him, in a friendly manner, not to make that noise. He answered me that the harp was his own, and he would play when he pleased. There was no great difference between us, for he had on one pair of irons, and I had two. I went up to him and snatched the jew's-harp from him, and broke the tongue out. He rose immediately, and we engaged; but in a few blows I was conqueror, and he fell down very quiet. My sick companion, when we began, tried to rise, but was so weak, that he fell back on his mat. He was full of joy, however, when he saw I had gained the victory. In three days after, he died, and was carried away to be buried. Then I was more distressed in mind than ever, thinking it would soon be my time to suffer the same fate. . . .

We so remained three or four days, when orders came that some of us were to be sent away, and I was one of them. The next day the governor came and told us that I and four of my companions were to be sent to the South Sea, to a place called Acapulco, and that we had first to go to Mexico.

The next morning horses were brought, and we started with a guard of twenty-five men, to guard five poor Americans, with two pairs of irons on each. The rest of our companions were set at liberty. Our journey to Mexico was nine hundred miles from Chihuahua. The officer commanding our guard favored us in giving us easy-going horses. The people, at every town through which we passed, would flock to see us, for they had never before seen an American so far in the interior. Of those that came to see us, some gave us money, and others sent us provisions. They were all mixed with Indian, and showed us real friendship, and seemed to have humanity in their hearts. The Spaniards were hard-hearted and barbarous, and seemed to have no other feeling than to make us as miserable as possible.

About two hundred miles from Mexico we came to a small town called Salamanca, where a number of people came flocking to see us. The place in which we stopped was a large square enclosed by houses and walls, so that we could either stay in our rooms, or walk about as we pleased. The stone walls were so high, that we were considered safe.

Among those who came to see us was a lady, who directed her conversation to me. She asked me slyly if I wished to make my escape. I answered her that it was a thing impossible, and I had resigned myself to my fate. She said she would free me from those irons I wore, and immediately left me. By this time night had come on us. I asked a man, who did not sit far from me, the name of that young lady. He told me her name was Maria Baldonada; that she was the wife of a very rich man; that he was very old, and had not long been married to her. This brought me to study what she meant by telling me that she would free me. But this soon left my mind, and I moved to my mat and blanket, and lay down to rest myself. But crowds of people kept coming and going. In a short time after I had laid down, I saw this woman returning, in company with a man who had on a cloak. She went to where I had sat down, and asked another lady where the American was who had sat there. Hearing her make these inquiries, I raised up and spoke to her. She came and sat by me on my mat, and told me the man with the cloak on had brought files for cutting off my irons; that I must walk out in the square to a horse stable, and he would cut them off; and then there was a man on the wall who would drop me a rope and pull me up to the top of the wall; that the same man would conduct me to where I should see her, and then I would be safe.

I could speak the Spanish language very well. I answered her that if I made my escape, my poor companions would perhaps suffer worse on my account, and it would be ungenerous in me to leave them. She said it would not be possible to get all out, but one she could; that she had a regard for me as soon as she saw me. "And," said she, "if I can be the cause of liberating you from your chains and confinement, I hope it will be the means of making you happy; for I am sure it will make me happy to think that I have been the means of setting you free."—"Madam," I answered, "it is very true I should be happy in being thus freed, but unhappy in thinking that my companions would still suffer." She said, "You must take care of yourself, and let God take care of all."—"But, madam," said I, "I reckon when I reach Mexico, I shall get my liberty, and be sent home by way of Vera Cruz."—"You may think so," was her answer, "and not find it so; and when you think of this chance, you will, perhaps, remember me."

"But, madam," said I, "if I were to be turned loose here in the center of your country, I could not escape without being taken again, and then my sufferings would be increased." She said, "I have horses and money, and you can have anything without exposing yourself to be retaken. I have several haciendas, in any of which you can stay without its being known."

By this time supper was ready, and I was called to eat. She said to me, "Now it is too late to do anything; but in the morning you can get your horse saddled, and come with a soldier to my house, which is three doors from this place."

Then I parted with the lady; but during all that night my mind was so much occupied with what I would have done had I been by myself, that I could not sleep. I thought of all that my companions might suffer if I were to take such a step. I also reflected that the lady was married; and if her husband should find out that she was the means of getting me away, it might make them unhappy, and be the cause of my being retaken.

In thoughts of this description I passed the night; and, as soon as day broke, I went and asked the officer to let a soldier saddle my horse, and go with me to a store, that I might buy a handkerchief. He ordered it to be done. Instead of going to the store, I went where the lady had directed me the night before. I found her sitting by an open window. I alighted from my horse by placing my foot on the window-sill; and gave the soldier a dollar, and told him to go and buy some bitters—that I would wait for him.

So soon as the soldier left me, she said: "Now is the time for your freedom. I will send my servant to the end of the town with your horse; and when the soldier comes, I will tell him you mounted your horse, and took such a street. So, if he follows, he will find your horse, and not you, and be afraid to show himself again to his officer, but will desert. And I have a safe place to hide you, and will give the soldier money to make him desert, and you must know that I can do it, for they all love money, and have none."

I answered her, and said: "Madam, you are a married lady, and I should be a most unhappy man to receive such favors from one of your rank, and then be compelled to leave you without any hope of seeing you again. But if, by the king's order, I should get free, I could then come and spend my days in this town, where I should have the happiness of seeing you, and perhaps be sometimes in your company, if admissible."

"Sir," said she, "you need not think, because I am married, I am bound. I do not so consider it. About a year since, I was married to a man fifty-five years old, in order not to displease my father and mother. He is a man of great property; but I can venture to tell you I do not love him. He is not now in town, but is at some silver mines he is working, and will be absent two weeks. Before he comes, I promise you to go with you to your country, and spend my days with you. Although you are a stranger, I have formed too good an opinion of you to suppose that, after leaving all to go with you to your country, you would then abandon me for any other lady, however fair. Though I am mixed with Indian blood, I would trust to your honor not to cast me off."

These words made a deep impression on my mind. Yet I was uneasy, as I expected every moment to see the soldier return. I told her I was sure of my freedom when I reached Mexico; that my friends had informed me they would write in my behalf, which raised my hopes; and that I could not leave my companions. For the next three years I repented that I did not take this lady's advice, as the reader will see further on in this book.

I waited sometime for the soldier to come; and would not agree that my horse should be taken away, as she had desired. When she saw that I would not agree to it, she brought me a heavy package and a letter, and directed me to put them in my pocket, and not look at them till the end of that day's journey. While she was saying this, the soldier came up, and asked if it were not time for us to go. I told her if I was set at liberty, as I expected, in Mexico, I would return to that town without delay. The soldier then helped me on my horse, and I bid adieu to the lovely Maria Baldonada.

When I reached my company, all things were in readiness for our march, and we set out on our journey. We stopped that night at a place called Arcos; and as soon as we halted, being impatient to look into my package and letter, I sat down to examine them before the people of the village should crowd on us. In the package I found three Joes, in small gold pieces. The letter was as follows:—

"About three days since, the news reached this town that some Americans were coming on as prisoners. I was very desirous to see them; but it has been an unhappy time for me since I first saw you. I hope you will obtain your freedom in a short time, and not forget one who is not ashamed to own that the love she has for you is more than she can bear. Sir, perhaps you may ask how this can be, when you are bound in irons; you may think a woman crazy who could love one in that situation. Perhaps so; but when I first saw you, I was touched with compassion; then I found my heart distressed; and, when I came to examine myself, I found it to be in love.

"I can write no more. If you leave Mexico, you will let me know where you go, as it will give me some satisfaction.

"In this letter is a ring from my finger. I hope you will keep it in remembrance of your love.   MARIA BALDONADA."

After reading the letter, I went into the room where my companions were; but I was unhappy, and could not pass off the time as usual. The next morning we set out, and in a few days arrived in Mexico. Here I was cast into a prison yard, in which there were about three hundred others, some of whom were negroes and Indians.

I remained here but a week, when I was taken to Acapulco. This is a seaport town, where vessels come once a year from the East Indies. It has a strong fortification. The castle is built of stone, and has about a hundred guns of the largest caliber. The walls of the fort are twelve feet thick.

When I arrived at this place, they called over our names; and, when I answered to mine, they told me to step to the front. I did so. They then directed me to follow an officer, which I also did, but slowly, as I had on two pairs of irons. The officer took me to the side of the castle, and, opening a small door, told me to go in. I did so; and, when the door was shut, I found myself between two stone walls, about three feet apart, and in a room seven feet long. At the far end of the room I could just discern light through a small opening in the twelve-foot wall, which was grated with iron bars. In the door was another opening of three inches square, also grated. Looking through this last opening, I saw that there was a soldier at the door. I asked him what he had done with my companions. He said they were all put together in a large room. In the evening the officer came and opened the door, and brought me some old clothes I had left with my companions; also a mat for my bed, and some beef and bread, and a pot of water. I asked him why I was separated from my companions. He said it was because something was written from Chihuahua, to the effect that great care should be taken of me; but he could not tell why.

The next day, about nine o'clock, when the relief guard came round, my prison door was opened, and my irons searched. I then asked the officer if it was possible that I could be put with my companions. He said I could not, as the governor of that place had ordered that I should be kept by myself. I tried to content myself as well as I could, though there was but little happiness to be found here.

I remember that Baron Trenck, when he was moved from his first prison to the second, thought how he should escape. So I began to think I should get free; but seeing the strength of the walls, and having nothing to work with, I concluded it was impossible for me ever to escape; and, should I succeed, I would have to travel three thousand miles through their country to get to the nearest part of the United States. As for the distance, I cared nothing about it, if I could only break through those walls.

In about ten days after I was put in there, a soldier on guard spoke very friendly to me. I asked him if he would sell me a small knife. He said he would give me one that night. Accordingly, at night, he slipped through the hole in the door the blade of a knife, for which I paid him a dollar. I began to work on the wall, but found it of stones of such large size, that I could do nothing. Still my spirits did not fail me, and I had a hope that I would make my escape in some way or other, though I could form no idea in what way it was to be done.

For about three months I was in this situation. Every day they gave me a pot of water, and some beef and bread. But I was not allowed to have any conversation with others.

This place lies in sixteen degrees of north latitude, and is very warm. There is here a lizard—which the Spaniard call *quija*—which is about nine or ten inches long and about three inches thick. It is as white as snow, and, if you hold it between you and the light, you may see the bones in its limbs and body. One day, as I was lying on my mat, I saw one of them, for the first time, on the wall. Watching him, I saw that he was trying to catch the flies that had come into the prison when the door was opened, to get out of the sun. I did not know whether he was poisonous or not, but I determined to feed him. So I caught some flies, and put them on the end of a straw I had pulled out of my mat; these I slipped up the wall to him, and found he would take them off the straw. This was my amusement for some days, when he became so gentle, that he would take the flies off my hand. Every morning, as he came down the wall, he would sing like a frog, by which means I had notice that he was coming. In about a week he was so gentle, that he did not leave me at night, but stayed with me all the time. Every day, when they would open the door to come and examine my irons, he would get frightened, and hide himself under my blanket. When the door was again shut, he would come out and stay with me. I found that he was sincerely my friend: in fact, he was my only companion and amusement. . . .

I thought I would try to escape on the road to the castle, for there were but two soldiers guarding me, and they were armed only with sabers. I started off with them, and had got about three hundred yards from the hospital, when we came by a house on the outside of the town, having a large garden. In this house the woman sold a kind of small beer. As I had money with me, I asked the soldiers if they would drink some. They quickly agreed to it. We went in the house, and called for some. She brought it out, and we drank it, and called for some more. I asked one of them to go with me into the garden, which he did. I walked with him to the back of the garden, and found a large bunch of pinks, which grow in that country as large as roses. I asked him to come and see those fine pinks. He came, and, in handing him one, with the same hand I caught him by the neck, presenting my knife blade, which I had held ready in my other hand, and told him if he did not give up his sword, I would kill him. He quickly obeyed, and asked me what I meant. I told him I was going off, and, if he would go with me, there would be no danger of being retaken. He said he must do so, or he would be put in prison in my place. I saw, however, that he was unwilling. I then gave him a dollar, and started, telling him to go and buy the worth of it in bread for the journey, as we had no provisions; and that I would wait for him at the burying ground outside of the town. So I left him, and went out at the back of the garden, and, before he could let the officer of the fort know it, I was safe in the woods.

By means of a steel I had to strike fire, I cut off my irons, and ascended the side of a mountain, so that I could see all the town and castle. I sat down in a shady grove, where the singing of birds and the thought of being at liberty so charmed me, that I was as happy as any monarch. The sweet-smelling blossoms, interwoven with the shade, formed for me a palace; and, though I had been starved in the hospital, I did not feel hungry, nor was I weak. I felt strong and happy, and sat in that pleasant shade till night.

I then made my way into the town, and went to a shop, where I supplied myself with bread, bacon, cheese, and a large gourd of brandy. As I was passing near the door of another shop, I heard two men speaking English in the house. As they came out, I spoke to them, and found that they were Irishmen, who belonged to a privateer, which had that day come into port from the city of Lima. I asked them what sort of a man their captain was, and if they thought I could talk to him. They said they would conduct me to the house, and ask him if he would be kind enough to have some conversation with me. They did so. He sent me word to come to his room; and when I went in, he asked me of what country I was. I told him I was an American. He could hardly believe me, as I spoke Spanish as well as he could. I told him I wanted to go in the brig with him, and that I had been a prisoner such a time. He said he would clear me from that place, but there we had no time to talk about it; that I must go away and take care of myself till the next night, and then go on board the brig and hide myself well: he would then sail, and I would be safe.

I went to the woods that night, and spent all the next day in listening to the songsters of the forest, being greatly pleased. When night came, I went where the sailors were to meet me, and found them waiting for me. They gave me sailors' clothes, and I went on board like a jolly tar, thinking I was safe. That night we broke the head out of a water-pipe, and at daybreak I took up my abode in it. There were about three hundred such pipes on board.

About ten o'clock next day a guard came and searched the vessel, and, as I was not to be found on board, they returned to the shore. The vessel was to sail in about two hours. There was on board an old Portuguese cook, who knew I was concealed, though he did not know where. The old wretch fell out with some of the Irish sailors, and went ashore, and told the governor I was hid on board the vessel; that he saw me, and heard them knocking on the hoops of a barrel. The poor Irishman was arrested, and told that I was a king's prisoner, and, if he did not show where I was, they would send him to prison. They frightened the poor coward so, that he told them I was on board, and he would tell where I was. They came with him on board, and he showed them the water-cask in which I was concealed. It was rolled out, and I was well tied, so that I could not move. I was then thrown from the vessel down into the boat, which bruised me badly, though no bones were broken. I was then landed and carried to the castle again, where my two pairs of irons were put on me, and I was placed again in my little cell. I consoled myself with the thought that I had enjoyed a few hours of liberty, and had heard the birds sing and perhaps might hear them again.

After some reflections upon my hard fortune, my mind became easy, and I thought of my poor companion, the lizard. As I had just come out of the light, it was so dark I could not see anything. The next day my lizard came down the wall, and, as soon as I saw him, I reached out my hand for him to come on it, but he was afraid to come into my hand as he had done before my departure. I gave him some boiled beef, and he ate it; but when I wanted to take him, he ran up the wall. It was four or five days before I could get him to know me; then he was as friendly as ever, and was the only companion I had.

One day I began to twist me a small string out of the palmetto of my mat. This was my work for four or five days, when I had a small cord about ten yards long. I laid it aside; and a short time afterward, I went to look out through the small hole in the thick wall. I saw a woman pass by—I called her. She stopped, and said, "Where are you?" I said: "You can't see me; I am a prisoner, and I want you to do me one favor." She asked me what it was. I told her to bring me some spirits. She said if she could get them to me, she would do it. I told her I had a string, and, if she would bring it, I would put out my string, so that she could tie it to the end, and I could pull it into my cell. I had yet some money, and threw some out at the hole, which she took and went on. I got a small piece of mortar out of the wall, and tied it to the end of the string, as a weight. I threw it out at the hole, and when I felt that it struck bottom outside, I tied it to my arm, and sat like a fisherman waiting for a bite. After sometime, I felt my string move: then I heard the woman say, "Pull"; then she said, "I am going." So she left me pulling up my line, which I did with great caution. When it came in sight, I saw that it was a cow's bladder. As it was soft, I got it in with great ease, although the hole was small.

When I got it in, I took a drink, and put the bladder under my head. I lay for sometime, when my door began to open. I took my bladder and put in my pot of water, and covered it with my old hat. It was an old priest, who had come out of curiosity to see if it was true that I had a gentle lizard. He asked to see it, and said the officers of the guard had told him of it. I called him Bill; he was in my bed. I took him in my hand and played with him. The old man observed that it was in the power of man to do anything, if he would but turn his attention to it. He then gave me some money, and left me.

I then took another drink, and lay down; and, though I found I was drunk, I took care to hide the bladder. I can truly say that, during the year and five months I stayed in this cell the last time, the hour I was drunk, and unconscious of everything, was the only happy time I saw.

CHAPTER XXXV

THE FAR Southwest drew thousands of settlers in the years following the romantic exploits of Bean and the other adventurers. The
portion of Mexico called Texas became not only a stretch of American homesteads but a battleground wherein revolution and war
determined boundaries and allegiances. A stream of immigrants
from the east flowed into the territory during the twenties under
such leaders as Stephen F. Austin; in the thirties, under the leadership of Sam Houston, the Texans won their independence from
Mexico. Annexation by the United States was to come later; but
meanwhile further west there was the movement of trade along a
route which ran from St. Louis to Santa Fé.

Before railroads were thought of in the Far West there were trails
along which trains of covered wagons toiled their way, at first with
traders, then with ever increasing thousands of homeseekers. The
two great thoroughfares were the Santa Fé Trail and the Oregon
Trail, which went together from St. Louis through Independence,
Missouri, as far as eastern Kansas, where they diverged. The Oregon
Trail, following up the rivers northwest, branched once more in what
is now southern Idaho, one line proceeding northwest into Oregon
and the other line bearing southwest for California. The Santa Fé
Trail went southwest from Kansas to its terminus, Santa Fé. Josiah
Gregg, who took the latter course on more than one occasion, has
drawn a detailed picture of the course as he knew it in 1831.

IT was on the 15th of May, 1831, and one of the brightest and
most lovely of all the days in the calendar, that our little party
set out from Independence. The general rendezvous at Council
Grove was our immediate destination. It is usual for the traders to
travel thus far in detached parties, and to assemble there for the
purpose of entering into some kind of organization, for mutual
security and defense during the remainder of the journey. It was
from thence that the formation of the *Caravan* was to be dated, and
the chief interest of our journey to commence: therefore, to this
point we all looked forward with great anxiety. As the wagons had

gone before us, and we were riding in a light carriage, we were able to reach the Round Grove, about thirty-five miles distant, on the first day, where we joined the rear division of the caravan, comprising about thirty wagons.

After leaving this spot the troubles and vicissitudes of our journey began in good earnest; for on reaching the narrow ridge which separates the Osage and Kansas waters (known as "the Narrows"), we encountered a region of very troublesome quagmires. On such occasions it is quite common for a wagon to sink to the hubs in mud, while the surface of the soil all around would appear perfectly dry and smooth. To extricate each other's wagons we had frequently to employ double and triple teams, with "all hands to the wheels" in addition—often led by the proprietors themselves up to the waist in mud and water.

Three or four days after this, and while crossing the head branches of the Osage river, we experienced a momentary alarm. Conspicuously elevated upon a rod by the roadside, we found a paper purporting to have been written by the Kansas agent, stating that a band of Pawnees were said to be lurking in the vicinity! The first excitement over, however, the majority of our party came to the conclusion that it was either a hoax of some of the company in advance, or else a stratagem of the Kaws (or Kansas Indians), who, as well as the Osages, prowl about those prairies, and steal from the caravans, during the passage, when they entertain the slightest hope that their maraudings will be laid to others. They seldom venture further, however, than to seize upon an occasional stray animal, which they frequently do with the view alone of obtaining a reward for returning it to its owner. As to the Pawnees, the most experienced traders were well aware that they had not been known to frequent those latitudes since the commencement of the Santa Fé trade. But what contributed as much as anything else to lull the fears of the timid, was an accession to our forces of seventeen wagons which we overtook the same evening.

Early on the 26th of May we reached the long-looked-for rendezvous of Council Grove, where we joined the main body of the caravan. Lest this imposing title suggest to the reader a snug and thriving village, it should be observed, that, on the day of our departure from Independence, we passed the last human abode upon our route; therefore, from the borders of Missouri to those of New Mexico not even an Indian settlement greeted our eyes.

The designation of "Council Grove," after all, is perhaps the most appropriate that could be given to this place; for *we* there held a "grand council," at which the respective claims of the different "aspirants to office" were considered, leaders selected, and a system of government agreed upon,—as is the standing custom of these promiscuous caravans. One would have supposed that electioneering and "party spirit" would hardly have penetrated so far into the wilderness: but so it was. Even in our little community we had our "office-seekers" and their "political adherents," as earnest and as devoted as any of the modern school of politicians in the midst of civilization. After a great deal of bickering and wordy warfare, however, all the "candidates" found it expedient to decline, and a gentleman by the name of Stanley, without seeking, or even desiring the "office," was unanimously proclaimed "Captain of the Caravan." The powers of this officer were undefined by any "constitutional provision," and consequently vague and uncertain: orders being only viewed as mere requests, they are often obeyed or neglected at the caprice of the subordinates. It is necessary to observe, however, that the captain is expected to direct the order of travel during the day, and to designate the camping-ground at night; with many other functions of a general character, in the exercise of which the company find it convenient to acquiesce. But the little attention that is paid to his commands in cases of emergency, I will leave the reader to become acquainted with, as I did, by observing their manifestations during the progress of the expedition.

But after this comes the principal task of organizing. The proprietors are first notified by "proclamation" to furnish a list of their men and wagons. The latter are generally apportioned into four "divisions," particularly when the company is large—and ours consisted of nearly a hundred wagons, besides a dozen of dearborns and other small vehicles, and two small cannons (a four and six pounder), each mounted upon a carriage. To each of these divisions, a "lieutenant" was appointed, whose duty it was to inspect every ravine and creek on the route, select the best crossings, and superintend what is called in prairie parlance, the "forming" of each encampment.

Upon the calling of the roll, we were found to muster an efficient force of nearly two hundred men without counting invalids or other disabled bodies, who, as a matter of course, are exempt from duty. There is nothing so much dreaded by inexperienced travelers as the ordeal of guard duty. But no matter what the condition or employment of the individual may be, no one has the smallest chance of evading the "common law of the prairies." The amateur tourist and the listless loafer are precisely in the same wholesome predicament—they must all take their regular turn at the watch. There is usually a set of genteel idlers attached to every caravan, whose wits are forever at work in devising schemes for whiling away their irksome hours at the expense of others. By embarking in these "trips of pleasure," they are enabled to live without expense; for the hospitable traders seldom refuse to accommodate even a loafing companion with a berth at their mess without charge. But then these lounging *attachés* are expected at least to do good service by way of guard duty. None are even permitted to furnish a substitute, as is frequently done in military expeditions, for he that would undertake to stand the tour of another besides his own, would scarcely be watchful enough for the dangers of the prairies. Even the invalid must be able to produce unequivocal proofs of his inability, or it is a chance if the plea is admitted. For my own part, although I started on the "sick-list," and though the prairie sentinel must stand fast and brook the severest storm (for then it is that the strictest watch is necessary), I do not remember ever having missed my post but once during the whole journey.

The usual number of watches is eight, each standing a fourth of every alternate night. When the party is small the number is generally reduced; while in the case of very small bands, they are sometimes compelled for safety's sake to keep one watch on duty half the night. With large caravans the captain usually appoints eight "sergeants of the guard," each of whom takes an equal portion of men under his command.

The heterogeneous appearance of our company, consisting of men from every class and grade of society, with a little sprinkling of the softer sex, would have formed an excellent subject for an artist's pencil. It may appear, perhaps, a little extraordinary that females should have ventured across the prairies under such forlorn auspices. Those who accompanied us, however, were members of a Spanish family who had been banished in 1829, in pursuance of a decree of the Mexican congress, and were now returning to their homes in consequence of a suspension of the decree. Other females, however, have crossed the prairies to Santa Fé at different times, among whom I have known two respectable French ladies, who now reside in Chihuahua.

The wild and motley aspect of the caravan can be but imperfectly conceived without an idea of the costumes of its various members. The most "fashionable" prairie dress is the fustian frock of the city-bred merchant furnished with a multitude of pockets capable of accommodating a variety of "extra tackling." Then there is the backwoodsman with his linsey or leather hunting-shirt—the farmer with his blue jean coat—the wagoner with his flannel-sleeve vest—

besides an assortment of other costumes which go to fill up the picture.

In the article of firearms there is also an equally interesting medley. The frontier hunter sticks to his rifle, as nothing could induce him to carry what he terms in derision "the scatter-gun." The sportsman from the interior flourishes his double-barreled fowling-piece with equal confidence in its superiority. The latter is certainly the most convenient description of gun that can be carried on this journey; as a charge of buckshot in night attacks (which are the most common), will of course be more likely to do execution than a single rifle-ball fired at random. The "repeating" arms have lately been brought into use upon the prairies, and they are certainly very formidable weapons, particularly when used against an ignorant savage foe. A great many were furnished beside with a bountiful supply of pistols and knives of every description, so that the party made altogether a very brigand-like appearance.

During our delay at the Council Grove, the laborers were employed in procuring timber for axle-trees and other wagon repairs, of which a supply is always laid in before leaving this region of substantial growths; for henceforward there is no wood on the route fit for these purposes; not even in the mountains of Santa Fé do we meet with any serviceable timber. The supply procured here is generally lashed under the wagons, in which way a log is not unfrequently carried to Santa Fé, and even sometimes back again.

Owing to the delays of organizing and other preparations, we did not leave the Council Grove camp till May 27th. Although the usual hour of starting with the prairie caravans is after an early breakfast, yet, on this occasion, we were hindered till in the afternoon. The familiar note of preparation, "Catch up! catch up!" was now sounded from the captain's camp, and reëchoed from every division and scattered group along the valley. On such occasions, a scene of confusion ensues, which must be seen to be appreciated. The woods and dales resound with the gleeful yells of the light-hearted wagoners, who, weary of inaction, and filled with joy at the prospect of getting under way, become clamorous in the extreme. Scarcely does the jockey on the race-course ply his whip more promptly at that magic word "Go," than do these emulous wagoners fly to harnessing their mules at the spirit-stirring sound of "Catch up." Each teamster vies with his fellows who shall be soonest ready; and it is a matter of boastful pride to be the first to cry out—"All's set!"

The uproarious bustle which follows—the hallooing of those in pursuit of animals—the exclamations which the unruly brutes call forth from their wrathful drivers; together with the clatter of bells —the rattle of yokes and harness—the jingle of chains—all conspire to produce a clamorous confusion, which would be altogether incomprehensible without the assistance of the eye; while these alone would hardly suffice to unravel the labyrinthian maneuvers and hurly-burly of this precipitate breaking up. It is sometimes amusing to observe the athletic wagoner hurrying an animal to its post—to see him "heave upon" the halter of a stubborn mule, while the brute as obstinately "sets back," determined not to "move a peg" till his own good pleasure thinks it proper to do so—his whole manner seeming to say, "Wait till your hurry's over!" I have more than once seen a driver hitch a harnessed animal to the halter, and by that process haul "his mulishness" forward, while each of his four projected feet would leave a furrow behind; until at last the perplexed master would wrathfully exclaim, "A mule will be a mule anyway you can fix it!"

"All's set!" is finally heard from some teamster—"All's set," is directly responded from every quarter. "Stretch out!" immediately vociferates the captain. Then, the "heps!" of drivers—the crackling of whips—the trampling of feet—the occasional creak of wheels— the rumbling of wagons—form a new scene of exquisite confusion, which I shall not attempt further to describe. "Fall in!" is heard from headquarters, and the wagons are forthwith strung out upon the long inclined plain, which stretches to the heights beyond Council Grove.

All were busily occupied when some objects were seen moving in the distance, which at first were mistaken for buffalo; but were speedily identified as horsemen. Anxiety was depicted in every countenance. Could it be possible that the party of Capt. Sublette, which was nearly a month ahead of us, had been lost in these dreary solitudes? or was it the band of Capt. Bent, who was expected to follow sometime after us? This anxious suspense, however, lasted only for a few minutes; and the cry of "Indians!" soon made the welkin ring. Still they appeared to approach too slowly for the western prairie tribes. A little nearer, and we soon perceived that they carried a flag, which turned out to be that of the United States. This welcome sight allayed at once all uneasiness; as it is well known that most savages, when friendly, approach the whites with a hoisted flag, provided they have one. It turned out to be a party of about eighty Sioux, who were on a tour upon the prairies for the purpose of trading with, stealing from or marauding upon the southwestern nations. Our communications were carried on entirely by signs; yet we understood them perfectly to say, that there were immense numbers of Indians ahead, upon the Cimarron river, whom they described by symbolic language to be Blackfeet and Comanches; a most agreeable prospect for the imagination to dwell upon!

We now moved on slowly and leisurely, for all anxiety on the subject of water had been happily set at rest by frequent falls of rain. But imagine our consternation and dismay, when, upon descending into the valley of the Cimarron, on the morning of the 19th of June, a band of Indian warriors on horseback suddenly appeared before us from behind the ravines—an imposing array of death-dealing savages! There was no merriment in this! It was a genuine alarm—a tangible reality! These warriors, however, as we soon discovered, were only the vanguard of a "countless host," who were by this time pouring over the opposite ridge, and galloping directly toward us.

The wagons were soon irregularly "formed" upon the hillside: but in accordance with the habitual carelessness of caravan traders, a great portion of the men were unprepared for the emergency. Scores of guns were "empty," and as many more had been wetted by the recent showers, and would not "go off." Here was one calling for balls—another for powder—a third for flints. Exclamations, such as, "I've broke my ramrod"—"I've spilt my caps"—"I've rammed down a ball without powder"—"My gun is 'choked'; give me yours" —were heard from different quarters; while a timorous "greenhorn" would perhaps cry out, "Here, take my gun, you can outshoot me!" The more daring bolted off to encounter the enemy at once, while the timid and cautious took a stand with presented rifle behind the wagons. The Indians who were in advance made a bold attempt to press upon us, which came near costing them dearly; for some of our fiery backwoodsmen more than once had their rusty but unerring rifles directed upon the intruders, some of whom would inevitably have fallen before their deadly aim, had not a few of the more prudent traders interposed. The savages made demonstrations no less hostile, rushing with ready sprung bows, upon a portion of our men who had gone in search of water; and mischief would, perhaps, have ensued, had not the impetuosity of the warriors been checked by the wise men of the nation.

The Indians were collecting around us, however, in such great numbers, that it was deemed expedient to force them away, so as to resume our march, or at least to take a more advantageous position. Our company was therefore mustered and drawn up in "line of battle"; and, accompanied by the sound of a drum and fife, we marched toward the main group of the Indians. The latter seemed far more delighted than frightened with this strange parade and music, a spectacle they had, no doubt, never witnessed before, and perhaps looked upon the whole movement rather as a complimentary salute than a hostile array; for there was no interpreter through whom any communication could be conveyed to them. But, whatever may have been their impressions, one thing is certain,—that the principal chief (who was dressed in a long red coat of strouding, or coarse cloth) appeared to have full confidence in the virtues of his calumet; which he lighted, and came boldly forward to meet our warlike corps, serenely smoking the "pipe of peace." Our captain, now taking a whiff with the savage chief, directed him by signs to cause his warriors to retire. This most of them did, to rejoin the long train of squaws and papooses with the baggage, who followed in the rear, and were just then seen emerging from beyond the hills. Having slowly descended to the banks of the stream, they pitched their wigwams or lodges; over five hundred of which soon bespeckled the ample valley before us, and at once gave to its recently meager surface the aspect of an immense Indian village. The entire number of the Indians, when collected together, could not have been less than from two to three thousand—although some of our company insisted that there were at least four thousand souls. In such a case they must have mustered nearly a thousand warriors, while we were but little over two hundred strong. Still, our superior arms and the protection afforded by the wagons, gave us considerably the advantage, even supposing an equality in point of valor. However, the appearance of the squaws and children soon convinced us, that, for the present, at least, they had no hostile intentions; so we also descended into the valley and formed our camp a few hundred yards below them. The "capitanes," or head men of the whites and Indians, shortly after met, and, again smoking the calumet, agreed to be friends.

Although we were now on the very banks of the Cimarron, even the most experienced traders of our party, whether through fright or ignorance, seemed utterly unconscious of the fact. Having made our descent, far below the usual point of approach, and there being not a drop of water found in the sandy bed of the river, it was mistaken for Sand creek, and we accordingly proceeded without noticing it. Therefore, after our "big talk" was concluded, and dinner dispatched, we again set out southward, in search of the Cimarron. As we were starting warriors, squaws and papooses now commenced flocking about us, gazing at our wagons with amazement; for many of them had never, perhaps, seen such vehicles before. A few chiefs and others followed us to our next encampment; but these were sent away at night.

Our guards were now doubled, as a night attack was apprehended; for although we were well aware that Indians never commit outrages with their families at hand, yet it was feared that they might either send them away or conceal them during the night. A little after dark, these fears seemed about to be realized; as a party of thirty or forty Indians were seen coming up toward the encampment. Immediate preparations were made to attack them, when they turned out to be a band of squaws, with merely a few men as gallants—all of whom were summarily turned adrift, without waiting to speculate upon the objects of their visit. The next morning a few others made their appearance, which we treated in precisely the same manner, as a horse was missing, which it was presumed the Indians had stolen.

We continued our march southward in search of the "lost river." After a few miles' travel we encountered a ledge of sandhills, which obstructed our course, and forced us to turn westward and follow their border for the rest of the day. Finding but little water that night, and none at all the next day, we began by noon to be sadly frightened; for nothing is more alarming to the prairie traveler than a "water-scrape." The impression soon became general that we were *lost*—lost on that inhospitable desert, which had been the theater of so many former scenes of suffering! and our course impeded by sandhills! A council of the veteran travelers was called to take our emergency into consideration. It was at once resolved to strike in a northwesterly direction in search of the "dry ravine" we had left behind us, which was now supposed to have been the Cimarron.

We had just set out, when a couple of Indians approached us, bringing the horse we had lost the night before; an apparent demonstration of good faith which could hardly have been anticipated. It was evidently an effort to ingratiate themselves in our favor, and establish an intercourse—perhaps a traffic. But the outrages upon Major Riley, as well as upon a caravan, not two years before, perpetrated probably by the same Indians, were fresh in the memory of all; so that none of us were willing to confide in their friendly professions. On inquiring by means of signs for the nearest water, they pointed to the direction we were traveling: and finally taking the lead, they led us, by the shortest way, to the valley of the long-sought Cimarron, which, with its delightful green-grass glades and flowing torrent (very different in appearance from where we had crossed it below), had all the aspect of an "elysian vale," compared with what we had seen for sometime past. We pitched our camp in the valley, much rejoiced at having again "made a port." . . .

We were now entering a region of rough, and in some places, rocky road, as the streams which intervene from this to the mountains are all bordered with fine sandstone. These rugged passes acted very severely upon our wagons, as the wheels were by this time becoming loose and "shackling," from the shrink of the wood, occasioned by the extreme dryness and rarity of this elevated atmosphere. The spokes of some were beginning to reel in the hubs, so that it became necessary to brace them with "false spokes," firmly bound with "buffalo tug." On some occasions, the wagon tires have become so loose upon the felloes as to tumble off while traveling. The most effective mode of tightening slackened tires (at least that most practiced on the plains, as there is rarely a portable forge in company), is by driving strips of hoop-iron around between the tire and felloe—simple wedges of wood are sometimes made to supply the place of iron. During halts I have seen a dozen wheels being repaired at the same time, occasioning such a clitter-clatter of hammers, that one would almost fancy himself in a shipyard.

In descending to the Rio Colorado, we met a dozen or more of our countrymen from Taos, to which town (sixty or seventy miles distant) there is a direct but rugged route across the mountains. It was a joyous encounter, for among them we found some of our old acquaintances whom we had not seen for many years. During our boyhood we had "spelt" together in the same country school, and roamed the wild woods with many a childish glee. They turned about with us, and the remainder of our march was passed in answering their inquiries after their relatives and friends in the United States.

Before reaching the stream, we encountered another party of visitors, being chiefly customhouse agents or clerks, who, accompanied by a military escort, had come out to guard the caravan to the Capital. The ostensible purpose of this escort was to prevent smuggling,—a company of troops being thus dispatched every year, with strict injunctions to watch the caravans. This custom appears since to have nearly grown out of use: and well might it be discontinued altogether, for any one disposed to smuggle would find no difficulty in securing the services of these preventive guards, who, for a trifling *douceur* would prove very efficient auxiliaries, rather than obstacles to the success of any such designs. As we were forming in the valley opposite where the escort was encamped, Col. Vizcarra, the commandant, honored us with a salute from his artillery, which was promptly responded to by our little cannon.

Considering ourselves at last out of danger of Indian hostilities (although still nearly a hundred and forty miles from Santa Fé) ; and not unwilling to give our "guard" as much trouble as possible, we abandoned the organization of our caravan a few miles beyond the Colorado; its members wending their way to the Capital in almost as many detached parties as there were proprietors. The road from this to San Miguel (a town nearly a hundred miles distant), leads in a southwestern direction along the base of and almost parallel with, that spur of snow-clad mountains, which has already been mentioned, bearing down east of the Rio del Norte.

Some distance beyond the Colorado, a party of about a dozen (which I joined) left the wagons to go ahead to Santa Fé. Fifty miles beyond the main branch of this stream we passed the last of the Canadian waters, known to foreigners as the *Mora*. From thence to the *Gallinas,* the first of the Rio del Norte waters, the road stretches over an elevated plain, unobstructed by any mountainous ridge. At Gallinas creek, we found a large flock of sheep grazing upon the adjacent plain; while a little hovel at the foot of a cliff showed it to be a *rancho*. A swarthy *ranchero* soon made his appearance, from whom we procured a treat of goat's milk, with some dirty ewe's milk "curdle cheese" to supply the place of bread.

Some twenty miles from this place we entered San Miguel, the first settlement of any note upon our route. This consists of irregular clusters of mud-wall huts, and is situated in the fertile valley of Rio Pecos, a silvery little river which ripples from the snowy mountains of Santa Fé—from which city this frontier village is nearly fifty miles to the southeast. The road makes this great southern bend, to find a passway through the broken extremity of the spur of mountains before alluded to, which from this point south is cut up into detached ridges and table plains. This mountain section of the road, even in its present unimproved condition, presents but few difficult passes, and might, with little labor, be put in good order.

A few miles before reaching the city, the road again emerges into an open plain. Ascending a table ridge, we spied in an extended valley to the northwest, occasional groups of trees, skirted with verdant corn and wheat fields, with here and there a square block-like protuberance reared in the midst. A little further, and just ahead of us to the north, irregular clusters of the same opened to our view. "Oh, we are approaching the suburbs!" thought I, on perceiving the cornfields, and what I supposed to be brick-kilns scattered in every direction. These and other observations of the same nature becoming audible, a friend at my elbow said, "It is true those are heaps of unburnt bricks, nevertheless, they are *houses*—this is the city of SANTA FÉ."

Five or six days after our arrival, the caravan at last hove in sight, and wagon after wagon was seen pouring down the last declivity at about a mile distance from the city. To judge from the clamorous rejoicings of the men, and the state of agreeable excitement which the muleteers seemed to be laboring under, the spectacle must have been as new to them as it had been to me. It was truly a scene for the artist's pencil to revel in. Even the animals seemed to participate in the humor of their riders, who grew more and more merry and obstreperous as they descended towards the city. I doubt, in short, whether the first sight of the walls of Jerusalem were beheld by the crusaders with much more tumultuous and soul-enrapturing joy.

The arrival produced a great deal of bustle and excitement among the natives. *"Los Americanos!"*—*"Los carros!"*—*"La entrada de la caravana!"* were to be heard in every direction; and crowds of women and boys flocked around to see the newcomers; while crowds of *léperos* hung about as usual to see what they could pilfer. The wagoners were by no means free from excitement on this occasion. Informed of the "ordeal" they had to pass, they had spent the previous morning in "rubbing up"; and now they were prepared with clean faces, sleek combed hair, and their choicest Sunday suit, to meet the "fair eyes" of glistening black that were sure to stare at them as they passed. There was yet another preparation to be made in order to "show off" to advantage. Each wagoner must tie a brand new "cracker" to the lash of his whip; for, on driving through the streets and the *plaza pública,* every one strives to outvie his comrades in the dexterity with which he flourishes this favorite badge of his authority.

Our wagons were soon discharged in the ware-rooms of the Customhouse; and a few days' leisure being now at our disposal, we had time to take that recreation which a fatiguing journey of ten weeks had rendered so necessary. The wagoners, and many of the traders, particularly the novices, flocked to the numerous fandangoes, which are regularly kept up after the arrival of a caravan. But the merchants generally were anxiously and actively engaged in their affairs—striving who should first get his goods out of the customhouse, and obtain a chance at the "hard chink" of the numerous country dealers, who annually resort to the capital on these occasions.

CHAPTER XXXVI

IN 1852 young Ezra Meeker started for the Oregon Country in a covered wagon with his wife and baby, striking the Trail at a point Westward from Eddyville, Iowa, where his little expedition started, after another journey that had been made from Indiana. His account takes him all the way to the Northwest.

WHEN we drove out of Eddyville, headed for the Oregon Country, our train consisted of but one wagon, two yoke of four-year-old steers, and one yoke of cows. We also had one extra cow. This cow was the only animal we lost on the whole journey; she strayed away in the river bottom before we crossed the Missouri.

Now as to the members of our little party. William Buck, who had joined us as partner for the expedition, was a man six years my senior. He had had some experience on the Plains, and he knew what outfit was needed; but he had little knowledge in regard to a team of cattle. He was an impulsive man, and to some extent excitable; yet withal a man of excellent judgment and honest as God makes men. No lazy bones occupied a place in Buck's body. He was scrupulously neat and cleanly in all his ways; courteous to every one; always in good humor and always looking upon the bright side of things. A better trail mate could not have been found.

Buck's skill in camp work and his lack of ability to handle the team naturally settled the division of the work between us. It was he who selected the outfit to go into the wagon, while I fitted up the wagon and bought the team. We had butter packed in the center of the flour, which was in double sacks; eggs packed in corn meal or flour, enough to last us nearly five hundred miles; fruit in abundance, and dried pumpkins; a little jerked beef, not too salt. Last though not least, there was a demijohn of brandy "for medicinal purposes only," as Buck said.

The first day's drive out from Eddyville was a short one. When we got to plodding along over the Plains, we made from fifteen to twenty miles a day. That was counted a good day's drive, without unusual accidents or delays.

As I now remember, this was the only day on the entire trip when the cattle were allowed to stand in the yoke at noontime, while the owners lunched and rested. When it was near nightfall we made our first camp. Buck excitedly insisted that we must not unyoke the cattle.

"What shall we do?" I asked. "They can't live in the yoke always."

"Yes, but if you unyoke here you will never catch them again," he said.

One word brought on another until we were almost in a dispute, when a stranger, Thomas McAuley, who was camped near by, stepped in. He said his own cattle were gentle; there were three men of his party, and they would help us yoke up in the morning. I gratefully accepted his offer and unyoked, and we had no trouble in starting off the next morning. After that, never a word with the least semblance of contention to it passed between Buck and me.

Scanning McAuley's outfit in the morning, I was quite troubled to start out with him. His teams, principally cows, were light, and they were thin in flesh; his wagons were apparently light and as frail as the teams. But I soon found that his outfit, like ours, carried no extra weight, and he knew how to care for a team. He was, besides, an obliging neighbor, which was fully demonstrated on many trying occasions, as we traveled in company for more than a thousand miles, until his road to California parted from ours at the big bend of the Bear River.

Of the trip through Iowa little remains to be said further than that the grass was thin and washy, the roads muddy and slippery, and the weather execrable, although May had been ushered in long before we reached the little Mormon town of Kanesville (now Council Bluffs), a few miles above the place where we were to cross the Missouri River. Here my brother Oliver joined us, having come from Indianapolis with old-time comrades and friends. Now, with the McAuleys and Oliver's party, we mustered a train of five wagons.

It was here at Kanesville that the last purchases were made, the last letter sent back to anxious friends. Once across the Missouri and headed westward, we should have to cross the Rocky Mountains to find a town again.

We had now come to the beginning of the second stage of our long journey. We had reached the Missouri River. From the western bank of the river we should strike out across the Plains, through what is now Nebraska and Wyoming, to the crest of the continent. We should follow the ox-team trail along the north bank of the

Platte, and then up the north fork of the Platte to the mountains. But first we must get across the Missouri.

"What on earth is that?" exclaimed one of the women, as we approached the landing for the ferry which crossed the river to a point a few miles below where Omaha now stands.

"It looks for all the world like a big white flatiron," answered another.

We drivers had little time for looking and for making comparisons. All our attention had to be given to our teams, for as we neared the landing we found the roads terribly cut up on account of the concentrated travel.

It was indeed a sight long to be remembered. The "white flatiron" proved to be wagons with their tongues pointing to the landing. A center train with other parallel trains extended back in the rear, gradually covering a wider range the farther back from the river it went. Several hundred wagons were thus closely interlocked, completely blocking the approach to the landing.

All about were camps of every kind, some without any covering at all, others with comfortable tents. Nearly everybody appeared to be intent on merrymaking, and the fiddlers and dancers were busy; but here and there were small groups engaged in devotional services. These camps contained the outfits, in great part, of the wagons in line; some of them had been there for two weeks with still no prospect of securing any early crossing. Two scows only were engaged in crossing the wagons and teams.

The muddy waters of the Missouri had already swallowed up two victims. On the first day we were there, I saw a third victim go under the drift of a small island within sight of his shrieking wife. The stock had rushed to one side of the boat, submerging the gunwale, and had precipitated the whole load into the dangerous river. One yoke of oxen that had reached the farther shore deliberately reëntered the river with a heavy yoke on, and swam to the Iowa side; there they were finally saved by the helping hands of the assembled emigrants.

"What shall we do?" was the question passed around in our party, without answer. Tom McAuley was not yet looked upon as a leader, as was the case later.

"Build a boat," said his sister Margaret, a most determined maiden lady, the oldest of the party and as resolute and brave as the bravest.

But of what should we build it? While a search for material was being made, one of our party, who had got across the river in search of timber, discovered a scow, almost completely buried, on the sandpit opposite the landing. The report seemed too good to be true.

The next thing to do was to find the owner. We discovered him eleven miles down the river.

"Yes, if you will agree to deliver the boat safely to me after crossing your five wagons and teams, you may have it," said he.

The bargain was closed then and there. By morning we could begin to see the end of the job. Then, while busy hands began to cut a landing on the perpendicular sandy bank of the Iowa side, others were preparing sweeps. All was bustle and stir. . . .

We were now across the river, and it might almost be said that we had left the United States. When we set foot upon the right bank of the Missouri River we were outside the pale of law. We were within the Indian country, where no organized civil government existed.

The greater body of the emigrants formed themselves into large companies and elected captains. These combinations soon began to dissolve and reform, only to dissolve again, with a steady accompaniment of contentions. I would not enter into any organized company, but neither could I travel alone. By tacit agreement our party and the McAuleys traveled together, the outfit consisting of four wagons and thirteen persons—nine men, three women, and the baby. Yet although we kept apart as a separate unit, we were all the while in one great train, never out of sight and hearing of others. In fact, at times the road would be so full of wagons that all could not travel in one track, and this fact accounts for the double roadbeds seen in so many places on the trail.

We crossed the Missouri on the seventeenth and eighteenth of May. The next day we made a short drive, and camped within hearing of the shrill steamboat whistle that resounded far over the prairie.

The whistle announced the arrival of a steamer. This meant that a dozen or more wagons could be carried across the river at a time, and that a dozen or more trips could be made during the day, with as many more at night. Very soon we were overtaken by this throng of wagons. They gave us some troubles, and much discomfort.

The rush for the West was then at its height. The plan of action was to push ahead and make as big a day's drive as possible; hence it is not to be wondered at that nearly all the thousand wagons that crossed the river after we did soon passed us.

"Now, fellers, jist let 'em rush on. If we keep cool, we'll overcatch 'em afore long," said McAuley.

And we did. We passed many a team, broken down as a result of those first few days of rush. People often brought these and other ills upon themselves by their own indiscretion.

The traveling had not progressed far until there came a general outcry against the heavy loads and unnecessary articles. Soon we began to see abandoned property. First it might be a table or a cupboard, or perhaps a bedstead or a cast-iron cookstove. Then feather beds, blankets, quilts, and pillows were seen. Very soon, here and there would be an abandoned wagon; then provisions, stacks of flour and bacon being the most abundant—all left as common property.

It was a case of help yourself if you would; no one would interfere. In some places such a sign was posted,—"Help yourself." Hundreds of wagons were left and hundreds of tons of goods. People seemed to vie with each other in giving away their property. There was no chance to sell, and they disliked to destroy their goods.

Long after the end of the mania for getting rid of goods to lighten loads, the abandonment of wagons continued, as the teams became weaker and the ravages of cholera among the emigrants began to tell. It was then that many lost their heads and ruined their teams by furious driving, by lack of care, and by abuse. There came a veritable stampede—a strife for possession of the road, to see who should get ahead. It was against the rule to attempt to pass a team ahead; a wagon that had withdrawn from the line and stopped beside the trail could get into the line again, but on the march it could not cut ahead of the wagon in front of it. Yet now whole trains would strive, often with bad blood, for the mastery of the trail, one attempting to pass the other. Frequently there were drivers on both sides of the team to urge the poor, suffering brutes forward.

During the ox-team days a mighty army of pioneers went West. In the year that we crossed (1852), when the migration was at its height, this army made an unbroken column fully five hundred miles long. We knew by the inscribed dates found on Independence Rock and elsewhere that there were wagons three hundred miles ahead of us, and the throng continued crossing the river for more than a month after we had crossed it.

How many people this army comprised cannot be known; the roll was never called. History has no record of a greater number of emigrants ever making so long a journey as did these pioneers. There must have been three hundred and fifty thousand in the years of the great rush overland, from 1843 to 1857. Careful estimates of the total migration westward from 1843 to 1869, when the first railroad across the continent was completed, make the number nearly half a million.

The animals driven over the Plains during these years were legion. Besides those that labored under the yoke, in harness, and under saddle, there was a vast herd of loose stock. A conservative estimate would be not less than six animals to the wagon, and surely there were three loose animals to each one in the teams. Sixteen hundred wagons passed us while we waited for Oliver to recover. With these teams must have been nearly ten thousand beasts of burden and thirty thousand head of loose stock.

Is it any wonder that the old trail was worn so deep that even now in places it looks like a great canal? At one point near Split Rock, Wyoming, I found the road cut so deep in the solid sandstone that the kingbolt of my wagon dragged on the high center.

The pioneer army was a moving mass of human beings and dumb brutes, at times mixed in inextricable confusion, a hundred feet wide or more. Sometimes two columns of wagons, traveling on parallel lines and near each other, would serve as a barrier to prevent loose stock from crossing; but usually there would be a confused mass of cows, young cattle, horses, and men afoot moving along the outskirts. Here and there would be the drivers of loose stock, some on foot and some on horseback: a young girl, maybe, riding astride and with a younger child behind her, going here and there after an intractable cow, while the mother could be seen in the confusion lending a helping hand. As in a thronged city street, no one seemed to look to the right or to the left, or to pay much attention, if any, to others, all being bent only on accomplishing the task in hand.

The dust was intolerable. In calm weather it would rise so thick at times that the lead team of oxen could not be seen from the wagon. Like a London fog, it seemed thick enough to cut. Then again, the steady flow of wind through the South Pass would hurl the dust and sand like fine hail, sometimes with force enough to sting the face and hands.

Sometimes we had trying storms that would wet us to the skin in no time. One such I remember well, being caught in it while out on watch. The cattle traveled so fast that it was difficult to keep up with them. I could do nothing but follow, as it would have been impossible to turn them. I have always thought of this storm as a cloudburst. Anyhow, in an incredibly short time there was not a dry thread left on me. My boots were as full of water as if I had been wading over boot-top depths, and the water ran through my hat as though it were a sieve. I was almost blinded in the fury of the wind and water. Many tents were leveled by this storm. One of our neighboring trains suffered great loss by the sheets of water on the ground floating away camp equipage, ox yokes, and all loose articles; and they narrowly escaped having a wagon engulfed in the raging torrent that came so unexpectedly upon them.

Fording a river was usually tiresome, and sometimes dangerous. I remember fording the Loup fork of the Platte with a large number of wagons fastened together with ropes or chains, so that if a wagon got into trouble the teams in front would help to pull it out. The quicksand would cease to sustain the wheels so suddenly that the wagon would drop a few inches with a jolt, and up again the wheel would come as new sand was struck; then down again it would go, up and down, precisely as if the wagons were passing over a rough corduroy road that "nearly jolted the life out of us," as the women folks said after it was over, and no wonder, for the river at this point was half a mile wide.

Many of the pioneers crossed rivers in their wagon boxes and very few lost their lives in doing so. The difference between one of these prairie-schooner wagon boxes and that of a scow-shaped, flat-bottomed boat is that the wagon box has the ribs on the outside, while in a boat they are on the inside.

The number of casualties in that army of emigrants I hesitate to guess at. Shall we say that ten per cent fell on the way? Many old plainsmen would think that estimate too low; yet ten per cent would give us five thousand lives as one year's toll paid for the peopling of the Oregon Country. Mrs. Cecilia McMillen Adams, late of Hillsboro, Oregon, kept a painstaking diary when she crossed the Plains in 1852. She counted the graves passed and noted down the number. In this diary, published in full by the Oregon Pioneer Association, I find the following entries:

June 14. Passed seven new-made graves.
June 16. Passed eleven new graves
June 17. Passed six new graves.
June 18. We have passed twenty-one new graves to-day.
June 19. Passed thirteen graves to-day.
June 20. Passed ten graves.
June 21. No report.
June 22. Passed seven graves. If we should go by the camping grounds, we
          should see five times as many graves as we do.

This report of Mrs. Adams's, coupled with the facts that a parallel column from which we have no report was traveling up the south side of the river, and that the outbreak of cholera had taken place originally in this column coming from the southeast, fully confirms the estimate of five thousand deaths on the Plains in 1852. It is probably under rather than over the actual number.

To the emigrants the fact that all the graves were new-made brought an added touch of sadness. The graves of previous years had disappeared, leveled by the storms of wind or rain, by the hoofs of the stock, or possibly by ravages of the hungry wolf. Many believed that the Indians had robbed the graves for the clothing on the bodies. Whatever the cause, all, or nearly all, graves of previous years were lost, and we knew that the last resting places of those that we might leave behind would also be lost by the next year.

One of the incidents that made a profound impression upon the minds of all was the meeting with eleven wagons returning, and not a man left in the entire train. All the men had died and had been buried on the way, and the women and children were returning to their homes alone from a point well up on the Platte, below Fort Laramie. The difficulties of the return trip were multiplied on account of the throng moving westward. How those women succeeded in their attempt, or what became of them, we never knew.

Our trail led straight across the Indian lands most of the way. The redmen naturally resented this intrusion into their territory; but they did not at this time fight against it. Their attitude was rather one of expecting pay for the privilege of using their land, their grass, and their game.

On the whole, we did not have much trouble with the Indians in 1852. The great numbers of the emigrants, coupled with the superiority of their arms, made them comparatively safe. It must be remembered, also, that this was before the treaty-making period, and the Indians of the Plains were not yet incensed against white men in general.

Herds of buffalo were more often seen than bands of Indians. The buffalo trails generally followed the water courses or paralleled them. But sometimes they would lead across the country with scarcely any deviation from a direct course. When on the road a herd would persistently follow their leader, whether in the wild tumult of a stampede or in leisurely grazing as they traveled.

Well up on the Platte, but below Fort Laramie, we had the experience of a night stampede that struck terror to the heart of man and beast. It so happened that we had brought our cattle into camp that evening, a thing we did not usually do. We had driven the wagons into a circle, with the tongue of each wagon chained to the hind axletree of the wagon ahead. The cattle were led inside the circle and the tents were pitched outside.

Usually I would be out on the range with the oxen at night, and if I slept at all, snuggled up close to the back of my good ox, Dandy; but that night, with the oxen safe inside the enclosure, I slept in the wagon. William Buck and my brother Oliver were in a tent near by, sleeping on the ground.

Suddenly there was a sound like an approaching storm. Almost instantly every animal in the corral was on its feet. The alarm was given and all hands turned out, not yet knowing what caused the general commotion. The roar we heard was like that of a heavy railroad train passing at no great distance on a still night. As by instinct all seemed to know suddenly that it was a buffalo stampede. The tents were emptied of their inmates, the weak parts of the corral guarded, the frightened cattle looked after, and every one in the camp was on the alert to watch what was coming.

In the darkness of the night we could see first the forms of the leaders, and then such dense masses that we could not distinguish one buffalo from the other. How long they were in passing we forgot to note; it seemed like an age. When daylight came the few stragglers yet to be seen fell under the unerring aim of the frontiersman's rifle.

We were lucky, but our neighbors in camp did not escape loss. Some were detained for days, gathering up their scattered stock, while others were unable to find their teams. Some of the animals never were recovered.

When not on the road, the buffalo were shy, difficult to approach, and hard to bag, even with the long-range rifles of the pioneers. But for over six hundred miles along the trail, a goodly supply of fresh meat was obtainable.

As the column of wagons passed up the Platte in what is now western Nebraska, there was some relief from the dust. The throng was visibly thinned out; some had pushed on beyond the congested district, while others had lagged behind. The dead, too, had left room upon the road.

When we reached the higher lands of Wyoming, our traveling became still more pleasant. The nights were cooler, and we had clearer, purer water. As we gradually ascended the Sweetwater, life grew more tolerable and discomfort less acute.

We were now nearing the crest of the continent. The climb was so gradual, however, as to be hardly observable. The summit of the Rocky Mountains, through the South Pass, presents a wide, open, undulating country. The Pass offers, therefore, an easy gateway to the West.

Passing Pacific Springs at the summit, we rolled over to Big Sandy Creek. At this point we left the Salt Lake Trail (known also as the Mormon Trail) and took the Sublette Cut-off over to Bear River. This was a shorter trail to the Oregon Country, made by William Sublette, one of the American fur traders of the early days. The earlier emigrants to Oregon went on to Fort Bridger before leaving the Salt Lake route.

Just after leaving Soda Springs our little company of friends separated. The McAuleys and William Buck took the trail to California, while with Oliver and the Davenport brothers we went northwest to Oregon. Jacob, the younger of the brothers, fell sick and gradually grew worse as the journey grew harder. Shortly after reaching Portland the poor boy died.

When Snake River was reached, and in fact even before that, the heat again became oppressive, the dust stifling, and the thirst at times almost maddening. In some places we could see the water of the Snake winding through the lava gorges; but we could not reach it, as the river ran in the inaccessible depths of the canyon. Sickness again became prevalent, and another outbreak of cholera claimed many victims.

There were but few ferries, and none at all in many places where crossings were to be made. Even where there was a ferry, the charges were so high that they were out of reach of most of the emigrants. As for me, all my funds had been absorbed in procuring my outfit at Eddyville, in Iowa. We had not dreamed that there would be use for money on the Plains, where there were neither supplies nor people. But we soon found out our mistake.

The crossing of the Snake River, although late in the journey, gave us the opportunity to mend matters. About thirty miles below Salmon Falls the dilemma confronted us of either crossing the Snake River or having our teams starve on the trip down the river on the south bank. We found that some emigrants had calked two wagon beds and lashed them together, and were using this craft for crossing. But they would not help others across for less than three to five dollars a wagon, the party swimming their own stock.

If others could cross in wagon beds, why couldn't we do likewise? Without more ado all the old clothing that could possibly be spared was assembled, and tar buckets were scraped. Old chisels and broken knives were hunted up, and a boat repairing and calking campaign began. Very soon the wagon box rode placidly, even if not gracefully, on the waters of the Snake River.

My boyhood experience at playing with logs and leaky old skiffs in the waters of White River now served me well; I could row a boat. My first venture across the Snake River was with the wagon gear run over the wagon box, the whole being gradually worked out into deep water. The load was so heavy that a very small margin was left to prevent the water from breaking over the sides, and some water did enter as light ripples on the surface struck the *Mary Jane*—for we had duly named our craft. I got over safely, but after that I took lighter loads, and I really enjoyed the work, with the change from the intolerable dust to the clear atmosphere of the river.

We had no trouble to get the cattle across, although the river was wide. Dandy would do almost anything I asked of him; so, leading him to the water's edge, with a little coaxing I got him into swimming water and guided him across with the wagon bed. The others all followed, having been driven into deep water after the leader. It seems almost incredible how passively obedient cattle will become after long training on such a journey. Indeed, the ox is always patient, and usually quite obedient; but when oxen get heated and thirsty, they become headstrong and reckless, and won't obey. I have known them to take off the road to a water hole, when apparently nothing could stop them till they had gone so far into the mud and water that it was a hard job for them to get out again.

We had not finished crossing when tempting offers came from others to cross them; but all our party said, "No, we must travel." The rule had been adopted to travel some distance every day that it was possible. "Travel, travel, travel," was the watchword, and nothing could divert us from that resolution. On the third day we were ready to pull out from the river, with the cattle rested by the enforced wait.

Now the question was, what about the lower crossing? Those who had crossed over the river must somehow get back. It was less than a hundred and fifty miles to the place where we must again cross to the south side (the left bank) of the river. I could walk that distance in three days, while it would take our teams ten. Could I go on ahead, procure a wagon box, and start a ferry of my own? The thought brought an affirmative answer at once.

With only food and a small blanket for load, I walked to the lower crossing. It may be ludicrous, but it is true, that the most I remember about that tramp is the jack rabbits. Such swarms, as I traveled down the Boise valley, I had never seen before and I never saw again.

I soon obtained a wagon bed, and all day long for several days I was at work crossing people. I continued at this till our teams came up, and for a few days after that. I left the river with a hundred and ten dollars in my pocket. All but two dollars and seventy-five cents of this was gone before I arrived in Portland.

But we could not delay longer, even to make money. I thought I could see signs of failing strength in my young wife and baby. Not for mountains of gold would we jeopardize their lives.

All along the way the baby and the little mother had been tenderly cared for. We used to clear away a space in the wagon bed for them to take a nap together. The slow swaying of the wagon over smooth, sandy stretches made a rock-a-by movement that would lull them off to dreamland and make them forget the weary way.

When we left the lower crossing, the mother and baby were placed in a small wagon. A sprightly yoke of oxen was hitched to it that they might get an early start and keep out of the dust. What few delicacies the pioneers had were given to them. By this tender care the mother and child were enabled to continue to the end of the long journey, though the brave little mother was frail and weak from the wearisome struggle before we reached a resting place at last.

After leaving the Snake River we had one of the worst stretches of the trying journey. From the lower crossing of the Snake River at old Fort Boise to The Dalles is approximately three hundred and fifty miles over mountains and deserts. It became a serious question with many travelers whether there would be enough provisions left to keep them from starvation and whether their teams could muster strength to take the wagons in. Many wagons were left by the way-side. Everything that could possibly be spared shared the same fate. Provisions, and provisions only, were religiously cared for. Considering the weakened condition of both man and beast, it was small wonder that some ill-advised persons should take to the river in their wagon beds, many thus going to their death.

The dust got deeper every day. Going through it was like wading in water as to resistance. Often it would lie in the road fully six inches deep, so fine that a person wading through it would scarcely leave a track. And when disturbed, such clouds! No words can describe it.

At length, after we had endured five long months of soul-trying travel and had covered about eighteen hundred miles, counting from the crossing of the Missouri, we dragged ourselves on to the end of the Overland Trail at The Dalles on the Columbia River. From here my wife and I, with the baby, went by boat down the river, while Oliver took the ox team on to Portland by the land way.

On the September day in 1852 when we reached The Dalles, we found there a great crowd of travel-worn people. This assemblage was constantly changing. It was a coming-and-going congregation.

The appearance of this crowd of emigrants beggars description. Their dress was as varied as pieces in a crazy quilt. Here was a matronly dame in clean apparel, but without shoes; her husband perhaps lacked both shoes and hat. Youngsters of all sizes were running about with scarcely enough clothing to cover their nakedness. Some suits and dresses were so patched that it was impossible to tell what was the original cloth. The color of practically everybody's clothing was that of desert dust.

Every little while other sweat-streaked, motley-dressed home-seekers would straggle up to this end of the long trail. Their thoughts went back to their old homes, or to the loved ones that they had laid away tenderly in the shifting sands of the Plains. Most of them faced the future with fortitude; the difficulties they had met and mastered had but steeled them to meet the difficulties ahead. There was an undercurrent of gladness in their souls with the thought that they had achieved the end of the Overland Trail. They were ready now to go on down the Columbia to find their new homes in this great, unknown Land of Promise.

Almost every nationality was represented among them. All traces of race peculiarity and race prejudice, however, had been ground away in the mill of adversity. The trying times through which these pioneers had just passed had brought all to a kinship of feeling such as only trial and danger can beget.

We camped but two days on the bank of the Columbia River. When I say "we," let it be understood that I mean myself, my young wife, and the baby boy who was but seven weeks old when the start was made from Eddyville.

I do not remember the embarking on the great scow for our trip down the Columbia to the Cascades. But incidents of the voyage come to me as vividly as if they had happened but yesterday.

Those who took passage felt that the journey was ended. The cattle had been unyoked for the last time; the wagons had been rolled to the last bivouac; the embers of the last campfire had died out. We were entering now upon a new field with new present experiences, and with new expectancy for the morrow.

The scow, or lighter, upon which we took passage was decked over, but without railing, offering a smooth surface upon which to pile our belongings. These, in the majority of cases, made but a very small showing. The whole deck surface of the scow was covered with the remnants of the homeseekers' outfits, which in turn were covered by the owners, either sitting or reclining upon their possessions, with but scant room to change position or move about in any way. There must have been a dozen families or more on the boat, or about sixty persons. These were principally women and children; the young men and some of the older ones were still struggling on the mountain trail to get the teams through to the west side of the Cascade Mountains.

As we went floating down that wonderful old river, the deep depression of spirits that, for lack of a better name, we call "the blues," seized upon us. Do you wonder why? We were like an army that had burned the bridges behind it. We had scant knowledge of what lay in the track before us. Here we were, more than two thousand miles from home,—separated from it by a trackless, uninhabited waste of country. It was impossible for us to retrace our steps. Go ahead we must, no matter what we were to encounter.

Then, too, we had for months borne the burden of duties that could not be avoided or delayed, until many were on the verge of collapse from strain and overwork. Some were sick, and all were reduced in flesh from the urgent toil at camp duty and from lack of variety of food. Such was the condition of the motley crowd of sixty persons as we slowly neared that wonderful channel through which the great Columbia flows while passing the Cascade range.

As we neared Portland we felt that a long task had been completed. Yet reaching the end of the Overland Trail did not mean that our pioneer struggles were over. Before us lay still another task —the conquest of the new land. And it was no easy work, we were to learn, to find a home or make one in the western wilderness.

CHAPTER XXXVII

MOST OF the wagons which left the Oregon Trail for California were bound for the gold fields which had been discovered in 1849, one year after a treaty with Mexico, following war, had given California to the United States. The lure of gold brought swarms of men across the desert and the mountains and in clipper ships around Cape Horn. The valleys filled with bearded men in red shirts who sweated for the fabulous wealth that came after all only to a few of them. Their rough and violent world was seen at close range by Mrs. Louise Amelia Knapp Smith Clappe, a doctor's wife who went with her husband from San Francisco and lived during 1851-2 at Rich and Indian "bars." Her letters, under the pseudonym Dame Shirley, were printed in California in 1854-5.

THROUGH the middle of Rich Bar runs the street, thickly planted with about forty tenements, among which figure round tents, square tents, plank hovels, log cabins, etc., the residences varying in elegance and convenience from the palatial splendor of "The Empire" down to a "local habitation" formed of pine boughs and covered with old calico shirts.

Today I visited the "office," the only one on the river. I had heard so much about it from others, as well as from F., that I really *did* expect something extra. When I entered this imposing place the shock to my optic nerves was so great that I sank helplessly upon one of the benches, which ran, divan-like, the whole length (ten feet!) of the building, and laughed till I cried. There was, of course, no floor. A rude nondescript, in one corner, on which was ranged the medical library, consisting of half a dozen volumes, did duty as a table. The shelves, which looked like sticks snatched hastily from the woodpile, and nailed up without the least alteration, contained quite a respectable array of medicines. The white-canvas window stared everybody in the face, with the interesting information painted on it, in perfect grenadiers of capitals, that this was Dr. ——'s office.

During my call at the office I was introduced to one of the *finders* of Rich Bar,—a young Georgian,—who afterwards gave me a full description of all the facts connected with its discovery. This unfortunate had not spoken to a woman for two years, and, in the elation of his heart at the joyful event, he rushed out and invested capital in some excellent champagne, which I, on Willie's principle of "doing in Turkey as the Turkeys do," assisted the company in drinking, to the honor of my own arrival. I mention this as an instance that nothing can be done in California without the sanctifying influence of the *spirit,* and it generally appears in a much more "questionable shape" than that of sparkling wine. Mr. H. informed me that on the 20th of July, 1850, it was rumored at Nelson's Creek —a mining station situated at the Middle Fork of the Feather River, about eighty miles from Marysville—that one of those vague "Somebodies," a near relation of the "They-Says," had discovered mines of a remarkable richness in a northeasterly direction, and about forty miles from the first-mentioned place. Anxious and immediate search was made for "Somebody," but, as our Western brethren say, he "wasn't thar'." But his absence could not deter the miners when once the golden rumor had been set afloat. A large company packed up their goods and chattels, generally consisting of a pair of blankets, a frying-pan, some flour, salt pork, brandy, pickax and shovel, and started for the new Dorado. On arriving at Rich Bar, part of the adventurers camped there, but many went a few miles farther down the river. The next morning, two men turned over a large stone, beneath which they found quite a sizable piece of gold. They washed a small panful of the dirt, and obtained from it two hundred and fifty-six dollars. Encouraged by this success, they commenced staking off the legal amount of ground allowed to each person for mining purposes, and, the remainder of the party having descended the hill, before night the entire bar was "claimed." In a fortnight from that time, the two men who found the first bit of gold had each taken out six thousand dollars. Two others took out thirty-three pounds of gold in eight hours, which is the best day's work that has been done on this branch of the river. The largest amount ever taken from one panful of dirt was fifteen hundred dollars. In a little more than a week after its discovery, five hundred men had settled upon the Bar for the summer. Such is the wonderful alacrity with which a mining town is built. Soon after was discovered, on the same side of the river, about half a mile apart, and at nearly the same distance from this place, the two bars, Smith and Indian, both very rich, also another, lying across the river, just opposite Indian, called Missouri Bar. There are several more, all within a few miles of here, called Frenchman's, Taylor's, Brown's, The Junction, Wyandott, and Muggin's; but they are, at present, of little importance as mining stations.

Those who worked in these mines during the fall of 1850 were extremely fortunate, but, alas! the monte fiend ruined hundreds. Shall I tell you the fate of two of the most successful of these gold-hunters? From poor men, they found themselves, at the end of a few weeks, absolutely rich. Elated with their good fortune, seized with a mania for monte, in less than a year these unfortunates, so lately respectable and intelligent, became a pair of drunken gamblers. One of them, at this present writing, works for five dollars a day, and boards himself out of that; the other actually suffers for the necessaries of life,—a too common result of scenes in the mines.

It seems indeed awful, dear M., to be compelled to announce to you the death of one of the four women forming the female population of this Bar. I have just returned from the funeral of poor Mrs. B., who died of peritonitis (a common disease in this place), after an illness of four days only. Our hostess herself heard of her sickness but two days since. On her return from a visit which she had paid to the invalid, she told me that although Mrs. B.'s family did not seem alarmed about her, in her opinion she would survive but a few hours. Last night we were startled by the frightful news of her decease. I confess that, without being very egotistical, the death of one, out of a community of four women, might well alarm the remainder.

Her funeral took place at ten this morning. The family reside in a log cabin at the head of the Bar, and although it has no window, all the light admitted entering through an aperture where there *will* be a door when it becomes cold enough for such a luxury, yet I am told, and can easily believe, that it is one of the most *comfortable* residences in the place. I observed it particularly, for it was the first log cabin that I had ever seen. Everything in the room, though of the humblest description, was exceedingly clean and neat.

On a board, supported by two butter-tubs, was extended the body of the dead woman, covered with a sheet. By its side stood the coffin, of unstained pine, lined with white cambric. You, who have alternately laughed and scolded at my provoking and inconvenient deficiency in the power of observing, will perhaps wonder at the minuteness of my descriptions; but I know how deeply you are interested in everything relating to California, and therefore I take pains to describe things exactly as I *see* them, hoping that thus you will obtain an idea of life in the mines *as it is*.

The bereaved husband held in his arms a sickly babe ten months old, which was moaning piteously for its mother. The other child, a handsome, bold-looking little girl six years of age, was running gayly around the room, perfectly unconscious of her great bereavement. A sickening horror came over me, to see her, every few moments, run up to her dead mother and peep laughingly under the handkerchief that covered her moveless face. Poor little thing! It was evident that her baby-toilet had been made by men. She had on a new calico dress, which, having no tucks in it, trailed to the floor, and gave her a most singular and dwarf-womanly appearance.

About twenty men, with the three women of the place, had assembled at the funeral. An extempore prayer was made, filled with all the peculiarities usual to that style of petition. Ah, how different from the soothing verses of the glorious burial service of the church!

As the procession started for the hillside graveyard, a dark cloth cover, borrowed from a neighboring monte-table, was flung over the coffin. Do not think that I mention any of these circumstances in a spirit of mockery. Far from it. Every observance usual on such occasions, that was *procurable*, surrounded this funeral. All the gold on Rich Bar could do no more; and should I die to-morrow, I should be marshaled to my mountain-grave beneath the same monte-table-cover pall which shrouded the coffin of poor Mrs. B.

I almost forgot to tell you how painfully the feelings of the assembly were shocked by the sound of the nails (there being no screws at any of the shops) driven with a hammer into the coffin while closing it. It seemed as if it *must* disturb the pale sleeper within.

To-day I called at the residence of Mrs. R. It is a canvas house containing a suite of three "apartments," as Dick Swiveller would say, which, considering that they were all on the ground-floor, are kept surprisingly neat. There is a barroom blushing all over with red calico, a dining-room, kitchen, and a small bed-closet. The little sixty-eight-pounder woman is queen of the establishment. By the way, a man who walked home with us was enthusiastic in her praise. "Magnificent woman, that, sir," he said, addressing my husband; "a wife of the right sort, *she* is. Why," he added, absolutely rising into eloquence as he spoke, "she earnt her *old man*" (said individual twenty-one years of age, perhaps) "nine hundred dollars in nine weeks, clear of all expenses, by washing! Such women ain't common, I tell *you*. If they were, a man might marry, and make money by the operation."

This Bar is so small that it seems impossible that the tents and cabins scattered over it can amount to a dozen. There are, however, twenty in all, including those formed of calico shirts and pine boughs. With the exception of the paths leading to the different tenements, the entire level is covered with mining-holes, on the edges of which lie the immense piles of dirt and stones which have been removed from the excavations. There is a deep pit in front of our cabin, and another at the side of it, though they are not worked, as, when "prospected," they did not "yield the color."

At present the sun does not condescend to shine upon Indian Bar at all, and the old settlers tell me that he will not smile upon us for the next three months, but he nestles lovingly in patches of golden glory all along the brows of the different hills around us, and now and then stoops to kiss the topmost wave on the opposite shore of the Río de las Plumas.

The first artificial elegance which attracts your vision is a large rag shanty, roofed, however, with a rude kind of shingles, over the entrance of which is painted, in red capitals ("to what base uses do we come at last"), the name of the great Humboldt spelt without the *d*. This is the only hotel in this vicinity, and as there is a really excellent bowling-alley attached to it, and the barroom has a floor upon which the miners can dance, and, above all, a cook who can play the violin, it is very popular. But the clinking of glasses, and the swaggering air of some of the drinkers, remind us that it is no place for a lady, so we will pass through the dining-room, and, emerging at the kitchen, in a step or two reach our log cabin. Enter, my dear; you are perfectly welcome. Besides, we could not keep you out if we would, as there is not even a latch on the canvas door, though we really intend, in a day or two, to have a hook put onto it.

The room into which we have just entered is about twenty feet square. It is lined over the top with white cotton cloth, the breadths of which, being sewed together only in spots, stretch gracefully apart in many places, giving one a bird's-eye view of the shingles above. The sides are hung with a gaudy chintz, which I consider a perfect marvel of calico-printing. The artist seems to have exhausted himself on *roses*. From the largest cabbage down to the tiniest Burgundy, he has arranged them in every possible variety of wreath, garland, bouquet, and single flower. They are of all stages of growth, from earliest budhood up to the ravishing beauty of the "last rose of summer." Nor has he confined himself to the colors usually worn by this lovely plant, but, with the daring of a great genius soaring above nature, worshiping the ideal rather than the real, he has painted them brown, purple, green, black, and blue. It would need a floral catalogue to give you the names of *all* the varieties which bloom upon the calico, but, judging by the shapes, which really are much like the originals, I can swear to moss-roses, Burgundies, York and Lancaster, tea-roses, and multifloras.

A curtain of the above-described chintz (I shall hem it at the first opportunity) divides off a portion of the room, behind which stands a bedstead that in ponderosity leaves the Empire couches far behind. But before I attempt the furniture let me finish describing the cabin itself.

The fireplace is built of stones and mud, the chimney finished off with alternate layers of rough sticks and this same rude mortar. Contrary to the usual custom, it is built inside, as it was thought that arrangement would make the room more comfortable, and you may imagine the queer appearance of this unfinished pile of stones, mud, and sticks. The mantelpiece (remember that on this portion of a great building some artists, by their exquisite workmanship, have become world-renowned) is formed of a beam of wood covered with strips of tin procured from cans, upon which still remain, in black hieroglyphics, the names of the different eatables which they formerly contained. Two smooth stones (how delightfully primitive!) do duty as fire-dogs. I suppose that it would be no more than civil to call a hole two feet square, in one side of the room, a window, although it is as yet guiltless of glass. F. tried to coax the proprietor of the Empire to let him have a window from that pine-and-canvas palace, but he, of course, declined, as to part with it would really inconvenience himself. So F. has sent to Marysville for some glass, though it is the general opinion that the snow will render the trail impassable for mules before we can get it. In this case we shall tack up a piece of cotton cloth, and should it chance at any time to be very cold, hang a blanket before the opening. At present the weather is so mild that it is pleasanter as it is, though we have a fire in the mornings and evenings, more, however, for luxury than because we really need it. For my part, I almost hope that we shall not be able to get any glass, for you will perhaps remember that it was a pet habit of mine, in my own room, to sit by a great fire, in the depth of winter, with my window open.

One of our friends had nailed up an immense quantity of unhemmed cotton cloth—very coarse—in front of this opening, and as he evidently prided himself upon the elegant style in which he had arranged the drapery, it went to my heart to take it down and suspend in its place some pretty blue linen curtains which I had brought from the valley. My toilet-table is formed of a trunk elevated upon two claret-cases, and by draping it with some more of the blue linen neatly fringed, it really will look quite handsome, and when I have placed upon it my rosewood workbox, a large cushion of crimson brocade, some Chiness ornaments of exquisitely carved ivory, and two or three Bohemian-glass cologne-stands, it would not disgrace a lady's chamber at home.

The looking-glass is one of those which come in paper cases for dolls' houses. How different from the full-length psyches so almost indispensable to a dressing-room in the States!

The washstand is another trunk, covered with a towel, upon which you will see, for bowl, a large vegetable-dish, for ewer, a common-sized dining-pitcher. Near this, upon a small cask, is placed a pail which is daily filled with water from the river. I brought with me from Marysville a handsome carpet, a hair mattress, pillows, a profusion of bed-linen, quilts, blankets, towels, etc., so that, in spite of the oddity of most of my furniture, I am, in reality, as thoroughly comfortable here as I could be in the most elegant palace.

We have four chairs, which were brought from the Empire. I seriously proposed having three-legged stools. With my usual desire for symmetry, I thought that they would be more in keeping; but as I was told that it would be a great deal of trouble to get them made, I was fain to put up with mere chairs. So you see that even in the land of gold itself one cannot have everything that she desires. An ingenious individual in the neighborhood, blessed with a large bump for mechanics, and good nature, made me a sort of wide bench, which, covered with a neat plaid, looks quite sofa-like. A little pine table, with oilcloth tacked over the top of it, stands in one corner of the room, upon which are arranged the chess and cribbage boards. There is a larger one for dining purposes, and as unpainted pine has always a most dreary look, F. went everywhere in search of oilcloth for it, but there was none at any of the bars. At last, "Ned," the Humboldt Paganini, remembered two old monte-table covers which had been thrown aside as useless. I received them thankfully, and, with my planning and Ned's mechanical genius, we patched up quite a respectable covering. To be sure, the ragged condition of the primitive material compelled us to have at one end an extra border, but that only agreeably relieved the monotony. I must mention that the floor is so uneven that no article of furniture gifted with four legs pretends to stand upon but three at once, so that the chairs, tables, etc., remind you constantly of a dog with a sore foot.

At each end of the mantelpiece is arranged a candlestick, not, much to my regret, a block of wood with a hole in the center of it, but a real britanniaware candlestick. The space between is gayly ornamented with F.'s meerschaum, several styles of clay pipes, cigars, cigarritos, and every procurable variety of tobacco, for, you know, the aforesaid individual is a perfect devotee of the Indian weed.

How would you like to winter in such an abode? in a place where there are no newspapers, no churches, lectures, concerts, or theaters; no fresh books; no shopping, calling, nor gossiping little tea-drinkings; no parties, no balls, no picnics, no tableaus, no charades, no latest fashions, no daily mail (we have an express once a month), no promenades, no rides or drives; no vegetables but potatoes and onions, no milk, no eggs, no *nothing?* Now, I expect to be very happy here. This strange, odd life fascinates me. As for churches, "the groves were God's first temples," "and for the strength of the hills, the Swiss mountains bless him"; and as to books, I read Shakespeare, David, Spenser, Paul, Coleridge, Burns, and Shelley, which are never old.

I little thought, dear M., that here, with the "green watching hills" as witnesses, amid a solitude so grand and lofty that it seems as if the faintest whisper of passion must be hushed by its holy stillness, I should have to relate the perpetration of one of those fearful deeds which, were it for no other peculiarity than its startling suddenness, so utterly at variance with all *civilized* law, must make our beautiful California appear to strangers rather as a hideous phantom than the flower-wreathed reality which she is.

Whether the life which a few men, in the impertinent intoxication of power, have dared to crush out was worth that of a fly, I do not know,—perhaps not,—though God alone, methinks, can judge of the value of the soul upon which he has breathed. But certainly the effect upon the hearts of those who played the principal parts in the revolting scene referred to—a tragedy, in my simple judgment, so utterly useless—must be demoralizing in the extreme.

The facts in this sade case are as follows: Last fall, two men were arrested by their partners on suspicion of having stolen from them eighteen hundred dollars in gold-dust. The evidence was not sufficient to convict them, and they were acquitted. They were tried before a meeting of the miners, as at that time the law did not even *pretend* to wave its scepter over this place.

The prosecutors still believed them guilty, and fancied that the gold was hidden in a coyote-hole near the camp from which it had been taken. They therefore watched the place narrowly while the suspected men remained on the Bar. They made no discoveries, however, and soon after the trial the acquitted persons left the mountains for Marysville.

A few weeks ago, one of these men returned, and has spent most of the time since his arrival in loafing about the different barrooms upon the river. He is said to have been constantly intoxicated. As soon as the losers of the gold heard of his return, they bethought themselves of the coyote-hole, and placed about its entrance some brushwood and stones in such a manner that no one could go into it without disturbing the arrangement of them. In the meanwhile the thief settled at Rich Bar, and pretended that he was in search of some gravel-ground for mining purposes.

A few mornings ago he returned to his boarding-place, which he had left some hour earlier, with a spade in his hand, and, as he laid it down, carelessly observed that he had been out prospecting. The losers of the gold went, immediately after breakfast, as they had been in the habit of doing, to see if all was right at the coyote-hole. On this fatal day they saw that the entrance had been disturbed, and going in, they found upon the ground a money-belt which had apparently just been cut open. Armed with this evidence of guilt, they confronted the suspected person and sternly accused him of having the gold in his possession. Singularly enough, he did not attempt a denial, but said that if they would not bring him to a trial (which of course they promised) he would give it up immediately. He then informed them that they would find it beneath the blankets of his bunk, as those queer shelves on which miners sleep, ranged one above another somewhat like the berths of a ship, are generally called. There, sure enough, were six hundred dollars of the missing money, and the unfortunate wretch declared that his partner had taken the remainder to the States.

By this time the exciting news had spread all over the Bar. A meeting of the miners was immediately convened, the unhappy man taken into custody, a jury chosen, and a judge, lawyer, etc., appointed. Whether the men who had just regained a portion of their missing property made any objections to the proceedings which followed, I know not. If they had done so, however, it would have made no difference, as the *people* had taken the matter entirely out of their hands.

At one o'clock, so rapidly was the trial conducted, the judge charged the jury, and gently insinuated that they could do no less than to bring in with their verdict of guilty a sentence of death! Perhaps you know that when a trial is conducted without the majesty of the law, the jury are compelled to decide not only upon the guilt of the prisoner, but the mode of his punishment also. After a few minutes' absence, the twelve men, who had consented to burden their souls with a responsibility so fearful, returned, and the foreman handed to the judge a paper, from which he read the will

of the *people,* as follows: That William Brown, convicted of stealing, etc., should, in *one hour* from that time, be hung by the neck
until he was dead.

By the persuasions of some men more mildly disposed, they
granted him a respite of *three hours* to prepare for his sudden
entrance into eternity. He employed the time in writing, in his native
language (he is a Swede), to some friends in Stockholm. God help
them when that fatal post shall arrive, for, no doubt, *he* also, although a criminal, was fondly garnered in many a loving heart.

He had exhibited, during the trial, the utmost recklessness and
nonchalance, had drank many times in the course of the day, and
when the rope was placed about his neck, was evidently much intoxicated. All at once, however, he seemed startled into a consciousness
of the awful reality of his position, and requested a few moments for
prayer.

The execution was conducted by the jury, and was performed by
throwing the cord, one end of which was attached to the neck of
the prisoner, across the limb of a tree standing outside of the Rich
Bar graveyard, when all who felt disposed to engage in so revolting
a task lifted the poor wretch from the ground in the most awkward
manner possible. The whole affair, indeed, was a piece of cruel
butchery, though *that* was not intentional, but arose from the ignorance of those who made the preparations. In truth, life was only
crushed out of him by hauling the writhing body up and down,
several times in succession, by the rope, which was wound round a
large bough of his green-leaved gallows. Almost everybody was surprised at the severity of the sentence, and many, with their hands
on the cord, did not believe even *then* that it would be carried into
effect, but thought that at the last moment the jury would release
the prisoner and substitute a milder punishment.

It is said that the crowd generally seemed to feel the solemnity
of the occasion, but many of the drunkards, who form a large part
of the community on these bars, laughed and shouted as if it were
a spectacle got up for their particular amusement. A disgusting
specimen of intoxicated humanity, struck with one of those luminous
ideas peculiar to his class, staggered up to the victim, who was praying at the moment, and, crowding a dirty rag into his almost unconscious hand, in a voice broken by a drunken hiccough, tearfully
implored him to take his "hankercher," and if he were *innocent* (the
man had not denied his guilt since first accused), to drop it as soon
as he was drawn up into the air, but if *guilty,* not to let it fall on
any account.

The body of the criminal was allowed to hang for some hours

after the execution. It had commenced storming in the earlier part of the evening, and when those whose business it was to inter the remains arrived at the spot, they found them enwrapped in a soft white shroud of feathery snowflakes, as if pitying nature had tried to hide from the offended face of Heaven the cruel deed which her mountain-children had committed.

I have heard no one approve of this affair. It seems to have been carried on entirely by the more reckless part of the community. There is no doubt, however, that they seriously *thought* they were doing right, for many of them are kind and sensible men. They firmly believed that such an example was absolutely necessary for the protection of this community. Probably the recent case of Little John rendered this last sentence more severe than it otherwise would have been. The Squire, of course, could do nothing (as in criminal cases the *people* utterly refuse to acknowledge his authority) but protest against the whole of the proceedings, which he did in the usual legal manner.

If William Brown had committed a murder, or had even attacked a man for his money; if he had been a quarrelsome, fighting character, endangering lives in his excitement,—it would have been a very different affair. But, with the exception of the crime for which he perished (he *said* it was his first, and there is no reason to doubt the truth of his assertion), he was a harmless, quiet, inoffensive person.

I wish that it were possible, dear M., to give you an idea of the perfect saturnalia which has been held upon the river for the last three weeks, without at the same time causing you to think *too* severely of our good mountains. In truth, it requires not only a large intellect, but a large heart, to judge with becoming charity of the peculiar temptations of riches. A more generous, hospitable, intelligent, and industrious people than the inhabitants of the half-dozen bars, of which Rich Bar is the nucleus, never existed, for you know how proverbially wearing it is to the nerves of manhood to be entirely without either occupation or amusement, and that has been preëminently the case during the present month.

Imagine a company of enterprising and excitable young men, settled upon a sandy level about as large as a poor widow's potato-patch, walled in by sky-kissing hills, absolutely *compelled* to remain on account of the weather, which has vetoed indefinitely their exodus, with no place to ride or drive even if they had the necessary vehicles and quadrupeds; with no newspapers nor politics to interest them; deprived of all books but a few dog-eared novels of the poorest class,—churches, lectures, lyceums, theaters, and (most unkind-est cut of all!) pretty girls, having become to these unhappy men mere myths; without *one* of the thousand ways of passing time peculiar to civilization, most of them living in damp, gloomy cabins, where heaven's dear light can enter only by the door; and when you add to all these disagreeables the fact that, during the never-to-be-forgotten month, the most remorseless, persevering rain which ever set itself to work to drive humanity mad has been pouring doggedly down, sweeping away bridges, lying in uncomfortable puddles about nearly all of the habitations, wickedly insinuating it-self beneath unumbrella-protected shirt-collars, generously treating to a shower-bath *and* the rheumatism sleeping bipeds who did not happen to have an india-rubber blanket and, to crown all, rendering mining utterly impossible,—you cannot wonder that even the most moral should have become somewhat reckless.

The saturnalia commenced on Christmas evening, at the Hum-boldt, which, on that very day, had passed into the hands of new proprietors. The most gorgeous preparations were made for cele-brating the *two* events. The bar was retrimmed with red calico, the bowling-alley had a new lining of the coarsest and whitest cotton cloth, and the broken lamp-shades were replaced by whole ones. All day long, patient mules could be seen descending the hill, bending beneath casks of brandy and baskets of champagne, and, for the first time in the history of that celebrated building, the floor (won-derful to relate, it *has* a floor) was *washed,* at a lavish expenditure of some fifty pails of water, the using up of one entire broom, and the melting away of sundry bars of the best yellow soap, after which I am told that the enterprising and benevolent individuals who had undertaken the herculean task succeeded in washing the boards through the hopeless load of dirt which had accumulated upon them during the summer and autumn. All these interesting particulars were communicated to me by Ned when he brought up dinner. That distinguished individual himself was in his element, and in a most intense state of perspiration and excitement at the same time.

About dark we were startled by the loudest hurrahs, which arose at the sight of an army of india-rubber coats (the rain was falling in riverfuls), each one enshrouding a Rich Barian, which was rapidly descending the hill. This troop was headed by the "General," who, lucky man that he is, waved on high, instead of a banner, a *live* lantern, actually composed of tin and window-glass, and evidently intended by its maker to act in no capacity but that *of* a lantern. The General is the largest and tallest and with one exception I think the oldest, man upon the river. He is about fifty, I should fancy, and wears a snow-white beard of such immense dimensions, in both length and thickness, that any elderly Turk would expire with envy at the mere sight of it. Don't imagine that *he* is a reveler. By no means. The gay crowd followed *him,* for the same reason that the king followed Madam Blaize,—because she went before.

At nine o'clock in the evening they had an oyster-and-champagne supper in the Humboldt, which was very gay with toasts, songs, speeches, etc. I believe that the company danced all night. At any rate, they were dancing when I went to sleep, and they were dancing when I woke the next morning. The revel was kept up in this mad way for three days, growing wilder every hour. Some never slept at all during that time. On the fourth day they got past dancing, and, lying in drunken heaps about the barroom, commenced a most unearthly howling. Some barked like dogs, some roared like bulls, and others hissed like serpents and geese. Many were too far gone to imitate anything but their own animalized selves. The scene, from the description I had of it, must have been a complete illustration of the fable of Circe and her fearful transformations. Some of these bacchanals were among the most respectable and respected men upon the river. Many of them had resided here for more than a year, and had never been seen intoxicated before. It seemed as if they were seized with a reckless mania for pouring down liquor, which, as I said above, everything conspired to foster and increase.

Of course there were some who kept themselves aloof from these excesses, but they were few, and were not allowed to enjoy their sobriety in peace. The revelers formed themselves into a mock vigilance committee, and when one of these unfortunates appeared outside, a constable, followed by those who were able to keep their legs, brought him before the court, where he was tried on some amusing charge, and *invariably* sentenced to "treat the crowd." The prisoners had generally the good sense to submit cheerfully to their fate.

Towards the latter part of the week, people were compelled to be a little more quiet, from sheer exhaustion, but on New Year's Day, when there was a grand dinner at Rich Bar, the excitement broke out, if possible, worse than ever. The same scenes, in a more or less aggravated form, in proportion as the strength of the actors held out, were repeated at Smith's Bar and The Junction.

Nearly every day I was dreadfully frightened by seeing a boatload of intoxicated men fall into the river, where nothing but the fact of their *being* intoxicated saved many of them from drowning. One morning about thirty dollars' worth of bread (it must have been tipsy-cake), which the baker was conveying to Smith's Bar, fell overboard, and sailed merrily away towards Marysville. People passed the river in a boat, which was managed by a pulley and a rope that was strained across it from Indian Bar to the opposite shore.

Of the many acquaintances who had been in the habit of calling every evening, three, only, appeared in the cabin during as many weeks. Now, however, the saturnalia is about over. Ned and Chock have nearly fiddled themselves into their respective graves, the claret (a favorite wine with miners) and oysters are exhausted, brandied fruits are rarely seen, and even port-wine is beginning to look scarce. Old callers occasionally drop in, looking dreadfully sheepish and subdued, and *so* sorry, and people are evidently arousing themselves from the bacchanal madness into which they were so suddenly and so strangely drawn.

We have lived through so much of excitement for the last three weeks, dear M., that I almost shrink from relating the gloomy events that have marked their flight. But if I leave out the darker shades of our mountain life, the picture will be very incomplete. In the short space of twenty-four days we have had murders, fearful accidents, bloody deaths, a mob, whippings, a hanging, an attempt at suicide, and a fatal duel.

I think that, even among these beautiful hills, I never saw a more perfect bridal of the earth and sky than that of Sunday, the 11th of July. On that morning I went with a party of friends to the head of the ditch, a walk of about three miles in length. We returned about three in the evening, loaded with fragrant bundles, which, arranged in jars, tumblers, pitchers, bottles, and pails (we are not particular as to the quality of our vases in the mountains, and love our flowers as well in their humble chalices as if their beautiful heads lay against a background of marble or porcelain) made the dark old cabin a bower of beauty for us.

Shortly after our arrival, a perfectly deafening volley of shouts and yells elicited from my companion the careless remark that the customary sabbath-day's fight was apparently more serious than usual. Almost as he spoke there succeeded a deathlike silence, broken in a minute after by a deep groan at the corner of the cabin, followed by the words, "Why, Tom, poor fellow, are you really wounded?" Before we could reach the door, it was burst violently open by a person who inquired hurriedly for the Doctor, who, luckily, happened at that very moment to be approaching. The man who called him then gave us the following excited account of what had happened. He said that in a mêlée between the Americans and the foreigners, Domingo, a tall, majestic-looking Spaniard, a perfect type of the novelistic bandit of Old Spain, had stabbed Tom Somers, a young Irishman, but a naturalized citizen of the United States, and that, at the very moment, said Domingo, with a Mexicana hanging upon his arm, and brandishing threateningly the long, bloody knife with which he had inflicted the wound upon his victim, was parading up and down the street unmolested. It seems that when Tom Somers fell, the Americans, being unarmed, were seized with a sudden panic and fled. There was a rumor (unfounded, as it afterwards proved) to the effect that the Spaniards had on this day conspired to kill all the Americans on the river. In a few moments, however, the latter rallied and made a rush at the murderer, who immediately plunged into the river and swam across to Missouri Bar. Eight or ten shots were fired at him while in the water, not one of which hit him. He ran like an antelope across the flat, swam thence to Smith's Bar, and escaped by the road leading out of the mountains from The Junction. Several men went in pursuit of him, but he was not taken, and without doubt is now safe in Mexico.

In the meanwhile the consternation was terrific. The Spaniards, who, with the exception of six or eight, knew no more of the affair than I did, thought that the Americans had arisen against them, and our own countrymen, equally ignorant, fancied the same of the foreigners. About twenty of the latter, who were either sleeping or reading in their cabins at the time of the *émeute*, aroused by the cry of "Down with the Spaniards!" barricaded themselves in a drinking-saloon, determined to defend themselves as long as possible against the massacre which was fully expected would follow this appalling shout. In the bakeshop, which stands next door to our cabin, young Tom Somers lay straightened for the grave (he lived but fifteen minutes after he was wounded), while over his dead body a Spanish woman was weeping and moaning in the most piteous and heartrending manner. The Rich Barians, who had heard a most exaggerated account of the rising of the Spaniards against the Americans, armed with rifles, pistols, clubs, dirks, etc., were rushing down the hill by hundreds. Each one added fuel to his rage by crowding into the little bakery to gaze upon the blood-bathed bosom of the victim, yet warm with the life which but an hour before it had so triumphantly worn. Then arose the most fearful shouts of "Down with the Spaniards!" "Drive every foreigner off the river!" "Don't let one of the murderous devils remain!" "Oh, if you have a drop of American blood in your veins, it must cry out for vengeance upon the cowardly assassins of poor Tom!" All this, mingled with the most horrible oaths and execrations, yelled up as if in mockery into that smiling heaven, which, in its fair sabbath calm, bent unmoved over the hell which was raging below.

After a time the more sensible and sober part of the community succeeded in quieting, in a partial degree, the enraged and excited multitude. During the whole affair I had remained perfectly calm, —in truth, much more so than I am now, when recalling it. The entire catastrophe had been so unexpected, and so sudden in its consummation, that I fancy I was stupefied into the most exemplary good behavior. F. and several of his friends, taking advantage of the lull in the storm, came into the cabin and entreated me to join the two women who were living on the hill. At this time it seemed to be the general opinion that there would be a serious fight, and they said I might be wounded accidentally if I remained on the Bar. As I had no fear of anything of the kind, I pleaded hard to be allowed to stop, but when told that my presence would increase the anxiety of our friends, of course, like a dutiful wife, I went on to the hill.

We three women, left entirely alone, seated ourselves upon a log overlooking the strange scene below. The Bar was a sea of heads, bristling with guns, rifles, and clubs. We could see nothing, but fancied from the apparent quiet of the crowd that the miners were taking measures to investigate the sad event of the day. All at once we were startled by the firing of a gun, and the next moment, the crowd dispersing, we saw a man led into the log cabin, while another was carried, apparently lifeless, into a Spanish drinking-saloon, from one end of which were burst off instantly several boards, evidently to give air to the wounded person. Of course we were utterly unable to imagine what had happened, and, to all our perplexity and anxiety, one of the ladies insisted upon believing that it was her own husband who had been shot, and as she is a very nervous woman, you can fancy our distress. It was in vain to tell her—which we did over and over again—that that worthy individual wore a *blue* shirt, and the wounded person a *red* one. She doggedly insisted that her dear M. had been shot, and, having informed us confidentially, and rather inconsistently, that she should never see him again, never, never, plumped herself down upon the log in an attitude of calm and ladylike despair, which would have been infinitely amusing had not the occasion been so truly a fearful one. Luckily for our nerves, a benevolent individual, taking pity upon our loneliness, came and told us what had happened.

It seems that an Englishman, the owner of a house of the vilest description, a person who is said to have been the primary cause of all the troubles of the day, attempted to force his way through the

line of armed men which had been formed at each side of the street.
The guard very properly refused to let him pass. In his drunken
fury he tried to wrest a gun from one of them, which, being accidentally discharged in the struggle, inflicted a severe wound upon a
Mr. Oxley, and shattered in the most dreadful manner the thigh of
Señor Pizarro, a man of high birth and breeding, a porteño of
Buenos Aires. This frightful accident recalled the people to their
senses, and they began to act a little less like madmen than they
had previously done. They elected a vigilance committee, and
authorized persons to go to The Junction and arrest the suspected
Spaniards.

The first act of the committee was to try a Mexicana who had
been foremost in the fray. She has always worn male attire, and
upon this occasion, armed with a pair of pistols, she fought like a
very fury. Luckily, inexperienced in the use of firearms, she wounded
no one. She was sentenced to leave the Bar by daylight,—a perfectly
just decision, for there is no doubt that she is a regular little demon.
Some went so far as to say she ought to be hanged, for she was the
indirect cause of the fight. You see, always it is the old cowardly
excuse of Adam in Paradise,—the *woman* tempted me, and I did
eat,—as if the poor frail head, once so pure and beautiful, had not
sin enough of its own, dragging it forever downward, without being
made to answer for the wrong-doing of a whole community of men.

The next day the committee tried five or six Spaniards, who were
proven to have been the ring-leaders in the sabbath-day riot. Two
of them were sentenced to be whipped, the remainder to leave the
Bar that evening, the property of all to be confiscated to the use of
the wounded persons. O Mary! imagine my anguish when I heard
the first blow fall upon those wretched men. I had never thought
that I should be compelled to hear such fearful sounds, and, although I immediately buried my head in a shawl, nothing can
efface from memory the disgust and horror of that moment. I had
heard of such things, but heretofore had not realized that in the
nineteenth century men could be beaten like dogs, much less that
other men not only could sentence such barbarism, but could actually stand by and see their own manhood degraded in such disgraceful manner. One of these unhappy persons was a very gentlemanly young Spaniard, who implored for death in the most moving
terms. He appealed to his judges in the most eloquent manner, as
gentlemen, as men of honor, representing to them that to be deprived of life was nothing in comparison with the never-to-be-
effaced stain of the vilest convict's punishment to which they had
sentenced him. Finding all his entreaties disregarded, he swore a

most solemn oath, that he would murder every American that he should chance to meet alone, and as he is a man of the most dauntless courage, and rendered desperate by a burning sense of disgrace which will cease only with his life, he will doubtless keep his word.

Although, in my very humble opinion, and in that of others more competent to judge of such matters than myself, these sentences were unnecessarily severe, yet so great was the rage and excitement of the crowd that the vigilance committee could do no less. The mass of the mob demanded fiercely the death of the prisoners, and it was evident that many of the committee took side with the people. I shall never forget how horror-struck I was (bombastic as it *now* sounds) at hearing no less a personage than the Whig candidate for representative say that the condemned had better fly for their lives, for the "Avenger of Blood" was on their tracks! I am happy to say that said very worthy but sanguinary individual, the Avenger of Blood, represented in this case by some half-dozen gambling rowdies, either changed his mind or lost scent of his prey, for the intended victims slept about two miles up the hill quite peacefully until morning.

The following facts, elicited upon the trial, throw light upon this unhappy affair. Seven miners from Old Spain, enraged at the cruel treatment which their countrymen had received on the Fourth, and at the illiberal cry of "Down with the Spaniards," had united for the purpose of taking revenge on seven Americans, whom they believed to be the originators of their insults. All well armed, they came from The Junction, where they were residing at the time, intending to challenge each one his man, and in fair fight compel their insolent aggressors to answer for the arrogance which they had exhibited more than once towards the Spanish race. Their first move, on arriving at Indian Bar, was to go and dine at the Humboldt, where they drank a most enormous quantity of champagne and claret. Afterwards they proceeded to the house of the Englishman whose brutal carelessness caused the accident which wounded Pizarro and Oxley, when one of them commenced a playful conversation with one of his countrywomen. This enraged the Englishman, who instantly struck the Spaniard a violent blow and ejected him from the shanty. Thereupon ensued a spirited fight, which, through the exertion of a gentleman from Chile, a favorite with both nations, ended without bloodshed. This person knew nothing of the intended duel, or he might have prevented, by his wise counsels, what followed. Not suspecting for a moment anything of the kind, he went to Rich Bar. Soon after he left, Tom Somers, who is said always to have been a dangerous person when in liquor, without any apparent provocation struck Domingo (one of the original seven) a violent blow, which nearly felled him to the earth. The latter, a man of "dark antecedents" and the most reckless character, mad with wine, rage, and revenge, without an instant's pause drew his knife and inflected a fatal wound upon his insulter. Thereupon followed the chapter of accidents which I have related.

On Tuesday following the fatal sabbath, a man brought news of the murder of a Mr. Bacon, a person well known on the river, who kept a ranch about twelve miles from Rich Bar. He was killed for his money by his servant, a negro, who, not three months ago, was our own cook. He was the last one anybody would have suspected capable of such an act.

A party of men, appointed by the vigilance committee, left the Bar immediately in search of him. The miserable wretch was apprehended in Sacramento, and part of the gold found upon his person. On the following Sunday he was brought in chains to Rich Bar. After a trial by the miners, he was sentenced to be hanged at four o'clock in the evening. All efforts to make him confess proved futile. He said very truly that whether innocent or guilty they would hang him, and so he "died and made no sign" with a calm indifference, as the novelists say, worthy of a better cause. The dreadful crime and death of Josh, who, having been an excellent cook, and very neat and respectful, was a favorite servant with us, added to the unhappiness which you can easily imagine that I was suffering under all these horrors.

The state of society here has never been so bad as since the appointment of a committee of vigilance. The rowdies have formed themselves into a company called the "Moguls," and they parade the streets all night, howling, shouting, breaking into houses, taking wearied miners out of their beds and throwing them into the river, and, in short, "murdering sleep" in the most remorseless manner. Nearly every night they build bonfires fearfully near some rag shanty, thus endangering the lives (or, I should rather say, the property, for, as it is impossible to sleep, lives are emphatically safe) of the whole community. They retire about five o'clock in the morning, previously to this blessed event posting notices to that effect, and that they will throw any one who may disturb them into the river. I am nearly worn out for want of rest, for, truly, they "make night hideous" with their fearful uproar. Mr. Oxley, who still lies dangerously ill from the wound received on what we call the "fatal Sunday," complains bitterly of the disturbances; and when poor Pizarro was dying, and one of his friends gently requested

that they be quiet for half an hour and permit the soul of the
sufferer to pass in peace, they only laughed and yelled and hooted
louder than ever in the presence of the departing spirit, for the
tenement in which he lay, being composed of green boughs only,
could, of course, shut out no sounds. Without doubt, if the Moguls
had been sober, they would never have been guilty of such horrible
barbarity as to compel the thoughts of a dying man to mingle with
curses and blasphemies, but, alas! they were intoxicated, and may
God forgive them, unhappy ones, for they knew not what they did.
The poor, exhausted miners—for even well people cannot sleep in
such a pandemonium—grumble and complain, but they, although
far outnumbering the rioters, are too timid to resist. All say, "It is
shameful," "Something ought to be done," "Something *must* be
done," etc., and in the meantime the rioters triumph. You will wonder that the committee of vigilance does not interfere. It is said
that some of that very committee are the ringleaders among the
Moguls.

CHAPTER XXXVIII

TEN YEARS after gold was discovered in California silver was discovered in Nevada, then a part of the same state. The silver fever proved to be as virulent an infection as the gold fever of '49 had been, and no less a person than Mark Twain, come to Nevada in 1861, contracted it. Some pages in "Roughing It" communicate all that needs to be known concerning the behavior of men afflicted with the disease.

BY and by I was smitten with the silver fever. "Prospecting parties" were leaving for the mountains every day, and discovering and taking possession of rich silver-bearing lodes and ledges of quartz. Plainly this was the road to fortune. The great "Gould and Curry" mine was held at three or four hundred dollars a foot when we arrived; but in two months it had sprung up to eight hundred. The "Ophir" had been worth only a mere trifle, a year gone by, and now it was selling at nearly *four thousand dollars a foot!* Not a mine could be named that had not experienced an astonishing advance in value within a short time. Everybody was talking about these marvels. Go where you would, you heard nothing else, from morning till far into the night. Tom So-and-So had sold out of the "Amanda Smith" for $40,000—hadn't a cent when he "took up" the ledge six months ago. John Jones had sold half his interest in the "Bald Eagle and Mary Ann" for $65,000, gold coin, and gone to the States for his family. The widow Brewster had "struck it rich" in the "Golden Fleece" and sold ten feet for $18,000—hadn't money enough to buy a crape bonnet when Sing-Sing Tommy killed her husband at Baldy Johnson's wake last spring. The "Last Chance" had found a "clay casing" and knew they were "right on the ledge"—consequence, "feet" that went begging yesterday were worth a brick house apiece to-day, and seedy owners who could not get trusted for a drink at any bar in the country yesterday were roaring drunk on champagne to-day and had hosts of warm personal friends in a town where they had forgotten how to bow or shake hands from long-continued want of practice. Johnny Morgan, a common loafer, had gone to sleep in the gutter and waked up worth a hundred thousand dollars, in consequence of the decision in the "Lady Franklin and Rough and Ready" lawsuit. And so on—day in and day out the talk pelted our ears and the excitement waxed hotter and hotter around us.

I would have been more or less than human if I had not gone mad like the rest. Cart-loads of solid silver bricks, as large as pigs of lead, were arriving from the mills every day, and such sights as that gave substance to the wild talk about me. I succumbed and grew as frenzied as the craziest.

Every few days news would come of the discovery of a brand-new mining region; immediately the papers would teem with accounts of its richness, and away the surplus population would scamper to take possession. By the time I was fairly inoculated with the disease, "Esmeralda" had just had a run and "Humboldt" was beginning to shriek for attention. "Humboldt! Humboldt!" was the new cry, and straightway Humboldt, the newest of the new, the richest of the rich, the most marvelous of the marvelous discoveries in silver-land, was occupying two columns of the public prints to "Esmeralda's" one. I was just on the point of starting to Esmeralda, but turned with the tide and got ready for Humboldt. . . .

On the fifteenth day we completed our march of two hundred miles and entered Unionville, Humboldt County, in the midst of a driving snowstorm. Unionville consisted of eleven cabins and a liberty pole. Six of the cabins were strung along one side of a deep cañon, and the other five faced them. The rest of the landscape was made up of bleak mountain walls that rose so high into the sky from both sides of the cañon that the village was left, as it were, far down in the bottom of a crevice. It was always daylight on the mountain-tops a long time before the darkness lifted and revealed Unionville.

We built a small, rude cabin in the side of the crevice and roofed it with canvas, leaving a corner open to serve as a chimney, through which the cattle used to tumble occasionally, at night, and mash our furniture and interrupt our sleep. It was very cold weather and fuel was scarce. Indians brought brush and bushes several miles on their backs; and when we could catch a laden Indian it was well—and when we could not (which was the rule, not the exception), we shivered and bore it.

I confess, without shame, that I expected to find masses of silver lying all about the ground. I expected to see it glittering in the sun on the mountain summits. I said nothing about this, for some instinct told me that I might possibly have an exaggerated idea about it, and so if I betrayed my thought I might bring derision upon myself. Yet I was as perfectly satisfied in my own mind as I could be of anything, that I was going to gather up, in a day or two, or at furthest a week or two, silver enough to make me satisfactorily wealthy—and so my fancy was already busy with plans for spending this money. The first opportunity that offered, I sauntered carelessly away from the cabin, keeping an eye on the other boys, and stopping and contemplating the sky when they seemed to be observing me; but as soon as the coast was manifestly clear, I fled away as guiltily as a thief might have done and never halted till I was far beyond sight and call. Then I began my search with a feverish excitement that was brimful of expectation—almost of certainty. I crawled about the ground, seizing and examining bits of stone, blowing the dust from them or rubbing them on my clothes, and then peering at them with anxious hope. Presently I found a bright fragment and my heart bounded! I hid behind a bowlder and polished it and scrutinized it with a nervous eagerness and a delight that was more pronounced than absolute certainty itself could have afforded. The more I examined the fragment the more I was convinced that I had found the door to fortune. I marked the spot and carried away my specimen. Up and down the rugged mountainside I searched, with always increasing interest and always augmenting gratitude that I had come to Humboldt and come in time. Of all the experiences of my life, this secret search among the hidden treasures of silver-land was the nearest to unmarred ecstasy. It was a delirious revel. By and by, in the bed of a shallow rivulet, I found a deposit of shining yellow scales, and my breath almost forsook me! A gold-mine, and in my simplicity I had been content with vulgar silver! I was so excited that I half believed my overwrought imagination was deceiving me. Then a fear came upon me that people might be observing me and would guess my secret. Moved by this thought, I made a circuit of the place, and ascended a knoll to reconnoiter. Solitude. No creature was near. Then I returned to my mine, fortifying myself against possible disappointment, but my fears were groundless—the shining scales were still there. I set about scooping them out, and for an hour I toiled down the windings of the stream and robbed its bed. But at last the descending sun warned me to give up the quest, and I turned homeward laden with wealth. As I walked along I could not help smiling at the thought of my being so excited over my fragment of silver when a nobler metal was almost under my nose. In this little time the former had so fallen in my estimation that once or twice I was on the point of throwing it away.

The boys were as hungry as usual, but I could eat nothing. Neither could I talk. I was full of dreams and far away. Their conversation interrupted the flow of my fancy somewhat, and annoyed me a little, too. I despised the sordid and commonplace things they talked about. But as they proceeded, it began to amuse me. It grew to be rare fun to hear them planning their poor little economies and sighing over possible privations and distresses when a gold-mine, all our own, lay within sight of the cabin, and I could point it out at any moment. Smothered hilarity began to oppress me, presently. It was hard to resist the impulse to burst out with exultation and reveal everything; but I did resist. I said within myself that I would filter the great news through my lips calmly and be serene as a summer morning while I watched its effect in their faces. I said:

"Where have you all been?"

"Prospecting."

"What did you find?"

"Nothing."

"Nothing? What do you think of the country?"

"Can't tell, yet," said Mr. Ballou, who was an old gold-miner, and had likewise had considerable experience among the silver-mines.

"Well, haven't you formed any sort of opinion?"

"Yes, a sort of a one. It's fair enough here, maybe, but overrated. Seven-thousand-dollar ledges are scarce, though. That Sheba may be rich enough, but we don't own it; and, besides, the rock is so full of base metals that all the science in the world can't work it. We'll not starve, here, but we'll not get rich, I'm afraid."

"So you think the prospect is pretty poor?"

"No name for it!"

"Well, we'd better go back, hadn't we?"

"Oh, not yet—of course not. We'll try it a riffle, first."

"Suppose, now—this is merely a supposition, you know—suppose you could find a ledge that would yield, say, a hundred and fifty dollars a ton—would that satisfy you?"

"Try us once!" from the whole party.

"Or suppose—merely a supposition, of course—suppose you were to find a ledge that would yield two thousand dollars a ton—would *that* satisfy you?"

"Here—what do you mean? What are you coming at? Is there some mystery behind all this?"

"Never mind. I am not saying anything. You know perfectly well there are no rich mines here—of course you do. Because you have been around and examined for yourselves. Anybody would know that, that had been around. But just for the sake of argument, suppose—in a kind of general way—suppose some person were to tell you that two-thousand-dollar ledges were simply contemptible—contemptible, understand—and that right yonder in sight of this very cabin there were piles of pure gold and pure silver—oceans of it!—enough to make you all rich in twenty-four hours! Come!"

"I should say he was as crazy as a loon!" said old Ballou, but wild with excitement, nevertheless.

"Gentlemen," said I, "I don't say anything—*I* haven't been around, you know, and of course don't know anything—but all I ask of you is to cast your eye on *that*, for instance, and tell me what you think of it!" and I tossed my treasure before them.

There was an eager scramble for it, and a closing of heads together over it under the candlelight. Then old Ballou said:

"Think of it? I think it is nothing but a lot of granite rubbish and nasty glittering mica that isn't worth ten cents an acre!"

So vanished my dream. So melted my wealth away. So toppled my airy castle to the earth and left me stricken and forlorn. . . .

True knowledge of the nature of silver-mining came fast enough. We went out "prospecting" with Mr. Ballou. We climbed the mountain-sides, and clambered among sage-brush, rocks, and snow till we were ready to drop with exhaustion, but found no silver—nor yet any gold. Day after day we did this. Now and then we came upon holes burrowed a few feet into the declivities and apparently abandoned; and now and then we found one or two listless men still burrowing. But there was no appearance of silver. These holes were the beginnings of tunnels, and the purpose was to drive them hundreds of feet into the mountain, and some day tap the hidden ledge where the silver was. Some day! It seemed far enough away, and very hopeless and dreary. Day after day we toiled, and climbed, and searched, and we younger partners grew sicker and still sicker of the promiseless toil. At last we halted under a beetling rampart of rock which projected from the earth high, upon the mountain. Mr. Ballou broke off some fragments with a hammer, and examined them long and attentively with a small eyeglass; threw them away and broke off more; said this rock was quartz, and quartz was the sort of rock that contained silver. *Contained* it! I had thought that at least it would be caked on the outside of it like a kind of veneering. He still broke off pieces and critically examined them, now and then wetting the piece with his tongue and applying the glass. At last he exclaimed:

"We've got it!"

We were full of anxiety in a moment. The rock was clean and

white, where it was broken, and across it ran a ragged thread of blue. He said that that little thread had silver in it, mixed with base metals, such as lead and antimony, and other rubbish, and that there was a speck or two of gold visible. After a great deal of effort we managed to discern some little fine yellow specks, and judged that a couple of tons of them massed together might make a gold dollar, possibly. We were not jubilant, but Mr. Ballou said there were worse ledges in the world than that. He saved what he called the "richest" piece of the rock, in order to determine its value by the process called the "fire-assay." Then we named the mine "Monarch of the Mountains" (modesty of nomenclature is not a prominent feature in the mines), and Mr. Ballou wrote out and stuck up the following "notice," preserving a copy to be entered upon the books in the mining recorder's office in the town.

NOTICE

We the undersigned claim three claims, of three hundred feet each (and one for discovery), on this silver-bearing quartz lead or lode, extending north and south from this notice, with all its dips, spurs, and angles, variations and sinuosities, together with fifty feet of ground on either side for working the same.

We put our names to it and tried to feel that our fortunes were made. But when we talked the matter all over with Mr. Ballou, we felt depressed and dubious. He said this surface quartz was not all there was of our mine; but that the wall or ledge of rock called the "Monarch of the Mountains" extended down hundreds and hundreds of feet into the earth—he illustrated by saying it was like a curbstone, and maintained a nearly uniform thickness—say twenty feet—away down into the bowels of earth, and was perfectly distinct from the casing rock on each side of it; and that it kept to itself, and maintained its distinctive character always, no matter how deep it extended into the earth or how far it stretched itself through and across the hills and valleys. He said it might be a mile deep and ten miles long, for all we knew; and that wherever we bored into it above ground or below, we would find gold and silver in it, but no gold or silver in the meaner rock it was cased between. And he said that down in the great depths of the ledge was its richness, and the deeper it went the richer it grew. Therefore, instead of working here on the surface, we must either bore down into the rock with a shaft till we came to where it was rich—say a hundred feet or so—or else we must go down into the valley and bore a long tunnel into the mountain-side and tap the ledge far under the earth. To do either was plainly the labor of months; for we could blast and bore only a few feet a day—some five or six. But this was not all. He said that after we got the ore out it must be hauled in wagons to a distant silver-mill, ground up, and the silver extracted by a tedious and costly process. Our fortune seemed a century away!

But we went to work. We decided to sink a shaft. So, for a week we climbed the mountain, laden with picks, drills, gads, crowbars, shovels, cans of blasting-powder and coils of fuse, and strove with might and main. At first the rock was broken and loose, and we dug it up with picks and threw it out with shovels, and the hole progressed very well. But the rock became more compact, presently, and gads and crowbars came into play. But shortly nothing could make an impression but blasting-powder. That was the weariest work! One of us held the iron drill in its place and another would strike with an eight-pound sledge—it was like driving nails on a large scale. In the course of an hour or two the drill would reach a depth of two or three feet, making a hole a couple of inches in diameter. We would put in a charge of powder, insert half a yard of fuse, pour in sand and gravel and ram it down, then light the fuse and run. When the explosion came and the rocks and smoke shot into the air, we would go back and find about a bushel of that hard, rebellious quartz jolted out. Nothing more. One week of this satisfied me. I resigned. Claggett and Oliphant followed. Our shaft was only twelve feet deep. We decided that a tunnel was the thing we wanted.

So we went down the mountainside and worked a week; at the end of which time we had blasted a tunnel about deep enough to hide a hogshead in, and judged that about nine hundred feet more of it would reach the ledge. I resigned again, and the other boys only held out one day longer. We decided that a tunnel was not what we wanted. We wanted a ledge that was already "developed." There were none in the camp.

We dropped the "Monarch" for the time being. Meantime the camp was filling up with people, and there was a constantly growing excitement about our Humboldt mines. We fell victims to the epidemic and strained every nerve to acquire more "feet." We prospected and took up new claims, put "notices" on them and gave them grandiloquent names. We traded some of our "feet" for "feet" in other people's claims. In a little while we owned largely in the "Gray Eagle," the "Columbiana," the "Branch Mint," the "Maria Jane," the "Universe," the "Root-Hog-or-Die," the "Samson and Delilah," the "Treasure Trove," the "Golconda," the "Sultana," the "Boomerang," the "Great Republic," the "Grand Mogul," and fifty other "mines" that had never been molested by a shovel or scratched with a pick. We had not less than thirty thousand "feet" apiece in the "richest mines on earth" as the frenzied cant phrased it—and were in debt to the butcher. We were stark mad with excitement—drunk with happiness—smothered under mountains of prospective wealth—arrogantly compassionate toward the plodding millions who knew not our marvelous cañon—but our credit was not good at the grocer's.

It was the strangest phase of life one can imagine. It was a beggars' revel. There was nothing doing in the district—no mining—no milling—no productive effort—no income—and not enough money in the entire camp to buy a corner lot in an eastern village, hardly; and yet a stranger would have supposed he was walking among bloated millionaires. Prospecting parties swarmed out of town with the first flush of dawn, and swarmed in again at nightfall laden with spoil—rocks. Nothing but rocks. Every man's pockets were full of them; the floor of his cabin was littered with them; they were disposed in labeled rows on his shelves.

I now come to a curious episode—the most curious, I think, that had yet accented my slothful, valueless, heedless career. Out of a hillside toward the upper end of the town, projected a wall of reddish-looking quartz croppings, the exposed comb of a silver-bearing ledge that extended deep down into the earth, of course. It was owned by a company entitled the "Wide West." There was a shaft sixty or seventy feet deep on the under side of the croppings, and everybody was acquainted with the rock that came from it—and tolerably rich rock it was, too, but nothing extraordinary. I will remark here, that although to the inexperienced stranger all the quartz of a particular "district" looks about alike, an old resident of the camp can take a glance at a mixed pile of rock, separate the fragments and tell you which mine each came from, as easily as a confectioner can separate and classify the various kinds and qualities of candy in a mixed heap of the article.

All at once the town was thrown into a state of extraordinary excitement. In mining parlance the Wide West had "struck it rich!" Everybody went to see the new developments, and for some days there was such a crowd of people about the Wide West shaft that a stranger would have supposed there was a mass-meeting in session there. No other topic was discussed but the rich strike, and nobody thought or dreamed about anything else. Every man brought away a specimen, ground it up in a hand-mortar, washed it out in his horn spoon, and glared speechless upon the marvelous result. It was not hard rock, but black, decomposed stuff which could be crumbled in the hand like a baked potato, and when spread out on a paper exhibited a thick sprinkling of gold and particles of "native" silver. Higbie brought a handful to the cabin, and when he had washed it out his amazement was beyond description. Wide West stock soared skyward. It was said that repeated offers had been made for it at a thousand dollars a foot, and promptly refused. We have all had the "blues"—the mere skyblues—but mine were indigo, now—because I did not own in the Wide West. The world seemed hollow to me, and existence a grief. I lost my appetite, and ceased to take an interest in anything. Still I had to stay, and listen to other people's rejoicings, because I had no money to get out of the camp with.

The Wide West company put a stop to the carrying away of "specimens," and well they might, for every handful of the ore was worth a sum of some consequence. To show the exceeding value of the ore, I will remark that a sixteen-hundred-pounds parcel of it was sold, just as it lay, at the mouth of the shaft, at *one dollar a pound;* and the man who bought it "packed" it on mules a hundred and fifty or two hundred miles, over the mountains, to San Francisco, satisfied that it would yield at a rate that would richly compensate him for his trouble. The Wide West people also commanded their foreman to refuse any but their own operatives permission to enter the mine at any time or for any purpose. I kept up my "blue" meditations and Higbie kept up a deal of thinking, too, but of a different sort. He puzzled over the "rock," examined it with a glass, inspected it in different lights and from different points of view, and after each experiment delivered himself, in soliloquy, of one and the same unvarying opinion in the same unvarying formula:

"It is *not* Wide West rock!"

He said once or twice that he meant to have a look into the Wide West shaft if he got shot for it. I was wretched, and did not care whether he got a look into it or not. He failed that day, and tried again at night; failed again; got up at dawn and tried, and failed again. Then he lay in ambush in the sage-brush hour after hour, waiting for the two or three hands to adjourn to the shade of a bowlder for dinner; made a start once, but was premature—one of the men came back for something; tried it again, but when almost at the mouth of the shaft, another of the men rose up from behind the bowlder as if to reconnoiter, and he dropped on the ground and lay quiet; presently he crawled on his hands and knees to the mouth of the shaft, gave a quick glance around, then seized the rope and slid down the shaft. He disappeared in the gloom of a "side drift" just as a head appeared in the mouth of the shaft and somebody shouted "Hello!"—which he did not answer. He was not disturbed any more. An hour later he entered the cabin, hot, red, and ready to burst with smothered excitement, and exclaimed in a stage whisper:

"I knew it! We are rich! It's A BLIND LEAD!"

I thought the very earth reeled under me. Doubt—conviction—doubt again—exultation—hope, amazement, belief, unbelief—every emotion imaginable swept in wild procession through my heart and brain, and I could not speak a word. After a moment or two of this mental fury, I shook myself to rights, and said:

"Say it again!"

"It's a blind lead!"

"Cal, let's—let's burn the house—or kill somebody! Let's get out where there's room to hurrah! But what is the use? It is a hundred times too good to be true."

"It's a blind lead for a million!—hanging wall—foot wall—clay casings—everything complete!" He swung his hat and gave three cheers, and I cast doubt to the winds and chimed in with a will. For I was worth a million dollars, and did not care "whether school kept or not!"

But perhaps I ought to explain. A "blind lead" is a lead or ledge that does not "crop out" above the surface. A miner does not know where to look for such leads, but they are often stumbled upon by accident in the course of driving a tunnel or sinking a shaft. Higbie knew the Wide West rock perfectly well, and the more he had examined the new developments the more he was satisfied that the ore could not have come from the Wide West vein. And so had it occurred to him alone, of all the camp, that there was a blind lead down in the shaft, and that even the Wide West people themselves did not suspect it. He was right. When he went down the shaft, he found that the blind lead held its independent way through the Wide West vein, cutting it diagonally, and that it was inclosed in its own well-defined casing-rocks and clay. Hence it was public property. Both leads being perfectly well defined, it was easy for any miner to see which one belonged to the Wide West and which did not.

We thought it well to have a strong friend, and therefore we brought the foreman of the Wide West to our cabin that night and revealed the great surprise to him. Higbie said:

"We are going to take possession of this blind lead, record it and establish ownership, and then forbid the Wide West company to take out any more of the rock. You cannot help your company in this matter—nobody can help them. I will go into the shaft with you and prove to your entire satisfaction that it *is* a blind lead.

Now we propose to take you in with us, and claim the blind lead in our three names. What do you say?"

What could a man say who had an opportunity to simply stretch forth his hand and take possession of a fortune without risk of any kind and without wronging any one or attaching the least taint of dishonor to his name? He could only say, "Agreed."

The notice was put up that night, and duly spread upon the recorder's books before ten o'clock. We claimed two hundred feet each—six hundred feet in all—the smallest and compactest organization in the district, and the easiest to manage.

No one can be so thoughtless as to suppose that we slept that night. Higbie and I went to bed at midnight, but it was only to lie broad awake and think, dream, scheme. The floorless, tumble-down cabin was a palace, the ragged gray blankets silk, the furniture rosewood and mahogany. Each new splendor that burst out of my visions of the future whirled me bodily over in bed or jerked me to a sitting posture just as if an electric battery had been applied to me. We shot fragments of conversation back and forth at each other. Once Higbie said:

"When are you going home—to the States?"

"To-morrow!"—with an evolution or two, ending with a sitting position. "Well—no—but next month, at furthest."

"We'll go in the same steamer."

"Agreed."

A pause.

"Steamer of the 10th?"

"Yes. No, the 1st."

"All right."

Another pause.

"Where are you going to live?" said Higbie.

"San Francisco."

"That's me!"

Pause.

"Too high—too much climbing"—from Higbie.

"What is?"

"I was thinking of Russian Hill—building a house up there."

"Too much climbing? Sha'n't you keep a carriage?"

"Of course. I forgot that."

Pause.

"Cal, what kind of a house are you going to build?"

"I was thinking about that. Three-story and an attic."

"But what *kind*?"

"Well, I don't hardly know Brick, I suppose "

"Brick—bosh."

"Why? What is your idea?"

"Brownstone front—French plate-glass—billiard-room off the dining-room—statuary and paintings—shrubbery and two-acre grass-plat—greenhouse—iron dog on the front stoop—gray horses—landau, and a coachman with a bug on his hat!"

"By George!"

A long pause.

"Cal, when are you going to Europe?"

"Well—I hadn't thought of that. When are you?"

"In the spring."

"Going to be gone all summer?"

"All summer! I shall remain there three years."

"No—but are you in earnest?"

"Indeed I am."

"I will go along too."

"Why, of course you will."

"What part of Europe shall you go to?"

"All parts. France, England, Germany—Spain, Italy, Switzerland, Syria, Greece, Palestine, Arabia, Persia, Egypt—all over—everywhere."

"I'm agreed."

"All right."

"Won't it be a swell trip!"

"We'll spend forty or fifty thousand dollars trying to make it one, anyway."

Another long pause.

"Higbie, we owe the butcher six dollars, and he has been threatening to stop our—"

"Hang the butcher!"

"Amen."

And so it went on. By three o'clock we found it was no use, and so we got up and played cribbage and smoked pipes till sunrise. It was my week to cook. I always hated cooking—now, I abhorred it.

The news was all over town. The former excitement was great—this one was greater still. I walked the streets serene and happy. Higbie said the foreman had been offered two hundred thousand dollars for his third of the mine. I said I would like to see myself selling for any such price. My ideas were lofty. My figure was a million. Still, I honestly believe that if I had been offered it, it would have had no other effect than to make me hold off for more.

I found abundant enjoyment in being rich. A man offered me a three-hundred-dollar horse, and wanted to take my simple, unindorsed note for it. That brought the most realizing sense I had yet had that I was actually rich, beyond shadow of doubt. It was followed by numerous other evidences of a similar nature—among which I may mention the fact of the butcher leaving us a double supply of meat and saying nothing about money.

By the laws of the district, the "locators" or claimants of a ledge were obliged to do a fair and reasonable amount of work on their new property within ten days after the date of the location, or the property was forfeited, and anybody could go and seize it that chose. So we determined to go to work the next day. About the middle of the afternoon, as I was coming out of the post-office, I met a Mr. Gardiner, who told me that Capt. John Nye was lying dangerously ill at his place (the "Nine-Mile Ranch"), and that he and his wife were not able to give him nearly as much care and attention as his case demanded. I said if he would wait for me a moment, I would go down and help in the sick-room. I ran to the cabin to tell Higbie. He was not there, but I left a note on the table for him, and a few minutes later I left town in Gardiner's wagon.

When I had been nursing the captain nine days he was somewhat better, but very feeble. During the afternoon we lifted him into a chair and gave him an alcoholic vapor bath, and then set about putting him on the bed again. We had to be exceedingly careful, for the least jar produced pain. Gardiner had his shoulders and I his legs; in an unfortunate moment I stumbled and the patient fell heavily on the bed in an agony of torture. I never heard a man swear so in my life. He raved like a maniac, and tried to snatch a revolver from the table—but I got it. He ordered me out of the house, and swore a world of oaths that he would kill me wherever he caught me when he got on his feet again. It was simply a passing fury, and meant nothing. I knew he would forget it in an hour, and maybe be sorry for it, too; but it angered me a little, at the moment. So much so, indeed, that I determined to go back to Esmeralda. I thought he was able to get along alone, now, since he was on the war-path. I took supper, and as soon as the moon rose, began my nine-mile journey, on foot. Even millionaires needed no horses, in those days, for a mere nine-mile jaunt without baggage.

As I "raised the hill" overlooking the town, it lacked fifteen minutes of twelve. I glanced at the hill over beyond the cañon, and in the bright moonlight saw what appeared to be about half the population of the village massed on and around the Wide West croppings. My heart gave an exulting bound, and I said to myself, "They have made a new strike to-night—and struck it richer than ever, no

MARK TWAIN DREAMS OF RICHES

doubt." I started over there, but gave it up. I said the "strike" would keep, and I had climbed hills enough for one night.

It was a little after one o'clock. As I entered the cabin door, tired but jolly, the dingy light of a tallow candle revealed Higbie, sitting by the pine table gazing stupidly at my note, which he held in his fingers, and looking pale, old, and haggard. I halted, and looked at him. He looked at me, stolidly. I said:

"Higbie, what—what is it?"

"We're ruined—we didn't do the work—THE BLIND LEAD'S RELOCATED!"

It was enough. I sat down sick, grieved—broken-hearted, indeed. A minute before, I was rich and brimful of vanity; I was a pauper now, and very meek. We sat still an hour, busy with thought, busy with vain and useless self-upbraidings, busy with "Why *didn't* I do this, and why *didn't* I do that," but neither spoke a word. Then we dropped into mutual explanations, and the mystery was cleared away. It came out that Higbie had depended on me, as I had on him, and as both of us had on the foreman. The folly of it! It was the first time that ever staid and steadfast Higbie had left an important matter to chance or failed to be true to his full share of a responsibility.

But he had never seen my note till this moment, and this moment was the first time he had been in the cabin since the day he had seen me last. He, also, had left a note for me, on that same fatal afternoon—had ridden up on horseback, and looked through the window, and being in a hurry and not seeing me, had tossed the note into the cabin through a broken pane.

A year ago my esteemed and in every way estimable old millionaire partner, Higbie, wrote me from an obscure little mining-camp in California that after nine or ten years of buffetings and hard striving, he was at last in a position where he could command twenty-five hundred dollars, and said he meant to go into the fruit business in a modest way. How such a thought would have insulted him the night we lay in our cabin planning European trips and brownstone houses on Russian Hill!

CHAPTER XXXIX

FOURTEEN YEARS after Dame Shirley watched the procession of the heroes through Rich and Indian bars, the geologist Clarence King, mountaineering in the Sierra Nevada, ran upon a troupe of ragged citizens whose condition seemed to him to symbolize the quick descent already made in California from the golden heights of '49.

I PURPOSELY avoid telling by what route I entered the Sierras, because there lingers in my breast a desire to see once more that lovely region, and failing, as I do, to confide in the people, I fear lest, if the camp I am going to describe should be recognized, I might, upon revisiting the scene, suffer harm, or even come to an untimely end. I refrain, then, from telling by what road I found myself entering the region of the pines one lovely twilight evening, two days after leaving Visalia. Pines, growing closer and closer, from sentinels gathered to groups, then stately groves, and at last, as the evening wore on, assembled in regular forest, through whose open tops the stars shone cheerfully.

I came upon an open meadow, hearing in front the rush of a large brook, and directly reached two campfires, where were a number of persons. My two hirelings caught and unloaded the pack-horse, and set about their duties, looking to supper and the animals, while I prospected the two camps. That just below me, on the same side of the brook, I found to be the bivouac of a company of hunters, who, in the ten minutes of my call, made free with me, hospitably offering a jug of whisky, and then went on in their old eternal way of making bear-stories out of whole cloth.

I left with a belief that my protoplasm and theirs must be different, in spite of Mr. Huxley, and passed across the brook to the other camp. Under noble groups of pines smoldered a generous heap of coals, the ruins of a mighty log. A little way from this lay a confused pile of bedclothes, partly old and half-bald buffalo-robes, but, in the main, thick strata of what is known to irony as comforters, upon which, outstretched in wretched awkwardness of position, was a family, all with their feet to the fire, looking as if they had been blown over in one direction, or knocked down by a single bombshell. On the extremities of this common bed, with the air of having gotten as far from each other as possible, the mother and father of the Pike family reclined; between them were two small children—a girl and boy—and a huge girl, who, next the old man, lay flat upon her back, her mind absorbed in the simple amusement of waving one foot (a cowhide eleven) slowly across the fire, squinting, with half-shut eye, first at the vast shoe and thence at the fire, alternately hiding bright places and darting the foot quickly in the direction of any new display of heightening flame. The mother was a bony sister, in the yellow, shrunken, of sharp visage, in which were prominent two cold eyes and a positively poisonous mouth; her hair, the color of faded hay, tangled in a jungle around her head. She rocked jerkily to and fro, removing at intervals a clay pipe from her mouth in order to pucker her thin lips up to one side, and spit with precision upon a certain spot in the fire, which she seemed resolved to prevent from attaining beyond a certain faint glow.

I have rarely felt more in difficulty for an overture to conversation, and was long before venturing to propose, "You seem to have a pleasant camp-spot here." The old woman sharply, and in almost a tone of affront, answered, "They's wus, and then again they's better."

"Doos well for our hogs," inserted the old man. "We've a band of pork that make out to find feed."

"Oh! how many have you?" I asked.

"Nigh three thousand."

"Won't you set?" asked Madame; then, turning, "You, Susan, can't you try for to set up, and not spread so? Hain't you no manners, say?"

At this the massive girl got herself somewhat together, and made room for me, which I declined, however.

"Prospecting?" inquired Madame.

"I say huntin'," suggested the man.

"Maybe he's a cattle-feller," interrupted the little girl.

"Goin' somewhere, ain't yer?" was Susan's guess.

I gave brief account of myself, evidently satisfying the social requirements of all but the old woman, who at once classified me as not up to her standard. Susan saw this, so did her father, and it became evident to me in ten minutes' conversation that they two were always at one, and made it their business to be in antagonism to the mother. They were then allies of mine from nature, and I felt at once at home. I saw too that Susan, having slid back to her horizontal position when I declined to share her rightful ground, was watching with subtle solicitude that fated spot in the fire, opposing sympathy and squints accurately aligned by her shoe to the dull spot in the embers, which slowly went out into blackness before the well-directed fire of her mother's saliva.

The shouts which I heard proceeding from the direction of my camp were easily translated into summons for supper. Mr. Newty invited me to return later and be sociable, which I promised to do, and, going to my camp, supped quickly and left the men with orders about picketing the animals for the night, then, strolling slowly down to the camp of my friends, seated myself upon a log by the side of the old gentleman. Feeling that this somewhat formal atti- tude unfitted me for partaking to the fullest degree the social ease around me, and knowing that my buckskin trousers were impervious to dirt, I slid down in a reclined posture with my feet to the fire, in absolute parallelism with the rest of the family.

The old woman was in the exciting *dénouement* of a coon-story, directed to her little boy, who sat clinging to her skirt and looking in her face with absorbed curiosity. "And when Johnnie fired," she said, "the coon fell and busted open." The little boy had misplaced his sympathies with the raccoon, and having inquired plaintively, "Did it hurt him?" was promptly snubbed with the reply, "Of course it hurt him. What do you suppose coons is made for?" Then turning to me she put what was plainly enough with her a test- question: "I allow you have killed your coon in your day?" I saw at once that I must forever sink beneath the horizon of her stand- ards, but, failing in real experienced or accurate knowledge concern- ing the coon, knew no subterfuges would work with her. Instinct had taught her that I had never killed a coon, and she had asked me thus ostentatiously to place me at once and forever before the family in my true light. "No, ma'am," I said "now you speak of it, I realize that I never have killed a coon." This was something of a staggerer to Susan and her father, yet as the mother's pleasurable dissatisfaction with me displayed itself by more and more accurate salivary shots at the fire, they rose to the occasion, and began to palliate my past. "Maybe," ventured Mr. Newty, "that they don't have coon round the city of York"; and I felt that I needed no self-defense when Susan firmly and defiantly suggested to her mother that perhaps I was in better business.

Driven in upon herself for some time, the old woman smoked in silence, until Susan, seeing that her mother gradually quenched a larger and larger circle upon the fire, got up and stretched herself, and giving the coals a vigorous poke swept out of sight the quenched spot, thus readily obliterating the result of her mother's precise and prolonged expectoration; then flinging a few dry boughs upon the fire illumined the family with the ruddy blaze, and sat down again, leaning upon her father's knee with a faint light of triumph in her eye.

By half past nine the gates of conversation were fairly open, and our part of the circle enjoyed itself socially,—taciturnity and clouds of Virginia plug reigning supreme upon the other. The two little children crept under comforters somewhere near the middle of the bed, and subsided pleasantly to sleep. The old man at last stretched sleepily, finally yawning out, "Susan, I do believe I am too tired out to go and see if them corral bars are down. I guess you'll have to go. I reckon there ain't no bears round to-night." Susan rose to her feet, stretched herself with her back to the fire, and I realized for the first time her amusing proportions. In the region of six feet, tall, square-shouldered, of firm iron back and heavy mold of limb, she yet possessed that suppleness which enabled her as she rose to throw herself into nearly all the attitudes of the Niobe children. As her yawn deepened, she waved nearly down to the ground, and then, rising upon tiptoe, stretched up her clinched fists to heaven with a groan of pleasure. Turning to me, she asked, "How would you like to see the hogs?" The old man added, as an extra encouragement, "Pootiest band of hogs in Tulare County! There's littler of the real sissor-bill nor Mexican racer stock than any band I have ever seen in the State. I drive the original outfit from Pike County to Oregon in '51 and '52." By this time I was actually interested in them, and joining Susan we passed out into the forest.

The full moon, now high in the heavens, looked down over the whole landscape of clustered forest and open meadow with tranquil silvery light. It whitened measurably the fine spiry tips of the trees, fell luminous upon broad bosses of granite which here and there rose through the soil, and glanced in trembling reflections from the rushing surface of the brook. Far in the distance moonlit peaks towered in solemn rank against the sky.

We walked silently on four or five minutes through the woods, coming at last upon a fence which margined a wide circular opening in the wood. The bars, as her father had feared, were down. We stepped over them, quietly entered the enclosure, put them up behind us, and proceeded to the middle, threading our way among sleeping swine to where a lonely tree rose to the height of about two hundred feet. Against this we placed our backs, and Susan waved her hand in pride over the two acres of tranquil pork. The eye, after accustoming itself to the darkness, took cognizance of a certain ridgyness of surface which came to be recognized as the objects of Susan's pride.

Quite a pretty effect was caused by the shadow of the forest, which, cast obliquely downward by the moon, divided the corral into halves of light and shade.

The air was filled with heavy breathing, interrupted by here and there a snore, and at times by crescendos of tumult, caused by forty or fifty pigs doing battle for some favorite bed-place.

I was informed that Susan did not wish me to judge of them by dark, but to see them again in the full light of day. She knew each individual pig by its physiognomy, having, as she said, "growed with 'em."

As we strolled back toward the bars a dusky form disputed our way,—two small, sharp eyes and a wild crest of bristles were visible in the obscure light. "That's Old Arkansas," said Susan; "he's eight year old come next June, and I never could get him to like me." I felt for my pistol, but Susan struck a vigorous attitude, ejaculating, "S-S-oway, Arkansas!" She made a dash in his direction; a wild scuffle ensued, in which I heard the dull thud of Susan's shoe, accompanied by, "Take that, dog-on-you!" a cloud of dust, one shrill squeal, and Arkansas retreated into the darkness at a business-like trot.

When quite near the bars the mighty girl launched herself into the air, alighting with her stomach across the topmost rail, where she hung a brief moment, made a violent muscular contraction, and alighted upon the ground outside, communicating to it a tremor quite perceptible from where I stood. I climbed over after her, and we sauntered under the trees back to camp. . . .

When I had breakfasted I joined Mr. Newty in his trip to the corral, where we stood together for hours, during which I had mastered the story of his years since, in 1850, he left his old home in Pike of Missouri.

It was one of those histories common enough through this wide West, yet never failing to startle me with its horrible lesson of social disintegration, of human retrograde.

That brave spirit of Westward Ho! which has been the pillar of fire and cloud leading on the weary march of progress over stretches of desert, lining the way with graves of strong men; of new-born lives; of sad, patient mothers, whose pathetic longing for the new home died with them; of the thousand old and young whose last agony came to them as they marched with eyes strained on after the sunken sun, and whose shallow barrows scarcely lift over the drifting dust of the desert; that restless spirit which has dared to uproot the old and plant the new, kindling the grand energy of California, laying foundations for a State to be, that is admirable, is poetic, is to fill an immortal page in the story of America; but when, instead of urging on to wresting from new lands something better than old can give, it degenerates into mere weak-minded restlessness, killing the power of growth, the ideal of home, the faculty of repose, it results in that race of perpetual emigrants who roam as dreary waifs over the West, losing possessions, love of life, love of God, slowly dragging from valley to valley till they fall by the wayside, happy if some chance stranger performs for them the last rites,—often less fortunate, as blanched bones and fluttering rags upon too many hillsides plainly tell.

The Newtys were of this dreary brotherhood. In 1850, with a small family of that authentic strain of high-bred swine for which Pike County is widely known, as Mr. Newty avers, they bade Missouri and their snug farm good-by, and, having packed their household goods into a wagon drawn by two spotted oxen, set out with the baby Susan for Oregon, where they came after a year's march, tired, and cursed with a permanent discontent. There they had taken up a rancho, a quarter-section of public domain, which at the end of two years was "improved" to the extent of the "neatest little worm fence this side of Pike," a barn, and a smoke-house. "In another year," said my friend, "I'd have dug for a house, but we tuck ager and the second baby died." One day there came a man who "let on that he knowd" land in California much fairer and more worthy tillage than Oregon's best, so the poor Newtys harnessed up the wagon and turned their backs upon a home nearly ready for comfortable life, and swept south with pigs and plunder. Through all the years this story had repeated itself, new homes gotten to the edge of completion, more babies born, more graves made, more pigs, who replenished as only the Pike County variety may, till it seemed to me the mere multiplication of them must reach a sufficient dead weight to anchor the family; but this was dispelled when Newty remarked: "These yer hogs is awkward about moving, and I've pretty much made my mind to put 'em all into bacon this fall, and sell out and start for Montana."

Poor fellow! at Montana he will probably find a man from Texas who in half an hour will persuade him that happiness lies there.

As we walked back to their camp, and when Dame Newty hove in sight, my friend ventured to say, "Don't you mind the old woman and her coons. She's from Arkansas. She used to say no man could have Susan who couldn't show coonskins enough of his own killing to make a bedquilt, but she's over that mostly." In spite of this assurance my heart fell a trifle when, the first moment of our return, she turned to her husband and asked, "Do you mind what a dead-open-and-shut on coons our little Johnny was when he was ten years old?" I secretly wondered if the dead-open-and-shut had anything to do with his untimely demise at eleven, but kept silence.

Regarding her as a sad product of the disease of chronic emigration, her hard thin nature, all angles and stings, became to me one of the most depressing and pathetic spectacles, and the more when her fever-and-ague boy, a mass of bilious lymph, came and sat by her, looking up with great haggard eyes as if pleading for something, he knew not what, but which I plainly saw only death could bestow.

Noon brought the hour of my departure. Susan and her father talked apart a moment, then the old man said the two would ride along with me for a few miles, as he had to go in that direction to look for new hog-feed.

I despatched my two men with the pack-horse, directing them to follow the trail, then saddled my Kaweah and waited for the Newtys. The old man saddled a shaggy little mountain pony for himself, and for Susan strapped a sheepskin upon the back of a young and fiery mustang colt.

While they were getting ready, I made my horse fast to a stake and stepped over to bid good-by to Mrs. Newty. I said to her, in tones of deference, "I have come to bid you good-by, madam, and when I get back this way I hope you will be kind enough to tell me one or two really first-rate coon-stories. I am quite ignorant of that animal, having been raised in countries where they are extremely rare, and I would like to know more of what seems to be to you a creature of such interest." The wet, gray eyes relaxed, as I fancied, a trifle of their asperity; a faint kindle seemed to light them for an instant as she asked, "You never see coons catch frogs in a spring branch?"

"No, Madame," I answered.

"Well, I wonder! Well, take care of yourself, and when you come back this way stop along with us, and we'll kill a yearlin' and I'll tell you about a coon that used to live under grandfather's barn." She actually offered me her hand, which I grasped and shook in a friendly manner, chilled to the very bone with its damp coldness.

Mr. Newty mounted, and asked me if I was ready. Susan stood holding her prancing mustang. To put that girl on her horse after the ordinary plan would have required the strength of Samson, or the use of a step-ladder, neither of which I possessed; so I waited for events to develop themselves. The girl stepped to the left side of her horse, twisted one hand in the mane, laying the other upon his haunches, and, crouching for a jump, sailed through the air, alighting upon the sheepskin. The horse reared, and Susan, twisting herself around, came right side up with her knee upon the sheepskin, shouting, as she did so, "I guess you don't get me off, sir!" I jumped upon Kaweah, and our two horses sprang forward together, Susan waving her hand to her father, and crying, "Come along after, old man!" and to her mother, "Take care of yourself!" which is the Pike County for *Au revoir!* Her mustang tugged at the bit, and bounded wildly into the air. We reached a stream bank at full gallop, the horses clearing it at a bound, sweeping on over the green floor, and under the magnificent shadow of the forest. Newty, following us at an humble trot, slopped through the creek, and when I last looked he had nearly reached the edge of the wood.

Mr. Newty at last came alongside and remarked that he must stop about here; "but," he added, "Susan will go on with you about half a mile, and come back and join me here after I have taken a look at the feed." As he rode out into the forest a little way, he called me to him, and I was a little puzzled at what seemed to be the first traces of embarrassment I had seen in his manner.

"You'll take care of yourself, now, won't you?" he asked. I tried to convince him that I would.

A slight pause.

"You'll take care of yourself, won't you?"

He might rely on it, I was going to say.

He added, "That—thet—thet man what gits Susan *has half the hogs!*"

Then turning promptly away, he spurred the pony, and his words as he rode into the forest were, "Take good care of yourself!"

Susan and I rode on for half a mile, until we reached the brow of a long descent, which she gave me to understand was her limit.

We shook hands and I bade her good-by, and as I trotted off these words fell sweetly upon my ear, "Say, you'll take good care of yourself, won't you, say?"

I took pains not to overtake my camp-men, wishing to be alone; and as I rode for hour after hour the picture of this family stood before me in all its deformity of outline, all its poverty of detail, all its darkness of future, and I believe I thought of it too gravely to enjoy as I might the subtle light of comedy which plays about these hard, repulsive figures.

CHAPTER XL

MARK TWAIN FINDS HEROES AND VILLAINS IN THE WEST

THE FAR West proceeded to develop its own particular brands of human being, good and bad. There were the faithful, indefatigable scouts and explorers; and there were the desperadoes, inevitable products of a land so broad and lawless. Mark Twain, traveling out by stagecoach in 1861, had admired the pony riders who carried the mail before there were trains to do so. He had also admired, if the truth be known, the "bad man" Slade.

IN a little while all interest was taken up in stretching our necks and watching for the "pony-rider"—the fleet messenger who sped across the continent from St. Joe to Sacramento, carrying letters nineteen hundred miles in eight days! Think of that for perishable horse and human flesh and blood to do! The pony-rider was usually a little bit of a man, brimful of spirit and endurance. No matter what time of the day or night his watch came on, and no matter whether it was winter or summer, raining, snowing, hailing, or sleeting, or whether his "beat" was a level straight road or a crazy trail over mountain crags and precipices, or whether it led through peaceful regions or regions that swarmed with hostile Indians, he must be always ready to leap into the saddle and be off like the wind! There was no idling-time for a pony-rider on duty. He rode fifty miles without stopping, by daylight, moonlight, starlight, or through the blackness of darkness—just as it happened. He rode a splendid horse that was born for a racer and fed and lodged like a gentleman; kept him at his utmost speed for ten miles, and then, as he came crashing up to the station where stood two men holding fast a fresh, impatient steed, the transfer of rider and mail-bag was made in the twinkling of an eye, and away flew the eager pair and were out of sight before the spectator could get hardly the ghost of a look. Both rider and horse went "flying light." The rider's dress was thin, and fitted close; he wore a "roundabout," and a skull-cap, and tucked his pantaloons into his boot-tops like a race-rider. He carried no arms—he carried nothing that was not absolutely necessary, for even the postage on his literary freight was worth *five dollars a letter.* He got but little frivolous correspondence to carry—his bag had business letters in it, mostly. His horse was stripped of all unnecessary weight, too. He wore a little wafer of a racing-saddle, and no visible blanket. He wore light shoes, or none at all. The little flat mail-pockets strapped under the rider's thighs would each hold about the bulk of a child's primer. They held many and many an important business chapter and newspaper letter, but these were written on paper as airy and thin as gold-leaf, nearly, and thus bulk and weight were economized. The stagecoach traveled about a hundred to a hundred and twenty-five miles a day (twenty-four hours), the pony-rider about two hundred and fifty. There were about eighty pony-riders in the saddle all the time, night and day, stretching in a long, scattering procession from the Missouri to California, forty flying eastward, and forty toward the west, and among them making four hundred gallant horses earn a stirring livelihood and see a deal of scenery every single day in the year.

We had had a consuming desire, from the beginning, to see a pony-rider, but somehow or other all that passed us and all that met us managed to streak by in the night, and so we heard only a whiz and a hail, and the swift phantom of the desert was gone before we could get our heads out of the windows. But now we were expecting one along every moment, and would see him in broad daylight. Presently the driver exclaims:

"Here he comes!"

Every neck is stretched further, and every eye strained wider. Away across the endless dead level of the prairie a black speck appears against the sky, and it is plain that it moves. Well, I should think so! In a second or two it becomes a horse and rider, rising and falling, rising and falling—sweeping toward us nearer and nearer—growing more and more distinct, more and more sharply defined—nearer and still nearer, and the flutter of the hoofs comes faintly to the ear—another instant a whoop and a hurrah from our upper deck, a wave of the rider's hand, but no reply, and man and horse burst past our excited faces, and go winging away like a belated fragment of a storm!

So sudden is it all, and so like a flash of unreal fancy, that but for the flake of white foam left quivering and perishing on a mail-sack after the vision had flashed by and disappeared, we might have doubted whether we had seen any actual horse and man at all, maybe.

There was much magic in that name, Slade! Day or night, now, I stood always ready to drop any subject in hand, to listen to something new about Slade and his ghastly exploits. Even before we got to Overland City, we had begun to hear about Slade and his "division" (for he was a "division-agent") on the Overland; and from the hour we had left Overland City we had heard drivers and conductors talk about only three things—"Californy," the Nevada silver mines, and this desperado Slade. And a deal the most of the talk was about Slade. We had gradually come to have a realizing sense of the fact that Slade was a man whose heart and hands and soul were steeped in the blood of the offenders against his dignity; a man who awfully avenged all injuries, affronts, insults or slights, of whatever kind—on the spot if he could, years afterward if lack of earlier opportunity compelled it; a man whose hate tortured him day and night till vengeance appeased it—and not an ordinary vengeance either, but his enemy's absolute death—nothing less; a man whose face would light up with a terrible joy when he surprised a foe and had him at a disadvantage. A high and efficient servant of the Overland, an outlaw among outlaws and yet their relentless scourge, Slade was at once the most bloody, the most dangerous, and the most valuable citizen that inhabited the savage fastnesses of the mountains.

Really and truly, two-thirds of the talk of drivers, and conductors had been about this man Slade, ever since the day before we reached Julesburg. In order that the Eastern reader may have a clear conception of what a Rocky Mountain desperado is, in his highest state of development, I will reduce all this mass of overland gossip to one straight-forward narrative, and present it in the following shape:

Slade was born in Illinois, of good parentage. At about twenty-six years of age he killed a man in a quarrel and fled the country. At St. Joseph, Missouri, he joined one of the early California-bound emigrant trains, and was given the post of trainmaster. One day on the plains he had an angry dispute with one of his wagon-drivers, and both drew their revolvers. But the driver was the quicker artist, and had his weapon cocked first. So Slade said it was a pity to waste life on so small a matter, and proposed that the pistols be thrown on the ground and the quarrel settled by a fist-fight. The unsuspecting driver agreed, and threw down his pistol—whereupon Slade laughed at his simplicity, and shot him dead!

He made his escape, and lived a wild life for awhile, dividing his time between fighting Indians and avoiding an Illinois Sheriff, who had been sent to arrest him for his first murder. It is said that in one Indian battle he killed three savages with his own hand, and afterward cut their ears off and sent them, with his compliments, to the chief of the tribe.

Slade soon gained a name for fearless resolution, and this was sufficient merit to procure for him the important post of Overland division-agent at Julesburg, in place of Mr. Jules, removed. For sometime previously, the company's horses had been frequently stolen, and the coaches delayed, by gangs of outlaws, who were wont to laugh at the idea of any man's having the temerity to resent such outrages. Slade resented them promptly. The outlaws soon found that the new agent was a man who did not fear anything that breathed the breath of life. He made short work of all offenders. The result was that delays ceased, the company's property was let alone, and, no matter what happened or who suffered, Slade's coaches went through, every time! True, in order to bring about this wholesome change, Slade had to kill several men—some say three, others say four, and others six—but the world was the richer for their loss. The first prominent difficulty he had was with the ex-agent Jules, who bore the reputation of being a reckless and desperate man himself. Jules hated Slade for supplanting him, and a good fair occasion for a fight was all he was waiting for. By and by Slade dared to employ a man whom Jules had once discharged. Next, Slade seized a team of stage-horses which he accused Jules of having driven off and hidden somewhere for his own use. War was declared, and for a day or two the two men walked warily about the streets, seeking each other, Jules armed with a double-barreled shot gun, and Slade with his history-creating revolver. Finally, as Slade stepped into a store, Jules poured the contents of his gun into him from behind the door. Slade was pluck, and Jules got several bad pistol wounds in return. Then both men fell, and were carried to their respective lodgings, both swearing that better aim should do deadlier work next time. Both were bed-ridden a long time, but Jules got on his feet first, and gathering his possessions together, packed them on a couple of mules, and fled to the Rocky Mountains to gather strength in safety against the day of reckoning. For many months he was not seen or heard of, and was gradually dropped out of the remembrance of all save Slade himself. But Slade was not the man to forget him. On the contrary, common report said that Slade kept a reward standing for his capture, dead or alive!

After awhile, seeing that Slade's energetic administration had restored peace and order to one of the worst divisions of the road, the Overland Stage Company transferred him to the Rocky Ridge division in the Rocky Mountains, to see if he could perform a like miracle there. It was the very paradise of outlaws and desperadoes. There was absolutely no semblance of law there. Violence was the rule. Force was the only recognized authority. The commonest misunderstandings were settled on the spot with the revolver or the knife. Murders were done in open day, and with sparkling frequency, and nobody thought of inquiring into them. It was considered that the parties who did the killing had their private reasons for it; for other people to meddle would have been looked upon as indelicate. After a murder, all the Rocky Mountain etiquette required of a spectator was, that he should help the gentleman bury his game—otherwise his churlishness would surely be remembered against him the first time he killed a man himself and needed a neighborly turn in interring him.

Slade took up his residence sweetly and peacefully in the midst of this hive of horse-thieves and assassins, and the very first time one of them aired his insolent swaggerings in his presence he shot him dead! He began a raid on the outlaws, and in a singularly short space of time he had completely stopped their depredations on the stage stock, recovered a large number of stolen horses, killed several of the worst desperadoes of the district, and gained such a dread ascendency over the rest that they respected him, admired him, feared him, obeyed him! He wrought the same marvelous change in the ways of the community that had marked his administration at Overland City. He captured two men who had stolen Overland stock, and with his own hands he hanged them. He was supreme judge in his district, and he was jury and executioner likewise—and not only in the case of offenses against his employers, but against passing emigrants as well. On one occasion some emigrants had their stock lost or stolen, and told Slade, who chanced to visit their camp. With a single companion he rode to a ranch, the owners of which he suspected, and, opening the door, commenced firing, killing three, and wounding the fourth.

From a bloodthirsty interesting little Montana book * I take this paragraph:

While on the road, Slade held absolute sway. He would ride down to a station, get into a quarrel, turn the house out of windows, and maltreat the occupants most cruelly. The unfortunates had no means of redress, and were compelled to recuperate as best they could. On one of these occasions, it is said he killed the father of the fine little half-breed boy Jemmy, whom he adopted, and who lived with his widow after his execution. Stories of Slade's hanging men, and of innumerable assaults, shootings, stabbings, and beatings, in which he was a principal actor, form part of the legends of the stage line. As for minor quarrels and shootings, it is absolutely certain that a minute history of Slade's life would be one long record of such practices.

Slade was a matchless marksman with a navy revolver. The legends say that one morning at Rocky Ridge, when he was feeling

* "The Vigilantes of Montana," by Prof. Thos. J. Dimsdale.

comfortable, he saw a man approaching who had offended him some days before—observe the fine memory he had for matters like that —and, "Gentlemen," said Slade, drawing, "it is a good twenty-yard shot—I'll clip the third button on his coat!" Which he did. The bystanders all admired it. And they all attended the funeral, too.

On one occasion a man who kept a little whisky-shelf at the station did something which angered Slade—and went and made his will. A day or two afterward Slade came in and called for some brandy. The man reached under the counter (ostensibly to get a bottle—possibly to get something else), but Slade smiled upon him that peculiarly bland and satisfied smile of his which the neighbors had long ago learned to recognize as a death warrant in disguise, and told him to "none of that!—pass out the high-priced article." So the poor barkeeper had to turn his back and get the high-priced brandy from the shelf; and when he faced around again he was looking into the muzzle of Slade's pistol. "And the next instant," added my informant, impressively, "he was one of the deadest men that ever lived."

The stage drivers and conductors told us that sometimes Slade would leave a hated enemy wholly unmolested, unnoticed and un-mentioned, for weeks together—had done it once or twice, at any rate. And some said they believed he did it in order to lull the vic-tims into unwatchfulness, so that he could get the advantage of them, and others said they believed he saved up an enemy that way, just as a schoolboy saved up a cake, and made the pleasure go as far as it would by gloating over the anticipation. One of these cases was that of a Frenchman who had offended Slade. To the surprise of everybody Slade did not kill him on the spot, but let him alone for a considerable time. Finally, however, he went to the French-man's house very late one night, knocked, and when his enemy opened the door, shot him dead—pushed the corpse inside the door with his foot, set the house on fire and burned up the dead man, his widow and three children! I heard this story from several dif-ferent people, and they evidently believed what they were saying. It may be true, and it may not. "Give a dog a bad name," etc.

Slade was captured once, by a party of men who intended to lynch him. They disarmed him, and shut him up in a strong log-house, and placed a guard over him. He prevailed upon his captors to send for his wife, so that he might have a last interview with her. She was a brave, loving, spirited woman. She jumped on a horse and rode for life and death. When she arrived they let her in without searching her, and before the door could be closed she whipped out a couple of revolvers, and she and her lord marched forth defying the party. And then, under a brisk fire, they mounted double and galloped away unharmed!

In the fullness of time Slade's myrmidons captured his ancient enemy, Jules, whom they found in a well-chosen hiding-place in the remote fastnesses of the mountains, gaining a precarious livelihood with his rifle. They brought him to Rocky Ridge, bound hand and foot, and deposited him in the middle of the cattle-yard with his back against a post. It was said that the pleasure that lit Slade's face when he heard of it was something fearful to contemplate. He examined his enemy to see that he was securely tied and then went to bed, content to wait till morning before enjoying the luxury of killing him. Jules spent the night in the cattle-yard, and it is a region where warm nights are never known. In the morning Slade practiced on him with his revolver, nipping the flesh here and there, and occasionally clipping off a finger, while Jules begged him to kill him outright and put him out of his misery. Finally Slade reloaded, and walking up close to his victim, made some characteristic remarks and then dispatched him. The body lay there half a day, nobody venturing to touch it without orders, and then Slade detailed a party and assisted at the burial himself. But he first cut off the dead man's ears and put them in his vest pocket, where he carried them for sometime with great satisfaction. That is the story as I have frequently heard it told and seen it in print in California newspapers. It is doubtless correct in all essential particulars.

In due time we rattled up to a stage-station, and sat down to breakfast with a half-savage, half-civilized company of armed and bearded mountaineers, ranchmen and station employees. The most gentlemanly-appearing, quiet, and affable officer we had yet found along the road in the Overland Company's service was the person who sat at the head of the table, at my elbow. Never youth stared and shivered as I did when I heard them call him SLADE!

Here was romance, and I sitting face to face with it!—looking upon it—touching it—hobnobbing with it, as it were! Here, right by my side, was the actual ogre who, in fights and brawls and various ways, *had taken the lives of twenty-six human beings,* or all men lied about him! I suppose I was the proudest stripling that ever traveled to see strange lands and wonderful people.

He was so friendly and so gentle-spoken that I warmed to him in spite of his awful history. It was hardly possible to realize that this pleasant person was the pitiless scourge of the outlaws, the rawhead-and-bloody-bones the nursing mothers of the mountains terrified their children with. And to this day I can remember nothing remarkable about Slade except that his face was rather broad across the cheek bones, and that the cheek bones were low and the lips peculiarly thin and straight. But that was enough to leave something of an effect upon me, for since then I seldom see a face possessing these characteristics without fancying that the owner of it is a dangerous man.

The coffee ran out. At least it was reduced to one tin-cupful, and Slade was about to take it when he saw that my cup was empty. He politely offered to fill it, but although I wanted it, I politely declined. I was afraid he had not killed anybody that morning, and might be needing diversion. But still with firm politeness he insisted on filling my cup, and said I had traveled all night and better deserved it than he—and while he talked he placidly poured the fluid, to the last drop. I thanked him and drank it, but it gave me no comfort, for I could not feel sure that he would not be sorry, presently, that he had given it away, and proceed to kill me to distract his thoughts from the loss. But nothing of the kind occurred. We left him with only twenty-six dead people to account for, and I felt a tranquil satisfaction in the thought that in so judiciously taking care of No. 1 at that breakfast-table I had pleasantly escaped being No. 27. Slade came out to the coach and saw us off, first ordering certain rearrangements of the mailbags for our comfort, and then we took leave of him, satisfied that we should hear of him again, some day, and wondering in what connection.

CHAPTER XLI

AMONG THE heroes was one who in the '60's and '70's slaughtered and shot his way to universal fame. When railroads pushed beyond the Mississippi the knell was sounded of buffalo and Indian—two creatures who had needed a wide world within which to range, and who now found that world cut into segments. Millions of buffalo were massacred from trains and the backs of horses before the west seemed tame enough; and scores of Indian tribes, driven into smaller and smaller areas, fought their white pursuers before the final surrender which condemned them to reservation life. Colonel William F. Cody, or "Buffalo Bill," was both a buffalo hunter and a scout against the Indians, and he has left reminiscences of his twofold career.

THE western end of the Kansas Pacific was at this time in the heart of the buffalo country. Twelve hundred men were employed in the construction of the road. The Indians were very troublesome, and it was difficult to obtain fresh meat for the hands. The company therefore concluded to engage expert hunters to kill buffaloes.

Having heard of my experience and success as a buffalo hunter, Goddard Brothers, who had the contract for feeding the men, made me a good offer to become their hunter. They said they would require about twelve buffaloes a day—twenty-four hams and twelve humps, as only the hump and hindquarters of each animal were utilized. The work was dangerous. Indians were riding all over that section of the country, and my duties would require me to journey from five to ten miles from the railroad every day in order to secure the game, accompanied by only one man with a light wagon to haul the meat back to camp. I demanded a large salary, which they could well afford to pay, as the meat itself would cost them nothing. Under the terms of the contract which I signed with them, I was to receive five hundred dollars a month, agreeing on my part to supply them with all the meat they wanted.

Leaving Rose to complete our grading contract, I at once began my career as a buffalo hunter for the Kansas Pacific. It was not long before I acquired a considerable reputation, and it was at this time that the title "Buffalo Bill' was conferred upon me by the railroad hands. Of this title, which has stuck to me through life, I have never been ashamed.

During my engagement as hunter for the company, which covered a period of eighteen months, I killed 4,280 buffaloes and had many exciting adventures with the Indians, including a number of hairbreadth escapes, some of which are well worth relating. . . .

My companion at the time was Scotty, the butcher who accompanied me on my hunts, to cut up the meat and load it on the wagon for hauling to the railroad camp.

I had killed fifteen buffaloes, and we were on our way home with a wagonload of meat when we were jumped by a big band of Indians.

I was mounted on a splendid horse belonging to the company, and could easily have made my escape, but Scotty had only the mule team, which drew the wagon, as a means of flight, and of course I could not leave him.

To think was to act in those days. Scotty and I had often talked of what we would do in case of a sudden attack, and we forthwith proceeded to carry out the plan we had made.

Jumping to the ground, we unhitched the mules more quickly than that operation had ever been performed before. The mules and my horse we tied to the wagon. We threw the buffalo hams on the ground and piled them about the wheels so as to form a breastwork. Then, with an extra box of ammunition and three or four extra revolvers which we always carried with us, we crept under the wagon, prepared to give our visitors a reception they would remember.

On came the Indians, pell-mell, but when they got within a hundred yards of us we opened such a sudden and galling fire that they held up and began circling about us.

Several times they charged. Their shots killed the two mules and my horse. But we gave it to them right and left, and had the satisfaction of seeing three of them fall to the ground not more than fifty feet away.

When we had been cooped up in our little fort for about an hour we saw the cavalry coming toward us, full gallop, over the prairie. The Indians saw the soldiers almost as soon as we did. Mounting their horses, they disappeared down the cañon of the creek. When the cavalry arrived we had the satisfaction of showing them five Indians who would be "good" for all time. Two hours later we reached the camp with our meat, which we found to be all right, although it had a few bullets and arrows imbedded in it.

It was while I was hunting for the railroad that I became acquainted with Kit Carson, one of the most noted of the guides, scouts, and hunters that the West ever produced. He was going through our country on his way to Washington. I met him again on his return, and he was my guest for a few days in Hays City. He then proceeded to Fort Lyon, Colorado, near which his son-in-law, Mr. Boggs, resided. His health had been failing for some time, and shortly afterward he died at Mr. Boggs's residence on Picket Wire Creek.

Soon after the adventure with Scotty I had my celebrated buffalo shooting contest with Billy Comstock, a well-known guide scout, and interpreter. Comstock, who was chief of scouts at Fort Wallace, had a reputation of being a successful buffalo hunter, and his friends at the fort—the officers in particular—were anxious to back him against me.

It was arranged that I should shoot a match with him, and the preliminaries were easily and satisfactorily arranged. We were to hunt one day of eight hours, beginning at eight o'clock in the morning. The wager was five hundred dollars a side, and the man who should kill the greater number of buffaloes from horseback was to be declared the winner. Incidentally my title of "Buffalo Bill" was at stake.

The hunt took place twenty miles east of Sheridan. It had been well advertised, and there was a big "gallery." An excursion party, whose members came chiefly from St. Louis and numbered nearly a hundred ladies and gentlemen, came on a special train to view the sport. Among them was my wife and my little daughter Arta, who had come to visit me for a time.

Buffaloes were plentiful. It had been agreed that we should go into the herd at the same time and make our "runs," each man killing as many animals as possible. A referee followed each of us, horseback, and counted the buffaloes killed by each man. The excursionists and other spectators rode out to the hunting-grounds in wagons and on horseback, keeping well out of sight of the buffaloes, so as not to frighten them until the time came for us to dash into the herd. They were permitted to approach closely enough to see what was going on.

For the first "run" we were fortunate in getting good ground. Comstock was mounted on his favorite horse. I rode old Brigham. I felt confident that I had the advantage in two things; first, I had the best buffalo horse in the country; second, I was using what was known at the time as a needle-gun, a breech-loading Springfield rifle, caliber .50. This was "Lucretia." Comstock's Henry rifle, though it could fire more rapidly than mine, did not, I felt certain, carry powder and lead enough to equal my weapon in execution.

When the time came to go into the herd, Comstock and I dashed forward, followed by the referees. The animals separated. Comstock took the left bunch, I the right. My great forte in killing buffaloes was to get them circling by riding my horse at the head of the herd and shooting their leaders. Thus the brutes behind were crowded to the left, so that they were soon going round and round.

This particular morning the animals were very accommodating. I soon had them running in a beautiful circle. I dropped them thick and fast till I had killed thirty-eight, which finished my "run."

Comstock began shooting at the rear of the buffaloes he was chasing, and they kept on in a straight line. He succeeded in killing twenty-three, but they were scattered over a distance of three miles. The animals I had shot lay close together.

Our St. Louis friends set out champagne when the result of the first run was announced. It proved a good drink on a Kansas prairie, and a buffalo hunter proved an excellent man to dispose of it.

While we were resting we espied another herd approaching. It was a small drove, but we prepared to make it serve our purpose. The buffaloes were cows and calves, quicker in their movements than the bulls. We charged in among them, and I got eighteen to Comstock's fourteen.

Again the spectators approached, and once more the champagne went round. After a luncheon we resumed the hunt. Three miles distant we saw another herd. I was so far ahead of my competitor now that I thought I could afford to give an exhibition of my skill. Leaving my saddle and bridle behind, I rode, with my competitor, to windward of the buffaloes.

I soon had thirteen down, the last one of which I had driven close to the wagons, where the ladies were watching the contest. It frightened some of the tender creatures to see a buffalo coming at full speed directly toward them, but I dropped him in his tracks before he had got within fifty yards of the wagon. This finished my "run" with a score of sixty-nine buffaloes for the day. Comstock had killed forty-six.

It was now late in the afternoon. Comstock and his backers gave up the idea of beating me. The referee declared me the winner of the match, and the champion buffalo hunter of the Plains.

On our return to camp we brought with us the best bits of meat, as well as the biggest and best buffalo heads. The heads I always turned over to the company, which found a very good use for them. They were mounted in the finest possible manner and sent to the principal cities along the road, as well as to the railroad centers of the country. Here they were prominently placed at the leading hotels and in the stations, where they made an excellent advertisement for the road. To-day they attract the attention of travelers almost everywhere. Often, while touring the country, I see one of them, and feel reasonably certain that I brought down the animal it once ornamented. Many a wild and exciting hunt is thus called to my mind.

In May, 1868, the Kansas Pacific track was pushed as far as Sheridan. Construction was abandoned for the time, and my services as buffalo hunter were no longer required. A general Indian war was now raging all along the Western borders. General Sheridan had taken up headquarters at Fort Hays, in order to be on the job in person. Scouts and guides were once more in great demand, and I decided to go back to my old calling.

I did not wish to kill my faithful old Brigham by the rigors of a scouting campaign. I had no suitable place to leave him, and determined to dispose of him. At the suggestion of a number of friends, all of whom wanted him, I put him up at a raffle, selling ten chances at thirty dollars each, which were all quickly taken. Ike Bonham, who won him, took him to Wyandotte, Kansas, where he soon added fresh laurels to his already shining wreath. In the crowning event of a tournament he easily outdistanced all entries in a four-mile race to Wyandotte, winning $250 for his owner, who had been laughed at for entering such an unprepossessing animal.

I lost track of him after that. For several years I did not know what had become of him. But many years after, while in Memphis, I met Mr. Wilcox, who had once been superintendent of construction on the Kansas Pacific. He informed me that he owned Brigham, and I rode out to his place to take a look at my gallant old friend. He seemed to remember me, as I put my arms about his neck and caressed him like a long-lost child.

When I had received my appointment as guide and scout I was ordered to report to the commandant of Fort Larned, Captain Daingerfield Parker. I knew that it would be necessary to take my family, who had been with me at Sheridan, to Leavenworth and leave them there. This I did at once.

When I arrived at Larned, I found the scouts under command of Dick Curtis, an old-time scout of whom I have spoken in these reminiscences. Three hundred lodges of Kiowa and Comanche Indians were encamped near the fort. These savages had not yet gone on the warpath, but they were restless and discontented. Their leading chief and other warriors were becoming sullen and insolent. The Post was garrisoned by only two companies of infantry and one troop of cavalry. General Hazen, who was at the post, was endeavoring to pacify the Indians; I was appointed as his special scout.

Early one morning in August I accompanied him to Fort Zarrah, from which post he proceeded, without an escort, to Fort Harker. Instructions were left that the escort with me should return to Larned the next day. After he had gone I went to the sergeant in command of the squad and informed him I intended to return that afternoon. I saddled my mule and set out. All went well till I got about halfway between the two posts, when at Pawnee Rock I was suddenly jumped by at least forty Indians, who came rushing up, extending their hands and saying, "How?" "How?" These redskins had been hanging about Fort Larned that morning. I saw that they had on their warpaint, and looked for trouble.

As they seemed desirous to shake hands, however, I obeyed my first friendly impulse, and held out my hand. One of them seized it with a tight grip and jerked me violently forward. Another grabbed my mule by the bridle. In a few minutes I was completely surrounded.

Before I could do anything at all in my defense, they had taken my revolvers from the holsters and I received a blow on the head from a tomahawk which rendered me nearly senseless. My gun, which was lying across the saddle, was snatched from its place. Finally two Indians, laying hold of the bridle, started off in the direction of the Arkansas River, leading the mule, which was lashed by the other Indians who followed along after.

The whole crowd was whooping, singing, and yelling as only Indians can. Looking toward the opposite side of the river, I saw the people of a big village moving along the bank, and made up my mind that the redmen had left the Post, and were on the warpath in dead earnest.

My captors crossed the stream with me, and as we waded through the shallow water they lashed both the mule and me. Soon they brought me before an important-looking body of Indians, who proved to be the chiefs and principal warriors. Among them I recognized old Satanta and others whom I knew. I supposed that all was over with me.

All at once Satanta asked me where I had been, and I suddenly had an inspiration.

I said I had been after a herd of cattle or "Whoa-haws" as they called them. The Indians had been out of meat for several weeks, and a large herd of cattle which had been promised them had not arrived.

As soon as I said I had been after "Whoa-haws" old Satanta began questioning me closely. When he asked where the cattle were I replied that they were only a few miles distant and that I had been sent by General Hazen to inform him that the herd was coming, and that they were intended for his people. This seemed to please the old rascal. He asked if there were any soldiers with the herd. I said there were. Thereupon the chiefs held a consultation. Presently Satanta asked me if the general had really said they were to have the cattle. I assured him that he had. I followed this by a dignified inquiry as to why his young men had treated me so roughly.

He intimated that this was only a boyish freak, for which he was very sorry. The young men had merely wanted to test my courage. The whole thing, he said, was a joke. The old liar was now beating me at the lying game, but I did not care, since I was getting the best of it.

I did not let him suspect that I doubted his word. He ordered the young men to restore my arms and reprimanded them for their conduct. He was playing a crafty game, for he preferred to get the meat without fighting if possible, and my story that soldiers were coming had given him food for reflection. After another council the old man ask me if I would go and bring the cattle down. "Of course," I told him. "Such are my instructions from General Hazen."

In response to an inquiry if I wanted any of his young men to accompany me I said that it would be best to go alone. Wheeling my mule around, I was soon across the river, leaving the chief firmly believed that I was really going for the cattle, which existed only in my imagination.

I knew if I could get the river between me and the Indians I would have a good three-quarters of a mile start of them and could make a run for Fort Larned. But as I reached the river bank I looked about and saw ten or fifteen Indians who had begun to suspect that all was not as it should be.

The moment my mule secured a good foothold on the bank I urged him into a gentle lope toward the place where, according to my story, the cattle were to be brought.

Upon reaching the top of the ridge and riding down the other side out of view, I turned my mount and headed westward for Fort Larned. I let him out for all he was worth, and when I reached a little rise and looked back the Indian village lay in plain sight.

My pursuers were by this time on the ridge I had passed over, and were looking for me in every direction. Soon they discovered me, and discovered also that I was running away. They struck out in swift pursuit. In a few minutes it became painfully evident that they were gaining.

When I crossed Pawnee Fork, two miles from the Post, two or three of them were but a quarter of a mile behind. As I gained the opposite side of the creek I was overjoyed to see some soldiers in a Government wagon a short distance away. I yelled at the top of my lungs that the Indians were after me.

When Denver Jim, an old scout, who was with the party, was informed that there were ten or fifteen Indians in the pursuit he said:

"Let's lay for them."

The wagon was driven hurriedly in among the trees and low box-elder bushes, and secreted, while we waited. We did not wait long. Soon up came the Indians, lashing their horses, which were blowing and panting. We let two of them pass, then opened a lively fire on the next three or four, killing two at the first volley. The others, discovering that they had run into an ambush, whirled around and ran back in the direction from which they had come. The two who had passed heard the firing and made their escape.

The Indians that were killed were scalped, and we appropriated their arms and equipment. Then, after catching the horses, we made our way into the Post. The soldiers had heard us firing, and as we entered the fort drums were beating and the buglers were sounding the call to fall in. The officers had thought Satanta and his warriors were coming in to capture the fort.

There was much excitement at the Post. The guards had been doubled. Captain Parker had all the scouts at his headquarters. He was seeking to get one of them to take dispatches to General Sheridan at Fort Hays. I reported to him at once, telling him of my encounter and my escape.

"You were lucky to think of that cattle story, Cody," he said. "But for that little game your scalp would now be ornamenting a Kiowa lodge."

CHAPTER XLII

AMONG THE villains were Frank and Jesse James of almost mythical repute, and, still further to the southwest in a later day, cowboy bandits like "Billy the Kid" (Billy Bonney), who went from New York to continue the bad-man tradition in New Mexico. How the Kid lived, and how he died in the '8o's, is told by "Old Charley" Siringo, cowboy and author, whose career was spent up and down the plains from New Mexico and Texas to Iowa.

W HISKEY PETE was mounted early one morning for my two-hundred-and-twenty-five-mile lonely ride to the LX ranch. I arrived at the headquarters ranch late in the evening. A crowd of strangers were playing cards under a cottonwood tree near by. The cook informed me that they were Billy the Kid and his Lincoln County, New Mexico, warriors.

When the cook rang the supper bell, these strangers ran for the long table. After being introduced, I found myself seated by the side of good-natured Billy the Kid. Henry Brown, Fred White and Tom O'Phalliard are the only names of this outlaw gang that I can recall.

When supper was over, I produced a box of fine Havana cigars, brought from Chicago as a treat for the boys on the ranch. They were passed around. Then one was stuck into my new ten-dollar meerschaum cigar-holder, and I began to puff smoke toward the ceiling.

Now Billy the Kid asked for a trial of my cigar-holder. This was granted. He liked it so well that he begged me to present it to him, which I did. In return he presented me with a finely bound novel which he had just finished reading. In it he wrote his autograph, giving the date that it was presented to me. During the next few weeks Billy the Kid and I became quite chummy. After selling out the band of ponies, which he and his gang had stolen from the Seven River warriors, in New Mexico, he left the Canadian River country, and I never saw him again. Two of his gang, Henry Brown and Fred Waite—a half-breed Chickasaw Indian—quit the outfit and headed for the Indian Territory.

During his long stay around the LX ranch and Tascosa, Billy the Kid made one portly old capitalist from Boston, Massachusetts, sweat blood for a few minutes. Mr. Torey owned a large cattle ranch above Tascosa. On arriving from the east he learned that Billy the Kid and gang had made themselves at home on his ranch for a few days—hence he gave the foreman orders not to feed them, if they should make another visit. This order reached the Kid's ears.

While in Tascosa Billy the Kid saw old man Torey ride up to the hitching-rack in front of Jack Ryan's saloon. He went out to meet him, and asked if he had ordered his foreman not to feed them.

Mr. Torey replied yes, that he didn't want to give his ranch a bad name by harboring outlaws.

Then the Kid jerked his Colt's pistol and jabbed the old man several times in his portly stomach, at the same time telling him to say his prayers, as he was going to pump him full of lead. With tears in his voice Mr. Torey promised to countermand the order. Then war was declared off.

Thus did Mr. Torey, a former sea captain, get his eye-teeth cut in the ways of the wild and woolly West.

This story was told to me by Billy the Kid and Steve Arnold, who was an eye-witness to the affair. But the Kid said he had no intention of shooting Mr. Torey—that he just wanted to teach him a lesson.

About the first of September my steer herd was turned loose on the winter range. Then we started out to brand calves. When the branding season was over, Moore sent me onto the South Plains in charge of a scouting crew.

A month later a runner hunted me up to deliver a letter from Moore. In this letter I was instructed to turn the outfit over to James McClaugherty, and to bring three of my picked fighting cowboys with me to the headquarters ranch. I selected James H. East, Lee Hall, and Cal Polk as the fighting men.

On arriving at the ranch Moore outfitted me for a trip to New Mexico after Billy the Kid and LX cattle which he and his gang had been stealing.

I finally started up the river with four large mules hitched to a heavy mess-wagon, with Francisco as driver and cook. My fighting crew consisted of five men: Big-Foot Wallace (Frank Clifford), James East, Cal Polk, Lon Chambers and Lee Hall. In Tascosa we were joined by the Littlefield crew, in charge of Bob Roberson. He had a mess-wagon, a cook, and five riders.

We started out with only one horse apiece, with the exception of myself; I had two. As corn was scarce, it was thought best to buy more horses if we should need them.

On reaching San Lorenzo, New Mexico, I boarded a buckboard to Las Vegas, to buy a supply of corn, grub and ammunition, giving the outfit instructions to lie over in Anton Chico, on the Pecos River, until I got there.

I found Las Vegas to be a swift dance-hall town, and the first night of my arrival I went broke, playing monte—a Mexican game. I blew in all my expense money, about three hundred dollars, and about a hundred dollars which Bob Roberson had given me to buy ammunition and grub. A big-hearted merchant by the name of Houston gave me the goods I needed, he taking orders on the LX Company for pay.

On reaching the Anton Chico with the wagon load of supplies, I learned that Billy the Kid and gang had slipped into town one night and stolen some fresh horses. They had come from the White Oaks country, to the southwestward. We finally pulled out for White Oaks, and the next morning early Pat Garrett, the sheriff of Lincoln County, New Mexico, rode into our camp. He said he was making up a crowd to go down the Pecos River in search of Billy the Kid and gang.

After consulting together, Bob Roberson and I decided to furnish Garrett part of our crew. Hence I turned over to him Lee Hall, Jim East, and Lon Chambers. Roberson loaned him Tom Emory and Louis Bozeman. Frank Stewart also joined Pat Garrett, he being his own boss and not subject to Roberson's orders. In Anton Chico, Pat Garrett picked up a few of his own men, his brother-in-law, Barney Mason, being one of them. They then started down the Pecos River.

In the Mexican village of Puerto de Luna, Garrett proved his bravery. A drunken Mexican enemy fired a shot at him from the open door of a saloon. Garrett remarked that he didn't want to kill the fellow, so he would just break his right arm. This he did with a well-aimed shot.

Roberson and I struck out for White Oaks in a raging snowstorm. When within a day's ride of White Oaks we came to the still smoking ruins of the Jim Greathouse road-ranch, a saloon and store. Here a posse from White Oaks, under the leadership of Deputy Sheriff Jim Carlyle, had fought a battle, a few days previous, with Billy the Kid and his gang. While the posse had the gang surrounded in the Greathouse ranch, Jim Carlyle went in to have a talk with the Kid. For an hour or more the gang held Carlyle a prisoner, waiting for darkness to come so they could make their escape. They made him drink with them at the bar every time they took a drink.

Finally Jim Carlyle jumped through a window to make his escape. As he sprang through the window the Kid shot him. He fell on the outside and began crawling away. Then the Kid killed him with another shot from his pistol. In the darkest part of the night the gang made a break for liberty, and escaped.

The next day the posse set fire to the ranch, as it had become a rendezvous for outlaws. In following the gang's trail through the snow they came to the Spence ranch, where the gang had eaten breakfast. Now the posse burnt up Mr. Spence's buildings for feeding them.

By tramping all that day and part of the night the Kid gang reached Anton Chico, where they stole horses and saddles while my outfit was there waiting for me to return from Las Vegas.

We arrived in the new mining camp of White Oaks in a severe snowstorm. For a week we camped out in the open with the snow nearly two feet deep, then we rented a building to live in. Two of the leading merchants, Mr. Whiteman and Mr. Sweet, gave us unlimited credit for grub and horse feed. We concluded to make this our headquarters until Pat Garrett and crowd were heard from. He had felt sure that he would find Billy the Kid and gang down on the Pecos River.

At midnight our crowd ushered in the new year of 1881, in front of our picket shack. Each man emptied a Winchester rifle and a six-shooter in rapid succession. This was done to frighten the citizens of White Oaks, as we figured that they would think Billy the Kid had struck town. He had shot up the town a short time previous.

Our guess was correct, for it caused a regular stampede out of the saloons and billiard-hall. The town marshal, Pinto Tom, was playing billiards when the shooting began. He dropped his cue and broke for the back door, and took to the tall timber on the side of Carrizozo Mountain. It was noon next day when he returned. We had a man watching Pinto Tom to see what his actions would be.

The first word we had of Billy the Kid was when three of our boys, Lee Hall, Lon Chambers, and Louis Bozeman arrived from Fort Sumner, with the news that Billy the Kid and gang had been captured, two of the gang being killed.

They explained the fight as follows:

On arriving in Fort Sumner, Garrett learned that the Kid and his gang had been there and had ridden east for Portales Lake. Hence the sheriff surmised that they would soon return. Therefore camp was pitched in an old vacated adobe house, fronting the Fort

Sumner and Los Portales road. In front of this house there was an adobe fence, behind which one man was put on guard every night to give the alarm if men were seen coming toward Fort Sumner.

Several nights later, while Lon Chambers was on duty behind the adobe fence, a crowd of men was seen coming down the road. Chambers at once gave the alarm to Garrett and the boys who were playing poker. Then all lined themselves along the adobe fence.

When the man in the lead was opposite, Garrett stood up and called to him to throw up his hands. Instead he drew his pistol, and received two bullets through the body. These shots scattered the gang like a flock of quail. Many shots were fired at them as they took the back track from whence they had come. The dead man proved to be Tom O'Phalliard. He breathed a few times after being carried into the house.

Then Garrett and the posse took up the trail in the deep snow. Twelve miles out they came to a dead horse which had been wounded in the stomach the night previous.

From now on two of the gang were mounted on one pony, which made their progress slow. Toward midnight that night a one-room rock house loomed up ahead, and the trail in the snow ended there, showing that the gang were inside the cabin.

Now the posse rode behind a high hill and built a fire. Just before daylight Pat Garrett and Lee Hall lay down along the west wall, near the corner, from whence the door could be covered with their rifles. Outside of this door stood four shivering ponies, the ropes around their necks being on the inside.

At the first peep of day one man walked out of the cabin, and the sheriff commanded him to throw up his hands. He jumped back toward the door, and received two bullets through the body. Then with his hands up, he walked to Garrett and Hall saying, "I wish, I wish!" and fell over dead. This man proved to the Charlie Bowdre.

Now the gang inside began pulling one of the ponies inside through the doorway. When halfway in Garrett sent a bullet through the pony's heart. This blocked up the entrance.

Billy the Kid already had his little race mare inside, and it was their intention to pull the rest of the ponies inside, and then make a dash out of the doorway for liberty.

Now the sheriff and the Kid opened up a conversation passing jokes back and forth. There were no windows in the cabin, and the gang tried to pick portholes through the thick stone walls, with their guns and knives, but this proved a failure.

All that day the gang held out without food, water, or fire.

They finally decided to surrender. Billy the Kid was the last to come out with hands up. There were only four of them left: Billy Wilson, Tom Picket, Rudabaugh, and the Kid.

On arrival in Fort Sumner the sheriff sent part of our boys to White Oaks, while he took Jim East, Tom Emory, and Frank Stewart with him to the railroad, at Las Vegas. There they boarded a train for Santa Fé, where the prisoners were put in the penitentiary for safe-keeping. In Las Vegas a mob was formed to hang Billy the Kid, but they were stood off until the train could pull out.

After the return of Tom Emory and Jim East, Bob Roberson decided, as the Kid was behind prison walls, to return home. I had concluded to stay until spring, and gather up any LX cattle that might be in the country.

We started toward home, rounding up cattle on small ranches through the Patos Mountains, then the Van Sickle range, now the large Block ranch, on the north side of Capitan Mountains. On our way down the Pecos River we camped for dinner one day, on the west bank of the stream. The river was bank-full from melted snow at its head. We were sitting on the ground near the water's edge, with plates on our laps, eating dinner, when a man rode up on a black horse; he said, "Boys, did you hear the news?"

When I replied "No," he continued:

"Billy the Kid has killed his two guards in Lincoln and escaped."

At that moment Big-Foot Wallace gave a Comanche Indian yell, saying: "Hurrah for Billy the Kid!" Then he dived headlong into the muddy water of the Pecos. He had on his boots, spurs, leather leggins, and six-shooter, with a belt of cartridges. When he came to the surface he yelled again: "Hurrah for the Kid." Then he swam ashore and wrung the water from his clothes.

This stranger didn't know the full particulars of the Kid's escape, but on our return to Roswell, two weeks later, we found out all about it.

We finally started up the river with our ten LX steers, having found two near the Chisum home ranch. Six miles above the abandoned post of Fort Sumner, at Sunnyside, I went ahead with the mess-wagon to buy horse-feed and grub.

On riding up to the platform, in front of the store, I dismounted, and, pulling my Winchester rifle out of the saddle scabbard, I walked into the open door. I had lost a screw out of the rifle, and wanted to buy another that would fit. As I entered the door several men went running out of the rear entrance. There was no one left in the store but the proprietor, who seemed greatly excited. He said: "Well, I'll be d——d! We thought you was Billy the Kid. You look just like him." Then the store man went to the rear entrance and called out: "Come back, boys, it's a false alarm."

Others had previously told me that I looked like Billy the Kid. Now I felt convinced that it must be true. These men had heard of Billy the Kid's escape, after killing his two guards.

I then returned to Fort Sumner and lay over to attend a Mexican dance that night.

Mrs. Charlie Bowdre—whose husband was killed by Pat Garrett and Lee Hall—attended this dance. She was a good-looking young Mexican woman and I danced with her often. When the dance broke up before daylight, I accompanied Mrs. Bowdre to her two-room adobe house. I tried to persuade her to allow me to go inside and talk awhile. Then I bade her good-night. On meeting her the next fall she told me the reason for her not letting me enter the house. Billy the Kid was in hiding there at the time.

Now we struck out east for Portales Lake, on the west edge of the Staked Plains. We camped one night at Stinking Springs, and slept in the rock house where Billy the Kid and his gang held out without fire, food, or water. Lon Chambers and Tom Emory pointed out to "Big-Foot" and me the spot where Charlie Bowdre fell, when hit by bullets from Garrett's and Hall's rifles. The stone walls inside showed the marks of where the gang tried to pick portholes.

Arriving at Los Portales Lake—near where the thriving county-seat town of Portales, New Mexico, is now located—we pitched camp at Billy the Kid's "cave." It was here at a large fresh-water spring—the lake being salty—that the Kid and gang made their headquarters while stealing LX steers. This "cave" was not a cave —just an overhanging rock cliff, with a stone corral around it, on three sides.

From now on our misery began, gathering Canadian River cattle which in past winters had strayed away, drifting south with the buffaloes. They had become as wild as deer. Being short of horses we had to press the four work mules into service, to stand night-watch over the cattle. Farther east there was a chain of fresh-water lakes, on the head draws of the Yellow-House Canyon, a tributary of the Brazos River, and around them we found many cattle.

After leaving these lakes we were two days and nights without water. The first habitation we struck, after leaving Fort Sumner, was Walter Dyer's log house on the head of Paladuro Canyon, a distance of about two hundred miles.

Now over that same stretch of country dwell thousands of prosperous "fool hoe-men," and their happy families.

We arrived at the LX ranch on the twenty-second day of June, with twenty-five hundred head of cattle, after an absence of seven months.

About July 1, 1881, Pat Garrett received a letter from a Mr. Brazil stating that the Kid had been seen lately around Fort Sumner. The sheriff answered the letter telling Mr. Brazil to meet him at the mouth of the Tayban Arroyo, on the Pecos River, after dark on July 13th.

Now Garrett took his two deputies, John Poe and Kip McKinnie, and started, horseback, for the meeting place. These three officers watched and waited during the whole night of July 13th, but Brazil failed to show up. On the morning of the 14th they rode up the Pecos River. When opposite Fort Sumner the sheriff sent Poe into that abandoned fort, where lived many Mexican families, to see if anything could be learned about the Kid. Then Garrett and McKinnie rode six miles up the river to Sunnyside, to keep in hiding until the arrival of Poe.

About night John Poe reached Sunnyside and reported to Garrett that he couldn't find out a thing of importance about the Kid. Then the sheriff said they would ride into Fort Sumner, after dark, and see Pete Maxwell, a wealthy sheep man, and the son of the famous Land Grant Maxwell. The Kid was in love with Pete Maxwell's sister, hence Garrett thought that Pete might have seen him hanging around their home.

It was dark when the three officers started on their six-mile journey. Arriving in Fort Sumner their horses were tied in an old orchard. Then they walked into Pete Maxwell's large, grassy yard. The residence was a long adobe building fronting south, with a covered porch the full length of the adobe house. Garrett knew the room in which Pete generally slept. The door of this room was open. The sheriff told his two deputies to lie down in the grass, while he went in to talk with Pete.

The sheriff lay over on Mr. Maxwell's bed and began questioning him about the Kid. No one besides Garrett was to know what Pete told him.

In the rear of the Maxwell dwelling lived an old Mexican servant, who was a warm friend to the Kid. Previous to the arrival of the sheriff and his deputies, Billy the Kid had entered this old servant's adobe cabin. The old man had gone to bed. Billy lit the lamp; then he pulled off his boots and coat and began reading the newspapers, which had been brought there for his special benefit.

After glancing over the papers the Kid told the old man to get up and cook him some supper, as he was very hungry, having just walked in from the sheep camp. The old servant told him that he didn't have any meat in the house. Then the Kid replied: "I'll go and see Pete and get some." Now he picked up a butcher knife from the table and started, barefooted and bareheaded. As he walked along the porch to Peter's room, Kip McKinnie saw him coming, but supposed he was one of the servants.

When nearly opposite Pete's room, Kip raised up and his spur rattled, which attracted the Kid's attention. Pulling his pistol he asked in Spanish: "Quien es? Quien es?" (Who's there? Who's there?) Not getting an answer he backed into Pete's room and asked: "Pete, who's out there?"

Maxwell didn't reply. Now the Kid saw strange movements in the bed and asked: "Who in the h—l is in here?"

With the pistol raised in his right hand and the butcher knife in his left, he began backing across the room. Pete whispered in the sheriff's ear: "That's him, Pat."

By this time the Kid had backed to the dim moonlight coming through the south window, which shone directly on him, making him an easy target for the sheriff. Bang! went Garrett's Colt's pistol, and down went a once mother's darling, shot through the heart.

After the first shot, the sheriff cocked the pistol and it went off accidentally, putting a hole in the ceiling.

The next day Billy Bonney, alias "Billy the Kid," was buried by the side of his chum, Tom O'Phalliard, in the old military cemetery.

A few months later Pat Garrett had the body dug up to see if the Kid's trigger finger had been cut off, but it had not. A man in the East was showing the first finger of a man, preserved in alcohol. He claimed it was Billy the Kid's trigger finger. The newspapers had sensational accounts of it.

Book VIII

WHITE AND BLACK

CHAPTER XLIII

THE STORY turns back across the Mississippi to a conflict of ideas which raged throughout the first half of the nineteenth century and led at last to a crisis affecting and unifying all of the hitherto separate sections of American society.

East of the Mississippi and South of the Ohio were three million Negroes whose ancestors, in some cases not so far back in time, had been brought from Africa by slave ships. In the colonies slavery had existed everywhere, North and South; but the economic development of New England in particular had failed to keep the institution in favor, and now the ownership of blacks by whites was pretty well restricted to the Southeastern States, though there were to be fierce disputes concerning the extension of slavery Westward and Northward into the new territories; and these disputes were to be among the many causes for a great and terrible war. Other causes were economic, intellectual, and social; an issue had long been preparing between the restless, industrialized North and the traditionally ordered South. But discussion of slavery was everywhere to be heard, and charges were leveled by New England Abolitionists against the moral iniquity of such a system.

Reports naturally varied concerning the lot of the black man. On the one hand, for instance, there was the record of her father's ideal plantation written by Susan Dabney Smedes, whose recollections of a girlhood spent in Mississippi are all in favor of a decision that Thomas Dabney kept his Negroes happy.

HIS plantation was considered a model one, and was visited by planters anxious to learn his methods. He was asked how he made his negroes do good work. His answer was that a laboring man could do more work and better work in five and a half days than in six. He used to give the half of Saturdays to his negroes, unless there was a great press of work; but a system of rewards was more efficacious than any other method. He distributed prizes of money among his cotton-pickers every week during the season, which lasted four or five months. One dollar was the first prize, a Mexican coin valued at eighty-seven and a half cents the second, seventy-five cents the third, and so on, down to the smallest prize, a small Mexican coin called picayune, which was valued at six and a half cents. The decimal nomenclature was not in use there. The coins were spoken of as "bits." Eighty-seven and a half cents were seven bits, fifty cents four bits, twenty-five cents two bits. The master gave money to all who worked well for the prizes, whether they won them or not. When one person picked six hundred pounds in a day, a five-dollar gold-piece was the reward. On most other plantations four hundred pounds or three hundred and fifty or three hundred was considered a good day's work, but on the Burleigh place many picked five hundred pounds. All had to be picked free of trash. No one could do this who had not been trained in childhood. To get five hundred pounds a picker had to use both hands at once. Those who went into the cotton-fields after they were grown only knew how to pull out cotton by holding on to the stalk with one hand and picking it out with the other. Two hundred pounds a day would be a liberal estimate of what the most industrious could do in this manner. A very tall and lithe young woman, one of mammy's "brer Billy's" children, was the best cotton-picker at Burleigh. She picked two rows at a time, going down the middle with both arms extended and grasping the cotton-bolls with each hand. Some of the younger generation learned to imitate this. At Christmas Nelly's share of the prize-money was something over seventeen dollars. Her pride in going up to the master's desk to receive it, in the presence of the assembled negroes, as the acknowledged leader of the cotton-pickers, was a matter of as great interest to the white family as to her own race.

The negroes were helped in every way to gather the cotton, not being interrupted or broken down by any other work. Some of the men were detailed to carry the cotton-hampers to the wagons that the pickers might lift no weights. Water-carriers, with buckets of fresh water, went up and down the rows handing water to the pickers. They would get so interested and excited over the work that they had to be made to leave the fields at night, some of the very ambitious ones wishing to sleep at the end of their rows, that they might be up and at work in the morning earlier than their rivals. The cotton was weighed three times a day, and the number of pounds picked by each servant set down opposite to his or her name on a slate. Quite a remarkable feat of memory was exhibited by one of the negro men one day in connection with this. His duty was to help the overseer to weigh the cotton. One day the slate was caught in a rain and the figures were obliterated. This man came that night to the master's desk and gave from memory every record on the slate, the morning, midday, and evening weights of each picker. The negroes stood near enough to hear if he had made a mistake in any man's figures. It was the more remarkable as he could not have expected to be called on to do this. In addition to the cotton crop, corn was raised in such abundance that it was not an unusual thing to sell a surplus of a thousand or two bushels or more. A maxim with the master was that no animal grew fat on bought corn. In putting in his corn crop he made full allowance for a bad season, hence there was never a scarcity. A lock on a corn-crib was not known. After the mules and horses were fed in the evening the negroes carried home all that they cared to have. They raised chickens by the hundreds. One of the chicken-raisers, old Uncle Isaac, estimated that he raised five hundred, unless the season was bad. Uncle Isaac's boast was that he was a child of the same year as the master, and that the master's mother had given to him in her own arms some of the baby Thomas's milk, as there was more of it than he wanted. He would draw himself up as he added, "I called marster brother till I was a right big boy, an' I called his mother ma till I was old enough to know better an' to stop it myself. She never tole me to stop."

The thrifty negroes made so much on their chickens, peanuts, popcorn, molasses-cakes, baskets, mats, brooms, taking in sewing, and in other little ways, that they were able to buy luxuries. Some of the women bought silk dresses; many had their Sunday dresses made by white mantua-makers. Of course they had the clothes of the master and mistress in addition; and in later years, as the house grew full of young masters and young mistresses, theirs were added. As the family knew that the servants liked nothing so well as the well-made clothes that they laid aside, they wore their clothes but little. They justly considered that those who had labored for them had rights to them while still fresh. Under these circumstances it did not seem wasteful for a daughter of the house to distribute, at the end of a season, as many as a dozen or more dresses that had been made up but a few months before. It was quite funny to see among the gallants three or four swallow-tail coats of the master's come in at the gate for the grand promenade on Sunday evening, escorting the colored belles in all their bravery of hoop-skirts, and ruffles, and ribbons, and flowers.

For some years the master accompanied every wagon loaded with cotton that went to market from his plantation. He slept on these journeys under the wagons, and sometimes on awakening in the morning he found that his great-coat, in which he was wrapped, was frozen hard to the ground. His negro drivers were more heavily clad than himself, each one being provided with a thick woollen great-coat that reached to his heels, home-knit woollen socks and gloves, and an enormous comforter for the neck. No illness resulted from the exposure. In the morning a hot meal, cooked by one of the negroes—and all the race are admirable cooks—was shared by the master and his men.

Until over seventy years old, he was singularly indifferent to cold or heat, or to discomforts of any sort. But he felt compassion for his negroes. He knew that the warm African blood in their veins was not fitted to endure what he could stand. He never regarded the weather for himself, but was very careful about sending them out in bad weather, and never did it unless it seemed a necessity. On such occasions he wore an anxious look, and said that he could not go to bed until his servants had gotten home safely. They were always sure of finding a hot fire and a warm drink ready for them on their return.

Every other year he distributed blankets on the plantation, giving one apiece to each individual. Many of the families were large, and as the father would move off under a load of twelve or fourteen blankets, some, whose quivers were less full, would be heard to exclaim over the good fortune of the lucky ones. There were usually a dozen or so left over in these distributions, and they were thrown in for good measure to those who had the large families. "Poor things, they have so many children," seemed to my dear mother a sufficient explanation for special favors that she often bestowed on those who had no other claim. Some of the negro men with the big families of children had a funny little affectation of feigning not to know either the names or the number of their boys and girls. "I disremember, missis, dyar's so many on 'em," with a little pleased laugh, was considered a sufficient answer to inquiries on the subject on every-day occasions. But not so on the days when blankets were to be given out. Then their memories were fresh. Then the babies that had not been in their cradles more than a few days, mayhap hours, were remembered and mentioned in due turn, with no danger of being forgotten or overlooked because there were "so many on 'em."

In addition to the blankets, comforts were quilted in the house by the seamstresses for every woman who had a young baby. The every-day clothes of all the negroes were cut out and made in the house; two complete woollen suits for winter and two cotton ones for summer. For Sundays, a bright calico dress was given to each woman. The thrifty ones, and, with scarcely an exception, these negroes were thrifty, had more than they needed, and the clothes were in their chests a year before they were put on. The woollen socks and stockings for both men and women were knit in the cabins by old women, and in the "great house" by young girls. These last were set a task by the mistress, with the privilege of holiday the rest of the day when it was done. This had the desired effect of making them quick and industrious, and so interested that they would be at their work betimes in the morning. The clever ones sometimes get through with the allotted task before breakfast.

On rainy days all the plantation women were brought into the house. Then Mammy Maria, who was in her way a field-marshal on such occasions, gave out the work and taught them to sew. By word and action she stimulated and urged them on, until there was not on the Burleigh plantation a woman who could not make and mend neatly her own and her husband's and children's clothes.

Poor mammy! She dreaded these days of teaching and worrying over her big scholars. It gave her the headache, she said: some seemed so hopelessly dull and stupid and lazy,—so unlike herself. Hers was a case both of greatness thrust upon one and of greatness achieved. She had grown up at my mother's feet, having been about her ever since she could remember, and had come to love the white family better than her own blood and race. She resented their being deceived and imposed on by her fellow-servants, and did not fail to inform them when such was the case. This confidence was considered as sacred, but of course it grew to be known that Mammy Maria was a "white folks' servant."

She was far more severe in her judgment of misdemeanors than the master and mistress. The place that she had made for herself was one that would, in a character less true and strong, have brought on herself the hatred and the distrust of her race. But they knew her to be just, one who never assailed the innocent, and with so warm and compassionate a heart in real trouble that none were afraid to come to her. From being a confidential servant she grew into being a kind of prime minister, and it was well known that if she espoused a cause and took it to the master it was sure to be attended to at once, and according to her advice.

Her independence and fearlessness in the discharge of her duty, both to the master and to her fellow-servants, won for her the affection and esteem of both. In consequence of her popularity with her own color, her namesakes became so numerous that the master had to forbid any further increase of them, on account of the confusion to which it gave rise. This her admirers evaded by having the babies christened Maria, and another name adopted for every-day use.

The nurse who took care of the women when their babies were

born received a fee each time. The mothers themselves looked on these seasons as gala times. They were provided with flour, sugar, dried fruit, and often meals from the table, and a woman to do all their cooking, washing, and housework for a month. During the rest of the year they did little more than take care of the babies. Their cabins were clean and orderly, their beds gay with bright quilts, and often the pillows were snowy enough to tempt any head.

When we children were allowed to go to see some of the servants, they delighted in setting out a little feast. If they had nothing else, we were not allowed to go without a new-laid egg or two. Once at Christmas Mammy Harriet gave a "high tea" to us children. I was at that time about fourteen years of age, the oldest of the invited. A friend of my own age, Arabella Foote, the youngest daughter of Henry S. Foote (Governor and United States Senator), was spending her Christmas holidays with me. Mammy felt some modesty about inviting the young lady into her house, but I took Arabella, and she enjoyed it as much as any of us. Mammy had made a nice cake and hot biscuits and tea for the occasion, set out in choicest cups, some of rare old china, and with sugar in the sugar-bowl that she had inherited from her mother. She gave us besides, sweetmeats, nuts, raisins, fruits of several kinds,—indeed, a delightful tea. And she stood behind us waiting on the table, her bright bandanna kerchief towering aloft on her head, and she looking so pleased.

The children delighted in teaching the house-servants. One night the whole family were formally invited, the master, mistress, governess, and guests, by a twelve-year-old school-mistress to hear her pupils recite poetry. She had about a dozen of the maids, old and young, Mammy Maria among them. One of the guests was quite astonished to see his own servant, whom he had with him spending several months at Burleigh, get up and recite a piece of poetry that had been learned with pains for this occasion.

With negro slaves it seemed impossible for one of them to do a thing, it mattered not how insignificant, without the assistance of one or two others. It was often said with a laugh by their owners that it took two to help one to do nothing. It required a whole afternoon for Joe, the aspirant for historical knwledge, and another able-bodied man like himself, to butcher a sheep. On a plantation the work of the women and children, and of some of the men also, amounted to so little that but small effort was made to utilize it. Of course, some kind of occupation had to be devised to keep them employed a part of the time. But it was very laborious to find easy work for a large body of inefficient and lazy people, and at Burleigh the struggle was given up in many cases. The different departments would have been more easily and better managed if there had been fewer to work. Sometimes a friend would say to the master that he made smaller crops than his negroes ought to make. His reply was that he did not desire them to do all that they could.

The cook at Burleigh had always a scullion or two to help her, besides a man to cut her wood and put it on the huge andirons. The scullions brought the water and prepared the vegetables, and made themselves generally useful. The vegetables were gathered and brought from the garden by the gardener, or by one of the half-dozen women whom he frequently had to help him. A second cook made the desserts, sweetmeats, etc. As children, we thought that the main business of the head cook was to scold the scullion and ourselves, and to pin a dish-rag to us if we ventured into her kitchen. Four women and a boy were in charge of the dairy. As the cows sometimes wandered to pastures several miles away, this number did not seem excessive. The boy brought the cows up, sometimes with one of the women to help him. Two of the women milked; the third held the semi-sinecure office, taking charge of the milk; and the fourth churned.

Southern children were taught to call the colored people aunt and uncle as titles of respect. They resented being called by their names without the title, and considered that it spoke ill for the manners of a child who would do so rude a thing. They called each other "brer" and "sis." This referred, not to the natural relationship, but to their relationship in the church. On formal occasions they were "Mr." and "Mrs." Ignorance of this led me into sad disgrace one night with my usually indulgent Mammy Maria. She had taken me to see her brother married. I heard her address him as Mr. Ferguson, and at once asked, "Mammy, what makes you call Henry Mr. Ferguson?" "Do you think 'cause we are black that we cyarn't have no names?" was mammy's indignant reply. She could not be angry more than a minute with "her white chillun." She never went to wedding or party or quilting without bringing to us an apple or a cake or a bouquet,— whatever was given to her there. I do not think that her own children fared as well. The mistress had wet-nurses for her babies, chosen from among her negro servants. The devotion of the nurses to these foster-children was greater than their love for their own. One of them, with a baby at home very sick, left it to stay with the white child. This one she insisted on walking the night through, because he was roaring with the colic, though the mistress entirely disapproved, and urged her to go home to her own child, whose illness was more serious, if less noisy, than the white nursling with its colic.

CHAPTER XLIV

ON THE other hand there was the testimony of a Negro—who in his later life was to become a nationally known figure—that slaves, even in a border state like Maryland, could be profoundly discontented. Frederick Douglass, later a friend of Lincoln and orator for his race's cause, grew up in one of the decidedly less attractive forms of bondage.

THERE were certain secluded and out-of-the-way places, even in the State of Maryland, seldom visited by a single ray of healthy public sentiment, where slavery, wrapt in its own congenial darkness, could and did develop all its malign and shocking characteristics, where it could be indecent without shame, cruel without shuddering, and murderous without apprehension or fear of exposure or punishment. Just such a secluded, dark, and out-of-the-way place was the home plantation of Colonel Edward Lloyd, in Talbot county, eastern shore of Maryland. It was far away from all the great thoroughfares of travel and commerce, and proximate to no town or village. There was neither school-house nor townhouse in its neighborhood. The school-house was unnecessary, for there were no children to go to school. The children and grandchildren of Col. Lloyd were taught in the house by a private tutor (a Mr. Page from Greenfield, Massachusetts, a tall, gaunt sapling of a man, remarkably dignified, thoughtful, and reticent, and who did not speak a dozen words to a slave in a whole year). The overseer's children went off somewhere in the State to school, and therefore could bring no foreign or dangerous influence from abroad to embarrass the natural operation of the slave system of the place. Here, not even the commonest mechanics, from whom there might have been an occasional outburst of honest and telling indignation at cruelty and wrong on other plantations, were white men. Its whole public was made up of and divided into three classes, slaveholders, slaves, and overseers. Its blacksmiths, wheelwrights, shoemakers, weavers, and coopers were slaves. Not even commerce, selfish and indifferent to moral considerations as it usually is, was permitted within its secluded precincts. Whether with a view of guarding against the escape of its secrets, I know not, but it is a fact, that every leaf and grain of the products of this plantation and those of the neighboring farms belonging to Col. Lloyd were transported to Baltimore in his own vessels, every man and boy on board of which, except the captain, were owned by him as his property. In return, everything brought to the plantation came through the same channel. To make this isolation more apparent, it may be stated that the estates adjoining Col. Lloyd's were owned and occupied by friends of his, who were as deeply interested as himself in maintaining the slave system in all its rigor. These were the Tilgmans, the Gold-boroughs, the Lockermans, the Pacas, the Skinners, Gibsons, and others of lesser affluence and standing.

Public opinion in such a quarter, the reader must see, was not likely to be very efficient in protecting the slave from cruelty. To be a restraint upon abuses of this nature, opinion must emanate from humane and virtuous communities, and to no such opinion or influence was Col. Lloyd's plantation exposed. It was a little nation by itself, having its own language, its own rules, regulations, and customs. The troubles and controversies arising here were not settled by the civil power of the State. The overseer was the important dignitary. He was generally accuser, judge, jury, advocate, and executioner. The criminal was always dumb, and no slave was allowed to testify other than against his brother slave.

There were, of course, no conflicting rights of property, for all the people were the property of one man, and they could themselves own no property. Religion and politics were largely excluded. One class of the population was too high to be reached by the common preacher, and the other class was too low in condition and ignorance to be much cared for by religious teachers, and yet some religious ideas did enter this dark corner.

This, however, is not the only view which the place presented. Though civilization was, in many respects, shut out, nature could not be. Though separated from the rest of the world, though public opinion, as I have said, could seldom penetrate its dark domain, though the whole place was stamped with its own peculiar iron-like individuality, and though crimes, high-handed and atrocious, could be committed there with strange and shocking impunity, it was, to outward seeming, a most strikingly interesting place, full of life, activity, and spirit, and presented a very favorable contrast to the indolent monotony and languor of Tuckahoe. It resembled, in some respects, descriptions I have since read of the old baronial domains of Europe. Keen as was my regret and great as was my sorrow at leaving my old home, I was not long in adapting myself to this my new one. A man's troubles are always half disposed of when he finds endurance the only alternative. I found myself here, there was no getting away, and naught remained for me but to make the best of it. Here were plenty of children to play with and plenty of pleasant resorts for boys of my age and older. The little tendrils of affection, so rudely broken from the darling objects in and around my grandmother's home, gradually began to extend and twine themselves around the new surroundings. Here, for the first time, I saw a large windmill, with its wide-sweeping white wings, a commanding object to a child's eye. This was situated on what was called Long Point—a tract of land dividing Miles river from the Wye. I spent many hours here watching the wings of this wondrous mill. In the river, or what was called the "Swash," at a short distance from the shore, quietly lying at anchor, with her small row boat dancing at her stern, was a large sloop, the *Sally Lloyd,* called by that name in honor of the favorite daughter of the Colonel. These two objects, the sloop and mill, awakened as I remember, thoughts, ideas, and wondering. Then here were a great many houses, human habitations full of the mysteries of life at every stage of it. There was the little red house up the road, occupied by Mr. Sevier, the overseer. A little nearer to my old master's stood a long, low, rough building literally alive with slaves of all ages, sexes, conditions, sizes, and colors. This was called the long quarter. Perched upon a hill east of our house, was a tall, dilapidated old brick building, the architectural dimensions of which proclaimed its creation for a different purpose, now occupied by slaves, in a similar manner to the long quarters. Besides these, there were numerous other slave houses and huts scattered around in the neighborhood, every nook and corner of which were completely occupied.

Old master's house, a long brick building, plain but substantial, was centrally located, and was an independent establishment. Besides these houses there were barns, stables, store-houses, tobacco-houses, blacksmith shops, wheelwright shops, cooper shops; but above all there stood the grandest building my young eyes had ever beheld, called by every one on the plantation the *great* house. This was occupied by Col. Lloyd and his family. It was surrounded by numerous and variously shaped outbuildings. There were kitchens, wash-houses, dairies, summer-houses, green-houses, hen-houses, turkey-houses, pigeon-houses, and arbors of many sizes and devices, all neatly painted or whitewashed, interspersed with grand old trees, ornamental and primitive, which afforded delightful shade in summer and imparted to the scene a high degree of stately beauty. The *great* house itself was a large white wooden building with wings on three sides of it. In front, extending the entire length of the building and supported by a long range of columns, was a broad portico, which gave to the Colonel's home an air of great dignity and grandeur. It was a treat to my young and gradually opening mind to behold this elaborate exhibition of wealth, power and beauty.

The carriage entrance to the house was by a large gate, more than a quarter of a mile distant. The intermediate space was a beautiful lawn, very neatly kept and tended. It was dotted thickly over with trees and flowers. The road or lane from the gate to the great house was richly paved with white pebbles from the beach and in its course formed a complete circle around the lawn. Outside this select enclosure were parks, as about the residences of the English nobility, where rabbits, deer, and other wild game might be seen peering and playing about, with "none to molest them or make them afraid." The tops of the stately poplars were often covered with red-winged blackbirds, making all nature vocal with the joyous life and beauty of their wild, warbling notes. These all belonged to me as well as to Col. Edward Lloyd, and, whether they did or not, I greatly enjoyed them. Not far from the great house were the stately mansions of the dead Lloyds—a place of somber aspect. Vast tombs, embowered beneath the weeping willow and the fir tree, told of the generations of the family, as well as of their wealth. Superstition was rife among the slaves about this family burying-ground. Strange sights had been seen there by some of the older slaves, and I was often compelled to hear stories of shrouded ghosts, riding on great black horses, and of balls of fire which had been seen to fly there at midnight, and of startling and dreadful sounds that had been repeatedly heard. Slaves knew enough of the Orthodox theology of the time, to consign all bad slaveholders to hell, and they often fancied such persons wishing themselves back again to wield the lash. Tales of sights and sounds strange and terrible, connected with the huge black tombs, were a great security to the grounds about them, for few of the slaves had the courage to approach them during the daytime. It was a dark, gloomy, and forbidding place, and it was difficult to feel that the spirits of the sleeping dust there deposited reigned with the blest in the realms of eternal peace.

At Lloyd's, was transacted the business of twenty or thirty different farms, which, with the slaves upon them, numbering, in all, not less than a thousand, all belonged to Col. Lloyd. Each farm was under the management of an overseer, whose word was law.

Mr. Lloyd was, at this time, very rich. His slaves alone, numbering as I have said not less than a thousand, were an immense fortune, and though scarcely a month passed without the sale to the Georgia traders, of one or more lots, there was no apparent diminution in the number of his human stock. The selling of any to the State of Georgia was a sore and mournful event to those left behind, as well as to the victims themselves.

Among other slave notabilities, I found here one called by everybody, white and colored, "Uncle" Isaac Copper. It was seldom that a slave, however venerable, was honored with a surname in Maryland, and so completely has the south shaped the manners of the north in this respect that their right to such honor is tardily admitted even now. It goes sadly against the grain to address and treat a negro as one would address and treat a white man. But once in a while, even in a slave state, a negro had a surname fastened to him by common consent. This was the case with "Uncle" Isaac Copper. When the "Uncle" was dropped, he was called Doctor Copper. He was both our Doctor of Medicine and our Doctor of Divinity. Where he took his degree I am unable to say, but he was too well established in his profession to permit question as to his native skill or attainments. One qualification he certainly had. He was a confirmed cripple, wholly unable to work, and was worth nothing for sale in the market. Though lame, he was no sluggard. He made his crutches do him good service, and was always on the alert looking up the sick, and such as were supposed to need his aid and counsel. His remedial prescriptions embraced four articles. For diseases of the body, epsom salts and castor oil; for those of the soul, the "Lord's prayer," and a few stout hickory switches.

I was, with twenty or thirty other children, early sent to Doctor Isaac Copper, to learn the Lord's prayer. The old man was seated on a huge three-legged oaken stool, armed with several large hickory switches, and from the point where he sat, lame as he was, he could reach every boy in the room. After our standing a while to learn what was expected of us, he commanded us to kneel down. This done, he told us to say everything he said. "Our Father"—this we repeated after him with promptness and uniformity—"who art in Heaven," was less promptly and uniformly repeated, and the old gentleman paused in the prayer to give us a short lecture, and to use his switches on our backs.

I was not long in my new home before I found that the dread I had conceived of Captain Anthony was in a measure groundless. Instead of leaping out from some hiding-place and destroying me, he hardly seemed to notice my presence. He probably thought as little of my arrival there as of an additional pig to his stock. He was the chief agent of his employer. The overseers of all the farms composing the Lloyd estate were in some sort under him. The Colonel himself seldom addressed an overseer, or allowed himself to be addressed by one. To Captain Anthony, therefore, was committed the headship of all the farms. He carried the keys of all the store-houses, weighed and measured the allowances of each slave, at the end of each month; superintended the storing of all goods brought to the store-house; dealt out the raw material to the different handicraftsmen; shipped the grain, tobacco, and all other saleable produce of the numerous farms to Baltimore, and had a general oversight of all the workshops of the place. In addition to all this he was frequently called abroad to Easton and elsewhere in the discharge of his numerous duties as chief agent of the estate.

The family of Captain Anthony consisted of two sons—Andrew and Richard, and his daughter Lucretia and her newly married husband, Captain Thomas Auld. In the kitchen were Aunt Katy, Aunt Esther, and ten or a dozen children, most of them older than myself. Captain Anthony was not considered a rich slave-holder, though he was pretty well off in the world. He owned about thirty slaves and three farms in the Tuckahoe district. The more valuable part of his property was in slaves, of whom he sold one every year, which brought him in seven or eight hundred dollars, besides his yearly salary and other revenue from his lands.

Although my old master, Captain Anthony, gave me, at the first of my coming to him from my grandmother's, very little attention, and although that little was of a remarkably mild and gentle description, a few months only were sufficient to convince me that mildness and gentleness were not the prevailing or governing traits of his character. These excellent qualities were displayed only occasionally. He could, when it suited him, appear to be literally insensible to the claims of humanity. He could not only be deaf to the appeals of the helpless against the aggressor, but he could himself commit outrages deep, dark, and nameless. Yet he was not by nature worse than other men. Had he been brought up in a free state, surrounded by the full restraints of civilized society—restraints which are necessary to the freedom of all its members, alike and equally—Capt. Anthony might have been as humane a man as are members of such society generally. A man's character always takes its hue, more or less, from the form and color of things about him. The slaveholder, as well as the slave, was the victim of the slave system. Under the whole heavens there could be no relation more unfavorable to the development of honorable character than that sustained by the slaveholder to the slave. Reason is imprisoned here, and passions run wild. Could the reader have seen Captain Anthony gently leading me by the hand, as he sometimes did, patting me on the head, speaking to me in soft, caressing tones, and calling me his little Indian boy, he would have deemed him a kind-hearted old man, and really almost fatherly to the slave boy. But the pleasant moods of a slaveholder are transient and fitful. They neither come often nor remain long. The temper of the old man was subject to special trials; but since these trials were never borne patiently, they added little to his natural stock of patience. Aside from his troubles with his slaves and those of Mr. Lloyd, he made the impression upon me of being an unhappy man. Even to my child's eye he wore a troubled and at times a haggard aspect. His strange movements excited my curiosity and awakened my compassion. He seldom walked alone without muttering to himself, and he occasionally stormed about as if defying an army of invisible foes. Most of his leisure was spent in walking around, cursing and gesticulating as if possessed by a demon. He was evidently a wretched man, at war with his own soul and all the world around him. To be overheard by the children disturbed him very little. He made no more of our presence than that of the ducks and geese he met on the green. But when his gestures were most violent, ending with a threatening shake of the head and a sharp snap of his middle finger and thumb, I deemed it wise to keep at a safe distance from him.

One of the first circumstances that opened my eyes to the cruelties and wickedness of slavery and its hardening influences upon my old master, was his refusal to interpose his authority to protect and shield a young woman, a cousin of mine, who had been most cruelly abused and beaten by his overseer in Tuckahoe. This overseer, a Mr. Plummer, was, like most of his class, little less than a human brute; and, in addition to his general profligacy and repulsive coarseness, he was a miserable drunkard, a man not fit to have the management of a drove of mules. In one of his moments of drunken madness he committed the outrage which brought the young woman in question down to my old master's for protection. The poor girl, on her arrival at our house, presented a most pitiable appearance. She had left in haste and without preparation, and probably without the knowledge of Mr. Plummer. She had traveled twelve miles, barefooted, bare-necked, and bare-headed. Her neck and shoulders were covered with scars, newly made; and, not content with marring her neck and shoulders with the cowhide, the cowardly wretch had dealt her a blow on the head with a hickory club, which cut a horrible gash, and left her face literally covered with blood. In this condition the poor young woman came down to implore protection at the hands of my old master. I expected to see him boil over with rage at the revolting deed, and to hear him fill the air with curses upon the brutal Plummer; but I was disappointed. He sternly told her in an angry tone, "She deserved every bit of it, and if she did not go home instantly he would himself take the remaining skin from her neck and back." Thus the poor girl was compelled to return without redress, and perhaps to receive an additional flogging for daring to appeal to authority higher than that of the overseer.

The reader will have noticed that, among the names of slaves, that of Esther is mentioned. This was the name of a young woman who possessed that which was ever a curse to the slave girl—namely, personal beauty. She was tall, light-colored, well formed, and made a fine appearance. Esther was courted by "Ned Roberts," the son of a favorite slave of Col. Lloyd, and who was as fine-looking a young man as Esther was a woman. Some slaveholders would have been glad to have promoted the marriage of two such persons, but for some reason Captain Anthony disapproved of their courtship. He strictly ordered her to quit the society of young Roberts, telling her that he would punish her severely if he ever found her again in his company. But it was impossible to keep this couple apart. Meet they would and meet they did. Had Mr. Anthony himself been a man of honor, his motives in this matter might have appeared more favorably. As it was, they appeared as abhorrent as they were contemptible. It was one of the damning characteristics of slavery that it robbed its victims of every earthly incentive to a holy life. The fear of God and the hope of heaven were sufficient to sustain many slave women amidst the snares and dangers of their strange lot; but they were ever at the mercy of the power, passion and caprice of their owners. Slavery provided no means for the honorable perpetuation of the race. Yet, despite this destitution, there were many men and women among the slaves who were true and faithful to each other through life.

But to the case in hand. Abhorred and circumvented as he was, Captain Anthony, having the power, was determined on revenge. I happened to see its shocking execution, and shall never forget the scene. It was early in the morning, when all was still, and before any of the family in the house or kitchen had risen. I was, in fact, awakened by the heart-rending shrieks and piteous cries of poor Esther. My sleeping-place was on the dirt floor of a little rough closet which opened into the kitchen, and through the cracks in its unplaned boards I could distinctly see and hear what was going on, without being seen. Esther's wrists were firmly tied, and the twisted rope was fastened to a strong iron staple in a heavy wooden beam above, near the fireplace. Here she stood on a bench, her arms tightly drawn above her head. Her back and shoulders were perfectly bare. Behind her stood old master, cowhide in hand, pursuing his barbarous work with all manner of harsh, coarse, and tantalizing epithets. He was cruelly deliberate and protracted the torture as one who was delighted with the agony of his victim. Again and again he drew the hateful scourge through his hand, adjusting it with a view of dealing the most pain-giving blow his strength and skill could inflict. Poor Esther had never before been severely whipped. Her shoulders were plump and tender. Each blow, vigorously laid on, brought screams from her as well as blood. "Have mercy! Oh, mercy!" she cried. "I won't do so no more." But her piercing cries seemed only to increase his fury. The whole scene, with all its attendant circumstances, was revolting and shocking to the last degree, and when the motives for the brutal castigation are known, language has no power to convey a just sense of its dreadful criminality. After laying on I dare not say how many stripes, old master untied his suffering victim. When let down she could scarcely stand. From my heart I pitied her, and child as I was, and new to such scenes, the shock was tremendous. I was terrified, hushed, stunned and bewildered. The scene here described was often repeated, for Edward and Esther continued to meet, notwithstanding all efforts to prevent their meeting.

CHAPTER XLV

AS TIME went on and facilities for doing so presented themselves, slaves escaped from the south. It was dangerous business, as pursuit was almost certain; but negroes who for one reason or another found existence intolerable ran the great risk. There was Father Josiah Henson, for instance, who took a most remarkable and heroic means of escaping with all his family to Canada and freedom.

IT was not without long thought upon the subject that I devised a plan of escape. But at last I matured it. My mind fully made up, I communicated the intention to my wife. She was overwhelmed with terror. With a woman's instinct she clung to hearth and home. She knew nothing of the wide world beyond, and her imagination peopled it with unseen horrors. We should die in the wilderness,—we should be hunted down with blood-hounds,—we should be brought back and whipped to death. With tears and supplications she besought me to remain at home, contented. In vain I explained to her our liability to be torn asunder at any moment; the horrors of the slavery I had lately seen; the happiness we should enjoy together in a land of freedom, safe from all pursuing harm. She had not suffered the bitterness of my lot, nor felt the same longing for deliverance. She was a poor, ignorant, unreasoning slave-woman.

I argued the matter with her at various times, till I was satisfied that argument alone would not prevail. I then told her deliberately, that though it would be a cruel trial for me to part with her, I would nevertheless do it, and take all the children with me except the youngest, rather than remain at home, only to be forcibly torn from her, and sent down to linger out a wretched existence in the hell I had lately visited. Again she wept and entreated, but I was sternly resolute. The whole night long she fruitlessly urged me to relent; exhausted and maddened, I left her, in the morning, to go to my work for the day. Before I had gone far, I heard her voice calling me, and waiting till I came up, she said, at last, she would go with me. Blessed relief! my tears of joy flowed faster than had hers of grief.

497

Our cabin, at this time, was near the landing. The plantation itself extended the whole five miles from the house to the river. There were several distinct farms, all of which I was overseeing, and therefore I was riding about from one to another every day. Our oldest boy was at the house with Master Amos; the rest of the children were with my wife.

The chief practical difficulty that had weighed upon my mind, was connected with the youngest two of the children. They were of three and two years, respectively, and of course would have to be carried. Both stout and healthy, they were a heavy burden, and my wife had declared that I should break down under it before I had got five miles from home. Sometime previously I had directed her to make me a large knapsack of tow cloth, large enough to hold them both, and arranged with strong straps to go round my shoulders. This done, I had practiced carrying them night after night, both to test my own strength and accustom them to submit to it. To them it was fine fun, and to my great joy I found I could manage them successfully. My wife's consent was given on Thursday morning, and I resolved to start on the night of the following Saturday. Sunday was a holiday; on Monday and Tuesday I was to be away on farms distant from the house; thus several days would elapse before I should be missed, and by that time I should have got a good start.

It was about the middle of September, and by nine o'clock all was ready. It was a dark, moonless night, when we got into the little skiff, in which I had induced a fellow slave to set us across the river. It was an anxious moment. We sat still as death. In the middle of the stream the good fellow said to me, "It will be the end of me if this is ever found out; but you won't be brought back alive, Sir, will you?" "Not if I can help it," I replied; and I thought of the pistols and knife I had bought some time before of a poor white. "And if they're too many for you, and you get seized, you'll never tell my part in this business?" "Not if I'm shot through like a sieve." "That's all," said he, "and God help you."

In due time we landed on the Indiana shore. A hearty, grateful farewell, such as none but companions in danger can know, and I heard the oars of the skiff propelling him home. There I stood in the darkness, my dear ones with me, and the all unknown future before us. But there was little time for reflection. Before daylight should come on, we must put as many miles behind us as possible, and be safely hidden in the woods. We had no friends to look to for assistance, for the population in that section of the country was then bitterly hostile to the fugitive. If discovered, we should be seized and lodged in jail. In God was our only hope. Fervently did I pray to him as we trudged on cautiously and steadily, and as fast as the darkness and the feebleness of my wife and boys would allow. To her, indeed, I was compelled to talk sternly; she trembled like a leaf, and even then implored me to return.

For a fortnight we pressed steadily on, keeping to the road during the night, hiding whenever a chance vehicle or horseman was heard, and during the day burying ourselves in the woods. Our provisions were rapidly giving out. Two days before reaching Cincinnati they were utterly exhausted. All night long the children cried with hunger, and my poor wife loaded me with reproaches for bringing them into such misery. It was a bitter thing to hear them cry, and God knows I needed encouragement myself. My limbs were weary, and my back and shoulders raw with the burden I carried. A fearful dread of detection ever pursued me, and I would start out of my sleep in terror, my heart beating against my ribs, expecting to find the dogs and slave-hunters after me. Had I been alone I would have borne starvation, even to exhaustion, before I would have ventured in sight of a house in quest of food. But now something must be done; it was necessary to run the risk of exposure by daylight upon the road.

The only way to proceed was to adopt a bold course. Accordingly, I left our hiding-place, took to the road, and turned towards the south, to lull any suspicion that might be aroused were I to be seen going the other way. Before long I came to a house. A furious dog rushed out at me, and his master following to quiet him, I asked if he would sell me a little bread and meat. He was a surly fellow. "No, he had nothing for niggers!" At the next I succeeded no better, at first. The man of the house met me in the same style; but his wife, hearing our conversation, said to her husband, "How can you treat any human being so? If a dog was hungry I would give him something to eat." She then added, "We have children, and who knows but they may some day need the help of a friend." The man laughed, and told her that she might take care of niggers, he wouldn't. She asked me to come in, loaded a plate with vension and bread, and, when I laid it into my handkerchief, and put a quarter of a dollar on the table, she quietly took it up and put it in my handkerchief, with an additional quantity of vension. I felt the hot tears roll down my cheeks as she said, "God bless you;" and I hurried away to bless my starving wife and little ones.

A little while after eating the vension, which was quite salt, the children became very thirsty, and groaned and sighed so that I went off stealthily, breaking the bushes to keep my path, to find water. I found a little rill, and drank a large draught. Then I tried to carry some in my hat; but, alas! it leaked. Finally, I took off both shoes, which luckily had no holes in them, rinsed them out, filled them with water, and carried it to my family. They drank it with great delight. I have since then sat at splendidly furnished tables in Canada, the United States, and England; but never did I see any human beings relish anything more than my poor famishing little ones did that refreshing draught out of their father's shoes. That night we made a long run, and two days afterward we reached Cincinnati.

We followed the same course as before—traveling by night and resting by day—till we arrived at the Scioto, where we had been told we should strike the military road of General Hull, in the last war with Great Britain, and might then safely travel by day. We found the road, accordingly, by the large sycamore and elms which marked its beginning, and entered upon it with fresh spirits early in the day. Nobody had told us that it was cut through the wilderness, and I had neglected to provide any food, thinking we should soon come to some habitation, where we could be supplied. But we traveled on all day without seeing one, and lay down at night, hungry and weary enough. The wolves were howling around us, and though too cowardly to approach, their noise terrified my poor wife and children. Nothing remained to us in the morning but a little piece of dried beef, too little, indeed, to satisfy our cravings, but enough to afflict us with intolerable thirst. I divided most of this among us, and then we started for a second day's tramp in the wilderness. A painful day it was to us. The road was rough, the underbrush tore our clothes and exhausted our strength; trees that had been blown down blocked the way; we were faint with hunger; and no prospect of relief opened up before us. We spoke little, but steadily struggled along; I with my babes on my back, my wife aiding the two other children to climb over the fallen trunks and force themselves through the briers. Suddenly, as I was plodding along a little ahead of my wife and the boys, I heard them call me, and turning round saw my wife prostrate on the ground. "Mother's dying," cried Tom; and when I reached her it seemed really so. From sheer exhaustion she had fallen in surmounting a log. Distracted with anxiety, I feared she was gone. For some minutes no sign of life was manifest; but after a time she opened her eyes, and finally recovering enough to take a few mouthfuls of the beef, her strength returned, and we once more went bravely on our way. I cheered the sad group with hopes I was far from sharing myself. For the first time I was nearly ready to abandon myself to despair.

Starvation in the wilderness was the doom that stared me and mine in the face. But again, "man's extremity was God's opportunity."

We had not gone far, and I suppose it was about three o'clock in the afternoon, when we discerned some persons approaching us at no great distance. We were instantly on the alert, as we could hardly expect them to be friends. The advance of a few paces showed me they were Indians, with packs on their shoulders; and they were so near that if they were hostile it would be useless to try to escape. So I walked along boldly, till we came close upon them. They were bent down with their burdens, and had not raised their eyes till now; and when they did so, and saw me coming toward them, they looked at me in a frightened sort of way for a moment, and then, setting up a peculiar howl, turned round, and ran as fast as they could. There were three or four of them, and what they were afraid of I could not imagine, unless they supposed I was the devil, whom they had perhaps heard of as black. But, even then, one would have thought my wife and children might have reassured them. However, there was no doubt they were well frightened, and we heard their wild and prolonged howls, as they ran, for a mile or more. My wife was alarmed, too, and thought they were merely running back to collect more of a party, and then to come and murder us; and she wanted to turn back. I told her they were numerous enough to do that, if they wanted to, without help; and that as for turning back, I had had quite too much of the road behind us, and that it would be a ridiculous thing that both parties should run away. If they were disposed to run, I would follow. We did follow, and the noise soon ceased. As we advanced, we could discover Indians peeping at us from behind the trees, and dodging out of sight if they thought we were looking at them. Presently we came upon their wigwams, and saw a fine-looking, stately Indian, with his arms folded, waiting for us to approach. He was, apparently, the chief; and, saluting us civilly, he soon discovered we were human beings and spoke to his young men, who were scattered about, and made them come in and give up their foolish fears. And now curiosity seemed to prevail. Each one wanted to touch the children, who were as shy as partridges with their long life in the woods; and as they shrunk away, and uttered a little cry of alarm, the Indian would jump back too, as if he thought they would bite him. However, a little while sufficed to make them understand what we were, and whither we were going, and what we needed; and as little to set them about supplying our wants, feeding us bountifully, and giving us a comfortable wigwam for our night's rest. The next day we resumed our march, having ascertained from the Indians that we were only about twenty-five miles from the lake. They sent some of their young men to point out the place where we were to turn off, and parted from us with as much kindness as possible.

In passing over the part of Ohio near the lake, where such an extensive plain is found, we came to a spot overflowed by a stream, across which the road passed. I forded it first, with the help of a sounding-pole, and then taking the children on my back, first the two little ones, and then the others, one at a time, and, lastly, my wife, I succeeded in getting them safely across. At this time the skin was worn from my back to an extent almost equal to the size of the knapsack.

One night more was passed in the woods, and in the course of the next forenoon we came out upon the wide plain, without trees, which lies south and west of Sandusky city. The houses of the village were in plain sight. About a mile from the lake I hid my wife and children in the bushes, and pushed forward. I was attracted by a house on the left, between which and a small coasting vessel a number of men were passing and repassing with great activity. Promptly deciding to approach them, I drew near, and scarcely had I come within hailing distance, when the captain of the schooner cried out, "Hollo there, man! you want to work?" "Yes, sir!" shouted I. "Come along, come along; I'll give you a shilling an hour. Must get off with this wind." As I came near, he said, "Oh, you can't work; you're crippled." "Can't I?" said I; and in a minute I had hold of a bag of corn, and followed the gang in emptying it into the hold. I took my place in the line of laborers next to a colored man, and soon got into conversation with him. "How far is it to Canada?" He gave me a peculiar look, and in a minute I saw he knew all. "Want to go to Canada? Come along with us, then. Our captain's a fine fellow. We're going to Buffalo." "Buffalo; how far is that from Canada?" "Don't you know, man? Just across the river." I now opened my mind frankly to him, and told him about my wife and children. "I'll speak to the captain," said he. He did so, and in a moment the captain took me aside, and said, "The Doctor says you want to go to Buffalo with your family." "Yes, sir." "Well, why not go with me!" was his frank reply. "Doctor says you've got a family." "Yes, sir." "Where do you stop?" "About a mile back." "How long have you been here?" "No time," I answered, after a moment's hesitation. "Come, my good fellow, tell us all about it. You're running away, ain't you?" I saw he was a friend, and opened my heart to him. "How long will it take you to get ready?" "Be here in half an hour, sir." "Well, go along and get them." Off I started; but, before I had run fifty feet, he called me back. "Stop," says he; "you go on getting the grain in. When we get off, I'll lay to over opposite that island, and send a boat back. There's a lot of regular nigger-catchers in the town below, and they might suspect if you brought your party out of the bush by daylight." I worked away with a will. Soon the two or three hundred bushels of corn were aboard, the hatches fastened down, the anchor raised, and the sails hoisted.

I watched the vessel with intense interest as she left her moorings. Away she went before the free breeze. Already she seemed beyond the spot at which the captain agreed to lay to, and still she flew along. My heart sunk within me; so near deliverance, and again to have my hopes blasted, again to be cast on my own resources. I felt that they had been making a mock of my misery. The sun had sunk to rest, and the purple and gold of the west were fading away into gray. Suddenly, however, as I gazed with weary heart, the vessel swung round into the wind, the sails flapped, and she stood motionless. A moment more, and a boat was lowered from her stern, and with steady stroke made for the point at which I stood. I felt that my hour of release had come. On she came, and in ten minutes she rode up handsomely on to the beach.

My black friend and two sailors jumped out, and we started off at once for my wife and children. To my horror, they were gone from the place where I left them. Overpowered with fear, I supposed they had been found and carried off. There was no time to lose, and the men told me I would have to go alone. Just at the point of despair, however, I stumbled on one of the children. My wife, it seemed, alarmed at my absence, had given up all for lost, and supposed I had fallen into the hands of the enemy. When she heard my voice, mingled with those of the others, she thought my captors were leading me back to make me discover my family, and in the extremity of her terror she had tried to hide herself. I had hard work to satisfy her. Our long habits of concealment and anxiety had rendered her suspicious of every one; and her agitation was so great that for a time she was incapable of understanding what I said, and went on in a sort of paroxysm of distress and fear. This, however, was soon over, and the kindness of my companions did much to facilitate the matter.

And now we were off for the boat. It required little time to embark our baggage—one convenience, at least, of having nothing. The men bent their backs with a will, and headed steadily for a light hung from the vessel's mast. I was praising God in my soul. Three hearty cheers welcomed us as we reached the schooner and never till my dying day shall I forget the shout of the captain—he was a

Scotchman—"Coom up on deck, and clop your wings and craw like a rooster; you're a free nigger as sure as the devil." Round went the vessel, the wind plunged into her sails as though inoculated with the common feeling—the water seethed and hissed passed her sides. Man and nature, and, more than all, I felt the God of man and nature, who breathes love into the heart and maketh the winds his ministers, were with us. My happiness, that night, rose at times to positive pain. Unnerved by so sudden a change from destitution and danger to such kindness and blessed security, I wept like a child.

The next evening we reached Buffalo, but it was too late to cross the river that night. "You see those trees," said the noble-hearted captain next morning, pointing to a group in the distance; "they grow on free soil, and as soon as your feet touch that you're a *mon*. I want to see you go and be a freeman. I'm poor myself, and have nothing to give you; I only sail the boat for wages; but I'll see you across. Here Green," said he to a ferryman; "what will you take this man and his family over for—he's got no money?" "Three shillings." He then took a dollar out of his pocket and gave it to me. Never shall I forget the spirit in which he spoke. He put his hand on my head and said, "Be a good fellow, won't you?" I felt streams of emotion running down in electric courses from head to foot. "Yes," said I; "I'll use my freedom well; I'll give my soul to God." He stood waving his hat as we pushed off for the opposite shore. God bless him! God bless him eternally! Amen!

It was the 28th of October, 1830, in the morning, when my feet first touched the Canada shore. I threw myself on the ground, rolled in the sand, seized handfuls of it and kissed them, and danced round till, in the eyes of several who were present, I passed for a madman. "He's some crazy fellow," said a Colonel Warren, who happened to be there. "Oh, no master! don't you know? I'm free!" He burst into a shout of laughter. "Well, I never knew freedom make a man roll in the sand in such a fashion." Still I could not control myself. I hugged and kissed my wife and children, and, until the first exuberant burst of feeling was over, went on as before.

CHAPTER XLVI

NOT ONLY were fugitive slaves pursued across the Ohio; the national laws encouraged their capture and return. Hence the Underground Railroad, a series of friendly stations in the North—cellars, barns, and kitchens of friendly householders—along which escaping slaves could be passed by night or in concealment to the Canadian border. Levi Coffin, removed in 1826 from North Carolina to Indiana, became active in the services of the Railroad, and in time was reputed to be its "president." He explains how the work was done.

IN the year 1836, I built an oil mill and manufactured linseed oil. Notwithstanding all this multiplicity of business, I was never too busy to engage in Underground Railroad affairs. Soon after we located at Newport, I found that we were on a line of the U. G. R. R. Fugitives often passed through that place, and generally stopped among the colored people. There was in that neighborhood a number of families of free colored people, mostly from North Carolina, who were the descendants of slaves who had been liberated by Friends many years before, and sent to free States at the expense of North Carolina Yearly Meeting. I learned that the fugitive slaves who took refuge with these people were often pursued and captured, the colored people not being very skillful in concealing them, or shrewd in making arrangements to forward them to Canada. I was pained to hear of the capture of these fugitives, and inquired of some of the Friends in our village why they did not take them in and secrete them, when they were pursued, and then aid them on their way to Canada? I found that they were afraid of the penalty of the law. I was willing to receive and aid as many fugitives as were disposed to come to my house. I knew that my wife's feelings and sympathies regarding this matter were the same as mine, and that she was willing to do her part. It soon became known to the colored people in our neighborhood and others, that our house was a depot where the hunted and harassed fugitive journeying northward, on the Underground Railroad, could find succor and sympathy. It also became known at other depots on the various lines that converged at Newport.

In the winter of 1826-27, fugitives began to come to our house, and as it became more widely known on different routes that the slaves fleeing from bondage would find a welcome and shelter at our house, and be forwarded safely on their journey, the number increased. Friends in the neighborhood, who had formerly stood aloof from the work, fearful of the penalty of the law, were encouraged to engage in it when they saw the fearless manner in which I acted, and the success that attended my efforts. They would contribute to clothe the fugitives, and would aid in forwarding them on their way, but were timid about sheltering them under their roof; so that part of the work devolved on us. Some seemed really glad to see the work go on, if somebody else would do it. Others doubted the propriety of it, and tried to discourage me, and dissuade me from running such risks. They manifested great concern for my safety and pecuniary interests, telling me that such a course of action would injure my business and perhaps ruin me; that I ought to consider the welfare of my family; and warning me that my life was in danger, as there were many threats made against me by the slave-hunters and those who sympathized with them.

Many of my pro-slavery customers left me for a time, my sales were diminished, and for a while my business prospects were discouraging, yet my faith was not shaken, nor my efforts for the slaves lessened. New customers soon came in to fill the places of those who had left me. New settlements were rapidly forming to the north of us, and our own was filling up with emigrants from North Carolina, and other States. My trade increased, and I enlarged my business. I was blessed in all my efforts and succeeded beyond my expectations. The Underground Railroad business increased as time advanced, and it was attended with heavy expenses, which I could not have borne had not my affairs been prosperous. I found it necessary to keep a team and a wagon always at command, to convey the fugitive slaves on their journey. Sometimes, when we had large companies, one or two other teams and wagons were required. These journeys had to be made at night, often through deep mud and bad roads, and along byways that were seldom traveled. Every precaution to evade pursuit had to be used, as the hunters were often on the track, and sometimes ahead of the slaves. We had different routes for sending the fugitives to depots, ten, fifteen, or twenty miles distant, and when we heard of slave-hunters having passed on one road, we forwarded our passengers by another.

In some instances where we learned that the pursuers were ahead of them, we sent a messenger and had the fugitives brought back to my house to remain in concealment until the bloodhounds in human shape had lost the trail and given up the pursuit.

I soon became extensively known to the friends of the slaves, at different points on the Ohio River, where fugitives generally crossed, and to those northward of us on the various routes leading to Canada. Depots were established on the different lines of the Underground Railroad, south and north of Newport, and a perfect understanding was maintained between those who kept them. Three principal lines from the South converged at my house; one from Cincinnati, one from Madison, and one from Jeffersonville, Indiana. The roads were always in running order, the connections were good, the conductors active and zealous, and there was no lack of passengers. Seldom a week passed without our receiving passengers by this mysterious road. We found it necessary to be always prepared to receive such company and properly care for them. We knew not what night or what hour of the night we would be roused from slumber by a gentle rap at the door. That was the signal announcing the arrival of a train of the Underground Railroad, for the locomotive did not whistle, nor make any unnecessary noise. I have often been awakened by this signal, and sprang out of bed in the dark and opened the door. Outside in the cold or rain, there would be a two-horse wagon loaded with fugitives, perhaps the greater part of them women and children. I would invite them, in a low tone, to come in, and they would follow me into the darkened house without a word, for we knew not who might be watching and listening. When they were all safely inside and the door fastened, I would cover the windows, strike a light and build a good fire. By this time my wife would be up and preparing victuals for them, and in a short time the cold and hungry fugitives would be made comfortable. I would accompany the conductor of the train to the stable, and care for the horses, that had, perhaps, been driven twenty-five or thirty miles that night, through the cold and rain. The fugitives would rest on pallets before the fire the rest of the night. Frequently, wagon-loads of passengers from the different lines have met at our house, having no previous knowledge of each other. The companies varied in number, from two or three fugitives to seventeen.

The care of so many necessitated much work and anxiety on our part, but we assumed the burden of our own will and bore it cheerfully. It was never too cold or stormy, or the hour of night too late, for my wife to rise from sleep, and provide food and comfortable lodging for the fugitives. Her sympathy for those in distress never tired, and her efforts in their behalf never abated. This work was kept up during the time we lived at Newport, a period of more than twenty years. The number of fugitives varied considerably in different years, but the annual average was more than one hundred. They generally came to us destitute of clothing, and were often barefooted. Clothing must be collected and kept on hand, if possible, and money must be raised to buy shoes, and purchase goods to make garments for women and children. The young ladies in the neighborhood organized a sewing society, and met at our house frequently, to make clothes for the fugitives.

Sometimes when the fugitives came to us destitute, we kept them several days, until they could be provided with comfortable clothes. This depended on the circumstances of danger. If they had come a long distance and had been out several weeks or months—as was sometimes the case—and it was not probable that hunters were on their track, we thought it safe for them to remain with us until fitted for traveling through the thinly settled country to the North. Sometimes fugitives have come to our house in rags, foot-sore and toil-worn, and almost wild, having been out for several months traveling at night, hiding in canebrakes or thickets during the day, often being lost and making little headway at night, particularly in cloudy weather, when the north star could not be seen, sometimes almost perishing for want of food, and afraid of every white person they saw, even after they came into a free State, knowing that slaves were often captured and taken back after crossing the Ohio River.

Such as these we have kept until they were recruited in strength, provided with clothes, and able to travel. When they first came to us they were generally unwilling to tell their stories, or let us know what part of the South they came from. They would not give their names, or the names of their masters, correctly, fearing that they would be betrayed. In several instances fugitives came to our house sick from exhaustion and exposure, and lay several weeks.

CHAPTER XLVII

AS THE issue more and more complicated itself, more and more confused impressions prevailed concerning the nature of Southern life. In the later '50's some very brilliant reporting, destined to be influential in England as well as in the United States, was done by Frederick Law Olmsted, now known as one of the most distinguished of landscape architects. He traveled through all the sections of the South and made many close and human observations of both black and white society. We see him stopping overnight in shabby houses, and through him discover the existence of a peculiar, though perhaps inevitable, custom in New Orleans. First he stops for a night at the run-down house of a Virginia slave-owner and tobacco-grower.

ZIGZAG fences up to a large, square yard, growing full of Lombardy poplar sprouts, from the roots of eight or ten old trees, which were planted some fifty years ago, I suppose, in a double row, on two sides of the house. At the further end of this yard, beyond the house, a gate opened on the road, and out of this was just then coming a black man.

I inquired of him if there was a house, near by, at which I could get accommodation for the night. Reckoned his master'd take me in, if I'd ask him. Where was his master? In the house: I could go right in here (at a place where a panel of the paling had fallen over) and see him if I wanted to. I asked him to hold my horse, and went in.

It was a simple two-story house, very much like those built by the wealthier class of people in New England villages, from fifty to a hundred years ago, except that the chimneys were carried up outside the walls. There was a porch at the front door, and a small wing at one end, in the rear: from this wing to the other end extended a broad gallery.

A dog had been barking at me after I had dismounted; and just as I reached the steps of the gallery, a vigorous, middle-aged man, with a rather sullen and suspicious expression of face, came out without any coat on, to see what had excited him.

Doubting if he were the master of the house, I told him that I had come in to inquire if it would be convenient to allow me to spend the night with them. He asked where I came from, where I was going to, and various other questions, until I had given him an epitome of my day's wanderings and adventures; at the conclusion of which he walked to the end of the gallery to look at my horse; then, without giving me any answer, but muttering indistinctly something about servants, walked into the house, shutting the door behind him!

Well, thought I, this is not overwhelmingly hospitable. What can it mean?

While I was considering whether he expected me to go without any further talk—his curiosity being, I judged, satisfied—he came out again, and said, "Reckon you can stay, sir, if you'll take what we'll give." (The good man had been in to consult his wife.) I replied that I would do so thankfully, and hoped they would not give themselves any unnecessary trouble, or alter their usual family arrangements. I was then invited to come in, but I preferred to see my horse taken care of first. My host called for "Sam," two or three times, and then said he reckoned all his "people" had gone off, and he would attend to my horse himself. I offered to assist him, and we walked out to the gate, where the negro, not being inclined to wait for my return, had left Jane fastened to a post. Our host conducted us to an old square log-cabin which had formerly been used for curing tobacco, there being no room for Jane, he said, in the stables proper.

The floor of the tobacco-house was covered with lumber, old plows, scythes and cradles, a part of which had to be removed to make room for the filly to stand. She was then induced, with some difficulty, to enter it through a low, square doorway; saddle and bridle were removed, and she was fastened in a corner by a piece of old plow-line. We then went to a fodder-stack, and pulled out from it several small bundles of maize leaves. Additional feed and water were promised when "some of the niggers" came in; and, after righting up an old door that had fallen from one hinge, and setting a rail against it to keep it in its place, we returned to the house.

My host (whom I will call Mr. Newman) observed that his building and fences were a good deal out of order. He had owned the place but a few years, and had not had time to make much improvement about the house yet.

Entering the mansion, he took me to a large room on the first floor, gave me a chair, went out and soon returned (now wearing a coat) with two negro girls, one bringing wood and the other some flaming brands. A fire was made with a great deal of trouble, scolding of the girls, bringing in more brands, and blowing with the mouth. When the room had been suffocatingly filled with smoke, and at length a strong bright blaze swept steadily up the chimney, Mr. Newman again went out with the girls, and I was left alone for nearly an hour, with one interruption, when he came in and threw some more wood upon the fire, and said he hoped I would make myself comfortable.

It was a square room, with a door from the hall on one side, and two windows on each of the other sides. The lower part of the walls was wainscoted, and the upper part, with the ceiling, plastered and whitewashed. The fireplace and mantelpiece were somewhat carved, and were painted black; all the woodwork lead color. Blue paper curtains covered the windows; the floor was uncarpeted, and the only furniture in the room was some strong plain chairs, painted yellow, and a Connecticut clock, which did not run. The house had evidently been built for a family of some wealth, and, after having been deserted by them, had been bought at a bargain by the present resident, who either had not the capital or the inclination to furnish and occupy it appropriately.

When my entertainer called again, he merely opened the door and said, "Come! get something to eat!" I followed him out into the gallery, and thence through a door at its end into a room in the wing—a family room, and a very comfortable homely room. A bountifully spread supper-table stood in the center, at which was sitting a very neat, pretty little woman, of as silent habits as her husband, but neither bashful nor morose. A very nice little girl sat at her right side, and a peevish, ill-behaved, whining glutton of a boy at her left. I was requested to be seated adjoining the little girl, and the master of the house sat opposite me. The fourth side of the table was unoccupied, though a plate and chair were placed there, as if some one else had been expected.

The two negro girls waited at table, and a negro boy was in the room, who, when I asked for a glass of water, was sent to get it. An old negro woman also frequently came in from the kitchen, with hot biscuit and corn-cake. There was fried fowl, and fried bacon and eggs, and cold ham; there were preserved peaches, and preserved quinces and grapes; there was hot wheaten biscuit, and hot short-cake, and hot corn-cake, and hot griddle cakes, soaked in butter; there was coffee, and there was milk, sour or sweet, whichever I preferred to drink. I really ate more than I wanted, and extolled the corn-cake and the peach preserve, and asked how they were made; but I evidently disappointed my pretty hostess, who said she was afraid there wasn't anything that suited me—she feared there wasn't anything on the table I could eat; and she was sorry I couldn't make out a supper. And this was about all she would say. I tried to get a conversation started, but could obtain little more than very laconic answers to my questions.

Except from the little girl at my side, whose confidence I gained by taking an opportunity, when her mother was engaged with young Hopeful t'other side the coffee-pot, to give her a great deal of quince and grape, and by several times pouring molasses very freely on her cakes and bacon; and finally by feeding Pink out of my hand. (Hopeful had done this first, and then kicked him away, when he came round to Martha and me.) She told me her name, and that she had got a kitten, and that she hated Pink; and that she went to a Sunday-school at the Court House, and that she was going to go to an every-day school next winter—she wasn't big enough to walk so far now, but she would be then. But Billy said he didn't mean to go, because he didn't like to, though Billy was bigger nor she was, a heap. She reckoned when Billy saw Wash Baker going past every day, and heard how much fun he had every day with the other boys at the school, he would want to go too, wouldn't he? etc., etc. When supper was ended, I set back my chair to the wall, and took her on my knee; but after she had been told twice not to trouble the gentleman, and I had testified that she didn't do it, and after several mild hints that I would perhaps find it pleasanter in the sitting-room—(the chairs in the supper-room were the easiest, being country-made, low, and seated with undressed calf-skin), she was called to, out of the kitchen, and Mr. Newman said—going to the door and opening it for me—"Reckon you'd better walk into the sittin'-room, sir."

I walked out at this, and said I would go and look at the filly. Mr. Newman called "Sam'" again, and Sam, having at that moment arrived at the kitchen door, was ordered to go and take care of this gentleman's horse. I followed Sam to the tobacco-house, and gave him to know that he would be properly remembered for any attentions he could give to Jane. He watered her, and brought her a large supply of oats in straw, and some maize on the cob; but he could get no litter, and declared there was no straw on the plantation, though the next morning I saw a large quantity in a heap (not a stack), at a little greater distance than he was willing to go for it, I suppose, at a barn on the opposite side of the road. Having seen her rubbed clean and apparently well contented with her quarters and her supper, I bade her good-night, and returned to the house.

I did not venture again into the supper-room, but went to the sitting-room, where I found Miss Martha Ann and her kitten; I was having a good time with her, when her father came in and told her she was "troubling the gentleman." I denied it, and he took a seat by the fire with us, and I soon succeeded in drawing him into a conversation on farming, and the differences in our methods of work at the North and those he was accustomed to.

I learned that there were no white laboring men here who hired themselves out by the month. The poor white people that had to labor for their living, never would work steadily at any employment. "They generally followed boating"—hiring as hands on the bateaus that navigate the small streams and canals, but never for a longer term at once than a single trip of a boat, whether that might be long or short. At the end of the trip they were paid by the day. Their wages were from fifty cents to a dollar, varying with the demand and individual capacities. They hardly ever worked on farms except in harvest, when they usually received a dollar a day, sometimes more. In harvest-time, most of the rural mechanics closed their shops and hired out to the farmers at a dollar a day, which would indicate that their ordinary earnings are considerably less than this. At other than harvest-time, the poor white people, who had no trade, would sometimes work for the farmers by the job; not often any regular agricultural labor, but at getting rails or shingles, or clearing land.

He did not know that they were particular about working with negroes, but no white man would ever do certain kinds of work (such as taking care of cattle, or getting water or wood to be used in the house); and if you should ask a white man you had hired, to do such things, he would get mad and tell you he wasn't a nigger. Poor white girls never hired out to do servants' work, but they would come and help another white woman about her sewing and quilting, and take wages for it. But these girls were not very respectable generally, and it was not agreeable to have them in your house, though there were some very respectable ladies that would go out to sew. Farmers depended almost entirely upon their negroes; it was only when they were hard pushed by their crops, that they ever got white hands to help them.

Negroes had commanded such high wages lately, to work on railroads and in tobacco-factories, that farmers were tempted to hire out too many of their people, and to undertake to do too much work with those they retained; and thus they were often driven to employ white men, and to give them very high wages by the day, when they found themselves getting much behind hand with their crops. He had been driven very hard in this way this last season; he had been so unfortunate as to lose one of his best women, who died in child-bed just before harvest. The loss of the woman and her child, for the child had died also, just at that time, came very hard upon him. He would not have taken a thousand dollars of any man's money for them. He had had to hire white men to help him, but they were poor sticks, and would be half the time drunk, and you never know what to depend upon with them. One fellow that he had hired, who had agreed to work for him all through harvest, got him to pay him some wages in advance (he said it was to buy him some clothes with, so that he could go to meeting on Sunday, at the Court House), and went off the next day, right in the middle of harvest, and he had never seen him since. He had heard of him—he was on a boat—but he didn't reckon he should ever get his money again.

Of course, he did not see how white laborers were ever going to come into competition with negroes here, at all. You never could depend on white men, and you couldn't *drive* them any; they wouldn't stand it. Slaves were the only reliable laborers—you could command them and make them do what was right.

From the manner in which he talked of the white laboring people, it was evident that, although he placed them in some sort of an equality with himself, and that in his intercourse with them he wouldn't think of asserting for himself any superior dignity, or even feel himself to be patronizing them in not doing so, yet he, all the time, recognized them as a distinct and a rather despicable class, and wanted to have as little to do with them as he conveniently could.

I have been once or twice told that the poor white people, meaning those, I suppose, who bring nothing to market to exchange for money but their labor, although they may own a cabin and a little furniture, and cultivate land enough to supply themselves with (maize) bread, are worse off in almost all respects than the slaves. They are said to be extremely ignorant and immoral, as well as indolent and unambitious. That their condition is not so unfortunate by any means as that of negroes, however, is most obvious, since from among them, men sometimes elevate themselves to positions and habits of usefulness, and respectability. They are said to "corrupt" the negroes, and to encourage them to steal, or to work for them at night and on Sundays, and to pay them with liquor, and also to constantly associate licentiously with them. They seem, nevertheless, more than any other portion of the community, to hate and despise the negroes.

In the midst of our conversation, one of the black girls had come into the room and stood still with her head dropped forward, staring at me from under her brows, without saying a word. When she had waited, in this way, perhaps two minutes, her master turned to her and asked what she wanted.

"Miss Matty says Marta Ann go to bed now."

But Martha Ann refused to budge; after being told once or twice by her father to go with Rose, she came to me and lifted up her hands, I supposed to kiss me and go, but when I reached down, she took hold of my shoulders and climbed up on to my knees. Her father seemed to take no notice of this proceeding, but continued talking about guano; Rose went to a corner of the fireplace, dropped down upon the floor, and presently was asleep, leaning her head against the wall. In about half an hour the other negro girl came to the door, when Mr. Newman abruptly called out, "Girl! take that child to bed!" and immediately got up himself and walked out. Rose roused herself, and lifted Martha Ann out of my arms, and carried her off fast asleep. Mr. Newman returned holding a small candle, and, without entering the room, stood at the door and said, "I'll show you your bed if you are ready, sir." As he evidently meant, "I am ready to show you to bed if you will not refuse to go." I followed him upstairs.

Into a large room, again, with six windows, with a fireplace, in which a few brands were smoking, with some wool spread thinly upon the floor in a corner; with a dozen small bundles of tobacco leaves; with a lady's saddle; with a deep feather-bed, covered with a bright patch-work quilt, on a maple bedstead, and without a single item of any other furniture whatever. Mr. Newman asked if I wanted the candle to undress by; I said yes, if he pleased, and waited a moment for him to set it down: as he did not do so, I walked towards him, lifting my hand to take it. "No—I'll hold it," said he, and I then perceived that he had no candlestick, but held the lean little dip in his hand: I remembered also that no candle had been brought into the "sitting-room," and that while we were at supper only one candle had stood upon the table, which had been immediately extinguished when we rose, the room being lighted only from the fire.

I very quickly undressed and hung my clothes upon a bed-post: Mr. Newman looked on in silence until I had got into bed, when, with an abrupt "Good-night, sir," he went out and shut the door.

It was not until after I had consulted Sam the next morning that I ventured to consider that my entertainment might be taken as a mere business transaction, and not as "genuine planter's hospitality," though this had become rather a ridiculous view of it, after a repetition of the supper, in all respects, had been eaten for breakfast, with equal moroseness on the part of my host and equal quietness on the part of his kind-looking little wife. I was, nevertheless, amused at the promptness with which he replied to my rather hesitating inquiry—what I might pay him for the trouble I had given him—"I reckon a dollar and a quarter will be right, sir."

Then Olmstead reaches New Orleans, and discovers an interesting social situation rising out of the neighborhood of white and black.

There is one, among the multitudinous classifications of society in New Orleans, which is a very peculiar and characteristic result of the prejudices, vices, and customs of the various elements of color, class, and nation, which have been there brought together.

I refer to a class composed of the illegitimate offspring of white men and colored women (mulattoes or quadroons), who, from habits of early life, the advantages of education, and the use of wealth, are too much superior to the negroes, in general, to associate with them, and are not allowed by law, or the popular prejudice, to marry white people. The girls are frequently sent to Paris to be educated, and are very accomplished. They are generally pretty, often handsome. I have rarely, if ever, met more beautiful women than one or two whom I saw by chance, in the streets. They are better formed, and have a more graceful and elegant carriage than Americans in general, while they seem to have commonly inherited or acquired much of the taste and skill, in the selection and arrangement, and the way of wearing dresses and ornaments, that is the especial distinction of the women of Paris. Their beauty and attractiveness being their fortune, they cultivate and cherish with diligence every charm or accomplishment they are possessed of.

Of course, men are attracted by them, associate with them, are captivated, and become attached to them, and, not being able to marry them legally, and with the usual forms and securities for constancy, make such arrangements "as can be agreed upon." When a man makes a declaration of love to a girl of this class, she will admit or deny, as the case may be, her happiness in receiving it; but, supposing she is favorably disposed, she will usually refer the applicant to her mother. The mother inquires, like the "Countess of Kew," into the circumstances of the suitor; ascertains whether he is able to maintain a family, and, if satisfied with him, in these and other respects, requires from him security that he will support her daughter in a style suitable to the habits in which she had been bred, and that, if he should ever leave her, he will give her a certain sum for her future support, and a certain additional sum for each of the children she shall then have.

The wealth, thus secured, will, of course, vary—as in society with higher assumptions of morality—with the value of the lady in the market; that is, with her attractiveness, and the number and value of other suitors she may have, or may reasonably expect. Of course, I do not mean that love has nothing at all to do with it; but love is sedulously restrained, and held firmly in hand, until the road of competency is seen to be clear, with less humbug than our English custom requires about it. Everything being satisfactorily arranged, a tenement in a certain quarter of the town is usually taken, and the couple move into it and go to housekeeping—living as if they were married. The woman is not, of course, to be wholly deprived of the society of others—her former acquaintances are continued, and she sustains her relations as daughter, sister, and friend. Of course, too, her husband (she calls him so) will be likely to continue, also, more or less in, and form a part of, this kind of society. There are parties and balls—*bals masqués*—and all the movements and customs of other fashionable society, which they can enjoy in it, if they wish.* The women of this sort are represented to be exceedingly affectionate in disposition, and constant beyond reproach.

During all the time a man sustains this relation, he will commonly be moving, also, in reputable society on the other side of the town; not improbably, eventually he marries, and has a family establishment elsewhere. Before doing this, he may separate from his *placée* (so she is termed). If so, he pays her according to agreement, and as much more, perhaps, as his affection for her, or his sense of the cruelty of the proceeding, may lead him to; and she has the world before her again, in the position of a widow. Many men continue for

---

* "THE GLOBE BALL ROOM

Corner of St. Claude and St. Peter Streets, abreast of the Old Basin

WILL OPEN THIS EVENING, October 16, when a Society Ball will be given. No ladies admitted without masks.

Gentlemen, fifty cents—Ladies, gratis.

Doors open at 9½ o'clock. Ball to commence at 10 o'clock.

No person admitted with weapons, by order of the Council.

A superior orchestra has been engaged for the season.

The public may be assured of the most strict order, as there will be at all times an efficient police in attendance.

Attached to the establishment is a superior Bar, well stocked with wines and liquors; also, a Restaurant, where may be had all such delicacies as the market affords.

All ladies are requested to procure free tickets in the Mask Room, as no lady will be admitted into the ball-room without one.

A. WHITLOCK, Manager."

a long time, to support both establishments—particularly if their legal marriage is one *de convenance*. But many others form so strong attachments, that the relation is never discontinued, but becomes, indeed, that of marriage, except that it is not legalized or solemnized. These men leave their estate, at death, to their children, to whom they may have previously given every advantage of education they could command. What becomes of the boys, I am not informed; the girls, sometimes, are removed to other countries, where their color does not prevent their living reputable lives; but, of course, mainly continue in the same society, and are fated to a life similar to that of their mothers.

I have described this custom as it was described to me; I need hardly say, in only its best aspects. The crime and heart-breaking sorrow that must frequently result from it, must be evident to every reflective reader.

A gentleman, of New England education, gave me the following account of his acquaintance with the quadroon society. On first coming to New Orleans, he was drawn into the social circles usually frequented by New England people, and some time afterwards was introduced by a friend to a quadroon family, in which there were three pretty and accomplished young women. They were intelligent and well informed; their musical taste was especially well cultivated; they were well read in the literature of the day, and their conversation upon it was characterized by good sense and refined discrimination. He never saw any indication of a want of purity of character or delicacy of feeling. He was much attracted by them, and for some time visited them very frequently. Having then discontinued his intimacy, at length one of the girls asked him why he did not come to see them as often as he had formerly done. He frankly replied, that he had found their society so fascinating, that he had thought it best to restrict himself in the enjoyment of it, lest it should become necessary to his happiness; and out of regard to his general plans of life, and the feelings of his friends, he could not permit himself to indulge the purpose to be united to one of them, according to the usual custom with their class. The young woman was evidently much pained, but not at all offended, and immediately acknowledged and commended the propriety and good sense of his resolution.

One reason which leads this way of living to be frequently adopted by unmarried men, who come to New Orleans to carry on business is, that it is much cheaper than living at hotels and boarding-houses. As no young man ordinarily dare think of marrying, until he has made a fortune to support the extravagant style of housekeeping and gratify the expensive tastes of young women, as fashion is now educating them, many are obliged to make up their minds never to marry. Such a one undertook to show me that it was cheaper for him to *placer* than to live in any other way which could be expected of him in New Orleans. He hired, at a low rent, two apartments in the older part of the town; his *placée* did not, except occasionally, require a servant; she did the marketing and performed all the ordinary duties of housekeeping herself; she took care of his clothes, and in every way was economical and saving in her habits; it being her interest, if her affection for him were not sufficient, to make him as much comfort and as little expense as possible, that he might be the more strongly attached to her, and have the less occasion to leave her. He concluded by assuring me that whatever might be said against it, it certainly was better than the way in which most young men lived who depended on salaries in New York.

Olmsted's detour through the poor white districts of upper Mississippi was not reassuring with respect to the state of happiness there.

I counted about ten plantations, or negro-cultivated farms, in twenty miles. A planter, at whose house I called after sunset, said it was not convenient for him to accommodate me, and I was obliged to ride until it was quite dark. The next house at which I arrived was one of the commonest sort of cabins. I had passed twenty like it during the day, and I thought I would take the opportunity to get an interior knowledge of them. The fact that a horse and wagon were kept, and that a considerable area of land in the rear of the cabin was planted with cotton, showed that the family were by no means of the lowest class, yet, as they were not able even to hire a slave, they may be considered to represent very favorably, I believe, the condition of the poor whites of the plantation districts. The whites of the county, I observe, by the census, are three to one of the slaves; in the nearest adjoining county, the proportion is reversed; and within a few miles the soil was richer, and large plantations occurred.

It was raining, and nearly nine o'clock. The door of the cabin was open, and I rode up and conversed with the occupant as he stood within. He said that he was not in the habit of taking in travelers, and his wife was about sick, but if I was a mind to put up with common fare, he didn't care. Grateful, I dismounted and took the seat he had vacated by the fire, while he led away my horse to an open shed in the rear—his own horse ranging at large, when not in use, during the summer.

The house was all comprised in a single room, twenty-eight by twenty-five feet in area, and open to the roof above. There was a large fireplace at one end and a door on each side—no windows at all. Two bedsteads, a spinning-wheel, a packing-case, which served as a bureau, a cupboard, made of rough hewn slabs, two or three deerskin-seated chairs, a Connecticut clock, and a large poster of Jayne's patent medicines, constituted all the visible furniture, either useful or ornamental in purpose. A little girl, immediately, without having had any directions to do so, got a frying-pan and a chunk of bacon from the cupboard, and cutting slices from the latter, set it frying for my supper. The woman of the house sat sulkily in a chair tilted back and leaning against the logs, spitting occasionally at the fire, but took no notice of me, barely nodding when I saluted her. A baby lay crying on the floor. I quieted it and amused it with my watch till the little girl, having made "coffee" and put a piece of corn-bread on the table with the bacon, took charge of it.

I hoped the woman was not very ill.

"Got the headache right bad," she answered. "Have the headache a heap, I do. Knew I should have it to-night. Been cuttin' brush in the cotton this arternoon. Knew't would bring on my headache. Told him so when I begun."

As soon as I had finished my supper and fed Jude, the little girl put the fragments and the dishes in the cupboard, shoved the table into a corner, and dragged a quantity of quilts from one of the bedsteads, which she spread upon the floor, and presently crawled among them out of sight for the night. The woman picked up the child—which, though still a suckling, she said was twenty-two months old—and nursed it, retaking her old position. The man sat with me by the fire, his back towards her. The baby having fallen asleep was laid away somewhere, and the woman dragged off another lot of quilts from the bed, spreading them upon the floor. Then taking a deep tin pan, she filled it with alternate layers of corn-cobs and hot embers from the fire. This she placed upon a large block, which was evidently used habitually for the purpose, in the center of the cabin. A furious smoke arose from it, and we soon began to cough. "Most *too* much smoke," observed the man. "Hope 'twill drive out all the gnats, then," replied the woman. (There is a very minute flying insect here, the bite of which is excessively sharp.)

The woman suddenly dropped off her outer garment and stepped from the midst of its folds, in her petticoat; then, taking the baby from the place where she had deposited it, lay down and covered herself with the quilts upon the floor. The man told me that I could take the bed which remained on one of the bedsteads, and kicking off his shoes only, rolled himself into a blanket by the side of his wife. I ventured to take off my cravat and stockings, as well as my boots, but almost immediately put my stockings on again, drawing their tops over my pantaloons. The advantage of this arrangement was that, although my face, eyes, ears, neck, and hands, were immediately attacked, the vermin did not reach my legs for two or three hours. Just after the clock struck two, I distinctly heard the man and woman, and the girl and the dog scratching, and the horse out in the shed stamping and gnawing himself. Soon afterward the man exclaimed, "Good God Almighty—mighty! mighty! mighty!" and jumping up pulled off one of his stockings, shook it, scratched his foot vehemently, put on the stocking, and lay down again with a groan. The two doors were open, and through the logs and the openings in the roof, I saw the clouds divide and the moon and stars reveal themselves. The woman, after having been nearly smothered by the smoke from the pan which she had originally placed close to her own pillow, rose and placed it on the sill of the windward door, where it burned feebly and smoked lustily, like an altar to the Lares, all night. Fortunately the cabin was so open that it gave us little annoyance, while it seemed to answer the purpose of keeping all flying insects at a distance.

When, on rising in the morning, I said that I would like to wash my face, water was given me for the purpose in an earthen pie-dish. Just as breakfast, which was of exactly the same materials as my supper, was ready, rain began to fall, presently in such a smart shower as to put the fire out and compel us to move the table under the least leaky part of the roof.

At breakfast occurred the following conversation:

"Are there many niggers in New York?"

"Very few."

"How do you get your work done?"

"There are many Irish and German people constantly coming there who are glad to get work to do."

"Oh, and you have them for slaves?"

"They want money and are willing to work for it. A great many American-born work for wages, too."

"What do you have to pay?"

"Ten or twelve dollars a month."

"There was a heap of Irishmen to work on the railroad; they was paid a dollar a day; there was a good many Americans, too, but mostly they had little carts and mules, and hauled dirt and sich like. They was paid twenty-five or thirty dollars a month and found."

"What did they find them?"

"Oh, blanket and shoes, I expect; they put up kind o' tents like for 'em to sleep in altogether."

"What food did they find them?"

"Oh, common food; bacon and meal."

"What do they generally give the niggers on the plantations here?"

"A peck of meal and three pound of bacon is what they call 'lowance, in general, I believe. It takes a heap o' meat on a big plantation. I was on one of William R. King's plantations over in Alabamy, where there was about fifty niggers, one Sunday last summer, and I see 'em weighin' outen the meat. Tell you, it took a powerful heap on it. They had an old nigger to weigh it out, and he warn't no ways partickler about the weight. He just took and chopped it off, middlins, in chunks, and he'd throw them into the scales, and if a piece weighed a pound or two over he wouldn't mind it; he never took none back. Ain't niggers all-fired sassy at the North?"

"No, not particularly."

"Ain't they all free, there? I hearn so."

"Yes."

"Well, how do they get along when they's free?"

"I never have seen a great many, to know their circumstances very well. Right about where I live they seem to me to live quite comfortably; more so than the niggers on these big plantations do, I should think."

"Oh, they have a mighty hard time on the big plantations. I'd rather be dead than to be a nigger on one of these big plantations."

"Why, I thought they were pretty well taken care of on them."

The man and his wife both looked at me as if surprised, and smiled.

"Why, they are well fed, are they not?"

"Oh, but they work 'em so hard. My God, sir, in pickin' time on these plantations they start 'em to work 'fore light, and they don't give 'em time to eat."

"I supposed they generally gave them an hour or two at noon."

"No, sir; they just carry a piece of bread and meat in their pockets and they eat it when they can, standin' up. They have a hard life on 't, that's a fact. I reckon you can get along about as well withouten slaves as with 'em, can't you, in New York?"

"In New York there is not nearly so large a proportion of very rich men as here. There are very few people who farm over three hundred acres, and the greater number—nineteen out of twenty, I suppose—work themselves with the hands they employ. Yes, I think it's better than it is here, for all concerned, a great deal. Folks that can't afford to buy niggers get along a great deal better in the Free States, I think; and I guess that those who could afford to have niggers get along better without them."

"I no doubt that's so. I wish there warn't no niggers here. They are a great cuss to this country, I expect. But 'twouldn't do to free 'em; that wouldn't do nohow!"

"Are there many people here who think slavery a curse to the country?"

"Oh, yes, a great many. I reckon the majority would be right glad if we could get rid of the niggers. But it wouldn't never do to free 'em and leave 'em here. I don't know anybody, hardly, in favor of that. Make 'em free and leave 'em here and they'd steal everything we made. Nobody couldn't live here then."

These views of slavery seem to be universal among people of this class. They were repeated to me at least a dozen times.

"Where I used to live [Alabama], I remember when I was a boy—must ha' been about twenty years ago—folks was dreadful frightened about the niggers. I remember they built pens in the woods where they could hide, and Christmas time they went and got into the pens, 'fraid the niggers was risin'."

"I remember the same time where we was in South Carolina," said his wife; "we had all our things put up in bags, so we could tote 'em, if we heerd they was comin' our way."

They did not suppose the niggers ever thought of rising now, but could give no better reason for not supposing so than that "everybody said there warn't no danger on 't now."

Hereabouts the plantations were generally small, ten to twenty negroes on each; sometimes thirty or forty. Where he used to live they were big ones—forty or fifty, sometimes a hundred on each. He had lived here ten years. I could not make out why he had not accumulated wealth, so small a family and such an inexpensive style of living as he had. He generally planted twenty to thirty acres, he said; this year he had sixteen in cotton and about ten, he thought, in corn. Decently cultivated, this planting should have produced him five hundred dollars' worth of cotton, besides supplying him with bread and bacon—his chief expense, apparently. I suggested that this was a very large planting for his little family; he would need some help in picking time. He ought to have some now, he said; grass and bushes were all overgrowing him; he had to work just like a nigger; this durnation rain would just make the weeds jump, and he didn't expect he should have any cotton at all. There warn't much use in a man's trying to get along by himself; everything seemed to set in agin him. He'd been trying to hire somebody, but he couldn't, and his wife was a sickly kind of a woman.

His wife reckoned he might hire some help if he'd look round sharp.

My horse and dog were as well cared for as possible, and a "snack" of bacon and cornbread was offered me for noon, which has been unusual in Mississippi. When I asked what I should pay, the man hesitated and said he reckoned what I had had wasn't worth much of anything; he was sorry he could not have accommodated me better. I offered him a dollar, for which he thanked me warmly. It is the first instance of hesitation in charging for a lodging which I have met with from a stranger at the South.

CHAPTER XLVIII

THE ISSUE between north and south had other than moral aspects. Out of the political questions which it raised came the machinery of war. There was the question, for instance, of the admission of new states into the Union. Should they be slave or free? Texas, California, Kansas were the occasions of fierce debate; and in Kansas there was local war in 1855-6. Antislavery settlers from New England fought with proslavery settlers from Missouri; for a time there were two state governments presenting rival claims to Washington for admission into the federal system.

In 1855 John Brown burst into Kansas from the east, where, failing in more than one kind of business, he had at last decided to throw his energies into the cause of abolition. This fanatical old New Englander, aided by his sons and a few other followers, contributed outrages of a special kind to the Kansas chaos. On a night in 1856 his band entered the homes of five proslavery men along Pottawatomie Creek, called them out, and butchered them with knives. The thing was done deliberately as a measure of intimidation; but retaliation followed, and it has been estimated that 200 lives were taken on both sides as a result of the little massacre. Statements by spectators of the deed reveal how it was performed.

STATEMENT OF JAMES TOWNSLEY AFTER POTTAWATOMIE

ABOUT two miles south of Middle Creek we were joined by the Osawatomie company, under Captain Dayton, and proceeded to Mount Vernon, where we waited about two hours until the moon rose. We then marched all night, camping the next morning (the 22d) for breakfast, near Ottawa Jones's. Before we arrived at this point news had been received that Lawrence had been destroyed, and a question was raised whether we should return or go on. During the forenoon, however, we proceeded up Ottawa Creek to within about five miles of Palmyra, and went into camp near the residence of Captain Shore. Here we remained undecided over night. About noon the next day, the 23d, old John Brown came to me and said he had just received information that trouble was expected on the Pottawatomie, and wanted to know if I would take my team and take him and his boys back, so that they could keep watch of what was going on. I told him I would do so. The party—consisting of John Brown, Frederick Brown, Owen Brown, Watson Brown, Oliver Brown, Henry Thompson (John Brown's son-in-law), and Mr. Wiener—were soon ready for the trip, and we started, as near as I can remember, about two o'clock P.M. All of the party except Mr. Wiener, who rode a pony, rode with me in my wagon. When within two or three miles of the Pottawatomie Creek we turned off the main road to the right, drove down into the edge of the timber between two deep ravines, and camped about one mile above Dutch Henry's Crossing. After my team was fed and the party had taken supper, John Brown told me for the first time what he proposed to do. He said he wanted me to pilot the company up to the forks of the creek, some five or six miles above, into the neighborhood in which I lived, and show them where all the pro-slavery men resided; that he proposed to sweep the creek as he came down of all the pro-slavery men living on it. I positively refused to do it. He insisted upon it; but when he found that I would not go he decided to postpone the expedition until the following night. I then wanted to take my team and go home, but he refused to let me do so, and said I should remain with them. We remained in camp that night and all day the next day. Sometime after dark we were ordered to march.

STATEMENT OF MRS. DOYLE

My husband got up and went to the door. Those outside inquired for Mr. Wilkson [Wilkinson] and where he lived. My husband told them that he would tell them. Mr. Doyle, my husband, opened the door, and several came into the house, and said that they were from the army. My husband was a pro-slavery man. They told my husband that he and the boys must surrender, they were their prisoners. These men were armed with pistols and large knives. They first took my husband out of the house, then they took two of my sons—the two oldest ones, William and Drury —out, and then took my husband and these two boys, William and Drury, away. My son John was spared, because I asked them in tears to spare him. In a short time afterward I heard the report of pistols.

Statement of Mrs. Wilkinson

I was sick with the measles, and woke up Mr. Wilkinson, and asked if he heard the noise and what it meant? He said it was only some one passing about, and soon after was again asleep. It was not long before the dog raged and barked furiously, awakening me once more; pretty soon I heard footsteps as of men approaching; saw one pass by the window, and some one knocked at the door. I asked, who is that? No one answered. I awoke my husband, who asked, who is that? Some one replied, "I want you to tell me the way to Dutch Henry's." He commenced to tell them, and they said to him, "Come out and show us." He wanted to go, but I would not let him; he then told them it was difficult to find his clothes, and could tell them as well without going out of doors. The men out of doors, after that, stepped back, and I thought I could hear them whispering; but they immediately returned, and, as they approached, one of them asked of my husband, "Are you a northern armist?" He said, "I am!" I understood the answer to mean that my husband was opposed to the northern or freesoil party. I cannot say that I understood the question. My husband was a pro-slavery man, and was a member of the territorial legislature held at Shawnee Mission. When my husband said "I am," one of them said, "You are our prisoner. Do you surrender?" He said, "Gentlemen, I do." They said, "Open the door." Mr. Wilkinson told them to wait till he made a light; and they replied, "if you don't open it, we will open it for you." He opened the door against my wishes, and four men came in, and my husband was told to put on his clothes, and they asked him if there were not more men about; they searched for arms, and took a gun and powder flask, all the weapon that was about the house. I begged them to let Mr. Wilkinson stay with me, saying that I was sick and helpless, and could not stay by myself. My husband also asked them to let him stay with me until he could get some one to wait on me; told them that he would not run off, but would be there the next day, or whenever called for. The old man, who seemed to be in command, looked at me and then around at the children, and replied, "You have neighbors." I said, "So I have, but they are not here, and I cannot go for them." The old man replied, "it matters not." I [he?] told him to get ready. My husband wanted to put on his boots and get ready, so as to be protected from the damp and night air, but they wouldn't let him. They then took my husband away. One of them came back and took two saddles; I asked him what they were going to do with him, and he said, "take him a prisoner to the camp." I wanted one of them to stay with me. He said he would, but "they would not let him." After they were gone, I thought I heard my husband's voice, in complaint, but do not know; went to the door, and all was still. Next morning Mr. Wilkinson was found about one hundred and fifty yards from the house in some dead brush. A lady who saw my husband's body, said that there was a gash in his head and in his side; others said that he was cut in the throat twice.

STATEMENT OF JAMES HARRIS

On last Sunday morning, about two o'clock, (the 25th of May last,) whilst my wife and child and myself were in bed in the house where we lived, we were aroused by a company of men who said they belonged to the northern army, and who were each armed with a saber and two revolvers, two of whom I recognized, namely, a Mr. Brown, whose given name I do not remember, commonly known by the appellation of "old man Brown," and his son, Owen Brown. They came in the house and approached the bedside where we were lying, and ordered us, together with three other men who were in the same house with me, to surrender; that the northern army was upon us, and it would be no use for us to resist. The names of these other three men who were then in my house with me are, William Sherman, John S. Whiteman, the other man I did not know. They were stopping with me that night. They had bought a cow from Henry Sherman, and intended to go home the next morning. When they [the Browns] came up to the bed, some had drawn sabers in their hands, and some revolvers. They then took into their possession two rifles and a Bowie knife, which I had there in the room—there was but one room in my house—and afterward ransacked the whole establishment in search of ammunition. They then took one of these three men, who were staying in my house, out. (This was the man whose name I did not know.) He came back. They then took me out, and asked me if there were any more men about the place. I told them there were not. They searched the place, but found none others but we four. They asked me where Henry Sherman was. Henry Sherman was a brother to William Sherman. I told them that he was out on the plains in search of some cattle which he had lost. They asked if I had ever taken any hand in aiding pro-slavery men in coming to the Territory of Kansas, or had ever taken any hand in the last troubles at Lawrence, and asked me whether I had ever done the free State party any harm or ever intended to do that party any harm; they asked me what made me live at such a place. I then answered that

I could get higher wages there than anywhere else. They asked me if there were any bridles or saddles about the premises. I told them there was one saddle, which they took, and they also took possession of Henry Sherman's horse, which I had at my place, and made me saddle him. They then said if I would answer to all questions which they had asked me, they would let [me?] loose. Old Mr. Brown and his son then went into the house with me. The other three men, Mr. William Sherman, Mr. Whiteman, and the stranger were in the house all this time. After old man Brown and his son went into the house with me, old man Brown asked Mr. Sherman to go out with him, and Mr. Sherman then went out with old Mr. Brown, and another man came into the house in Brown's place. I heard nothing more for about fifteen minutes. Two of the northern army, as they styled themselves, stayed on with us until we heard a cap burst, and then these two men left. That morning about ten o'clock I found William Sherman dead in the creek near my house. I was looking for Mr. Sherman, as he had not come back, I thought he had been murdered. I took Mr. William Sherman out of the creek and examined him. Mr. Whiteman was with me. Sherman's skull was split open in two places and some of his brains was washed out by the water. A large hole was cut in his breast, and his left hand was cut off except a little piece of skin on one side. We buried him.

NOT CONTENT with this contribution to the cause, Brown toured the east raising funds for abolition in Kansas; returned and led a little group of slaves to freedom in Canada; and then planned his great and final action. The scheme through which he became a martyr was a scheme to seize and fortify a stronghold in the Virginia or Maryland mountains whence he could conduct operations toward the liberation of slaves in large numbers. Hitting upon Harper's Ferry, West Virginia, as the point of strategy, he and his handful of henchmen occupied a neighboring farm until one night in October, 1859, when they sallied into Harper's Ferry, seized the United States arsenal there, took citizens captive, and the next day were captured themselves by marines under Colonel Robert E. Lee. The execution of Brown in December seemed a symbol to the antislavery enthusiasts of the north, and stimulated a new burst of zeal. A description by Annie Brown of her father's behavior before Harper's Ferry reveals the sense of dedication which he felt; his own speeches and letters after the capture tell why he fanned his sympathizers into flame.

Annie Brown had this to say of her father's headquarters before the raid:

My father encouraged debating and discussions on all subjects among the men, often taking a lively part in the debate himself. Sometimes it would commence between two in the dining-room, then others would join, those who were upstairs coming down into the room to listen or take a part, some sitting on the stairs ready to jump and run back out of sight, if the danger signal was given that some one was approaching. Although he did not always agree with them, he encouraged them to discuss religious questions with him, and to express themselves freely on the subject.

After breakfast Father usually read a chapter in the Bible and made a plain, short, sensible prayer, standing while praying. (I have seen him kneel, but not often.) This was his custom both at home and at Kennedy Farm. Evenings he usually sat on a stool in the kitchen because it was warm there, and he once told me he did not wish to disturb the "boys," or spoil their enjoyment and fun by his presence in the living-room. He thought they did not feel quite so free when he was there.

As the table was not large enough for all to sit down at one time and the supply of dishes quite limited, Martha and I usually ate alone after all the rest were done. She "dished up" the victuals and washed dishes while I carried things into the room and waited on the table. There was no door between the kitchen and dining-room then, both rooms opened on to the porch, making a great deal of walking back and forth. After the meals I cleared off the table and washed the dishes and swept the floors of the room and porch, constantly on the look out for Mrs. Huffmaster, our nearest neighbor. She was a worse plague than the fleas. Of our supplies of food a few things were occasionally bought at Harper's Ferry when the men went to the post-office after *The Baltimore Sun,* which father subscribed for. Most of the mail was sent to Kagi at Chambersburg —merely for appearance sake. The rest of our food supplies was purchased at the towns and all along the road from Chambersburg down, a few things at a time or place so as not to arouse suspicion. Owen brought a barrel of eggs at one time because they were cheaper than meat. We had potatoes, onions and bacon. Then Martha was an extra good "light bread" maker. . . . We had a cookstove in the small kitchen off the porch upstairs, where we did our cooking. We used the basement kitchen and other cemented room on the ground floor only for storing purposes.

The middle room in the second story was used for dining and

general living room as the stairway from above came down into that room. The men came down and took their meals at the table, except on special occasions when some stranger or neighbor was calling there. If he or she stayed too long something was carried up the ladder at the back end of the house and passed into the window to the men. Sometimes Mrs. Huffmaster with her brood of little ones would be seen coming while the men were at the table eating. They would then gather up all the things, tablecloth and all, and go so quietly upstairs that no one would believe they existed, finish their meal up there and come back down bringing the things, when the visitor had gone. We did not have any stove or way of warming any of the rooms except the kitchen. The white men most of them, would watch their chance, when no one was in sight and skulk into the kitchen and stay and visit Martha awhile to relieve the monotony. If any one came they would climb the ladder into the loft over the kitchen and stay there until Mrs. Huffmaster (usually) was gone. The colored men were never allowed to be seen by daylight outside of the dining-room. After Mrs. Huffmaster saw Shields Green in that room, they stayed upstairs closely.

I was there to keep the outside world from discovering that John Brown and his men were in their neighborhood. I used to help Martha with the cooking all she would let me. Father would often tell me that I *must* not let any work interfere with my *constant watchfulness*. That others could help to do the housework, but he *depended* on me to watch. When I sat on the porch or just inside the door, in the daytime, I either read or sewed, to appear occupied if any one came near. When I washed the dishes I stood at the end of the table, where I could see out of the window and open door if any one was approaching the house. I was constantly on the look-out while carrying the victuals across the porch, from the kitchen, and while I was sweeping and tidying the rooms, and always at my post on the porch while the men ate their meals, when not passing in and out from the kitchen with food, or waiting on them in other ways at the table. My evenings were spent on the porch or sitting on the stairs, watching, and listening.

The men did nearly all the washing; we spread the clothes on the fence and on the ground to dry. Martha and I would bring them in as fast as they dried, but Mrs. Huffmaster would have some excuse to come to the garden, which she had rented before we went there, and then she would notice the clothes and tell us "Your men folks has a right smart lot of shirts." No one can ever imagine the pestering torment that little barefooted woman and her four little children were to us. Martha called them the little hen and chickens.

We were in constant fear that people would become suspicious enough to attempt an investigation and try to arrest the men. The rifles were in boxes called "furniture" and were used to sit on and kept standing against the walls in the dining-room, one box of pistols being in one bedroom near Martha's bed. She used it for a stand, table or dressing case, whatever name you wish to call it by. I had to tell people who called that: "My mother was coming soon and that she was very particular and had requested us to not unpack her furniture until she arrived," to account for the boxes in the room.

At Kennedy Farm, my father wore a short beard, an inch or an inch and a half long. He had made this change as a disguise, on his return from Kansas, thinking it more likely to disguise him than a clean face or than the long beard.

Hazlett and Leeman were the hardest ones to keep caged of all of "my invisibles," as I called them. They would get out and wander off in the woods and even go down to Harper's Ferry, going to Cook's home and back in daylight. We were so self-conscious that we feared danger when no man pursued or even thought of it. Watson, Oliver, Leeman and Kagi were all a little more than six feet in height, J. G. Anderson and Dauphin Thompson were next them in height but a little less than six feet; William Thompson and Stewart Taylor were above or about medium height but not quite as tall as the two last. Dangerfield Newby was I think above medium size, spare and showed the Scotch blood plainly in his looks and ways. His father was a Scotchman, who took his family of mulatto children into Ohio and gave them their freedom. Newby was quiet, sensible and very unobtrusive. Stevens and Stewart Taylor were the only ones who believed in "spiritualism" and their belief was more theoretical than otherwise. The latter was nearer to a "born crank" than any other man in the company. He believed in dreams and all sorts of "isms," and predicted his own death, which really came true. He talked as coolly about it as if he were going into another room. He considered it his duty to go to Harper's Ferry and go he did, although he knew he was going to his end. He was all the time studying and "improving his mind" as he called it. He had learned to write shorthand. O. P. Anderson was accustomed to being confined in the house, being a printer by trade, so that he was not so restive as some of the others.

William Thompson was an easy-going, good-natured person who enjoyed telling funny stories, mimicking old people for the amusement of any company he was in. But for all his nonsense he possessed an abundance of good common sense. When the occasion seemed to demand it, he knew how to use it to advantage. He was kind hearted and generous to a fault. Dauphin Thompson was the youngest one of a family of eighteen children. He was a quiet person, read a good deal, said little. He was a perfect blond, with yellow, curly hair and blue eyes, innocent as a baby, nearly six feet high, good size, well proportioned—a handsome young man. I heard Hazlett and Leeman, one day, saying that "Barclay Coppoc and Dauphin Thompson were too nearly like good girls to make soldiers"; that they ought to have gone to Kansas and "roughed it" awhile to toughen them, before coming down there. To while away the time the men read magazines, sang, told stories, argued questions, played cards and checkers, studied military tactics, and drilled under Stevens. When there was a thunderstorm they would jump about and play, making all kinds of noise to rest themselves, as they thought no one could hear them then.

The plan failed, the capture came, and Brown's trial proceeded swiftly. These were his last stirring words to the court on November 2, 1859:

I have, may it please the Court, a few words to say.

In the first place, I deny everything but what I have all along admitted,—the design on my part to free the slaves. I intended certainly to have made a clean thing of that matter, as I did last winter, when I went into Missouri and there took slaves without the snapping of a gun on either side, moved them through the country, and finally left them in Canada. I designed to have done the same thing again, on a larger scale. That was all I intended. I never did intend murder, or treason, or the destruction of property, or to excite or incite slaves to rebellion, or to make insurrection.

I have another objection; and that is, it is unjust that I should suffer such a penalty. Had I interfered in the manner which I admit, and which I admit has been fairly proved (for I admire the truthfulness and candor of the greater portion of the witnesses who have testified in this case),—had I so interfered in behalf of the rich, the powerful, the intelligent, the so-called great, or in behalf of any of their friends,—either father, mother, brother, sister, wife, or children, or any of that class,—and suffered and sacrificed what I have in this interference, it would have been all right; and every man in this court would have deemed it an act worthy of reward rather than punishment.

This court acknowledges, as I suppose, the validity of the law of God. I see a book kissed here which I supposed to be the Bible, or at least the New Testament. That teaches me that all things whatsoever I would that men should do to me, I should do even so to them. It teaches me, further, to "remember them that are in bonds, as bound with them." I endeavored to act up to that instruction. I say, I am yet too young to understand that God is any respecter of persons. I believe that to have interfered as I have done—as I have always freely admitted I have done—in behalf of His despised poor, was not wrong, but right. Now, if it is deemed necessary that I should forfeit my life for the furtherance of the ends of justice, and mingle my blood further with the blood of my children and with the blood of millions in this slave country whose rights are disregarded by wicked, cruel, and unjust enactments,—I submit; so let it be done!

Let me say one word further.

I feel entirely satisfied with the treatment I have received on my trial. Considering all the circumstances, it has been more generous than I expected. But I feel no consciousness of guilt. I have stated from the first what was my intention, and what was not. I never had any design against the life of any person, nor any disposition to commit treason, or excite slaves to rebel, or make any general insurrection. I never encouraged any man to do so, but always discouraged any idea of that kind.

Let me say, also, a word in regard to the statements made by some of those connected with me. I hear it has been stated by some of them that I have induced them to join me. But the contrary is true. I do not say this to injure them, but as regretting their weakness. There is not one of them but joined me of his own accord, and the greater part of them at their own expense. A number of them I never saw, and never had a word of conversation with, till the day they came to me; and that was for the purpose I have stated.

Now I have done.

During his trial and after it, while he was awaiting execution, Brown wrote the following letters to his family and friends:

CHARLESTOWN, JEFFERSON COUNTY, VA., Oct. 31, 1859.

My dear Wife and Children, every one,—I suppose you have learned before this by the newspapers that two weeks ago to-day we were fighting for our lives at Harper's Ferry; that during the fight Watson was mortally wounded, Oliver killed, William Thompson killed, and Dauphin slightly wounded; that on the following day I was taken prisoner, immediately after which I received several saber-cuts on my head and bayonet-stabs in my body. As nearly as I can learn, Watson died of his wound on Wednesday, the second—or on Thursday, the third—day after I was taken. Dauphin was killed when I was taken, and Anderson I suppose also. I have since been tried, and found guilty of treason, etc., and of murder in the first degree. I have not yet received my sentence. No others of the company with whom you were acquainted were, so far as I can learn, either killed or taken. Under all these terrible calamities I feel quite cheerful in the assurance that God reigns and will overrule all for his glory and the best possible good. I feel no consciousness of guilt in the matter, nor even mortification on account of my imprisonment and irons; and I feel perfectly sure that very soon no member of my family will feel any possible disposition to "blush on my account." Already dear friends at a distance, with kindest sympathy, are cheering me with the assurance that posterity, at least, will do me justice. I shall commend you all together, with my beloved but bereaved daughters-in-law, to their sympathies, which I do not doubt will soon reach you. I also commend you all to Him "whose mercy endureth forever,"—to the God of my fathers, "whose I am, and whom I serve." "He will never leave you nor forsake you," unless you forsake Him. Finally, my dearly beloved, be of good comfort. Be sure to remember and follow my advice, and my example, too, so far as it has been consistent with the holy religion of Jesus Christ,—in which I remain a most firm and humble believer. Never forget the poor, nor think anything you bestow on them to be lost to you, even though they may be black as Ebedmelech, the Ethiopian eunuch, who cared for Jeremiah in the pit of the dungeon; or as black as the one to whom Philip preached Christ. Be sure to entertain strangers, for thereby some have—"Remember them that are in bonds as bound with them."

I am in charge of a jailer like the one who took charge of Paul and Silas; and you may rest assured that both kind hearts and kind faces are more or less about me, while thousands are thirsting for my blood. "These light afflictions, which are but for a moment, shall work out for us a far more exceeding and eternal weight of glory." I hope to be able to write you again. Copy this, Ruth, and send it to your sorrow-stricken brothers to comfort them. Write me a few words in regard to the welfare of all. God Almighty bless you all, and make you "joyful in the midst of all your tribulations!" Write to John Brown, Charlestown, Jefferson County, Va., care of Captain John Avis.

Your affectionate husband and father,
JOHN BROWN.

P.S.—Yesterday, November 2, I was sentenced to be hanged on December 2 next. Do not grieve on my account. I am still quite cheerful. God bless you!

Yours ever,
JOHN BROWN.

CHARLESTOWN, JEFFERSON COUNTY, VA., Nov. 29, 1859.

MRS. GEORGE L. STEARNS, Boston, Mass.

My dear Friend,—No letter I have received since my imprisonment here has given me more satisfaction or comfort than yours of the 8th instant. I am quite cheerful, and was never more happy. Have only time to write a word. May God forever reward you and all yours! My love to all who love their neighbors. I have asked to be spared from having any weak or hypocritical prayers made over me when I am publicly murdered, and that my only religious attendants be poor little dirty, ragged, bareheaded and barefooted slave boys and girls, led by some old gray-headed slave mother.

Farewell! Farewell!

Your friend,
JOHN BROWN.

CHARLESTOWN PRISON, JEFFERSON COUNTY, VA., Nov. 30, 1859.

My dearly beloved Wife, Sons, and Daughters, every one,—As I now begin probably what is the last letter I shall ever write to any of you, I conclude to write to all at the same time. I will mention some little matters particularly applicable to little property concerns in another place.

I recently received a letter from my wife, from near Philadelphia, dated November 22, by which it would seem that she was about giving up the idea of seeing me again. I had written her to come on if she felt equal to the undertaking, but I do not know that she will get my letter in time. It was on her own account, chiefly, that I asked her to stay back. At first I had a most strong desire to see her again, but there appeared to be very serious objections; and should we never meet in this life, I trust that she will in the end be satisfied it was for the best at least, if not most for her comfort.

I am waiting the hour of my public murder with great composure of mind and cheerfulness; feeling the strong assurance that in no other possible way could I be used to so much advantage to the cause of God and of humanity, and that nothing that either I or all my family have sacrificed or suffered will be lost. The reflection that a wise and merciful as well as just and holy God rules not only the affairs of this world, but of all worlds, is a rock to set our feet upon under all circumstances,—even those more severely trying ones in which our own feelings and wrongs have placed us. I have now no doubt but that our seeming disaster will ultimately result in the most glorious success. So, my dear shattered and broken family, be of good cheer, and believe and trust in God with all your heart and with all your soul; for he doeth all things well. Do not feel ashamed on my account, nor for one moment despair of the cause or grow weary of well-doing. I bless God I never felt stronger confidence in the certain and near approach of a bright morning and glorious day than I have felt, and do now feel, since my confinement here. I am endeavoring to return, like a poor prodigal, as I am, to my Father, against whom I have always sinned, in the hope that he may kindly and forgivingly meet me, though a very great way off.

Oh, my dear wife and children, would to God you could know how I have been travailing in birth for you all, that no one of you may fail of the grace of God through Jesus Christ; that no one of you may be blind to the truth and glorious light of his Word, in which life and immortality are brought to light. I beseech you, every one, to make the Bible your daily and nightly study, with a child-like, honest, candid, teachable spirit of love and respect for your husband and father. And I beseech the God of my fathers to open all your eyes to the discovery of the truth. You cannot imagine how much you may soon need the consolations of the Christian religion. Circumstances like my own for more than a month past have convinced me, beyond all doubt, of my own great need of some theories treasured up, when our prejudices are excited, our vanity worked up to the highest pitch. Oh, do not trust your eternal all upon the boisterous ocean, without even a helm or compass to aid you in steering! I do not ask of you to throw away your reason; I only ask you to make a candid, sober use of your reason.

My dear young children, will you listen to this last poor admonition of one who can only love you? Oh, be determined at once to give your whole heart to God, and let nothing shake or alter that resolution. You need have no fears of regretting it. Do not be vain and thoughtless, but sober-minded; and let me entreat you all to love the whole remnant of our once great family. Try and build up again your broken walls, and to make the utmost of every stone that is left. Nothing can so tend to make life a blessing as the consciousness that your life and example bless and leave others stronger. Still, it is ground of the utmost comfort to my mind to know that so many of you as have had the opportunity have given some proof of your fidelity to the great family of men. Be faithful unto death:

from the exercise of habitual love to man it cannot be very hard to love his Maker.

I must yet insert the reason for my firm belief in the divine inspiration of the Bible, notwithstanding I am, perhaps, naturally skeptical,—certainly not credulous. I wish all to consider it most thoroughly when you read that blessed book, and see whether you cannot discover such evidence yourselves. It is the purity of heart, filling our minds as well as work and actions, which is everywhere insisted on, that distinguishes it from all the other teachings, that commends it to my conscience. Whether my heart be willing and obedient or not, the inducement that it holds out is another reason of my conviction of its truth and genuineness; but I do not here omit this, my last argument on the Bible, that eternal life is what my soul is panting after this moment. I mention this as a reason for endeavoring to leave a valuable copy of the Bible, to be carefully preserved in remembrance of me, to so many of my posterity, instead of some other book at equal cost.

I beseech you all to live in habitual contentment with moderate circumstances and gains of worldly store, and earnestly to teach this to your children and children's children after you, by example as well as precept. Be determined to know by experience, as soon as may be, whether Bible instruction is of divine origin or not. Be sure to owe no man anything, but to love one another. John Rogers wrote to his children, "Abhor that arrant whore of Rome." John Brown writes to his children to abhor, with undying hatred also, that sum of all villanies,—slavery. Remember, "he that is slow to anger is better than the mighty," and "he that ruleth his spirit than he that taketh a city." Remember also that "they being wise shall shine, and they that turn many to righteousness, as the stars for ever and ever."

And now, dearly beloved family, to God and the work of his grace I commend you all.

Your affectionate husband and father,

JOHN BROWN.

The day of his death arrived, Brown marched to the gallows; but handed to one of his guards a slip of paper containing these prophetic words:

CHARLESTOWN, VA., Dec. 2, 1859.

I, John Brown, am now quite *certain* that the crimes of this *guilty land* will never be purged away but with *blood*. I had, as I now think vainly, flattered myself that without very much bloodshed it might be done.

Book IX
CIVIL WAR AND RECONSTRUCTION

CHAPTER XLIX

BROWN'S LAST words were prophetic indeed. The issue had become national and political. Washington lived in a state of ferment throughout the years immediately preceding the first hostilities. The election of Abraham Lincoln as president in 1860 seemed, since Lincoln in 1858 had taken the stand he did against Stephen A. Douglas in the Illinois debates, evidence enough that there was to be no compromise between north and south. The question of the south's secession from the union, long agitated, became acute; political circles at the capital buzzed with threats, predictions, plans. Charles Francis Adams, grandson of John Quincy Adams, happened to be in Washington during the winter following Lincoln's election; and he set down, then as well as later, his impressions of Seward, Sumner, and Lincoln.

THAT winter * I went on to Washington on the 18th of February, and remained until the 13th of March, staying over Lincoln's inauguration, of which I was a witness. An intensely interesting period, we all in a way realized its nature. And yet I now wonder at our lack of prescience and general incapacity, North and South, to realize even in a remote degree the imminence as well as magnitude of the impending catastrophe. Something would surely happen to avert it! We didn't know what—we couldn't even suggest a "something"; but we clung to the childish belief all the same. Consequently, neither as a whole nor as individuals did we make any preparation. Perhaps it was just as well; and yet there was the flag flying over Fort Sumter, with the eyes of the whole country directed that way! Still, I cannot now but wonder at my own purblindness; for I was at the time in position to know fairly well what was going on, being in close contact with prominent men, and an interested if not a keen observer. Of course I had no share in events or influence over them—no one that I know of did. We were, as I now see, drifting—drifting into an inevitable and close impending war; but this we could not realize, and every day

* 1860.

brought with it reports, doubts, hopes and fears. My father and Governor Seward had by this time been brought into close cooperation. Their policy was simple, and, as I still see it, eminently sensible—though based on an entire misapprehension of the facts, and fore-doomed to failure. Their scheme was to divide the South, by conciliating the northern tier of Slave States, including Virginia especially; and, holding them loyal until the tide of reaction, setting in, should drive the seceding States into a false position from which they would ultimately be compelled to recede. All winter the immediate effort had been to gain time until the Government had been transferred to the newly elected Administration. This essential point had been practically assured through the Virginia election. The peaceful inauguration of Lincoln was now practically certain; the next question was as to the policy he would adopt when he became President. The working theory of my father and of Seward was that the less extreme Slave States—notably Virginia—were in a condition of senseless panic from fear of something terrible intended—some invasion of their constitutional rights, they did not well know what; but, if Lincoln could be safely inaugurated and his Administration set quietly in motion without any overt act of force having taken place on either side, it was not unreasonable to hope this groundless fear would gradually subside, and a strong and rising Union reaction could be anticipated. The question would then settle itself, without bloodshed; and once for all. Wholly mistaken, as the result showed, it was still, at that stage of trouble-development, the only sound theory to work on, at any rate until the possession of the Government was secured. Meanwhile, Lincoln's attitude was wholly unknown. His every movement was jealously watched; his utterances closely followed. In Washington, the Republican party was divided between the extremists and coercionists —of whom Sumner and Chase were the exponents; and the conciliators and opportunists—of whom Seward and my father were chief. With which side would Lincoln be allied? That, North and South, was the question.

That winter I saw in Washington a great deal of Seward, and I still think he was then at his best—truly a statesman. The secession movement had by its force, volume and intensity taken him by surprise. Failing correctly to appreciate conditions, he had shown that he was not a statesman of the first order; but still his attitude, bearing and utterances were statesmanlike. Awaiting final developments, he was conciliatory, patient, and, outwardly, cool and confident. He had formulated a policy based on the careful avoidance of a collision and bloodshed until there had been ample time allowed for reflection and the saving second-thought. The course of subsequent events showed that he was wholly wrong in basing any hopes on this misconception of the real attitude and feelings of the South; but, on the other hand, they also showed that the day of compromise was over, and that the attitude of conciliation, while it might gain valuable time, endangered nothing.

In point of fact, as was found out in the following April, Seward was laboring under a total misconception of the real facts in the case and of the logic of events. If, however, he had been endowed with the prophetic gift and read the future as an open book, I do not now see that his policy or line of conduct at this juncture would have been other than they were in any essential aspect. It was a period of crystallization, North and South; and any attempt at decisive action on either side would have been premature and disastrous. A more far-seeing statesman would, perhaps, have occupied himself, very quietly, in the work of preparation, observing the course of events and—biding his time! But this again was, practically, the course pursued; the Executive Government was still in the old hands—untransferred; Congress was composed largely of future Confederates; and whatever was done had to be done through the States. So, even now, I cannot see any error or weakness in Seward's attitude and policy. My father acted in close harmony with him; totally misapprehending, he also, the nature of the situation, and wholly failing to realize the intensity of the forces at work. Since the election, Lincoln had hitherto maintained a Sphinx-like silence. He was still at Springfield, while Seward, understood to be the coming Secretary of State, had found himself compelled to formulate such a policy as he might, without any means of knowing the mind of his future chief, or forecasting his policy and action.

Thus when, in February, 1861, I reached my father's house there, the situation in Washington was about as chaotic as was possible. I see it all now; then it was inscrutable to the best informed or the wisest. The simple fact was that the ship was drifting on the rocks of a lee shore; nothing could save it; this, however, was something none of us could bring ourselves to believe. We still clung to a delusive hope that the coming change of commanders would alter the whole aspect of the situation, and we would work clear. Meanwhile, where and what sort of a man was the new commander? That conundrum was foremost in all minds. Abraham Lincoln was an absolutely unknown quantity; and yet he was the one possible *Deus ex machina!*

The President-elect had left Springfield on the 11th. In the interim his silence had been broken; he had been doing a good deal of talking.

I reached Washington on the afternoon of Tuesday, the 19th of February. My father's house on K Street Northwest, near Pennsylvania Avenue, was full; so I was quartered in lodgings at Jost's, on Pennsylvania Avenue—the place, by the way, where Russell, of the London *Times*, lived shortly after, and from the windows of which he observed the condition of Washington's main thoroughfare in the days succeeding Bull Run. My brother Henry was acting as secretary to my father, and he also was living at Jost's, where he met me on my arrival.

My own narrative begins at my meeting him on that Tuesday afternoon in February, 1861. It ran thus: "Hardly daring to put to him a question, I prepared for dinner. We all sat down [at my father's house] but, somehow or other, while the talking was fast, all present were evidently blue as indigo. Evil was in the air; and I felt it. I finally got a clew to the trouble in a feminine outburst on the mention of our President-elect's name, and it became at once apparent that his recent peripatetic oratory on his route to Washington had by no means served to elevate him in the estimation of the Adams family circle. Little was said, however, until dinner was over; when, at last, my father gave mouth. Temporarily, it then appeared, the fat was all in the fire. He did not hesitate to say that, ten days before, the whole game was in Seward's hands; but now it was surrendered again to the chapter of accidents. The difficulty was wholly owing to Lincoln's folly in not consulting with his official advisers, but saying whatever came into his head. Thus he was dividing his party deplorably—destroying the chance of union in action. Seward's position had thus been made lamentable; for, with his strength exhausted, he was surrounded by opponents, friends and foes; and here now was Lincoln, without consultation or understanding with Seward, and with no apparent regard for the policy indicated by him, showing an ignorance as complete as lamentable of the position of public affairs, fomenting dissensions and jealousies already too formidable. Jeopardizing, in fact, the only hope of the country's salvation. The present indications were that the extremists—the Sumners and Greeleys—had prevailed, and that Seward had been thrown overboard. In which case, my father did not hesitate to say that he expected war within sixty days."

In point of fact, and as afterwards appeared, Seward was not thrown over, and Lincoln had not joined the extremists; but we did have war in exactly fifty-three days from that talking. My record then goes on: "Later in the evening I had quite a long talk to the same effect. He [my father] told me that a few days before Governor Hicks, of Maryland, Andrew Johnson, and Cassius M. Clay had offered to answer for their States on the basis of the propositions of the Committee of Thirty-three; and that Mr. Rives, of the Virginia State Senate, had told him that, upon those propositions, they could carry every Virginia district in the spring election; but, in consequence of the developments of the last few days the whole aspect of affairs had changed, and Seward was at that time more depressed than he had been previously during the whole Winter—in fact no man in Washington then knew where he was standing: I walked home, blue enough. The very knowledge of the military preparations going on all about gave me in the darkness a feeling almost approaching fear. In my letters I had all winter long noted the sudden and violent transitions from extreme exultation to the depths of despair; but I had not learnt from experience. I now felt as much in doubt as if this had been my first experience of a panic, and asked myself in vain—Where is it all to end? The issue seemed made up, and the result in the worst possible hands—those of the Virginia Convention. We sat in Jost's discussing the gloomy aspect of affairs until long after midnight; but, though I felt that my nerves had received a considerable shock, I did not notice that my night's sleep was troubled."

I had gone on to Washington in company with Arthur Dexter of Boston (H. U. 1851), a grandson of Samuel Dexter, Secretary of War in the Cabinet of John Adams, and then on intimate terms with my family generally. Two days after our arrival we went together to the Capitol, and I sent in my cards to Mr. Sumner and Governor Seward, not having seen the last since I left his house at Auburn, in the previous October. "Summer came out almost immediately, greeting me most cordially, and at once invited us round to the cloakroom. On the way we passed a rather tall, strongly built man, with black hair and a swarthy complexion, who, Sumner said, was Andrew Johnson, of Tennessee, and immediately introduced me to him. Mr. Johnson shook hands with me, and at once referred to the fact that he had formerly sat next to my grandfather in the House of Representatives, occupied his seat during his first illness, and seen him fall in his last. Mr. Johnson's manners are quite gentle, though slightly formal. He has a deep, black eye, and, with his somewhat neat black clothes and clean-shaven face, looks, physically and intellectually, like a strong man. While talking with him, I turned round and my eyes fell on Seward, just coming out of one of the side doors in the lobby. There he was, the same small, thin, sallow man, with the pale, wrinkled, strongly marked face—plain and imperturbable—the thick, guttural voice and the everlasting cigar. Yet it was immediately apparent that his winter's cares had told on him, for he looked thin and worn, and ten years older than when I had left him at Auburn. I went into the cloakroom, and sat down with Sumner; but, seeing Wilkinson, of Minnesota, in the Senate-chamber, I sent in for him. The conversation soon turned on the one topic of the day, and for the first time I realized that I was in Washington, and how intense was the excitement and how bitter the feeling. It was immediately apparent that all these men had been brooding over the questions at issue and dwelling on them till their minds had lost their tone, and become morbid. They were in fact now the last men in the country to be entrusted with responsibility. The conversation was long, interesting and excited. Wilkinson was riding the high blood-and-thunder horse; but, after uttering one or two excited platitudes about Major Anderson and 'the traitors,' and looking somewhat surprised when I remarked that 'all that might do very well for the hustings but wouldn't go down with me,' he subsided." I ought, by the way, to say here that, while in the Northwest with Seward in September, I had seen a great deal of Wilkinson, and quite intimately; and had "sized him up." He was no grave or potent Senator to me; and he knew it well enough. But to return to my diary. Wilkinson subsided; but "not so Sumner. I had heard that he was excited, but his manner and language amazed me. He talked like a crazy man, orating, gesticulating, rolling out deep periods in theatrical, whispered tones,—repeating himself, and doing everything but reason. He began by remarking in a deep, low voice and with earnest gestures that 'the session was drawing to a close, and the only question of real practical statesmanship before it had not been touched and would not be touched—that was the treatment to be accorded to the seceding States—the only question of true statesmanship.' I suggested that this question was not at all a new one; that secession was but another name for revolution; and, accordingly, it was but the old question of the treatment of revolution, and nothing more! This idea seemed rather to stagger him, and he passed on to talk of what he called 'the compromisers'—meaning Seward and my father. In less than five minutes, however, he was back on his old topic of 'the one true question of real statesmanship'; and this he kept reiterating, each time more excitedly until our conversation came to a close. I soon saw that reason was out of the question, and the only course for me was to hold my tongue, letting him run down. Still, I could not resist the temptation now and again to put a spoke in his wheel; but it was not possible to throw him off the track, he merely gave a bump and a jerk, and went on fiercer in his utter disregard of logic and policy. His attack was on Seward and 'the compromisers'; 'he had thought of this matter in the daytime, and lay awake over it whole nights; it was all clear to him; to him, his path was as clear as day,' and then he reverted with a jolt to 'the one question.' 'Seward,' he went on, 'did not realize the true position of affairs; he had been demented all the session, and the film had not yet cleared from his eyes. He was demoralizing the North. If he had but held firmly to his position, and refused all parley with secessionists, all would have been well. An appeal should have been made to the loyal, Union-loving feeling of the border Slave States, and all would have been well.' 'Seward,' he said, 'had read to him his speech, and to him only of the Senate,' and he then proceeded to orate; with intense feeling and animated gesticulation, he described how he 'had pleaded with him, he had prayed him, besought him, implored him by his past record, his good name, his memory hereafter' to omit certain passages. Had he done so, 'assuming the pure ground of his party, the whole North would have rallied to him;—but now—too late!—too late!' Then he would reiterate: 'I am sure—I am certain—I see my way so clearly; such a glorious victory was before us; right was with us, God was with us—our success was sure did we only hold firmly to our principles.' Once I lost my patience, and attempted to stop the conversation as not likely to lead to any good result; but at this he got angry, and said that I was discussing, not he; that I began it; and then he went straight on, for, evidently, he could think of nothing else. It was very painful. The man talked so without reason, and almost without connection; and yet he gave me distinctly to understand that he alone could now guide affairs; that Seward was a mere politician vainly trying to deal with great issues. I was disgusted, shocked and mortified; the more because of Dexter's presence, who entertains for Sumner a pet aversion. Finally Seward came out; and what a relief it was! Thin and pale, but calm, gentle and patient, he was as philosophical as ever, as pleasant and companionable; and I now realized his position. With a formidable enemy in front and such allies around—foolish, positive, angry—it was a general-of-division in battle, his reserves used up and waiting for reënforcements—praying for night or Blücher. And meanwhile, Lincoln, his Blücher, was perambulating the country, kissing little girls and growing whiskers! We talked for a few moments only, as he was quite busy. He said that half the men there—indicating the Senate-chamber—were intent on pulling the house down, and he was merely trying to prevent them; that he was very much occupied, for the women and children of the whole South were writing to him, and looking to him for protection.

"As we walked home, we passed the artillery. It was the first time I had seen them. Washington is almost in a state of siege. Every morning and evening I hear from my room the bugles and drums of no less than three companies quartered almost within a stone's throw of us."

Even now I can see Sumner's eyes gleaming with something distinctly suggestive of insanity, as he rolled out his oratorical periods. He was plainly off his balance, nor did I ever again feel towards him as before. What policy did he propose? What course of action was it that was so clear to him?—that would result so immediately in a glorious victory? It is most unfortunate that when then in Washington I was not a little older, and did not have a good deal more tact and objectiveness. Had I been so blessed, I might have learned and recorded—for I was industrious enough with my pen, recording indeed at great length—many things now of interest. Sumner's brain was at that time super-heated, his nervous system overloaded. When he got in that condition, and in February, 1861, he was so almost continuously, he seemed surcharged with rhetoric. His voice vibrated with a tremulous depth, he orated, he laid down the law. Had I only had the sense to invite him to do so, he would have disclosed the heart of his mystery. As it is I have had to piece together a plausible hypothesis.

I understood the position of Wilkinson at that crisis. It was as simple as it was senseless. He wanted to fight "the traitors" then and there, regardless of conditions. That the machinery of government was still in the hands of the old régime, that we had neither army nor navy, that a precipitate act would bring on a premature crisis— none of these things did he take into account. He was just mad; and he wanted to get at the "traitors." The course he suggested was not sensible; but it could be understood. Not so Sumner. What curious hallucination did he then have in his head? What was he driving at when he orated and reiterated his "one question of true statesmanship, which had not even been touched"? What was that proposed mysterious treatment of the seceding States? This question has interested me, because it was here that my father broke with Sumner, and their intimacy ceased for good. After that, I never met him again on the old footing. Either he had become perverted or I had developed. Possibly both.

That Sumner was an agitator, a rhetorician and a theorist—in a word, an egotistical doctrinaire—is well understood. As such he was devoid of hard common sense and true sagacity of insight. He saw every situation through his feelings, often overexcited, and he evolved his facts from his inner consciousness. His mind had dwelt on the issues which now presented themselves, waking and sleeping, until he had ceased to be a reasoning being; and his friends at times feared for his sanity. His mission was to denounce Seward, and, if possible, force him from public life. He openly declared Seward ready to sell us out. In February, 1861, he was actually haunted with fear of some compromise. In point of fact the time for compromise was past; *that* any clear-sighted, well-informed man should have seen, and ceased to concern himself with the thought of it. Sumner still regarded it as the one great danger. The policy he had in mind—concerning the results of which he felt such absolute certainty of conviction—was in reality based on an hallucination and a complete misapprehension of the facts of the situation.

His idea was that the Republican party should take what he called a lofty moral stand. Firm, absolutely unyielding, it should use no word of conciliation, much less make any suggestion of compromise. It should, on the contrary, go straight forward in its course; and then came in his utter inability to comprehend the slave-holding character and the situation in the South. He fully believed that "firmness," as he called it, was all that was necessary; in its presence they would yield, like petulant, passionate children, prone to violence. He looked upon the whole slave-holding class as a combination of ruffianism and bluster, whisky-drinking and tobacco-chewing. In dealing with them "firmness" was essential; by them, any word of concession would be construed into an indication of fear or symptom of weakness, and do infinite mischief. When, in June, 1861, Russell, of the *Times*, got back to Washington from his trip through the Confederacy he pronounced Mr. Sumner as "ignorant of the whole condition of things below Mason and Dixon's line as he was of the politics of Timbuctoo." So in February—three months previous—he derived his confidence from the wholly imaginary condition of affairs, evolved from his own inner consciousness. As he implied in his talk with me, he believed fully in the existence of a strong Union sentiment—a really predominating sentiment—in all the border Slave States. That sentiment he considered was "debauched," as he expressed it, or, more properly, demoralized by any word of conciliation. Those entertaining it "besought us" not so to weaken them. If, on the contrary, the "slaveocracy" was met with absolutely unyielding firmness the people now cowed by it would assert themselves, and the "slaveocracy" would yield. But how about the seceding States—those below South Carolina and bordering on the Gulf? There was where his question—"the only question"—of "true statesmanship" came in; and there was my cause of mystification. He never intimated to me, but his solution of that difficulty was "to let them go," he "would not lift a finger to retain them." We would be well rid of them and their slavery. This explanation of his theory never suggested itself to me at the time of our conversation, and I only became aware of it recently in reading Russell's *Diary* and Yarnall's *Recollections,* but it accounts for all he said in the talk I have narrated. His theory was that, in presence of a display of absolute firmness at Washington, the border States would, in the end, adhere to the Union, and the Gulf States, after a sufficient exhibition of bluster and rhodomontade, resulting in their secession, would come back into the Union on our own terms. So, let them go; there need be no war. Only be "firm" and it would in the near future be a complete and glorious triumph; only Seward's and my father's weakness now jeopardized it. No sillier figment ever gained footing in agitator's imagination; *that* subsequent events demonstrated to him. The supposed Union sentiment did not exist in the border Slave States; it was both the intention and in the power of the extreme Slave States to precipitate a conflict; the possession of the National Capital would, as he well knew, be in dispute. Such, however, was in February, 1861, the policy which Charles Sumner felt absolutely certain would afford a plain and easy way to glorious and permanent victory!

As I look back on it—recalling those days of doubt and pain—we were all wrong; a band of men—anxious, excited, blind or blindfolded—some passionate and vindictive; ready, ripe for blows, all groping their way to a dreaded result; but Sumner was the most wrong and the blindest of the whole throng; though by all odds the most certain in his own clearness of vision and knowledge of the facts. Seward and my father were in his belief wrong; for they fixed their eyes on the change of administration, and looked no further, confidently believing that a reaction would then set in, and reason reassert itself. Seward so told Russell, of the *Times,* speaking with perfect confidence only five days before Sumter: "the States would come back at the rate of one a month." The "compromisers," as Sumner called them, referring always to Seward and my father, but who in reality were Crittenden and the supporters of his East-and-West line project, were so very wrong as to call for no comment; for the Southern extremists—let alone the Northern Republicans—would not consider it, and were intent on a separate, slave-holding nationality, and nothing short of that. The day for compromise on that basis was wholly past. On the other hand, the Northern extremists were wrong, for they, after the manner of my friend, Wilkinson, wholly underestimated their enemy. On the whole, there-fore, up to this point—the change of administration—Seward and my father were the coolest and wisest counselors. They were wrong in their understanding of the ultimate and fundamental facts of the situation; but their error implied no consequences. They proposed to get possession of the machinery of the Government; that was abso-lutely essential. That secured, they counted on a sullen but un-demonstrative attitude on the part of the seceded States, and a strong and increasing reaction in the border States; and, if in this they proved mistaken, a policy of another character must then be shaped to meet events as they developed. In such case the true course could not yet be foreseen. That was the only statesmanship possible in the situation as it then was; and the event fully justified it.

Unfortunately for Seward, following this wise policy until the close of April, when he then at last found his hopes vanishing; when, plainly, no reaction in the border States was to be longer hoped for, and the problem of the Southern forts pressed for an immediate solution—could, indeed, no longer be deferred—then, one day, Seward lost his head. He found himself fairly beyond his depth; and he plunged! The foreign-war panacea took possession of him; and he yielded to it. Then, once for all, he showed himself unequal to the great occasion; his limitations became apparent. The fact is, as I now see him, Seward was an able, a specious and adroit, and a very versatile man; but he escaped being really great. He made a parade of philosophy, and by it I was very effectually de-ceived; but it was not the genuine article. It was, on the contrary, something else—stuff of a very flimsy texture. Seward was not well grounded either in learning or in the facts surrounding him—did not have a strong, firm grasp. He was, after all, as men instinctively felt, more of a politician than a statesman. Perhaps my own im-pression could best be conveyed—looking back on him now through the perspective of forty years—by saying that he was an adroit politician and pseudo-statesman, having in him a dash of the phi-losopher. He was patient, good-tempered, tolerant, and a great be-liever in his countrymen and their institutions. Sumner, on the other hand, I knew better. He was a very considerable historical figure—the most considerable in Massachusetts during my time. As I have already said, a theorist, agitator and rhetorician, a doc-trinaire with no real insight into men and conditions, Sumner was a tremendous egotist and woefully lacking in plain common sense. Strange to say, by no means a bad politician, he was no statesman. Intolerant to the last degree when any issue he had at heart was involved, he was as a Senator great, and, in many respects, ideal. He was there essentially a round peg in a round hole; and he filled the hole, also, though by no means a small one.

I left off on the 21st of February. On the 22d, a dull, murky day, Henry and I dined at Arlington, with the family of General Lee. He was not there, and I never had even a glance at him; though, possibly, I may have seen him one day shortly after, as I was riding away from Arlington after a morning call. If I did, he was going up the Avenue in a carriage, just returned from Texas; and he looked at my sister and myself from the window—curiously —a military, handsome man, with a short, gray beard. The dinner at Arlington was interesting, and I remember it well. One of General Lee's sons had been a classmate of Henry's at Harvard. A daughter, Miss Agnes, I thought extremely attractive. We had some young officers of artillery there. A few months later we were all arrayed against each other; and I fancy there must have been fully half-a-dozen future generals and colonels about the Arlington table that day.

The evening of the 28th I passed with Andrew Johnson, whose acquaintance I had made in the Senate waiting-room a few days before. Johnson was then at the highest point of his reputation. A Southern Unionist, a "poor white" of Eastern Tennessee, who, by native energy, had elevated himself to the Senate, he was holding his own there against Davis and all the representatives of Sumner's "Slaveocracy," who were trying in vain to dragoon him. It was not given us to look into the future, and see Andrew Johnson as he later on exhibited himself from the unfortunate altitude to which Booth's pistol elevated him. In February, 1861, he bore himself very gallantly in a most trying position. And so I wisely called on him, with a view to better acquaintance. "I found him at home in his hotel, stived up in one miserable room, littered with folded speeches and copies of public documents, and otherwise containing a bed and some scanty chamber furniture. He received me cordially, and introduced me to his son, a by no means distinguished-looking specimen of the young Tennesseean. As we talked, he paced slowly up and down the room, or sat facing me, speaking slowly and very carefully, with force though not with much feeling. We first discussed a convention election which had just been held in North Carolina, with the result of which he was greatly elated, though to evince feeling one way or the other is evidently no part of his philosophy. The great thing about the man is evidently his nerve— his apparent force and coolness in a position of danger. I spoke to him of his colleague, Nicholson. 'I can't,' he said, 'speak with freedom of my colleague because of our position; but when I became convinced that this conspiracy existed, it seemed to me very desirable that we should act together, and I consulted him. But I soon found that he had been swept away in the general current. When I spoke to him, Sir, there was dismay depicted on that man's countenance.' 'But,' he went on to add, 'though I can't speak of him personally, I will make a general remark, with no particular application: there are, you know, some men of a nature so selfish and conceited that they can't take a broad, generous view of any subject; and so mean and cowardly that they dare not pursue it if they could.' Of Sumner, he said that he knew him slightly—enough to exchange ordinary civilties; but he seemed to him on the present issues to be morbid and diseased, in fact, actually crazy. The feeling towards him on the Democratic side of the Senate he described as one of rather 'contempt' than anything else. He talked freely of political questions, agreeing with me that no remark had ever been more ingeniously misconstrued and misrepresented than Seward's 'irrepressible conflict'; and he admitted that slavery was, as an institution, opposed to the spirit of Christianity. The constitutional amendment framed by my father [and which Lincoln expressly approved in his inaugural of the following week] he said was enough for him to go home on, and sustain himself in Tennessee. He then went off on the secession conspiracy. He declared that nearly all the Senators from the South were parties to it, and he was afraid that Breckenridge and 'Joe' Lane were both of them in it. He was most amusingly severe over the secession of Florida. 'There's that Yulee,' he said, 'miserable little cuss! I remember him in the House—the contemptible little Jew—standing there and begging us—yes! begging us to let Florida in as a State. Well! we let her in, and took care of her, and fought her Indians; and now that despicable little beggar stands up in the Senate and talks about *her* rights.' Towards Jews, he evidently felt a strong aversion; for, after finishing with Yulee he began on Benjamin, exclaiming: 'There's another Jew—that miserable Benjamin! He looks on a country and a government as he would on a suit of old clothes. He sold out the old one; and he would sell out the new if he could in so doing make two or three millions.' The seceded States, he said, must come back; the remote and northern portions of the States would, he declared, pass other ordinances, and bring them back. He denounced Wigfall, of Texas, as 'a damned blackguard,' who hadn't a cent, and 'that's his way! the strongest secessionists never owned the hair of a nigger.' His conclusion was that somebody would be, and ought to be, hanged for all this. I was with him about an hour and a half, and left, considerably edified by Andrew Johnson."

On Sunday, March 3d, the day preceding Lincoln's inauguration, I called on the Sewards in the afternoon. Seward then said, referring to Lincoln and his intercourse with him: "The President has a curious vein of sentiment running through his thought, which is his most valuable mental attribute." Long subsequent events gave a noticeable significance to those words, and caused me to bear them freshly in recollection. They showed, in my opinion, not only considerable insight, but a most creditable spirit of appreciation on Seward's part. Few men in public life, then or now, would have noticed the attribute at all; and the few who did would, most of them, have taken it as an element of weakness. It was one of not a few casual remarks of Seward in those days which have caused me to realize that, with all his "outs," he was after all a man of finer fiber than the rest.

Lincoln's inauguration (Monday) came with a sudden change of weather. The sun shone brightly, but a strong wind carried on its clouds of that Washington dust, which, then much more than now—for the streets were not yet asphalted—was wont to render walking detestable on days of early March. From the Senate gallery I saw Lincoln walk in, arm in arm with Buchanan, and the two seated themselves in front of the desk of the Vice-President. And, "in spite of the wry neck and dubious eye, the outgoing President was," to my mind, "undeniably the more presentable man of the two; his tall, large figure, and white head, looked well beside Mr. Lincoln's lank, angular form and hirsute face; and the dress of the President-elect did not indicate that knowledge of the proprieties of the place which was desirable." Then followed the inaugural, delivered from "the miserable scaffold" on the east front before "a vast sea, not exactly of upturned human faces, but of hats and shirt-bosoms of all descriptions." Of the inaugural, I did not hear one word; for I was standing on a projection of the unfinished Senate wing of the Capitol, watching the scene, and was thus too far removed. But "Mr. Lincoln's delivery struck me as good; for it was quiet, with but little gesture and small pretense of oratory; the audience did not strike me as very enthusiastic—not such as they tell us hailed Jackson when he stood on the same steps on the occasion of the first invasion of Washington by the hordes of the youthful West—but it was silent, attentive, appreciative, and wonderfully respectable and orderly. At length a louder and more prolonged cheer announced that the inaugural was delivered. The Chief Justice administered the oath of office, and the long, eager, anxious struggle was over. A Republican President was safely inaugurated.

"Not until the ceremony was over did the curious cease to speculate as to the probabilities of 'a bead being drawn on Mr. Lincoln,' and the chances of assassination; and the question was curiously discussed whether the whole South would not yet furnish one Ravaillac." Now the procession was reformed, and the new President was escorted to the White House. I started for home. As I walked up by way of F Street and the Patent Office, parallel with Pennsylvania Avenue, the procession's route, I chanced to meet Mr. Sumner, and joined him. "He seemed satisfied with the inaugural, and remarked of it: 'I do not suppose Lincoln had it in his mind, if indeed he ever heard of it; but the inaugural seems to me best described by Napoleon's simile of "a hand of iron and a velvet glove."'" At home, on the other hand, I found my father in high glee over the endorsement that same inaugural gave him, and he was declaring the party saved. I also met Winter Davis, who pronounced himself as ready to stand on the President's position. Thus, that day, every one was, as Seward predicted they would be, "satisfied."

Returning to my walk home with Mr. Sumner; "all day I had looked in vain for the tall, commanding figure of General Scott; he was not in the procession; he was not in the Senate. As I left the Capitol" and was walking homeward in company with Mr. Sumner, I came, at one of the intersecting avenues where a view was obtained in several directions, "upon a small carriage, drawn by a single horse and surrounded by mounted staff officers and orderlies, the whole the center of a crowd of idlers. It was Scott's carriage, and in it sat the old General himself, in full uniform, anxiously observing the procession as it passed in the street beyond, and holding himself ready for any emergency. What was now dreaded was, of course, assassination followed by riot and panic, and an immediate necessity for a display of force; the fear of a *coup de main* was passed." Mr. Sumner stopped, and exchanged greetings with Scott through the open window of his carriage. The old General shook hands with us, and seemed in high spirits and greatly relieved, as he watched intently the perfectly quiet progress of events below, on Pennsylvania Avenue. In his staff were several officers destined soon to have high rank and participate in great movements; they also were now in high spirits—satisfied with themselves, and feeling that the situation was well in hand. We walked in a street converging with the movement of the procession, which, at length, "enveloped in its cloud of dust, reached the White House, and I drew a long breath when I saw Mr. Lincoln leave his carriage; and turned away confident that the last danger was passed."

We all, the hope being father of the thought, had then nursed ourselves into a feverish faith, and anxious rather than real belief that, with a peaceful inauguration, the crisis would be really in safety "passed," and I closed this letter of mine in that spirit. "From this time," I wrote, "the secession experiment, I believe, will die away, and the Union feeling rise almost visibly, day by day, unless again the secession feeling is revived by some sort of strange folly on the part of the Administration. Within the last few days I have conversed with many men from the South, including even South Carolina, and all announce a better, kinder state of feeling, needing only gentleness and concilation to ripen into Union." The one fact to which we then pinned our faith in an ultimate peaceful solution was in the avoidance as yet of any act of overt violence resulting in the shedding of blood. Until this should actually occur we nourished a hope, amounting almost to faith, that, somehow or other, it was fated not to occur. Yet all the time we were conscious that we were drifting with neither guidance nor control. It was a period of anxious suspense; a fading reliance on "something."

A few days later, I attended the new President's first evening levee. "A pretty business it was. Such a crush was, I imagine, never seen in the White House before, on a similar, or any other occasion. After two vain attempts to get into the reception room, Dexter and I resolutely set ourselves in the main current, and were pushed and squeezed along. It was a motley crowd. There they were—the sovereigns; some in evening dress, others in morning suits; with gloves and without gloves; clean and dirty; all pressing in the same direction, and all behaving with perfect propriety. There was no ill temper; no vulgarity or noise; no rudeness; in spite of the crowd and discomfort, everything was respectful and decorous. The sight was one not pleasant to see, and even less pleasant to participate in; but still good of its kind. Here, as everywhere, the people governed themselves. At last, after the breath was nearly out of our bodies, Dexter and I came in sight of the President—the tall, rapidly bobbing head of the good 'Abe,' as he shook hands with his guests, and quickly passed them along. The vastly greater number he hurried by him; but, when any one he knew came along, he bent himself down to the necessary level, and seemed to whisper a few words in the ear, in pleasant, homely fashion; though not exactly in one becoming our President. I hurried by as quickly as I could, and retreated into the rear of the room, there to observe. I stayed about an hour and a half, meeting Mr. Sumner, Mr. and Mrs. S. A.

Douglas and others, and subsequently, leaving by the south front, reached home with 'tir'd eyelids upon tir'd eyes.' "

Presently Sumner came, and that was the last time he ever sat at my father's table—he who, for over a dozen years, had been the guest most constant at it. It was, and to my mind, still is a great pity; and there was no sufficient reason for a break. However, that day I got Mr. Sumner there once more, and, as it proved, for the last time. "He was in great feather. Such a wonderful change I never saw in mortal man. The excitement and other peculiarities, which had so disgusted me in our previous interviews during this visit to Washington, had disappeared. They had vanished wholly under the soothing influence of success, and beneath the calm dignity of the chairmanship of the Senate Committee on Foreign Affairs. He now aired his new importance; and, in place of his former fierceness, he roared as gently as a sucking dove. The pleasant way in which he looked upon propositions, which, only the week before, were 'compromises' with Hell, was, indeed, beautiful to behold. To-day he was great! He talked of Seward and the diplomatic corps; and told us all the secrets of the Cabinet, so far as he knew them; how Mrs. Lincoln wanted to make a Collector of the Port of Boston, on account of her son 'Bobby,' and *had* made a naval officer; how disgusted the diplomatic corps was at the possible nomination of Schurz to Turin; how Lincoln and Seward had a conversation about Schurz, in which Seward convinced Lincoln that Schurz ought not to be sent, and Lincoln sent him to Seward, for them to fight the matter out together; how the Western barbarians had invaded the White House, and Mr. Lincoln was meddling with every office in the gift of the Executive. Finally I took myself off, leaving him in my father's hands."

That evening I went to the reception at Mrs. Eames's. "If the President caught it at dinner, his wife caught it at the reception. All manner of stories about her were flying around; she wanted to do the right thing, but, not knowing how, was too weak and proud to ask; she was going to put the White House on an economical basis, and, to that end, was about to dismiss 'the help' as she called the servants; some of whom, it was asserted, had already left because 'they must live with gentlefolks'; she had got hold of newspaper reporters and railroad conductors, as the best persons to go to for advice and direction. Numberless stories of this sort were current; and, while Mrs. Lincoln was in a stew, it was obvious that her friends, the Illinoisans, were in a rumpus. Much fun is brewing in Washington." It was now the dead season in Washington, or rather, that year, the season of lull before the fierce bursting of the storm.

Congress had dispersed; and expectancy was in the air, with greedy office-seekers thronging streets and corridors. And such streets and such corridors! The unheroic was much in evidence.

We all left Washington on the 13th. By the 10th of the month the Cabinet complications, which reached a climax three weeks later, had begun to develop. The question of mastery was yet to be settled. The President was an absolutely unknown quantity; so much so that a little later, as subsequently appeared, Seward invited him practically to abdicate, delegating full authority to himself. We, of my father's house, were all ardent Sewardites. We thought that in him, and the pursuance of the policy he either had devised, or at the proper time would devise, lay the single chance of peace and the preservation of the Union. As I now see it, his usefulness was, however, in fact then over. He had been of great service, during the interim period, holding things together and tiding over dangerous shoals. This he had done; but he had done it under an entire misapprehension of the real facts of the situation and with an absolutely impossible result in view. As I have said, he believed in the existence of a strong underlying Union sentiment in the South; he looked forward with confidence to a sharp reaction of sentiment there, as soon as the people of those States realized that no harm was intended them; and he nourished the delusive belief that a recourse to force could be avoided; that, if it was avoided or postponed, the secession movement would languish, and gradually die out. Thus he was now exerting all his influence, greater by far than that of any other man, in a wrong direction. The possession of the Government having been secured, the true policy to be pursued, it is now obvious, was to let events take their course, inducing or compelling the seceded States to put themselves in the wrong by assuming the initiative, striking the first blow. A statesman equal to the occasion and grasping the situation in its full scope, would undoubtedly have pursued this course. Gathering his resources, he would have bided his time, perhaps covertly provoking the blow. But Seward was no Bismarck, and this was just the course Seward did not wish to have pursued.

That evening, the 11th, he talked freely. Talking in his offhand way, Seward then expressed to us, as four weeks later he did to Mr. Russell, "the fullest confidence that things were coming out right; but he at the same time admitted that, three months before, it was in no way impossible that Jefferson Davis might, at the time he was speaking to us, have been in possession of Washington. 'Ever since Congress met,' he said, 'we have been on a lee shore. The sails have been flapping, and more than once we have thugged on the bottom; but we have been making offing all the time, and are now getting safely off shore and into deep water.' " As Russell the moment he got into the Confederacy afterwards became satisfied, Seward knew nothing of the real state of feeling in the South. He derived what little knowledge he had from local and unreliable, or misinformed, sources. So, this evening, he did not hesitate to assert that "the fever of secession" was "fast disappearing, before the strong reaction for Union. The political traitors of that region," he said—"the Hunters, Masons, Wises, Clingmans and Garnetts—are trembling for their lives, and their only chance, and they know it, of retaining their power, lies in the revival of the excitement." The abandonment of Fort Sumter, he argued, would therefore not be taken by the South as a sign of weakness, but, on the contrary, would give "a new and tremendous emphasis to the now rapidly reviving Union spirit. The true men of Virginia will, at the close of the coming April, sweep every representative, even suspected of treason, from the National Congress, and forewarn the chuckle-headed Mason and sophistical Hunter of their impending fate; and Virginia would but set an example to other States. To hold Fort Sumter longer" was, therefore, "to stop the mouth and palsy the arm of every Union man, and there are many of them, throughout the seceded States, for no important end." The abandonment of Sumter he considered, therefore, "a mere question of time. It might be done then, and made the basis of a claim of gratitude by the Administration; or it might be done thirty days hence as a matter of necessity, and no credit gained. If we set out to reënforce it, we must join battle at our weakest point, and the enemy's strongest; our loss might be heavy, while our gain could not be great." Thus at this stage of the development of affairs—with a crisis immmediately impending— Seward was pursuing an impossible result in pursuance of a policy devised under an entire misapprehension of facts. Meanwhile, to abandon the Tortugas or Fort Pickens was no part of Mr. Seward's plan. Those could be held and defended; what he had in mind was to avoid a collision at a point where we could not hope to escape defeat.

Accompanied by his family, my father left Washington and returned home, all of us nourishing this delusive hope of peace and a restored Union. Once in Boston, we heard nothing. On the 19th came the telegraphic announcement of my father's nomination to the English Mission.

Presently my father was summoned on to Washington to confer with the Secretary. He was there during the closing days of March, getting home on the 1st of April. I well remember his return. It then lacked only four days of a full month since the inauguration of

Lincoln, and there were no visible signs of that reaction in the sentiment of the South which Seward had looked for with such confidence. On the contrary, though the new Administration did not threaten to resort to coercion, the Confederacy seemed to be fast consolidating. Nor in the border States did the aspect of affairs improve; on the contrary, it day by day grew unmistakably menacing. My diary read as follows: "My father, summoned by Seward to Washington a week ago, got home last night. For several days, now, I have been conscious of a vague presentiment that things were not going well. Instead of righting itself and coming up into the wind as soon as it was free of the incubus of a Democratic Administration—as I all along had so confidently hoped and predicted—the ship seemed, on the contrary, to be steadily and helplessly drifting upon the rocks, Secession and Reconstruction. So strongly had this feeling got a hold on me, that, when my father came into the breakfast-room, I feared to ask him any question on the subject. I did at last; and, at first, he seemed to deny that any change for the worse was apparent. Yet a few more inquiries were enough. It was at once apparent that my apprehensions were not only well founded, but that the real truth was worse than I supposed. We are drifting; and drifting fearfully. Our last card has proved a low one; the card on which we relied for everything. It is not the ace of trumps, but only the deuce; if, indeed, it be a trump card at all."

Whether my father then still clung to the hope of a peaceable solution of the troubles, I cannot say. On that point I never satisfied myself. In immediate presence of the inevitable, I think we were all, and he especially, in a state approaching mental bewilderment; we would not acknowledge that of which we could not help being inwardly conscious. We were, in fact, exactly in the position of people, passengers and landsmen, on some battered hulk drifting slowly but surely on the reefs that outlined a menacing lee shore. The ship had not yet struck, but we waited breathlessly to hear and feel her strike. Seward had in Washington evidently still talked to my father in the old, optimistic, hopeful vein; just as, a week later, he still talked in it to Russell. That, however, would not longer pass current; and for myself, I can only say that, from the moment I saw my father after he got back, I ceased to hope. War, I felt, confronted us. As I wrote, it was a bitter day—"without, a furious snowstorm raging; within, for me at least, doubt, hesitation and gloom." Three days later I wrote: "Fast day! and never did this country stand in greater need of aid from above than now. Still drifting—drifting—drifting! Our case resembles nothing so much as that of a ship, which, close on a lee shore, has only just weathered a violent storm. Morning has broken, not fresh and bright, but murky and sullen. The wind has died away, but a strong undertow is bearing us imperceptibly nearer and nearer those rocks over which tremendous seas are dashing. Unless God helps us, we shall in a few moments be in the breakers." Then follow the usual weak observations and objurgations over the absence of a guiding hand at the helm, useless to repeat now, though natural enough then. Ten days afterwards, on the 14th, I wrote: "The war has begun! Fort Sumter is taken! Two bad announcements together. Yet strangely enough no drop of blood has yet been shed; or rather no life has been lost. Still, the first gun in civil war is fired, and its echoes will reverberate through years."

CHAPTER L

AT THE end of 1860 South Carolina seceded. Within a few months Georgia, Alabama, Mississippi, Louisiana, and Florida had followed suit, and The Confederate States of America came into existence with Jefferson Davis as its president. Still there were efforts to preserve peace between the sections; but war came steadily nearer, and when in April, 1861, the Confederates fired on Fort Sumter at Charleston the Civil War had begun. Both sides prepared; Lincoln called for volunteers to preserve the Union; and Northern armies marched into the south.

The general plan called for an attack in two areas, one to the west and one to the east of the Allegheny mountains. The western attack succeeded before the eastern one did, and furnished the leader who three years later was to supplant a succession of inadequate generals in the main theater of war and bring the Union effort to a successful conclusion.

The issue was long doubtful, and no one knew this better than Charles Francis Adams, who, enlisting at the commencement of the war, served with the Northern cavalry until the end. The letters which he wrote, chiefly to his mother in Massachusetts and to his father and brother Henry at the Court of St. James in England, expressed alternate fear and hope; nor were they always complimentary to the ruling powers.

Quincy, November 26, 1861.

I DON'T know whether you will be surprised or disgusted or annoyed or distressed by the information that I have gone into the army, but such is the fact. Before this reaches you I shall be an officer of the 1st Mass. Cavalry and probably in Carlisle Barracks. You know it now and I am glad of it! You ask what has impelled me to this unadvised and sudden step. Many reasons, I answer; a few of which I will now give you. But in the first place let me say that I have not felt sure of my appointment until within the last five days and that I would have notified you of it before had not former false alarms made me timid of present ones. Now I feel reasonably sure and will give you the reasons of my action. You will say, of course, that the arguments which were decisive against my going two months ago are decisive now in no less degree; but this is not so. I have all along felt that it was my place to represent our family in the army in this struggle, but a higher sense of public duty kept me at home while I was useful to you; and when that usefulness was gone, the argument which had justified my staying at home became one for my going away. I can be of little future use to you here....

For going I have many reasons. I do not think myself a soldier by nature. I am not sure I am doing that which is best for myself; but I feel that, if I go, I shall be better satisfied with myself, and, as I said to you before, I do not think it right that our family, so prominent in this matter while it is a contest of words, should be wholly unrepresented when it has grown to be a conflict of blows. You say there is neither glory nor honor to be won in civil strife. I answer, that it cannot be otherwise than right for me to fight to maintain that which my ancestors passed their whole lives in establishing. These however are general arguments which I have advanced to you before, but there are others nearer home. I have completely failed in my profession and I long to cut myself clear of it. I have indeed derived an income this summer from my office, but not from the law, and that I have made up my mind to give up. This mortifies me and the army must cover my defeat. My future must be business and literature, and I do not see why the army should not educate me for both, for its routine is that of business and it will go hard if my pen is idle while history is to be written or events are to be described. Thus my decision not only closes one career in which I have failed, but it opens others in which experience teaches me I can succeed if at all. . . .

Milne Plantation, Port Royal Island, Monday, April 6, 1862.

Yours of the 14th of February reminds me of our long interrupted correspondence. My last to you, if I remember right, was from on shipboard nearly three months ago, and was of a savage tenor. This is from an old South Carolina plantation, the headquarters of our cavalry pickets, and is likely to be of an eminently pacific tone. Here I am surrounded by troopers, missionaries, contrabands, cotton fields and serpents, in a summer climate, riding immensely every day, dreadfully sick of the monotony of my present existence, disgusted with all things military and fighting off malaria with whiskey and tobacco. So far, the island of Port Royal is a small Paradise, and no men were ever so fortunate in the inception of a military career, barring the immense labor of organizing such a regiment as this and our peculiarly rigid discipline, than we have been. So far our privations have been next to nothing and our career has been more that of a winter picnic than anything else. The future I fear has less agreeable things in store for us.

Cotton fields, pine barrens, contrabands, missionaries and soldiers are before me and all around me. A sick missionary is in the next room, a dozen soldiers are eating their suppers in the yard under my window and some twenty negroes of every age, lazy, submissive and as the white man has made them, are hanging about the plantation buildings just as though they were not the *teterrima causa* of this consuming *bella*. The island is now just passing into its last stage of spring. The nights are cool, but the days are hot enough to make the saddle no seat of comfort. The island, naturally one of the most delightful places in the world, is just now at its most delightful season. The brown unhappy wastes of cotton fields unplanted this year and with the ragged remnants of last year's crop, still fluttering in the wind, do not add to its beauty, but nothing can destroy the charm of the long plantation avenues with the heavy gray moss drooping from branches fresh with young leaves, while the natural hedges for miles along are fragrant with wild flowers.

One can ride indefinitely over this island and never exhaust its infinite cross-roads and out-of-the-way plantations, but you cannot ride fifteen minues in any direction, however new, without stumbling over the two great facts of the day, pickets and contrabands. The pickets are recruits in active service without models—excellent material for soldiers and learning the trade, but scarcely soldiers yet. The contrabands were slaves yesterday and may be again tomorrow, and what slaves are any man may know without himself seeing who will take the trouble to read Olmsted's books. No man seems to realize that here, in this little island, all around us, has begun the solution of this tremendous "nigger" question.

The war here seems to rest and, for the present, Port Royal is thrown into the shade, and yet I am much mistaken if at this minute Port Royal is not a point of greater interest than either Virginia or Kentucky. Here the contraband question has arisen in such proportions that it has got to be met and the Government is meeting it as best it may. Some ten thousand *quondam* slaves are thrown upon the hands of an unfortunate Government; they are the forerunners of hundreds of thousands more, if the plans of the Government succeed, and so the Government may as well now decide what it will do in case of the success of its war plans. While Government has sent agents down here, private philanthropy has sent missionaries, and while the first see that the contrabands earn their bread, the last teach them the alphabet. Between the two I predict diverse results, among which are numerous jobs for agents and missionaries, small comfort to the Negroes and heavy loss to the Government. Doubtless the world must have cotton and must pay for it, but it does not yet know what it is to pay for it if the future hath it in store that the poor world shall buy the next crop of Port Royal at prices remunerative to Government. The scheme, so far as I can see any, seems to be for the Government, recognizing and encouraging private philanthropy and leaving to it the task of educating the slaves to the standard of self-support, to hold itself a sort of guardian to the slave in his indefinite state of transition, exacting from him that amount of labor which he owes to the community and the cotton market. The plan may work well; if it does, it will be the first of the kind that ever has. Certainly I do not envy the slaves its operation. The position of the Government is certainly a most difficult one. Something must be done for these poor people and done at once. They are indolent, shiftless, unable to take care of themselves and plundered by every comer—in short, they are slaves. For the present they must be provided for. It is easy to find fault with the present plan. Can any one suggest a better? For me, I must confess that I cannot. I think it bad, very bad, and that it must end in failure, but I can see no other more likely to succeed.

That this is the solution of the Negro question I take it no one but the missionaries and agents will contend. That is yet to come, and here as elsewhere we are looking for it, and trying to influence it. My own impression is that the solution is coming—may already in some degree be shadowed out; but that it is a solution hurried on by this war, based on simple and immutable principles of economy and one finally over which the efforts of Government and individuals can exercise no control.

This war is killing slavery. Not by any legal quibble of contrabands or doubtful theory of confiscation, but by stimulating free trade. Let any man ride as I do over this land. Let him look at the cotton fields and the laborers. Let him handle their tools and examine their implements, and if he comes from any wheat-growing country, he will think himself amid the institutions and implements of the middle ages—and so he would be. The whole system of cotton growing—all its machinery from the slave to the hoe in his hand—is awkward, cumbrous, expensive and behind the age.

That the cultivation of cotton is so behind that of all the other great staples is the natural result of monopoly, but it is none the less disgraceful to the world, and to give it an impulse seems to have been the mission of this war. The thorough and effectual breaking up of its so much prized monopoly will be the greatest blessing which could happen to the South, and it seems to be the one probable result of this war. Competition involves improvement in ruin, and herein lies the solution of this slavery question. Northern men with Northern ideas of economy, agriculture and improvement, are swarming down onto the South. They see how much behind the times the country is and they see that here is money to be made. If fair competition in the growth of cotton be once established a new system of economy and agriculture must inevitably be introduced here in which the slave and his hoe will make room for the free laborer and the plow, and the change will not be one of election but a sole resource against utter ruin. The men to introduce this change or any other are here and are daily swarming down in the armies of the Government, soon to become armies of occupation. A new tide of emigration has set in before which slavery has small chance.

But how is it for the African? Slavery may perish and no one regret it, but what is to become of the unfortunate African? When we have got thus far we have just arrived at the real point of interest in the "nigger" question. The slaves of whom I see so much here may be taken as fair specimens of their race as at present existing in this country. They have many good qualities. They are good tempered, patient, docile, willing to learn and easily directed; but they are slavish and all that the word slavish implies. They will lie and cheat and steal; they are hypocritical and cunning; they are not brave, and they are not fierce—these qualities the white man took out of them generations ago, and in taking them deprived the African of the capacity for freedom. My views of the future of those I see about me here are not therefore encouraging. That they will be free and free soon by the operation of economic laws over which Government has no control, I thoroughly believe; but their freedom will be the freedom of antiquated and unprofitable machines, the freedom of the hoes they use which will be swept aside to make way for better implements. The slave, however, cannot be swept aside and herein lies the difficulty and the problem. My impression from what I see is that emancipation as a Government measure would be a terrible calamity to the blacks as a race; that rapid emancipation as the result of an economic revolution destroying their value as agricultural machines would be a calamity, though less severe; and finally, that the only transition to freedom absolutely beneficial to them as a race would be one proportioned in length to the length of their captivity, such a one in fact as destroyed villeinage in the wreck of the feudal system. Were men and governments what they should be instead of what they are, the case would be different and all would combine in the Christian and tedious effort to patiently undo the wrongs they had done, and to restore to the African his attributes. Then the work could be done well and quickly; but at present, seeing what men are, and how remorselessly they throw aside what has ceased to be useful, I cannot but regard as a doubtful benefit to the African anything which by diminishing his value increases his chances of freedom.

A revolution in cotton production springing from competition may work differently by gradually changing the *status* of the African from one of forced to one of free labor, but I do not regard this as probable. The census already shows not only that cotton can everywhere be cultivated by free labor, but also that the best cotton now is so cultivated, and the most probable result of a permanent reduction in the price of cotton would seem to me to be a sudden influx of free white emigration into the cotton fields of the South. Such a result would produce untold advantages to the South, to America and to the white race; but how about the blacks? Will they be educated and encouraged and cared for; or will they be challenged to compete in the race, or go to the wall, and finally be swept away as a useless rubbish? Who can answer those queries? I for one cannot; but one thing I daily see and that is that no spirit exists among the contrabands here which would enable them to care for themselves in a race of vigorous competition. The blacks must be cared for or they will perish, and who is to care for them when they cease to be of value? I do not pretend to solve these questions or do more than raise them, and their solution will come, I suppose, all in good time with the emergency which raises them. But no man who dreams at all of the future can wander over Port Royal Island at present and mark the character and condition of its inhabitants, without having all these questions and many more force themselves upon his mind.

John's Island, S. C., June 18, 1862.
You have probably heard, through Southern sources and with their usual degree of truth, of the action yesterday and you may have been anxious for my safety, though I hope you were sufficiently ignorant of all the facts not to be apprehensive for me personally.

The amount of the whole story is that we had a severe action and were repulsed with very heavy loss. This much you know; and for myself, General Williams' brigade was in the advance of one of the attacking columns, was under fire about four hours, during the whole of which time the danger of his men was fully shared by the General and his staff. I would not have missed it for anything. I had never been really under fire before and the sensation was glorious. There we were, mounted officers, either standing right before the enemy's works, while the shells went shrieking and hurtling just over our heads and sometimes broke close to us, or else carrying orders to all parts of the line, feeling that you carried life and death in your hands. I was frightened of course—every one is, except a few who don't know what danger is; but my fear was not what I had imagined it might be. My face was a little fixed I imagine. I knew that my nerves were a little braced, but my mind was never clearer or more easily made up on points of doubt, and altogether the machine worked with a vigor and power which, under the circumstances, I had never hoped it possessed. To all his staff, collectively and individually, General Williams has expressed the highest satisfaction, saying that he was perfectly satisfied and that a difficult and dangerous work could not have been better executed; and if you knew General Bob, and had seen how recklessly he exposed himself, and were aware how he does snub and how he doesn't praise, you would allow that this was something. In a word I don't care if I'm never in action again, and I would rather not run its risk, though I should like once to join in the shouts of victory; but I would not for anything have lost the experience of yesterday and, without affectation, it was one of the most enjoyable days I ever passed.

I don't pretend to give you a history of the engagement. You will get that from the lying prints, and a very false one it will be; but being on the staff I saw all the Generals and all the movements. There was Benham, an old hen, cackling round, insulted by messages from angry Brigadiers sent through boyish aids, and he himself mainly anxious for cover, indecisive, and, many thought, frightened. There was Wright, a little excited at times but growing genial and kindly as the fire grew hot. There was your friend, Stevens, dirty and excited, but clear headed and full of fight, with a dirty straw hat on his head and his trousers above his knees from the friction of riding. And finally, there was handsome Bob Williams astride of his big horse, defiantly planted in front of the battery in open field, full of all sorts of humors—the long saber hanging from the saddle-bow and his eyes beaming, sparkling and snapping according to the turn of the fight. In the hottest fire he grew genial and took the occasion of a shell splashing us with mud to tell me an old and not very good story. Then the retreat was ordered and he grew savage, though not to us; and finally I thought old Benham would have to put him under arrest, he treated him with such undisguised contempt. My rides round the battle-field too were curious. Here was a long line of wounded men toiling to the rear, and the different ways in which they bore their wounds, from the coward limping off untouched to the plucky fellow with his leg hanging by the skin making faces that he might not yell. There were knots of men behind hedges and in the ditches, strag-glers and cowards, men who could not be shamed to the front. To talk of the horrors of a battlefield is a misnomer. The hospital is horrid and so are the stretchers and ambulances running blood; but in the heat of battle a corpse becomes a bundle of old clothes and you pass the most fearful wounds with a mere glance and without a thought.

There was nothing disgraceful in our repulse, and our retreat was a model of good order and regularity. The regiments when over-come retired in column in common step and with their colors flying and formed exactly where their officers ordered. There was no running, no panic, and I felt proud of New England as I saw the 3d N. H. coolly hold their position between two murderous fires. We should have whipped them dreadfully had they fol-lowed us. . . .

Hilton Head, S. C., July 16, 1862.

. . . .

McClellan's reverses fell on us with sufficient weight here and 10,000 of our troops are being hurried to the north, destroying all chance of operations here and leaving only artillery to hold these points. For artillery and cavalry they say they do not need, so our poor regiment seems likely to go into garrison duty in the midst of active war, and that too when all the operations of the war in Virginia indicate the vital necessity of good cavalry and this regi-ment is here considered the best in our volunteer service. However personal consideration don't amount to much and I want to dis-cuss the news and its effects. How do you look at this terrible fighting in Virginia? Not, I mean, in a military or even immediate point of view, but in its remote bearing on our country's future? For myself I must confess I begin to be frightened. The questions of the future seem to me too great for us to grapple with success-fully and I have really begun to fear anarchy and disorganization for years to come. If we succeed in our attempt at subjugation, I see only an immense territory and a savage and ignorant populace to be held down by force, the enigma of slavery to be settled by us somehow, right or wrong, and, most dangerous of all, a spirit of blind, revengeful fanaticism in the North, of which Sumner has come in my mind to be typical, which, utterly deficient in practical wisdom, will, if it can, force our country into any position—be it bankrupt, despotic, anarchical, or what not—in its blind efforts to destroy slavery and the South. These men, and they will always in troubulous times obtain temporary supreme control, will bankrupt the nation, jeopard all liberty by immense standing armies, debauch the morality of the nation by war, and undermine all our republican foundations to effect the immediate destruction of the one institution of slavery. Do you not think that this is so? . . .

Willard's Hotel, Washington, August 27, 1862.

Here I am once more in the city of Washington. Since I last wrote the first detachment of our regiment has arrived at Fortress Monroe, and is now in camp at Acquia Creek, while I have come up here to see about this business of Pope's staff. I find the old city much as usual, but still not the same. It was indeed pleasant for me to get here and at least to see something familiar once more, and I looked at all the public buildings and even at Willard's as at old friends. Once more I have really slept in a bed and I really never enjoyed anything in my life, in its kind, more than the delicious little supper which Gautier got up for me. You don't know how much eight months of coarse fare improve one's faculties for gastronomic enjoyment, and last evening I experienced a new sensation.

Here I am though, and what next? Shall I go onto Pope's staff? I think not. This is a very different place from Hilton Head and here I am learning many strange things which make me open my eyes very wide, which make me sorrow over our past and do not encourage me for the future. Here I have access to certain means of information and I think I can give you a little more light than you now have. Do you know that just before leaving the Peninsula McClellan offered to march into Richmond on his own responsibility? Do you know that in the opinion of our leading military men Washington is in more danger than it ever yet has been? Do you know that but for McDowell's jealousy we should have triumphantly marched into Richmond? Do you know that Pope is a humbug and known to be so by those who put him in his present place? Do you know that to-day he is so completely outgeneraled as to be cut off from Washington? Yet these are not rumors, but facts, doled out to me by members of McClellan's and Halleck's staffs.

Our rulers seem to me to be crazy. The air of this city seems thick with treachery; our army seems in danger of utter demoralization and I have not since the war begun felt such a tug on my nerves as to-day in Washington. Everything is ripe for a terrible panic, the end of which I cannot see or even imagine. I always mean to be one of the hopeful, but just now I cast about in vain for something on which to hang my hopes. I still believe in McClellan, but I *know* that the nearest advisers of the President—among them Mr. Holt—distrust his earnestness in this war. Stanton is jealous of him and he and Pope are in bitter enmity. All pin their hope on Halleck and we must do as the rest do; but it is hinted to me that Stanton is likely to be a block in Halleck's way, and the jealousies of our generals are more than a new man can manage. We need a head and we must have it; a man who can keep these jealousies under subordination; and we must have him or go to the wall. Is Halleck going to supply our need? I hope he is, but while the question is in doubt we may lose Washington. You will think that I am in a panic and the most frightened man in Washington. I assure you it is not so. I do consider the outside condition of affairs very critical, but it is my glimpse behind the scenes, the conviction that small men with selfish motives control the war without any central power to keep them in bounds, which terrifies and discourages me.

Take the history of the Peninsular campaign. My authorities are one aid of McClellan's and Halleck's Assistant Adjutant General, but the facts speak for themselves, and the inferences any man may draw. Stanton, contrary to the first principle of strategy and for motives not hard to comprehend, divides Virginia into four independent departments. McClellan takes charge of one and a column is taken from him to form another under charge of McDowell. It is solemnly promised McClellan that McDowell shall join him before Richmond, and meanwhile he is retained where he is to protect Washington. Mark the result. McClellan fights the battle of Hanover Court House, with all its loss of life and time, simply to open the road for McDowell to join him and he does open it. McDowell's advance guard hears his cannon on that day, but McDowell does not stir, and McClellan, still looking for him, forms that fatal Chickahominy front of twenty miles. Doubtless McDowell was kept back by orders, but in how far was he instrumental in procuring these orders to suit himself? McClellan's staff do not hesitate to say that he dictated them on pretense of danger to Washington, in reality because his advance would have absorbed his command in that of McClellan. Take the pretense. Jackson makes his raid in the valley of the Shenandoah, and again McDowell's advance hears the sound of his guns. Washington is in danger now. As before he does not move and Jackson escapes and returns to attack McClellan. Had McDowell done his duty either for McClellan or against Jackson, we should now have Richmond and McClellan would now be the conquering hero. He did neither and is now in disgrace, as subordinated to Pope; but McClellan is not the conquering hero. Not half an hour ago Halleck's nephew and private secretary told me that I could not imagine the trouble these jealousies gave his uncle. Said he, "McDowell and Sigel will not fight under Pope. McClellan and Pope are not in sympathy"; and he added an intimation that McClellan was most restive under Halleck.

Under these circumstances what can we expect? What can we hope for? Sigel stands well, but all our army officers are bitter and jealous against him. In Burnside there is indeed hope. He has been true and generous and, what is much, successful. He did not hesitate to award to McClellan the credit of planning his Carolina campaign, and, unlike McDowell, when told to send to McClellan all the troops he could spare, he at once sent him twenty-eight regiments and six batteries, leaving himself and the Major General under him some 3000 men in all. We have some grim old fighters who do their work and do not scheme. Such they tell me are Sumner and Heintzelman; but even of these the last is outspoken against McClellan because he will not fight with more energy. The simple truth is the man has not come and now we mean to supply his place with vast numbers of undrilled recruits. Shall we succeed? You can judge as well as I.

Thus the war is gloomily enough approaching its last and bloodiest stage. Unless Halleck is the man of iron who can rule, it will be discordant numbers against compact strategy. We must face the music, though we do not like the tune....

Camp of 1st Mass. Cav'y, Potomac Run, Va., January 8, 1863.

It was clear that we were not going to the bridge, as Chamberlain of our regiment had charge of that party. I had the rear of the column and a ripping headache, otherwise I should have enjoyed the thing immensely, for it was a clear, cold, moonlight night and we went floundering through the marshes at a tremendous gait. All I could see was dissolving views of the rear of the column as we pelted through woods and across broad white marshes, intersected by creeks which we had to ford. Presently Ben [Crowninshield] came down the column and informed me that we were going up the railroad to destroy some smaller bridges and, if it took us long, we were to let the column go and find our own way home. Of course we lost the way and after riding up the road two miles and finding no bridge, we rode down two miles and a half, cutting down the telegraph poles as we went along, and then there was a halt and I heard the sound of the axes. "Ah," thought I, "here is the bridge," and my headache felt better.

So I rode up and looked at a miserable little culvert, about three yards long, on which some twenty destroyers were at work. This was, then, the greatest humbug of all. We had come with artillery and cavalry and infantry, through rain and snow and ice, without shelter or forage, all the way up here to cut up a miserable little culvert which ten men could rebuild in five hours. It would have been very amusing had I felt well. There we were, a hundred of us, some eighty in line and ready to fire into any unsuspecting train which might come along, and the other twenty, without direction, or system or tools, tugging away at a remarkably well-built railroad which resisted their utmost efforts. Ye Gods! how the mismanagement did stick out!! Our tools were six axes and the ground was hard frozen. Every one directed and every one worked on his own hook. My second Lieutenant, a son of Judge Parsons, was ordered to do the work and he bellowed and swore, and the men laughed and minded him or not as they chose. White, quite nervous and anxious to get through, complained that too many orders were given and did nothing to remedy it. Ben Crowninshield, very anxious to get the job done while yet there was time, seeing that the men had worked an hour without getting up a single rail, encouraged them by dancing round in high excitement, exhorting them somewhat generally to "do *something* to turn the whole thing over at once, *somehow*," and I sat on my horse in amused despair.

At length with immense effort we got up one rail and threw it into the creek, and White at once declared the bridge used up and we started back along the railroad. It was eleven o'clock now and the last half hour we had heard a spattering fire of carbines and musquetry toward the river, indicating that Chamberlain was at work, but no artillery, which seemed to indicate that it wasn't much of a job after all. As for us we went rapidly along the track and the first thing we knew we came to a bridge, as was a bridge. It was clear at once we had been at work on the wrong bridge hitherto, so we went to work again. It was the same old story, only a little better, for this time we made cleaner work, pulling up the track, cutting through the uprights and main beams and finally setting the middle pier on fire; having done which we mounted and went off better pleased.

Through the whole thing I must confess I felt like a fool. It was a small job and badly done; slight resistance would have turned us back and I haven't as yet gotten over an old prejudice against going round destroying property which no one tries to protect. Anyhow it was done and the fire of the burning bridge threw a bright light across the marsh as we rode away. We rejoined the main body and waited for Chamberlain, who had been at work on the main bridge and had, after some slight resistance, resulting in nothing, destroyed about one hundred and twenty feet of it. The whole party was in by three o'clock, and we at once started back and, as I rode along in the clear, cold moonlight, I very soon made up my mind as to the whole affair.

I don't know, but I imagine a newspaper success—"dashing raid" and all that—will be manufactured out of this. If it is I can only say it is a clap-trap and a humbug and was intended as such. It is, I fear, pure Joe Hookerism and wire pulling. The bridge was of no real value to the rebels or to us and was not protected. Even if it had been, Ned Flint, who is an engineer, said he would contract to repair with forty men all the damage done in four days. Anyhow, value or no value, two hundred cavalry could have done it twice as surely and effectually and in just half the time, and so Chamberlain had previously reported. But no! that wouldn't answer for political effect, and so the sledge is brought out to crush the fly, and infantry, artillery and cavalry are paraded out in the depth of winter to burn a bridge which no one used or means to use, and I expect to see an immense pow-wow over it. If there is, rest assured it's all a humbug. The thing amounted to nothing, was very badly done after no end of blunders and mismanagement, and was and is intended solely for political effect and has about as much bearing on the ends of the war as would the burning of Neponset Bridge or our barn at Quincy....

At last, at half past one, we marched into camp and were dismissed. This was Saturday afternoon. I had been on continuous duty for thirty-four hours and in the saddle twenty-eight; my horse had not eaten for thirty hours. I had last washed my face and hands on Wednesday morning, and in this week, the first in January and by far the most severe of the winter, I had passed two nights in my tent and five in bivouac. I got something to eat and washed my face and hands and then went out to see that the horses were cared for, but that night my blankets felt like a bed of down and I slept like an infant.

Aldie, Va., June 25, 1863.

. . . .

But what is coming? I fear that universal lack of confidence in every one, from the President through General Hooker downwards, is the distinguishing feature of the army now. Things are certainly much changed for the worse since our regiments first arrived in Virginia ten months ago. Lack of confidence has steadily grown upon us. In Hooker not one soul in the army that I meet puts the slightest, though it may be that I meet only one class. All whom I do see seem only to sadly inquire of themselves how much disaster and slaughter this poor army must go through before the Government will consider the public mind ripe for another change. Meade or Reynolds seems to be the favorite for the rising man and either is respectable and would be a great improvement on the drunk-murdering-arson dynasty now prevailing, of Hooker, Sickles and Butterfield. Meanwhile the golden moments are flying and we are lying here doing nothing. . . .

Camp of 1st Mass. Cav. near St. James College, Md., July 12, 1863.

One more line to be forwarded to London to tell you I am still safe, well and sound. Once more we are with the cavalry and in the front and under the command of the damndest fool I ever saw or read of, one ———. For two days we have been skirmishing gently with trifling casualties, but I think our share of the fighting for this bout is pretty much over and now the infantry will walk in for a few field days of slaughter and then "to-morrow to new fields and pastures new" over in Virginia. Of course you know well enough that your newspapers tell you nothing but lies and that "the cavalry" as depicted by them is all a figment of the poet's brain. If you don't I tell you so now and know it in future. We have done our work decently, but Pleasonton is, next to Hooker, the greatest humbug of the war, and Kilpatrick is a brave injudicious boy, much given to blowing and who will surely come to grief. The army has done nobly and is in fine condition, but as to Lee's being routed, he has lots of fight left and this war is not over yet, and there will still be many shrewd blows. Though not elated I am confident and most happy in that novel sensation. All is going well and day, I believe, breaks at last. . . .

I tell you the Army of the Potomac is a magnificent army, but what shall we say of the great State of Pennsylvania? They left that army to fight it out, and win or lose with Lee, without the aid of a man or a musket, and before the battle devoted their energies to running away, or buying immunity for their precious goods by giving aid and comfort to the enemy and, after the battle, turned to with all their souls to make money out of their defenders by selling soldiers bread at twenty-five cents a loaf and milk at fifteen cents a canteen—in one case charging a hospital $19.00 for forty loaves of bread. Facts, John, facts. They are a great people! ...

Camp of the 1st Mass. Cav'y, Hillsboro, Va., July 22, 1863.

. . . . . .

Here we are and we enjoy this as more of a settled rest than we have had since the 30th of May. So I pulled out your old letters and read them over, reread them with Gettysburg, Vicksburg, Port Hudson and Morris Island still ringing in my ears, and with our wondrous successes of July absorbing my thoughts. Does Europe want more? If it does I think it will get more, but I am lost in astonishment at the strength the North is developing. Can the South stand up against it? War is a dangerous game and the South has all that desperate courage which makes one a majority; so, while there is a single chance left I feel no safety. But for the last few days I had dwelt much during long marches on our relative positions as compared with two years ago. Two years ago at this time we fought the stampede of Bull-Run, and the two years that have passed have proved exactly the time necessary to develop our strength. Do you realize what prodigious victories we have won this summer? Men and money are the sinews of war. While we have reduced gold fifty per cent in five months, we have settled the question of a Negro soldiery, and at last enforced the draft, thus opening an unlimited supply of recruits. Two years have thus brought us to just what we never had before, plenty of money and plenty of men. The Negro regiment question is our greatest victory of the war so far, and, I can assure you, that in the army, these are so much of a success that they will soon be the fashion. General Andrews, formerly of the 2nd Massachusetts and one of the bravest and most reliable officers in the service, is organizing a corps of these soldiers in South Carolina, and he writes to officers here that, though he went out with all a conservative's prejudices against their use, he has seen them do well under indifferent officers and he is confident that under good officers they will make troops equal to the best. This is a great deal from Andrews. I almost wish I had gone into that movement, but perhaps it's just as well.

As to the conscription, the army is delighted with that and only regrets that it had no chance to discuss the matter with the gentlemen of New York. We, who have borne the heat and burden of the day, are tired and disgusted at seeing men bought by immense bounties, leaving home one day to return a hero the next, ovations to regiments with unthinned ranks. The three years men received no bounty. Now we do so much want to see all those who kiss our Lady Peace at home come in for a share of our laurels. So the army feels none the less pleased because it sees an iron hand on the rioters at home.

But having finished with our moral victories, I have not begun on our physical. Probably I can tell you little about those except that I really at last believe that we are learning to outfight the rebels on even fields, in spite of their dash and fanatical desperation. Does Europe want more? Europe, however, seems to me now out of the question. I may look at these things from too much of an army point of view, just as you take everything from your London watch-tower; but it does now seem to me that if any European nation, and especially England, and next to her France, wants hard knocks with little gain, they need only to meddle with us. Two years ago our soldiers would have dreaded foreign armies and especially French *"Zouaves."* That's played out. If the Mexicans can make a fight, we can win a victory. Eighty thousand French soldiers might *now* make an impression through a campaign which would use them up; but in case of a war with us the whole English standing army could not save Canada from being overrun. How I would like to raid it through Canada, and how we would astonish the regular cavalry of Europe.

You will laugh at all this and say: "Why, victory has turned his head! How he does crow!! And that too before he's out of the woods." Not at all. It is not success in the field which delights me, it is feeling and seeing the strength behind me which this rebellion has just sufficed to call forth. Europe looked to see us exhausted and calling for mediation, without money and without recruits, and behold! the whole African race comes forward to fill our ranks at just the moment when by a wise conscription we are for the first time strong enough without them, and all this time the very war which was to destroy us reduces gold from 175 to 125. At last, oh Lord! at last!! Three months ago powerful and energetic foreign intervention would have saved Vicksburg to the South, cost us New Orleans and cost us the Mississippi. To-day we have all these and will not lose them easily and, if European nations care to interfere, they may injure us in a small degree as we shall injure them; but, thank God! we have secured the material issues of this great struggle. For the rest I would the South East might have its own way and depart in peace. I am tired equally of them and of this war.

July 23.

As we still continue here I may as well lucubrate a little further. I notice that you and Henry dwell a great deal upon the apparent exhaustion of the rebel resources and their lack of men and supplies. As I yesterday dwelt on our successes, I will to-day give my experiences on their reverses, and that experience is by no means that of the newspaper reporters. I have lately seen and talked with considerable numbers of rebel prisoners, beside passing over some rebel territory, and that, too, in "desolated" Virginia. That the rebels have no money or currency is very apparent, but I see no evidence that they are either starving or destitute. Wherever we have been in Virginia we find cattle and corn in abundance, and the people seem comfortable. We find few men and few blacks but no suffering. I see that all accounts agree in placing the flower of the rebel army in Virginia. This may well be, for finer fighting material it would be hard to find. I am struck by their immensely improved condition since a year ago at Antietam. Judging by my means of observation, and I saw great numbers of prisoners, having myself at one time charge of a squad of five hundred from every Southern State, I should say that Lee's army at Gettysburg was in every respect superior to the Army of the Potomac, superior in numbers, better officered, a better fighting material, as well armed, better clothed and as well fed. The spirit of his army was much better than that of ours, and I saw no evidence of their ever having been on short rations or demoralized by want or misfortune. Their tone was the very best. All said they were sick of the war, but scouted the idea of going home or giving it up until they had won their cause. I must say my opinion of the confederates and Southrons improved on near acquaintance in the early days of July.

You will ask why we were not defeated then at Gettysburg? We just escaped it by the skin of our teeth and the strength of our position. This regiment came into the field on the evening of the second day and in the midst of the battle. At sunset we were whipped and night saved the army. I never felt such sickening anxiety. We went into camp a mile and a half from the front and in rear of the right wing, in a wood. At sunset the enemy outflanked us and our men began to give way. Presently they came swarming through our camp in demoralized squads—wounded and well, officers and men—so that we were forced out and obliged to move back. Then it was resolved to fall back that night twenty miles, but fortunately at midnight this determination was reconsidered, our position was strengthened and next day the enemy were fairly whipped out.

Now, for the future, how do things stand? I *guess* Lee has 60,000 men left, but he is outflanked at the South West and at Charleston, and he must still make head against the large and now confident army. Southern affairs do seem desperate. They seem to me in just that condition from which genius alone could restore them and here is where, to my mind, the rebels have sustained their most vital loss. Stonewall Jackson would have given them this chance had he lived. In Virginia alone since the war began have they held their own, and what have they done in Virginia which they did not owe to Jackson? Now his loss to them seems to me to be irreparable and almost decisive. In a single campaign the South has lost Jackson and Vicksburg, and if they are not desperate, I do not know what can bring them to it. I do believe Jackson had genius and in that respect stands alone in the annals of this most stupid and uninspired of struggles. Certainly his death excited throughout this army a deep regret which was lost only in a sense of intense relief. To-day I am sure, as Americans, this army takes a pride in "Stonewall" second only to that of the Virginians and confederates. To have fought against him is next to having fought under him.

As for Lee, how can we have faith in him? He might have crushed Burnside at Fredericksburg and yet he let him escape. Hooker got away, but then Lee was glad enough to let him go, for, at the start, Lee was surprised, outgeneraled, and on the verge of utter destruction. Jackson seemed to have saved the army which Lee jeopardized. As to Lee's two invasions, he cannot brag much on Antietam, for Jackson almost destroyed Pope only to enable Lee to get pounded to a mummy in Maryland. And now finally at Gettysburg, with every chance in his favor, and against a dispirited army and a new General, he has incurred a disaster to the Southern army which belittles our defeat at Fredericksburg or their own at Malvern Hill. Thus I cannot share in the general admiration of Lee, Jackson was his right-hand man and his right hand is gone. For the rest I do not see that they are stronger in Generals than we....

H. Q. Army of Potomac, Hanover Town, Va., April [May] 29, 1864.

The campaign to us here gradually unfolds itself. Grant and Meade discuss and decide, but keep their own counsel, and no one knows whether to-morrow the Army is to fight, to march, or to rest. Meanwhile marching now seems to be the order of the day, and since day before yesterday Head Quarters have moved thirty odd miles, turning all the exterior lines of Richmond and bringing us down to the interior line of the Chickahominy. Here we rest for to-day. Up to this time General Grant seems to have looked on this campaign in Virginia as one necessarily to be made up of the hardest kind of fighting, combined with all the generalship which he could command, and, as we were numerically the strongest, we might as well do the fighting first as last, pounding and maneuvering at the same time. If this was his idea, I think the wisdom of it is becoming apparent. I cannot believe that his operations have been or now are conducted on any fixed plan. He seems to have one end in view—the capture of Richmond and the destruction of Lee's army; but I imagine his means to that end undergo daily changes and no man in this Army, but Meade perhaps, is even able to give grounds for a guess as to whether we are to approach Richmond from this side or from the other. Meanwhile, though Grant expected hard fighting, I have no idea that he expected anything like the fighting and the slaughter which took place in the Wilderness and at Spottsylvania. He had never seen anything like it in the West, and the fierce, stubborn resistance we met far surpassed his expectation. Meade knew better what he had to expect and in fighting for him those battles were, I imagine, of incalculable assistance to Grant. To-day, as near as I can see, results stand as follows: these two great armies have pounded each other nearly to pieces for many days; neither has achieved any real success over the other on the field of battle. Our loss has probably been greater than theirs, for ours has been the offensive; but we have a decided balance of prisoners and captured artillery in our favor. The enemy, I think, outfight us, but we outnumber them, and, finally, within the last three days one witnesses in this Army as it moves along all the results of a victory, when in fact it has done only barren fighting. For it has done the one thing needful before the enemy—it has advanced. The result is wonderful. Hammered and pounded as this Army has been; worked, marched, fought and reduced as it is, it is in better spirits and better fighting trim to-day than it was in the first day's fight in the Wilderness. Strange as it seems to me, it is, I believe, yet the fact, that this Army is now just on its second wind, and is more formidable than it ever was before. This I see on every march and I attribute it to movement in advance after heavy, though barren, fighting.

With the enemy it is otherwise. Heavier fighting, harder marching, and greater privations—for with them deficiency in numbers was only to be made good by redoubled activity—two men with them have done the work of three with us—all these have led only to movements to the rear, to the abandonment of line after line until now they find themselves with their backs against Richmond. Naturally this discourages troops, particularly coming after as hard fighting as they know how to do, and as a result we now get, as I am informed, from all sources but one story, and that of discouragement and exhaustion. The enemy is getting off his fight. What is to come next? Will Lee try to revive the spirits of his men and the fortunes of his Army by taking the offensive? Will he try to repeat the story of the Chickahominy and the six days' fighting? What does Grant mean next to do? I have always noticed that when I try to divine the future of military operations I am invariably wrong, and so I long ago gave up trying. Of a few things though I feel pretty sure. Stonewall Jackson is dead, Grant is not McClellan, nor is Meade McDowell. Grant will not let his Army be idle, nor will he allow the initiative to be easily taken out of his hands, and if he can outfight Meade, he will do more than he was ever able to do yet when his troops were more numerous, in better heart and much fresher than they now are. Accordingly we find ourselves approaching the climax of the campaign, under circumstances which certainly seem to me hopeful. The next few days will probably develop Grant's final move, the line on which he means to approach Richmond and the point at which he means, unless Lee outgenerals him, to have the final fight. I don't believe he will allow time to slip away or Lee to repair damages. I do believe that while the Army is resting to-day, it is drawing breath for the great struggle and on the eve of great movements and decisive results.

Things meanwhile work in the Army charmingly. Grant is certainly a very extraordinary man. He does not look it and might pass well enough for a dumpy and slouchy little subaltern, very fond of smoking. Neither do I know that he shows it in his conversation, for he never spoke to me and doesn't seem to be a very talkative man anyhow. They say his mouth shows character. It may, but it is so covered with beard that no one can vouch for it. The truth is, he is in appearance a very ordinary looking man, one who would attract attention neither in the one way or the other. Not knowing who it is, you would not pronounce him insignificant, and knowing who it is, it would require some study to find in his appearance material for hero worship, though there is about his face no indication of weakness or lack of force. He has not nearly so strong a head and face as Humphreys', for instance, who at once strikes you as a man of force. In figure Grant is comical. He sits a horse well, but in walking he leans forward and toddles. Such being his appearance, however, I do not think that any intelligent person could watch him, even from such a distance as mine, without concluding that he is a remarkable man. He handles those around him so quietly and well, he so evidently has the faculty of disposing of work and managing men, he is cool and quiet, almost stolid and as if stupid, in danger, and in a crisis he is one against whom all around, whether few in number or a great army as here, would instinctively lean. He is a man of the most exquisite judgment and tact. See how he has handled this Army. He took command under the most unfavorable circumstances —jealousy between East and West; the Army of the Potomac and the Army of the Southwest; that general feeling that the officers from the West were going to swagger over those here and finally that universal envy which success creates and which is always ready to carp at it. The moment I came to Head Quarters I saw that, though nothing was said, yet the materials were all ready for an explosion at the first mistake Grant made. All this has passed away and now Grant has this army as firmly as ever he had that of the Southwest. He has effected this simply by the exercise of tact and good taste. He has humored us, he has given some promotions, he has made no parade of his authority, he has given no orders except through Meade, and Meade he treats with the utmost confidence and deference. The result is that even from the most jealously disposed and most indiscreet of Meade's staff, not a word is heard against Grant. The result is of inestimable importance. The army has a head and confidence in that head. It has leaders and there is no discord among those leaders. We seem to have gotten rid of jealousy and all now seem disposed to go in with a will to win.

At last we have gotten out of the Wilderness. That interminable outline of pines of all sizes which it seemed never would end has given way to a clearer and more cultivated country, and now we come across the old Virginia plantation houses and can now and then see a regular clearing. The Wilderness was a most fearfully discouraging place—an enemy always in front, against whom the fiercest attack we could make made no impression; incessant fighting day after day; no progress forward, and the hospitals cleared out only to be filled again, while the country was becoming peopled with graves. There the Army got very much discouraged and took blue views of life. The straggling became terrible and you saw men the whole time and officers sometimes living in the woods or wandering round the country. At that time I take it Lee had accomplished his object and the Army of the Potomac was crippled. It could not effectively have advanced. At that time, however, it experienced the great advantage of Grant's presence and power, for he at once reënforced it by every available man round Washington, thus at once restoring its efficiency, while but for his power and name the Administration would, as heretofore, doubtless have defended Washington at the cost of all the fruits of this Army's fighting. Thus Lee found himself again opposed by a fresh army and every new man who came up from the rear served to revive the spirits of those who had been here before. Now the Army is in capital condition and I feel once more sanguine; but the telegraphs of the steamer which brings this will tell the whole story.

Washington, D. C., August 20, 1864.

Here I find myself once more in Washington, and that city as low-toned and unattractive as ever, looking much the same as ever, except that I see in it fewer uniforms. I came up here to try and carry out a plan I have for mounting the 5th Cavalry, to which I have already got General Grant's assent and I shall leave the instant I can finish my business. I met John here and we passed a couple of days pleasantly together.... He and I went to call on Governor Seward and passed an hour with your chief. He probably will write you his impressions, mine were not cheerful. The old Governor didn't seem to feel firm about the future and retired himself largely into his philosophy. His tone was very different from that of last spring, when he seemed to me so buoyant and confident of the future. Then he evidently thought he saw his way through; now, as evidently, his future is obscured and dangerous. He had none of his crowing confidence of last spring, and I was pained to feel how discouraged he was. He too gave me the impression which all here do, of "going it wild," and not seeing where this thing is going to come out; but while others have a reckless and excited manner of going it, he, on the contrary, looked like a thoughtful and wise man, troubled at seeing the machine passing beyond control.

Newport, R. I., March 7, 1865.

. . . .

What do you think of the inaugural? That rail-splitting lawyer is one of the wonders of the day. Once at Gettysburg and now again on a greater occasion he has shown a capacity for rising to the demands of the hour which we should not expect from orators or men of the schools. This inaugural strikes me in its grand simplicity and directness as being for all time the historical keynote of this war; in it a people seemed to speak in the sublimely simple utterance of ruder times. What will Europe think of this utterance of the rude ruler, of whom they have nourished so lofty a contempt? Not a prince or minister in all Europe could have risen to such an equality with the occasion....

CHAPTER LI

IN WASHINGTON there was often confusion and despair, what with the failures of generals and the difficulties of wartime politics. In his most trying moments President Lincoln found it necessary to unbend—as on the occasion of the Cabinet meeting in 1862 at which he read a proclamation freeing the slaves. His Secretary of the Treasury, Salmon P. Chase, entered in his diary for that day an account of how the president began with the reading of light literature.

MONDAY, *Sept.* 22d., 1862.

TO Department about nine. State Department messenger came, with notice to Heads of Department to meet at 12.—Received sundry callers.—Went to White House.

All the members of the Cabinet were in attendance. There was some general talk; President mentioned that Artemus Ward had sent him his book. Proposed to read a chapter which he thought very funny. Read it, and seemed to enjoy it very much—the Heads also (except Stanton) of course. The chapter was "High-handed Outrage at Utica."

The President then took a graver tone and said:—

"Gentlemen: I have, as you are aware, thought a great deal about the relation of this war to Slavery: and you all remember that, several weeks ago, I read to you an Order I had prepared on this subject, which, on account of objections made by some of you, was not issued. Ever since then, my mind has been much occupied with this subject, and I have thought all along that the time for acting on it might very probably come. I think the time has come now. I wish it were a better time. I wish that we were in a better condition. The action of the army against the rebels has not been quite what I should have best liked. But they have been driven out of Maryland, and Pennsylvania is no longer in danger of invasion. When the rebel army was at Frederick, I determined, as soon as it should be driven out of Maryland, to issue a Proclamation of Emancipation such as I thought most likely to be useful.

I said nothing to any one: but I made the promise to myself, and (hesitating a little)—to my Maker. The rebel army is now driven out, and I am going to fulfill that promise. I have got you together to hear what I have written down. I do not wish your advice about the main matter—for that I have determined for myself. This I say without intending anything but respect for any one of you. But I already know the views of each on this question. They have been heretofore expressed, and I have considered them as thoroughly and carefully as I can. What I have written is that which my reflections have determined me to say. If there is anything in the expressions I use, or in any other minor matter, which any one of you thinks had best be changed, I shall be glad to receive the suggestions. One other observation I will make. I know very well that many others might, in this matter, as in others, do better than I can: and if I were satisfied that the public confidence was more fully possessed by any one of them than by me, and knew of any Constitutional way in which he could be put in my place, he should have it. I would gladly yield it to him. But though I believe that I have not so much of the confidence of the people as I had some time since, I do not know that, all things considered, any other person has more: and, however this may be, there is no way in which I can have any other man put where I am. I am here. I must do the best I can, and bear the responsibility of taking the course which I feel I ought to take."

The President then proceeded to read his Emancipation Proclamation, making remarks on the several parts as he went on, and showing that he had fully considered the whole subject, in all the lights under which it had been presented to him.

CHAPTER LII

AS THE war went on almost exclusively in Southern territory, it was the civilian south which suffered most in the way of deprivation and despair. Particularly in Virginia was this true, since Virginia was first and last the scene of critical, prolonged engagements. Within the stricken area behind the Confederate lines women resorted to many devices in order to keep body and pride together; Mrs. Roger A. Pryor, wife of one of Lee's generals, has described those devices in the course of a narrative dealing with her exile from a captured and pillaged home.

HAVING no longer a home of my own, it was decided that I should go to my people in Charlotte County. One of my sons, Theo, and two of my little daughters were already there, and there I expected to remain until the end of the war.

But repeated attempts to reach my country home resulted in failure. Marauding parties and guerillas were flying all over the country. There had been alarm at a bridge over the Staunton near the Oaks, and the old men and boys had driven away the enemy. I positively *could* not venture alone.

So it was decided that I should return to my husband's old district, to Petersburg, and there find board in some private family.

I reached Petersburg in the autumn and wandered about for days seeking refuge in some household. Many of my old friends had left town. Strangers and refugees had rented the houses of some of these, while others were filled with the homeless among their own kindred. There was no room anywhere for me, and my small purse was growing so slender that I became anxious. Finally my brother-in-law offered me an overseer's house on one of his "quarters." The small dwelling he placed at my disposal was to be considered temporary only; some one of his town houses would soon be vacant. When I drove out to the little house, I found it hardly better than a hovel. We entered a rude, unplastered kitchen, the planks of the floor loose and wide apart, the earth beneath plainly visible. There were no windows in this smoke-blackened kitchen. A door opened into a tiny room with a fireplace, window, and outdoor of its own; and a short flight of stairs led to an unplastered attic, so that the little apartment was entered by two doors and a staircase. It was already cold, but we had to beat a hasty retreat and sit outside while a colored boy made a "smudge" in the house, to dislodge the wasps that had tenanted it for many months. My brother had lent me bedding for the overseer's pine bedstead and the low trundle-bed underneath. The latter, when drawn out at night, left no room for us to stand. When that was done, we had to go to bed. For furniture we had only two or three wooden chairs and a small table. There were no curtains, neither carpet nor rugs, no china. There was wood at the woodpile, and a little store of meal and rice, with a small bit of bacon in the overseer's grimy closet. This was to be my winter home.

Petersburg was already virtually in a state of siege. Not a tithe of the food needed for its army of refugees could be brought to the city. Our highway, the river, was filled, except for a short distance, with Federal gunboats. The markets had long been closed. The stores of provisions had been exhausted, so that a grocery could offer little except a barrel or two of molasses made from the domestic sorghum sugar-cane—an acrid and unwholesome sweet used instead of sugar for drink with water or milk, and for eating with bread. The little boys at once began to keep house. They valiantly attacked the woodpile, and found favor in the eyes of Mary and the man, whom I never knew as other than "Mary's husband." He and Mary were left in charge of the quarter and had a cabin near us.

I had no books, no newspapers, no means of communicating with the outside world; but I had one neighbor, Mrs. Laighton, a daughter of Winston Henry, granddaughter of Patrick Henry. She lived near me with her husband—a Northern man. Both were very cultivated, very poor, very kind. Mrs. Laighton, as Lucy Henry,—a brilliant young girl,—had been one of the habitués of the Oaks. We had much in common, and her kind heart went out in love and pity for me.

She taught me many expedients: that to float tea on the top of a cup of hot water would make it "go farther" than when steeped in the usual way; also that the herb, "life everlasting," which grew in the fields would make excellent yeast, having somewhat the property of hops; and that the best substitute for coffee was not the dried cubes of sweet potato, but parched corn or parched meal, making a nourishing drink, not unlike the "postum" of to-day.

From the beginning of the war to its last year Petersburg had remained in a state of comparative repose, broken only by the arrival and departure of the troops passing from the South to the Army of Northern Virginia. These, as we have said, were always welcomed, if they passed through by day, with gifts of flowers, fruit, and more substantial refreshment.

To continue this greeting, Petersburg women denied themselves every luxury. The tramp of soldiers was a familiar sound in our streets, but no hostile footsteps had ever resounded there, no hostile gun had yet been fired within its limits. It is true the low muttering of distant artillery as it came up the James and the Appomattox from the field of Big Bethel had caught the ears of the citizens, and they had listened with heightened interest in its louder booming as it told of Seven Pines, and the seven days' struggle around Richmond, just twenty miles away. But when the baffled army of McClellan retired in the direction of Washington, and General Lee moved away beyond the Potomac, the old men, women, and children (for there were no men left capable of bearing arms) settled down to their daily avocations.

John was installed as cook and commissary-general. He had no material except flour, rice, peas, and dried apples, such grease or "shortening" as he could extract from bones he purchased of the quartermaster, and sorghum molasses. He made yeast of "life everlasting" I brought from the country,—and he gave us waffles and pancakes. John's pancakes, compared with the ordinary article, were as the fleecy cloud to the dull, heavy clod beneath. Butter could be had at eight dollars a pound; meat was four and five dollars a pound—prices we learned very soon afterward to regard as extremely cheap; bargains, indeed, of the first water. From Agnes's letters I have reason to suppose that Petersburg suffered more from scarcity than did Richmond. There, dinners were given by the members of the Cabinet, and wine was served as of old. In Petersburg we had already entered upon our long season of want. The town was drained by its generous gifts to the army; regiments were constantly passing, and none ever departed without the offer of refreshment.

On January the 30th Agnes wrote from Richmond:—

"How can you be even dreaming of new cups and saucers? Mend your old ones, my dear, with white lead. That is what we are doing here; and when the cup is very much broken, the triangular, rectangular, and other 'angular' lines of white give it quite a Japanesque effect. There is not a bit of china for sale in the capital of the Confederacy. A forlorn little chipped set—twelve odd pieces —sold last week at auction for $200—and as to hats and bonnets!

We are washing the old ones and plaiting straw for the new. I'll
send you a package of straw I gleaned and dyed for you last
summer. Did I tell you about that straw? I asked my host at the
farmhouse to give me a few sheaves, but he shook his head and
opined it would be 'sinful in these hard times to take good vittles
and convert it into hats.' I could not see clearly that straw came
under the generic term 'vittles'—unless indeed the straw fed the
animal that fed the soldier. However, I meekly borrowed a sun-
bonnet and gleaned my straw. Half of it I popped into the kettle
of boiling black dye behind the kitchen,—when the lady of the
manor was looking another way,—and we will mix the black and
white for the boys' hats. But mark the quick and sure grinding of
the mills of the gods. After the wheat was all stacked there came a
mighty rain with fog and warm mist. One day my host brought in
what seemed to be a feathery bouquet of delicate green. It was a
bunch of wheat, every grain of which had sprouted. He had lost
his crop!

"President and Mrs. Davis gave a large reception last week, and
all the ladies looked positively gorgeous. Mrs. Davis is in mourning
for her father. We should not expect suppers in these times, but we
do have them! Champagne is $350 a dozen, but we sometimes have
champagne! The confectioners charge $15 for cake, but we have
cake. My flounced gray silk is behaving admirably, but I am afraid
my Washington friends remember it as an old acquaintance. I never
go out without meeting them. I have seen Dr. Garnett and Judge
Scarborough and Mr. Dimitri on the street, and often meet Mr.
Hunter, running about, in his enthusiasm, like a boy. But what do
you think? I never could bear that Lord Lyons, with his red face
and small eyes like ferrets'; and now we have reason to suppose
that England would have recognized us but for his animosity against
us. He says 'the Confederacy is on its last legs.' We have heard
from dear old Dudley Mann; but of course *he* can do nothing for
us in England, and he had as well come home and go with me to
receptions. Mrs. Davis receives every Tuesday, and Mr. Mann is a
better squire of dames than he is a diplomat."

My Petersburg beauties were all wearing hats of their own manufacture, the favorite style being the Alpine with a pointed crown.
For trimming, very soft and lovely flowers were made of feathers,
the delicate white feather with a tuft of fleecy marabout at its
stem. The marabout tuft would be carefully drawn off, to be made
into swan's-down trimming. A wire was prepared and covered with
green paper for a stem, a little ball of wax fastened on the end,

and covered with a tiny tuft of the down for a center, and around this the feathers were stuck—with incurving petals for apple blossoms and half-open roses,—and reversed for camelias. Neatly trimmed and suitably tinted, these flowers were handsome enough for anybody, and were in great demand. Cocks' plumes were also used on hats, iridescent, and needing no coloring. With the downy breast of a goose which came into my possession I essayed the making of a powder-puff for my baby, but alas! the oil in the cuticle proved a perennial spring which could not be dried up by soda or sunning, and finally I saw my powder-puff disappearing in a hole, drawn downward by a vigorous and hungry rat.

It had not been many years since every Virginia farm owned a house for a great cumbrous loom, with beams supported against the ceiling. The door of the loom-house was again opened, and the weaver installed upon her high bench. Cotton cloth was woven and dyed yellow with butternut, black with walnut-bark, gray with willow. A mordant to "set the dye" was unattainable—but at last rusty iron, nails, old horseshoes, old clamps and hinges, were found to be effective. Every atom of black silk was a treasure. It was shredded to mix with the cotton before carding. Even now the cells of my brain waken at the sight of a bundle of old black silk, and my fingers would fain respond.

Pins became scarce. People walked about with downcast eyes; they were looking for pins! Thorns were gathered and dried to use as pins. Dentists' gold soon disappeared. The generation succeeding the war period had not good teeth. Anæsthetics—morphine, chloroform, opium—were contraband of war. This was our great grief. Our soldier boys, who had done nothing to bring the war upon the country, must suffer every pang that followed the disasters of battle. The United States gave artificial limbs to its maimed soldiers. Ours had only their crutches, and these of rude home manufacture. The blockade-running, for which our women were so much blamed, was often undertaken to bring morphine and medicine to our hospitals. The fashions of the day included a small round cushion worn at the back of a lady's belt, to lift the heavy hoop and many petticoats then in vogue. It was called "a bishop," and was made of silk. These were brought home from "a visit to friends at the North" filled with quinine and morphine. They were examined at the frontier by a long pin stuck through them. If the pin met no resistance, they were allowed to pass.

The famine moved on apace, but its twin sister, fever, never visited us. Never had Petersburg been so healthy. No garbage was decaying in the streets. Every particle of animal or vegetable food was consumed, and the streets were clean. Flocks of pigeons would follow the children who were eating bread or crackers. Finally the pigeons vanished having been themselves eaten. Rats and mice disappeared. The poor cats staggered about the streets, and began to die of hunger. At times meal was the only article attainable except by the rich. An ounce of meat daily was considered an abundant ration for each member of the family. To keep food of any kind was impossible—cows, pigs, bacon, flour, everything, was stolen, and even sitting hens were taken from the nest.

The question that pressed upon me day and night was: How, where, can I earn some money? to be answered by the frightful truth that there could be no opening for me anywhere, because I could not leave my children.

One wakeful night, while I was revolving these things, a sudden thought darted, unbidden, into my sorely oppressed mind:—

"Why not open the trunk from Washington? Something may be found there which can be sold."

At an early hour next morning John and Alick brought the trunk from the cellar. Aunt Jinny, Eliza, and the children gathered around. It proved to be full of my old Washington finery. There were a half-dozen or more white muslin gowns, flounced and trimmed with Valenciennes lace, many yards; there was a rich bayadere silk gown trimmed fully with guipure lace; a green silk dress with gold embroidery; a blue and silver brocade,—these last evening gowns. There was a paper box containing the shaded roses I had worn to Lady Napier's ball, the ball at which Mrs. Douglas and I had dressed alike in gowns of tulle. Another box held the garniture of green leaves and gold grapes which had belonged to the green silk; and still another the blue and silver feathers for the brocade. An opera cloak trimmed with fur; a long purple velvet cloak; a purple velvet "coalscuttle" bonnet, trimmed with white roses; a point lace handkerchief; Valenciennes lace; Brussels lace; and at the bottom of the trunk a package of *ciel* blue zephyr, awakening reminiscences of a passion which I had cherished for knitting shawls and "mariposas" of zephyr,—such was the collection I had discovered.

The velvet cloak had come to grief. Somebody had put the handsome books President Pierce had given me into this box, for special safe-keeping; and all these years the cloak had cushioned the books so that they made no inroads upon the other articles, and had given up its own life in their protection. Not an inch of the garment was ever fit for use. It was generously printed all over with the large cords and tassels of its own trimming.

These were my materials. I must make them serve for the support of my family.

I ripped all the lace from the evening gowns, and made it into collars and undersleeves. John found an extinct drygoods store where clean paper boxes could be had.

My first installment of lace collars was sent to Price's store in Richmond and promptly sold. Mr. Price wrote me that all of my articles would find purchasers. There were ladies in Richmond who could afford to buy, and the Confederate court offered opportunities for display.

One day I consulted Eliza about the manufacture of a Confederate candle. We knew how to make it—by drawing a cotton rope many times through melted wax, and then winding it around a bottle. We could get wax, but our position was an exposed one. Soldiers' tents were close around us, and we scrupulously avoided any revelation of our needs, lest they should deny themselves for our sakes. Eliza thought we might avail ourselves of the absence of the officers, and finish our work before they returned. We made our candle; but that night, as I sat sewing beside its dim, glow-worm light, I heard a step in the hall, and a hand, hastily thrust out, placed a brown paper parcel on the piano near the door. It was a soldier's ration of candles!

After I had converted all my laces into collars, cuffs, and sleeves, and had sold my silk gowns, opera cloak, and point lace handkerchiefs, I devoted myself to trimming the edges of the artificial flowers, and separating the long wreaths and garlands into clusters for hats and *bouquets de corsage*.

When I had stripped the pretty muslin gowns of their trimmings, what could be done with the gowns themselves? Finally I resolved to embroider them with the blue zephyr. I rolled the edges of the flounces, and edged them delicately with a spiral line of blue. I traced with blue a dainty vine of forget-me-nots on bodice and sleeves, with a result that was simply ravishing!

My first purchase was a barrel of flour, for which I paid thirteen hundred dollars. John made hot biscuits three times a day thereafter. As the winter wore on, and the starvation became stern in the army, a soldier would occasionally bring to the kitchen his ration of a small square of beef to be cooked, or *eight grains of coffee* to trade with John for a few biscuits. I sternly forbade the trade, and ordered John to grind the coffee in the owner's presence, mix it with our toasted corn, and give him the biscuits, with a good, strengthening drink. Often a brown hand would place a tiny bundle on the piano, as the donor passed through the hall, and my heart would ache to find it contained a soldier's ration of coffee. My dear father had friends among his old parishioners who never allowed him to do without his coffee—a necessity for a man who never, under any circumstances, fortified his strength with ardent spirits. He was almost fanatical on the total abstinence subject.

Of course I could not command shoes for my boys. I made them of carpet lined with flannel for my baby. I could in one day make a pair which she wore out in three! A piece of bronze morocco fell into my hands, of which I made a pair of boots for my little daughter, Mary, and out of an old leather pocket-book and two or three leather bags which Alick found in his prowling over the fields, a soldier-shoemaker contrived shoes for each of the boys.

My own prime necessity was for the steel we women wear in front of our stays. I suffered so much for want of this accustomed support, that Captain Lindsay had a pair made for me by the government gunsmith.

The time came when the salable contents of the Washington trunk were all gone. I then cut up my husband's dress-coat, and designed well-fitting ladies' gloves, with gauntlets made of the watered silk lining. Of an interlining of gray flannel I made gray gloves, and this glove manufacture yielded me hundreds of dollars. Thirteen small fragments of flannel were left after the gloves were finished. Of these, pieced together, I made a pair of drawers for my Willy— my youngest boy.

When Mrs. Pryor did finally manage a return to the house out of which she had been driven, this is what she found:

When I reached Cottage Farm I found a home that no soldier, however forlorn, could have envied me. A scene of desolation met my eyes. The earth was plowed and trampled, the grass and flowers were gone, the carcasses of six dead cows lay in the yard, and filth unspeakable had gathered in the corners of the house. The evening air was heavy with the sickening odor of decaying flesh. As the front door opened, millions of flies swarmed forth.

Within was dirt and desolation. Pieces of fat pork lay on the floors, molasses trickled from the library shelves, where bottles lay uncorked. Filthy, malodorous tin cans were scattered on the floors. Nothing, not even a tin dipper to drink out of the well, was left in the house, except one chair out of which the bottom had been cut, and one bedstead fastened together with bayonets. Picture frames were piled against the wall. I eagerly examined them. Every one was empty. One family portrait of an old lady was hanging on the wall with a saber-cut across her face.

The guard, a great, tall fellow, came to me for orders. I felt nervous at his presence and wished I had not brought him. I directed him to watch all night at the roadside of the house, while I would sit up and keep watch in the opposite direction. The children soon slept upon the floor.

As the night wore on, I grew extremely anxious about the strange negroes. Aunt Jinny thought there were not more than fifty. They had filled every outhouse except the kitchen. Suppose they should overpower the guard and murder us all.

Everything was quiet. I had not the least disposition to sleep—thinking, thinking, of all the old woman had told me of the sacking of the house, of the digging of the cellar in search of treasure, of the torch that had twice been applied to the house, and twice withdrawn because some officer wanted the shaded dwelling for a temporary lodging. Presently I was startled by a shrill scream from the kitchen, a door opened suddenly and shut, and a voice cried, "Thank Gawd! Thank Gawd A'mighty." Then all was still.

Was this a signal? I held my breath and listened, then softly rose, closed the shutters and fastened them, crept to the door, and bolted it inside. I might defend my children till the guard could come.

Evidently he had not heard! He was probably sleeping the sleep of an untroubled conscience on the bench in the front porch. And with untroubled consciences my children were sleeping. It was so dark in the room I could not see their faces, but I could touch them, and push the wet locks from their brows, as they lay in the close and heated atmosphere.

I resumed my watch at the window, pressing my face close to the slats of the shutters. A pale half-moon hung low in the sky, turning its averted face from a suffering world. At a little distance I could see the freshly made soldier's grave which Alick had discovered and reported. A heavy rain had fallen in the first hours of the night, and a stiff arm and hand now protruded from the shallow grave. To-morrow I would reverently cover the appealing arm, be it clad in blue or in gray, and would mark the spot.

The sun was rising when I saw my good old friend emerge from her kitchen, and I opened the shutters to greet her. She had brought me a cup of delicious coffee, and was much distressed because I had not slept. Had I heard anything?

"Course I know you were bleeged to hear," said Aunt Jinny, as she bustled over the children. "That was Sis' Winny! She got happy in the middle of the night, an' Gawd knows what she would have done, if Frank hadn't ketched hold of her and pulled her back in the kitchen! Frank an' me is pretty nigh outdone an' discouraged 'bout Sis' Winny. She prays constant all day; but Gawd A'mighty don't count on bein' bothered all night. Ain' He 'ranged for us all to sleep, an' let Him have a little peace? Sis' Winny must keep her happiness to herself, when folks is trying to git some res'."

The guard now came to my window to say he "guessed" he'd "have to put on some more harness. Them blamed niggers refused to leave. They might change their minds when they saw the pistols."

"Oh, you wouldn't shoot, would you?" I said, in great distress. "Call them all to the back door and let me speak with them." I found myself in the presence of some seventy-five negroes, men, women, and children, all with upturned faces, keenly interested in what I should say to them.

I talked to them kindly, and told them I was sorry to see so many of them without homes. One of them, an intelligent-looking man, interrupted me.

"We are not without homes," he said. "I planted and worked on this place for years before the war. It is right I should have some choice in the land the government promises us, and I have come here because I shall ask for the land I have worked."

"You are mistaken, I am sure," I said. "This farm belongs to my brother, not to me. I am here through his kindness, and I am perfectly willing you should remain through mine until you find other shelter, provided you consider my husband master here, give no trouble, and help me clean up this place. All who are not willing to do this must leave. You must distinctly understand this is private property which will be protected by the government."

"That's so!" said the guard, emphatically. Thereupon an old, gray-haired man stepped forth and said:

"My name's Abram! I'se toted Marse Roger on my back to school many a time. Me an' my family will stay an' clean up, an' thank you, Mistis! Come now! You all hear what the Yankee gentleman say! Git to work now on them dead cows—hurry up!"

I sent Abram to the quartermaster, and borrowed a team to haul away the filth and the dead animals. My faithful old friend in the kitchen lent me chairs and a table, and before night we were comparatively clean, having had a score or more scrubbers, and as many out-of-door laborers at work. My husband returned to us, and we commenced our new life of hopeless destitution.

CHAPTER LIII

THE END came when General Grant's forces, closing in upon Virginia from north and south and west, took Richmond, the Southern capital, and pursued the forces of Lee to Appomattox, where in April, 1865, they surrendered. Grant has placed on record the preliminary letters between himself and Lee, and has told of the meeting at which the two of them arranged terms of peace.

These three letters preceded the famous meeting:

April 7, 1865.

GENERAL:—
The result of the last week must convince you of the hopelessness of further resistance on the part of the Army of Northern Virginia in this struggle. I feel that it is so, and regard it as my duty to shift from myself the responsibility of any further effusion of blood, by asking of you the surrender of that portion of the Confederate States army known as the Army of Northern Virginia.

U. S. GRANT, Lieutenant-General.

April 7, 1865.

GENERAL:—
I have received your note of this date. Though not entertaining the opinion you express on the hopelessness of further resistance on the part of the Army of Northern Virginia, I reciprocate your desire to avoid useless effusion of blood, and therefore, before considering your proposition, ask the terms you will offer on condition of its surrender.

R. E. LEE, General.

April 8, 1865.

GENERAL:—
Your note of last evening, in reply to mine of same date, asking conditions on which I will accept the surrender of the Army of Northern Virginia, is just received. In reply, I would say that *peace* being my great desire, there is but one condition I would insist

upon—namely, That the men and officers surrendered shall be disqualified for taking up arms again against the Government of the United States until properly exchanged. I will meet you, or will designate officers to meet any officers you may name for the same purpose, at any point agreeable to you, for the purpose of arranging definitely the terms upon which the surrender of the Army of Northern Virginia will be received.

U. S. GRANT, Lieutenant-General.

Then Grant takes up the tale of the conference itself.

When I had left camp that morning [April 9] I had not expected so soon the result that was then taking place, and consequently was in rough garb. I was without a sword, as I usually was when on horseback on the field, and wore a soldier's blouse for a coat, with the shoulder straps of my rank to indicate to the army who I was. When I went into the house I found General Lee. We greeted each other, and after shaking hands took our seats. I had my staff with me, a good portion of whom were in the room during the whole of the interview.

What General Lee's feelings were I do not know. As he was a man of much dignity, with an impassive face, it was impossible to say whether he felt inwardly glad that the end had finally come, or felt sad over the result and was too manly to show it. . . . I felt like anything rather than rejoicing at the downfall of a foe who had fought so long and valiantly, and had suffered so much for a cause, though that cause was, I believe, one of the worst for which a people ever fought, and one for which there was the least excuse. I do not question, however, the sincerity of the great mass of those who were opposed to us.

General Lee was dressed in a full uniform which was entirely new, and was wearing a sword of considerable value, very likely the sword which had been presented by the State of Virginia.

We soon fell into a conversation about old army times [in the Mexican War]. He remarked that he remembered me very well in the old army. . . . Our conversation grew so pleasant that I almost forgot the object of our meeting . . . when General Lee again interrupted the course of the conversation by suggesting that the terms I proposed to give his army ought to be written out. I called to General Parker, Secretary on my staff, for writing materials, and commenced writing out the following terms:

Appomattox C. H., Va.
Ap'l 9th, 1865.

Gen. R. E. Lee,
 Comd'g C.S.A.

GEN : In accordance with the substance of my letter to you of the 8th inst., I propose to receive the surrender of the Army of N. Va. on the following terms, to wit: Rolls of all the officers and men to be made in duplicate. One copy to be given to an officer designated by me, the other to be retained by such officer or officers as you may designate. The officers to give their individual paroles not to take up arms against the Government of the United States until properly exchanged, and each company or regimental commander sign a like parole for the men of their commands. The arms, artillery and public property to be parked and stacked, and turned over to the officer appointed by me to receive them. This will not embrace the side-arms of the officers, nor their private horses or baggage. This done, each officer and man will be allowed to return to their homes, not to be disturbed by United States authority so long as they observe their paroles and the laws in force where they may reside.

Very respectfully
U. S. GRANT
Lt. Gen.

. . . I then said to him that I thought this would be about the last battle of the war—I sincerely hoped so; and I said further I took it that most of the men in the ranks were small farmers. The whole country had been so raided by the two armies that it was doubtful whether they would be able to put in a crop to carry themselves and their families through the next winter without the aid of the horses they were then riding. The United States did not want them, and I would therefore instruct the officers I left behind to receive the paroles of his troops to let every man of the Confederate army who claimed to own a horse or mule take the animal to his home. Lee remarked again that this would have a happy effect. He then sat down and wrote out the following letter:

Headquarters Army of Northern Virginia
April 9, 1865.

GENERAL :—

I received your letter of this date containing the terms of the surrender of the Army of Northern Virginia as proposed by you. As they are substantially the same as those expressed in your letter of the 8th inst., they are accepted. I will proceed to designate the proper officers to carry the stipulations into effect.

R. E. LEE, General.

While duplicates of the two letters were being made, the Union Generals present were severally presented to General Lee.

The much talked of surrendering of Lee's sword and my handing it back, this and much more that has been said about it is purest romance.

General Lee, after all was completed, and before taking his leave, remarked that his army was in a very bad condition for want of food, and that they were without forage; that his men had been living for some days on parched corn exclusively, and that he would have to ask me for rations and forage. I told him "certainly," and asked for how many men he wanted rations. His answer was "about twenty-five thousand": and I authorized him to send his own commissary and quartermaster to Appomattox Station, two or three miles away, where he could have, out of the trains we had stopped, all the provisions wanted.

When news of the surrender first reached our lines our men commenced firing a salute of a hundred guns in honor of the victory. I at once sent word, however, to have it stopped. The Confederates were now our prisoners, and we did not want to exult over their downfall.

I suggested to General Lee that there was not a man in the Confederacy whose influence with the soldiery and the whole people was as great as his, and that if he would now advise the surrender of all the armies I had no doubt his advice would be followed with alacrity. But Lee said, that he could not do that without consulting the President first. I knew that there was no use urging him to do anything against his ideas of what was right.

When Lee and I separated he went back to his lines and I returned to the house of Mr. McLean. Here the officers of both armies came in great numbers, and seemed to enjoy the meeting as much as though they had been friends separated for a long time while fighting battles under the same flag.

CHAPTER LIV

PEACE HAVING arrived, there was immediate necessity for a policy which should restore as much as possible of the south's existence to her. For she had suffered in all senses from a devastating conflict fought on her own ground. There was not merely her poverty now, but the problem which arose out of the freeing of the slaves. The assassination of Lincoln five days after Appomattox delayed and perhaps perverted what might have been a speedy Reconstruction. For at least a decade there was soreness in the south over the presence of Northern agents—"carpet baggers"—come down to settle things. The Freedmen's Bureau, created to assist the Negro find himself, worked sometimes well and sometimes blunderingly. A secret society, the Ku Klux Klan, formed in Tennessee to protect the ancient privileges of white men against anticipated outrages by former slaves, served its purpose too well and spread terror over some of the districts it was supposed to protect. Many a plantation was for years in confusion, its Negroes ranging helplessly between the extremes of industry and insurrection.

On one such plantation lived Frances Butler Leigh, who went with her father to his Georgia land immediately after the war, and within a few years was herself in control of the estate. Her experiences with the Negroes are preserved in letters sent north.

THE morning after our arrival in Savannah, my father came into my room to say he was off to the plantation at once, having seen some gentlemen the evening before, who told him if he wished to do anything at all in the way of planting this season, that he must not lose an hour, as it was very doubtful even now if a crop could be got in. So off he went, promising to return as soon as possible, and report what state of things he found on the island. I consoled myself by going off to church to hear Bishop Elliott, who preached one of the most beautiful sermons I ever heard, on the Resurrection, the one thought that can bring hope and comfort to these poor heart-broken people. There was hardly any one at church out of deep mourning, and it was piteous to see so many mere girls' faces, shaded by deep crape veils and widows' caps.

I can hardly give a true idea of how crushed and sad the people are. You hear no bitterness towards the North; they are too sad to be bitter; their grief is overwhelming. Nothing can make any difference to them now; the women live in the past, and the men only in the daily present, trying, in a listless sort of way, to repair their ruined fortunes. They are like so many foreigners, whose only interest in the country is their own individual business. Politics are never mentioned, and they know and care less about what is going on in Washington than in London. They received us with open arms, my room was filled with flowers, and crowds of people called upon me every day, and overwhelmed me with thanks for what I did for their soldiers during the war, which really did amount to but very little. I say this, and the answer invariably is, "Oh, yes, but your heart was with us," which it certainly was.

We had, before leaving the North, received two letters from Georgia, one from an agent of the Freedmen's Bureau, and the other from one of our neighbors, both stating very much the same thing, which was that our former slaves had all returned to the island and were willing and ready to work for us, but refused to engage themselves to any one else, even to their liberators, the Yankees; but that they were very badly off, short of provisions, and would starve if something were not done for them at once, and, unless my father came directly (so wrote the agent of the Freedmen's Bureau), the negroes would be removed and made to work elsewhere.

On Wednesday, when my father returned, he reported that he had found the negroes all on the place, not only those who were there five years ago, but many who were sold three years before that. Seven had worked their way back from the up country. They received him very affectionately, and made an agreement with him to work for one-half the crop, which agreement it remained to be seen if they would keep. Owing to our coming so late, only a small crop could be planted, enough to make seed for another year and clear expenses. I was sorry we could do no more, but too thankful that things were as promising as they were. Most of the finest plantations were lying idle for want of hands to work them, so many of the negroes had died; 17,000 deaths were recorded by the Freedmen's Bureau alone. Many had been taken to the Southwest, and others preferred hanging about the towns, making a few dollars now and then, to working regularly on the plantations; so most people found it impossible to get any laborers, but we had as many as we wanted, and nothing could induce our people to go anywhere else.

The negroes seem perfectly happy at getting back to the old place and having us there, and I have been deeply touched by many instances of devotion on their part. On Sunday morning, after their church, having nothing to do, they all came to see me, and I must have shaken hands with nearly four hundred. They were full of their troubles and sufferings up the country during the war, and the invariable winding up was, "T'ank the Lord, missus, we's back, and sees you and massa again." I said to about twenty strong men, "Well, you know you are free and your own masters now," when they broke out with, "No, missus, we belong to you; we be yours as long as we lib."

Nearly all who have lived through the terrible suffering of these past four years have come back, as well as many of those who were sold seven years ago. Their good character was so well known throughout the State that people were very anxious to hire them and induce them to remain in the "up country," and told them all sorts of stories to keep them, among others that my father was dead, but all in vain. One old man said, "If massa be dead, den I'll go back to the old place and mourn for him." So they not only refused good wages, but in many cases spent all they had to get back, a fact that speaks louder than words as to their feeling for their old master and former treatment.

Our overseer, who was responsible for all our property, has little or nothing to give us back, while everything that was left in charge of the negroes has been taken care of and given back to us without the hope or wish of reward. One old man has guarded the stock so well from both Southern and Northern marauders, that he has now ninety odd sheep and thirty cows under his care. Unfortunately they are on a pine tract some twelve miles away up the river, and as we have no means of transporting them we cannot get them until next year.

One old couple came up yesterday from St. Simon's, Uncle John and Mum Peggy, with five dollars in silver half-dollars tied up in a bag, which they said a Yankee captain had given them the second year of the war for some chickens, and this money these two old people had kept through all their want and suffering for three years because it had been paid for fowls belonging to us. I wonder whether white servants would be so faithful or honest! My father was much moved at this act of faithfulness, and intends to have something made out of the silver to commemorate the event, having returned them the same amount in other money.

One of the great difficulties of this new state of things is, what is to be done with the old people who are too old, and the children who are too young, to work? One Northern General said to a planter, in answer to this question, "Well, I suppose they must die," which, indeed, seems the only thing for them to do. To-day Mr. J—— tells me my father has agreed to support the children for three years, and the old people till they die, that is, feed and clothe them. Fortunately, as we have some property at the North we are able to do this, but most of the planters are utterly ruined and have no money to buy food for their own families, so on their plantations I do not see what else is to become of the negroes who cannot work except to die.

The prospect of getting in the crop did not grow more promising as time went on. The negroes talked a great deal about their desire and intention to work for us, but their idea of work, unaided by the stern law of necessity, is very vague, some of them working only half a day and some even less. I don't think one does a really honest full day's work, and so of course not half the necessary amount is done and I am afraid never will be again, and so our properties will soon be utterly worthless, for no crop can be raised by such labor as this, and no negro will work if he can help it, and is quite satisfied just to scrape along doing an odd job here and there to earn money enough to buy a little food.* They are affectionate and often trustworthy and honest, but so hopelessly lazy as to be almost worthless as laborers.

My father was quite encouraged at first, the people seemed so willing to work and said so much about their intention of doing so; but not many days after they started he came in quite disheartened, saying that half the hands had left the fields at one o'clock and the rest by three o'clock, and this just at our busiest time. Half a day's work will keep them from starving, but won't raise a crop. Our contract with them is for half the crop; that is, one-half to be divided among them, according to each man's rate of work, we letting them have in the meantime necessary food, clothing, and money for their present wants (as they have not a penny) which is to be deducted from whatever is due to them at the end of the year.

This we found the best arrangement to make with them, for if we paid them wages, the first five dollars they made would have seemed like so large a sum to them, that they would have imagined their fortunes made and refused to work any more. But even this arrange-

---

* N.B. I was mistaken. In the years 1877 and 1880 upwards of thirty thousand bushels of rice was raised on the place by these same negroes.

ment had its objections, for they told us, when they missed working two or three days a week, that they were losers by it as well as ourselves, half the crop being theirs. But they could not see that this sort of work would not raise any crop at all, and that such should be the result was quite beyond their comprehension. They were quite convinced that if six days' work would raise a whole crop, three days' work would raise half a one, with which they as partners were satisfied, and so it seemed as if we should have to be too.

Christmas, 1868.

Dearest M——, You have heard of our safe arrival, and how much more comfortable the traveling was than last year. We arrived about a month ago, and I have been hard at work ever since. The negroes do not seem to be in a very satisfactory condition, but it is owing in a great measure, I think, to its being Christmas time. They are all prepared again to make their own, and different, terms for next year, but except for the bother and trouble I don't feel very anxious about it, for we have a gang of Irishmen doing the banking and ditching, which the negroes utterly refuse to do any more at all, and therefore, until the planting begins, we can do without the negro labor.

Last year they humbugged me completely by their expressions of affection and desire to work for me, but now that the novelty of their getting back once more to their old home has entirely worn off and they have lost their old habits of work, the effects of freedom are beginning to tell, and everywhere sullen unwillingness to work is visible, and all round us people are discussing how to get other laborers in the place of negroes. But alas! on the rice lands white labor is impossible, so that I really don't know what we shall do, and I think things look very gloomy for the planters. Our Northern neighbors on St. Simon's, the D——s, who were most hopeful last year, are now perfectly discouraged with the difficulties they have to encounter with their labor, and of course having to lose two or three months every year while the negroes are making up their minds whether they will work or not, obliges us to plant much less ground than we should otherwise do. However, there is no use taking evil on account, and when we are ruined will be time enough to say free labor here is a failure, and I still hope that when their Christmas excitement is over, the people will settle down to work.

We had a small excitement about this time, owing to a report which went the round of the plantations, that there was to be a general negro insurrection on the 1st of the year. I did not much believe it, but as I had promised my friends at the North, who were very anxious about me, to run no risks and to take every precaution against danger, I thought it best to seek some means of protection. I first asked my friend whether she felt nervous and would rather leave the Island, but she, being a true soldier's daughter, said no, she would stay and take her chance with me. We then agreed to say nothing about it to my maid, who was a new English maid, thinking that if we did not mind having *our* throats cut, neither need she—particularly as she now spent most of her time weeping at the horrors which surrounded her.

I wrote therefore to our nearest military station and asked that a guard of soldiers might be sent over for a day or two, which was done. But as they came without any officer, and conducted themselves generally disagreeably, stealing the oranges, worrying the negroes, and making themselves entirely at home even to the point of demanding to be fed by me, I packed them off, preferring to take my chance with my negroes than with my protectors. I don't believe that there was the least foundation for the report of the insurrection, but we had trouble enough the whole winter in one form or other.

The negroes this year and the following seemed to reach the climax of lawless independence, and I never slept without a loaded pistol by my bed. Their whole manner was changed; they took to calling their former owners by their last name without any title before it, constantly spoke of my agent as old R——, dropped the pleasant term of "Mistress," took to calling me "Miss Fanny," walked about with guns upon their shoulders, worked just as much and when they pleased, and tried speaking to me with their hats on, or not touching them to me when they passed me on the banks. This last rudeness I never permitted for a moment, and always said sharply, "Take your hat off instantly," and was obliged to take a tone to them generally which I had never done before. One or two, who seemed rather more inclined to be insolent than the rest, I dismissed, always saying, "You are free to leave the place, but not to stay here and behave as you please, for I am free, too, and moreover own the place, and so have a right to give my orders on it, and have them obeyed."

I felt sure that if I relaxed my discipline for one moment all was up, and I never could control the negroes or plant the place again; and to this unerring rule I am sure I owe my success, although for that year, and the two following, I felt the whole time that it was touch-and-go whether I or the negroes got the upper hand.

A new trouble came upon us, too, or rather an old trouble in a new shape. Negro adventurers from the North, finding that politics was such a paying trade at the South, began pouring in, and were really worse than the whites, for their Southern brethren looked upon their advent quite as a proof of a new order of things, in which the negroes were to rule and possess the land.

We had a fine specimen in one Mr. Tunis Campbell, whose history is rather peculiar. Massachusetts had the honor of giving him birth, and on his first arrival in Georgia he established himself, whether with or without permission I know not, on St. Catherine's Island, a large island midway between Savannah and Darien, which was at that time deserted. The owner, without returning, rented it to a Northern party, who on coming to take possession found Mr. Campbell established there, who declined to move, on some pretended permission he had from the Government to occupy it, and it was necessary to apply to the authorities at Darien to remove him, which was done by sending a small armed force. He then came to Darien, and very soon became a leader of the negroes, over whom he acquired the most absolute control, and managed exactly as he pleased, so that when the first vote for State and county authorities was cast, he had no difficulty in having himself elected a magistrate, and for several years administered justice with a high hand and happy disregard of law, there being no one to oppose him.

Happily, he at last went a little too far, and arrested the captain of a British vessel, which had come to Darien for timber, for assault and battery, because he pushed Campbell's son out of the way on the deck of his own ship. The captain was brought before Campbell, tried, and sentenced to pay a heavy fine, from which he very naturally appealed to the English Consul in Savannah, who of course ordered his release at once. This and some other equally lawless acts by which Mr. Campbell was in the habit of filling his own pockets, drew the attention of the authorities to him, and a very good young judge having just been put on our circuit, he was tried for false imprisonment, and sentenced to one year's imprisonment himself, which not only freed us from his iniquitous rule, against which we had had no appeal, but broke the spell which he held over the negroes, who up till the time of his downfall, had believed his powers omnipotent, and at his instigation had defied all other authority; which state of things had driven the planters to despair, for there seemed to be no remedy for this evil, the negroes throwing all our authority to the wind, and following Campbell wherever he chose to lead them.

So desperate were some of the gentlemen, that at one time they entertained the idea of seeing if they could not buy Campbell over, and induce him by heavy bribes to work for us, or rather to use his influence over our negroes to make them work for us. And this proposition was made to me, but I could not consent to such a plan. In the first place it was utterly opposed to my notions of what was right, and my pride revolted from the idea of making any such bargain with a creature like Campbell; besides which I felt sure it was bad policy, that if we bought him one day he would sell us the next. So I refused to have anything to do with the project, and it was fortunately never carried out, for although during the next three or four years Campbell gave us infinite trouble, he would have given us far more had we put ourselves in his power by offering him a bribe.

My agent unfortunately was not much assistance to me, being nervous, timid, and irresolute. Naturally his first thought was to raise the crops by any means that he could, but feeling himself powerless to enforce his orders, owing to the fact that we had no proper authorities to appeal to, should our negroes misbehave themselves, these representatives of the Government pandering to the negroes in every way, in order to secure their votes for themselves, he was obliged to resort to any means he could, to get any work out of the negroes at all, often changing his tactics and giving different orders from day to day. In vain I implored him to be firm, and if he gave an order to stand to it; but the invariable answer was, "It's of no use, Miss B——, I should only get myself into trouble, and have the negro sheriff sent over by Campbell to arrest me." And every one went on the same principle. One of the negroes committed a brutal murder, but no notice was taken of it by any of the authorities, until, with much personal trouble, I had him arrested and shut up. Shortly afterwards, greatly to my astonishment and indignation, I met him walking about the place, and on inquiring how he had got out, was coolly informed that "a gentleman had hired him, from the agent of the Freedmen's Bureau, to work on his plantation." I went at once to the agent, and told him that if the man was not rearrested at once and kept confined, I would report him to the higher authorities.

A few days afterwards I visited the same negro in his prison (!) which turned out to be a deserted warehouse, with no fastening upon the door, and here I found him playing the fiddle to a party who were dancing. He did meet his fate, however, poor fellow, at last, but not for three years, when our own courts were reëstablished, and he was tried, sentenced, and hanged.

On another occasion I had to insist upon two of my own negroes being sent off the place, as they had been caught stealing rice. No one would try them, and my agent proposed to let them off for the present, as he needed their labor just then.

Finding things so unsettled and unsatisfactory, I determined to remain at the South during the summer, fearing that we might after all lose the crops we had with so much difficulty got planted; and part of the hot weather I passed at St. Simon's, and part in South Carolina, with the same friends I had been with the winter before.

On St. Simon's I found as usual a very different state of things from that on Butler's Island. The people were working like machinery, and gave no trouble at all, which was owing perhaps somewhat to the fact that there were only fifty, instead of three hundred, and at the head of the fifty was Bram, with eight of his family at work under him. He was really a remarkable man, and gave the tone to the whole place. And oh! the place was so beautiful; each day it seemed to me to grow more so. All the cattle had come down, and it was a pretty sight to see first the thirty cows, then the sheep, of which there were over a hundred, with their lambs, come in for the night, and then the horses led out to water before going to bed. I used to go round every evening to visit them in their different pens and places, where they were all put up for the night. The stable I visited several times a day, as I had not much faith in my groom, and once when I was telling him how to rub one of the horses down with a wisp of straw when he came in hot, he said, "Yis, so my ole missus (my mother) taught me, and stand dere to see it done." To which I could only say, "You seem to have forgotten the lesson pretty thoroughly."

In July I went to South Carolina, and found my friends moved from the rice plantation to a settlement about fifteen miles distant in the pine woods, which formerly had been occupied entirely by the overseers, when the gentlemen and their families could afford to spend their summer at the North, a thing they no longer could afford, nor wished to do. The place and the way of living were altogether queerer than anything I had ever imagined. The village consisted of about a dozen houses, set down here and there among the tall pine trees, which grew up to the very doors, almost hiding one house from another. The place was very healthy and the sanitary laws very strict. No two houses were allowed to be built in a line, no one was allowed to turn up the soil, even for a garden, and no one, on pain of death, to cut down a pine tree; in which way they succeeded in keeping it perfectly free from malaria, and the air one breathed was full of the delicious fragrance of the pines, which in itself is considered a cure for most ills. In front of each house was a high mound of sand, on which at night a blazing pine fire was lit to drive away malaria that might come from the dampness of the night. These fires had the most picturesque effect, throwing their glare upon the red trunks of the pines and lighting the woods for some distance around.

The houses were built in the roughest possible manner, many of them being mere log-houses. The one we were in was neither plastered nor lined inside, one thickness of boards doing for both inside and outside walls. M—— and I slept literally under the shingles, between which and the walls of the house, we could lie and watch the stars; but I liked feeling the soft air on my face, and to hear it sigh softly through the tall pines outside, as I lay in bed. Occasionally bats came in, which was not so pleasant, and there was not one room in the house from which you could not freely discourse with any one in any other part of the building. Hampton Point, which I had always regarded as the roughest specimen of a house any one could live in, was a palace compared with this. We were nevertheless perfectly comfortable, and it was really pretty, with numbers of easy-chairs and comfortable sofas about, and the pretty bright chintz curtains and covers, which looked very well against the fresh whitewashed boards; and there was an amusing incongruity between a grand piano and fine embroidered sheets and pillow cases, relics of past days of wealth and luxury, and our bare floors and walls.

Most of the people were very poor, which created a sort of commonwealth, as there was a friendly feeling among them all, and desire to share anything good which one got with his neighbors; so that, constantly through the day, negro servants would be seen going about from one house to another, carrying a neatly covered tray, which contained presents of cakes or fruit, or even fresh bread that some one had been baking. There was a meat club, which every one belonged to, and to which every one contributed in turn, either an ox or a sheep a week, which was then divided equally, each house receiving in turn a different part, so that all fared alike, and one week we feasted sumptuously off the sirloin, and the next, not so well, from the brisket.

Mrs. P—— was most energetic, directing the affairs of the estate with a masterly hand, and at the same time devoting herself to the comfort and happiness of her children; reading French or German, or practicing music with her daughter in the mornings, and being always ready to receive her boys on their return from their hard day's work on the plantation, to which they rode fifteen miles every morning, and back the same distance in the evening, with interest and sympathy in the day's work, and a capital good dinner, which especially excited my admiration, as half the time there really seemed nothing to make it of. But they were better off than most of the people, who were very wretched. Many of them had their fine plantation houses, with everything in them, burnt to the ground during the war, and had no money and very little idea of how to help themselves. In the next house to us was Mrs. M——, an elegant, refined, and cultivated old lady, with soft silver gray hair and delicate features that made her look like a picture on Sèvres china and as unable as a Sèvres cup to bear any rough handling, but who lived without many of the ordinary necessaries of life, and was really starving to death because she could not eat the coarse food which was all she could get.

Poor people! they were little used to such hardships, and seemed as helpless as children, but nevertheless were patient and never complained.

CHAPTER LV

THE BITTEREST pill for Southern pride to swallow was the enfranchisement of the Negro. Millions who only a few years before had composed an utterly subject race now came by act of Congress into the rights of citizenship—were sovereigns equally with their old owners. The south found means eventually to control elections; but in the late '60's the spectacle was presented of Negroes voting— and not only that, being elected to state legislatures, where in certain cases they held the balance of power. Wholesale corruption entered some of the Southern capitals, or if not that, confusion and incompetence. The situation in South Carolina was reported by James S. Pike in a book called, significantly, "The Prostrate State."

YESTERDAY, about 4 P.M., the assembled wisdom of the State, whose achievements are illustrated on that theater, issued forth from the State House. About three-quarters of the crowd belonged to the African race. They were of every hue, from the light octoroon to the deep black. They were such a looking body of men as might pour out of a market-place or a courthouse at random in any Southern State. Every negro type and physiognomy was here to be seen, from the genteel serving-man to the rough-hewn customer from the rice or cotton field. Their dress was as varied as their countenances. There was the second-hand black frock-coat of infirm gentility, glossy and threadbare. There was the stove-pipe hat of many ironings and departed styles. There was also to be seen a total disregard of the properties of costume in the coarse and dirty garments of the field; the stub-jackets and slouch hats of soiling labor. In some instances, rough woolen comforters embraced the neck and hid the absence of linen. Heavy brogans, and short, torn trousers, it was impossible to hide. The dusky tide flowed out into the littered and barren grounds, and, issuing through the coarse wooden fence of the inclosure, melted away into the street beyond. These were the legislators of South Carolina.

In conspicuous bas-relief over the door of exit, on the panels of the stately edifice, the marble visages of George McDuffie and

Robert Y. Hayne overlooked the scene. Could they veritably witness it from their dread abode? What then? "I tremble," wrote Jefferson, when depicting the character of Southern slavery, "I tremble when I reflect that God is just." But did any of that old band of Southern Revolutionary patriots who wrestled in their souls with the curse of slavery ever contemplate such a descent into barbarism as this spectacle implied and typified? "My God, look at this!" was the unbidden ejaculation of a low-country planter, clad in homespun, as he leaned over the rail inside the House, gazing excitedly upon the body in session. "This is the first time I have been here. I thought I knew what we were doing when we consented to emancipation. I knew the negro, and I predicted much that has happened, but I never thought it would come to this. Let me go."

Here, then, is the outcome, the ripe, perfected fruit of the boasted civilization of the South, after two hundred years of experience. A white community, that had gradually risen from small beginnings, till it grew into wealth, culture, and refinement, and became accomplished in all the arts of civilization; that successfully asserted its resistance to a foreign tyranny by deeds of conspicuous valor, which achieved liberty and independence through the fire and tempest of civil war, and illustrated itself in the councils of the nation by orators and statesmen worthy of any age or nation—such a community is then reduced to this. It lies prostrate in the dust, ruled over by this strange conglomerate, gathered from the ranks of its own servile population. It is the spectacle of a society suddenly turned bottom-side up. The wealth, the intelligence, the culture, the wisdom of the State, have broken through the crust of that social volcano on which they were contentedly reposing, and have sunk out of sight, consumed by the subterranean fires they had with such temerity braved and defied.

In the place of this old aristocratic society stands the rude form of the most ignorant democracy that mankind ever saw, invested with the functions of government. It is the dregs of the population habilitated in the robes of their intelligent predecessors, and asserting over them the rule of ignorance and corruption, through the inexorable machinery of a majority of numbers. It is barbarism overwhelming civilization by physical force. It is the slave rioting in the halls of his master, and putting that master under his feet. And, though it is done without malice and without vengeance, it is nevertheless none the less completely and absolutely done. Let us approach nearer and take a closer view. We will enter the House of Representatives. Here sit one hundred and twenty-four members. Of these, twenty-three are white men, representing the remains of the old civilization. These are good-looking, substantial citizens. They are men of weight and standing in the communities they represent. They are all from the hill country. The frosts of sixty and seventy winters whiten the heads of some among them. There they sit, grim and silent. They feel themselves to be but loose stones, thrown in to partially obstruct a current they are powerless to resist. They say little and do little as the days go by. They simply watch the rising tide, and mark the progressive steps of the inundation. They hold their places reluctantly. They feel themselves to be in some sort martyrs, bound stoically to suffer in behalf of that still great element in the State whose prostrate fortunes are becoming the sport of an unpitying Fate. Grouped in a corner of the commodious and well-furnished chamber, they stolidly survey the noisy riot that goes on in the great black Left and Center, where the business and debates of the House are conducted, and where sit the strange and extraordinary guides of the fortunes of a once proud and haughty State. In this crucial trial of his pride, his manhood, his prejudices, his spirit, it must be said of the Southern Bourbon of the Legislature that he comports himself with a dignity, a reserve, and a decorum, that command admiration. He feels that the iron hand of Destiny is upon him. He is gloomy, disconsolate, hopeless. The gray heads of this generation openly profess that they look for no relief. They see no way of escape. The recovery of influence, of position, of control in the State, is felt by them to be impossible. They accept their position with a stoicism that promises no reward here or hereafter. They are the types of a conquered race. They staked all and lost all. Their lives remain, their property and their children do not. War, emancipation, and grinding taxation, have consumed them. Their struggle now is against complete confiscation. They endure, and wait for the night.

This dense negro crowd they confront do the debating, the squabbling, the law-making, and create all the clamor and disorder of the body. These twenty-three white men are but the observers, the enforced auditors of the dull and clumsy imitation of a deliberative body, whose appearance in their present capacity is at once a wonder and a shame to modern civilization.

Deducting the twenty-three members referred to, who comprise the entire strength of the opposition, we find one hundred and one remaining. Of this one hundred and one, ninety-four are colored, and seven are their white allies. Thus the blacks outnumber the whole body of whites in the House more than three to one. On the mere basis of numbers in the State the injustice of this disproportion is manifest, since the black population is relatively four to three of the whites. A just rectification of the disproportion, on the basis of population merely, would give fifty-four whites to seventy black members. And the line of race very nearly marks the line of hostile politics. As things stand, the body is almost literally a Black Parliament, and it is the only one on the face of the earth which is the representative of a white constituency and the professed exponent of an advanced type of modern civilization. But the reader will find almost any portraiture inadequate to give a vivid idea of the body, and enable him to comprehend the complete metamorphosis of the South Carolina Legislature, without observing its details. The Speaker is black, the Clerk is black, the door-keepers are black, the little pages are black, the chairman of the Ways and Means is black, and the chaplain is coal-black. At some of the desks sit colored men whose types it would be hard to find outside of Congo; whose costume, visages, attitudes, and expression, only befit the forecastle of a buccaneer. It must be remembered, also, that these men, with not more than half a dozen exceptions, have been themselves slaves.

A large, well-built, showy kind of white man, with a good voice and fluent speech, was addressing the House yesterday. Standing beside me on the floor, near the Speaker's chair, was a snug-built, round-headed, young black man, of perhaps one-quarter white blood. He had full eyes, thick lips, and woolly hair, and was brusque and lively. I asked who was the speaker. "Oh," replied he, with a toss of the head and a scornful air, "that is a chuckle-head from ——. He has got about as much brains as you can hold in your hand." My pride of race was incontinently shocked. Here was a new view. It was no longer the white man deriding the incapacity of the negro. The tables were emphatically turned. It was Sambo proclaiming the white man's inferiority. Here, then, is something suggestive. "Soho! my friend," I said, "you know these people, then; give us your judgment of them."

He replied: "We have all sorts here, good, bad, and indifferent." "Parsons among them?" "No, only a few. Not so many as formerly. When I was on the stump at the last election, I advised the people not to send the parsons. They gave us a great deal of trouble. They had been the most corrupt rascals we had in the Legislature. Now they are less plenty. We are improving. But see that darkey now talking. Isn't it ridiculous that people should send such representatives? They don't know anything, and haven't even decent manners. There is another big fool, sitting there. Look at him. Why don't they keep such chaps at home? They are a disgrace to the colored people." It was my snug-built, thick-lipped, woolly-headed, small-brained, black friend, you see, who was making these fruitful comments. The scene grew interesting. "How about this Senator Patterson business?" "Well, we sha'n't know anything certain about it till it is investigated. A member was boasting the other day at a public table, before twenty fellow-boarders and members, of his intentions. He said that, where there was money going, a member was a fool who did not get his share. For his part, he intended to make all he could. He was here for that purpose. A while after Patterson's election, this man was flush of money. He deposited $250 in bank, and displayed $150 more, which he said he must reserve for current expenses. Where he got his money nobody knows. All we know is this, that he had none when he came here." Then our colored friend added, with great *naïveté,* "Everybody is aware that the senatorial election is the only money measure that has been before the Legislature at this session."

"Who is this Whittemore, just elected by the Legislature as one of the trustees of the State Agricultural College?" "Oh, he is that white member of Congress who was turned out for selling his cadetship. He may do well enough for a place like that, but I should not vote for him if I had a seat here. I am a young man, just entered on a political career, and have a record to make, and I don't want to be mixed up with such fellows as Whittemore."

Here, again, we have virtuous Sambo on the corrupt white man. This is even more edifying. Whittemore is a white parson. Our friend is a black layman. We cordially sympathize in his youthful, praiseworthy resolutions. Who knows he will not hold to them steadfastly to the end? Let us hope. There is need he should. He bears one of the most honored names in South Carolina, and there is a good sprinkling of white blood in his veins. May he live long and illustrate the virtues of both races!

He continued: "You have heard of Beverly Nash? There he sits. A full-blooded black man, six feet high. He is a good-looking man, with pleasing manners. He was formerly a slave of W. C. Preston, and afterward a bootblack at one of our hotels. He is now a substantial citizen, and a prominent leader in the Senate and in the State. He handles them all. The lawyers and the white chivalry, as they call themselves, have learned to let him alone. They know more of law and some other things than he does; but he studies them all up, and then comes down on them with a good story or an anecdote, and you better believe he carries the audience right along with him. All the laugh and all the ridicule is on his side. And when he undertakes a thing, he generally puts it through, I tell you. No, sir, there is now nobody who cares to attack Beverly Nash. They let him alone right smart."

"They were mostly slaves, these people in the Legislature?" "Yes, nearly all, including the Speaker of the House: not more than five or six were freeborn." "And you?" "No, sir, I never was a slave. I was raised in Charleston. My parents were free and my grandparents before them."

"You have United States troops in Columbia." "Yes, but we don't need them. The Ku-klux did not bother anybody down here. We can take care of ourselves. Things are in rather a bad fix in the State, financially, but they will all come out right in the end. This town has suffered greatly, but it is fast recovering. Sherman's troops burnt the city. There is no doubt about that. I myself lost a house, and I ought to be paid for it; for if ever the sun shone on a loyal man I am one. It cost $600 or $700, and could not be rebuilt for twice the money. I am sure I ought to be paid." It was evident our bright belligerent black friend was not only bent on a political "career," but also had a thrifty eye to the main chance. But why not? Who shall reproach him for that? "There were many black mercenaries in the Legislature. Nobody could dispute that. But the same thing existed elsewhere, didn't it, where things were whiter?" I declined to contest that view of the case.

Turning to a solitary white man on my way out of the crowd, he replied, to some remark, that "to take the State of South Carolina away from the intelligent white men and hand it over bodily to ignorant negroes just escaped from slavery, because there happened to be four blacks to three whites throughout the State, was nothing less than flat burglary on the theory and practice of representative government." I suggested, in reply, that the system of cumulative voting might very much relieve the problem. If the whites had their fair proportion of the representation, say three to four, would not energy, talent, and resolution, do the rest? But he was disinclined to any hopeful view of the case. He said "the darkey was not going to let up on any of the advantages he had. He was more inclined to be aggressive than yielding. He was improving, but he was already getting too big for his breeches. Instead of giving the whites a show, he was rather thinking of Africanizing the State. He felt he could go alone. He was beginning to show the cold shoulder to the white man. What did he want of the white man? The white man put on airs. He would not associate socially with the colored brethren, neither would he introduce them to his daughters. This thing could not last. Genuine political equality means social equality with the governing classes. If the white man could not fraternize with them, then the white man may go hang. Sambo will go it alone. Why not? The white walking-stick will be dispensed with. The white figurehead will be removed. Congo is sufficient unto itself. Everything was tending that way. It appeared like ingratitude to their white emancipators, and perhaps this consideration would operate to retard the movement. But look at the evidence. Here were 101 Republicans in the Legislature. Out of the whole number only seven were white men; 94 were colored. Did not this look like Africanizing things? In the executive government, to be sure, the Governor was white. He got his place by dancing at negro balls and speculating in negro delegates. But the Lieutenant-Governor was colored, and the President of the Senate, and the Speaker of the House, and the Treasurer of the State, and nearly all the rest of the officials. Here was Columbia. Half the population was white, but its Senator was colored, and its Representatives in the Legislature and in the city government were nearly all colored men. So were its policemen and its market-men. Everybody in office was a darkey. As for the white carpet-baggers, they were getting shoved out all round." My informant was undoubtedly well informed. He was more alive to the facts than another less interested might have been. For he was an office-holder and a carpet-bagger. His species have had their day in South Carolina. This he foresees, and naturally quakes in his shoes. His track in the State has been one of robbery and desolation, and there is none to lament his final expulsion, whoever follows.

CHAPTER LVI

THE CIVIL War was followed in the north by a period of nervous, reckless expansion. The victory had seemed to vindicate an already powerful tendency for America to industrialize and commercialize herself; and now there was the wealth with which to do it. A huge, self-conscious, and growing society had to accommodate itself to the possession of an almost embarrassing power. East and west there were evidences of a people trying to express itself, often crudely enough, in terms of this power.

Grant had scarcely stepped into the presidency which his military achievements had won for him when a financial scandal engaged the attention of the country—a scandal into which he had almost allowed himself to be drawn, and which was only the first of a series that blackened his administration. Henry Adams, writing for the English press, told the full story of Jim Fisk and Jay Gould, representatives of a ruthless type destined to dominate the American scene throughout the century.

THE civil war in America, with its enormous issues of depreciating currency, and its reckless waste of money and credit by the government, created a speculative mania such as the United States, with all its experience in this respect, had never before known. Not only in Broad Street, the center of New York speculation, but far and wide throughout the Northern States, almost every man who had money at all employed a part of his capital in the purchase of stocks of gold, of copper, of petroleum, or of domestic produce, in the hope of a rise in prices, or staked money on the expectation of a fall. To use the jargon of the street, every farmer and every shopkeeper in the country seemed to be engaged in "carrying" some favorite security "on a margin." Whoever could obtain five pounds sent it to a broker with orders to buy fifty pounds' worth of stocks, or whatever amount the broker would consent to purchase. If the stock rose, the speculator prospered; if it fell until the five pounds of deposit or margin were lost, the broker demanded a new deposit, or sold the stock to protect himself. By means of this simple and smooth machinery, which differs in no essential respect from the processes of *roulette* or *rogue-et-noir*, the whole nation flung itself into the Stock Exchange, until the "outsiders," as they were called, in opposition to the regular brokers of Broad Street, represented nothing less than the entire population of the American Republic. Every one speculated, and for a time every one speculated successfully.

The inevitable reaction began when the government, abut a year after the close of the war, stopped its issues and ceased borrowing. The greenback currency had for a moment sunk to a value of only 37 cents to the dollar. It is even asserted that on the worst day of all, the 11th of July, 1864, one sale of £20,000 in gold was actually made at 310, which is equivalent to about 33 cents in the dollar. At this point, however, the depreciation stopped; and the paper which had come so near falling into entire discredit steadily rose in value, first to 50 cents, then to 60, to 70, and within the present year to more than 90 cents. So soon as the industrious part of the public felt the touch of this return to solid values, the whole fabric of fictitious wealth began to melt away under their eyes.

Thus it was not long before the so-called "outsiders," the men who speculated on their own account, and could not act in agreement or combination, began to suffer. One by one, or in great masses, they were made the prey of the larger operators; their last margins were consumed, and they dropped down to the solid level of slow, productive industry. Some lost everything; many lost still more than they had, and there are few families of ordinary connection and standing in the United States which cannot tell, if they choose, some dark story of embezzlement, or breach of trust, committed in these days. Some men, who had courage and a sense of honor, found life too heavy for them; others went mad. But the greater part turned in silence to their regular pursuits, and accepted their losses as they could. Almost every rich American could produce from some pigeon-hole a bundle of worthless securities, and could show check-books representing the only remaining trace of margin after margin consumed in vain attempts to satisfy the insatiable broker. A year or two of incessant losses swept the weaker gamblers from the street.

But even those who continued to speculate found it necessary to change their mode of operations. Chance no longer ruled over the Stock Exchange and the gold market. The fate of a battle, the capture of a city, or the murder of a President, had hitherto been the influences which broke through the plans of the strongest combinations, and put all speculators, whether great or small, on fairly even ground; but as the period of sudden and uncontrollable disturbing elements passed away, the market fell more and more completely into the hands of cliques which found a point of adhesion in some great mass of incorporated capital. Three distinct railways, with all their enormous resources, became the property of Cornelius Vanderbilt, who, by means of their credit and capital, again and again swept millions of dollars into his pocket by a process curiously similar to gambling with loaded dice. But Vanderbilt was one of the most respectable of these great operators. The Erie Railway was controlled by Daniel Drew, and while Vanderbilt at least acted in the interests of his corporations, Drew cheated equally his corporation and the public. Between these two men and the immense incorporated power they swayed, smaller operators, one after another, were crushed to pieces, until the survivors learned to seek shelter within some clique sufficiently strong to afford protection. Speculation in this manner began to consume itself, and the largest combination of capital was destined to swallow every weaker combination which ventured to show itself in the market.

Thus, between the inevitable effect of a currency which steadily shrank the apparent wealth of the country, and the omnipotence of capital in the stock market, a sounder and healthier state of society began to make itself felt. Nor could the unfortunate public, which had been robbed with such cynical indifference by Drew and Vanderbilt, feel any sincere regret when they saw these two cormorants reduced to tearing each other. In the year 1867 Mr. Vanderbilt undertook to gain possession of the Erie Road, as he had already obtained possession of the New York Central, the second trunk line between New York and the West. Mr. Vanderbilt was supposed to own property to the value of some £10,000,000, all of which might be made directly available for stock operations. He bought the greater part of the Erie stock; Drew sold him all he could take, and then issued as much more as was required in order to defeat Vanderbilt's purpose. After a violent struggle, which overthrew all the guaranties of social order, Drew triumphed, and Mr. Vanderbilt abandoned the contest. The Erie corporation paid him a large sum to reimburse his alleged losses. At the same time it was agreed that Mr. Drew's accounts should be passed, and he obtained a release in full, and retired from the direction. And the Erie Road, almost exhausted by such systematic plundering, was left in the undisturbed, if not peaceful, control of Mr. Jay Gould and Mr. James Fisk, Jr., whose reign began in the month of July, 1868.

Mr. Jay Gould was a partner in the firm of Smith, Gould, & Martin, brokers, in Wall Street. He had been engaged before now in railway enterprises, and his operations had not been of a nature likely to encourage public confidence in his ideas of fiduciary relations. He was a broker, and a broker is almost by nature a gambler, perhaps the very last profession suitable for a railway manager. In character he was strongly marked by his disposition for silent intrigue. He preferred as a rule to operate on his own account, without admitting other persons into his confidence, and he seemed never to be satisfied except when deceiving every one as to his intentions. There was a reminiscence of the spider in his nature. He spun huge webs, in corners and in the dark, which were seldom strong enough to resist a serious strain at the critical moment. His disposition to this subtlety and elaboration of intrigue was irresistible. It is scarcely necessary to say that he had not a conception of a moral principle. In speaking of this class of men it must be fairly assumed at the outset that they do not and cannot understand how there can be a distinction between right and wrong in matters of speculation, so long as the daily settlements are punctually effected. In this respect Mr. Gould was probably as honest as the mass of his fellows, according to the moral standard of the street; but without entering upon technical questions of roguery, it is enough to say that he was an uncommonly fine and unscrupulous intriguer, skilled in all the processes of stock-gambling, and passably indifferent to the praise or censure of society.

James Fisk, Jr., was still more original in character. He was not yet forty years of age, and had the instincts of fourteen. He came originally from Vermont, probably the most respectable and correct State in the Union, and his father had been a pedler who sold goods from town to town in his native valley of the Connecticut. The son followed his father's calling with boldness and success. He drove his huge wagon, made resplendent with paint and varnish, with four or six horses, through the towns of Vermont and Western Massachusetts; and when his father remonstrated in alarm at his reckless management, the young man, with his usual bravado, took his father into his service at a fixed salary, with the warning that he was not to put on airs on the strength of his new dignity. A large Boston firm which had supplied his goods on credit, attracted by his energy, took him into the house; the war broke out; his influence drew the firm into some bold speculations which were successful; in a few years he retired with some £20,000, which he subsequently lost. He formed a connection with Daniel Drew in New York, and a new sign, ominous of future trouble, was raised in Wall Street, bearing the names of Fisk & Belden, brokers.

Personally Mr. Fisk was coarse, noisy, boastful, ignorant; the type of a young butcher in appearance and mind. Nothing could be more striking than the contrast between him and his future associate Gould. One was small and slight in person, dark, sallow, reticent, and stealthy, with a trace of Jewish origin. The other was large, florid, gross, talkative, and obstreperous. Mr. Fisk's redeeming point was his humor, which had a strong flavor of American nationality. His mind was extraordinary fertile in ideas and expedients, while his conversation was filled with unusual images and strange forms of speech, which were caught up and made popular by the New York press. In respect to honesty as between Gould and Fisk, the latter was, perhaps, if possible, less deserving of trust than the former. A story not without a keen stroke of satirical wit is told by him, which illustrates his estimate of abstract truth. An old woman who had bought of the elder Fisk a handkerchief which cost ninepence in the New England currency, where six shillings are reckoned to the dollar, complained to Mr. Fisk, Jr., that his father had cheated her. Mr. Fisk considered the case maturely, and gave a decision based on *a priori* principles. "No!" said he, "the old man wouldn't have told a lie for ninepence"; and then, as if this assertion needed some reasonable qualification, he added, "though he would have told eight of them for a dollar!" The distinction as regards the father may have been just, since the father seems to have held old-fashioned ideas as to wholesale and retail trade; but in regard to the son even this relative degree of truth cannot be predicated with any confidence, since, if the Investigating Committee of Congress and its evidence are to be believed, Mr. Fisk seldom or never speaks truth at all.

An intrigue equally successful and disreputable brought these two men into the Erie Board of Directors, whence they speedily drove their more timid predecessor Drew. In July, 1868, Gould made himself President and Treasurer of the corporation. Fisk became Comptroller. A young lawyer, named Lane, became counsel. These three directors made a majority of the Executive Committee, and were masters of Erie. The Board of Directors held no meetings. The Executive Committee was never called together, and the three men—Fisk, Gould, and Lane—became from this time the absolute, irresponsible owners of the Erie Railway, not less than if it had been their personal property and plaything.

This property was in effect like all the great railway corporations, an empire within a republic. It consisted of a trunk line of road 459 miles in length, with branches 314 miles in extent, or 773 miles of road in all. Its capital stock amounted to about £7,000,000.

Its gross receipts exceeded £3,000,000 per annum. It employed not less than 15,000 men, and supported their families. Over all this wealth and influence, greater than that directly swayed by any private citizen, greater than is absolutely and personally controlled by most kings, and far too great for the public safety either in a democracy or in any other form of society, the vicissitudes of a troubled time placed two men in irresponsible authority; and both these men belonged to a low and degraded moral and social type. Such an elevation has been rarely seen in modern history. Even the most dramatic of modern authors, even Balzac himself, who so loved to deal with similar violent alternations of fortune, or Alexandre Dumas, with all his extravagance of imagination, never have reached a conception bolder or more melodramatic than this, nor have they ever ventured to conceive a plot so enormous, or a catastrophe so original, as was now to be developed.

One of the earliest acts of the new rulers was precisely such as Balzac or Dumas might have predicted and delighted in. They established themselves in a palace. The old offices of the Erie Railway were in the lower part of the city, among the wharves and warehouses; a situation, no doubt, convenient for business, but by no means agreeable as a residence; and the new proprietors naturally wished to reside on their property. Mr. Fisk and Mr. Gould accordingly bought a huge building of white marble, not unlike a European palace, situated about two miles from the business quarter, and containing a large theater or opera-house. They also purchased several smaller houses adjoining it. The opera-house cost about £140,000, and a large part of the building was at once leased, by the two purchasers, to themselves as the Erie corporation, to serve as offices. This suite of apartments was then furnished by themselves, as representing the corporation, at an expense of some £60,000, and in a style which, though called vulgar, is certainly not more vulgar than that of the President's official residence, and which would be magnificent in almost any palace in Europe. The adjoining houses were connected with the main building; and in one of these Mr. Fisk had his private apartments, with a private passage to his opera-box. He also assumed direction of the theater, of which he became manager-in-chief. To these royal arrangements he brought tastes which have been commonly charged as the worst results of royal license. The atmosphere of the Erie offices was not supposed to be disturbed with moral prejudices; and as the opera itself supplied Mr. Fisk's mind with amusement, so the opera *troupe* supplied him with a permanent harem. Whatever Mr. Fisk did was done on an extraordinary scale.

These arrangements, however, regarded only the pleasures of the American Aladdin. In the conduct of their interests the new directors showed a capacity for large conceptions, and a vigor in the execution of their schemes, such as alarmed the entire community. At the annual election in 1868, when Gould, Fisk, and Lane, having borrowed or bought proxies for the greater part of the stock, caused themselves to be elected for the ensuing year, the respectable portion of the public throughout the country was astonished and shocked to learn that the new Board of Directors contained two names peculiarly notorious and obnoxious to honest men,—the names of William M. Tweed and Peter B. Sweeney. To English ears these commonplace, not to say vulgar, titles do not seem singularly alarming; but to every honest American they conveyed a peculiar sense of terror and disgust. The State of New York in its politics is much influenced, if not controlled, by the city of New York. The city politics are so entirely in the hands of the Democratic party as to preclude even the existence of a strong minority. The party organization centers in a political club, held together by its patronage and the money it controls through a system of jobbery unequaled elsewhere in the world. And the Tammany Club, thus swaying the power of a small nation of several million souls, is itself ruled by William M. Tweed and Peter B. Sweeney, absolute masters of this terrible system of theft and fraud, and to American eyes the incarnation of political immorality.

The effect of this alliance was felt in the ensuing winter in the passage of a bill through the State legislature, and its signature by the Governor, abolishing the former system of annual elections of the entire board of Erie directors, and authorizing the board to classify itself in such a manner that only a portion should be changed each year. The principle of the bill was correct. Its practical effect, however, was to enable Gould and Fisk to make themselves directors for five years, in spite of any attempt on the part of the stockholders to remove them. The formality of annual reëlection was spared them; and so far as the stockholders were concerned, there was no great injustice in the act. The Erie Road was in the peculiar position of being without an owner. There was no *cestui que trust,* unless the English stockholders could be called such. In America the stock was almost exclusively held for speculation, not for investment; and in the morals of Wall Street speculation means, or had almost come to mean, disregard of intrinsic value. In this case society at large was the injured party, and society knew its risk.

This step, however, was only a beginning. The Tammany ring,

as it is called, exercised a power far beyond politics. Under the existing constitution of the State, the judges of the State courts are elected by the people. There are thirty-three such judges in New York, and each of the thirty-three is clothed with equity powers running through the whole State. Of these judges Tammany Hall elected several, and the Erie Railway controlled others in country districts. Each of these judges might forbid proceedings before any and all the other judges, or stay proceedings in suits already commenced. Thus the lives and the property of the public were in the power of the new combination; and two of the city judges, Barnard and Cardozo, had already acquired a peculiarly infamous reputation as so-called "slaves to the ring," which left no question as to the depths to which their prostitution of justice would descend.

The alliance between Tammany and Erie was thus equivalent to investing Mr. Gould and Mr. Fisk with the highest attributes of sovereignty; but in order to avail themselves to the utmost of their judicial powers, they also required the ablest legal assistance. The degradation of the bench had been rapidly followed by the degradation of the bar. Prominent and learned lawyers were already accustomed to avail themselves of social or business relations with judges to forward private purposes. One whose partner might be elevated to the bench was certain to be generally retained in cases brought before this special judge; and litigants were taught by experience that a retainer in such cases was profitably bestowed. Others found a similar advantage resulting from known social relations with the court. The debasement of tone was not confined to the lower ranks of advocates; and it was probably this steady demoralization of the bar which made it possible for the Erie ring to obtain the services of Mr. David Dudley Field as its legal adviser. Mr. Field, a gentleman of European reputation, in regard to which he is understood to be peculiarly solicitous, was an eminent law reformer, author of the New York Code, delegate of the American Social Science Association to the European International Congress, and asserted by his partner, Mr. Shearman, in evidence before a committee of the New York legislature, to be a man of quixotic sense of honor. Mr. Shearman himself, a gentleman of English parentage, had earned public gratitude by arranging and deploring, with unsurpassed courage and point, the condition of the New York judiciary, in an admirable essay which will be found in the *North American Review* for July, 1867. The value of Mr. Field's services to Messrs. Fisk and Gould was not to be measured even by the enormous fees their generosity paid him. His power over certain judges became so absolute as to impress the popular imagination; and the gossip of Wall Street insists that he has a silken halter round the neck of Judge Barnard, and a hempen one round that of Cardozo. It is certain that he who had a year before threatened Barnard on his own bench with impeachment now appeared in the character of Barnard's master, and issued as a matter of course the edicts of his court.

One other combination was made by the Erie managers to extend their power, and this time it was credit that was threatened. They bought a joint-stock bank in New York City, with a capital of £200,000. The assistance thus gained was purchased at a very moderate price, since it was by no means represented by the capital. The great cliques and so-called "operations" of Wall Street and Broad Street carry on their transactions by a system of credits and clearing-houses with a very limited use of money. The banks certify their checks, and the certified checks settle all balances. Nominally and by law the banks only certify to the extent of *bona fide* deposits, but in reality the custom of disregarding the strict letter of the law is not unknown, and in regard to the bank in question, the Comptroller of the Currency, an officer of the National Treasury, testifies that on an examination of its affairs in April, 1869, out of fifteen checks deposited in its hands as security for certifications made by it, selected at hazard for inquiry, and representing a nominal value of £300,000, three only were good. The rest represented accommodation extended to brokers and speculators without security. As an actual fact it is in evidence that this same bank on Thursday, September 24, 1869, certified checks to the amount of nearly £1,500,000 for Mr. Gould alone. What sound security Mr. Gould deposited against this mass of credit may be left to the imagination. His operations, however, were not confined to this bank alone, although this was the only one owned by the ring.

Thus Mr. Gould and Mr. Fisk created a combination more powerful than any that has been controlled by mere private citizens in America or in Europe since society for self-protection established the supreme authority of the judicial name. They exercised the legislative and the judicial powers of the State; they possessed almost unlimited credit, and society was at their mercy. One authority alone stood above them, beyond their control; and this was the distant but threatening figure of the National Government.

Nevertheless, powerful as they were, the Erie managers were seldom in funds. The huge marble palace in which they lived, the theater which they supported, the reckless bribery and profusion of management by which they could alone maintain their defiance of public opinion, the enormous schemes for extending their operations into which they rushed with utter recklessness, all required greater resources than could be furnished even by the wholesale plunder of the Erie Road. They were obliged from time to time to issue from their castle and harry the industrious public or their brother freebooters. The process was different from that known to the dark ages, but the objects and the results were equally robbery. At one time Mr. Fisk is said to have ordered heavy speculative sales of stock in an express company which held a contract with the Erie Railway. The sales being effected, the contract was declared annulled. The stock naturally fell, and Mr. Fisk realized the difference. He then ordered heavy purchases, and having renewed the contract the stock rose again, and Mr. Fisk a second time swept the street. In the summer and autumn of 1869 the two managers issued and sold 235,000 new shares of Erie stock, or nearly as much as its entire capital when they assumed power in July, 1868. With the aid of the money thus obtained, they succeeded in withdrawing about £2,500,000 in currency from circulation at the very moment of the year when currency was most in demand in order to harvest the crops. For weeks the whole nation writhed and quivered under the torture of this modern rack, until the national government itself was obliged to interfere and threaten a sudden opening of the treasury. But whether the Erie speculators operated for a rise or operated for a fall, whether they bought or sold, and whether they were engaged in manipulating stocks, or locking up currency, or cornering gold, they were always a public nuisance and scandal.

In order to explain the operation of a so-called corner in gold to ordinary readers with the least possible use of slang or technical phrases, two preliminary statements are necessary. In the first place it must be understood that the supply of gold immediately available for transfers is limited within distinct bounds in America. New York and the country behind it contain an amount usually estimated at about £4,000,000. The national government commonly holds from £15,000,000 to £20,000,000, which may be thrown bodily on the market if the President orders it. To obtain gold from Europe or other sources requires time.

In the second place, gold in America is a commodity bought and sold like stocks in a special market or gold-room which is situated next the Stock Exchange in Broad Street and is practically a part of it. In gold as in stocks, the transactions are both real and speculative. The real transactions are mostly purchases or loans made by importers who require coin to pay customs on their imports. This legitimate business is supposed to require from £1,000,000 to £1,500,000,000 per day. The speculative transactions are mere wagers on the rise or fall of price, and neither require any actual transfer of gold, nor even imply its existence, although in times of excitement hundreds of millions nominally are bought, sold, and loaned.

Under the late administration Mr. McCulloch, then Secretary of the Treasury, had thought it his duty at least to guarantee a stable currency, although Congress forbade him to restore the gold standard. During four years gold had fluctuated little, and principally from natural causes, and the danger of attempting to create an artificial scarcity in it had prevented the operators from trying an experiment which would have been sure to irritate the government. The financial policy of the new administration was not so definitely fixed, and the success of a speculation would depend on the action of Mr. Boutwell, the new secretary, whose direction was understood to have begun by a marked censure on the course pursued by his predecessor.

Of all financial operations, cornering gold is the most brilliant and the most dangerous, and possibly the very hazard and splendor of the attempt were the reasons of its fascination to Mr. Jay Gould's fancy. He dwelt upon it for months, and played with it like a pet toy. His fertile mind even went so far as to discover that it would prove a blessing to the community, and on this ingenious theory, half honest and half fraudulent, he stretched the widely extended fabric of the web in which all mankind was to be caught. This theory was in itself partially sound. Starting from the principle that the price of grain in New York is regulated by the price in London and is not affected by currency fluctuations, Mr. Gould argued that if it were possible to raise the premium on gold from thirty to forty cents at harvest-time, the farmers' grain would be worth $1.40 instead of $1.30, and as a consequence the farmer would hasten to send all his crop to New York for export, over the Erie Railway, which was sorely in need of freights. With the assistance of another gentleman, Mr. Gould calculated the exact premium at which the Western farmer would consent to dispose of his grain, and thus distance the three hundred sail which were hastening from the Danube to supply the English market. Gold, which was then heavy at 34, must be raised to 45.

This clever idea, like all the other ideas of these gentlemen of Erie, seems to have had the single fault of requiring that some one, somewhere, should be swindled. The scheme was probably feasible;

but sooner or later the reaction from such an artificial stimulant must have come, and whenever it came some one must suffer. Nevertheless, Mr. Gould probably argued that so long as the farmer got his money, the Erie Railway its freights, and he himself his small profits on the gold he bought, it was of little consequence who else might be injured; and, indeed, by the time the reaction came, and gold was ready to fall as he expected, Mr. Gould would probably have been ready to assist the process by speculative sales in order to enable the Western farmer to buy his spring goods cheap as he had sold his autumn crops dear. He himself was equally ready to buy gold cheap and sell it dear on his private account; and as he proposed to bleed New York merchants for the benefit of the Western farmer, so he was willing to bleed Broad Street for his own. The patriotic object was, however, the one which for obvious reasons Mr. Gould preferred to put forward most prominently, and on the strength of which he hoped to rest his ambitious structure of intrigue.

In the operation of raising the price of gold from 133 to 145, there was no great difficulty to men who controlled the resources of the Erie Railway. Credit alone was needed, and of credit Mr. Gould had an unlimited supply. The only serious danger lay in the possible action of the national government, which had not taken the same philanthropic view of the public good as was peculiar to the managers of Erie. Secretary Boutwell, who should have assisted Mr. Gould in "bulling" gold, was gravely suspected of being a bear, and of wishing to depress the premiums to nothing. If he were determined to stand in Mr. Gould's path, it was useless even for the combined forces of Erie and Tammany to jostle against him; and it was therefore essential that Mr. Gould should control the government itself, whether by fair means or foul, by persuasion or by purchase. He undertook the task; and now that his proceedings in both directions have been thoroughly drawn into light, it is well worth while for the public to see how dramatic and how artistically admirable a conspiracy in real life may be, when slowly elaborated from the subtle mind of a clever intriguer, and carried into execution by a band of unshrinking scoundrels.

The first requisite for Mr. Gould's purpose was some channel of direct communication with the President; and here he was peculiarly favored by chance. Mr. Abel Rathbone Corbin, formerly lawyer, editor, speculator, lobby-agent, familiar, as he claims, with everything, had succeeded, during his varied career, in accumulating from one or another of his hazardous pursuits a comfortable fortune, and he had crowned his success, at the age of sixty-seven or thereabouts, by contracting a marriage with General Grant's sister, precisely at the moment when General Grant was on the point of reaching the highest eminence possible to an American citizen. To say that Mr. Corbin's moral dignity had passed absolutely pure through the somewhat tainted atmosphere in which his life had been spent, would be flattering him too highly; but at least he was now no longer engaged in any active occupation, and he lived quietly in New York, watching the course of public affairs, and remarkable for an eminent respectability which became the President's brother-in-law. Mr. Gould enjoyed a slight acquaintance with Mr. Corbin, and he proceeded to improve it. He assumed, and he asserts that he really felt, a respect for Mr. Corbin's shrewdness and sagacity. It is amusing to observe that Mr. Corbin claims to have first impressed the famous crop theory on Mr. Gould's mind; while Mr. Gould testifies that he himself indoctrinated Mr. Corbin with this idea, which became a sort of monomania with the President's brother-in-law, who soon began to preach it to the President himself. On the 15th of June, 1869, the President came to New York, and was there the guest of Mr. Corbin, who urged Mr. Gould to call and pay his respects to the Chief Magistrate. Mr. Gould had probably aimed at precisely this result. He called; and the President of the United States not only listened to the president of Erie, but accepted an invitation to Mr. Fisk's theater, sat in Mr. Fisk's private box, and the next evening became the guest of these two gentlemen on their magnificent Newport steamer, while Mr. Fisk, arrayed, as the newspapers reported, "in a blue uniform, with a broad gilt cap-band, three silver stars on his coat-sleeve, lavender gloves, and a diamond breastpin as large as a cherry, stood at the gangway, surrounded by his aids, bestarred and bestriped like himself," and welcomed his distinguished friend.

It had been already arranged that the President should on this occasion be sounded in regard to his financial policy; and when the selected guests—among whom were Mr. Gould, Mr. Fisk, and others—sat down at nine o'clock to supper, the conversation was directed to the subject of finance. "Some one," says Mr. Gould, "asked the President what his view was." The "some one" in question was, of course, Mr. Fisk, who alone had the impudence to put such an inquiry. The President bluntly replied, that there was a certain amount of fictitiousness about the prosperity of the country, and that the bubble might as well be tapped in one way as another. The remark was fatal to Mr. Gould's plans, and he felt it, in his own words, as a wet blanket.

Meanwhile the post of assistant-treasurer at New York had become vacant, and it was a matter of interest to Mr. Gould that some person friendly to himself should occupy this position, which, in its relations to the public, is second in importance only to the secretaryship of the treasury itself. Mr. Gould consulted Mr. Corbin, and Mr. Corbin suggested the name of General Butterfield,—a former officer in the volunteer army. The appointment was not a wise one; nor does it appear in evidence by what means Mr. Corbin succeeded in bringing it about. There is a suggestion that he used Mr. A. T. Stewart, the wealthy importer, as his instrument for the purpose; but whatever the influence may have been, Mr. Corbin appears to have set it in action, and General Butterfield entered upon his duties toward the 1st of July.

The elaborate preparations thus made show that some large scheme was never absent from Mr. Gould's mind, although between the months of May and August he made no attempt to act upon the markets. But between the 20th of August and the 1st of September, in company with Messrs. Woodward and Kimber, two large speculators, he made what is known as a pool, or combination, to raise the premium on gold, and some ten or fifteen millions were bought, but with very little effect on the price. The tendency of the market was downwards, and it was not easily counteracted. Perhaps under ordinary circumstances he might have now abandoned his project; but an incident suddenly occurred which seems to have drawn him headlong into the boldest operations.

Whether the appointment of General Butterfield had any share in strengthening Mr. Gould's faith in Mr. Corbin's secret powers does not appear in evidence, though it may readily be assumed as probable. At all events, an event now took place which would have seemed to authorize an unlimited faith in Mr. Corbin, as well as to justify the implicit belief of an Erie treasurer in the corruptibility of all mankind. The unsuspicious President again passed through New York, and came to breakfast at Mr. Corbin's house on the 2d of September. He saw no one but Mr. Corbin while there, and the same evening at ten o'clock departed for Saratoga. Mr. Gould declares, however, that he was told by Mr. Corbin that the President, in discussing the financial situation, had shown himself a convert to the Erie theory about marketing the crops, and had "stopped in the middle of a conversation in which he had expressed his views, and written a letter" to Secretary Boutwell. This letter is not produced; but Secretary Boutwell testifies as follows in regard to it:—

"I think on the evening of the 4th of September I received a letter from the President dated at New York, as I recollect it; I am not sure where it is dated. I have not seen the letter since the night I received it. I think it is now in my residence in Groton. In that letter he expressed an opinion that it was undesirable to force down the price of gold. He spoke of the importance to the West of being able to move their crops. His idea was that if gold should fall, the West would suffer, and the movement of the crops would be retarded. The impression made on my mind by the letter was that he had rather a strong opinion to that effect.... Upon the receipt of the President's letter on the evening of the 4th of September, I telegraphed to Judge Richardson [Assistant Secretary at Washington] this dispatch: 'Send no order to Butterfield as to sales of gold until you hear from me.' "

Mr. Gould had therefore succeeded in reversing the policy of the national government; but this was not all. He knew what the government would do before any officer of the government knew it. Mr. Gould was at Corbin's house on the 2d of September; and although the evidence of both these gentlemen is very confused on this point, the inference is inevitable that Gould saw Corbin privately, unknown to the President, within an hour or two after this letter to Mr. Boutwell was written, and that it was at this interview, while the President was still in the house, that Mr. Corbin gave him the information about the letter; perhaps showed him the letter itself. Then followed a transaction worthy of the French stage. Mr. Corbin's evidence gives his own account of it:—

"On the 2d of September (referring to memoranda) Mr. Gould offered to let me have some of the gold he then possessed.... He spoke to me as he had repeatedly done before, about taking a certain amount of gold owned by him. I finally told Mr. Gould that for the sake of a lady, my wife, I would accept $500,000 of gold for her benefit, as I shared his confidence that gold would rise.... He afterwards insisted that I should take a million more, and I did so on the same conditions for my wife. He then sent me this paper."

The paper in question is as follows:—

"Smith, Gould, Martin, & Co., Bankers,
"Mr. ——   11 Broad Street, New York, September 2, 1869.

"Dear Sir: we have bought for your account and risk—
500,000, gold, 132, R.
1,000,000, gold, 133⅝, R.
which we will carry on demand with the right to use.
"SMITH, GOULD, MARTIN, & CO."

This memorandum meant that for every rise of one per cent in the price of gold Mr. Corbin was to receive £3,000, and his name nowhere to appear. If the inference is correct that Gould had seen Corbin in the morning and had learned from him what the President had written, it is clear that he must have made his bargain on the spot, and then going directly to the city, he must in one breath have ordered this memorandum to be made out and large quantities of gold to be purchased, before the President had allowed the letter to leave Mr. Corbin's house.

No time was lost. On this same afternoon, Mr. Gould's brokers bought large amounts in gold. One testifies to buying $1,315,000 at 134⅛. On the 3d the premium was forced up to 36; on the 4th, when Mr. Boutwell received his letter, it had risen to 37. Here, however, Mr. Gould seems to have met a check, and he describes his own position in nervous Americanisms as follows:—

"I did not want to buy so much gold. In the spring I put gold up from 32 to 38 and 40, with only about seven millions. But all these fellows went in and sold short, so that in order to keep it up I had to buy, or else to back down and show the white feather. They would sell it to you all the time. I never intended to buy more than four or five millions of gold, but these fellows kept purchasing it on, and I made up my mind that I would put it up to 40 at one time. ... We went into it as a commercial transaction, and did not intend to buy such an amount of gold. I was forced into it by the bears selling out. They were bound to put it down. I got into the contest. All these other fellows deserted me like rats from a ship. Kimber sold out and got short. ... He sold out at 37. He got short of it, and went up" (or, in English, he failed).

It was unfortunate that the bears would not consent to lie still and be flayed, but this was unquestionably the fact. They had the great operators for once at a disadvantage, and they were bent on revenge. Mr. Gould's position was very hazardous. When Mr. Kimber sold out at 37, which was probably on the 7th of September, the market broke; and on the 8th the price fell back to 35. Nor was this all. At the same moment, when the "pool" was ended by Mr. Kimber's desertion, Mr. Corbin, with his eminent shrewdness and respectability, told Mr. Gould "that gold had gone up to 37," and that he "should like to have this matter realized," which was equivalent to saying that he wished to be paid something on account. This was on the 6th; and Gould was obliged this same day to bring him a check for £5,000, drawn to the order of Jay Gould, and indorsed in blank by him with a touching regard for Mr. Corbin's modest desire not to have his name appear. There are few financiers in the world who will not agree that this transaction does great credit to Mr. Corbin's sagacity. It indicates at least that he was acquainted with the men he dealt with. Undoubtedly it placed Mr. Gould in a difficult position; but as Mr. Gould already held some fifteen millions of gold and needed Mr. Corbin's support, he preferred to pay £5,000 outright rather than allow Corbin to throw his gold on the market. Yet the fabric of Gould's web had now been so seriously injured that, for a whole week, from the 8th to the 15th of September, he was at a loss what to do, unable to advance and equally unable to retreat without very severe losses. He sat at his desk in the opera-house, silent as usual, and tearing little slips of paper which he threw on the floor in his abstraction, while he revolved new combinations in his mind.

Down to this moment Mr. James Fisk, Jr., has not appeared in the affair. Gould had not taken him into his confidence; and it was not until after the 10th of September that Gould appears to have decided that there was nothing else to be done. Fisk was not a safe ally in so delicate an affair, but apparently there was no choice. Gould approached him; and, as usual, his touch was like magic. Mr. Fisk's evidence begins here, and may be believed when very strongly corroborated:

"Gold having settled down to 35, and I not having cared to touch it, he was a little sensitive on the subject, feeling as if he would rather take his losses without saying anything about it.... One day he said to me, 'Don't you think gold has got to the bottom?' I replied that I did not see the profit in buying gold unless you have got into a position where you can command the market. He then said he had bought quite a large amount of gold, and I judged from his conversation that he wanted me to go into the movement and help strengthen the market. Upon that I went into the market and bought. I should say that was about the 15th or 16th of September. I bought at that time about seven or eight millions, I think."

The market responded slowly to these enormous purchases; and on the 16th the clique was still struggling to recover its lost ground.

Meanwhile Mr. Gould had placed another million and a half of gold to the account of General Butterfield, and notified him of the purchase. So Mr. Gould swears in spite of General Butterfield's denial. The date of this purchase is not fixed. Through Mr. Corbin a notice was also sent by Gould about the middle of September to the President's private secretary, General Porter, informing him that half a million was placed to his credit. General Porter instantly wrote to repudiate the purchase, but it does not appear that Butterfield took any notice of Gould's transaction on his account. On the

10th of September the President had again come to New York, where he remained his brother-in-law's guest till the 13th; and during this visit Mr. Gould appears again to have seen him, although Mr. Corbin avers that on this occasion the President intimated his wish to the servant that this should be the last time Mr. Gould obtained admission. "Gould was always trying to get something out of him," he said; and if he had known how much Mr. Gould had succeeded in getting out of him, he would have admired the man's genius, even while shutting the door in his face. On the morning of the 13th the President set out on a journey to the little town of Washington, situated among the mountains of Western Pennsylvania, where he was to remain a few days. Mr. Gould, who now consulted Mr. Corbin regularly every morning and evening, was still extremely nervous in regard to the President's policy; and as the crisis approached, this nervousness led him into the fatal blunder of doing too much. The bribe offered to Porter was a grave mistake, but a greater mistake yet was made by pressing Mr. Corbin's influence too far. He induced Mr. Corbin to write an official article for the New York press on the financial policy of the government, an article afterwards inserted in the New York *Times* through the kind offices of Mr. James McHenry, and he also persuaded or encouraged Mr. Corbin to write a letter directly to the President himself. This letter, written on the 17th under the influence of Gould's anxiety, was instantly sent away by a special messenger of Fisk's to reach the President before he returned to the capital. The messenger carried also a letter of introduction to General Porter, the private secretary, in order to secure the personal delivery of this important dispatch.

We have now come to the week which was to witness the explosion of all this elaborately constructed mine. On Monday, the 20th, gold again rose. Throughout Tuesday and Wednesday Fisk continued to purchase without limit, and forced the price up to 40. At this time Gould's firm of Smith, Gould & Martin, through which the operation was conducted, had purchased some $50,000,000; and yet the bears went on selling, although they could only continue the contest by borrowing Gould's own gold. Gould, on the other hand, could no longer sell and clear himself, for the very reason that the sale of $50,000,000 would have broken the market to nothing. The struggle had become intense. The whole country was looking on with astonishment at the battle between the bulls and the bears. All business was deranged, and all values unsettled. There were indications of a panic in the stock market; and the bears in their emergency were vehemently pressing the government to intervene.

Gould now wrote to Mr. Boutwell a letter so inconceivably impudent that it indicates desperation and entire loss of his ordinary coolness. He began:—

"Sir,—There is a panic in Wall Street, engineered by a bear combination. They have withdrawn currency to such an extent that it is impossible to do ordinary business. The Erie Company requires eight hundred thousand dollars to disburse. . . . Much of it in Ohio, where an exciting political contest is going on, and where we have about ten thousand employed, and the trouble is charged on the administration. . . . Cannot you, consistently, increase your line of currency?"

From a friend such a letter would have been an outrage; but from a member of the Tammany ring, the principal object of detestation to the government, such a threat of bribe—whichever it may be called—was incredible. Mr. Gould was, in fact, at his wits' end. He dreaded a panic, and he felt that it could no longer be avoided.

The scene now shifts for a moment to the distant town of Washington, among the hills of Western Pennsylvania. On the morning of the 19th of September, President Grant and his private secretary, General Porter, were playing croquet on the grass, when Fisk's messenger, after twenty-four hours of travel by rail and carriage, arrived at the house, and sent in to ask for General Porter. When the President's game was ended, General Porter came, received his own letter from Corbin, and called the President, who entered the room and took his brother-in-law's dispatch. He then left the room, and after some ten or fifteen minutes' absence returned. The messenger, tired of waiting, then asked, "Is it all right?" "All right," replied the President; and the messenger hastened to the nearest telegraph station, and sent word to Fisk, "Delivered; all right."

The messenger was, however, altogether mistaken. Not only was all not right, but all was going hopelessly wrong. The President, it appears, had at the outset supposed the man to be an ordinary post-office agent, and the letter an ordinary letter which had arrived through the post-office. Nor was it until Porter asked some curious question as to the man, that the President learned of his having been sent by Corbin merely to carry this apparently unimportant letter of advice. The President's suspicions were at once excited; and the same evening, at his request, Mrs. Grant wrote a hurried note to Mrs. Corbin, telling her how greatly the President was distressed at the rumor that Mr. Corbin was speculating in Wall Street, and how much he hoped that Mr. Corbin would "instantly disconnect himself with anything of that sort."

This letter, subsequently destroyed or said to have been destroyed by Mrs. Corbin, arrived in New York on the morning of Wednesday the 22d, the same day on which Gould and his enemies the bears were making their simultaneous appeals to Secretary Boutwell. Mrs. Corbin was greatly excited and distressed by her sister-in-law's language. She at once carried the letter to her husband, and insisted that he should instantly abandon his interest in the gold speculation. Mr. Corbin, although he considered the scruples of his wife and her family to be highly absurd, assented to her wish; and when Mr. Gould came that evening as usual, with $50,000,000 of gold on his hands, and extreme anxiety on his mind, Corbin read to him two letters: the first, written by Mrs. Grant to Mrs. Corbin; the second, written by Mr. Corbin to President Grant, assuring him that he had not a dollar of interest in gold. The assurance of this second letter was, at any sacrifice, to be made good.

Mr. Corbin proposed that Mr. Gould should give him a check for £20,000, and take his $1,500,000 off his hands. A proposition more calmly impudent than this can scarcely be imagined. Gould had already paid Corbin £5,000, and Corbin asked for £20,000 more, at the very moment when it was clear that the £5,000 he had received had been given him under a misunderstanding of his services. He even had the impudence to represent himself as doing Gould a favor by letting him have a million and a half more gold at the highest market price, at a time when Gould had fifty millions which it was clear he must sell or be ruined. What Gould might, under ordinary circumstances, have replied, may be imagined; but at this moment he could say nothing. Corbin had but to show this note to a single broker in Wall Street, and the whole fabric of Gould's speculation would have fallen to pieces. Gould asked for time and went away. He consulted no one. He gave Fisk no hint of what had happened. The next morning he returned to Corbin, and made him the following offer:—

" 'Mr. Corbin, I cannot give you anything if you will go out. If you will remain in, and take the chances of the market, I will give you my check [for £20,000].' 'And then,' says Mr. Corbin, 'I did what I think it would have troubled almost any other business man to consent to do,—refuse one hundred thousand dollars on a rising market. If I had not been an old man married to a middle-aged woman, I should have done it (of course with her consent) just as sure as the offer was made. I said, 'Mr. Gould, my wife says "No!" Ulysses thinks it wrong, and that it ought to end.' So I gave it up. . . . He looked at me with an air of severe distrust, as if he was afraid of treachery in the camp. He remarked, 'Mr.

Corbin, I am undone if that letter gets out.' ... He stood there for a little while looking very thoughtful, exceedingly thoughtful. He then left and went into Wall Street, ... and my impression is that he it was, and not the government, that broke that market.' "

Mr. Corbin was right; throughout all these transactions his insight into Mr. Gould's character was marvelous.

It was the morning of Thursday, the 3d; Gould and Fisk went to Broad Street together, but as usual Gould was silent and secret, while Fisk was noisy and communicative. There was now a complete separation in their movements. Gould acted entirely through his own firm of Smith, Gould, & Martin, while Fisk operated principally through his old partner, Belden. One of Smith's principal brokers testifies:—

" 'Fisk never could do business with Smith, Gould, & Martin very comfortably. They would not do business for him. It was a very uncertain thing of course where Fisk might be. He is an erratic sort of genius. I don't think anybody would want to follow him very long. I am satisfied that Smith, Gould, & Martin controlled their own gold, and were ready to do as they pleased with it without consulting Fisk. I do not think there was any general agreement.... None of us who knew him cared to do business with him. I would not have taken an order from him nor had anything to do with him.' Belden was considered a very low fellow. 'I never had anything to do with him or his party,' said one broker employed by Gould. 'They were men I had a perfect detestation of; they were no company for me. I should not have spoken to them at all under any ordinary circumstances.' Another says, 'Belden is a man in whom I never had any confidence in any way. For months before that, I would not have taken him for a gold transaction.' "

And yet Belden bought millions upon millions of gold. He himself says he had bought twenty millions by this Thursday evening, and this without capital or credit except that of his brokers. Meanwhile Gould, on reaching the city, had at once given secret orders to sell. From the moment he left Corbin, he had but one idea, which was to get rid of his gold as quietly as possible. "I purchased merely enough to make believe I was a bull," says Gould. This double process continued all that afternoon. Fisk's wild purchases carried the price up to 144, and the panic in the street became more and more serious as the bears realized the extremity of their danger. No one can tell how much gold which did not exist they had contracted to deliver or pay the difference in price. One of the clique brokers swears that on this Thursday evening the street had sold the clique one hundred and eighteen millions of gold, and every rise of one per cent on this sum implied a loss of more than £200,000 to the bears. Naturally the terror was extreme, for half Broad Street and thousands of speculators would have been ruined if compelled to settle gold at 150 which they had sold at 140. It need scarcely be said that by this time nothing more was heard in regard to philanthropic theories of benefit to the Western farmer.

Mr. Gould's feelings can easily be imagined. He knew that Fisk's reckless management would bring the government upon his shoulders, and he knew that unless he could sell his gold before the order came from Washington he would be a ruined man. He knew, too, that Fisk's contracts must inevitably be repudiated. This Thursday evening he sat at his desk in the Erie offices at the opera-house, while Fisk and Fisk's brokers chattered about him.

"I was transacting my railway business. I had my own views about the market, and my own fish to fry. I was all alone, so to speak, in what I did, and I did not let any of those people know exactly how I stood. I got no ideas from anything that was said there. I had been selling gold from 35 up all the time, and I did not know till the next morning that there would probably come an order about twelve o'clock to sell gold."

He had not told Fisk a word in regard to Corbin's retreat, nor his own orders to sell.

When the next day came, Gould and Fisk went together to Broad Street, and took possession of the private back office of a principal broker, "without asking the privilege of doing so," as the broker observes in his evidence. The first news brought to Gould was a disaster. The government had sent three men from Washington to examine the bank which Gould owned, and the bank sent word to Mr. Gould that it feared to certify for him as usual, and was itself in danger of a panic, caused by the presence of officers, which created distrust of the bank. It barely managed to save itself. Gould took the information silently, and his firm redoubled sales of gold. His partner, Smith, gave the orders to one broker after another,— "Sell ten millions!" "The order was given as quick as a flash, and away he went," says one of these men. "I sold only eight millions." "Sell, sell, sell! do nothing but sell!—only don't sell to Fisk's brokers," were the orders which Smith himself acknowledges. In the gold-room Fisk's brokers were shouting their rising bids, and the packed crowd grew frantic with terror and rage as each successive rise showed their increasing losses. The wide streets outside were thronged with excited people; the telegraph offices were overwhelmed with messages ordering sales or purchases of gold or stocks; and the whole nation was watching eagerly to see what the result of this convulsion was to be. All trade was stopped, and even the President felt that it was time to raise his hand. No one who has not seen the New York gold-room can understand the spectacle it presented; now a perfect pandemonium, now silent as the grave. Fisk, in his dark back office across the street, with his coat off, swaggered up and down, "a big cane in his hand," and called himself the Napoleon of Wall Street. He really believed that he directed the movement, and while the street outside imagined that he and Gould were one family, and that his purchases were made for the clique, Gould was silently flinging away his gold at any price he could get for it.

Whether Fisk really expected to carry out his contract, and force the bears to settle, or not, is doubtful; but the evidence seems to show that he was in earnest, and felt sure of success. His orders were unlimited. "Put it up to 150," was one which he sent to the gold-room. Gold rose to 150. At length the bid was made—"160 for any part of five millions," and no one any longer dared take it. "161 for five millions,"— "162 for five millions." No answer was made, and the offer was repeated,—"162 for any part of five millions." A voice replied, "Sold one million at 62." The bubble suddenly burst, and within fifteen minutes, amid an excitement without parallel even in the wildest excitements of the war, the clique brokers were literally swept away, and left struggling by themselves, bidding still 160 for gold in millions which no one would any longer take their word for; while the premium sank rapidly to 135. A moment later the telegraph brought from Washington the government order to sell, and the result was no longer possible to dispute. Mr. Fisk had gone too far, while Mr. Gould had secretly weakened the ground under his feet.

Gould, however, was saved. His fifty millions were sold; and although no one yet knows what his gains or losses may have been, his firm was now able to meet its contracts and protect its brokers. Fisk was in a very different situation. So soon as it became evident that his brokers would be unable to carry out their contracts, every one who had sold gold to them turned in wrath to Fisk's office. Fortunately for him it was protected by armed men whom he had brought with him from his castle of Erie; but nevertheless the excitement was so great that both Mr. Fisk and Mr. Gould thought it best to retire as rapidly as possible by a back entrance leading into another street, and to seek the protection of the opera-house. There nothing but an army could disturb them; no civil mandate was likely to be served without their permission within these walls, and few men would care to face Fisk's ruffians in order to force an entrance.

The subsequent winding up of this famous conspiracy may be stated in few words. But no account could possibly be complete which failed to reproduce in full the story of Mr. Fisk's last interview with Mr. Corbin, as told by Fisk himself.

"I went down to the neighborhood of Wall Street, Friday morning, and the history of that morning you know. When I got back to our office, you can imagine I was in no enviable state of mind, and the moment I got up street that afternoon I started right round to old Corbin's to rake him out. I went into the room, and sent word that Mr. Fisk wanted to see him in the dining-room. I was too mad to say anything civil, and when he came into the room, said I, 'You damned old scoundrel, do you know what you have done here, you and your people?' He began to wring his hands, and, 'Oh!' he says, 'this is a horrible position. Are you ruined?' I said I didn't know whether I was or not; and I asked him again if he knew what had happened? He had been crying, and said he had just heard; that he had been sure everything was all right; but that something had occurred entirely different from what he had anticipated. Said I, 'That don't amount to anything; we know that gold ought not to be at 31, and that it would not be but for such performances as you have had this last week; you know damned well it would not if you had not failed.' I knew that somebody had run a saw right into us, and said I, 'This whole damned thing has turned out just as I told you it would.' I considered the whole party a pack of cowards, and I expected that when we came to clear our hands they would sock it right into us. I said to him, 'I don't know whether you have lied or not, and I don't know what ought to be done with you.' He was on the other side of the table, weeping and wailing, and I was gnashing my teeth. 'Now,' he says, 'you must quiet yourself.' I told him I didn't want to be quiet. I had no desire to ever be quiet again, and probably never should be quiet again. He says, 'But, my dear sir, you will lose your reason.' Says I, 'Speyers [a broker employed by him that day] has already lost his reason; reason has gone out of everybody but me.' I continued, 'Now what are you going to do? You have got us into this thing, and what are you going to do to get out of it?' He says, 'I don't know. I will go and get my wife.' I said, 'Get her down here!' The soft talk was all over. He went upstairs and they returned, tottling into the room, looking older than Stephen Hopkins. His wife and he both looked like death. He was tottling just like that. [Illustrated by a trembling movement of his body.] I have never seen him from that day to this."

This is sworn evidence before a committee of Congress; and its humor is perhaps the more conspicuous, because there is every reason to believe that there is not a word of truth in the story from beginning to end. No such interview ever occurred, except in the unconfined apartments of Mr. Fisk's imagination. His own previous statements make it certain that he was not at Corbin's house at all that day, and that Corbin did come to the Erie offices that evening, and again the next morning. Corbin himself denies the truth of the account without limitation; and adds, that when he entered the Erie offices the next morning Fisk was there. "I asked him how Mr. Gould felt after the great calamity of the day before." He remarked, "Oh, he has no courage at all. He has sunk right down. There is nothing left of him but a heap of clothes and a pair of eyes." The internal evidence of truth in this anecdote would support Mr. Corbin against the world.

In regard to Mr. Gould, Fisk's graphic description was probably again inaccurate. Undoubtedly the noise and scandal of the moment were extremely unpleasant to this silent and impenetrable intriguer. The city was in a ferment, and the whole country pointing at him with wrath. The machinery of the gold exchange had broken down, and he alone could extricate the business community from the pressing danger of a general panic. He had saved himself, it is true; but in a manner which could not have been to his taste. Yet his course from this point must have been almost self-evident to his mind, and there is no reason to suppose that he hesitated.

His own contracts were all fulfilled. Fisk's contracts, all except one, in respect to which the broker was able to compel a settlement, were repudiated. Gould probably suggested to Fisk that it was better to let Belden fail, and to settle a handsome fortune on him, than to sacrifice something more than £1,000,000 in sustaining him. Fisk therefore threw Belden over, and swore that he had acted only under Belden's order; in support of which statement he produced a paper to the following effect:—

"September 24.

"DEAR SIR,—I hereby authorize you to order the purchase and sale of gold on my account during this day to the extent you may deem advisable, and to report the same to me as early as possible. It is to be understood that the profits of such order are to belong entirely to me, and I will, of course, bear any losses resulting.

"Yours,   "WILLIAM BELDEN.

"JAMES FISK, JR."

This document was not produced in the original, and certainly never existed. Belden himself could not be induced to acknowledge the order; and no one would have believed him if he had done so. Meanwhile the matter is before the national courts, and Fisk may probably be held to his contracts: but it will be far more difficult to execute judgment upon him, or to discover his assets.

One of the first acts of the Erie gentlemen after the crisis was to summon their lawyers, and set in action their judicial powers. The object was to prevent the panic-stricken brokers from using legal process to force settlements, and so render the entanglement inextricable. Messrs. Field and Shearman came, and instantly prepared a considerable number of injunctions, which were sent to their judges, signed at once, and immediately served. Gould then was able to dictate the terms of settlement; and after a week of complete paralysis, Broad Street began at last to show signs of returning life. As a legal curiosity, one of these documents, issued three months after the crisis, may be reproduced in order to show the powers wielded by the Erie managers:—

"SUPREME COURT.

H. N. SMITH, JAY GOULD, H. H. MARTIN, and J. B. BACH, Plaintiffs,

against

JOHN BONNER and ARTHUR L. SEWELL, Defendants,

} Injunction by order.

"It appearing satisfactorily to me by the complaint duly verified by the plaintiffs that sufficient grounds for an order of injunction exist, I do hereby order and enjoin.... That the defendants, John Bonner and Arthur L. Sewell, their agents, attorneys, and servants, refrain from pressing their pretended claims against the plaintiffs, or either of them, before the Arbitration Committee of the New York Stock Exchange, or from taking any proceedings thereon, or in relation thereto, except in this action.

"GEORGE G. BARNARD, J. S. C.

"NEW YORK, December 29, 1869."

Mr. Bonner had practically been robbed with violence by Mr. Gould, and instead of his being able to bring the robber into court as the criminal, the robber brought him into court as criminal, and the judge forbade him to appear in any other character. Of all Mr. Field's distinguished legal reforms and philanthropic projects, this injunction is beyond a doubt the most brilliant and the most successful.

The fate of the conspirators was not severe. Mr. Corbin went to Washington, where he was snubbed by the President, and at once disappeared from public view, only coming to light again before the Congressional Committee. General Butterfield, whose share in the transaction is least understood, was permitted to resign his office without an investigation. Speculation for the next six months was at an end. Every person involved in the affair seemed to have lost money, and dozens of brokers were swept from the street. But Mr. Jay Gould and Mr. James Fisk, Jr., continued to reign over Erie, and no one can say that their power or their credit was sensibly diminished by a shock which for the time prostrated all the interests of the country.

CHAPTER LVII

HARDLY HAD the country recovered from the shock of Fisk and Gould when scandal of another sort struck their ears. It rose out of the relations—whatever those may have been—between the most popular of American preachers, Henry Ward Beecher, and the wife of one of his congregation in Brooklyn, New York. The early '70's were agog over a declaration by Theodore Tilton that Beecher had committed adultery with Elizabeth Tilton, his wife. The sensation was enormous, and continued so even after the acquittal of Beecher at the end of a long trial. The New York *Times* goes over the evidence and finds against Beecher.

THE counsel on the part of Mr. Beecher have treated the charge as one which originated entirely with Tilton and the Moultons. They apparently overlooked the fact that the real accusers are not Theodore Tilton and the Moultons, but Mrs. Tilton and Henry Ward Beecher. It is these two persons who have supplied the evidence which has produced the deepest impressions upon the public mind.

Mrs. Tilton made the first confession of her guilt on the 3d of July, 1870. The paper signed by Mrs. Tilton on the 29th of December, 1870, was a partial repetition of her original confession, and it is alleged that this—the only "confession" acknowledged by the defendant's counsel—was extorted from Mrs. Tilton by her husband. The improbabilities which surround the coercion theory are overwhelming. As a general rule, a husband would find it no easy task to compel his wife to take any course which would bring the slightest discredit on herself or her household. But that the mother of several children, a deeply religious and pious woman (as she is represented by Mr. Beecher to be), should be coerced into writing a charge against her pastor that he had "solicited her to be a wife to him, together with all that this implied," there not being the slightest ground for such an accusation—such a story will seem to every woman in the world to be unnatural and monstrous. But, apart from theories or conjectures, it is clear that, if any undue influence was brought to bear upon Mrs. Tilton, it was when she was made to *retract* her confession. This statement we have from the woman herself, in a document which has never been challenged. It incidentally admits that the original confession was made, not in December, 1870, but in the previous July. The statement is so important that we must print it entire. It is dated December 16, 1872:

"In July, 1870, prompted by my duty, I informed my husband that H. W. Beecher, my friend and pastor, had solicited me to be a wife to him, together with all that this implied. Six months afterwards my husband felt impelled by the circumstances of a conspiracy against him, in which Mrs. Beecher had taken part, to have an interview with Mr. Beecher.

"In order that Mr. B. might know exactly what I had said to my husband, I wrote a brief statement (I have forgotten in what form), which my husband showed to Mr. Beecher. Late the same evening Mr. B. came to me (lying very sick at the time), *and filled me with distress, saying I had ruined him*—and wanting to know if I meant to appear against him. This I certainly did not mean to do, *and the thought was agonizing to me*. I then signed a paper *which he wrote*, to clear him in case of a trial. In this instance, as in most others, when absorbed by one great interest or feeling, the harmony of my mind is entirely disturbed, and I found on reflection that this paper was so drawn as to place me most unjustly against my husband, and on the side of Mr. Beecher. So, in order to repair *so cruel a blow to my long suffering husband*, I wrote an explanation of the first paper and my signature. Mr. Moulton procured from Mr. B. the statement which I gave to him in my agitation and excitement, and now holds it.

"This ends my connection with the case.

(Signed) "ELIZABETH R. TILTON."

This remarkable statement seems, in itself, sufficient to settle three things—first, that the woman retracted her confession unwillingly, and then not because it was untrue, but because Mr. Beecher had worked upon her feelings; secondly, that Mr. Beecher taxed her with having ruined him, which it is scarcely supposable he could or would have done had he been an innocent man; thirdly, that even at this late date Mrs. Tilton regarded her husband as "long-suffering," and repented of a "cruel blow" she had dealt him. Would it have been a cruel blow to have withdrawn a wholly unjust charge against her pastor, which had been extorted from her? Or would a wife, who had been the victim of her husband's cruelties and base conspiracies, be likely to describe him as a "long-suffering" man?

That the retraction which she gave to Mr. Beecher was actually *dictated* by him is proved by another highly important document. It is a letter from Mrs. Tilton to her husband, dated Dec. 30, 1870 —the night of the day on which Mr. Beecher obtained the retraction of the original charge:

"MIDNIGHT.

"MY DEAR HUSBAND: I desire to leave with you before going to sleep a statement that Mr. Henry Ward Beecher called upon me this evening and asked me if I would defend him against any accusations in a council of ministers, and I replied solemnly that I would, in case the accuser was any other than my husband. *He dictated the letter, which I copied as my own,* to be used by him *against any other accuser than my husband.*

"This letter was designed to vindicate Mr. Beecher against all other persons save only my husband. I was ready to give him this letter because he said that upon that matter the letter in your hands addressed to him, dated Dec. 29, had struck him dead and ended his usefulness. You and I both are pledged to do our best to avoid publicity. God send a speedy end to all further anxieties.

"Affectionately,

"ELIZABETH."

Mrs. Tilton not only made the charge against Mr. Beecher, but she invariably adopted a tone of penitence for her own crime and sympathy for her husband when he was at a distance from home. In one of these letters she says of Mr. Beecher: "He has been the guide of our youth, and until the three last dreadful years, when our confidence was shaken in him, we trusted him as no other human being." A letter which makes a still more unmistakable reference to some terrible event in her life, known and admitted by herself and her husband, is that dated from Marietta, Ohio, November, 1870. It is impossible for any person to read it carefully without seeing that it involves an admission of her own grave misconduct in every line. She is writing to her husband:

"When, by your threats, my mother cried out in agony to me, 'Why, what have you done, Elizabeth, my child?' her worst suspicions were aroused, and I laid bare my heart then, that from my lips, and not yours, she might *receive the dagger into her heart.*"

Could such language as this apply to an ordinary domestic quarrel? Or to any transaction such as Mr. Beecher now says alone marked his intercourse with the Tiltons? What sense or meaning could there be in a woman using it who had merely been the victim of her husband's neglect or brutality? The letter goes on:

"Did not my dear child (Florence) learn enough by insinuation, that her sweet, pure soul agonized in secret, *till she broke out with the dreadful question? I know not but it hath been her death blow.*"

Are we to regard this passage as destitute of any meaning whatever? What was the dreadful question, and why should the mother's answer to it have been of such a nature as that she feared it would kill her child? She continues thus:

"When you say to my beloved brother, 'Mr. B.' preaches to forty of his mistresses every Sunday, then follow with the remark that after my death *you have a dreadful secret to reveal,* need he be told any more ere the sword pass into his soul?"

There is no pretense here that the "secret" was merely a false charge—no complaint of injustice, no defense of herself, even when she had been accused to her own mother and brother. Nor is it denied that Tilton really had a "dreadful secret" to reveal. The ground assumed is that the husband was ungenerous in disclosing the secret, not that he was guilty of falsehood, for Mrs. Tilton says that she herself elected to tell the secret to her mother; and taken in connection with the allusion to the forty mistresses, it is difficult to conjecture what she could mean except one thing. Indeed, she substantially declares her love for Mr. Beecher. She says: "Would you suffer were I to cast a shadow on any lady whom you love? Certainly, if you have any manliness you would. Even so, every word, look, or intimation *against Mr. B.,* though I be in no wise brought in, is an agony beyond the piercing of myself a hundred times." She adds a postcript for her mother, in which she says: "I should mourn greatly if my life was to be made yet known to father; *his head would be bowed indeed to the grave.*" Is it possible that these are merely the expressions of a perfectly pure and innocent woman—the victim of a husband's cruelty? Again, when on July 4, 1871, Mrs. Tilton wrote a letter in which she said that she had been "misled by a good man," we see no other explanation of the passage than that she *had* been misled—though to what extent the letter itself does not say. Read in connection with the woman's other letters and "confessions," it seems scarcely possible to ascribe two meanings to it.

The charge itself, then, unquestionably originated with Mrs. Tilton, in a confession made voluntarily to her husband, and repeated, as she tells us, to her mother. Her own letters down to a certain date substantially repeat her confession over and over again.

The knowledge that such letters were in existence as those from which we have just quoted early convinced Mr. Beecher's friends that it would be indispensable to admit the existence of some peculiar or unusual intimacy between Mr. Beecher and Mrs. Tilton. It could not be pretended that they were all written under coercion, because, in every instance save one, they were written to the husband when he was at a distance from the wife. The explanation which was offered in this dilemma was that Mrs. Tilton really had been in love with Mr. Beecher, but that he never returned her affection, and was shocked when he discovered its existence.

Mr. Beecher's admissions in his evidence proved that he was on terms of extreme intimacy with Mrs. Tilton—an intimacy which cannot be usual between pastors and the female members of their congregations, or husbands would hesitate to admit ministers to their households. It rather resembles the position once taken up by the Romish priesthood toward the family, and which led to the scandals that did so much to bring about the Reformation. One incident connected with this long intimacy was related by a man who could have had no motive for seeking to injure either Mr. Beecher or Mrs. Tilton. Mr. Richards, the brother of Mrs. Tilton (who gave his evidence with manifest pain and reluctancy), testified that on a certain occasion, when he visited his sister's, he was the witness of a strange scene. He thus describes it:

"I called at the house, and was in the upper story—the second story, I think. I descended to the parlor floor, and opened the door of the parlor, which was closed, and I saw Mr. Beecher seated in the front room, and Mrs. Tilton making a very hasty motion, and with a highly-flushed face, away from the position that Mr. Beecher occupied. It was such a situation as left an indelible impression on my mind."

It is hard to believe that a brother would perjure himself in order to make such a statement about an only sister.

Mr. Beecher himself tells us that, prior to the close of 1870, he had been in the habit of making the Tilton dwelling a sort of second home. "I was glad to resort to it," he said; "it was where people could not find me." He admits, too, that he brought the powerful art of flattery to bear upon Mrs. Tilton. "I spoke to her in great admiration of some letters which she showed me which she had written, one in particular, and a variety of such things; *it was entering into her life, and, in some sense, giving her an interest in my own.*" He describes in these words a relationship which a man usually reserves for his own wife, and which he can seldom transfer to another man's wife without danger. Mr. Beecher also stated in his evidence (April 13) that he was in the habit of kissing Mrs.

Tilton. Whereupon Mr. Fullerton asked him, "Were you in the habit of kissing her when you went to her house in the absence of her husband?" and Mr. Beecher replied, "Sometimes I did and sometimes I did not." Again, in his letter to Plymouth Church (July 15, 1874), he admits that there had been indiscretions on his part which caused him the "sharpest pangs of sorrow," while he denied there was actual guilt. Those, therefore, who say that there never was anything unusual in the intimacy between Mr. Beecher and Mrs. Tilton, go far beyond Mr. Beecher himself. They set up a defense (as in other material parts of the case) which the defendant has emphatically contradicted. There was love—but it was unrequited love. In Mr. Beecher's own version of his conversation with Mrs. Moulton on the subject, given in evidence on the 12th of April, he said he had then admitted having "wrought in that good little woman a smoldering fire; that it had burned unknown to me within her, and finally it broke out with such infinite mischief." He also said (April 3) that when Moulton made the statement to him that Mrs. Tilton loved "his [Beecher's] little finger better than Theodore Tilton's whole body," "*I accepted it;* I had no means of contradicting it." Yet it must seem to the ordinary observer that an innocent man, placed in such a position, would naturally have received such a statement with infinite surprise. Mr. Beecher further admitted that Mrs. Tilton had "allowed the tendrils of her affection to grow up upon him." Whether Mrs. Tilton did indeed act in the way which is alleged on the part of Mr. Beecher—whether she immodestly forced a love upon him which he did not want, and could not return—may be doubted from the evidence, but it is the imputation which the defendant has deliberately fastened upon her. Supposing it to be well founded, it then becomes hard to understand how Mrs. Tilton can be called the stainless saint and the model of purity which Mr. Beecher himself has described her at various subsequent periods.

There were other parties to the case besides Mrs. Tilton with whom Mr. Beecher was on remarkable terms of friendship. It is true that they are now denounced as conspirators and perjurers—but not by Mr. Beecher himself, as we shall see farther on. That Mr. and Mrs. Moulton were frequently consulted by Mr. Beecher throughout these troubled years, concerning some great and difficult trouble, cannot be questioned, seeing that it rests upon evidence supplied by Mr. Beecher's own hand and from his own mouth.

In his letter to Moulton of June 1st, 1873, he wrote, "Your noble wife, too, has been to me one of God's comforters. It is such as she that renews a waning faith in womanhood." And he went on in a strain which it is difficult to make applicable to the ordinary relationships or intercourse of life:

"For a thousand encouragements—for service that no one can appreciate who has not been as sore-hearted as I have been, for your honorable delicacy, for confidence and affection—I owe you so much that I can neither express nor pay it. Not the least has been the great-hearted kindness and trust which your noble wife has shown, and which have lifted me out of despondencies often, though sometimes her clear truthfulness has laid me pretty flat."

These ardent acknowledgments of "service" to a "sore heart" accord, it must be admitted, rather with Mrs. Moulton's version of Mr. Beecher's confidences in her than with the theory of Mr. Beecher's counsel, that she is a low and degraded conspirator and perjurer. In explanation of the above letter, Mr. Beecher himself said in his evidence, "My whole intercourse with Mrs. Moulton was one which inspired in me a sense of affectionate respect and of gratitude." And again he said (April 12): "Mrs. Moulton was a lady—thoroughbred, to my apprehension; and I never heard her say a word that jarred upon my sense of the delicacy and propriety of a lady's tongue." In the same day's evidence he declared that Mrs. Moulton "was like a bank of spring flowers" to him. And yet all this time, according to the present theory of the defense, she was planning with others a deep-laid and devilish plot against his honor.

Another person with whom he was on curious terms, and whom he permitted to address him in a tone which most men would never have tolerated for a moment, was the mother of Mrs. Tilton—Mrs. Morse. She constantly assumed the position towards him of a woman who had some strong hold and claim upon him through her knowledge of a damning secret. She wrote a letter to Mr. Beecher (dated October 24, no year, cited in evidence April 14), in which she uses this remarkable language: "Do come and see me. I will promise that the 'secret of her life,' as she calls it, shall not be mentioned. I know it's hard to bring it up, as you must have suffered intensely, and we all will, I fear, till released by death." Here again, is an allusion to a "secret" which could not possibly have been unknown to Mr. Beecher, because Mrs. Morse says she knows he has "suffered intensely" on account of it. What was the secret thus referred to by mother and daughter? Mr. Beecher had asked Mrs. Morse to call him her son, and she writes, "When I have told darling, I felt if you could in *safety to yourself* and all concerned, you would be to me all this endearing name. Am I mistaken?" This letter was handed by Mr. Beecher to Moulton, in common with other papers bearing upon the case. "It was a dangerous letter to have around," said Mr. Beecher when he gave Moulton the letter.

There is a still more startling letter from Mrs. Morse to Mr. Beecher, produced in evidence January 14, after a prolonged and earnest resistance on the part of defendant's counsel. It was evidently written in the first week of November, 1870, and its authenticity has never been questioned. It begins by reproaching Mr. Beecher for not having "attended to the request I [Mrs. Morse] left at your house over two weeks since," and then proceeds to berate him for not having done anything for "Elizabeth." Presently she goes on thus: "You say, keep quiet. I have all through her married life done so, and we now see our error. . . . The publicity he has given to this recent and most crushing of all trouble is what's taken the life out of her. I know of twelve persons whom he has told, and they in turn have told others." Told what? At this period— November, 1870—Mr. Beecher says he had no idea that even a suspicion was entertained in reference to him and Mrs. Tilton. And yet, here is Mrs. Tilton's own mother writing to him in reference to a secret which was manifestly known to him and to her. But mark the extraordinary language which she proceeds to use: "Do you know, when I hear of you cracking your jokes from Sunday to Sunday, and think of the misery you have brought upon us, I think with the Psalmist, 'There is no God'?" She goes on to say that, admitting it all to be the "invention of his [Tilton's] half-drunken brain, the effect is the same, for everybody believes it." She complains of him for not getting her brother into the custom-house, and says "Elizabeth was as disappointed" as herself. And then, referring to Tilton, she says: "He swears as soon as her breath leaves her body, *he will make this whole thing public,* and this prospect, I think, is one thing which keeps her living."

Now, no specific charge is made in this letter; but the whole tone of it is clearly that of a woman who knows that a man has done her daughter a great injury, and feels that she has a claim upon that man. If we ask, "Is it likely that a mother would thus assume her daughter's guilt?" we are met by another inquiry, "Is it likely that a minister of the gospel would allow a woman to address him in this threatening and insolent strain, if he did not, in some way or other, feel that he was at her mercy?" Mr. Beecher handed this letter over to Moulton. Mr. Fullerton asked him why he had done so? He answered (April 19) that Mr. Moulton was "the depositary of all the papers that related in any way, directly or indirectly, to the case." He thus admitted that the letter did relate to the case. His answer to the letter was cautious, but by no means that which any one might have supposed he would have returned to so impudent a series of demands and reproaches.

Let us now recapitulate the events of five days—five memorable days. How do Mr. Beecher's actions and conduct on those days accord with the theory of his innocence?

Monday, Dec. 26.—Tilton sends a note to Beecher demanding his retirement from Plymouth Church and Brooklyn. The following is the document—an extraordinary one for an innocent man to receive without taking instant steps to punish or expose the person who sent it:

"DEC. 26, 1870, BROOKLYN.

"HENRY WARD BEECHER—*Sir:* I demand that, for reasons which you explicitly understand, you immediately cease from the ministry of Plymouth Church, and that you quit the City of Brooklyn as a resident.

(Signed,)   "THEODORE TILTON."

Thursday, Dec. 29.—Mrs. Tilton writes her confession.

Friday, Dec. 30.—Mr. Beecher receives a peremptory summons to go to Moulton's house to meet Tilton. He goes. Mr. Fullerton puts this question to him: "Then you went off at the beck of the man who had insulted you on the 26th, to know what he wanted?" Mr. Beecher answered, "I did, sir." He is told of Mrs. Tilton's confession, and charged with the adultery. After leaving Moulton's house, Mr. Beecher goes to Tilton's, and induces Mrs. Tilton to retract her charge.

Saturday, Dec. 31.—Moulton goes to Beecher's house and tells him he has acted basely in forcing the retraction from Mrs. Tilton. Thereupon, Beecher hands over the retraction to Moulton.

Sunday, Jan. 1, 1871.—Beecher dictates the celebrated letter of contrition, in which he "humbles himself before Theodore Tilton as before his God," and pleads for forgiveness.

But now we are face to face with another extraordinary fact. On the 7th of February, 1871—more than a month after Tilton had accused Beecher of a crime which his counsel says would have justified him in "burying a knife" in Tilton's heart—he writes to Moulton an urgent request that he will make him and Tilton friends again. And he adds: "Theodore will have the *hardest task in such a case,* but has he not proved himself capable of the noblest things?" So that we are to understand that to accuse an intimate friend and a pastor of adultery is a "noble thing." And the wrongfully accused man is to go to his accuser and beg his forgiveness. And the false accuser—traitor, villain, perjurer—is to be conceded to have the hardest part to play in the reconciliation. These are startling propositions to lay down—and yet they are the only deductions to be drawn from the theory of the defense. Another difficult fact to explain is that whenever Mr. Beecher wrote a letter on this subject, he always referred to Tilton as an ill-used man. Thus, in his letter denouncing Dr. Storrs, he says: "I am in hopes that Theodore, *who has borne so much,* will be unwilling to be a flail in Storrs' hand to strike at a friend." Always there is the same fear of Tilton, and the same anxiety to induce him to be silent. In his letter of February 7th, 1871, to Moulton, he says: "Of course I can never speak with her [Mrs. Tilton] again, except with his permission." Why should he assume that this condition would be imposed by the husband? He says that there was nothing wrong between himself and the wife.

On the 20th of May, 1871, Mr. Beecher, according to his own evidence (given on the 5th of April last), went to Tilton's house—not for the purpose of "burying a knife in his heart," but in order to plead again for forgiveness. He thus describes what took place—we purposely follow Mr. Beecher's own narrative:

"I only know that when I went in Mr. Tilton received me moodily, and that after a little conversation and explanation which took place he became gracious, and that he fell into an easy and unbusiness-like chat; and that in the course of it, sitting there in the old-fashioned way in his house, I went up and argued the matter—sat down on his knee in order to make the appeal closer, and when I was sitting there Mrs. Tilton came into the room and burst out laughing; I recollect the interview, and I think when she came into the room she came up and kissed me very cordially."

Thus, the victim of a charge which is enough to ruin any man, to say nothing of a great minister, never seeks to clear or defend himself—he merely "appeals" to his accusers, and sits down on his accuser's knee to "make the appeal closer."

We are unable to discover any time at which Mr. Beecher attempted to defend himself until the charge against him had been made public through the newspapers. Then something had to be said and done. From the 30th December, 1870, down to last summer,* he was incessantly engaged in a despairing effort to conceal something which, if made known, he felt sure would ruin him. The Moultons evidently knew the secret; and his piteous appeals to Mr. Moulton to help him are on record in his own letters. In all this correspondence, Mr. Beecher constantly represented himself as the offender.

* 1874.

Down to so late a period as June 1, 1873, Mr. Beecher wrote to Moulton a letter in which his own culpability and Tilton's past generosity are assumed as perfectly well understood between all the parties. He says in the course of the letter: "He [Tilton] had condoned his wife's fault." Very strange language, considering that the wife had committed *no* fault. Of course this fatal passage could not be reconciled with the general theory of the defense—that Mr. Beecher and Mrs. Tilton were both ill-used persons, and perfectly innocent of all wrong. Consequently, Mr. Evarts suggested that the "fault" in Mrs. Tilton above referred to was that of having divided her affections between her husband and Mr. Beecher. But in a previous part of his speech Mr. Evarts declared that she had never acted thus—that Mr. Beecher had been "imposed upon" when he was led to believe that she had. One of the most curious features of the defense is the rapidity with which Mr. Beecher's legal advisers have from time to time substituted one theory for another— constructing elaborate chains of explanations, then repudiating them, then returning to them, then discarding them again, and so on *ad infinitum*. Every theory which Mr. Beecher put forward to account for his conduct *before* the trial was expressly contradicted by himself or his counsel *upon* the trial. Every theory advanced by Mr. Beecher during the trial is expressly contradicted by his own former admissions and letters.

Mr. Beecher knew, after the 30th December, 1870, that he was accused of adultery. He must have known, months before, that Tilton accused him of it; but it was not until December that he found out that the charge *rested on Mrs. Tilton's own confession*. The letters, conversations, and negotiations which from that time forth passed between all the chief personages in this miserable tragedy obviously proceeded upon the understanding that Mr. Beecher had committed some grave offense, the consequences of which would be utter destruction to him, so that rather than face them he cried out for death. That was the common ground on which all these persons met. It is the key, and apparently the only key, to the long series of letters, compromises, and interviews. The fact of guilt was taken for granted on all sides. It was acknowledged in all Mr. Beecher's interviews with Moulton and Mrs. Moulton, it had been confessed to Mrs. Tilton's mother by *herself* (as the Marietta letter conclusively shows), and it was proclaimed by Mr. Beecher in all his letters. On the 7th of February, 1871, he implores Mrs. Tilton to trust implicitly to Mr. Moulton's guidance. "His hand it was," he says, "that tied up the storm that was ready to burst upon our heads." What necessity was there for using language of this sort to a woman who had done no wrong, and could have no reason to fear any storm? In February, 1872—exactly a year later—Mr. Beecher offers to abandon his church and position altogether if Tilton felt disposed to exact such a penalty. "If my destruction," he wrote, "would place him, Theodore, all right, that shall not stand in the way. I am willing to step down and out. . . . I do not think that anything would be gained by it. I should be destroyed, but he would not be saved. E. and the children would have their future clouded." The last sentence is full of dreadful meaning. It is a plain admission that something had taken place which, if known, would not only ruin Mr. Beecher, but *cloud the future* even of Tilton's children. What was there to *destroy* Mr. Beecher in his having advised Bowen to discharge Tilton, or suggesting a separation between man and wife—even if he had done these things? Or how many acts can a mother commit which will "cloud the future" of her children? The same kind of reference to the children appears in Mr. Beecher's letter to Moulton on June 1, 1873. Referring to Tilton, he says: "He had enjoined upon me with the utmost earnestness and solemnity *not to betray his wife, nor leave his children to a blight*. I had honestly and earnestly joined in the purpose." Supposing Mr. Beecher to be innocent, how *could* he have betrayed Tilton's wife? What was there to reveal? The language which he declares that Tilton used to him exactly coincides with the position described by the witnesses—namely that the adultery was admitted, but that Tilton wished to keep the fact a secret for the sake of his wife and children, and did so keep it until he was accused of conspiracy by Plymouth Church. Mr. Beecher went on in the same letter to declare that he was suffering "the torments of the damned," and that he was living "on the sharp and ragged edge of anxiety, remorse, fear, despair." Why remorse? And above all, why *fear?* Supposing that he advised the wife to leave her husband—which is purely a supposition—why fear *for himself?* He protests that he had done all he could "to allay prejudices against Tilton," and to suppress "tendencies which, if not stopped, *would break out into* ruinous defense of me." How could the defense of Tilton ruin Beecher? And why should Mr. Beecher have been so anxious to keep all his friends from defending him, unless from the fear of provoking Tilton to make public explanations—the very catastrophe which afterwards happened?

Even when Tilton reproached Beecher for forcing Mrs. Tilton to retract her charge, what was the minister's attitude? Did he turn upon his accuser in indignation? No—he simply complained that he thought "an unfair advantage had been taken of him." Tilton rejoined that it was he who had acted unfairly, in extorting the retraction. *"I argued the point with him,"* says Mr. Beecher. (Evidence, April 15.) It is difficult to imagine a man, who had been innocently accused of adultery, condescending to argue such a "point" with the scoundrel who had trumped up the charge. Mr. Beecher had obtained a retraction to which, on his own version of the affair, he was thoroughly entitled. He then apologized for having obtained it, and *handed it back to Moulton.* The ordinary principles or motives upon which human conduct can be explained utterly fail to reconcile such a course as this with conscious innocence.

It is impossible to feel surprise that all the ingenuity of Mr. Beecher's counsel failed to convince the jury, and has failed to convince the public, that Mr. Beecher's method of meeting this charge was worthy of a Christian minister, or could have been prompted by a "conscience void of offense." Mr. Beecher has told a dozen different stories in explanation of his letters and conduct—and every one of them crushes the other. Apart, moreover, from the versions of the affair given by the witnesses on the trial, there are the letters of the principal persons in the case; and the endless efforts which have been made to place an innocent construction upon these letters fail to reduce them to a level with ordinary correspondence. The following quotations clearly relate to the same transaction, whatever that may have been, and they demand the most careful attention. We bring them together here for the purpose of comparison:

Mrs. Tilton to Her Husband

"Oh, my dear husband, may you never need the discipline of being misled by a good woman as I have been by a good man."

"When, by your threats, my mother cried out in agony to me, 'Why, what have you done, Elizabeth, my child?' her worst suspicions were aroused, and I laid bare my heart then, that from my lips, and not yours, she might *receive the dagger into her heart.*"

"Did not my dear child, Florence, learn enough by insinuation, that her sweet, pure soul agonized in secret, *till she broke out with the dreadful question?* I know not but it hath been her death-blow."

"When you say to my beloved brother, 'Mr. B.' preaches to forty of his mistresses every Sunday, then follow with the remark that after my death *you have a dreadful secret to reveal,* need he be told any more ere the sword passes into his soul!"

"Would you suffer were I to cast a shadow on any lady whom you love? Certainly, if you have any manliness you would. Even so, every word, look, or intimation *against Mr. B.*, though I be in no wise brought in, is an agony beyond the piercing of myself a hundred times."

(To her mother.) "I should mourn greatly if my life was to be made yet known to my father; *his head would be bowed indeed to the grave.*"

BEECHER TO MOULTON

"I ask, through you, Theodore Tilton's forgiveness, and I humble myself before him as I do before my God."

"He [Tilton] has condoned his wife's fault. He had enjoined upon me with the utmost earnestness and solemnity *not to betray his wife, nor leave his children to a blight.*"

"If my destruction would place him all right, that shall not stand in the way. I am willing to step down and out. I do not think that anything would be gained by it. *I should be destroyed*, but he would not be saved. *E. and the children would have their future clouded.*"

"To live on the sharp and ragged edge of anxiety, remorse, fear, despair, and yet to put on all the appearance of serenity and happiness, cannot be endured much longer."

"Would to God, who orders all hearts, that by your kind mediation, Theodore, Elizabeth, and I could be made friends again. Theodore will have the hardest task in such a case; but has he not proved himself capable of the noblest things? I wonder if Elizabeth knows how generously he has carried himself towards me."

MRS. MORSE TO MR. BEECHER

"Do come and see me. I will promise *that the secret of her life,* as she calls it, shall not be mentioned. I know it's hard to bring it up, as you must have suffered intensely, and we all will, I fear, till released by death."

"The publicity he [Tilton] has given to this recent and most crushing of all trouble is what's taken the life out of her. I know of twelve persons whom he has told, and they in turn have told others."

"Do you know, when I hear of you cracking your jokes from Sunday to Sunday, and think of the misery you have brought upon us, I think with the Psalmist, 'There is no God'?"

"He [Tilton] swears, as soon as her breath leaves her body he will *make this whole thing public,* and this prospect, I think, is one thing which keeps her living."

It cannot be pretended that these extraordinary letters are without meaning. Then what do they mean? To what "secret" do these three persons, writing to or of each other, thus constantly refer in a spirit of alarm or remorse? Can it be supposed that they were merely pursuing shadows?

CHAPTER LVIII

THE TRIAL of Beecher was attended by many significant circumstances. For instance, two radical and charming women of New York, Virginia Woodhull and Tennessee Claflin, were arrested for publishing in their Wall Street paper, *Woodhull and Claflin's Weekly*, a free and intelligent discussion of Beecher's conduct. The instigator of the arrest was Anthony Comstock, who was to become notorious for his crusades against "vice." His charge was that the article in question had been obscene. George Francis Train, taking the trouble to deny this publicly, was in turn arrested. He tells the story.

IN November, '72, I was making a speech from Henry Clew's steps in Wall Street, partly to quiet a mob, when a paper was thrust into my hand. I glanced at it, thinking it had to do with myself, and saw that Victoria C. Woodhull and Tennie C. Claflin had been arrested for publishing in their paper in Brooklyn an account of a scandal about a famous clergyman in that city. The charge was "obscenity," and they had been arrested at the instance of Anthony Comstock. I immediately said: "This may be libel, but it is not obscenity."

That assertion, with what I soon did to establish its truth, got me into jail, with the result that six courts in succession—afraid to bring me to trial for "obscenity"—declared me a "lunatic," and prevented my enjoyment of property in Omaha, Nebraska, which is now worth millions of dollars.

From Wall Street I hurried to Ludlow Street Jail, where I found Victoria C. Woodhull and Tennie C. Claflin in a cell about eight by four feet. I was indignant that two women, who had merely published a current rumor, should be treated in this way, and took a piece of charcoal and wrote on the newly whitewashed walls of the cell a couplet suggesting the baseness of this attack upon their reputations. It is sufficient to say here that public feeling was so aroused that these women were soon set free; but I got myself deeper and deeper into the toils of the courts.

In order to prove that the publication was not obscene, if judged by Christian standards of purity, I published in my paper, called *The Train Ligue,* three columns of quotations from the Bible. Every verse I used was worse than anything published by these women. I was immediately arrested on a charge of "obscenity," and taken to the Tombs. I was never tried on this charge, but was kept in jail as a lunatic, and then dismissed, under the ban of declared lunacy, and have so remained for thirty years. Although the public pretended to be against me, it was very eager to buy the edition of my paper that gave these extracts from the Bible. The price of the paper rose from five cents a copy to twenty, forty, sixty cents, and even to one dollar. In a few days it was selling surreptitiously for two dollars a copy.

I was put in Tweed's cell, number 56, in "Murderers' Row," in the Tombs, where at that time were twenty-two men imprisoned under the charge of murder. I made the twenty-third inhabitant of that ghastly "Row." It is remarkable that not one of these men was hanged. All were either acquitted, or tried and sentenced and got off with varying terms of service.

It was not a select, but it was at least a famous, group of men in "Murderers' Row." Across the narrow hallway, just opposite my cell, was Edward S. Stokes, who had killed James Fisk, Jr. Next to me were John J. Scannell and Richard Croker, both of whom have been prominent in the city administration in late years. There was, also, the famous Sharkey, who might have got into worse trouble than any of us, but who escaped through the pluck and ingenuity of Maggie Jordan. Maggie happened to be about the same size as her lover, and changed clothes with him in the cell. The warden, one morning, found he had a woman in his cage instead of Sharkey. This was the last ever heard of Sharkey, so far as I know.

My chief purpose in jail was not to get out, but to be tried on the charge of obscenity. I had been arrested for that offense, and determined that I would be either acquitted or convicted. But I have never had a trial to this day. I do not believe that any court in the land would face the danger of trying to convict a man of publishing obscenity for quoting from the standard book on morality read throughout Christendom.

However this may be, I was offered a hundred avenues of escape from jail, every conceivable one, except the honest and straightforward one of a fair trial by jury. Men offered to bail me out; twice I was taken out on proceedings instituted by women; but I would not avail myself of this way to freedom. Several times I was left alone in the courthouse or in hallways, or other places, where access to the street was easy, entirely without guards, in the vain hope that I would walk off with my liberty. I was discharged by the courts; and I was offered freedom if I would sign certain papers that were brought to me, but I invariably refused to look at them. In all cases I merely turned back and took my place in the cell, and waited for justice.

In '73 I was finally taken before Judge Davis in the Court of Oyer and Terminer. William F. Howe, who died this year, was one of my counsel, and Clark Bell was another. Howe took the ground, first, that obviously there could be nothing obscene in the publication of extracts from the Bible, and, second, if there were, that I was insane at the time of the publication. The judge hastily said that he would instruct the jury to acquit me if the defense took this position. Mr. Bell then asked that a simple verdict of "not guilty" be rendered; but the judge insisted upon its form being "Not guilty, on the ground of insanity." This verdict was taken.

I rose immediately, and said: "I protest against this whole proceeding. I have been four months in jail; and I have had no trial for the offense with which I am charged." I felt that I was in the same plight as Paul. The Bible and the Church, surely, could not condemn me for quoting Scripture; and I had appealed unto Cæsar; but Cæsar refused, out of sheer cowardice, to hear me and try me. I was not even listened to when I made this protest, and I shouted, so that all must hear me: "Your honor, I move your impeachment in the name of the people!"

The sensation was tremendous. "Sit down!" roared the judge. He evidently thought that I would attack him. An order committing me to the State Lunatic Asylum was issued, and I was taken back to the Tombs. But I did not go to the asylum. Another writ of habeas corpus took me out of jail, and I at last turned my back on the Tombs—a lunatic by judicial decree. I hope that the courts, inasmuch as I am their ward, and have been for thirty years, have protected me in my rights, and have safeguarded those interests in Omaha where some millions of dollars depend upon the question of my sanity.

The moment I was taken out of the Tombs, I went down town, had a bath, got a good meal, put on better clothes, and bought passage for England. I went to join my family at Hamburg, as my sons were then in Germany, studying at Frankfort.

This Woodhull-Claflin affair had far-reaching effects. Besides leaving me for thirty years in the grip of the court, it affected many other persons. I shall refer here only to one of these, the publisher of a newspaper in Toledo, who printed some of the matter that I had printed in New York. He was prosecuted, and his paper and press were seized. The poor fellow asked me to lecture in his interest. I could not do this, but helped him to raise some money to buy a new printing-press.

CHAPTER LIX

SOON THE wealth which poured into New York had created millionaires, whose families, like that of Commodore Vanderbilt—once the owner of a line of ferries across the Hudson River but now a king of railroads—quickly achieved power in metropolitan society. The country now began to speak of New York's "high" society, seeing in it a symbol of all that is extravagantly expensive and conspicuously fine. It was an age of dowagers and diamonds, and the age took itself with an amusing seriousness; as may be seen by glancing at the memoirs of that rather heavy glass of fashion, Ward McAllister, who in the '70's and '80's flourished as gentleman manager of select affairs both in New York itself and in the famous social colony of Newport.

NEWPORT was now at its best. The most charming people of the country had formed a select little community there; the society was small, and all were included in the gayeties and festivities. Those were the days that made Newport what it was then and is now, the most enjoyable and luxurious little island in America. The farmers of the island even seemed to catch the infection, and they were as much interested in the success of our picnics and country dinners, as we were ourselves. They threw open their houses to us, and never heeded the invasion, on a bright sunshiny day, of a party of fifty people, who took possession of their dining-room, in fact of their whole house, and frolicked in it to their hearts' content. To be sure, I had often to pacify a farmer when a liveried groom robbed his hen roost, but as he knew that this fashionable horde paid their way, he was easily soothed. I always then remarked that in Newport, at that time, you could have driven a four-in-hand of camels or giraffes, and the residents of the island would have smiled and found it quite the thing. The charm of the place then was the simple way of entertaining; there were no large balls; all the dancing and dining were done by daylight, and in the country. I did not hesitate to ask the very *crème de la crème* of New York society to lunch and dine at my farm, or to a fishing party on the rocks. My little farm dinners gained such a reputation that my friends would say to me: "Now, remember, leave me out of your ceremonious dinners as you choose, but always include me in those given at your farm, or I'll never forgive you." But to convey any idea of our country parties, one must in detail give the method of getting them up: Riding on the Avenue on a lovely summer's day, I would be stopped by a beautiful woman, in gorgeous array, looking so fascinating that if she were to ask you to attempt the impossible, you would at least make the effort. She would open on me as follows: "My dear friend, we are all dying for a picnic. Can't you get one up for us?"

"Why, my dear lady," I would answer, "you have dinners every day, and charming dinners too; what more do you want?"

"Oh, they're not picnics. Any one can give dinners," she would reply; "what we want is one of your picnics. Now, my dear friend, do get one up."

This was enough to fire me, and set me going. So I reply:

"I will do your bidding. Fix on the day at once, and tell me what is the best dish your cook makes."

Out comes my memorandum book, and I write: "Monday, 1 P.M., meet at Narragansett Avenue, bring *filet de bœuf piqué*," and with a bow am off in my little wagon, and dash on, to waylay the next cottager, stop every carriage known to contain friends, and ask them, one and all, to join our country party, and assign to each of them the providing of a certain dish and a bottle of champagne. Meeting young men, I charge them to take a bottle of champagne, and a pound of grapes, or order from the confectioner's a quart of ice cream to be sent to me. My pony is put on its mettle; I keep going the entire day getting recruits; I engage my music and servants, and a carpenter to put down a dancing platform, and the florist to adorn it, and that evening I go over in detail the whole affair, map it out as a general would a battle, omitting nothing, not even a salt spoon; see to it that I have men on the road to direct my party to the farm, and bid the farmer put himself and family, and the whole farm, in holiday attire.

On one occasion, as my farmer had just taken unto himself a bride, a young and pretty woman, I found that at midday, to receive my guests, she had dressed herself in bridal array; she was *décolleté*, and seemed quite prepared to sing the old ballad of "Coming through the rye"; but as her husband was a stalwart young fellow, and extremely jealous, I advised the young men in the party to confine their attentions to their own little circle and let Priscilla, the Puritan, alone.

When I first began giving picnics at my farm, I literally had no stock of my own. I felt that it would never do to have a gathering of the brightest and cleverest people in the country at my place with the pastures empty, neither a cow nor a sheep; so my Yankee wit came to my assistance. I at once hired an entire flock of South-down sheep, and two yoke of cattle, and several cows from the neighboring farm, for half a day, to be turned into my pasture lots, to give the place an animated look. I well remember some of my knowing guests, being amateur farmers, exclaiming:

"Well, it is astonishing! Mc has but fifty acres, and here he is, keeping a splendid flock of Southdowns, two yoke of cattle, to say nothing of his cows!"

I would smile and say:

"My friend, I am not a fancy farmer, like yourself; I farm for profit."

At that time, I was out of pocket from three to four thousand dollars a year by my farm, but must here add, for my justification, that finding amateur farming an expensive luxury, I looked the matter squarely in the face, watched carefully the Yankee farmers around me, and satisfied myself that they knew more about the business than I did, and at once followed in their footsteps, placed my farm on shares, paying nothing out for labor, myself paying the running expenses, and dividing the profits with my farmer. Instead of losing three or four thousand dollars a year by my farm, it then paid me, and continues to pay me seven to eight hundred dollars a year clear of all expenses. We sell off of fifty acres of land, having seventeen additional acres of pasturage, over three thousand dollars of produce each year. I sell fifty Southdown lambs during the month of April and May, at the rate of eight to ten dollars each, to obtain which orders are sent to me in advance, and my winter turkeys have become as famous as my Southdown lambs. The farm is now a profit instead of a loss. I bought this place in 1853; if I had bought the same amount of land south of Newport, instead of north of the town, it would have been worth a fortune to-day.

To return to our picnic. The anxiety as to what the weather would be, was always my first annoyance, for of course these country parties hinge on the weather. After making all your preparations, everything ready for the start, then to look out of your window in the morning, as I have often done, and see the rain coming down in torrents, is far from making you feel cheerful. But, as a rule, I have been most fortunate in my weather. We would meet at Narragansett Avenue at 1 P.M., and all drive out together. On reaching the picnic grounds, I had an army of skirmishers, in the way of servants, thrown out, to take from each carriage its contribution to the country dinner. The band would strike up, and off the whole party would fly in the waltz, while I was directing the icing of the champagne, and arranging the tables; all done with marvelous celerity. Then came my hour of triumph, when, without giving the slightest signal (fearing some one might forestall me, and take off the prize), I would dash in among the dancers, secure our society queen, and lead with her the way to the banquet. Now began the fun in good earnest. The clever men of the party would assert their claims to the best dishes, proud of the efforts of their cook, loud in their praise of their own game pie, which most probably was brought out by some third party, too modest to assert and push his claim. Beauty was there to look upon, and wit to enliven the feast. The wittiest of men was then in his element, and I only wish I dared quote here his brilliant sallies. The beauty of the land was also there, and all feeling that they were on a frolic, they threw hauteur, ceremonial, and grand company manners aside, and, in place, assumed a spirit of simple enjoyment. Toasts were given and drunk, then a stroll in pairs, for a little interchange of sentiment, and then the whole party made for the dancing platform, and a cotillon of one hour and a half was danced, till sunset. As at a "Meet," the arrivals and departures were a feature of the day. Four-in-hands, tandems, and the swellest of Newport turnouts rolled by you. At these entertainments you formed lifetime intimacies with the most cultivated and charming men and women of this country.

These little parties were then, and are now, the stepping-stones to our best New York society. People who have been for years in mourning and thus lost sight of, or who having passed their lives abroad and were forgotten, were again seen, admired, and liked, and at once brought into society's fold. Now, do not for a moment imagine that all were indiscriminately asked to these little fêtes. On the contrary, if you were not of the inner circle, and were a newcomer, it took the combined efforts of all your friends' backing and pushing to procure an invitation for you. For years, whole families sat on the stool of probation, awaiting trial and acceptance, and many were then rejected, but once received, you were put on an intimate footing with all. To acquire such intimacy in a great city like New York would have taken you a lifetime. A fashionable woman of title from England remarked to me that we were one hundred years behind London, for our best society was so small, every one in it had an individuality. This, to her, was charming, "for," said she, "one could have no such individuality in London." It was accorded only to the highest titled people in all England, while here any one in society would have every movement chronicled.

Your *"personnel,"* she added, "is daily discussed, your equipage is the subject of talk, as well as your house and household." Another Londoner said to me, "This Newport is no place for a man without fortune." There is no spot in the world where people are more *en evidence*. It is worth while to do a thing well there, for you have people who appreciate your work, and it tells and pays. It is the place of all others to take social root in.

The first Patriarch Balls were given * in the winters of 1872 and 1873. At this period, a great personage (representing a silent power that had always been recognized and felt in this community, so long as I remember, by not only fashionable people, but by the solid old quiet element as well) had daughters to introduce into society, which brought her prominently forward and caused her at once to take a leading position. She possessed great administrative power, and it was soon put to good use and felt by society. I then, for the first time, was brought in contact with this *grande dame*, and at once recognized her ability, and felt that she would become society's leader, and that she was admirably qualified for the position.

It was not long before circumstances forced her to assume the leadership, which she did, and which she has held with marked ability ever since, having all the qualities necessary,—good judgment and a great power of analysis of men and women, a thorough knowledge of all their surroundings, a just appreciation of the rights of others, and, coming herself from an old Colonial family, a good appreciation of the value of ancestry; always keeping it near her, and bringing it in, in all social matters, but also understanding the importance and power of the new element; recognizing it, and fairly and generously awarding to it a prominent place. Having a great fortune, she had the ability to conceive and carry out social projects; and this she has done, always with success, ever ready to recognize ability and worth, and give to it advice and assistance. Above all things, a true and loyal friend in sunshine or shower. Deeply interested in the welfare of this city, she lent herself to any undertaking she felt worthy of her support, and once promising it her aid, she could be always relied on and always found most willing to advance its interests. With such a friend, we felt the Patriarchs had an additional social strength that would give them the solidity and lasting powers which they have shown they possess. Whenever we required advice and assistance on or about them, we went to her, and always found ourselves rewarded in so doing by receiving suggestions that were invaluable. Quick to criticize any defect of lighting or ornamentation, or arrangement, she was not backward in chiding the

* In New York.

management for it, and in this way made these balls what they were in the past, what they are in the present, and what we hope they may be in the future.

The Patriarchs, from their very birth, became a great social feature. You could but read the list of those who gave these balls, to see at a glance that they embraced not only the smart set, but the old Knickerbocker families as well; and that they would, from the very nature of the case, representing the best society of this great commercial city, have to grow and enlarge. Applications to be made Patriarchs poured in from all sides; every influence was brought to bear to secure a place in this little band, and the pressure was so great that we feared the struggle would be too fierce and engender too much rancor and bad feeling, and that this might of itself destroy them. The argument against them, the one most strongly urged, was that they were overturning all old customs; that New Yorkers had been in the habit of taking an active part in society only when they had daughters to bring out, *lancée-ing* their daughters, and they themselves taking a back seat. But that here in this new association, the married women took a more prominent place than the young girls; *they* were the belles of the balls, and not the young girls. This was Europeanizing New York too rapidly.

Hearing all this, and fearing we would grow unpopular, to satisfy the public we at once got up a new association, wholly for the young girls, and called it The Family Circle Dancing Class. Its name would in itself explain what it was, a small gathering of people in a very small and intimate way, so that unless one was in close intimacy with those getting up these dances, they would have no possible claim to be included in them. Any number of small subscription parties had been formed, such as "The Ancient and Honorables," "The New and Notables," "The Mysterious," and "The Fortnightlies." All had been most enjoyable, but short-lived. The F. C. D. C.'s were to be, in fact, "Junior Patriarchs," under the same management, and were to be cherished and nourished by the same organization. They were given at first in six private houses. The first was held at Mr. William Butler Duncan's; the second at Mr. Ward McAllister's; the third at Mr. De Lancey Kane's; the fourth at Mr. William Astor's; the fifth at Mr. George Henry Warren's, and the sixth at Mr. Lewis Colford Jones's. I gave mine in my house in West Nineteenth Street, and then saw what it was to turn a house inside out for a ball, and how contracted everything must necessarily be in a twenty-five foot house, to receive guests in it, give them a *salle de danse* and a supper room, and then concluded that we must go in most cases to a good-sized ballroom to give an enjoyable dance.

From the first, these dances were very popular. They gave the Patriarch balls the relief they required, and were rapidly growing in favor and threatened in the end to become formidable rivals of the Patriarchs. The same pains were taken in getting them up, as were given to the Patriarchs. We had them but for one season in private houses, and then gave them at Dodworth's, now Delmonico's. Later on, when this house changed hands and became Delmonico's, we gave them all there, with the exception of one winter when we gave them in the foyers of the Metropolitan Opera House. We made the subscription to them an individual subscription, each lady and gentleman subscribing $12.00 for the three balls. One of them at Delmonico's we made a "Mother Goose" Ball. It was a species of fancy dress ball, powered hair being *de rigueur* for all ladies who did not wear fancy costumes, and the feature of the occasion was the "Mother Goose" Quadrille, which had been planned and prepared with much skill and taste. This Quadrille was made up of sixteen couples and was danced at eleven o'clock. As those who danced in it passed you as they marched from the hall into the ballroom, you found it a beautiful sight truly. Many of the men wore pink. Some of the characters were droll indeed. Among others, "Tom, Tom, the Piper's son," with his traditional pig; "A man in the moon, who had come down too soon"; one lady as "Twinkle, twinkle, little star"; "Mother Hubbard," in an artistic costume of scarlet chintz; "Mary, Mary, quite contrary; "Little Bo-Peep," "The Maid in the garden hanging out the clothes," "Punch and Judy"; "Oranges and Lemons"; while M. de Talleyrand appeared as a *mignon* of Henry the Second. "Mother Goose" herself was also there. The feature of the evening was the singing of the nursery rhymes. The second was the "Pinafore" Quadrille introducing the music of that operetta. All the men who danced in it were in sailor's dress. Then followed a Hunting Quadrille, in which every man wore a scarlet coat.

I little knew what I was undertaking when I started these F. C. D. C. Balls. From the giving of the first of these dances, out of a private house, to the time of my giving them up, I had no peace either at home or abroad. I was assailed on all sides, became in a sense a diplomat, committed myself to nothing, promised much and performed as little as possible. I saw at once the rock on which we must split: that the pressure would be so great to get in, no one could resist it; that our parties must become too general, and that in the end the smart set would give up going to them. I knew that when this occurred, they were doomed; but I fought for their existence manfully, and if I could here narrate all I went through to keep these small parties select, I would fill a volume. My mornings were given up to being interviewed of and about them; mothers would call at my house, entirely unknown to me, the sole words of introduction being, "Kind sir, I have a daughter." These words were cabalistic; I would spring up, bow to the ground, and reply: "My dear madam, say no more, you have my sympathy; we are in accord; no introduction is necessary; you have a daughter, and want her to go to the F. C. D. C.'s. I will do all in my power to accomplish this for you; but my dear lady, please understand, that in all matters concerning these little dances I must consult the powers that be. I am their humble servant; I must take orders from them." All of which was a figure of speech on my part. "May I ask if you know any one in this great city, and whom do you know? for to propitiate the powers that be, I must be able to give them some account of your daughter." This was enough to set my fair visitor off. The family always went back to King John, and in some instances to William the Conqueror. "My dear madam," I would reply, "does it not satisfy any one to come into existence with the birth of one's country? In my opinion, four generations of gentlemen make as good and true a gentleman as forty. I know my English brethren will not agree with me in this, but, in spite of them, it is my belief." With disdain, my fair visitor would reply, "You are easily satisfied, sir." And so on, from day to day, these interviews would go on; all were Huguenots, Pilgrims, or Puritans. I would sometimes call one a Pilgrim in place of a Puritan, and by this would uncork the vials of wrath. If they had ever lived south of Mason and Dixon's line, their ancestor was always a near relative of Washington, or a Fairfax, or of the "first families of Virginia." Others were more frank, and claimed no ancestry, but simply wished to know "how the thing was to be done." When our list was full, all comers were told this, but this did not stop them. I was then daily solicited and prayed to give them the first vacancy. I did the best in my power, found out who people were, and if it was possible asked them to join.

The little dances were most successful. Year by year they improved. They were handsomer each season. We were not content with the small buffet in the upper ballroom at Delmonico's, but supped, as did the Patriarchs, in the large room on Fifth Avenue and Twenty-sixth Street, and literally had equally as good suppers, leaving out terrapin and canvasback. But when the ladies organized Assembly Balls, we then thought that there would perhaps be too many subscription balls, and the F. C. D. C. was given up.

Just at this time a man of wealth, who had accumulated a fortune here, resolved to give New Yorkers a sensation; to give them a banquet which should exceed in luxury and expense anything before seen in this country. As he expressed it, "I knew it would be a folly, a piece of unheard-of extravagance, but as the United States Government had just refunded me $10,000, exacted from me for duties upon importations (which, being excessive, I had petitioned to be returned me, and had quite unexpectedly received this sum back), I resolved to appropriate it to giving a banquet that would always be remembered." Accordingly, he went to Charles Delmonico, who in turn went to his cuisine classique to see how they could possibly spend this sum on this feast. Success crowned their efforts. The sum in such skillful hands soon melted away, and a banquet was given of such beauty and magnificence, that even New Yorkers, accustomed as they were to every species of novel expenditure, were astonished at its lavishness, its luxury. The banquet was given at Delmonico's, in Fourteenth Street. There were seventy-two guests in the large ballroom, looking on Fifth Avenue. The table covered the whole length and breadth of the room, only leaving a passageway for the waiters to pass around it. It was a long extended oval table, and every inch of it was covered with flowers, excepting a space in the center, left for a lake, and a border around the table for the plates. This lake was indeed a work of art; it was an oval pond, thirty feet in length, by nearly the width of the table, inclosed by a delicate golden wire network, reaching from table to ceiling, making the whole one grand cage; four superb swans, brought from Prospect Park, swam in it, surrounded by high banks of flowers of every species and variety, which prevented them from splashing the water on the table. There were hills and dales; the modest little violet carpeting the valleys, and other bolder sorts climbing up and covering the tops of those miniature mountains. Then, all around the inclosure, and in fact above the entire table, hung little golden cages, with fine songsters, who filled the room with their melody, occasionally interrupted by the splashing of the waters of the lake by the swans, and the cooing of these noble birds, and at one time by a fierce combat between these stately, graceful, gliding white creatures. The surface of the whole table, by clever art, was one unbroken series of undulations, rising and falling like the billows of the sea, but all clothed and carpeted with every form of blossom. It seemed like the abode of fairies; and when surrounding this fairyland with lovely young American womanhood, you had indeed an unequaled scene of enchantment. But this was not to be alone a feast for the eye; all that art could do, all that the cleverest men could devise to spread before the guests, such a feast as the gods should enjoy, was done, and so well done that all present felt, in the way of feasting, that man could do no more! The wines were perfect. Blue seal Johannisberg flowed like water. Incomparable '48 claret, superb Burgundies, and amber-colored Madeira, all were there to add to the intoxicating delight of the scene. Then, soft music stole over one's senses; lovely women's eyes sparkled with delight at the beauty of their surroundings, and I felt that the fair being who sat next to me would have graced Alexander's feast.

> "Sitting by my side,
> Like a lovely Eastern bride,
> In flower of youth and beauty's pride."

CHAPTER LX

MICHAEL PUPIN IMMIGRATES FROM EUROPE

AT THE other social extreme were the hundreds of thousands of Scandinavians, Irish, Germans, Russian Jews, Italians, and—on the Pacific coast—Chinese who poured into the country every year in the hope of a better living than they had been able to earn in their older worlds. In 1875, when Michael Pupin ventured here from Serbia, there were six million foreign-born people in the United States. Michael Pupin was destined to become a famous inventor in the generation of Thomas A. Edison, who, four years after the coming of Pupin, completed his experiments on the first incandescent light; but in this place he tells merely of his somewhat typical entry as a stranger into New York.*

IT was a clear, mild, and sunny March morning, and as we approached New York Harbor the warm sun rays seemed to thaw out the chilliness which I had accumulated in my body by continuous exposure to the wintry blasts of the North Atlantic. I felt like a new person, and saw in every new scene presented by the New World as the ship moved into it a new promise that I should be welcome. Life and activity kept blossoming out all along the ship's course, and seemed to reach full bloom as we entered New York Harbor. The scene which was then unfolded before my eyes was most novel and bewildering. The first impressions of Budapest and of Prague seemed like pale-faced images of the grand realities which New York Harbor disclosed before my eager eyes. A countless multitude of boats lined each shore of the vast river; all kinds of craft plowed hurriedly in every direction through the waters of the bay; great masses of people crowded the numerous ferry-boats, and gave me the impression that one crowd was just about as anxious to reach one shore of the huge metropolis as the other was to reach the other shore; they all must have had some important thing to do, I thought. The city on each side of the shore seemed to throb with activity. I did not distinguish between New York and Jersey City. Hundreds of other spots like the one I beheld, I thought, must be

* By permission of the publishers, Charles Scribner's Sons.

scattered over the vast territories of the United States, and in these seething pots of human action there must be some one activity, I was certain, which needed me. This gave me courage. The talk which I had listened to during two weeks on the immigrant ship was rather discouraging, I thought. One immigrant was bragging about his long experience as a cabinetmaker, and informed his audience that cabinetmakers were in great demand in America; another one was telling long tales about his skill as a mechanician; a third one was spinning out long yarns about the fabulous agricultural successes of his relatives out West, who had invited him to come there and join them; a fourth confided to the gaping crowd that his brother, who was anxiously waiting for him, had a most prosperous bank in some rich mining camp in Nevada where people never saw any money except silver and gold and hardly ever a coin smaller than a dollar; a fifth one, who had been in America before, told us in a rather top-lofty way that no matter who you were or what you knew or what you had you would be a greenhorn when you landed in the New World, and a greenhorn has to serve his apprenticeship before he can establish his claim to any recognition. He admitted, however, that immigrants with a previous practical training, or strong pull through relatives and friends, had a shorter apprenticeship. I had no practical training, and I had no relatives nor friends nor even acquaintances in the New World. I had nothing of any immediate value to offer to the land I was about to enter. That thought had discouraged me as I listened to the talks of the immigrants; but the activity which New York Harbor presented to my eager eyes on that sunny March day was most encouraging.

Presently the ship passed by Castle Garden, and I heard some one say: "There is the Gate to America." An hour or so later we all stood at the gate. The immigrant ship, *Westphalia*, landed at Hoboken and a tug took us to Castle Garden. We were carefully examined and cross-examined, and when my turn came the examining officials shook their heads and seemed to find me wanting. I confessed that I had only five cents in my pocket and had no relatives here, and that I knew of nobody in this country except Franklin, Lincoln, and Harriet Beecher Stowe, whose "Uncle Tom's Cabin" I had read in a translation. One of the officials, who had one leg only, and walked with a crutch, seemed much impressed by this remark, and looking very kindly into my eyes and with a merry twinkle in his eye he said in German: "You showed good taste when you picked your American acquaintances." I learned later that he was a Swiss who had served in the Union army during the Civil War. I confessed also to the examining officials that I had no training in the arts and crafts, but that I was anxious to learn, and that this desire had brought me to America. In answer to the question why I had not stayed at home or in Prague to learn instead of wandering across the sea with so little on my back and nothing in my pocket, I said that the Hungarian and Austrian authorities had formed a strong prejudice against me on account of my sympathies with people, and particularly with my father, who objected to being cheated out of their ancient rights and privileges which the emperor had guaranteed to them for services which they had been rendering to him loyally for nearly two hundred years. I spoke with feeling, and I felt that I made an impression upon the examiners, who did not look to me like officials such as I was accustomed to see in Austria-Hungary. They had no gold and silver braid and no superior airs but looked very much like ordinary civilian mortals. That gave me courage and confidence, and I spoke frankly and fearlessly, believing firmly that I was addressing human beings who had a heart which was not held in bondage by cast-iron rules invented by their superiors in authority. The Swiss veteran who walked on crutches, having lost one of his legs in the Civil War, was particularly attentive while I was being cross-examined, and nodded approvingly whenever I scored a point with my answers. He whispered something to the other officials, and they finally informed me that I could pass on, and I was conducted promptly to the Labor Bureau of Castle Garden. My Swiss friend looked me up a little later and informed me that the examiners had made an exception in my favor and admitted me, and that I must look sharp and find a job as soon as possible.

As I sat in the Labor Bureau waiting for somebody to come along and pick me out as a worthy candidate for some job, I could not help surveying those of my fellow immigrants who, like myself, sat there waiting for a job. I really believed that they were in a class below me, and yet they had had no trouble in being admitted. They had not needed favors on the part of the officials in order to be admitted. I had, and therefore, I inferred, they must have appeared to the officials to be more desirable. It was true, I said, arguing with myself, that they had a definite trade; they undoubtedly had some money; and they certainly looked more prosperous than I did, judging by their clothes. But why should the possession of a trade, of money, or of clothes stand so much higher in America than it did in Idvor, my native village? We had a blacksmith, a wheelwright, and a barber in Idvor; they were our craftsmen; and we had a Greek storekeeper who had a lot of money and wore expensive city-made clothes, but there was not one respectable Serb peasant in Idvor, no matter how poor, who did not think that he was superior to these people who had only a transient existence in our historic village. The knowledge of our traditions and our implicit belief in them made us feel superior to people who wandered about like gypsies with no traditions, and with nothing to anchor them to a definite place. A newcomer to our village was closely scrutinized, and he was judged not so much by his skill in a craft, nor by his money, nor by his clothes, but by his personality, by the reputation of his family, and by the traditions of the people to whom he belonged. The examiners at Castle Garden seemed to attach no importance to these things, because they did not ask me a single question concerning my family, the history of my village, or the history of the military frontier and of the Serb race. It was no wonder, said I, consoling myself, that I appeared to them less desirable than many of the other immigrants who would never have been allowed to settle in Idvor, and whose society on the immigrant ship had interested me so little, and, in fact, had often been repulsive to me, because I could not help considering many of them a sort of spiritual muckers. My admission by a special favor of the examiners was a puzzle and a disappointment to me, but it did not destroy the firmness of my belief that I brought to America something which the examiners were either unable or did not care to find out, but which, nevertheless, I valued very highly, and that was: a knowledge of and a profound respect and admiration for the best traditions of my race. My mother and the illiterate peasants at the neighborhood gatherings in Idvor had taught me that; no other lesson had ever made a deeper impression upon me.

My first night under the Stars and Stripes was spent in Castle Garden. It was a glorious night, I thought; no howling of the gales, no crashing of the waves, and no tumbling motion of the world beneath my feet, such as I had experienced on the immigrant ship. The feeling of being on *terra firma* sank deep into my consciousness and I slept the sound sleep of a healthy youth, although my bed was a bare floor. The very early morning saw me at my breakfast, enjoying a huge bowl of hot coffee and a big chunk of bread with some butter, supplied by the Castle Garden authorities at Uncle Sam's expense. Then I started out, eager to catch a glimpse of great New York, feeling, in the words of the psalmist, "as a strong man ready to run a race." An old lady sat near the gate of Castle Garden offering cakes and candies for sale. A piece of prune pie caught my eye, and no true Serb can resist the allurements of prunes. It is a national sweetmeat. I bought it, paying five cents for it, the only money I had, and then I made a bee-line across Battery Park, at the same time attending to my pie. My first bargain in America proved a failure. The prune pie was a deception; it was a prune pie filled with prune pits, and I thought of the words of my fellow passenger on the immigrant ship who had said: "No matter who you are or what you know or what you have you will be a greenhorn when you land in America." The prune-pie transaction whispered into my ear: "Michael, you are a greenhorn; this is the first experience in your life as a greenhorn. Cheer up! Get ready to serve your apprenticeship as a greenhorn before you can establish your claim to any recognition," repeating the words of my prophetic fellow passenger who had served his apprenticeship in America. No prophet ever uttered a truer word.

The old Stevens House, a white building with green window-shutters, stood at the corner of Broadway and Bowling Green. When I reached this spot and saw the busy beehive called Broadway, with thousands of telegraph-wires stretching across it like a cobweb between huge buildings, I was overawed, and wondered what it meant. Neither Budapest, nor Prague, nor Hamburg had looked anything like it. My puzzled and panicky expression and the red fez on my head must have attracted considerable attention, because suddenly I saw myself surrounded by a small crowd of boys of all sizes, jeering and laughing and pointing at my fez. They were news-boys and bootblacks, who appeared to be anxious to have some fun at my expense. I was embarrassed and much provoked, but con-trolled my Serbian temper. Presently one of the bigger fellows walked up to me and knocked the fez off my head. I punched him on the nose and then we clinched. My wrestling experiences on the pasturelands of Idvor came to my rescue. The bully was down in a jiffy, and his chums gave a loud cheer of ringing laughter. I thought it was a signal for general attack, but they did not touch me nor interfere in any way. They acted like impartial spectators, anxious to see that the best man won. Suddenly I felt a powerful hand pull-ing me up by the collar, and when I looked up I saw a big official with a club in his hand and a fierce expression in his eye. He looked decidedly unfriendly, but after listening to the appeals of the news-boys and bootblacks who witnessed the fight he softened and handed me my fez. The boys who a little while before had jeered and tried to guy me, evidently appealed in my behalf when the policeman interfered. They had actually become my friends. When I walked away toward Castle Garden, with my red fez proudly cocked up on my head, the boys cheered. I thought to myself that the unpleasant incident was worth my while, because it taught me that I was in a country where even among the street urchins there was a strong sentiment in favor of fair play even to a Serbian greenhorn. America was different from Austria-Hungary. I never forgot the lesson and never had a single reason to change my opinion.

A gentleman who had witnessed the fight joined me on my return trip to Castle Garden, and when we reached the employment bureau he offered me a job. When I learned that one of my daily duties would be to milk a cow, I refused. According to Serb traditions, milking a cow is decidedly a feminine job. Another gentleman, a Swiss foreman on a Delaware farm, offered me another job, which was to drive a team of mules and help in the work of hauling things to the field preparatory for spring planting. I accepted gladly, feeling confident that I knew all about driving animals, although I had never even seen a mule in all my experiences in Idvor. We left for Philadelphia that forenoon and caught there the early afternoon boat for Delaware City, where we arrived late in the afternoon.

Jim * had a relative attending classes at Cooper Union and encouraged me to join several of its evening classes, which I did. I reported to him regularly the new things which I learned there. This practice benefited me even more than it did Jim, because in trying to explain to him the laws of heat phenomena, which were explained to me in the evening lectures at Cooper Union, I got a very much better hold of them. The first ideas of sound and light I caught on the pasture-lands of my native village; the first ideas of the phenomena of heat I caught in the boiler-room in Cortlandt Street and at Cooper Union lectures. These lectures, supplemented by Jim's boiler-room demonstrations, proved much more effective than the instruction which I had received from my teacher Kos, in Panchevo. Kos was a Slovene, a native of that beautiful valley in Carniola, in the very bosom of the Dolomites; it is nearer to being an ideal dreamland than any other spot in Europe. To Kos, as to every true Slav, and particularly to the Slovenes of Carniola, the poetical side of physical phenomena appealed most strongly. Hence his patient listening to my enthusiastic professions of the belief that sound and light were different forms of the language of God. But as I watched the busy flames under Jim's boilers, and understood how they were sustaining the strenuous efforts of steam to supply every hustling wheel in the factory with driving power, I understood for the first time that there is also a prose in physics not a bit less impressive than its poetry. It is this prose which interested Jim, the fireman, just as it did the Cooper Union lecturer. Their chief concern was what heat can do and not what it is. My Slavonic craving for know-

* The name of a friend Pupin had made.

ing what heat is was soon satisfied by reading a poem in prose concerning the nature of heat. But of that later.

During my very first visits to the Cooper Union Library I saw a great painting hung up in the northwest corner of its large reading-room. It was called "Men of Progress," and represented a group of very learned-looking men. I admired the painting, but took no pains to find out its meaning. One day, while reading in the Cooper Union Library, I saw quite near me an old gentleman standing and carefully scrutinizing what was going on. I imagined at first that he had stepped out of that painting. I looked again and found that the figure in the painting which I fancied had walked out was still there and that the old gentleman near me was undoubtedly the original from which the artist had painted that figure. The ambidextrous youth behind the library-desk told me afterward that the old gentleman was Peter Cooper, the founder of Cooper Union, and that he was one of the group of famous men represented in the great painting. He looked as I imagined the Patriarch of Karlovci must have looked. He was a striking resemblance to St. Sava, the Educator, as he is represented on an ikon in our church in Idvor. The same snowy locks and rosy complexion of saintly purity, and the same benevolent look from two luminous blue eyes. Peter Cooper was then eighty-five years of age, but he looked as lively as if he were going to live another eighty-five years. His personality as revealed by his appearance inspired me with awe, and I read everything I could lay my hands on concerning his life; then I read about the lives of the other great men who were associated with Peter Cooper in that historical painting. Some of these men were: Morse, the first promoter of the electric telegraph; Joseph Henry, the great physicist, head of the Smithsonian Institution, and founder of scientific bureaus in Washington; McCormick, the inventor of the reaper; Howe, the inventor of the sewing-machine; Ericsson, the engineer of the *Monitor,* and so forth. My study of their lives was a timely preparation for my visit to Philadelphia, to see the Centennial Exposition, the preparatory work for which I had seen two years prior to that time, when, returning from the Delaware farm, I stopped at Philadelphia to search for opportunities.

The work of those great captains of industry forming the group in the great painting, "Men of Progress," was in evidence in every nook and corner of the Centennial Exposition. This great show impressed me as a splendid glorification of all kinds of wonderful mechanisms, driven by steam and animal power, which helped to develop the great resources of the United States. All scientific efforts exhibited there concerned themselves with the question of what things can do, rather than what they are. The show was also a glorification of the great men who first formulated, clearly stated, and fought for the ideals of the United States. I saw that fact proclaimed in many of the historical features of the exposition, and I did not fail to understand clearly that the show took place in Philadelphia because the Liberty Bell and the Declaration of Independence were first heard in Philadelphia. When I left Philadelphia and its show I carried away in my head a good bit of American history. The Americanization process which was going on within me was very much speeded up by what I saw at the Centennial Exposition.

One day, after leaving Cooper Union library, I walked along the upper Bowery, refreshing my memories of the hard winter of 1874-1875. In Broome Street near the Bowery I saw a store with a sign bearing the name of Lukanitch. The man of that name must be a Serb, thought I, and I walked in, longing to hear the language which I had not heard for over three years. It was a hardware store dealing principally in files and tools made of hardened steel. Behind the desk stood an elderly man, and he, much surprised, answered my Serbian greeting in the Serbian language with an accent reminding me of Kos, my Slovene teacher in Panchevo. Lukanitch told me that he was a Slovene and that in his young days he was a peddler, a Kranyats, as they called the Slovenian peddlers in my native village. His annual summer tours took him to my native Banat. A Kranyats travels on foot hundreds of miles, carrying on his back a huge case with numerous small drawers, each drawer containing a different line of goods; pins, needles, and threads; pens and pencils, cheap jewelry and gaily colored handkerchiefs; cotton, linen, silk, and all kinds of things which the peasants are apt to buy. A Kranyats was a familiar sight in my native village, and he was always welcome there, because he was a Slovene, a near kin to the Serb; and the Serb peasants of the Banat plains loved to hear a Kranyats describe the beauties of the mountainsides of little Slovenia on the eastern slope of the Dolomites. When I disclosed my name to Lukanitch he asked me for my father's name, and when I told him that it was Constantine and that he lived in Idvor, Banat, his eyes looked like two scintillating stars. He gave me a big hug and a big tear threatened to roll down his cheek when he said: "Ko che ko Bog?" (Who can fathom the will of God?) After relating to me that my father had befriended him nearly thirty years prior to that time and that he had often stayed as guest at my father's house whenever his annual tours as Kranyats took him through Idvor, he begged me to come to his house on the following Sunday and dine with his family. I did, and there I met his good wife, a fine Slavonic type, and also his son and daughter, who were born in this country and who looked like young Slavs with Americanism grafted upon them. His son was about to graduate from a high school, and his daughter was preparing for Normal College. They were both American in manner and sentiment, but father and mother, although deeply devoted to the United States, the native country of their children, were still sincerely attached to the beautiful customs of the Slovene land. The children preferred to speak English, but they delighted in Slovene music, which they cultivated with much enthusiasm. That made their parents most happy. Their home was a beautiful combination of American and Slovene civilization. Once they invited me to an anniversary party and I found the whole family dressed in most picturesque Slovenian costumes; but everybody in the party, including even old Lukanitch and his wife and all the Slovenian guests, spoke English. Most of the guests were Americans, but they enjoyed the Slovenian dishes and the Slovenian music, singing, and dancing as much as anybody. To my great surprise the American girls, friends of Miss Lukanitch, played Slovenian music exceedingly well, and I thought to myself that a sufficiently frequent repetition of parties of that kind would soon transform the American population in the vicinity of Prince Street into Slovenians. This interaction between two very different civilizations gave me food for thought, whch I am still digesting mentally.

Lukanitch and his family became my devoted friends, and they were just as interested in my plans and aspirations as if I had been a member of their family. The old lady had a tender heart, and she had shed many a tear listening to bits of my history from the time when I bade good-by to father and mother at the steamboat landing on the Danube, five years before. The disappearance of my roast goose at Karlovci, my first railroad ride from Budapest to Vienna, my dialogues with the train conductor and the gaudy station-master at Vienna, and my free ride in a first-class compartment from Vienna to Prague in company with American friends amused her and her husband hugely. I had to repeat the story many a time for the benefit of her Slovenian friends. She begged me repeatedly to tell the story of my crossing of the Atlantic and of my hardships as greenhorn, being evidently anxious to have her children hear it. I did it several times, scoring much success on each occasion, and as a reward she loaded me with many little gifts and with many enjoyable feasts on Sundays and holidays. My interpretation of the American theory of freedom, which I had derived from reading the lives and the utterances of the great men who made this country and from my three years' struggles as greenhorn, found a most appreciative audience in the Lukanitch family. They applauded Jim's sentiment, that this country is a monument to the great men who made it, and not to a single family like the Hapsburgs of Austria-Hungary. Old Lukanitch offered to engage me as his teacher in American history, and young Lukanitch offered to get me an invitation from the principal of his high school to deliver an oration on the Declaration of Independence. The offers were not meant very seriously, but there was enough sincerity in them to make me believe that my training in America was recognized as having substantial value by people whose opinion deserved respect. I saw in it the first real recognition referred to in the prophecy of my fellow passenger on the immigrant ship who said: "No matter who you are or what you know or what you have, you will be a greenhorn when you land in the New World, and a greenhorn has to serve his apprenticeship as greenhorn before he can establish his claim to any recognition." I said to myself: "Here is my first recognition, small as it may be, and I am certainly no longer a greenhorn."

No longer a greenhorn! Oh, what a confidence that gives to a foreign-born youth who has experienced the hardships of serving his apprenticeship as a greenhorn! Then there were other sources of confidence: I had a goodly deposit in the Union Dime Savings Bank and it was several thousand times as big as the nickel which I brought to Castle Garden when I landed. Besides, I had learned a thing or two in the evening classes at Cooper Union, and my English was considered good not only in vocabulary and grammar, but also in articulation, thanks to Bilharz. Young Lukanitch assured me that my knowledge of English, mathematics, and science would easily take me into college. He even prophesied a most successful college career, pointing at my big chest and broad shoulders and feeling my hard biceps. "You will make a splendid college oarsman," said he, "and they will do anything for you at Columbia if you are a good oarsman, even if you do not get from Bilharz so very much Greek or Latin." At that time Columbia stood very high in rowing. One of her crews won in the Henley Regatta, and its picture could be seen in every illustrated paper. I had seen it many a time and remembered the looks of every member of that famous crew. Young Lukanitch was so enthusiastic about it that he would have gone to Columbia himself if his father had not needed him so much in his steel-tool business. He did his best to turn my eyes from Nassau Hall to Columbia. He succeeded, but not so much on account of my prospects in rowing as on account of other things, and among them was the official name of that institution: "Columbia College in the City of New York." The fact that the college was located in the city of New York carried much weight, because New York appealed to my imagination more than any other place in the world. The impression which it made upon my mind as the immigrant ship moved into New York Harbor on that clear and sunny March day when I first passed through Castle Garden, the Gate of America, never faded. My first victory on American soil was won in New York when I fought for my right to wear the red fez.

CHAPTER LXI

MEANWHILE THE Middle West, the great granary of America, was profiting in its own way by the progress of wealth and invention. Cities like Chicago grew with bewildering rapidity; a wide, level world was subdued by improved plows and by the celebrated new reaper which vastly increased the output of wheat. The prairie states on both sides of the Mississippi were preparing a new life in the generation after the Civil War—a life lived often in struggle with cold and drouth, the failure of crops, and the hard influence of a meager environment, but a life which had its glories too. Hamlin Garland, a son of the Middle Border just beyond the Mississippi, recalls the prairie '70's with mingled affection and dismay.

IT burned deep into our memories, this wide, sunny, windy country. The sky so big, and the horizon line so low and so far away, made this new world of the plain more majestic than the world of the Coulee.—The grasses and many of the flowers were also new to us. On the uplands the herbage was short and dry and the plants stiff and woody, but in the swales the wild oat shook its quivers of barbed and twisted arrows, and the crow's foot, tall and sere, bowed softly under the feet of the wind, while everywhere, in the lowlands as well as on the ridges, the bleaching white antlers of bygone herbivora lay scattered, testifying to "the herds of deer and buffalo" which once fed there. We were just a few years too late to see them.

To the south the sections were nearly all settled upon, for in that direction lay the county town, but to the north and on into Minnesota rolled the unplowed sod, the feeding ground of the cattle, the home of foxes and wolves, and to the west, just beyond the highest ridges, we loved to think the bison might still be seen.

The cabin on this rented farm was a mere shanty, a shell of pine boards, which needed reënforcing to make it habitable and one day my father said, "Well, Hamlin, I guess you'll have to run the plow-team this fall. I must help neighbor Button wall up the house and I can't afford to hire another man."

This seemed a fine commission for a lad of ten, and I drove my horses into the field that first morning with a manly pride which added an inch to my stature. I took my initial "round" at a "land" which stretched from one side of the quarter section to the other, in confident mood. I was grown up!

But alas! my sense of elation did not last long. To guide a team for a few minutes as an experiment was one thing—to plow all day like a hired hand was another. It was not a chore, it was a job. It meant moving to and fro hour after hour, day after day, with no one to talk to but the horses. It meant trudging eight or nine miles in the forenoon and as many more in the afternoon, with less than an hour off at noon. It meant dragging the heavy implement around the corners, and it meant also many shipwrecks, for the thick, wet stubble matted with wild buckwheat often rolled up between the coulter and the standard and threw the share completely out of the ground, making it necessary for me to halt the team and jerk the heavy plow backward for a new start.

Although strong and active I was rather short, even for a ten-year-old, and to reach the plow handles I was obliged to lift my hands above my shoulders; and so with the guiding lines crossed over my back and my worn straw hat bobbing just above the cross-brace I must have made a comical figure. At any rate nothing like it had been seen in the neighborhood and the people on the road to town looking across the field, laughed and called to me, and neighbor Button said to my father in my hearing, "That chap's too young to run a plow," a judgment which pleased and flattered me greatly.

Harriet cheered me by running out occasionally to meet me as I turned the nearest corner, and sometimes Frank consented to go all the way around, chatting breathlessly as he trotted along behind. At other times he was prevailed upon to bring to me a cookie and a glass of milk, a deed which helped to shorten the forenoon. And yet, notwithstanding all these ameliorations, plowing became tedious.

The flies were savage, especially in the middle of the day, and the horses, tortured by their lances, drove badly, twisting and turning in their despairing rage. Their tails were continually getting over the lines, and in stopping to kick their tormentors from their bellies they often got astride the traces, and in other ways made trouble for me. Only in the early morning or when the sun sank low at night were they able to move quietly along their ways.

The soil was the kind my father had been seeking, a smooth dark sandy loam, which made it possible for a lad to do the work of a man. Often the share would go the entire "round" without striking a root or a pebble as big as a walnut, the steel running steadily with a crisp craunching ripping sound which I rather liked to hear. In truth work would have been quite tolerable had it not been so long drawn out. Ten hours of it even on a fine day made about twice too many for a boy.

Meanwhile I cheered myself in every imaginable way. I whistled. I sang. I studied the clouds. I gnawed the beautiful red skin from the seed vessels which hung upon the wild rose bushes, and I counted the prairie chickens as they began to come together in winter flocks running through the stubble in search of food. I stopped now and again to examine the lizards unhoused by the share, tormenting them to make them sweat their milky drops (they were curiously repulsive to me), and I measured the little granaries of wheat which the mice and gophers had deposited deep under the ground, storehouses which the plow had violated. My eyes dwelt enviously upon the sailing hawk, and on the passing of ducks. The occasional shadowy figure of a prairie wolf made me wish for Uncle David and his rifle.

On certain days nothing could cheer me. When the bitter wind blew from the north, and the sky was filled with wild geese racing southward, with swiftly-hurrying clouds, winter seemed about to spring upon me. The horses' tail streamed in the wind. Flurries of snow covered me with clinging flakes, and the mud "gummed" my boots and trouser legs, clogging my steps. At such times I suffered from cold and loneliness—all sense of being a man evaporated. I was just a little boy, longing for the leisure of boyhood.

Day after day, through the month of October and deep into November, I followed that team, turning over two acres of stubble each day. I would not believe this without proof, but it is true! At last it grew so cold that in the early morning everything was white with frost and I was obliged to put one hand in my pocket to keep it warm, while holding the plow with the other, but I didn't mind this so much, for it hinted at the close of autumn. I've no doubt facing the wind in this way was excellent discipline, but I didn't think it necessary then and my heart was sometimes bitter and rebellious.

The soldier did not intend to be severe. As he had always been an early riser and a busy toiler it seemed perfectly natural and good discipline, that his sons should also plow and husk corn at ten years of age. He often told of beginning life as a "bound boy" at nine, and these stories helped me to perform my own tasks without whining. I feared to voice my weakness.

At last there came a morning when by striking my heel upon

the ground I convinced my boss that the soil was frozen too deep for the mold-board to break. "All right," he said, "you may lay off this forenoon."

Finally the day came when the ground rang like iron under the feet of the horses, and a bitter wind, raw and gusty, swept out of the northwest, bearing gray veils of sleet. Winter had come! Work in the furrow had ended. The plow was brought in, cleaned and greased to prevent its rusting, and while the horses munched their hay in well-earned holiday, father and I helped farmer Button husk the last of his corn.

One night as we were all seated around the kerosene lamp my father said, "Well, Belle, I suppose we'll have to take these young ones down to town and fit 'em out for school." These words so calmly uttered filled our minds with visions of new boots, new caps and new books, and though we went obediently to bed we hardly slept, so excited were we, and at breakfast next morning not one of us could think of food. All our desires converged upon the wondrous expedition—our first visit to town.

Our only carriage was still the lumber wagon but it had now two spring seats, one for father, mother and Jessie, and one for Harriet, Frank and myself. No one else had anything better, hence we had no sense of being poorly outfitted. We drove away across the frosty prairie toward Osage—moderately comfortable and perfectly happy.

Osage was only a little town, a village of perhaps twelve hundred inhabitants, but to me as we drove down its Main Street, it was almost as impressive as LaCrosse had been. Frank clung close to father, and mother led Jessie, leaving Harriet and me to stumble over nail-kegs and dodge whiffle trees what time our eyes absorbed jars of pink and white candy, and sought out boots and buckskin mittens. Whenever Harriet spoke she whispered, and we pointed at each shining object with cautious care.—Oh! the marvelous exotic smells! Odors of salt codfish and spices, calico and kerosene, apples and gingersnaps mingle in my mind as I write.

Each of us soon carried a candy marble in his or her cheek (as a chipmunk carries a nut) and Frank and I stood like sturdy hitching posts whilst the storekeeper with heavy hands screwed cotton-plush caps upon our heads,—but the most exciting moment, the crowning joy of the day, came with the buying of our new boots.—If only father had not insisted on our taking those which were a size too large for us!

They were real boots. No one but a Congressman wore "gaiters" in those days. War fashions still dominated the shoe-shops, and high-topped cavalry boots were all but universal. They were kept in boxes under the counter or ranged in rows on a shelf and were of all weights and degrees of fineness. The ones I selected had red tops with a golden moon in the center but my brother's taste ran to blue tops decorated with a golden flag. Oh! that deliciously oily *new* smell! My heart glowed every time I looked at mine. I was especially pleased because they did *not* have copper toes. Copper toes belonged to little boys. A youth who had plowed seventy acres of land could not reasonably be expected to dress like a child.—How smooth and delightfully stiff they felt on my feet.

Then came our new books, a McGuffey reader, a Mitchell geography, a Ray's arithmetic, and a slate. The books had a delightful new smell also, and there was singular charm in the smooth surface of the unmarked slates. I was eager to carve my name in the frame. At last with our treasures under the seat (so near that we could feel them), with our slates and books in our laps we jolted home, dreaming of school and snow. To wade in the drifts with our fine high-topped boots was now our desire.

It is strange but I cannot recall how my mother looked on this trip. Even my father's image is faint and vague (I remember only his keen eagle-gray terrifying eyes), but I can see every acre of that rented farm. I can tell you exactly how the house looked. It was an unpainted square cottage and stood bare on the sod at the edge of Dry Run ravine. It had a small lean-to on the eastern side and a sitting-room and bedroom below. Overhead was a low unplastered chamber in which we children slept. As it grew too cold to use the summer kitchen we cooked, ate and lived in the square room which occupied the entire front of the two-story upright, and which was, I suppose, sixteen feet square. As our attic was warmed only by the stovepipe, we older children of a frosty morning made extremely simple and hurried toilets. On very cold days we hurried downstairs to dress beside the kitchen fire.

Our furniture was of the rudest sort. I cannot recall a single piece in our house or in our neighbors' houses that had either beauty or distinction. It was all cheap and worn, for this was the middle border, and nearly all our neighbors had moved as we had done in covered wagons. Farms were new, houses were mere shanties, and money was scarce. "War times" and "war prices" were only just beginning to change. Our clothing was all cheap and ill-fitting. The women and children wore home-made "cotton flannel" underclothing for the most part, and the men wore rough, ready-made suits over which they drew brown denin blouses or overalls to keep them clean.

Father owned a fine buffalo overcoat (so much of his song's promise was redeemed) and we possessed two buffalo robes for use in our winter sleigh, but mother had only a sad coat and a woollen shawl! How she kept warm I cannot now understand—I think she stayed at home on cold days.

All of the boys wore long trousers, and even my eight-year-old brother looked like a miniature man with his full-length overalls, high-topped boots and real suspenders. As for me I carried a bandanna in my hip pocket and walked with determined masculine stride.

My mother, like all her brothers and sisters, was musical and played the violin—or fiddle, as we called it,—and I have many dear remembrances of her playing. *Napoleon's March, Money Musk, The Devil's Dream* and half-a-dozen other simple tunes made up her repertoire. It was very crude music of course but it added to the love and admiration in which her children always held her. Also in some way we had fallen heir to a Prince melodeon—one that had belonged to the McClintocks, but only my sister played on that.

Once at a dance in neighbor Button's house, mother took the "dare" of the fiddler and with shy smile played *The Fisher's Horn-pipe* or some other simple melody and was mightily cheered at the close of it, a brief performance which she refused to repeat. Afterward she and my father danced and this seemed a very wonderful performance, for to us they were "old"—far past such frolicking, although he was but forty and she thirty-one!

At this dance I heard, for the first time, the local professional fiddler, old Daddy Fairbanks, as quaint a character as ever entered fiction, for he was not only butcher and horse doctor but a renowned musician as well. Tall, gaunt and sandy, with enormous nose and sparse projecting teeth, he was to me the most enthralling figure at this dance and his queer "Calls" and his "York State" accent filled us all with delight. *"Ally* man left," "Chassay *by* your pardners," "Dozy-*do"* were some of the phrases he used as he played *Honest John* and *Haste to the Wedding*. At times he sang his calls in high nasal chant, *"First* lady lead to the *right,* deedle, deedle dum-dum — *gent* foller after — dally-deedle-do-do — *three* hands round"—and everybody laughed with frank enjoyment of his words and action.

It was a joy to watch him "start the set." With fiddle under his chin he took his seat in a big chair on the kitchen table in order to command the floor. "Farm on, farm on!" he called disgustedly. "Lively now!" and then, when all the couples were in position, with one mighty No. 14 boot uplifted, with bow laid to strings he snarled, "Already—GELANG!" and with a thundering crash his foot came down, "Honors TEW your pardners—right and left FOUR!" And the dance was on!

I suspect his fiddlin' was not even "middlin'," but he beat time fairly well and kept the dancers somewhere near to rhythm, and so when his ragged old cap went round he often got a handful of quarters for his toil. He always ate two suppers, one at the beginning of the party and another at the end. He had a high respect for the skill of my Uncle David and was grateful to him and other better musicians for their noninterference with his professional engagements.

The school-house which was to be the center of our social life stood on the bare prairie about a mile to the southwest and like thousands of other similar buildings in the west, had not a leaf to shade it in summer nor a branch to break the winds of savage winter. "There's been a good deal of talk about setting out a windbreak," neighbor Button explained to us, "but nothing has as yet been done." It was merely a square pine box painted a glaring white on the outside and a desolate drab within; at least drab was the original color, but the benches were mainly so greasy and hacked that original intentions were obscured. It had two doors on the eastern end and three windows on each side.

A long square stove (standing on slender legs in a puddle of bricks), a wooden chair, and a rude table in one corner, for the use of the teacher, completed the movable furniture. The walls were roughly plastered and the windows had no curtains.

It was a barren temple of the arts even to the residents of Dry Run, and Harriet and I, stealing across the prairie one Sunday morning to look in, came away vaguely depressed. We were fond of school and never missed a day if we could help it, but this neighborhood center seemed small and bleak and poor.

With what fear, what excitement we approached the door on that first day, I can only faintly indicate. All the scholars were strange to me except Albert and Cyrus Button, and I was prepared for rough treatment. However, the experience was not so harsh as I had feared. True, Rangely Field did throw me down and wash my face in snow, and Jack Sweet tripped me up once or twice, but I bore these indignities with such grace as I could command, and soon made a place for myself among the boys.

I cannot recover much of that first winter of school. It was not an experience to remember for its charm. Not one line of grace, not one touch of color relieved the room's bare walls or softened its harsh windows. Perhaps this very barrenness gave to the poetry in our readers an appeal that seems magical, certainly it threw over the faces of Frances Babcock and Mary Abbie Gammons a lovelier halo.—They were "the big girls" of the school, that is to say, they were seventeen or eighteen years old,—and Frances was the special terror of the teacher, a pale and studious pigeon-toed young man who was preparing for college.

In spite of the cold, the boys played open air games all winter. "Dog and Deer," "Dare Gool" and "Fox and Geese" were our favorite diversions, and the wonder is that we did not all die of pneumonia, for we battled so furiously during each recess that we often came in wet with perspiration and coughing so hard that for several minutes recitations were quite impossible.—But we were a hardy lot and none of us seemed the worse for our colds.

There was not much chivalry in the school—quite the contrary, for it was dominated by two or three big rough boys and the rest of us took our tone from them. To protect a girl, to shield her from remark or indignity required a good deal of bravery and few of us were strong enough to do it. Girls were foolish, ridiculous creatures, set apart to be laughed at or preyed upon at will. To shame them was a great joke.—How far I shared in these barbarities I cannot say but that I did share in them I know, for I had very little to do with my sister Harriet after crossing the school-house yard. She kept to her tribe as I to mine.

This winter was made memorable also by a "revival" which came over the district with sudden fury. It began late in the winter —fortunately, for it ended all dancing and merry-making for the time. It silenced Daddy Fairbanks' fiddle and subdued my mother's glorious voice to a wail. A cloud of puritanical gloom settled upon almost every household. Youth and love became furtive and hypocritic.

The evangelist, one of the old-fashioned shouting, hysterical, ungrammatical, gasping sort, took charge of the services, and in his exhortations phrases descriptive of lakes of burning brimstone and ages of endless torment abounded. Some of the figures of speech and violent gestures of the man still linger in my mind, but I will not set them down on paper. They are too dreadful to perpetuate. At times he roared with such power that he could have been heard for half a mile.

And yet we went, night by night, mother, father, Jessie, all of us. It was our theater. Some of the roughest characters in the neighborhood rose and professed repentance, for a season, even old

Barton, the profanest man in the township, experienced a "change of heart."

We all enjoyed the singing, and joined most lustily in the tunes. Even little Jessie learned to sing *Heavenly Wings, There is a Fountain filled with Blood,* and *Old Hundred.*

As I peer back into that crowded like school-room, smothering hot and reeking with lamp smoke, and recall the half-lit, familiar faces of the congregation, it all has the quality of a vision, something experienced in another world. The preacher, leaping, sweating, roaring till the windows rattle, the mothers with sleeping babes in their arms, the sweet, strained faces of the girls, the immobile wondering men, are spectral shadows, figures encountered in the phantasmagoria of disordered sleep.

The movement of settlers toward Dakota had now become an exodus, a stampede. Hardly anything else was talked about as neighbors met one another on the road or at the Burr Oak schoolhouse on Sundays. Every man who could sell out had gone west or was going. In vain did the county papers and Farmer's Institute lecturers advise cattle raising and plead for diversified tillage, predicting wealth for those who held on; farmer after farmer joined the march to Kansas, Nebraska, and Dakota. "We are wheat raisers," they said, "and we intend to keep in the wheat belt."

Our own family group was breaking up. My uncle David of pioneer spirit had already gone to the far Missouri Valley. Rachel had moved to Georgia, and Grandad McClintock was with his daughters, Samantha and Deborah, in western Minnesota. My mother, thus widely separated from her kin, resigned herself once more to the thought of founding a new home. Once more she sang "O'er the hills in legions, boys," with such spirit as she could command, her clear voice a little touched with the huskiness of regret.

I confess I sympathized in some degree with my father's new design. There was something large and fine in the business of wheatgrowing, and to have a plague of insects arise just as our harvesting machinery was reaching such perfection that we could handle our entire crop without hired help, was a tragic, abominable injustice. I could not blame him for his resentment and dismay.

My personal plans were now confused and wavering. I had no intention of joining this westward march; on the contrary, I was looking toward employment as a teacher, therefore my last weeks at the Seminary were shadowed by a cloud of uncertainty and vague alarm. It seemed a time of change, and immense, far-reaching, portentous readjustment. Our homestead was sold, my world was broken up. "What am I to do?" was my question.

Father had settled upon Ordway, Brown County, South Dakota, as his future home, and immediately after my graduation, he and my brother set forth into the new country to prepare the way for the family's removal, leaving me to go ahead with the harvest alone. It fell out, therefore, that immediately after my flowery oration on *Going West* I found myself more of a slave to the cattle than ever before in my life.

Help was scarce; I could not secure even so much as a boy to aid in milking cows; I was obliged to work double time in order to set up the sheaves of barley which were in danger of moldering on the wet ground. I worked with a kind of bitter, desperate pleasure, saying, "This is the last time I shall ever lift a bundle of this accursed stuff."

And then, to make the situation worse, in raising some heavy machinery connected with the self-binder, I strained my side so seriously that I was unable to walk. This brought the harvesting to a stand, and made my father's return necessary. For several weeks I hobbled about, bent like a gnome, and so helped to reap what the chinch bugs had left, while my mother prepared to "follow the sunset" with her "Boss."

September first was the day set for saying good-by to Dry Run, and it so happened that her wedding anniversary fell close upon the same date and our neighbors, having quietly passed the word around, came together one Sunday afternoon to combine a farewell dinner with a Silver Wedding "surprise party."

Mother saw nothing strange in the coming of the first two carriages, the Buttons often came driving in that way,—but when the Babcocks, the Coles, and the Gilchrists clattered in with smiling faces, we all stood in the yard transfixed with amazement. "What's the meaning of all this?" asked my father.

No one explained. The women calmly clambered down from their vehicles, bearing baskets and bottles and knobby parcels, and began instant and concerted bustle of preparation. The men tied their horses to the fence and hunted up saw-horses and planks, and soon a long table was spread beneath the trees on the lawn. One by one other teams came whirling into the yard. The assembly resembled a "vandoo" as Asa Walker said. "It's worse than that," laughed Mrs. Turner. "It's a silver wedding and a 'send off' combined."

They would not let either the "bride" or the "groom" do a thing, and with smiling resignation my mother folded her hands and sank into a chair. "All right," she said. "I am perfectly willing to sit by

and see you do the work. I won't have another chance right away."
And there was something sad in her voice. She could not forget that
this was the beginning of a new pioneering adventure.

The shadows were long on the grass when at the close of the
supper old John Gammons rose to make a speech and present the
silver tea set. His voice was tremulous with emotion as he spoke
of the loss which the neighborhood was about to suffer, and tears
were in many eyes when father made reply. The old soldier's voice
failed him several times during his utterance of the few short sentences he was able to frame, and at last he was obliged to take his
seat, and blow his nose very hard on his big bandanna handkerchief
to conceal his emotion.

It was a very touching and beautiful moment to me, for as I
looked around upon that little group of men and women, rough-
handed, bent and worn with toil, silent and shadowed with the sorrow of parting, I realized as never before the high place my parents
had won in the estimation of their neighbors. It affected me still
more deeply to see my father stammer and flush with uncontrollable
emotion. I had thought the event deeply important before, but I
now perceived that our going was all of a piece with the West's
elemental restlessness. I could not express what I felt then, and I
can recover but little of it now, but the pain which filled my throat
comes back to me mixed with a singular longing to relive it.

There, on a low mound in the midst of the prairie, in the shadow
of the house we had built, beneath the slender trees we had planted,
we were bidding farewell to one cycle of emigration and entering
upon another. The border line had moved on, and my indomitable
Dad was moving with it. I shivered with dread of the irrevocable
decision thus forced upon me. I heard a clanging as of great gates
behind me and the field of the future was wide and wan.

From this spot we had seen the wild prairies disappear. On every
hand wheat and corn and clover had taken the place of the wild
oat, the hazelbush and the rose. Our house, a commonplace frame
cabin, took on grace. Here Hattie had died. Our yard was ugly, but
there Jessie's small feet had worn a slender path. Each of our lives
was knit into these hedges and rooted in these fields and yet, notwithstanding all this, in response to some powerful yearning call,
my father was about to set out for the fifth time into the still more
remote and untrodden west. Small wonder that my mother sat with
bowed head and tear-blinded eyes, while these good and faithful
friends crowded around her to say good-by.

She had no enemies and no hatreds. Her rich singing voice, her
smiling face, her ready sympathy with those who suffered, had

endeared her to every home into which she had gone, even as a momentary visitor. No woman in childbirth, no afflicted family within a radius of five miles had ever called for her in vain. Death knew her well, for she had closed the eyes of youth and age, and yet she remained the same laughing, bounteous, whole-souled mother of men that she had been in the valley of the Neshonoc. Nothing could permanently cloud her face or embitter the sunny sweetness of her creed.

One by one the women put their worn, ungraceful arms about her, kissed her with trembling lips, and went away in silent grief. The scene became too painful for me at last, and I fled away from it— out into the fields, bitterly asking, "Why should this suffering be? Why should mother be wrenched from all her dearest friends and forced to move away to a strange land?"

CHAPTER LXII

AS THE century drew nearer to its close there developed in centers of industry the problem of labor. Great fortunes might be coming to a few Vanderbilts, Rockefellers, and Carnegies; on farms there might be freedom; but in industrial plants there was exploitation of masses of men, and a growing consciousness of this on the part of wage earners. The Knights of Labor, founded in 1869 to enforce respect for the working class, was succeeded in 1881 by the Federation of Trades and Labor Unions, which eventually became the American Federation of Labor. Railroad strikes in the 1880's brought into relief the activities of such associations, and the great Chicago strike of freight handlers in 1886 was an episode of national importance. The police of Chicago, alarmed by Anarchist demonstrations in support of the strike, attempted to suppress a meeting, with the result that a bomb was thrown and seven persons were killed. Seven Anarchists were sentenced to be hanged, and the sentence was carried out on five; the other two, committed to imprisonment for life, were pardoned by the next governor of Illinois, John P. Altgeld, who never recovered the prestige he lost by this unpopular act. Brand Whitlock, newspaper man, knew Altgeld in the days of his "disgrace," and here recalls two meetings with him.

IT was on a cold raw morning that I met Joseph P. Mahony, then a Democratic member of the State Senate, who said:

"Come with me and I'll introduce you to the next governor of Illinois."

It was the time of year when one was meeting the next governor of Illinois in most of the hotel corridors, or men who were trying to look like potential governors of Illinois, so that such a remark was not to be taken too literally; but I went, and after ascending to an upper floor of a narrow little building in Adams Street, we entered a suite of law offices, and there in a very much crowded, a very much littered and a rather dingy little private room, at an odd little walnut desk, sat John P. Altgeld.

The figure was not prepossessing; he wore his hair close-clipped in ultimate surrender to an obstinate cowlick; his beard was closely trimmed, too, and altogether the countenance was one made for the hands of the cartoonists, who in the brutal fury that was so soon to blaze upon him and to continue to blaze until it had consumed him quite, could easily contort the features to the various purposes of an ugly partisanship; they gave it a peculiarly sinister quality, and it is one of the countless ironies of life that a face, sad with all the utter woe of humanity, should have become for a season, and in some minds remained forever, the type and symbol of all that is most abhorrent. There was a peculiar pallor in the countenance, and the face was such a blank mask of suffering and despair that, had it not been for the high intelligence that shone from his eyes, it must have impressed many as altogether lacking in expression. Certainly it seldom or never expressed enthusiasm, or joy, or humor, though he had humor of a certain mordant kind, as many a political opponent was to know.

He had been a judge of the Circuit Court, and was known by his occasional addresses, his interviews and articles, as a publicist of radical and humanitarian tendencies. He was known especially to the laboring classes and to the poor, who, by that acute sympathy they possess, divined in him a friend, and in the circles of sociological workers and students, then so small and obscure as to make their views esoteric, he was recognized as one who understood and sympathized with their tendencies and ideals. He was accounted in those days a wealthy man,—he was just then building one of those tall and ugly structures of steel called "sky-scrapers,"—and now that he was spoken of for governor this fact made him seem "available" to the politicians. Also he had a German name, another asset in Illinois just then, when Germans all over the state felt themselves outraged by legislation concerning the "little red schoolhouse," which the Republicans had enacted when they were in full power in the state.

But my paper did not share this enthusiasm about him; it happened to be owned by John R. Walsh, and between Walsh and Altgeld there was a feud, a feud that cost Altgeld his fortune, and lasted until the day that death found him poor and crushed by all the tragedy which a closer observer, one with a keener prescience of destiny than I, might have read in his face from the first.

The feeling of the paper, if one may so personalize a corporation as to endow it with emotion, was not corrected by his nomination, and *The Herald* had little to say of him, and what it did say was given out in the perfunctory tone of a party organ. But as the summer wore on, and I was able to report to my editors that all the signs pointed to Altgeld's election, I was permitted to write an article in which I tried to describe his personality and to give some impression of the able campaign he was making. Horace Taylor drew some pictures to illustrate it, and I had the satisfaction of knowing that it gave Altgeld pleasure, while at the same time to me at least it revealed for an instant the humanness of the man.

He sent for me—he was then in offices in his new sky-scraper— and asked if I could procure for him Horace Taylor's pictures; he hesitated a moment, and then, as though it were a weakness his Spartan nature was reluctant to reveal, he told me that he intended to have my article republished in a newspaper in Mansfield, Ohio, the town whence he had come, where he had taught school, and where he had met the gracious lady who was his wife. He talked for a while that afternoon about his youth, about his poverty and his struggles, and then suddenly lapsed into a silence, with his eyes fastened on me. I wondered what he was looking at; his gaze was disconcerting, and it made me self-conscious and uneasy, till he said:

"Where could one get a cravat like the one you have on?"

It was, I remember—because of the odd incident—an English scarf of blue, quite new. I had tried to knot it as Ben Cable of the Democratic National Committee knotted his, and it seemed that such a little thing should not be wanting to the happiness of a man who, by all the outward standards, had so much to gratify him as Altgeld had, and I said—with some embarrassment, and some doubt as to the taste I was exhibiting—"Why, you may have this one."

In a moment his face changed, the mask fell, and he shook his head and said: "No, it would not look like that on me."

After his election it was suggested to me that I might become his secretary, but I declined; in my travels over the state as a political correspondent I was always meeting aged men, seemingly quite respectable and worthy and entirely well meaning, who were introduced not so much by name as such and such a former governor's private secretary; though like the moor which Browning crossed, they had

. . . names of their own,
And a certain use in the world, no doubt.

My work in the office of the secretary of state involved the care of the state's archives. The oldest of these were stored in a vault in the cellar of the huge pile, and the discovery had just been made that some kind of insect, which the state entomologist knew all about, was riddling those records with little holes,—piercing them through and through. In consequence a new vault was prepared, and steel filing cases were set up in it, and the records removed to this safer sanctuary.

It was a tedious and stupid task, until we came one day to file what were called the papers in the anarchist case. Officially they related to the application for the commutation of the sentences of the four men, Spies, Engel, Fischer, and Parsons, who had been hanged, and for the pardon of the three who were then confined in the penitentiary at Joliet, Fielden and Schwab for life, and old Oscar Neebe for fifteen years. Fielden and Schwab had been sentenced to death with the four who had been killed, but Governor Oglesby had commuted their sentences to imprisonment for life; Neebe's original sentence had been for the fifteen years he was then serving. The papers consisted of communications to the governor, great petitions, and letters and telegrams, many sent in mercy, and some in the spirit of reason, asking for clemency, many in a wild hysteria of fear, and the hideous hate that is born of fear, begging the governor to let "justice" take its course.

But all these prayers had fallen on official ears that—to use a grotesque figure—were so closely pressed to the ground that they could not hear; and there was nothing to do, since they were so many and so bulky that no latest-improved and patented steel filing-case could hold them, but to have a big box made and lock them up in that for all time, forgotten, like so many other records of injustice, out of the minds of men.

But not entirely; injustice was never for long out of the mind of John P. Altgeld, and during all those first months of his administration he had been brooding over this notable instance of injustice, and he had come to his decision. He knew the cost to him; he had just come to the governorship of his state, and to the leadership of his party, after its thirty years of defeat, and he realized what powerful interests would be frightened and offended if he were to turn three forgotten men out of prison; he understood how partisanship would turn the action to its advantage.

It mattered not that most of the thoughtful men in Illinois would tell you that the "anarchists" had been improperly convicted, that they were not only entirely innocent of the murder of which they had been accused, but were not even anarchists; it was simply that the mob had convicted them in one of the strangest frenzies of fear that ever distracted a whole community, a case which all the psychologists of all the universities in the world might have tried, without getting at the truth of it—much less a jury in a criminal court.

And so, one morning in June, very early, I was called to the governor's office, and told to make out pardons for Fielden, Neebe, and Schwab. "And do it yourself," said the governor's secretary, "and don't say anything about it to anybody."

I cannot tell in what surprise, in what a haze, or with what emotions I went about that task. I got the blanks and the records, and, before the executive clerk, whose work it was, had come down, I made out those three pardons, in the largest, roundest hand I could command, impressed them with the Great Seal of State, had the secretary of state sign them, and took them over to the governor's office. I was admitted to his private room, and there he sat, at his great flat desk. The only other person in the room was Dreier, a Chicago banker, who had never wearied, it seems, in his effort to have those men pardoned. He was standing, and was very nervous; the moment evidently meant much to him. The Governor took the big sheets of imitation parchment, glanced over them, signed his name to each, laid down the pen, and handed the papers across the table to Dreier. The banker took them, and began to say something. But he only got as far as——

"Governor, I hardly"—when he broke down and wept. Altgeld made an impatient gesture; he was gazing out of the window in silence, on the elm-trees in the yard. He took out his watch, told Dreier he would miss his train—Dreier was to take the Alton to Joliet, deliver the pardons to the men in person, and go on into Chicago with them that night—and Dreier nervously rolled up the pardons, took up a little valise, shook hands, and was gone.

On the table was a high pile of proofs of the document in which Governor Altgeld gave the reasons for his action. It was an able paper; one might well rank it among state papers, and I suppose no one now, in these days, when so many of Altgeld's democratic theories are popular, would deny that his grounds were just and reasonable, or that he had done what he could to right a great wrong; though he would regret that so great a soul should have permitted itself to mar the document by expressions of hatred of the judge who tried the case. But perhaps it is not so easy to be calm and impersonal in the midst of the moving event, as it is given to others to be long afterward.

But whatever feelings he may have had, he was calm and serene ever after. I saw him as I was walking down to the Capitol the next morning. It was another of those June days which now and then are so perfect on the prairies. The Governor was riding his horse—he was a gallant horseman—and he bowed and smiled that faint, wan smile of his, and drew up to the curb a moment. There was, of course, but one subject then, and I said:

"Well, the storm will break now."

"Oh, yes," he replied, with a not wholly convincing air of throwing off a care, "I was prepared for that. It was merely doing right."

I said something to him then to express my satisfaction in the great deed that was to be so willfully, recklessly, and cruelly misunderstood. I did not say all I might have said, for I felt that my opinions could mean so little to him. I have wished since that I had said more,—said something, if that might have been my good fortune, that could perhaps have made a great burden a little easier for that brave and tortured soul. But he rode away with that wan, persistent smile. And the storm did break, and the abuse it rained upon him broke his heart; but I never again heard him mention the anarchist case.

CHAPTER LXIII

JACK LONDON BUMS HIS WAY

THE NINETEENTH century closed upon an immense and varied nation of people who had come an almost immeasurable distance from Jamestown and Plymouth. It was at such a moment that Jack London, not yet a novelist, tramped unknown the length and breadth of the land, stealing his way on trains, getting jailed for vagrancy, begging his meals when he could, and fraternizing with hosts of other knights of the open road who with him saw the country—rich and poor, cruel and kind—from its under side.

I RODE into Niagara Falls in a "side-door Pullman," or, in common parlance, a box-car. A flat-car, by the way, is known amongst the fraternity as a "gondola," with the second syllable emphasized and pronounced long. But to return. I arrived in the afternoon and headed straight from the freight train to the falls. Once my eyes were filled with that wonder-vision of down-rushing water, I was lost. I could not tear myself away long enough to "batter" the "privates" (domiciles) for my supper. Even a "set-down" could not have lured me away. Night came on, a beautiful night of moonlight, and I lingered by the falls until after eleven. Then it was up to me to hunt for a place to "kip."

"Kip," "doss," "flop," "pound your ear," all mean the same thing; namely, to sleep. Somehow, I had a "hunch" that Niagara Falls was a "bad" town for hoboes, and I headed out into the country. I climbed a fence and "flopped" in a field. John Law would never find me there, I flattered myself. I lay on my back in the grass and slept like a babe. It was so balmy warm that I woke up not once all night. But with the first gray daylight my eyes opened, and I remembered the wonderful falls. I climbed the fence and started down the road to have another look at them. It was early—not more than five o'clock—and not until eight o'clock could I begin to batter for my breakfast. I could spend at least three hours by the river. Alas! I was fated never to see the river nor the falls again.

The town was asleep when I entered it. As I came along the quiet street, I saw three men coming toward me along the sidewalk.

They were walking abreast. Hoboes, I decided, like myself, who had got up early. In this surmise I was not quite correct. I was only sixty-six and two thirds per cent correct. The men on each side were hoboes all right, but the man in the middle wasn't. I directed my steps to the edge of the sidewalk in order to let the trio go by. But it didn't go by. At some word from the man in the center, all three halted, and he of the center addressed me.

I piped the lay on the instant. He was a "fly-cop" and the two hoboes were his prisoners. John Law was up and out after the early worm. I was a worm. Had I been richer by the experiences that were to befall me in the next several months, I should have turned and run like the very devil. He might have shot at me, but he'd have had to hit me to get me. He'd have never run after me, for two hoboes in the hand are worth more than one on the get-away. But like a dummy I stood still when he halted me. Our conversation was brief.

"What hotel are you stopping at?" he queried.

He had me. I wasn't stopping at any hotel, and, since I did not know the name of a hotel in the place, I could not claim residence in any of them. Also, I was up too early in the morning. Everything was against me.

"I just arrived," I said.

"Well, you turn around and walk in front of me, and not too far in front. There's somebody wants to see you."

I was "pinched." I knew who wanted to see me. With that "fly-cop" and the two hoboes at my heels, and under the direction of the former, I led the way to the city jail.

From the office we were led to the "Hobo" and locked in. The "Hobo" is that part of a prison where the minor offenders are confined together in a large iron cage. Since hoboes constitute the principal division of the minor offenders, the aforesaid iron cage is called the Hobo. Here we met several hoboes who had already been pinched that morning, and every little while the door was unlocked and two or three more were thrust in on us. At last, when we totaled sixteen, we were led upstairs into the courtroom.

In the courtroom were the sixteen prisoners, the judge, and two bailiffs. The judge seemed to act as his own clerk. There were no witnesses. There were no citizens of Niagara Falls present to look on and see how justice was administered in their community. The judge glanced at the list of cases before him and called out a name. A hobo stood up. The judge glanced at a bailiff. "Vagrancy, your Honor," said the bailiff. "Thirty days," said his Honor. The hobo sat down, and the judge was calling another name and another hobo was rising to his feet.

The trial of that hobo had taken just about fifteen seconds. The trial of the next hobo came off with equal celerity. The bailiff said, "Vagrancy, your Honor," and his Honor said, "Thirty days." Thus it went like clockwork, fifteen seconds to a hobo—and thirty days.

We were a hungry lot in the Erie County Pen. Only the "long-timers" knew what it was to have enough to eat. The reason for this was that they would have died after a time on the fare we "short-timers" received. I know that the long-timers got more substantial grub, because there was a whole row of them on the ground floor in our hall, and when I was a trusty, I used to steal from their grub while serving them. Man cannot live on bread alone and not enough of it.

My pal delivered the goods. After two days of work in the yard I was taken out of my cell and made a trusty, a "hall-man." At morning and night we served the bread to the prisoners in their cells; but at twelve o'clock a different method was used. The convicts marched in from work in a long line. As they entered the door of our hall, they broke the lock-step and took their hands down from the shoulders of their line-mates. Just inside the door were piled trays of bread, and here also stood the First Hall-man and two ordinary hall-men. I was one of the two. Our task was to hold the trays of bread as the line of convicts filed past. As soon as the tray, say, that I was holding was emptied, the other hall-man took my place with a full tray. And when his was emptied, I took his place with a full tray. Thus the line tramped steadily by, each man reaching with his right hand and taking one ration of bread from the extended tray.

The task of the First Hall-man was different. He used a club. He stood beside the tray and watched. The hungry wretches could never get over the delusion that sometimes they could manage to get two rations of bread out of the tray. But in my experience that sometime never came. The club of the First Hall-man had a way of flashing out—quick as the stroke of a tiger's claw—to the hand that dared ambitiously. The First Hall-man was a good judge of distance, and he had smashed so many hands with that club that he had become infallible. He never missed, and he usually punished the offending convict by taking his one ration away from him and sending him to his cell to make his meal of hot water.

And at times, while all these men lay hungry in their cells, I have seen a hundred or so extra rations of bread hidden away in the cells of the hall-men. It would seem absurd, our retaining this bread. But it was one of our grafts. We were economic masters inside our hall, turning the trick in ways quite similar to the economic masters of civilization. We controlled the food-supply of the population, and, just like our brother bandits outside, we made the people pay through the nose for it. We peddled the bread. Once a week, the men who worked in the yard received a five-cent plug of chewing tobacco. This chewing tobacco was the coin of the realm. Two or three rations of bread for a plug was the way we exchanged, and they traded, not because they loved tobacco less, but because they loved bread more. Oh, I know, it was like taking candy from a baby, but what would you? We had to live. And certainly there should be some reward for initiative and enterprise. Besides, we but patterned ourselves after our betters outside the walls, who, on a larger scale, and under the respectable disguise of merchants, bankers, and captains of industry, did precisely what we were doing. What awful things would have happened to those poor wretches if it hadn't been for us, I can't imagine. Heaven knows we put bread into circulation in the Erie County Pen. Ay, and we encouraged frugality and thrift . . . in the poor devils who forewent their tobacco. And then there was our example. In the breast of every convict there we implanted the ambition to become even as we and run a graft. Saviours of society—I guess yes.

Here was a hungry man without any tobacco. Maybe he was a profligate and had used it all up on himself. Very good; he had a pair of suspenders. I exchanged half a dozen rations of bread for it—or a dozen rations if the suspenders were very good. Now I never wore suspenders, but that didn't matter. Around the corner lodged a long-timer, doing ten years for manslaughter. He wore suspenders, and he wanted a pair. I could trade them to him for some of his meat. Meat was what I wanted. Or perhaps he had a tattered, paper-covered novel. That was treasure-trove. I could read it and then trade it off to the bakers for cake, or to the cooks for meat and vegetables, or to the firemen for decent coffee, or to some one or other for the newspaper that occasionally filtered in, heaven alone knows how. The cooks, bakers, and firemen were prisoners like myself, and they lodged in our hall in the first row of cells over us.

In short, a full-grown system of barter obtained in the Erie County Pen. There was even money in circulation. This money was sometimes smuggled in by the short-timers, more frequently came from the barber-shop graft, where the newcomers were mulcted, but most of all flowed from the cells of the long-timers—though how they got it I don't know.

What with his preëminent position, the First Hall-man was reputed to be quite wealthy. In addition to his miscellaneous grafts, he grafted on us. We farmed the general wretchedness, and the First Hall-man was Farmer-General over all of us. We held our particular grafts by his permission, and we had to pay for that permission. As I say, he was reputed to be wealthy; but we never saw his money, and he lived in a cell all to himself in solitary grandeur.

But that money was made in the Pen I had direct evidence, for I was cell-mate quite a time with the Third Hall-man. He had over sixteen dollars. He used to count his money every night after nine o'clock, when we were locked in. Also, he used to tell me each night what he would do to me if I gave away on him to the other hall-men. You see, he was afraid of being robbed, and danger threatened him from three different directions. There were the guards. A couple of them might jump upon him, give him a good beating for alleged insubordination, and throw him into the "solitaire" (the dungeon); and in the mix-up that sixteen dollars of his would take wings. Then again, the First Hall-man could have taken it all away from him by threatening to dismiss him and fire him back to hard labor in the prison-yard. And yet again, there were the ten or us who were ordinary hall-men. If we got an inkling of his wealth, there was a large liability, some quiet day, of the whole bunch of us getting him into a corner and dragging him down. Oh, we were wolves, believe me—just like the fellows who do business in Wall Street.

He had good reason to be afraid of us, and so had I to be afraid of him. He was a huge, illiterate brute, an ex-Chesapeake-Bay-oyster-pirate, an "ex-con" who had done five years in Sing Sing, and a general all-around stupidly carnivorous beast. He used to trap sparrows that flew into our hall through the open bars. When he made a capture, he hurried away with it into his cell, where I have seen him crunching bones and spitting out feathers as he bolted it raw. Oh, no, I never gave away on him to the other hall-men. This is the first time I have mentioned his sixteen dollars.

But I grafted on him just the same. He was in love with a woman prisoner who was confined in the "female department." He could neither read nor write, and I used to read her letters to him and write his replies. And I made him pay for it, too. But they were good letters. I laid myself out on them, put in my best licks, and furthermore, I won her for him; though I shrewdly guess that she was in love, not with him, but with the humble scribe. I repeat, those letters were great.

Another one of our grafts was "passing the punk." We were the celestial messengers, the fire-bringers, in that iron world of bolt and

bar. When the men came in from work at night and were locked
in their cells, they wanted to smoke. Then it was that we restored
the divine spark, running the galleries, from cell to cell, with our
smoldering punks. Those who were wise, or with whom we did
business, had their punks all ready to light. Not every one got
divine sparks, however. The guy who refused to dig up, went spark-
less and smokeless to bed. But what did we care? We had the
immortal cinch on him, and if he got fresh, two or three of us would
pitch on him and give him "what-for."

You see, this was the working-theory of the hall-men. There were
thirteen of us. We had something like half a thousand prisoners in
our hall. We were supposed to do the work, and to keep order. The
latter was the function of the guards, which they turned over to us.
It was up to us to keep order; if we didn't, we'd be fired back to
hard labor, most probably with a taste of the dungeon thrown in.
But so long as we maintained order, that long could we work our
own particular grafts.

Bear with me a moment and look at the problem. Here were
thirteen beasts of us over half a thousand other beasts. It was a
living hell, that prison, and it was up to us thirteen there to rule.
It was impossible, considering the nature of the beasts, for us to
rule by kindness. We ruled by fear. Of course, behind us, backing
us up, were the guards. In extremity we called upon them for help;
but it would bother them if we called upon them too often, in
which event we could depend upon it that they would get more
efficient trusties to take our places. But we did not call upon them
often, except in a quiet sort of way, when we wanted a cell unlocked
in order to get at a refractory prisoner inside. In such cases all the
guard did was to unlock the door and walk away so as not to be a
witness of what happened when half a dozen hall-men went inside
and did a bit of man-handling.

As regards the details of this man-handling I shall say nothing.
And after all, man-handling was merely one of the very minor unprintable horrors of the Erie County Pen. I say "unprintable"; and
in justice I must also say "unthinkable." They were unthinkable to
me until I saw them, and I was no spring chicken in the ways of
the world and the awful abysses of human degradation. It would
take a deep plummet to reach bottom in the Erie County Pen, and
I do but skim lightly and facetiously the surface of things as I
there saw them.

At times, say in the morning when the prisoners came down to
wash, the thirteen of us would be practically alone in the midst of
them, and every last one of them had it in for us. Thirteen against

five hundred, and we ruled by fear. We could not permit the slightest infraction of rules, the slightest insolence. If we did, we were lost. Our own rule was to hit a man as soon as he opened his mouth—hit him hard, hit him with anything. A broom-handle, end-on, in the face, had a very sobering effect. But that was not all. Such a man must be made an example of; so the next rule was to wade right in and follow him up. Of course, one was sure that every hall-man in sight would come on the run to join in the chastisement; for this also was a rule. Whenever any hall-man was in trouble with a prisoner, the duty of any other hall-man who happened to be around was to lend a fist. Never mind the merits of the case—wade in and hit, and hit with anything; in short, lay the man out.

I remember a handsome young mulatto of about twenty who got the insane idea into his head that he should stand for his rights. And he did have the right of it, too; but that didn't help him any. He lived on the topmost gallery. Eight hall-men took the conceit out of him in just about a minute and a half—for that was the length of time required to travel along his gallery to the end and down five flights of steel stairs. He traveled the whole distance on every portion of his anatomy except his feet, and the eight hall-men were not idle. The mulatto struck the pavement where I was standing watching it all. He regained his feet and stood upright for a moment. In that moment he threw his arms wide apart and emitted an awful scream of terror and pain and heart-break. At the same instant, as in a transformation scene, the shreds of his stout prison clothes fell from him, leaving him wholly naked and streaming blood from every portion of the surface of his body. Then he collapsed in a heap, unconscious. He had learned his lesson, and every convict within those walls who heard him scream had learned a lesson. So had I learned mine. It is not a nice thing to see a man's heart broken in a minute and a half.

The following will illustrate how we drummed up business in the graft of passing the punk. A row of newcomers is installed in your cells. You pass along before the bars with your punk. "Hey, Bo, give us a light," some one calls to you. Now this is an advertisement that that particular man has tobacco on him. You pass in the punk and go your way. A little later you come back and lean up casually against the bars. "Say, Bo, can you let us have a little tobacco?" is what you say. If he is not wise to the game, the chances are that he solemnly avers that he hasn't any more tobacco. All very well. You condole with him and go your way. But you know that his punk will last him only the rest of that day. Next day you come by, and he says again, "Hey, Bo, give us a light." And you say, "You haven't any tobacco and you don't need a light." And you don't give him any, either. Half an hour after, or an hour or two or three hours, you will be passing by and the man will call out to you in mild tones, "Come here, Bo." And you come. You thrust your hand between the bars and have it filled with precious tobacco. Then you give him a light.

Sometimes, however, a newcomer arrives, upon whom no grafts are to be worked. The mysterious word is passed along that he is to be treated decently. Where this word originated I could never learn. The one thing patent is that the man has a "pull." It may be with one of the superior hall-men; it may be with one of the guards in some other part of the prison; it may be that good treatment has been purchased from grafters higher up; but be it as it may, we know that it is up to us to treat him decently if we want to avoid trouble.

We hall-men were middle-men and common carriers. We arranged trades between convicts confined in different parts of the prison, and we put through the exchange. Also, we took our commissions coming and going. Sometimes the objects traded had to go through the hands of half a dozen middle-men, each of whom took his whack, or in some way or another was paid for his service.

Sometimes one was in debt for services, and sometimes one had others in his debt. Thus, I entered the prison in debt to the convict who smuggled in my things for me. A week or so afterward, one of the firemen passed a letter into my hand. It had been given to him by a barber. The barber had received it from the convict who had smuggled in my things. Because of my debt to him I was to carry the letter on. But he had not written the letter. The original sender was a long-timer in his hall. The letter was for a woman prisoner in the female department. But whether it was intended for her, or whether she, in turn, was one of the chain of go-betweens, I did not know. All that I knew was her description, and that it was up to me to get it into her hands.

Two days passed, during which time I kept the letter in my possession; then the opportunity came. The women did the mending of all the clothes worn by the convicts. A number of our hall-men had to go to the female department to bring back huge bundles of clothes. I fixed it with the First Hall-man that I was to go along. Door after door was unlocked for us as we threaded our way across the prison to the women's quarters. We entered a large room where the women sat working at their mending. My eyes were peeled for the woman who had been described to me. I located her and worked near to her. Two eagle-eyed matrons were on watch. I held the letter in my palm, and I looked my intention at the woman. She knew I had something for her; she must have been expecting it, and had set herself to divining, at the moment we entered, which of us was the messenger. But one of the matrons stood within two feet of her. Already the hall-men were picking up the bundles they were to carry away. The moment was passing. I delayed with my bundle, making believe that it was not tied securely. Would that matron ever look away? Or was I to fail? And just then another woman cut up playfully with one of the hall-men—stuck out her foot and tripped him, or pinched him, or did something or other. The matron looked that way and reprimanded the woman sharply. Now I do not know whether or not this was all planned to distract the matron's attention, but I did know that it was my opportunity. My particular woman's hand dropped from her lap down by her side. I stooped to pick up my bundle. From my stooping position I slipped the letter into her hand, and received another in exchange. The next moment the bundle was on my shoulder, the matron's gaze had returned to me because I was the last hall-man, and I was hastening to catch up with my companions. The letter I had received from the woman I turned over to the fireman, and thence it passed through the hands of the barber, of the convict who had smuggled in my things, and on to the long-timer at the other end.

At last came the day of days, my release. It was the day of release for the Third Hall-man as well, and the short-timer girl I had won for him was waiting for him outside the wall. They went away blissfully together. My pal and I went out together, and together we walked down into Buffalo. Were we not to be together always? We begged together on the "main-drag" that day for pennies, and what we received was spent for "shupers" of beer—I don't know how they are spelled, but they are pronounced the way I have spelled them, and they cost three cents. I was watching my chance all the time for a get-away. From some bo on the drag I managed to learn what time a certain freight pulled out. I calculated my time accordingly. When the moment came, my pal and I were in a saloon. Two foaming shupers were before us. I'd have liked to say good-by. He had been good to me. But I did not dare. I went out through the rear of the saloon and jumped the fence. It was a swift sneak, and a few minutes later I was on board a freight and heading south on the Western New York and Pennsylvania Railroad.

In the course of my tramping I encountered hundreds of hoboes, whom I hailed or who hailed me, and with whom I waited at water-tanks, "boiled-up," cooked "mulligans," "battered" the "drag" or "privates," and beat trains, and who passed and were seen never again. On the other hand, there were hoboes who passed and re-passed with amazing frequency, and others still who passed like ghosts, close at hand, unseen, and never seen.

It was one of the latter that I chased clear across Canada over three thousand miles of railroad, and never once did I lay eyes on him. His "monica" was Skysail Jack. I first ran into it at Montreal. Carved with a jack-knife was the skysail-yard of a ship. It was perfectly executed. Under it was "Skysail Jack." Above was "B.W. 9-15-94." This latter conveyed the information that he had passed through Montreal bound west, on October 15, 1894. He had one day the start of me. "Sailor Jack" was my monica at that particular time, and promptly I carved it alongside of his, along with the date and the information that I, too, was bound west.

I had misfortune in getting over the next hundred miles, and eight days later I picked up Skysail Jack's trail three hundred miles west of Ottawa. There it was, carved on a water-tank, and by the date I saw that he likewise had met with delay. He was only two days ahead of me. I was a "comet" and "tramp-royal," so was Sky-sail Jack; and it was up to my pride and reputation to catch up with him. I "railroaded" day and night, and I passed him; then turn about he passed me. Sometimes he was a day or so ahead, and some-times I was. From hoboes, bound east, I got word of him occa-sionally, when he happened to be ahead; and from them I learned that he had become interested in Sailor Jack and was making inquiries about me.

We'd have made a precious pair, I am sure, if we'd ever got to-gether; but get together we couldn't. I kept ahead of him clear across Manitoba, but he led the way across Alberta, and early one bitter gray morning, at the end of a division just east of Kicking Horse Pass, I learned that he had been seen the night before between Kicking Horse Pass and Rogers' Pass. It was rather curious the way the information came to me. I had been riding all night in a "side-door Pullman" (box-car), and nearly dead with cold had crawled out at the division to beg for food. A freezing fog was drift-ing past, and I "hit" some firemen I found in the round-house. They fixed me up with the leavings from their lunch-pails, and in addition I got out of them nearly a quart of heavenly "Java" (coffee). I heated the latter, and, as I sat down to eat, a freight pulled in from the west. I saw a side-door open and a road-kid climb out. Through the drifting fog he limped over to me. He was stiff with cold, his lips were blue. I shared my Java and grub with him, learned about Skysail Jack, and then learned about him. Behold, he was from my own town, Oakland, California, and he was a member of the celebrated Boo Gang—a gang with which I had affiliated at rare intervals. We talked fast and bolted the grub in the half-hour that followed. Then my freight pulled out, and I was on it, bound west on the trail of Skysail Jack.

I was delayed between the passes, went two days without food, and walked eleven miles on the third day before I got any, and yet I succeeded in passing Skysail Jack along the Fraser River in British Columbia. I was riding "passengers" then and making time; but he must have been riding passengers, too, and with more luck or skill than I, for he got into Mission ahead of me.

Now Mission was a junction, forty miles east of Vancouver. From the junction one could proceed south through Washington and Oregon over the Northern Pacific. I wondered which way Skysail Jack would go, for I thought I was ahead of him. As for myself I was still bound west to Vancouver. I proceeded to the water-tank to leave that information, and there, freshly carved, with that day's date upon it, was Skysail Jack's monica. I hurried on into Vancouver. But he was gone. He had taken ship immediately and was still flying west on his world-adventure. Truly, Skysail Jack, you were a tramp-royal, and your mate was the "wind that tramps the world." I take off my hat to you. You were "blowed-in-the-glass" all right.

CHAPTER LXIV

AND THERE is the even more comprehensive record of John Wesley Gordon, Negro laborer and lover in thirty-eight States, as taken down from Gordon's own musical lips by a sociologist and edited for publication. Among all the notes on which the book might end, this one is not the least revealing of huge America in the twentieth century.*

I SEEN a lot of o' black boys an' girls in my day since I lef' home goin' on thirteen years old. I started travelin' when I was thirteen years old, an' now I'll be thirty-two this coming August, the twenty-sixth. I would work for folks an' sometimes I wouldn't like it an' sometimes they wouldn't treat me right, an' so I would move on. Take me till to-morrow night an' 'bout a dozen books to tell about all jobs I worked at an' all places I been. I never stays in one place mo' 'n four weeks, leastwise never mo' 'n five. Long lonesome road I been down. After workin' at all sorts o' little jobs with my father an' then my mother an' grandmother, I started out, an' since then I done most everything anybody ever do.

I been helper in maloominum plant, stirrin' pots at Bessemer, janitor for mayor of two towns, factory hand, porter an' butler on railroad, an' wipin' up engines of Great Northwestern railroad. I been waiter in hotels an' restaurants. I sold papers in mo' 'n one town. I worked as helper for carpenters an' layin' brick for masons. I worked in store brushin' furniture, worked in packin'-house, an' in engine-house. I been in government camp an' in Ford factory. I plowed hard-tail mule, cut wood to fire log engine, an' worked on green ends o' rollin' lumber. I worked as harves' han' out Wes'. I been driver of teams, pick an' shovel man, worker in concrete, an' laborer in log camp an' hard roads. I worked on railroad gangs, an' sho' could drive steel for section boss. I worked keepin' yards an' mowin' lawns, white-washin' fences, an' paintin' houses. I been yard an' house butler for white folks, traveled with white man, an' I been

* From RAINBOW ROUND MY SHOULDERS, by Howard W. Odum, copyright, 1928, Used by special permission of the publishers. The Bobbs-Merrill Company.

bootlegger, too. I worked in show, an' traveled over into Canada. I was hand on Mississippi Delta job, boatin' on Mississippi River an' on lake, diggin' in coal mine, an' workin' in steel foundry. I pressed clothes, helped in print-shop, an' seem like 'bout hundred mo' jobs which I try to tell 'bout later. An' been times I run up 'gainst the law. But mos' times all dirt I ever done I been lucky enough to git off.

Sometimes I works an' sometimes I don't. 'Long with work or travelin', I plays my box an' sings my Blues an' gits folks to help me out when I need 'em, mo' specially good-lookin' womens.

> I ain't no good-lookin' man,
> My teeth don't shine like pearls,
> But this nice disposition
> Take me on through this worl'.

Funny how I can't stay no place long. Always some other place better, some other work easier. Somebody thinkin' 'bout me, road callin' me on. When I come to new place I works while or maybe I hustles, an' then, lawd, I'll row here few days longer then I'll be gone. Don't stay long in states like Georgia and Mississippi. Folks in them states mighty ruffish an' don't give man no chance. Seems like they ain't civilized, leastwise like they ought to be.

I had some hard times in Louisiana an' Florida on sawmill an' roads. In Alabama, Iowa, Tennessee, West Virginia an' Pennsylvania I worked in mines. I worked on boats in Louisiana, Mississippi, Missouri, Baltimore an' New Haven. I had a little money an' so jes' had good time in Texas, Wyoming, Arizona an' Richmond. Had sister in Springfield an' 'nuther one in St. Louis an' stayed there while, sometimes workin', sometimes loafin'.

Had all sorts o' other jobs in Arkansas, Illinois, Nebraska, Michigan, Kansas, North Carolina, Arizona, South Carolina, Virginia, New York, Washington, Ohio, New Jersey, Wisconsin, Connecticut, Massachusetts, Rhode Island, North Dakota an' South Dakota. An' I worked in war camp in both South an' North, an' went little while overseas on boat with the boys in the war. Went up in Canada sometimes workin' across on boat an' jobs with show, an' since war been down across Mexico line some. I can get plenty of trouble down there. You ought to see me turnin' round when Mexican girl throw dagger at me. I been in 'bout fohty states, but I 'spects to go in all of 'em yet. I got one friend, fellow I tell you 'bout later, maybe been in mo' states than I has, but he turn to Pullman porter an' don't see much life like I do.

I been in heap o' towns. Take me till to-morrow night to count 'em. Can't name 'em. Been in Norfolk 'bout hundred times. Been in

St. Louis an' Chicago an' got stuck up, an' eve'y time I go to them towns, I'm leavin' an' ain't comin' back. New O'leans bes' place, feller find most kindest folks. Mos' freest-hearted womens. Hoboed through Birmingham two times, an' one time stayed while in steel works. Stayed while in Atlanta but soon comin' 'way from there. Always goin' back to Philadelphia. Had hard time in New York. Memphis, Tennessee, good place if feller knows how to git 'long. Been out to Los Angeles but never did go back. Work my way back to Detroit an' Kentucky an' Virginia and come back home. Take me till to-morrow night to tell 'bout all towns I been in. Good lawd, can't count 'em.

I see lots o' gamblers in my day. But sho' is fact, worst gambler I ever seen in all my time was big black nigger called Shine, carryin' black cat bones in his pocket. Seen him clean up whole camp here las' week. Mighty bad gamblers in these camps, but I ain't seen none so finish as this black boy.

Some o' these boys carry extra dice an' crooked dice so they can't lose no way they throw 'em, an' they have all sorts of hands to give 'em luck. Rabbit feet they carry a plenty. Some of 'em go to witchcrafters an' git baby hands an' carry 'em in their pockets, an' some of 'em carry scorpion heads, an' snake skins, and buckeyes, an' other sich things, but man carryin' black cat bones in his pocket can't lose.

Sho' is a fact if you stand test of black cat you can't lose. You take black cat an' put in a wash pot full o' cold water, build fire 'round pot an' set on top of lid while hot water boil all meat off cat. Then, you take bones to stream runnin' eas' an' wes' an' throw bones in runnin' stream. Actual fact, one of these bones goin' to swim against stream. You take that bone an' put it in yo' pocket, then you take yo' right hand an' set right foot in palm of right hand an' put left hand on top of yo' head an' swear by all the gods that made you what is between yo' two hands belong to the devil. An' that will rise a storm an' devil will appear to you in some form, such as cow or horse, or tree, or hisself. But you stay till all storm has ceasted an' then anything you want to do you can do. 'Nuther thing, reason nigger carrin' black cat bones is so mean, he knows he done sold his soul to the devil an' he have to stick it out, an' all the pleasure he gits he must git out of this life.

Well, las' Sat'day evening one of these fellows with black cat bones come to camp an' had big red dice, ponies with white spots on 'em. He didn't have no little pee-wee dice foolin' round with him. This fellow Shine was black as ace of spades. Well, he didn't have nothin' with him 'cept his ponies, an' so he borrowed two cents from a little boy driver an' in a little while won fifty cents.

So he come on over to the big game, an' so somebody faded him for fifty cents, an' he won with a lick an' picked up his dice and say, "Les' shoot the whole dollar." An' so he played that an' won, an' made another pass an' hit 'em a lick an' throwed seven. An' so he said, "Les' shoot the four," an' made another lick. An' then he say, "Les' shoot this whole dam' eight," when a fellow faded him with twelve. An' so he kept shootin' the whole works until he was ready to leave with one hundred and forty-two dollars. An' so he come over walking big an' give little boy fifty cents. An' so he rattled the black cat bones in his pocket an' left that camp singing like make cold chills run over you.

> Done sold my soul
> Done sold it to the devil
> An' my heart's done turned back to stone
> I'm goin' back home
> An' knock on my mama's do'
> No sign I'm dead
> Just ain't coming back here no more.

I was tellin' 'bout rough outlaw camps an' how I got in one first time I run off an' went to work in camp, an' worked in few more later. Well, the chiefest of big contractors runnin' outlaw camps was Big Billy Bob, white man who had graveyard o' his own. Reckon he had more'n five hundred mules an' he graded big roads, railroads, national highways, dug out big lakes an' big developments, dug big tunnels like Big Ben Tunnel where John Henry died, an' built big tunnel under Hudson River.

Boys work fer him from all over worl', come all way from Mississippi an' Louisiana an' Georgia an' Alabama an' Florida an' South Carolina an' Tennessee an' jes' eve'ywhere. He had small contractors takin' sub-contracts under him. Sometimes boys would git tired workin' in little camp an' take notion they wanted to go to big camp, but we was mighty sorry after we got in. So they made up song 'bout Big Billy Bob:

> When I was up bottom, was doin' pretty well;
> Now, I'm down here ketchin' Billy Bob Hell.

Eve'ybody skeered of Big Billy Bob. Reason I say he had graveyard of his own was when he kill a man or somebody else in camp, like bad nigger I told 'bout kill one, they jes' cover him up out in field, an' that's last of him. They say boys skeered to tell on 'em, skeered they be covered up too. Take all-day story to tell 'bout Big Billy Bob an' his camps.

One day Big Billy Bob got mad at driver of big team of six red mules an' pull out his gun to shoot him, but boy seen him an' dodge behin' mule, an' so he killed mule instead.

> If it hadn't been fer red mule's head,
> Big Bob Russell would 'a' kill me dead.
> Ain't but one man on job I fear,
> Big Billy Bob Russell don't stop by here.

I worked for man called Bill Smexer, used to be foreman for Big Billy Bob an' I seen him kill a fellow one day. Foreman an' driver fell out 'bout way he was drivin'. He spoke to boy 'bout drivin' on edge of field an' kep' cussin' boy. Boy took out gun an' shot at foreman but missed him. Then boss shot 'im an' hit in neck an' broke it jes' lak chicken's neck. They covered him up in field. Big Billy Bob had 'way o' saying:

> Kill a mule, buy another,
> Kill a nigger, hire another.

'Nuther foreman for Big Bob was fellow named Gaxton down in Mississippi, buildin' what is called lockin' dam, one o' Billy Bob's jobs. He didn't have no pay-day. Jes' work all time an' if you want clothes go to commissary an' get 'em. Would fit you out an' tell you to wear shoes an' if you didn't wear 'em charge 'em to you jes' same. Would say "Shoes an' clothes here, if you don't wear 'em ain't my fault." Then, he charge 'em jes' same. If boss wanted to give you little money to spend, all right; but sho' didn't have *no* pay-day. Had big nigger called shack-rouster go roun' with big stick wakin' you up, an' I'm tellin' you, you *better* git up. He would holler:

> Eatin' captain's good grub an' callin' it junk,
> Layin' in captain's warm bed an' callin' bunk,
> Say, big nigger, can't you rise?

Well, you *gonna* git up whether you want to or not. One big nigger called Bama come in wid stick an' say, "Now three of us in dis room—jes' three of us in here, you, me, an' dis stick. Ain't no room for all of us; hospital fer sick, graveyard fer the dead. Didn't send fer you nohow, you come round sayin' you could work. Sent for po'k an' beans an' you come pokin' round here, you got to git up." An' 'less'n you mean to kill somebody jes' well to git up.

> I don't want no trouble with de walker;
> I don't want no trouble with de walker;
> I jes' want to go home,
> Lawd, I jes' want to go home.

One time I worked for man name Bill Round who had shack-rouster from Atlanta, Georgia. One mo'nin' one boy say to others in shack:

"Well, boys, I'm gonna make it easy fer you an' hard fer me. I ain't goin' out to-day."

So when big shack-rouster come an' knock on door he say he ain't goin' to git up. So shack-rouster struck him on head with stick. An' he say:

"Don't hit me no mo' 'cause I ain't goin' out to-day."

So when shack-rouster hit him again he turn over an' snatch fohty-five out from under his pillow an' shoots him and then gits up from bed an' takes shack-rouster's gun an' shoots him five mo' times. He takes his pistol an' shack-rouster's pistol an' loads 'em both an' goes out in fiel' an' sets down an' says:

"Well, white folks, I knows you-all wants to have picnic."

He was signifyin' he knowed they wants to 'rest him. He says to white folks he knows they ain't gonna do nothin' 'cause he's gonna make it easy on other boys, hard on hisself. So he sets round all day smokin' an' sayin' nothin' an' holdin' his guns, an' 'bout sundown he puts pistol to his head an' blows his brains out. So they covered him up in field, too, an' that ended it 'cause nobody knowed where he come from an' who he was. So he made it a little easier for other boys an' hard for hisself, jes' like he said, 'cause nex' shack-rouster won't be so dam' iron-jawed.

I worked fer white man named June Heever, runnin' No. 2 crusher, an' he was principled up like this: eve'y colored man was no mo' than dog, jes' sumpin' out there to work. He was jes' cruel as he could be. An' was some boys workin' out there come from South Carolina was 'fraid of him. Some colored folks skeered of white man jes' to see him, no matter how kind he is. Well, if they find one rough they skeered to death. This man never had a kind word to speak, I know, 'cause I worked at that job from time it started till completed. That was befo' I got to travelin' so fast. One time Mr. Sockey sent truck an' fo' colored men down to git some rock dust, an' we had to load from big bend in crusher. Big bend was stopped up an' we couldn't git no dust. So colored driver ast him to send one of his men up to unstop big bend 'cause it was his business to do it. This colored man was called Frog Eye an' so he ast him again. So foreman cussed him out an' he say:

"Boss, ain't no use talkin' to me lak that."

Then big foreman hit him wid pick handle an' knock all skin off back of his head. Frog Eye started to pick up rock, an' foreman hit him again, an' so Frog Eye run off hard as he could back to camp.

One day I was workin' for this foreman helpin' him with belt an' belt slip. I couldn't help it an' he cussed me. Then I said to him:

"I'll do yo' work, but you don't have to cuss me. I ain't afraid of you like the other boys."

He says, "Who you talkin' to?"

I say, "I'm talkin' to you an' you can't be beatin' me up like you do other boys."

So he looks at me an' I looks at him. So he toted a twenty-five ortermatic, an' went over to his raincoat an' got his pistol an' come back. So I had mine already 'cause I carried it hid under belt under my shirt an' I said to him:

"If you can't treat me like a man even if I is black, I don't keer nothin' 'bout you, an' no other man ain't got no principle."

"You dam' nigger, you don't mean to talk back to white folks like that, do you?"

"Yes, you an' all other white men on this job come befo' me jes' like gourd vine 'cause if you try to beat me up one or t'other of us gwine eat breakfast or dinner in hell. Don't matter to me which one of us it is."

So I told him I was gonna quit anyway, I couldn't stand his junk. So he say he can't pay me till pay-day, end of week. So I say to him when he fire me he gonna pay me, he's gonna *make* me some money. Then foreman say:

"Well, ain't no use this dam' foolishness, you got fretted an' I got fretted. So you jes' come on an' work for me."

"That's all right long as you treat me like a man, but if you make move to beat me up I'm gonna knock the heart out o' you," I says.

An' so he told me to work on, an' we never had no troubles, an' he said I was as good hand as anybody he ever had. But I never did joke or make pleasant with him. If he spoke pleasant to me I spoke pleasant to him, an' if he speak short to me I speak short to him.

But lot o' boys he'd holler at an' kick around callin' 'em ole black scoundrels, ole tar barrels, ole knotty heads, treat 'em worse'n convicts. I tole him I had a name an' if he couldn't call my name don't say nothin' to me. An' so he always took time to call my name. Same ole foreman used to have pet named George, come from his home down in Georgia, an' he treat him fine 'cause he was home man an' anyway would do eve'ything foreman wanted.

Not all foremen like this one. Worked for Mr. Haplane in camp; was jes' fine man as I ever seen anywhere. He would call you by yo' name an' if he want you to hurry up a little he would come roun' an' say:

"Well, boys, guess we better hurry up, big boss comin' pretty soon. Big boss he gittin' after us. Don't want you to work too hard 'cause

I need you nex' week, but better for all of us if we hurry 'em up a little."

Sometimes he ast me if I was sick an' when I say, "No," well then, he say:

"Better pick 'em up. I got to hold my job same as you."

If I need any money he would loan it to me, an' if anything he could do he would do it. Would bring us cigarettes back from town an' if we didn't have none would let us smoke off'n him. He was mighty hard on you though if you cut up mules. He would say to us:

"Boys, you can't cut up my mules. Knee down to huff belong to you, but knee up belong to me. You can strike 'em wid leather below knee but if you can't drive mules without 'busin' 'em, drive 'em in shade an' let 'em be. 'Nuther man can drive 'em." He would make us curry mules every mo'nin' an' keep harness all greased up an' bright.

You ought to see crowd of us workin' on big road camp. Sometimes maybe would be as high as thirty or fohty wheelers steppin' in line, with three hooks an' six loaders, an' believe me we stepped about. One ole man, foreman, was so bad he didn't keer fer nothin', mules, men nor nothin' else, jes' so he could see dirt piled up. Used to have some hot times. He would yell an' cuss at boys.

"All right, boys, bring them wheelers here—goddam'. If you can't bring mules, stop an' unhitch 'em an' bring collars, got to have sumptin'.

> "Knock 'em an' chop 'em,
> Side-wheel 'em an' lock 'em,
> An' don't stop.

"Bring 'em here an' let wheelers roll—knock 'em in collar till they go stone blin'."

All day long boss walk up an' down, hat off, scratchin' his head an' hollerin':

"Bring 'em here, goddam', Jesus Chris', bring 'em in pace, take 'em back in gallup."

Mules an' men rushin' an' sweatin' an' clankin' an' knockin'. Thirty wheelers an' one loader for eve'y ten wheelers, an' many time seen 'em knock him out an' white-eye an' have to git 'nuther loader. Had to fill wheelers up full an' had to bring 'em full up an' some on Johnson bar, an' highball 'em 'cause that's captain's profit. "All right," he holler. "Stack 'em up, if man in front can't git out o' way drive over him. Dirt on field what I got to have." Used to have big teams, sometimes six mules, front pair bein' lead mules an' two nex' to wheelers swing mules. Boys could swing leather line whip an' knock mule off'n his feet easy lak lasso. Could hit lead mule wherever he want to, an' mules had hard time, too. Seen 'em put mules' eyes out that way. Boys used to sing:

> Hame string poppin', collar cryin',
> Knock 'em in collar till go stone blin'.
> Lead mule cripple, swing mule blin',
> Knocked 'em in collar till he went stone blind.

All day long in hot or rain, in dust or mud boys holler an' jaw at one another:

"Let dis team git mo' collar than yo's."

"Well, you have to unhook an' let me take yo' plugs."

"Dam it, put 'em in the shade, yo' team done rivered."

All day long jokin' an hollerin', jawin' an' cussin', singin' an' sighin', an' callin' eve'y name in God's worl': Bitin' Spider, Trottin' Sallie, Stewball, Mollie, Hikin' Jerry. Mike an' Jerry was one of Big Bob's hook teams. Was wild mules so full o' ambition—always took bes' mules in career fer hook teams.

See Mike an' Jerry kill boy one day. Boy had belt on with ring so he could hook on to belt so he wouldn't have to stoop down an' pick up hook. So he put hook in belt one day, an' team got skeered an' broke an' run away. Was on main line Southern—an' dragged po' boy till jes' wo' him out. So boys made song:

> Mike an' Jerry,
> Lawd, Mike an' Jerry;
> Mike an' Jerry,
> Yes, Lawdy, Mike an' Jerry;
> Didn't stop here to git no coal,
> Lawd, didn't stop here to git no coal.
> Well, dey hike from de Rome to Decatur,
> Well, dey hike from de Rome to Decatur,
> In one day, Lawd, in one day;
> Didn't stop git coal, neither water,
> Hiked on by, Lovin' Mamie,
> Well hiked on by, Lovin' Mamie.

Lovin' Mamie was boy got killed 's woman. Boys git hurt ridin' wheelers an' log truck, standin' in pan, and other ways. Sometimes mule kick 'em, an' sometimes git blowed up when blastin'. Sometimes git sick an' laid out an' keep you at camp, or some of buddies take keer o' you, or some of boys' women stayin' in camp help you out. If can't git 'way have to stay in camp till lice eat you up. I seen 'em lousy as hogs an' sick as buzzards.

I had some mighty fine women. Fust one was Abbie Jones, 'bout Ioway Street. Nex' was in Missouri, Jennie Baker, Susan Baker's daughter. Nex' one St. Louis, lady called Beulah Cotton, Pete Cotton's daughter. Nex' one was in Eas' St. Louis, her name Sylvia Brown. Nex' one I had in Poplar Bluff, one dat took my money an' went off. Nex' Laura, she's in Memphis, Tennessee, she's 'nuther took my money and gone. Jes' lay down, went to sleep, jes' took money and gone. Wake up sometimes broke an' hungry, they jes' naturally take my money. Nex' woman was at Columbia, South Carolina, 'bout las' regular one I had, Mamie Willard, mother and father dead. 'Co's these women I'm talkin' 'bout finer sort, an' 'scusin' them I married, an' tellin' 'bout later. Other kinds o' sweethearts I can git plenty of if I got money. If I ain't got none I'se sometimes lonesome, but not always, 'cause sometimes they feel sorry fer you an' treat you mighty fine anyway. Had so many can't count 'em. Take me till day after to-morrow to tell 'bout 'em. Find fifteen or twenty in different cities, an' I been in a heap o' cities. New Orleans best place to find most fastest, mo' freer women. Person find gang of 'em in minute. Everybody say New Orleans' womens kindes'-hearted an' most lovin'.

Most o' the fellers ramblin' around don't 'sociate with the best intelligent girls. Guess you can't call our low-down on that 'cause we sho' gonna need a lovin' babe to tell our troubles to. Lots o' times I be in strange city, jes' come to town. Ain't got no money, ain't got no friends. So I see nice-lookin' lady at station or on street on my way lookin' fer place to stay or maybe some work to do. So I ask her name an' street number an' address. Then I asks her if she's got a friend. Sometimes she say "yes" an' sometimes she say "no." So I say I'm in town, lonesome an' want a friend, so what about us bein' friends? I say I'm a man makes good money an' know how to get it, but jes' now jes' happen to be out an' lonesome boy.

> Pity po' boy 'way from home,
> Good old boy jes' ain't treated right.
> No need o' babe to throw me down,
> A po' little boy jes' come to town.

Well, if she let me be her friend I go stay with her. Easy to do 'cause nobody snoopin' round or mindin' our business as usual thing. Well, I stay with her while an' sweethearts with her. She ask me if I ever hustles any whisky. I says, "Yes, sometimes." Well, she say fer me to git her some an' maybe we pick up some easy money. So I asks her which way bootleggers come in. She say down on Ellers Street an' fer me to hang around and git some fer her. I say 'bout how much, an' she say 'bout a gallon an' gives me money fer it.

So I take her the gallon and maybe I'll git me a job or maybe I'll have good luck with my gamblin' spell. So I goes back an' I says, "Well, I had good luck. I told you I could git good money but you wouldn't believe me." So I may make fifty dollars or one hundred dollars, an' I gives her half o' this to show her what a fine feller I am.

Well, she says to me she ain't no slow poke herself. She taken three gallon whisky cost 'bout six or seven dollars an' caught some soft guys. She kiss 'em and love 'em an' git 'em all lit up an' throw 'em fer three or fo' dollars apiece an' still got most o' her liquor left. Well, we have good times over dat till I gits tired of her an' gits her money and moves on. Of course while I'se sweetheartin' with her I got to keep away from other women. If she find me foolin' round 'em, she likely to give me hot time, maybe cut me up.

One time I was in Greensboro on visit an' I met girl at station. She spoke to me. I spoke to her. I say I'm stranger. She ask me where I come from. I tell her Baltimore, 'cause they think heap mo' of you if you been travelin' 'bout. 'Co's I come from Durham, there 'cause I was jes' beginning to travel.

So I say I'd like a friend and place to stay. She say she like friends too. I say I may be here month. I'm a feller can do anything and capable of good money. So she say come on over to her room. Most womens have rooms to selves, so company can come in. So she fixed me nice bed an' all, an' I stayed round two days. Then I says how 'bout lettin' me have a nickel note or a double son. I means a five-dollar bill or ten-dollar bill, an' I tells her if I be lucky I come back. So I come back, an' she give me mo' money an' taken likin' to me. So I stayed there two or three weeks, an' didn't work none an' didn't do nothin' but drink whisky an' borrow money.

> Now good-lookin' man can git home anywhere he go;
> Reason why is the women tell me so.
> Reason I love my baby so,
> Eve'y time she make five dollars
> She give her daddy fo'.

Sometimes I ask 'em if they like to drink, an' they say yes. Well, I ask 'em if they ever practice bein' sweet to a person, an' maybe they say yes they like to be pleasant. So I says I'll do to be pleasant to, an' so they git pretty soft on me an' always anxious fer strange feller.

Then sometimes I don't find no friend an' so I go with feller to regular barrel club. Three or four girls have fifteen-twenty men callin' on 'em. One time I seen one woman drunk an' dozen niggers all callin' on her at one time. They starts to arguing, fightin', shootin', cuttin' an' sho' did have a hell of a mix-up that night. 'Nuther time was three girls and 'bout ten men an' they put one fellow out. He swore he'd set house on fire, started shootin', an' they put lights out an' had terrible time. That boy say woman was his woman an' he'd have her that night there else he'd have her in hell next night.

> Well, I'm gonna start graveyard of my own
> If you don't, ole nigger, let my woman alone.

Well, jes' lak I said—Lawd, hundred won't start 'em—hundreds an' hundreds. I was with eight different women one week an' I heard boys tell one day they had as high as fifteen-twenty in week. An' then again I knowed eight boys fightin' over one woman from sundown one day till nex' mornin'. Well, boys biddin' 'gainst one 'nuther an' womens mighty well off—maybe they take eighty or ninety dollars an' give it all to some other feller they taken a likin' to.

Well, I always have way with women, an' can keep up with the boys an' girls too. Seem lak they like you mo' if you been married. Leastwise didn't make no difference with 'em if you be married or if they be married, 'scusin' mo' better women like I told 'bout befo'. 'Co's heap o' fights an' shootin' goin' on, but I never did git caught 'cept one time ole wife of mine had man shoot me but didn't put me on no coolin' board, like I'll tell 'bout later.

Of course feller have to be on to these women 'cause they mighty slick. Beat you out your money an' steal it off'n you befo' you know it. One time woman took ten dollars off me. I wasn't drunk but she taken money out my pocket an' I don't no mo' know when she took it than nothin'. She lovin' me all sorts o' ways an' she sho' slick.

I tell her she got to give me my money. She lie to me an' swear she ain't got none o' my money. So I says to her if she don't give me my money I'm gonna frail very hell out o' her with chair. She say mighty sweet-like she know her daddy won't hurt her. I say no I won't hurt her, I jes' beat hell out o' her, an' I don't keer what they do to me. So I reaches out an' grabs chair an' start after her, an' she sho' give me back my ten dollars. 'Bout that time I'm leavin'.

Well, womens is mighty smart—hide money in their hair an' anywhere you can't find it. Sho' do git' way with country nigger jes' come to town. Got kind o' powder put on 'em so when country boy kiss or hug 'em goes clean crazy. Don't know where they git it, but sho' run feller crazy. Well, one o' these boys like myself when I started out come to town. Good-lookin' woman ask him if he don't want to have good time and so she gits him drunk an' say he beat anybody lovin' she ever see. An' so he falls for it, an' she take his money an' then say to him she need pair shoes. So he go gits some mo' money, an' maybe she keep him fooled for two or three months. At same time 'nuther man she givin' all this money to be foolin' her.

One kind of black lady I ought to tell 'bout, mos' freest-hearted, good-natured, but sho' got temper like whirlwind too. In my day I been knowin' heap of 'em. Large fat ladies an' black as ace o' spades. Always helpin' somebody out o' trouble, always laughin' an' smilin' an' eve'ywhere they is needed. Will take feller an' keep him an' love him. Will bring him food an' hide him when he's in trouble. Ain't no limit to trouble they do for you and amount of lovin' can give feller. Mos' colored folks, men an' women both, likes high browns an' yellows an' leaves the black women out. But they sho' got mo' endurance and mo' good to fellow than others. That's why I likes to keep 'em in my mind when I'm travelin' round. Always know where to find friend.

Some o' these creepers an' rounders more smarter 'n mos' women. Sho' do fool 'em. I done learned trick myself long time ago. I hides my money in bottom o' my shoe or some place. I out-talks 'em an' I plays all sorts o' tricks on 'em, how to beat 'em. Howsomever I done learned my tricks by loosin' heap first. One o' my bes' tricks is to flash Michigan roll o' bills on 'em. Way I do it is to take 'bout five one-dollar bills and one five-dollar bill, take newspaper or something an' cut same size as bills. Then I rolls three one-dollar bills on inside and five-dollar bill an' other dollar bills on outside. Looks like I got 'bout five hundred dollars.

So I say to woman she can see I knows how to throw my money. Well, I tears off couple one-dollar bills an' throws 'em at her an' leaves five-dollar bill showin'. She goes an' tells folks 'bout my money. I tell her I'se plasterer or maybe brick mason makin' big money. She say fer me to lend her 'nuther dollar, an' I say sho', an' shows her top five-dollar bill an' say that's smallest I got. So I got her fooled. She's good woman, hard workin' an' makin' good money, so she won't beg me for my money. So I tells her if I stay with her she can have that roll. She say she never do nothin' like that.

So I goes an' hires me nice-lookin' car an' tells her it belongs to me an' I'll sho' take keer of her if she needs me. So I keeps on and she jes' naturally fall for me. An' so I stays on with her asking her to let me keep her money. Then after I gits her money an' ruint her I'm gone from there.

Still I don't pay 'em no min' 'cause women can beat men double-crossin'—jes' won't be straight. Always do something crooked in spite of eve'ything. Las' week I seen man locked out his house by woman. He come whoopin' an' hollerin' an' cryin' like a baby, sayin' if she don't let him in he gonna kill some nigger. Well, she let man with her out back do' an' so sweet on her regular man sayin' she didn't know it was her sweet daddy tryin' to git in. Well, I'd ship that woman. Fool man standin' outside blubberin' like a little baby. She jes' do him anyway. I'd break her dam' neck if I was goin' with her. I'd put that thing on her an' she wouldn't monkey with me but once.

> Don't never git one woman on yo' min';
> Keep you in trouble all time.
> Buddy, let me tell you what nigger woman do,
> She have 'nuther man an' play sick on you.
> Well, oh my baby, you don't know my mind:
> When you think I'm lovin' you, I'm leavin' you behind.

THE END

BIBLIOGRAPHY

of Chapter Sources

Chapter I. The General History of Virginia. By Captain John Smith. Works, Ed. Edward Arber. London. 1884.

Chapter II. History of Plymouth Plantation. By William Bradford. 1856. Chronicles of the Pilgrim Fathers. Ed. Alexander Young. 1841-46.

Chapter III. The Wonders of the Invisible World. By the Reverend Cotton Mather. London. 1862.

Chapter IV. Samuel Sewall's Diary. Ed. Mark Van Doren. 1927.

Chapter V. The Autobiography of Benjamin Franklin.

Chapter VI. A Journey to the Land of Eden and Other Papers. By William Byrd. Ed. Mark Van Doren. 1928.

Chapter VII. Letters from an American Farmer. By Hector St.-John de Crèvecoeur. 1912.

Chapter VIII. Memoirs of an American Lady. By Anne Grant. London. 1808.

Chapter IX. Bundling: Its Origin, Progress, and Decline in America. By Henry Reed Stiles. Albany. 1871.

Chapter X. Memoirs of a Life Chiefly Passed in Pennsylvania. By Alexander Graydon. 1811.

Chapter XI. The Journal of Nicholas Cresswell, 1774-1777. Ed. Samuel Thornely. 1924.

Chapter XII. Letters and Journals Relating to the War of the American Revolution. By Mrs. General Riedesel. Translated by William L. Stone. Albany. 1867.

Chapter XIII. Collections of the New York Historical Society. 1872-3.

Chapter XIV. Journal and Letters of the Late Samuel Curwen. 1842.

Chapter XV. The Domestic Life of Thomas Jefferson. Ed. Sarah N. Randolph. 1871.

Chapter XVI. Life in a New England Town: 1787-1788. Diary of John Quincy Adams. 1903.

Chapter XVII. The Journal of William Maclay. Ed. Charles A. Beard. 1927.

Chapter XVIII. Letters of Mrs. Adams, the wife of John Adams. Ed. Charles Francis Adams. 1840.

Chapter XIX. The Writings of Thomas Jefferson. Ed. H. A. Washington. Vol. IX. 1854.

Chapter XX. The Works of Alexander Hamilton. Ed. Henry Cabot Lodge. Vol. VI. 1886.

Chapter XXI. Memoirs of Aaron Burr. By Matthew L. Davis. 2 Vols. 1869.

Chapter XXII. Perley's Reminiscences. By Benjamin Perley Poore. 2 Vols. 1886. John Randolph of Roanoke. By William Bruce. 2 Vols. 1922.

Chapter XXIII. Retrospections of America, 1797-1811. By John Bernard. Ed. Mrs. Bayle Bernard. 1887.

Chapter XXIV. Annual Report of the American Historical Association for the Year 1902. Vol. II. 1903.

Chapter LXI. A Son of the Middle Border. By Hamlin Garland. 1917.
Chapter LXII. Forty Years of It. By Brand Whitlock. 1914.
Chapter LXIII. The Road. By Jack London. 1907.
Chapter LXIV. Rainbow Round My Shoulder. The Blue Trail of Black Ulysses.
   By Howard W. Odum. Indianapolis. 1928.

INDEX